A Companion to Environmental Philosophy

Blackwell Companions to Philosophy

This outstanding student reference series offers a comprehensive and authoritative survey of philosophy as a whole. Written by today's leading philosophers, each volume provides lucid and engaging coverage of the key figures, terms, topics, and problems of the field. Taken together, the volumes provide the ideal basis for course use, representing an unparalleled work of reference for students and specialists alike.

Already published in the series:

The Blackwell Companion to Philosophy
Edited by Nicholas Bunnin and Eric Tsui-James

A Companion to Ethics
Edited by Peter Singer

A Companion to Aesthetics
Edited by David Cooper

A Companion to Epistemology
Edited by Jonathan Dancy and Ernest Sosa

A Companion to Contemporary Political Philosophy
Edited by Robert E. Goodin and Philip Pettit

A Companion to Philosophy of Mind
Edited by Samuel Guttenplan

A Companion to Metaphysics
Edited by Jaegwon Kim and Ernest Sosa

A Companion to Philosophy of Law and Legal Theory
Edited by Dennis Patterson

A Companion to Philosophy of Religion
Edited by Philip L. Quinn and Charles Taliaferro

A Companion to the Philosophy of Language
Edited by Bob Hale and Crispin Wright

A Companion to World Philosophies
Edited by Eliot Deutsch and Ron Bontekoe

A Companion to Continental Philosophy
Edited by Simon Critchley and William Schroeder

A Companion to Feminist Philosophy
Edited by Alison M. Jaggar and Iris Marion Young

A Companion to Cognitive Science
Edited by William Bechtel and George Graham

A Companion to Bioethics
Edited by Helga Kuhse and Peter Singer

A Companion to the Philosophers
Edited by Robert L. Arrington

A Companion to Business Ethics
Edited by Robert E. Frederick

A Companion to the Philosophy of Science
Edited by W. H. Newton-Smith

A Companion to Environmental Philosophy
Edited by Dale Jamieson

Forthcoming:

A Companion to African American Philosophy
Edited by Tommy Lott and John Pittman

A Companion to African Philosophy
Edited by Kwasi Wiredu

A Companion to Genethics
Edited by John Harris and Justine Burley

A Companion to Ancient Philosophy
Edited by Mary Louise Gill

A Companion to Analytic Philosophy
Edited by A. P. Martinich and David Sosa

A Companion to Early Modern Philosophy
Edited by Steven Nadler

A Companion to Philosophical Logic
Edited by Dale Jacquette

A Companion to Medieval Philosophy
Edited by Jorge J. E. Gracia, Greg Reichberg, and Timothy Noone

Blackwell Companions to Philosophy

A Companion to Environmental Philosophy

Edited by
DALE JAMIESON

Copyright © Blackwell Publishers Ltd 2001

First published 2001

2 4 6 8 10 9 7 5 3 1

Blackwell Publishers Inc.
350 Main Street
Malden, Massachusetts 02148
USA

Blackwell Publishers Ltd
108 Cowley Road
Oxford OX4 1JF
UK

Library of Congress Cataloging-in-Publication Data

A companion to environmental philosophy / [Dale Jamieson, editor].
        p.cm.—(Blackwell companions to philosophy)
    Includes bibliographical references and index.
    ISBN 1–55786–910–3 (alk. paper)
    1. Environmental sciences—Philosophy. I. Jamieson, Dale.   II. Series.

    GE40 .C66 2000
    363.7′001—dc21   00–039772

British Library Cataloguing in Publication Data
A CIP catalogue record for this book is available from the British Library.

Typeset in 10 on 12.5pt Photina
by Kolam Information Services Pvt Ltd. Pondicherry, India
Printed in Great Britain by TJ International, Padstow, Cornwall

This book is printed on acid-free paper.

For Richard Sylvan

In Memoriam

Contents

List of contributors   x

Preface   xv

PART I: CULTURAL TRADITIONS   1

1 Indigenous perspectives   3
LAURIE ANNE WHITT, MERE ROBERTS, WAERETE NORMAN, AND VICKI GRIEVES

2 Classical China   21
KARYN L. LAI

3 Classical India   37
O. P. DWIVEDI

4 Jainism and Buddhism   52
CHRISTOPHER KEY CHAPPLE

5 The classical Greek tradition   67
GABRIELA R. CARONE

6 Judaism   81
ERIC KATZ

7 Christianity   96
ROBIN ATTFIELD

8 Islam   111
S. NOMANUL HAQ

9 Early modern philosophy   130
CHARLES TALIAFERRO

10 Nineteenth- and twentieth-century philosophy   146
ANDREW BRENNAN

PART II: CONTEMPORARY ENVIRONMENTAL ETHICS   161

11 Meta-ethics   163
JOHN O'NEILL

12 Normative ethics   177
ROBERT ELLIOT

13   **Sentientism**   192
     GARY VARNER

14   **The land ethic**   204
     J. BAIRD CALLICOTT

15   **Deep ecology**   218
     FREYA MATHEWS

16   **Ecofeminism**   233
     VICTORIA DAVION

PART III: ENVIRONMENTAL PHILOSOPHY AND ITS NEIGHBORS   249

17   **Literature**   251
     SCOTT SLOVIC

18   **Aesthetics**   264
     JOHN ANDREW FISHER

19   **Economics**   277
     A. MYRICK FREEMAN III

20   **History**   291
     IAN SIMMONS

21   **Ecology**   304
     KRISTIN SHRADER-FRECHETTE

22   **Politics**   316
     ROBYN ECKERSLEY

23   **Law**   331
     SHEILA JASANOFF

PART IV: PROBLEMS IN ENVIRONMENTAL PHILOSOPHY   347

24   **Wilderness**   349
     MARK WOODS

25   **Population**   362
     CLARK WOLF

26   **Future generations**   377
     ERNEST PARTRIDGE

27   **Sustainability**   390
     ALAN HOLLAND

28   **Biodiversity**   402
     HOLMES ROLSTON III

29   **Animals**   416
     PETER SINGER

30 **Environmental justice**   **426**
ROBERT FIGUEROA AND CLAUDIA MILLS

31 **Technology**   **439**
LORI GRUEN

32 **Climate**   **449**
HENRY SHUE

33 **Land and water**   **460**
PAUL B. THOMPSON

34 **Consumption**   **473**
MARK SAGOFF

35 **Colonization**   **486**
KEEKOK LEE

36 **Environmental disobedience**   **498**
NED HETTINGER

Index   **510**

Contributors

Robin Attfield is Professor of Philosophy at Cardiff University, Philosophy Section, ENCAP, Cardiff University, P.O. Box 94, Cardiff CF10 3XB, United Kingdom. He has also taught in several places in Africa. His books include *The Ethics of Environmental Concern* (1983 and 1991), *Environmental Philosophy: Principles and Prospects* (1994), *Value, Obligation and Meta-Ethics* (1995), and *The Ethics of the Global Environment* (1999). He can be contacted on the internet at attfieldr@cardiff.ac.uk.

Andrew Brennan is Professor of Philosophy at the University of Western Australia, Perth, WA 6907, Australia. His most recent book is *Philosophical Dialogues: Arne Naess and the Progress of Ecophilosophy* (1999), co-edited with Nina Witoszek. He is presently working on a book on animals, ethics, and science. He can be contacted on the internet at abrennan@cyllene.uwa.edu.au.

J. Baird Callicott is Professor of Philosophy and Religion Studies at the University of North Texas, Denton, TX 76203. He is editor or author of a dozen books and more than a hundred book chapters, journal articles, and book reviews in environmental philosophy, the most recent of which is *Beyond the Land Ethic: More Essays in Environmental Philosophy* (1999). He can be contacted on the internet at callicott@unt.edu.

Gabriela R. Carone is Assistant Professor of philosophy at the University of Colorado at Boulder, CB 232, Boulder, CO 80309. She has published in both Spanish and English on Plato's cosmology and its relation to his ethics together with its impact on Neoplatonism. She has also published various articles on the moral philosophy of Socrates. Carone is working on a book on Plato's cosmology in relation to his ethics. She can be contacted on the internet at carone@stripe.colorado.edu.

Christopher Key Chapple is Professor of Theological Studies and Director of Asian and Pacific Studies at Loyola Marymount University, 7900 Loyola Blvd, Los Angeles, CA 90045. He has published eight books and is the editor of two forthcoming volumes: *Hinduism and Ecology* and *Jainism and Ecology*. He can be contacted on the internet at cchapple@lmu.edu. His home page is clawww.lmu.edu/faculty/cchapple/cchapple.html.

Victoria Davion is Associate Professor of Philosophy at the University of Georgia, Athens, GA 30602. She is the founding and current editor of the international journal *Ethics and the Environment* and is co-editor (with Clark Wolf) of *The Idea of a Political Liberalism: Essays on Rawls* (1999). She can be contacted on the internet at vdavion@arches.uga.edu.

O. P. Dwivedi is Professor of Public and Environmental Administration at the University of Guelph, Guelph, Ontario, Canada, N1G 2W1. He has published 29 books and many articles in refereed journals and chapters in books, and is a Fellow of the Royal Society of Canada. He can be contacted on the internet at odwivedi@uoguelph.ca.

Robyn Eckersley teaches in the School of Political and Social Inquiry, Monash University, Wellington Road, Clayton 3168, Victoria, Australia. She has published widely in the fields of environmental philosophy, green political theory, and environmental policy. She can be contacted on the internet at robyn. eckersley@arts.monash.edu.au.

Robert Elliot is Professor of Philosophy at University of the Sunshine Coast, Maroochydore DC, Queensland, Australia. He is the author of *Faking Nature* (1997). He can be contacted on the internet at elliot @usc.edu.au.

Robert Figueroa is Visiting Assistant Professor at Colgate University, 13 Oak Drive, Hamilton, NY 13346. He is currently working on comparative studies of environmental justice between global and domestic contexts, and is developing theoretical components of social justice on issues of climate affairs. He can be contacted on the internet at rfigueroa @mail.colgate.edu.

John Andrew Fisher is Professor of Philosophy at the University of Colorado at Boulder, CB 232, Boulder, CO 80309. He is the author of *Reflecting on Art* (1992). He has also written articles about animal minds and anthropomorphism and articles on various aesthetic themes, including rock music,

the ontology of recordings, and the aesthetics of nature. He can be contacted on the internet at jafisher@spot.colorado .edu.

A. Myrick Freeman III is William D. Shipman Research Professor at Bowdoin College, Department of Economics, 9700 College Station, Brunswick, Maine 04011. *The Economic Approach to Environmental Policy* (1998) is a selection of his essays. He can be contacted on the internet at rfreeman@bowdoin. edu.

Lori Gruen is Assistant Professor of Philosophy at Wesleyan University, 350 High Street, Middletown, CT 06459. She can be reached on the internet at lgruen@wesleyan.edu.

S. Nomanul Haq is Assistant Professor in the Department of Religion, Rutgers University, New Brunswick, NJ 08901, and a visiting scholar at the University of Pennsylvania in Philadelphia. He is General Editor of the Studies in Islamic Philosophy of Oxford University Press, and is currently working on Arabic metaphysical texts. Haq can be contacted on the internet at nomanhaq@rci. rutgers.edu.

Ned Hettinger teaches social, political, and environmental philosophy at the College of Charleston, Charleston, SC 29424. He is currently writing a book about respect for nature's autonomy that allows for a positive role for humans in nature. He can be contacted on the internet at hettingern@cofc.edu. His home page is http://www.cofc.edu/ ~philo/dept.htg/hettinger.htm.

Alan Holland is Professor of Applied Philosophy at Lancaster University, Furness College, Lancaster University,

Lancaster, LA1 4YG, United Kingdom, and is editor of *Environmental Values*. He recently co-edited *Animal Biotechnology and Ethics* (1998). He is a newly appointed member of the UK government's Animal Procedures Committee. He can be contacted on the internet at a.holland@lancaster. ac.uk.

Sheila Jasanoff is Professor of Science and Public Policy at Harvard University's John F. Kennedy School of Government, 79 John F. Kennedy Street, Cambridge, MA 02138. She is currently completing a book on biotechnology regulation in Europe and the USA. She can be contacted on the internet at sheila_jasanoff@ harvard.edu.

Eric Katz is Associate Professor of Philosophy and Director of the Science, Technology, and Society Program at the New Jersey Institute of Technology, University Heights, Newark, NJ 07102–1982. He has been an invited speaker at the United Nations and is the author of *Nature as Subject* (1997) and editor of *Environmental Pragmatism* (1996) and *Beneath the Surface: Critical Essays in the Philosophy of Deep Ecology* (2000). He can be contacted on the internet at katze@admin. njit.edu.

Karyn L. Lai lectures at the School of Philosophy at the University of New South Wales, PO Box 1, NSW 2052, Australia. She works in moral philosophy, applied ethics, environmental ethics, and Confucian and Daoist philosophy. She can be contacted on the internet at K.Lai@unsw.edu.au.

Keekok Lee is with the Philosophy Department, in a research position, at the University of Lancaster, Furness College, Lancaster University, Lancaster, LA1 4YG, United Kingdom. Her most recent book is *The Natural and the Artefactual: The Implications of Deep Science and Deep Technology for Environmental Philosophy* (1999). She can be contacted on the internet at keekok.lee@man. ac.uk.

Freya Mathews is Senior Lecturer in the School of Philosophy at La Trobe University, Bundoora VIC, 3083, Australia. Her most recent book is *Ecology and Democracy* (1996), and she is currently developing a theory of ecological "countermodernity." She can be contacted on the internet at philosophy @latrobe. edu.au. Her homepage is http://www. latrobe.edu.au/www/philosophy/.

Claudia Mills is Associate Professor of Philosophy at the University of Colorado at Boulder, CN 232, Boulder, CO 80309–0232. She writes on a wide range of topics in ethics, practical ethics, and social and political philosophy, and is also the author of 30 books for children. She can be contacted on the internet at cmills@colorado.edu.

John O'Neill is Professor of Philosophy at Lancaster University, Furness College, Lancaster, LA1 4YG, United Kingdom, before which he taught in Beijing and Sussex. His books include *The Market: Ethics, Knowledge and Politics* (1998) and *Ecology, Policy and Politics* (1993). He is currently working on a research project on the environmental dimensions of the socialist calculation debates. He can be contacted on the internet at j.oneill@ lancaster.ac.uk.

Ernest Partridge is a Research Philosopher at the University of California – Riverside, 900 University Ave., Riverside,

CA 92521, where he is currently studying ecological theory and ethics with a grant from the National Science Foundation. He can be contacted on the internet at gadfly@igc.org. His homepage is http://www.igc.org/gadfly.

Holmes Rolston III is University Distinguished Professor and Professor of Philosophy at Colorado State University, Fort Collins, CO 80523. His most recent book is *Genes, Genesis and God* (1999). He gave the Gifford Lectures at the University of Edinburgh in 1997–8. He can be contacted on the internet at rolston@lamar.colostate.edu. His homepage is http://lamar.colostate.edu/~rolston/.

Mark Sagoff is Senior Research Scholar at the Institute for Philosophy and Public Policy in the School of Public Affairs, 3111 Van Munching Hall, College Park, MD 20742. He is the author of *The Economy of the Earth* (1988) and has served as President of the International Society for Environmental Ethics. He can be reached on the internet at ms2@umail.umd.edu.

Kristin Shrader-Frechette is O'Neill Family Chair, Professor of Philosophy, and Concurrent Professor of Biological Sciences at the University of Notre Dame, Notre Dame, Indiana, 46556. Most of her 14 books and 280 articles are on quantitative risk assessment, philosophy of science, and environmental ethics. With Swedish physicist Lars Persson, she currently has a multi-year NSF grant to examine ethical and scientific problems with workplace standards for ionizing radiation. She can be contacted on the internet at kristin.shrader-frechette.1@nd.edu. Her home page is http://www.nd.edu/~kshrader.

Henry Shue is the Wyn and William Y. Hutchinson Professor of Ethics and Public Life, and Professor of Philosophy, at Cornell University in Ithaca, NY 14853–2801. Best-known for *Basic Rights* (1996), he has also recently written a series of ten articles on climate change and international justice. He can be contacted on the internet at hs23@cornell.edu.

Ian Simmons is a part-time Professor in the Department of Geography in the University of Durham, Durham DH1 3HP, United Kingdom. He has recently written an environmental history of Great Britain in the last 10,000 years and will soon embark on a similar book about the world. He can be contacted on the internet at i.g.simmons@durham.ac.uk.

Peter Singer is DeCamp Professor of Bioethics at Princeton University, Princeton, NJ 08544. His books include *Animal Liberation* (1990), *Practical Ethics* (1993), *How Are We to Live?* (1995), *Rethinking Life and Death* (1995), and *Ethics into Action* (1998).

Scott Slovic is Associate Professor of Literature and the Environment, and Director of the Center for Environmental Arts and Humanities at the University of Nevada – Reno, Reno, Nevada, 89557. He was the founding president of the Association for the Study of Literature and Environment, and currently he serves as editor of the journal *ISLE: Interdisciplinary Studies in Literature and Environment*. He can be contacted on the internet at slovic@unr.edu.

Charles Taliaferro is Professor of Philosophy and a member of the Environmental Studies Faculty at St. Olaf College, Northfield, MN 55057. His most recent book is *Contemporary*

Philosophy of Religion (1998), and he is the co-editor of the *Blackwell Companion to the Philosophy of Religion* (1998). He can be contacted on the internet at taliafer@stolaf.edu.

Paul B. Thompson holds the Joyce and Edward E. Brewer Chair of Applied Ethics at Purdue University, West Lafayette, IN 47907. Most recently, he co-edited a collection of essays called *The Agrarian Roots of Pragmatism*. He is starting the Center for Food Animal Productivity and Well-Being at Purdue which will examine issues of animal welfare within a livestock production context. He can be contacted on the internet at pault @purdue.edu.

Laurie Anne Whitt teaches philosophy in the Humanities Department at Michigan Technological University, Houghton, MI. **Mere Roberts** teaches Maori Environmental Perspectives at the School of Environmental and Marine Sciences, University of Auckland, New Zealand. **Waerete Norman** teaches Maori language and culture in the Maori Studies Department, University of Auckland, New Zealand. **Vicki Grieves** teaches Aboriginal history at Macquarie University, Sydney, NSW, Australia. They are, respectively, of Choctaw, Tainui (Ngati Apakura), Muriwhenua (Ngati Kuri), and Worimi-Kattang descent.

Clark Wolf is Associate Professor of Philosophy at the University of Georgia, Athens, GA 30602. He is currently writing a book on justice between generations. He can be contacted on the internet at cwolf@uga.edu. His home page is http://www.phil.uga.edu/faculty/wolf/.

Mark Woods is Assistant Professor in the Department of Philosophy at the University of San Diego, 5998 Alcala Park, San Diego, CA 92110–2492. Currently, he is writing a book on the concept of wilderness and the philosophy of wilderness preservation. He can be contacted on the internet at mwoods@acusd.edu.

Gary Varner is Associate Professor in the Department of Philosophy at Texas A&M University, College Station, Texas, 77843–4237. He is the author of *In Nature's Interests? Interests, Animal Rights, and Environmental Ethics* (1998) and numerous articles on environmental ethics, animal rights, and environmental law. He can be contacted on the internet at g-varner@tamu.edu. His home page is http://www-phil.tamu.edu/~gary/index.html.

Preface

The late French director, François Truffaut, once said that every time he begins a project he hopes that it will turn out to be the best film ever made; halfway through, he wants only to finish the movie with his sanity intact. For me, commissioning and editing 36 new essays in environmental philosophy was a little like that. However, I still harbor the hope that this is the best single volume collection on the subject that is currently available.

The first environmental philosophy courses were offered in the 1970s, and over the last two decades they have steadily proliferated. Nearly every university and college in North America, Britain, and Australia now offers at least one class in environmental philosophy. Through most of the 1980s good materials were hard to find for use in these courses but in the last three years more than a half dozen new environmental philosophy anthologies have been published. Several of these anthologies are excellent, but since they mainly reprint articles published in professional journals they are fundamentally different from this book.

After an anarchic quarter century, environmental philosophy has yet to become fully defined as a field. Indeed, it probably has more than its share of divisions and academic infighting. My purpose in editing this volume is both to present a snapshot of the field as it currently exists, and to contribute to consolidating the field. I have been guided by the following principles. First, I have tried to be as inclusive as possible, presenting the rich diversity of work characteristic of this field. Second, I have tried to bring environmental philosophy into conversation with other fields and disciplines such as economics, ecology, and law. Third, I have been concerned to connect environmental philosophy to the cultural traditions from which it springs. Fourth, I have tried to keep a firm focus on the environmental problems that motivate the enterprise in the first place. Finally, without neglecting my editorial responsibilities, I have tried to let the contributors speak in their own voices to the greatest extent possible. My hope is that this book will be used as a primary text in courses on environmental philosophy, as a secondary text for courses in related fields, and as a reference book for those who are working on related topics. Most of all I hope that this volume finds its way into the hands of readers who simply want to learn something about the subject.

A project like this necessarily involves so many complicated interactions with people that I'm not quite sure whether to have a paragraph of acknowledgements or one with apologies. I'll start with the easy stuff. Carleton College has supported this project in various ways. Thanks to the students who assisted me with this book: Matthew Varilek, Kelly Knutson, and especially Max Wilson, whose work on the proofs, index, and just about everything else relating to this volume went beyond the call of duty. Thanks to Paula Lackie, my computer guru, for turning various virus-infected floppies in obsolete word-processing programs into readable text. The folks at Blackwell, who seduced me into this project, were unfailingly supportive. Thanks especially to Sarah Dancy for her efficient copy-editing, Beth Remmes for her good humor, and Steve Smith for calmly presiding over the proceedings. (The subject of Blackwell reminds me that I should warn the reader that the text is governed by various conventions. Words that appear in small capitals refer to other chapters in the volume explicitly concerned with the topic to which the word refers. I leave it to the reader to decipher the other conventions.) So many of my colleagues in environmental philosophy provided me with helpful advice about who and what should be included in this book that I cannot even begin to acknowledge them here. And obviously, without the contributors, this book would not exist. I thank them all for putting up with a stream of hectoring phone calls and emails, punctuated by long silences, over a several-year period. I especially thank those who responded in a graceful and timely manner, making all of our lives a bit easier. While I feel honored by those who have contributed to this volume, I am also painfully aware that there are many people doing important work in this field who, for various reasons, did not contribute.

I have dedicated this book to Richard Sylvan, formerly Senior Research Fellow in the Research School of Social Sciences at the Australian National University, who died unexpectedly of a heart attack in Bali, Indonesia on June 16, 1996. His 1973 paper, "Is There a Need for a New, an Environmental, Ethic?", originally presented to the Fifteenth World Congress of Philosophy, subsequently published under the name "Richard Routley," marked the beginning of a new field. Not only is Richard's claim to be the founder of this field as strong as anyone's, but he also expressed many of the ideals of environmental philosophy in his life and work. There are many good "Richard stories" around, and I hope that this dedication will prompt those who knew him to pass a few on to those who continue to struggle with fundamental questions about the human relationship with the rest of nature.

Dale Jamieson
Northfield, Minnesota
May 2000

PART I
CULTURAL TRADITIONS

1

Indigenous perspectives

LAURIE ANNE WHITT, MERE ROBERTS, WAERETE NORMAN, AND VICKI GRIEVES

Some years ago, the Cherokee mounted fierce resistance to the construction of the Tellico Dam and the subsequent flooding of the Little Tennessee Valley. Many of their objections were based on the threat it posed to their cultural heritage. Ammoneta Sequoyah, a medicine man who gathered healing plants in the valley, explained that his people believe that all that a person knows is placed in the ground with that person at the time of burial. So flooding the valley, or digging up the Indian graves there, will destroy "the knowledge and beliefs of [the] people who are in the ground" (*Sequoyah* v. *Tennessee Valley Authority*, 1980). It will also destroy what they have taught. Consequently, he believes that if the valley were flooded, he would lose his knowledge of medicine.

That knowledge and land are intimately bound to one another is a belief widely shared among indigenous peoples, as is the accompanying belief that the natural world is alive, spiritually replete. Consider Alice Benally, a Diné woman who expresses the incomprehensibility of her removal from Big Mountain by commenting that in the proposed relocation site the plants and animals would not know her – nor would she know them. She says: "If we are to make our offerings at a new place, the spiritual beings would not know us. We would not know the mountains or the significance of them. We would not know the land and the land would not know us" (in Jenny Manybeads et al. 1989, p. 248). Indeed, in some native languages such relocations are literally unthinkable. There is no term for them; no concept by which they are known.

Knowledge is tied to the natural world in different ways within indigenous and western knowledge systems; so too is knowledge transmission. Ammoneta Sequoyah realizes that if the valley is flooded his *knowledge* of medicine – and not just the medicinal plants themselves – will be lost. This knowledge is the cultural heritage and responsibility of his people. He also realizes that when he is buried this knowledge returns with him to the land in which it is embedded, and so continues to be present within the land for others to experience. This may seem strange to someone deeply committed to certain prevailing convictions in western philosophy and the science which it sustains – e.g. "knowledge of nature is ultimately distinct, and separable from, nature" and "what is known are true propositions about reality." One way of capturing the contrast between such convictions and those of Sequoyah would be to say that western science, western knowledge of the natural world, is representational. Indigenous science, indigenous knowledge of the natural world, is (if Sequoyah's and Benally's comments are taken as typical) presentational. Its continuation, its transmission, its possibility turn vitally upon the presence of the natural world, and on the kind of experiences it offers.

We will say little more about this contrast, for it is the words of Sequoyah and Benally that concern us here. Spoken in the context of specific political struggles, they are not offered primarily as philosophical commentary, or as insight into the environmental ethics of their cultures. Nor should they be heard that way. They are part of political struggle. This essay ends as it begins, by reflecting on them. The words that lie in between belong to many different people(s). If they speak with one voice on any single issue, it may well be this: "We are indigenous people to this land...our brothers are all the natural world...remember that as long as [we] exist, so will you. But when we are gone, you too will go" (Oren Lyons, quoted in Dooling and Smith 1989, p. 274). Why this is so, how this is so, and the significance of granting that it is so, is what this essay relates.

Belonging and genealogical bonds

> *All around me are my ancestors,*
> *my unborn children.*
> *I am the tear between them*
> *and both sides live.*
>   (Linda Hogan)

Indigenous responsibilities to and for the natural world are based on an understanding of the relatedness, or affiliation, of the human and non-human worlds, which is best understood in its primary – genealogical – context. Genealogies provide stories of origins. They tell a person, or a people, where and from whom they are descended. In this sense they bind through time, showing how ancestors and descendants course together through a continuous, unfolding history. Properly told, they set out the changing contours and constitution of families, including how they have branched into and out of one another over time.

Genealogies need not, and for indigenous peoples typically do not, confine themselves to the human. Since they relate origins, they address themselves to specific places, and the non-human beings inhabiting them. So genealogies map affiliations spatially as well, placing individuals and families in relation to one another, and locating them in – by connecting them to – the earth. Insofar as everything has an origin, everything has a genealogy which situates it relationally in time – linking those who have been with those yet to be – and in space – linking everything to a particular place and to everything in that place. In this sense, genealogies are stories of temporal and spatial belonging. They relate how a person or a people belongs in a particular time and place, how the non-human things in that place have come to belong there, and how all of these belong to one another.

A genealogy draws a family or a people together, distinguishing them from others. It also acknowledges that members of a family or clan already are drawn together, and sets out how they are related to others. To recite a genealogy, to recall affiliational ties, is to affirm a reciprocal bonding. It has the powerful function of reminding members of a family or clan of who they are, individually and collectively, and with this of their moral responsibilities to one another.

Genealogies, then, are potent sources of knowledge about the past and present, about the natural world and the beings that inhabit it. Integral aspects of many indigenous cultures, they locate a people spatially, temporally, and spiritually, investing them in certain lands with certain responsibilities at a particular time. They are sources of identity, binding individuals and groups to others, past, present, and to come. They also serve to integrate, and to reflect the integration of, the human and non-human worlds.

The centrality of *whakapapa*, or genealogy, within Maori culture cannot be overstated. The eloquent formal introductions which Maori use to identify themselves by reference to their mountain and river, to their ancestral dwelling place within the tribal landscape, are illustrative. This relationship of the people to the land is expressed through *whakapapa*. To Maori, *whakapapa* is a most fundamental form of knowing; it functions as an epistemological template. Hence, to know something is to locate it in space and time, and knowledge of *whakapapa* is essential to this: "To 'know' oneself is to know one's *whakapapa*. To 'know' about a tree, a rock, the wind, or the fishes in the sea – is to know their *whakapapa*" (Roberts and Wills 1998, p. 45). All beings, human and non-human, share descent; they have the same origin. As Erenora Puketapu-Hetet explains, *harakeke* (flax) "is a descendant of the great god Tane-mahuta . . . today's Maori are related to *harakeke* and all the other plants: Tane is their common ancestor" (1989, p. 18).

Among the peoples of the Andes, a similar sense of the pervasiveness and significance of genealogical bonding is evident. An *ayllu* – a group of related persons who live in a particular place – includes the human and the non-human. It refers to relationships between humans and between "all members of the *Pacha*": "the stars, the sun, the moon, the hills, lakes . . . the plants and animals . . . along with the rocks and the human beings . . . they are all relatives and are at once children, parents, and siblings" (Apffel-Marglin and Rivera 1995, p. 25). Rembarrnga storyteller Paddy Wainburranga relates that talking and singing to the country is "the law for the center of Arnhem Land . . . The law about singing out was made . . . to make you notice that all the trees here are your countrymen, your relations. All the trees and birds are your relations" (1988, p. 46). The depth and intimacy of such affiliational ties is also reflected in the Mayan concept of a *nahual* – a protective spirit, usually an animal, with which every child is born. The *nahual*, according to Rigoberta Menchu, is "the representative of the earth, the animal world, the sun and water, and in this way the child communicates with nature. The *nahual* is our double, something very important to us" (in Hogan et al. 1998, p. 27).

When affiliational bonding among families and clans is broadly conceived, the notion of unbreachable boundaries between the human and non-human worlds has no place. Human animals assume non-human form, and non-humans assume human animal form; it is possible to "become animal, without ceasing to be a person" (Hogan et al. 1998, p. 27). What is not assumed is fundamental difference. The human and non-human interpenetrate: "Aboriginals see themselves as part of nature. We see all things natural as part of us. All the things on Earth we see as part human" (Neidjie 1986, p. 11). Given the interpenetration of the human and non-human, to speak of "pristine wilderness" (land devoid of humans) is to speak of something which does not, did not, and cannot exist, at least not on this planet.

The nature of a genealogy is such that individuals cannot appear in it without thereby assuming relational ties to all others within the genealogy; the Lakota prayer *mitakuye oyasin* ("I am related to all that is") reflects this. It is not possible to exist within genealogies and stand outside such affiliational ties, although one may fail to acknowledge their presence. Nor is it possible to exist in such genealogies and be "outside" of nature: "nature is not something apart from [the Native American . . . it is] an element in which he exists. He has existence within that element, much in the same way that we think of having existence within the element of air" (Momaday 1976, p. 84). An analogous perspective is evident in the Maori tendency to speak of themselves as mountains or rivers: "These cannot be objectified or externalized. They are not 'out there', but 'in here' . . . Maori cannot conceptualize an entity called 'Nature' as something separate from oneself and one's tribal identity" (Roberts and Wills 1998, p. 55). In a clear sense, it is simply not possible to exist outside a genealogy. Hence the psychological, spiritual, and physical trauma of tribal "relocations," which involve the severing of affiliational ties with the non-human world. ("Dislocations" would more accurately describe the wrenching, the pulling out of joint, that is involved in the removals of indigenous peoples from the lands to which they belong.)

The significance of human ties of affiliation with the non-human world is symbolically captured in many indigenous languages and practices. It can be seen in the Mayan custom of burying a newborn's umbilical cord in the parents' house "in the hope that when the baby reaches adulthood he or she will understand the importance of home and the dependence on land" (Chay 1993, p. 21). Or in the analogous Diné practice: "so the child will be familiar with the spiritual beings of the area . . . the woman offers the afterbirth to a young tree and buries the child's umbilical cord in Mother Earth. These things create spiritual ties between us and the land" (Jenny Manybeads et al. 1989, p. 230). It is captured by the Maori term *whenua* (meaning land as well as placenta), and *hapu* (meaning both pregnant and extended family or sub-tribe). The expression *te u kai po* refers to the area where you were brought up; it also means to be breast fed (Roberts et al. 1995, p. 10). As Waerete Norman notes, the burying of *whenua*

> was also seen as helping to sustain the land. The practice of burial reflects the importance of *tiaki whenua* and *tiaki taiao* [caring for the land and environment] to ensure a future sustained by *papatuanuku* [earth mother] . . . *whenua* and placenta is one and the same land. (unpublished ms., p. 136–7)

These practices reveal how crucial affiliational ties between the human and non-human are. As one senior Gumadji clan leader observes:

> Aboriginal belief systems based on affinity to land underpin Aboriginal existence. (Yunupingu 1997, pp. xv–xvi)

We believe the land is all life. We are part of the land and the land is part of us. It cannot be one or the other. We cannot be separated by anything or anybody. (Yunupingu 1996, p. 16)

Such practices affirm the presence and persistence of genealogical bonds which link the human and non-human. They are expressions of human belonging, of the intimate relationship between a people and a land. Aboriginal activist Mick Dodson comments that "our...reason for existence is the land...We have grown the land up...Removed from our lands, we are literally removed from ourselves (in Yunupingu 1997, p. 41). For Maori too, "People belong to earth. Earth is not a possession of the people" (Norman unpublished ms., p. 131).

If a people belongs to a land, and land inheres in a people, it cannot be alienated or disowned. It cannot be reduced to a commodity. It cannot be replaced or done without. Haunani-Kai Trask notes that the Hawaiian language has two ways of showing possession: the "a" possessive indicates acquired status and the "o" possessive indicates inherent status. While most material objects take the "a" form, land – like one's body and one's parents – takes the "o" form: "Thus, in our way of speaking, land is inherent to the people; it is like our bodies and our parents. The people cannot exist without the land, and the land cannot exist without the people" (1993, p. 152). A comparable observation is made by Aboriginal author Bill Neidjie:

> So I'm saying now,
> earth is my mother or father...
> Tree is mine.
> In my body that tree.
> (1989, p. 170)

And for Maori "land was not something that could be owned or traded. [They] did not seek to own or possess anything, but to belong. One belonged to a family that belonged to a hapu that belonged to a tribe. One did not own land. One belonged *to* the land" (Eddie Durie, in Phillips 1987, p. 78).

When possession or ownership is understood as an inherent, rather than acquired, status, the term "belong" becomes especially apt. To belong to land is to be attached or bound to it by birth, by allegiance, and by dependence. The resulting relationship of belonging may be characterized as one of intimacy, or inherency. The land is involved in the constitution of a people. It characterizes them, as they do it:

> The relationship between the crocodile and myself and all my clansmen is a very special relationship...I see a crocodile as an animal that is part of me and I belong to him, he belongs to me. It's a commonness of land ownership...Crocodile, he's the creator and the land giver to the Gumatj people...we have always treated crocodile in a way that it is part of a family. (Galarrwuy Yunupingu, in Watson and Chambers 1989, p. 26)

The land and living entities which make it up are not apart from, but part of, the people. Nor is "the environment" something surrounding a people. The relation of belonging is ontologically basic.

With inherent possession, agency is sometimes held to be reciprocal – a people belongs to/owns the land, and the land belongs to/owns a people. Sometimes it is the inverse of that implied by acquired possession – while a people belongs to the land or the land owns a people, a people do not own land nor does land belong to a people. Several Maori commentators, for example, reject the notion of stewardship as a translation of the term *kaitiaki* because it connotes guarding someone else's property: "ownership of property was a foreign concept . . . the earth did not belong to man, but rather man belonged to the earth" (Roberts et al. 1995, p. 14). Dell Wihongi concurs: "It is wrong to think that we humans act as '*kaitiaki*' (guardians) of nature . . . The earth *kaitiaki*'s us" (ibid, p. 14). According to the Muriwhenua Land Report: "Maori saw themselves as users of the land rather than its owners. While their use must equate with ownership for the purpose of English law, they saw themselves not as owning the land but as being owned by it" (1997, p. 23).

Belonging or inherent possession is the type of relationship that genealogical bonds affirm. As such, it endures; it does not cease to be as the result of "removals," nor is it ended by death. Progenitors and progeny continue to belong to, to inhere in, one another. When the constancy of affiliational ties is conjoined to widespread beliefs regarding the cyclical nature of time and of the natural order, the full sense of Linda Hogan's words at the start of this section becomes plain. It is a theme taken up by Darcy Nicholas as well:

> Nothing dies in the Maori world. Things merely move through different dimensions – the flax, for example, becomes a cloak of immense beauty. Those we love become part of the beautiful land around us. This is our bond with the land. It is our ancestor and as such part and parcel of what we are. It has sustained the life of our people for hundreds of years. (1980, p. 32)

Beholdenness and reciprocal relations

Because genealogies affirm affiliational ties that exist between individual beings and between generations, they also establish moral bonds. Individual beings are situated within a family, within a generation, and within a land filled with other beings – human and non-human. Genealogically embedded individuals are bound, and answerable, to one another. At the most fundamental level, they are responsible for one another, ontologically and morally.

The moral implications of genealogical bonding are expressed directly in the system of *gurrutu* embraced by the Yolngu people: "these precise relationships are those of kinship and thus entail certain obligations and responsibilities: certain types of beholdenness like those of sister to brother or parent to child" (Watson and Chambers 1989, p. 36). A stranger with whom Yolngu expect prolonged contact will be given a Yolngu name and instructed in his or her genealogical relations: "To be a 'real' entity in Yolngu life, a person or place must be named, and thus located within the genealogical order" (ibid). One of the most important functions of the *gurrutu* system is that it brings orderliness to individual and group relations, to the land and to everything in the Yolngu world: "At a general level, it is a formally articulated system of beholdenness: it orders degrees and types of indebtedness" (ibid, p. 37).

Such beholdenness is decidedly not limited to the human. The Lakota speak of the *Nagila* "that dwells in everything...[part of the] force that makes all things and beings relatives to each other and to their common ancestor" (Arthur Amiotte, in Dooling and Smith 1989, p. 171). This common ancestry of the human and non-human grounds Maori responsibilities of care, or guardianship, toward the environment and the ancestors:

> Everybody on this planet has a role to play as a guardian [*kaitiaki*]...to be a *kaitiaki* means looking after one's own blood and bones – literally. One's *whanaunga* (relatives) and *tupuna* (ancestors) include the plants and animals, rocks and trees. We are all descended from *Papatuanuku* (Earth Mother); she is our *kaitiaki* and we in turn are hers. (Carmen Kirkwood, in Roberts et al. 1995, p. 13)

Guardianship is a moral responsibility, an appropriate response to a sense of beholdenness in the presence of genealogical relatedness. It is the acknowledgement of a people that they are held by, and endebted to, their affiliational ties with the non-human world. These ties are as much prescriptive as descriptive; they suggest ways in which it is appropriate, or inappropriate, to behave. This idea of "appropriateness," Kiowa writer M. Scott Momaday suggests, "is central to the Indian experience of the natural world...[it] is a moral idea...a basic understanding of right within the framework of relationship" (1976, p. 82).

Like beholdenness, the moral responsibilities of genealogically-imbedded individuals also extend temporally beyond the present to include past and future generations. As the *Bining*, the community of traditional owners of the Kakadu National Park, have noted: "A main part of traditional culture is that *Bining* are responsible for caring for country – a responsibility with important obligations to past, current and future generations of traditional owners" (Kakadu 1996, p. 16). First Nations author Lee Maracle (1988, pp. 8–9) acknowledges this openly:

> I do know
> that the farther backward
> in time that I travel
> the more grandmothers
> and the farther forward
> the more grandchildren.
> I am obligated to both.

The injunction to act always to protect the seventh generation is a particularly compelling example of this. Onondaga spiritual leader Oren Lyons observes that the first mandate of traditional Haudenosaunee chiefs is to ensure that their decision-making is guided by consideration of the welfare and well-being of the seventh generation to come: "What about that seventh generation? Where are you taking them? What will they have?" (1980, p. 174). The seventh generation principle applies to the ancestors as well. In honoring the ancestors, one expresses gratitude to them as the seventh generation, which they kept foremost in their decision-making and for whom they sacrificed. As a general injunction to live responsibly and respectfully, and as a practical guide to specific moral decision-making, the seventh generation principle may be without equal:

> We say that the faces of the coming generations are looking up from the earth. So when you put your feet down, you put them down very carefully – because there are generations coming one after the other. If you think in these terms, then you'll walk a lot more carefully, be more respectful of this earth. (Lyons 1995)

Genealogical bonds are normative bonds, generating moral responsibilities to the natural world and the living beings it sustains; they give rise to "reciprocal relations" which define "responsibilities...between humans and the ecosystem" (LaDuke 1994, p. 128). Relations of reciprocity involve mutual exchange or co-respondence, something that is shared, felt, and shown by both (or all) sides. While one may be in such relations without responding, or acknowledging them, one remains beholden to them. There is no escaping the fact of interdependency, even when the attendant obligation of reciprocity is ignored. In the words of April Bright (1995): "It is part of our responsibility [to be] looking after our country. If you don't look after country, country won't look after you" (p. 59).

Within Australia, the term "traditional owners" is frequently used to designate the relationship between diverse Aboriginal communities and their homelands, although the English understanding of "ownership" is very different from the Arrernte term, *pmere-k-artweye*, used to translate it. The latter acknowledges the custodial role responsibilities of indigenous peoples and the genealogical-embeddedness on which they rely. *Pmere-k-artweye* refers to those with "inherited or acquired responsibilities for the proper care and treatment of a site," with "the rights to speak for that site and determine what constitutes proper use" of it (Wilkins 1993, p. 24). The Arrernte words for "the ancestors" ("those who have primary responsibility for looking after us properly") and for "parents" ("those who have primary responsibility for looking after a child properly") are linguistically parallel (ibid). As guardians, the Arrernte are charged with protecting and maintaining the lands they co-inhabit with the other beings that constitute the natural world.

That the human and non-human worlds are bound by relations of reciprocity has significant implications for appreciating the role responsibilities of indigenous peoples. They are obligated to provide their lands with sustenance, to sustain them by means of practices and ceremonies (and if needed, by protest and resistance), even as the land sustains them. Speaking from a Bundjalung perspective, Pauline Gordon notes:

> Aboriginal people dance the corroboree...they're doing a traditional thing – they're making something happen. So they dance and sing, and as they dance their powers dance up. The spirit of the land replenishes the land, all the animals...And it comes from the land, that power...that's why for Aboriginal people it's our obligation to protect the land, those sacred sites – it's our life. And our Law. (Ishtar 1994, p. 9)

Assuming responsibility for a sacred site involves being responsible for maintaining the power of the site, tending it, through observance of proper ceremonies (Thornton 1996, p. 11). One aboriginal man acknowledges that the Bandhamarr track is his track . . . his responsibility. He has to know the route and the purposes of following it in the order he takes – in the footsteps of the ancestors. He has to maintain it by acting in accordance with this knowledge, following practices and performing ceremonies in the course of everyday life. (in ibid, p. 20)

What such spirituality secures for the natural world is health, balance, and survival – the holding of disintegration at bay (ibid, p. 15). This, in turn, is what the natural world secures for its people. Maori lawyer Moana Jackson remarks that among the duties of traditional Maori law was "the ancestrally defined responsibility to maintain order and protect the land by ensuring a balance between the interlinked animal, plant, spirit and human worlds" (1988, p. 40).

The reciprocity of human and non-human relations, the mutuality of beholdenness, is aptly expressed by Jake Swamp's account of how the Mohawk are trained to gather medicinal herbs:

> What I was taught was that when you see that plant, to first see that it's the one you offer thanksgiving to, that plant is still here with us, still performing its duty and that you wish it to continue. You walk past it and you look for the other one, and that one you can pick. For if you take that first one, who is to know, maybe that's the last one that exists in the world. (Quoted in Barreiro 1992, p. 21)

Humans may, of course, interfere with a plant's, or the planet's, ability to continue performing its duty. Given the reciprocity of relations, however, when country is treated improperly and desecrated, the natural world becomes unbalanced and all within it are affected. For the Mayans, because every human has an animal counterpart and every animal has a human counterpart, to harm one is simultaneously to harm the other (Hogan et al. 1998, p. 27). Laguna Pueblo author Leslie Silko makes a comparable point:

> According to the elders, destruction of any part of the earth does immediate harm to all living things. Teachers at Indian School would ridicule these ideas; they would laugh and say, "how stupid you Indians are! How can the death of one tree in the jungle possibly affect a person in NYC? But isn't it far more obvious these days *how* important that single tree in the rain forest of Brazil is to the Manhattanite? (1996, pp. 131–2)

However desecrated a place, a people's custodial responsibilities remain. No matter how damaged, the land retains its power and significance:

> RF: the place that they've smashed to pieces, is it still a *tywerrenge* for you, is it still sacred to you?
> MC: It's gotta be. It's a *tywerrenge*, a sacred place right down to and inside the ground. It was created that way. (Wilkins 1993, p. 73)

The perspective from another people in another hemisphere is the same, warning of the danger of valuing only the "pristine" and of recognizing only some places as sacred:

No part of the earth is expendable... Those who claim to love and protect the Mother Earth have to love all of her, even the places that are no longer pristine. *Ma ah shra true ee*, the giant serpent messenger, chose the edge of the uranium mining tailings at Jackpile Mine for his reappearance; he was making this point when he chose that unlikely location. (Silko 1996, pp. 94–5)

The contrast between country that has been cared for by its people and country that has been either neglected or abused is captured by a Ngarinman distinction between "quiet" and "wild" country. Daly Pulkara, one of the senior custodians of Ngarinman land allocated by the Australian government to pastoral leaseholders for many years, was asked what he called the heavily cattle-eroded area:

He looked at it for a while and said, "It's the wild, just the wild"... where life is absent, where all the care, intelligence and respect that generations of Aboriginal people have put into the country have been eradicated in a matter of a few short years. (in Rose 1988, p. 386)

Quiet country is tame, domesticated: "country in which those who know how to read the signs see human action of the most responsible sort" (ibid). Frank Gurrmanamana, a Gidgingali man, had a similar response while visiting Australia's capital city. What he found in Canberra was barrenness and disorder. He said that once long ago, "Aborigines had lived there and that they would have known these attributes of the land which still existed somewhere, but that now, in his own words, 'this country bin lose 'im Dreaming.' He was disturbed by this" (in Donaldson and Donaldson 1985, p. 207).

The state of a land that has lost its guardians, and of a people who have lost their land, are comparable: abandonment and banishment. The words of Mary Tall Mountain (quoted in Hobson 1979, pp. 404–5) bring the two together – the last wolf in an abandoned city and an Athabascan Indian woman alone in an empty hospital room:

> the last wolf hurried toward me
> through the ruined city...
> baying his way eastward...
> through clutter and rubble of quiet blocks
>
> I heard his voice ascending the hill
> and at last his low whine as he came
> floor by empty floor to the room
> where I sat
> in my narrow bed looking west, waiting....
>
> he laid his long gray muzzle
> on the spare white spread
> and his eyes burned yellow
>   his small dotted eyebrows quivered
>
> Yes, I said,
> I know what they have done.

Respect, or the wish-to-be-appreciated

Truganinny, the last of the Tasmanians, had seen the stuffed and mounted body of her husband and it was her dying wish that she be buried in the outback or at sea for she did not wish her body to be subjected to the same indignities. Upon her death she was nevertheless stuffed and mounted and put on display for over eighty years. (Paul Coe, Aboriginal Activist)

We have seen that the genealogical bonds joining human to human, and human to non-human, have both descriptive and normative aspects. The concept of belonging helps to demonstrate the full significance of the former, while the notion of beholdenness captures the normative implications of relatedness. Since genealogical bonds acknowledge relations of reciprocity, they entail mutual obligations and responsibilities. They recognize that beings are related and endebted to one another, and are to respond to one another in ways which respect that fact. We can turn now to the concept of respect, the central and perhaps single most widely shared moral principle among indigenous peoples. The Iroquois also refer to it as the "wish-to-be-appreciated", the "fundamental shared perception – the first principle – of existence. As long as everything is appreciated for what it does and what it shares to sustain the cycles of Creation, the world will be in balance and life will continue" (Barreiro 1992, p. 28). It actively informs a vast number of diverse practices, teachings, and beliefs regarding how the natural world and its constituent beings are to be treated.

Respect, in this context, is best understood as a matter of appreciating the inherent value of some entity or activity, the value it has by virtue of the fact that it inheres in, or belongs to, the natural world. This involves realizing the vital role it plays in sustaining the natural world. "No part of the earth," Silko reminds us, "is expendable." To realize that (and how) some individual or group is integral to the completeness and continuation of the whole, and to appreciate that its contribution to the natural world is indispensable, requires intimate knowledge, familiarity with it. Respect consists of a continuum of behaviors informed by such knowledge, and ranges from avoiding inappropriate treatment of something to responding to it in ways that actively maintain its ability to continue performing its vital function.

Knowledge or familiarity may come from prolonged, intimate contact with a being or a place. The Diné translatation of "sense of place," *keʼtlʼóoʼl*, implies a rootedness in the earth, a familiarity "that breeds respect and symbiosis rather than contempt and exploitation" (Semken 1997, p. 2). Such familiarity extends to non-human beings. Kee Shay speaks of "the land where we are known": "Here on our land we are familiar with the springs, rocks, mountains, hills, etc., they are familiar with us...each day I come to know my relatives here a little better" (in Jenny Manybeads et al. 1989, pp. 228, 239).

Alternatively, the simple awareness of relatedness may ground respect. Among the Cree, for example, one of the main reasons for showing respect to game animals is that humans and non-humans are related. While respect involves avoiding acts that degrade or ignore the integral value of game, it also involves performing acts that reflect and sustain that value. The reciprocal relations between geese and hunters are honored by the practice of *pwaatikswaau*, or smoking to the game, which expresses gratitude for the gift of geese. When the hunter is successful and a goose falls, "the gift is respectfully admired by the hunter and later received as a guest into the lodge by the women of the hunter's household" (Scott 1996, p. 82).

That respect for the land involves acknowledgement of reciprocity and active observance of certain ritual activities is also evident in the practices of Andean peoples. The expression *"criar y dejarse criar"* ("to nurture and let oneself be nurtured") forms the basis of agricultural activities. According to Modesto Machaca (Apffel-Marglin 1995), to open a *chacra* "I must ask permission of the *Pachamama* so that she will allow me to work this soil. . . . I tell her that I will cultivate this soil with love, without mistreatment and the fruits she gives me we will all eat" (quoted in Apffel-Marglin and Rivera 1995, p. 25). All the activities that go on in the *chacra* (sowing, weeding, hilling, harvesting, and even the storage, transformation, and consumption of harvested products) are ritual activities that embrace and cultivate relatedness. These rituals express the Andeans' attitude of love, respect, and gratitude to the earth for its gifts, including the gifts of knowledge regarding how to cultivate a *chacra*. Cultivating a *chacra* is a reciprocal activity, necessarily involving both humans and the land. In this sense, Andean agricultural knowledge itself is tied or tethered to the land, or better perhaps, generated from it:

> To raise a *chacra* is not merely to domesticate plants and animals; it is to nurture lovingly and respectfully, in other words, to nurture ritually, together with plants and animals, the soils, waters, micro-climates and, in general, the whole land. (ibid, p. 24)

Given the affiliational ties that bind humans to the non-human, to the land and its constituent beings, respect is the most fitting and revealing moral response. It requires: constant attentiveness to the value of some thing or some one; appreciation of the fact that that individual has its own contribution to make which is vital to the natural order; awareness of the constraints and limitations which characterize and contextualize it; and gratitude for all of this. None of this is possible without careful thought and observation, so that one can better understand what its function or contribution is; what conditions are needed to permit its continuation; how not to interfere with it; and how best to enable it. This is to suggest that respect is as much a cognitive as it is a moral virtue, that knowing and valuing are integrated activities (Whitt 1995).

Maori weaving offers an example of the richness of the indigenous understanding of respect. According to Puketapu-Hetet, "we have a responsibility to this life force" (1989, p. 5):

> It is important to me as a weaver that I respect the *mauri* (life force) of what I am working with. Once I have taken [flax] from where it belongs, I must give another dimension to its life force so that it is still a thing of beauty. (Quoted in Nicholas 1980, p. 40)

The weaver must respect the materials used. One aspect of this consists in knowing where the materials come from and how they will be used; another lies in ensuring that they are put to proper use. Ensuring that that life force is respected and that the forest or river is able to continue to fulfill its vital role in the natural order are part of the Maori's *kaitiaki* (guardian) responsibilities:

> *kaitiaki* must ensure that the *mauri* or life force of their *taonga* [treasures] is healthy and strong. A *taonga* whose life force has been depleted . . . presents a major task for the *kaitiaki* . . . [they] must do all in their power to restore the *mauri* of the *taonga* to its original strength. (Roberts et al. 1995, p. 14)

One obvious way to fail to appreciate the value of something is to distort or diminish its value. The treatment of the bodies of Truganinny and her husband, described above, is a particularly egregious instance of disrespect. But there are others deserving of mention. The relation of belonging or inherent possession which binds a people to a land is at odds with the alienation and acquisition that accompanies commodification. Aboriginal writer Liz Johnson makes this point directly: "The land is our old people and those of us who are still here today are of that same land. When I take a handful of dirt and say 'This is ME,' it's true, the same as it was true when my early forefathers said it" (1981, p. 13). And land, as Maori would say, has its own *mauri*, or life force (Rangihau, in King 1992, p. 171). It is not a commodity whose value is determined by the marketplace; it is heritage, life itself. Many indigenous cultures recognize that the process of commodification distorts something's value and significance, and results in a failure to meet one's custodial responsibilities regarding it.

Knowledge, inherent value, and landkeeping

> *We cannot separate our place on earth from our lives on the earth, nor from our vision nor our meaning as a people.* (Jimmie Durham)

Respect, we have suggested, requires appreciating something's inherent value, the value which it has by virtue of the fact that it inheres in, or belongs to, the natural world. To treat something with respect involves knowledge – minimally, the knowledge that it plays an integral role in sustaining the natural order. To know more than this, to know something of what that role is and how it plays out, to know its limitations and constraints as well as its possibilities, positions one to be more respectful towards it, i.e. better situated to avoid behaviors that diminish it and to adopt those behaviors which enable its continued functioning. To come to know such things is to know better just how something inheres in, or belongs to, the natural order. But how does one come to know such things? How does one learn? And when one does, to return to Sequoyah and Benally – is it possible to separate that knowledge from what is, and from where it is, known?

It is by remembering and listening to stories that one learns. Vehicles for knowing and respecting the natural world, stories are vital components of indigenous knowledge and value systems. They are themselves generated from the land, and so are inseparable from it. Leslie Silko maintains that Laguna Pueblo stories are so much a part of the ancestral lands "that it is almost impossible for future generations to lose them":

there is a story connected with every place, every object in the landscape. Dennis Brutus has talked about the "yet unborn" as well as "those from the past," and how we are still all in this place, and language – the storytelling – is our way of passing through or being with them, of being together again. (1996, p. 59)

Storytelling is a form of conversing with the natural world, part of the way in which things come to be known. It transmits important information about the nature of that world, its beings and processes. Stories are a means of relating knowledge and of correlating behavior. They show how "those from the past" are bound to the land, to those from the present, and to those "yet unborn," and how those from the present should conduct themselves in light of this.

Since many stories relate accounts of humans listening, speaking to, and communicating with the non-human, they emphasize the importance of conversing with (etymologically, of "living or keeping company with") the natural world and its constituent beings. Andean agriculture testifies to a similar view by placing conversing and dialogue at the center of the process of mutual nurturance between humans and the non-human world: "We have great faith in what nature transmits to us . . . it is the voice of nature itself which announces to us the manner in which we must plant our crops" (Rengifo, quoted in Apffel-Marglin and Rivera 1995, p. 10).

The potency and significance of conversing with the natural world is also evident within Maori stories about ancestors claiming territory, naming landmarks after parts of their bodies and leaving these names behind: "most of the names evoke ancestral histories. A child would often be taught a particular account *in that place*, so that the place and its knowledge were one" (Salmond 1982, pp. 84–5). Tribal understanding is thereby "locked together . . . with the entities themselves so that a place and its knowledge could not be separated" (Roberts and Wills 1998, p. 49). One result of this is that the land itself serves as the repository of knowledge and place names function as "mnemonic devices whereby the narrative related to that particular place, and its meaning, can be recalled. Recounting the narrative at that very location enables the knowledge associated with the name to be experienced; to be felt as well as heard" (ibid, p. 55). It is in this sense that indigenous knowledge of the natural world is presentational. The presence of the natural world is a condition for the very possibility of knowledge. Knowledge is located in the world as much as it is located in a people or a person; it is part of what relates the human and non-human. And it is thoroughly contextualized: specific knowledge requires specific places whereby it can be recalled and experienced.

Thus, Ammoneta Sequoyah's knowledge cannot be severed from the natural world, and stored elsewhere – in libraries or data banks – for later "consumption". He is deeply aware that if his knowledge of medicinal herbs is to continue, the plants must remain in their familiar places, where he may continue to exercise his custodial responsibilities towards them. His knowledge depends on his continued appreciation of their inherent value, of how they belong to, contribute to, and function within, the natural order. And Alice Benally expresses how forced relocation constitutes dislocation – the disruption of the natural order and the severing of the affiliational ties that bind people to the land. To sever those ties is to sever the knowledge embedded in them, and to abandon one's role responsibilities as guardian of that portion of the natural world. It is to estrange, if not destroy, an entire knowledge and value system:

> When the white man talks of relocation he talks of finding a new place to live, a new job, a new place to pray to his God... The white man can practice his religion anywhere, he does not know the earth. The Diné are different, the land is sacred to us, we cannot practice our religion elsewhere, only on the land where we are known... It is like your family... You could not leave your relatives if they were sick – it is in this way that we must stay with this land, our relative. (in Jenny Manybeads et al. 1989, pp. 228, 230)

Jimmie Durham's statement that indigenous peoples cannot separate their place on earth from their life on earth, nor from their meaning or vision as a people, expresses a similar commitment to the duties inherent in belonging to land, to the responsibilities of landkeeping. This commitment is being vigorously embraced by an increasing number of indigenous peoples who are asserting their legal and moral rights as guardians, or keepers of the land. This chapter has offered one possible way of understanding the foundation of indigenous responsibilities as guardians of the land and of future generations. Insofar as a people inheres in or belongs to land, they are bound to it ontologically and morally. Their role as guardians of the land is indispensable; it is essential to the completeness and continuation of the natural world. To conclude with the words with which we began:

> We are indigenous people to this land. We are like a conscience... We are the landholders, we are the landkeepers... [It is] time to challenge the destruction of your grandchildren... and think about the coming generations. (Lyons, quoted in Dooling and Smith 1989, p. 274)

References

Apffel-Marglin, F. and Rivera, J. V. (1995) *Regeneration in the Andes* (Québec: Intercultural Institute of Montréal). [A discussion of traditional Andean agricultural knowledge and practices being regenerated today.]

Barreiro, J. (1992) "The search for lessons," *Akwe: kon* IX, pp. 18–39. [*Akwe: kon*, now called *Native Americas*, is a leading journal devoted to indigenous issues.

Bright, A. (1995) "Burn Grass," in *Country in Flames* (Canberra: Department of the Environment, Sport and Territories), pp. 59–62. [Yinirrakun, a MakMak Marranunggu woman, describes the practice, purpose and responsibilities of burning as a means of caring for country.]

Chay, R. Q. (1993) "The Corn Men have not forgotten their ancient gods," in *Story Earth*, ed. Inter-Press Service (San Francisco: Mercury House), pp. 19–30. [An anthology of indigenous responses to various aspects of the global environmental crisis.]

Donaldson, I. and Donaldson, T. (1985) *Seeing the First Australians* (Sydney: Allen and Unwin). [Frank Gurrmanamana's response to the chaos of Canberra is described in the essay "Ordering the Landscape."]

Dooling, D. M. and Smith, P. J., eds. (1989) *I Become Part of It* (New York: Harper Collins). [A collection of tribal stories, artwork, and essays from Native North America emphasizing the interconnectedness of the human and non-human world.]

Hobson, G. (1979) *The Remembered Earth* (Albuquerque: University of New Mexico Press). [One of the first major anthologies of work by American Indian writers and poets.]

Hogan, L., Metzger, D., and Peterson, B., eds. (1998) *Intimate Nature* (New York: Ballantine). [Reflections by indigenous and non-indigenous women writers and field scientists on the bond between women and animals.]

Ishtar, Z. (1994) *Daughters of the Pacific* (Melbourne: Spinifex). [Stories of survival and struggle against colonization and its effects by indigenous women from across the Pacific.]

Jackson, M. (1988) *The Maori and the Criminal Justice System*, Part 2 (Wellington: Department of Justice). [A well-known Maori lawyer and activist critiques the criminal justice system of Aotearoa/New Zealand.]

Jenny Manybeads et al. v. *United States of America et al.* (1989) 730 F. Supp. 1515 (US Dist. AZ) (No. 88–410) Affidavits of Alice Benally, Kee Shay, and Mae Tso. [A legal case prompted by the controversy surrounding the recent, federally mandated removal of some 10,000 Diné from their ancestral homelands on Big Mountain.]

Johnson, L. (1981) "Cultural revitalization," *Identity* 4, no. 2, pp. 13–14. [An Aboriginal woman discusses cultural revitalization and the role of the land therein.]

Kakadu Board of Management (1996) *Kakadu National Park Draft Plan of Management* (Canberra: Australian Nature Conservation Agency). [The Kakadu National Park is the site of an ongoing struggle against uranium mining led by the Mirrar people, the traditional owners of the affected areas.]

King, M., ed. (1992) *Te Ao Hurihuri: The World Moves On* (Auckland: Reed). [The 1975 edition of this influential book was the first published collection of writings on Maori issues by Maori writers.]

LaDuke, W. (1994) "Traditional ecological knowledge and environmental futures," *Colorado Journal of International Environmental Law and Policy* 5, pp. 127–48. [Winona LaDuke is one of the leading indigenous environmental activists in North America.]

Lyons, O. (1980) "An Iroquois perspective," in *American Indian Environments*, ed. C. Vecsey and R. Venables (Syracuse: Syracuse University Press), pp. 171–4. [A diverse collection of essays by native and non-native authors addressing changes in American Indian environmental experiences.]

—— (1995) *A Gathering for the Earth* (National Earth Day Video Conference) (Washington, DC: Project Earthlink). [A panel of American Indian elders discuss human impacts on the land and on present and future generations.]

Maracle, L. (1988) *I Am Woman* (Vancouver: Write-On Press). [One of many publications by this major contemporary First Nations writer and poet.]

Momaday, N. S. (1976) "Native American attitudes to the environment," *Seeing With a Native Eye*, ed. W. Copps (New York: Harper and Row), pp. 79–85. [Transcribed from oral remarks by a widely published Kiowa author and scholar.]

Muriwhenua Land Report (1997) *Report to the Waitangi Tribunal* (Wellington: GP Publications). [Official report regarding the seven land claims in the northernmost district of Aotearoa/New Zealand.]

Neidjie, B. (1986) *Kakadu Man* (Darwin: Resource Management Pty Ltd.). [A traditional owner of Kakadu National Park, Neidjie expresses his concern over threats to the Kakadu's culture and environment.

—— (1989) *Story About Feeling* (Perth: Magabala Books). [Neidjie's stories about the natural world and Aboriginal relations to it.]

Nicholas, D. (1980) *Seven Maori Artists* (Wellington: V. R. Ward). [In a series of personal interviews, seven well-known Maori artists describe the cultural dimensions and significance of their work.]

Norman, W. (unpublished ms.) "Tikanga Wahine In a Changing World." [This dissertation in process is a comprehensive study of Maori women and their cultural responsibilities both historically and today.]

Phillips, J. (1987) *Te Whenua Te Iwi: The Land and the People* (Wellington: Allen and Unwin). [A collection of essays exploring both the uses and the culture of the land in Maori and Pakeha society.]

Puketapu-Hetet, E. (1989) *Maori Weaving* (Auckland: Pitman). [A renowned Maori weaver explains the spiritual and philosophical aspects of her art.]

Roberts, M., Norman, W., Minhinnick, N., Wihongi, D., and Kirkwood, C. (1995) "Kaitiaki-tanga: Maori perspectives on conservation," *Pacific Conservation Biology* 2, pp. 7–20. [An introductory account of the Maori environmental concept of kaitiakitanga, or guardian-ship.]

Roberts, M., Norman, W., Minhinnick, N., Wihongi, D., Kirkwood, C., and Wills, P. R. (1998) "Understanding Maori epistemology," in *Tribal Epistemologies*, ed. H. Wautischer (Brookfield: Ashgate), pp. 43–77. [Maori epistemology is contrasted with that of western science.]

Rose, D. B. (1988) "Exploring an Aboriginal land ethic," *Meanjin* 47, 378–87. [Focuses on the Yarralin peoples' understanding of ecosystems.]

Salmond, A. (1982) "Theoretical landscapes," in *Semantic Anthropology*, ed. D. Parkin (London: Academic Press), pp. 65–87. [Addresses cross-cultural conceptions of knowledge.]

Scott, C. (1996) "Science for the West, myth for the rest?," in *Naked Science*, ed. L. Nader (New York: Routledge), pp. 69–86. [An account of knowledge construction and epistemology among the James Bay Cree.]

Semken, S. (1997) "Kéyah: a geological sense of place," Diné College Instructor's Guide, Tsaile, Arizona. [Attempts to integrate Diné concepts of the importance of the land and natural processes with those of western geological science.]

Sequoyah v. *Tennessee Valley Authority* (1980) 620 F. 2d 1159. [A lawsuit which states Cherokee objections to the flooding of their sacred lands along the Little Tennessee Valley.]

Silko, L. M. (1996) *Yellow Woman and a Beauty of the Spirit* (New York: Simon and Schuster). [Essays on diverse topics by one of Native America's foremost literary voices.]

Thornton, M. B. (1996) *Living Maths* (Melbourne: Boulder Valley Films). [A book of the video on Garma Living Maths which articulates the formal logical and mathematical concepts of the Yolngu people.]

Trask, H. (1993) *From a Native Daughter* (Maine: Common Courage Press). [A leader in the Native Hawaiian sovereignty movement discusses colonialism and sovereignty issues.]

Wainburranga, P. F. (1988) "Talking History," *Land Rights News* 2, p. 46. [*Land Rights News* is an excellent source for information regarding Australian Aboriginal activism with regard to land rights.]

Watson, H. and Chambers, W. (1989) *Singing the Land, Signing the Land* (Geelong, Victoria: Deakin University Press). [Analyzes the interaction of European and Aboriginal knowledge systems in a format intended to demonstrate the cultural dimensions of human perception of the environment.]

Whitt, L. A. (1995) "Indigenous peoples and the cultural politics of knowledge," in *Issues in American Indian Cultural Identity*, ed. M. Green (New York: Peter Lang), pp. 223–71. [Contrasts some of the distinctive features of indigenous knowledge systems with those of western cultures.]

Wilkins, D. P. (1993) "Linguistic evidence in support of a holistic approach to traditional ecological knowledge," in *Traditional Ecological Knowledge*, ed. N. Williams and G. Baines (Canberra: Australian National University), pp. 71–93. [A linguistic approach to understanding the ecological knowledge of the Mparntwe Arrernte.]

Yunupingu, G. (1996) "Land Rights Conference," *Land Rights News* 2, p. 16. [A formidable advocate for Aboriginal peoples and the chair of the Northern Land Council emphasizes the importance of defending land rights.]

——(1997) *Our Land Is Our Life* (Queensland: University of Queensland Press). [Some of indigenous Australia's most influential leaders speak to issues of social justice and land rights for their people.]

Further reading

LaDuke, W. (1999) *All Our Relations* (Cambridge: South End Press). [A series of essays by a well-known Anishinabe activist relating contemporary Native struggles for survival and sovereignty.]

Weaver, J. (1997) *Defending Mother Earth* (New York: Orbis Books). [A collection documenting Native North American resistance to environmental injustices by those engaged in the struggle.]

2

Classical China

KARYN L. LAI

Introduction

The schools of thought in ancient China varied widely in terms of their doctrines and teachings. Scholars belonging to the different schools were constantly engaged in debate about a wide range of issues. Such philosophical activity first flourished in a significant way during the Spring and Autumn period (722–481 BCE) and the Warring States period (403–221 BCE). This span of about five hundred years in Chinese intellectual history saw the formation of numerous different schools of thought. It has been characterized by many scholars as the first phase in Chinese philosophy, associated with influential thinkers, such as Confucius (Kongzi) (551–479 BCE), Laozi (ca. 6th or 4th century BCE?) Mozi (479–438 BCE), Zhuangzi (399–295 BCE), Hui Shi (380–305 BCE), Gongsun Long (b. 380 BCE?), Mencius (Mengzi) (371–289 BCE), Zou Yan (305–240 BCE), Xunzi (298–238 BCE) and Han Fei (b. 233 BCE). By the time of the Warring States period, so numerous, indeed, were the schools of thought in this first phase, that the era was dubbed the period of the hundred schools (*baijia*) (Fung 1951, Vol. 1, pp. 132–69).

The end of the Warring States period was a significant moment in Chinese history and had important implications for the development of philosophy. Existing feudal structures suffered a final blow through the efforts of the emperor Qin Shi Huangdi (259–210 BCE) to unify the empire. One of the methods by which Shi Huangdi sought to achieve the centralization of power and authority was to order the "Burning of the Books" in 213 BCE, an edict prohibiting the private possession of books of poetry, history, and philosophy. The burning of privately owned books greatly affected the development of Chinese thought in the existing schools, and possibly prevented the formation of new schools. It is significant that, beginning from this period, relatively few new doctrines and schools of thought were introduced, as compared with the 500 years immediately prior to it. From this period on, much philosophical activity centered around the study, explication, and analysis of theories and doctrines of existing schools of thought. Indeed, philosophy in the Han (206 BCE–CE 220), the period immediately following the Qin (221–206 BCE), consisted mainly of syntheses of existing doctrine and teaching. Since then, the method of synthesis has permeated Chinese philosophy such that it became common for thinkers to appropriate concepts from other schools and traditions and to adapt them to their own teachings.

This feature of classical Chinese philosophy renders it impractical to provide a systematic, chronological account of attitudes to nature in the different Chinese philosophical schools. For this reason, this survey is organized thematically, according to concepts, rather than chronologically: it involves an analysis of the range of concepts in Chinese philosophy which figure significantly in discussions of the natural world. These concepts include *tian* (heaven), *dao*, *zhiran* (natural, spontaneous), *wuxing* (five elements), *yin-yang*, and *qi* (stuff).

The background: correlative thinking

A prominent feature of the ancient Chinese world-view was the notion that human life is inextricably bound up with the rhythms, processes, and phenomena of the natural world. Since the Shang (1751–1112 BCE), belief that forces and powers which were beyond human control, which yet affected human life, has been a prominent feature of Chinese thinking. For many ancient Chinese people, life was, to varying extents, caught up in attempts to discern some of these forces and powers through divination processes. While some of these practices were religious, centering on pacifying spirit beings, many of them included a naturalistic aspect, focusing on the rhythms of the natural environment such as the seasons and the weather.

The philosophy of the early Chinese, which brought together the many different aspects of life, has been dubbed "correlative thinking" (Graham 1986). Correlative thinking was a significant part of the larger context within which much philosophical inquiry took place. Many of the schools of thought in classical China subscribed, in some way or other, to this belief. The view of correlative thinking was that it was not merely the case that there were similarities or analogies between the operations and processes of the natural world and those deriving from human design, but that changes in the natural world and events in the human world were interlocking.

Such a view was a feature of Chinese thought from the time of the earliest historical records – early Han thought, in particular, set out consciously to demonstrate that some of the correlations between human life and cosmic processes were regular and predictable (Major 1993, p. 31). For instance, some thinkers in this period posited correspondences between human communal and socio-political life and the processes of the cosmos. In addition, the interaction between different spheres and forms of life was explained in terms of groups and sets of numerical balances and contra-positions such as the four seasons, four directions, five colors, five sounds, five tastes, five smells, five phases, and eight trigrams and sixty-four hexagrams (Graham 1986, p. 1). For example, thinkers belonging to the Huang-Lao School (see Schwartz 1985, pp. 237–54), a prominent school of the Han period, postulated a unified system of cosmology based on mutual interaction between the human and natural worlds:

> In Huang-Lao cosmology, the principal means by which the ruler was advised to make his actions conform to the natural rhythms and processes of the cosmos emerged from a thorough understanding of systems of correspondence ... In this mode of thought, all things in the world can be grouped into numerical categories; things within a category resonate with each other more strongly, reliably and predictably than do things that are not in the same category ... Resonance (*ganying*) between or among things within a class is conveyed through *qi*, conceived of as both the basic stuff of concrete phenomena and as an intangible vibrating medium pervading empty space. (Major 1993, pp. 28–30)

As stated previously, while such systematic correlative thinking is a distinctive feature of early Han thought, elements of correlative thinking – balance, proportion, and harmony – though unarticulated, were already pervasive both in the content and methodology of ancient Chinese thought (Cheng 1977).

Tian

The term *tian* (heaven) had a variety of different meanings because it figured in popular religious beliefs as well as in somewhat more abstract philosophical systems. *Tian* was variously thought to be: a superhuman entity or force; a being with anthropomorphic features; an overseer and judge of human ethical conduct; and the origin or source of all existence including day and night, the four seasons, and flora and fauna (Forke 1925, pp. 62–7). In some other cases, however, *tian* simply meant the physical sky (Fung, 1951, Vol. 1, pp. 30ff).

Within the various schools of thought, *tian* was evoked to provide justification for a range of philosophies. Depending on the frameworks within which *tian* was used, it was functional in providing legitimation for rulership, in serving as the infrastructure upon which morality was grounded (and more narrowly as the source of human ethical conduct and of social order), and in justifying a naturalistic conception of the universe.

With regard to the idea of divine rulership, the concept *tian* became prominent towards the end of the Shang. In the context of the changeover of dynasties (from Shang to Zhou), the god-ruler of the Shang dynasty (Shangdi) needed replacement. Both philosophically and psychologically, *tian* served this purpose (Chan 1963, pp. 3–13).

The divine legitimation of ruling power gave much authority to the emperor. However, because he was, as it were, appointed by *tian*, he was also held responsible, at least indirectly, for almost every conceivable event and state of affairs in the life of the nation. For example, many social, economic, and political problems within the nation were explained in terms of the inappropriate behaviors or practices of the emperor; the latter were said to be the direct cause of the former (see, e.g., *Shujing*, Hongfan section in Legge (trans.) 1960, Vol. 3). In addition, the emperor was, in some cases, held responsible for natural disasters such as droughts and floods; these occurrences were thought to be due to the emperor's failure properly to coordinate or perform the sacrifices which were necessary for the maintenance of the various harmonies of life at different levels (See, e.g., *Shujing*, Shuntian section, in Legge (trans.) 1960, Vol. 3). Accordingly, the remedies to a range of problems faced by the nation lay in the rectification of the inappropriate behaviors or practices of the emperor. There was sometimes an ultimatum attached to this belief, that the emperor or the dynasty itself might lose divine sanction (Fung 1951, Vol. 1, p. 22ff).

The demystification of the notion of divine rulership gradually came about as a result of an enlightened conception of human capacities and abilities, and of the human situation. At the level of ideas, this demystification was sometimes expressed in terms of the view that there was a tripartite cooperation between *tian*, *di* (earth), and *ren* (man). On this view, *tian*, *di*, and *ren* each had specific spheres of activity, and the well-being of the universe depended on the successful cooperation of the three agents or forces in their respective spheres.

In the case of some variants of this view, *ren* was used to denote the emperor, and not the common person. In some other cases, *ren* was used generically to refer to all human beings. With regard to the former usage of *ren*, it is worth noting that, while the *tian–di–ren* view of the emperor resembles the notion of divine kingship, there was an essential difference between the two. The *tian–di–ren* view upholds the emperor's cooperation with *tian* and *di*, whereas the view of divine kingship holds that the emperor is a mere conduit or a representative of *tian*.

While, at first glance, it might seem that the *tian–di–ren* formulation is anthropo-centric, it was not always used to express the exclusivity of human beings. The relationships between the three agents or agencies, their comparative power and authority, and the responsibilities and obligations arising from the relationships posited varied according to the philosophies of the different schools. In particular, there was a primary difference between the schools of thought in the Daoist and the Confucianist traditions regarding the tripartite relationship. In the Confucian tradi-tion – which had an essentially humanistic focus – the main point of drawing the tripartite relationship was to emphasize the significance of human effort and action, and, hence, psychologically to empower human beings for socio-political activity. In the Daoist tradition, the tripartite relationship was evoked in order to emphasize that human beings should model themselves after *tian* and *di* which were, in turn, modeled according to the primordial and naturalistic *dao*.

In the Confucian tradition, the connection between *tian*, *di*, and *ren* are articulated in a number of earlier Confucian texts such as *Mengzi*, *Xiaojing*, *Liji*, *Zhongyong*, *Daxue*, and *Chunqiu Fanlu*, as well as in the works of Neo-Confucian thinkers, such as Li Ao (d. ca. 844), Zhang Zai (1020–77), Cheng Hao (1032–85), Cheng Yi (1033–1108), Zhu Xi (1130–1200), Lu Xiangshan (1139–93), Wang Yangming (1472–1529), Wang Fuzhi (1619–93) and Yan Yuan (1635–1746) (Fung 1953, Vol. 2; see also Legge (trans.) 1960).

In the *Liji*, the connection between *tian*, *di*, and *ren* is discussed in detail. Specifi-cally, the three are positioned according to a hierarchical structure, and parallel hierarchies are thought to exist amongst different species:

> Heaven is honorable, Earth is lowly, and likewise the positions of ruler and subject were both made definite . . . Animals are grouped according to their kind, and plants are divided according to their family. Thus the natures and endowments of things are not the same . . . The yin and the yang act upon one another, and the [*qian*] (heaven) and the [*kun*] (earth) agitate each other. They are drummed on by thunder, excited by wind and rain, moved by the four seasons, warmed by the sun and moon, and all the processes of change and growth vigorously proceed. (Legge (trans.) 1966, Vol. 28, pp. 102–5)

By contrast to the *Liji*, it seems that a hierarchical conception of *tian–di–ren* is not a primary concern in the *Xunzi* text. What is important, in the latter, is that, from a pragmatic and humanistic point of view, the ruler is the selected man on par with *tian* and *di*. For *Xunzi*, it is a mistake to attempt to be like *tian* or *di*, or to replicate their processes, because, while the three are connected, man has his own special needs and concerns. In that connection, *Xunzi* advocates a "division of labor" approach, setting out the boundaries of each sphere:

> Heaven has its seasons, Earth has its wealth, and man has his government. This is how they are able to form a triad. To neglect (human actions) which constitute man's part in the triad and put one's hope in those with which he forms a triad is indeed a mistake... The fixed stars rotate in succession, the sun and moon shine alternately, the four seasons follow one another, yin and yang effect their great transformations... Instead of regarding Heaven as great and admiring it, why not foster it as a thing and regulate it? Instead of obeying Heaven and singing praise to it, why not control the Mandate of Heaven and use it? (Section 17, Chan 1961, pp. 117–22; see Dubs 1928)

The *Xunzi* approach insists, as it were, that there are some affairs which rightly belong to humankind, and that these are the only affairs humans should concern themselves with; conversely, attempting to replicate the movements and processes of *tian* is not within the sphere of proper human action and will, if undertaken, prove deleterious to humankind. *Xunzi*'s view is interesting because it attempts to empower human beings both by establishing a connection between heaven, earth, and man in a special, triadic relationship, and by insisting on the relatively separate spheres of action of each of these three agencies such that the realm of human action should not be seen merely as epiphenomena of *tian*.

In the *Chunqiu Fanlu*, man's special (moral) capacities are emphasized: human beings are capable of manifesting humanity (*ren*) and rightness (*yi*), two distinctly Confucian values. These special capacities are an endowment from *tian*. Furthermore, man's superior status, compared with the status of other species, is upheld:

> Nothing is more refined than the (yin and yang) ethers, richer than Earth, or more spiritual than Heaven. Of the creatures born from the refined essence [*qing*] of Heaven and Earth, none is more noble than man. Man receives the Decree (*ming*) of Heaven, and therefore is loftier (than other) creatures. (Other) creatures suffer troubles and distress and are unable to practice love [*ren*] and righteousness [*yi*]; only man is capable of practicing them. (Other) creatures suffer trouble and distress and are unable to match themselves with Heaven and Earth; only man is capable of doing this. (Section 56, Fung 1953, Vol. 2, pp. 30–1)

From passages like this, it seems that the low status of non-human species is a corollary of the elevated status of the human species. Indeed, it could be said in general of the thought of the Confucian tradition that, in emphasizing humanism, it requires that clear distinctions and dichotomies be formulated in order to distinguish the human from the non-human. This is particularly true in the case of Mengzi, Confucius's most prominent disciple, who strongly asserted that human beings and other animal species are incomparable in a most important way: the latter, in not having human nature (*xing*) and the human heart-mind (*xin*), lack the capacity for morality (*yi*), humaneness (*ren*), propriety (*li*) and wisdom (*zhi*) (*Mengzi*, sections 2A, 6A).

Compared with the humanism of Confucian thought, Daoist thought is much more inclusive. In the *Laozi* and *Zhuangzi* texts, for instance, a perspective favoring the human is ridiculed and, to some extent, seen as morally reprehensible. In these texts, *tian*, and sometimes both *tian* and *di*, are variously portrayed as the source or origin of all existence or as an inscrutable judge of all (*Laozi*, sections 73, 74; *Zhuangzi*, sections 17, 18); both these views transcend the merely anthropocentric. An interesting aspect of Daoist philosophy with regard to *tian*, *di* and *ren* is that man learns from *tian* and *di* to not overvalue human concerns. In the *Laozi* (section 5, Chan 1961, p. 141) the rejection of anthropocentric (Confucian) institutions and structures as impermanent artefacts of civilization, is a lesson the Daoist sage learns from *tian* and *di*:

> Heaven and Earth are not humane [*ren*]
> They regard all things as straw dogs.
> The sage is not humane.
> He regards all people as straw dogs.
> How Heaven and Earth are like a bellows!
> While vacuous, it is never exhausted.

Straw dogs were items used in sacrificial rites, to be discarded after use; they had only instrumental value. In this passage, it is explicitly stated that the Daoist sage, modeling his behavior according to some characteristics of *tian* and *di*, is not humane in that he does not accord special priority to human life or human concerns. The impartiality of *tian* and *di* is upheld and human beings are called upon to be likewise.

The conception of the holistic interconnectedness of all things is somewhat fuller in the *Zhuangzi* than in the *Laozi*. While both are critical of anthropocentricism, the *Zhuangzi* text takes an additional step to challenge even the value placed on human life. An often-quoted passage (section 18, Chan 1961, pp. 204, 209), regarding Zhuangzi's attitude to the death of his wife, is expressive of such a stance:

> When she died, how could I help being affected? But as I think the matter over, I realize that originally she had no life; and not only no life, she had no form; not only no form, she had no material force [*qi*] . . . The material force was transformed to be form, form was transformed to become life, and now birth has transformed to become death. This is like the rotation of the four seasons, spring, summer, fall and winter . . . Man again goes back into the originative process of Nature. All things come from the originative process of Nature and return to the originative process of Nature.

In this chapter, Zhuangzi's sorrow over the death of his wife is mediated by his ability to move beyond what is seen as the excessive value placed on human life by human beings. This is one of the lessons he has learnt from observing the processes of nature. Zhuangzi likens the course of human life and death to the movement of the four seasons. In the context of Daoist naturalism, Zhuangzi, in his appreciation of matters of (human) life and death, is applauded for having successfully transcended the merely human perspective.

Comparing Confucian and Daoist thought, it is interesting to observe that the notion of the tripartite relationship between *tian*, *di* and *ren* is utilized as a justification for two exactly opposite world-views. In the context of Confucian humanism, the tripartite relationship affirms man's position within the universe as central or apical. By contrast, Daoist philosophy views all forms of existence as ontologically equal. This equality is seen to derive from the fact that everything is "formed by a process of self- and mutual transformation" (Cheng 1997, p. 121), where nothing can be seen to have intrinsic value in and of itself (see DEEP ECOLOGY). In emphasizing impartiality, Daoist philosophy is non-hierarchical in its conceptualization of differences between species; in emphasizing mutuality and connectedness, Daoist philosophy upholds an inclusive and holistic view of all forms of existence.

Wuxing (five elements) and *yin-yang* (yin and yang)

The concept *wuxing* refers to the five natural elements of water, fire, wood, metal, and earth. It has been argued that the idea of a set of five categories dates back to the Shang dynasty, with the four directions (north, south, east, and west) plus, implicitly, the center (Allan 1991, pp. 74–111). In its usage, the concept *wuxing* was not primarily understood literally, that is, to signify some physical or material composition of existing things. Rather, it was a metaphysical concept to do with balance and proportion, suggesting harmony (*he*) as opposed to identity (*tong*). As such, it was applied variously to a range of human concerns and activities (in particular, those relating to government and to social relationships), as well as to non-human states of affairs (for instance, the weather, the seasons, and to some extent the heavenly bodies). Thus, for instance, in the *Zuozhuan*, the idea of balancing proportions is seen as central to the ways of *tian*, *di*, government, social norms, and institutions, the categories used in discrimination, and the processes and structures of the natural world. In addition, all these different spheres were seen to be intertwined:

> Heaven and Earth have their standards, and men take these for their pattern, imitating the brilliant bodies of Heaven and according with the natural diversities of Earth. (Heaven and Earth) produce the six atmospheric conditions and men make use of the Five Elements. These conditions produce the five tastes, make manifest the five colors, and make evident the five notes ... The duties of government, requisitions of labour, and conduct of affairs were made to accord with the four seasons. Punishments and penalties, and the terrors of legal proceedings were instituted to make the people stand in awe, resembling the destructive forces of thunder and lightning. Mildness and gentleness, kindness and harmony, were made in imitation of the creating and nourishing action of Heaven. The people had feelings of love and hatred, pleasure and anger, grief and joy, produced by the six atmospheric conditions. (Legge (trans.) 1960, Vol. 5, pp. 708–9)

Apart from the idea that particular and appropriate proportions of each of the five elements were required, it was also believed that these elements, engaged in constant flux, took turns in being ascendant and flourishing. This meant that when a particular element was in its ascendancy, processes and events ran according to that element. For example, in the *Lushi Chunqiu*, it is recorded that when the element earth is ascendant, yellow, the color correlated with earth, is adopted by the Yellow Emperor, who models himself according to earth (Fung 1951, Vol. 1, pp. 161f; see also de Bary et al. 1960).

In many of the classical Chinese texts, the emperor is seen to have primary responsibility for the coordination of this delicate juggling act. For example, in the *Hongfan* section of the *Shujing*, the earliest recorded mention of *wuxing*, he is advised to be heedful of *wuxing* and its correlations in his handling of various affairs. Thus, he must be careful to ensure that his actions properly coordinate and balance the different proportions of the five elements and their respective correlations, together with the transformations that occur between them (Forke 1925, pp. 227–42). Many examples are given of inappropriate actions and behaviors of the emperor which were believed to have sent both human affairs and natural processes into disarray (see Legge (trans.) 1966, Vol. 3, pp. 138–41; Fung 1951, Vol. 1, pp. 164–5).

The best-known early interpretation of the *wuxing* theory was by Zou Yan (350–270 BCE). He attempted to account for the rise and fall of dynasties by reference to the ascendancy of one of the five elements at particular historical periods. Furthermore, he propounded a theory of the flux and interplay of *wuxing* and other aspects of existence which involved not only the topography of the earth, fauna, flora, and the effects of the movements of the soil and waters, but also the continents and the seas (Day 1962, p. 19).

Zou Yan's discussions of *wuxing* often included references to *yin-yang* as well; this dual reference seems to be a feature of thinkers of the Yin-Yang School. It has been argued that there was another school called the School of Five Elements and that, from the Han period, the phrases "Yin-Yang School" or "School of Five Elements" referred to one set of teachings, or a group of thinkers associated with such teachings. Indeed, this school was at times referred to as the "Yin-Yang and Five Elements School" (Fung 1953, Vol. 2, pp. 7–8).

It appears, however, that *wuxing* and *yin-yang* were not always thought of as connected theories or concepts. Indeed, prior to the period of the former Han (206 BCE–CE 8), the *wuxing* and *yin-yang* theories were referred to as mutually exclusive. In the Yueling section of the *Lushi Chunqiu*, a work of the late fourth or third century BCE, there is mention of *wuxing* but not of *yin-yang*. Conversely, in the *Shiyi* (Appendices to the Book of Changes), a work dated at third century BCE, *yin-yang* is mentioned, but not *wuxing* (Day 1962, p. 8).

It needs to be noted that, even within the context of the Yin-Yang School, *wuxing* and *yin-yang* were retained as separate concepts and each was irreducible to the other, though many theorists maintained that their movements and processes were intricately intertwined. Significantly, the concepts *yin* and *yang* were used, like the concept *wuxing*, to signify balance and proportion. While there was also some reference to *yin-yang* as the primary elements associated with *tian* and *di*, the sun and moon, the seasons and the weather, these references are relatively few (Forke, 1925, pp. 163–200). On the whole, it is quite clear that *yin-yang* was treated differently from *wuxing* in that, while the two concepts are often referred to in a particular passage, the terms were not used co-extensively or synonymously.

It seems that *yin-yang* entered the Chinese vocabulary sometime during the early to mid-Warring States period, with the original meanings "the shady and sunny sides of a hill side" and "cool and warm." Both uses imply gradients on a scale rather than polar opposites. As employed by Zou Yan and others in the Yin-Yang School, *yin* and *yang* became paradigms of a complementary (non-antagonistic) dualism, whereby phenomena could be analyzed in terms of shifting proportions of *yin* and *yang*; a predominantly *yin* phenomenon always contained at least a germ of *yang* and vice versa (Major 1993, pp. 28f).

Thinkers belonging to the Yin-Yang School, in keeping with a trend set by others before them, practiced divination using the *yin-yang* and *wuxing* concepts (Fung 1951, Vol. 1, ch. 7, esp. pp. 159–69). It is apparent why these thinkers took on the practice of divination. Believing in a correlative cosmology, it would have been integral to their perspective on existence, to decipher and interpret the workings of *wuxing*, *yin-yang*, their respective correlations, and their transformations.

Perhaps the most prominent text of the Han period which expounded on such correlative thinking, involving *yin-yang* and *wuxing*, as well as a range of processes, species, forces, and events, was the *Huainanzi*. The *Huainanzi* is thought to be a compilation which included ideas that were relatively more mature than many other works from the same period (Major 1993, pp. 30f). In this regard, it presents fairly explicit descriptions of interconnectedness between the different forms and modes of life, articulating rather clearly the origin of form, matter, and species.

Chapter 4 of the *Huainanzi* focuses on topography in a broad and general way, discussing how the various aspects of the earth (such as the nine continents, the eight winds, and the six rivers) combine to have different effects on different creatures and on the formation of minerals. Further, the chapter contains a discussion of the origin and taxonomy of minerals and species, specifically regarding how *yin* and *yang* variously combine to generate difference:

> birds (feathered creatures) are correlated with phase fire [one of the five elements]; they are *yang*, in that they fly, but *yin*, in that they are oviparous. In modern terms, the set of living creatures has a subset, creatures correlated with phase fire; this subset is intersected by a set of *yin* attributes and a set of *yang* attributes. The small area where the sets are congruent yields the category "birds." (Major 1993, pp. 30f)

In addition to discussions of the connection between diets and characteristic features of different species, the *Huainanzi* propounds an evolutionary theory of different animal and plant species (ibid, pp. 141–215).

The idea of correlative cosmology was so pervasive during the Han period that even thinkers associated with the Confucian tradition – noted for its humanistic emphasis – engaged fully in debates regarding such issues. For instance, an important point of debate between members of the New Text School (Jinwenjia) and the Old Text School (Kuwenjia) was the topic of divination and prognostication. Members of each school claimed that their respective ideas were closer in spirit to early Confucianism than those of the other. Dong Zhongshu (?179–?104 BCE), a prominent member of the New Text School, upheld the notion of a unified and interconnected cosmology, as well as divination practices associated with that cosmology. In opposition, members of the Old Text School, such as Wang Chong (CE 27–100) argued that the superstitions and supernatural beliefs of those in the New Text School seem incommensurable to early Confucianism (Fung 1953, Vol. 2, pp. 152ff).

If there is a need to pick a "winning side" in this debate, it might be noted that many thinkers of the Han period accepted correlative cosmology. Indeed, this view was so popular and pervasive in this period that it has been commented, regarding philosophy during this period of Chinese intellectual history, that, "[i]t makes no difference whether the thinkers of that era regarded themselves as Taoists or as Confucianists; all the viewpoints embodied the viewpoint of the Yin Yang School and its essential spirit" (Fung 1947, p. 116).

While there were subtle differences in the ways the concepts *wuxing* and *yin-yang* were used in various philosophical systems in ancient China, they were always used to provide the metaphysical infrastructure for a cosmological theory of interdependence between processes and events in the natural and human worlds.

At the level of popular belief, correlative cosmology was manifest in superstitious beliefs regarding the consequences of certain human actions for the natural world and its processes, and vice versa. Indeed, in some cases the correlation between states of affairs in the natural and human worlds was thought to be so strongly causal in either or both directions that little action was carried out prior to the undertaking of some divination procedure (Fung 1951, Vol. 1, pp. 159–69). Such a strong view of correlation and interdependence would render distinctions between the human and the non-human, or the human and the natural, meaningless.

Dao

Within the Daoist tradition, the concept *dao* figures significantly in discussions about the natural world. The term was used variously to signify ultimate reality, or some principle of reality, by the early Daoists in reference to an all-encompassing and inclusive cosmology and ontology.

The usage of *dao* by the Daoists to refer to a reality set well beyond human life and concerns stands in clear contrast to the classical Confucian *dao*. In the *Lunyu* (section 15: 29; see Legge (trans.) 1960), the primary classical Confucian text, Confucius purportedly articulates the view that *dao* is the process of *human* self-cultivation, and is fully defined by human beings: "It is not *dao* that makes man great; it is man that makes *dao* great."

Here, Confucius could be understood to be refuting the Daoist conception of *dao*. The point is made, rather emphatically, that a transcendent *dao* so defined, abstracted, and independent of lived human reality, has nothing useful to offer as far as human cultivation and development are concerned. Similarly, in another Confucian text, the *Mengzi*, *dao* has the rather plain meaning of "teaching"; there is, for example, Mozi's *dao*, Yangzhu's *dao* and the undesirable *dao* of the contemporary world (sections 3B: 9.9 and 3B: 2; see Legge (trans.) 1960).

By contrast, *dao* in the Daoist tradition is not restricted merely to the socio-political dimension. While there are chapters both in the *Laozi* and *Zhuangzi* texts which discuss only this aspect of *dao*, it would be reductionist to conceive the Daoist enterprise solely in these terms. Thus, in most chapters of the Daoist texts, such as chapter 77 of the *Laozi*, many aspects of *dao* emerge:

> Heaven's [*dao*] is indeed like the bending of a bow.
> When (the string) is high, bring it down.
> When it is low, raise it up.
> When it is excessive, reduce it.
> When it is insufficient, supplement it.
> The [*dao*] of Heaven reduces whatever is excessive and
>   supplements whatever is insufficient.
> The [*dao*] of man is different.
> It reduces the insufficient to offer to the excessive.
> Who is able to have excess to offer to the world?
> Only the man of Tao.

Two important aspects of *dao* are alluded to in this chapter. The first is that the *dao* of man, in embodying a goal contrary to that of Heaven, falls short of the mark. Specifically, while *tian* seeks to balance and reduce differences between the excessive and the insufficient, the *dao* of man – plainly manifest in government and other human institutions – serves to widen the gap (between superior and inferior and great and small). The values of the then contemporary Chinese society, by comparison, are inadequate and hence rejected.

The other important point is the contrast made between the *dao* of man and the man of *dao*: the former is ridiculed as being impermanent, shallow, and inequitable while the latter is upheld as the proper approach of the Daoist sage. This man of *dao* is antithetical to the Confucian gentleman (*junzi*), who creates his own *dao*. These two approaches to human existence project different values, goals, and methodologies. The *dao* of man is a constructed, impermanent goal which has a narrow, restricted (anthropocentric) focus; the way to attain that goal is through the implementation of structures and institutions which allow men to strive towards those goals. By contrast, the tenor of the *Laozi* is that a more complete life for all forms of existence can be achieved only through a full appreciation of the connectedness of all beings. Hence, the man of *dao* attempts to replicate the aims of *tian* and *dao* and, in so doing, sees himself as merely a part of the permanent, enduring, holistic reality. From the Daoist point of view, the only perspective that properly reflects the nature of reality is a view that all forms of existence are connected and, correspondingly, that reality is holistically comprised by the continuous interaction of all forms of being. In this connection, it has been argued that Daoist philosophy provides the basis for an aesthetic structure of the world (Ames 1986; see also AESTHETICS).

The metaphysical, ethical, and ontological aspects of Daoist philosophy call for attention. In the first instance, there is a call to human beings to observe and follow the ways of nature. This is articulated in terms of Daoist counter-values such as non-assertiveness, weakness, and spontaneity; *dao* is sometimes presented as a principle of spontaneity, modeled according to the natural (*zhiran*) (*Laozi*, sections 17, 25; cf. Schwartz 1985, pp. 203ff).

For the Daoist sage to act in a manner in accord with *zhiran* is for him not to create and facilitate, and perhaps to demolish, man-made, artificial norms, values, and institutions which, when superimposed on to human lives, forcibly alienate human beings both from other human beings and from their natural context (*Laozi*, sections 2, 28, 30, 32; see Chan 1961). In fact, the Daoist dictum requiring human beings to act according to the principle of spontaneity can be seen as an encouragement to take "lessons" from the natural world. Within this framework, striking images and metaphors of water, the infant, and the female are utilized in the *Laozi* to illustrate the necessity of non-assertive spontaneity in one's actions (e.g., *Laozi*, sections 36, 55, 66, 76, 78; see Chan 1961). In the *Zhuangzi*, too, such imagery is expressed through the personification of the processes of nature:

> "Then what shall I do?" asked Uncle River. "What shall I not do? Should I accept or reject, advance or withdraw?"
> The Spirit of the North Sea said, "From the point of view of Tao, what is noble and what is humble? They all merge into one. Never stick to one's own intention and thus handicap the operation of Tao. What is much and what is little? They replace and apply to each other. Never follow one stubborn course of action and thus deviate from Tao." (Section 17; see Chan 1961, p. 206)

It needs to be noted, too, that while *zhiran* was often used to refer to style or method or *modus operandi*, some discussions of *zhiran* dealt with the concept at a metaphysical level. This is true especially of later commentaries on the *Laozi* and *Zhuangzi* texts by thinkers belonging to the neo-Daoist school, such as Xiang Xiu (ca. CE 221–300) (Fung 1953, Vol. 2, p. 208), and even by those belonging to the Confucianist Old Text School, such as Yang Xiong (53 BCE–CE 18) (Fung 1953, Vol. 2, pp. 139ff).

Another important feature of the Daoist *dao* is its ontology of holistic connectedness, reflected in the Daoist ideal to "identify all things as one" (Chan 1961, p. 184). In some chapters of the *Laozi* and *Zhuangzi* texts, the ideal of holistic connectedness is associated with an evaluative judgment concerning the equality of all forms of being. For instance, the *Zhuangzi* points out the unjustified exploitation of other animals by human beings as a manifestation of the artificially-constructed power hierarchy:

> "What do you mean by Heaven [*tian*] and what do you mean by man?"
> "A horse or a cow has four feet. That is [*tian*]. Put a halter around the horse's head and put a string through the cow's nose, that is man. Therefore it is said, 'Do not let man destroy [*tian*]. Do not let cleverness destroy destiny [*ming*]. And do not sacrifice your name for gain.' Guard carefully your [*tian*] and do not let it go astray. This is called returning to one's true nature." (Section 17; see Chan 1961, p. 207; see also *Zhuangzi*, sections 1, 12, and 33; Fung 1933)

One is invited in this chapter to adopt a standpoint that transcends the anthropocentric and to see each form of existence as equal to all other forms. A neo-Daoist text, the *Liezi*, is explicit in its criticism of a hierarchy of existence imposed by human beings upon all other species:

> Mr. T'ien of Ch'i was holding an ancestral banquet in his hall, to which a thousand guests were invited, some of whom came forward with presents of fish and geese. Eying them, Mr T'ien exclaimed: "How generous is Heaven to man! It causes the five kinds of grain to grow, and creates fish and birds, especially for our use." . . . The twelve year old son of a Mr Pao, who, regardless of seniority, came forward and said: "It is not as you say, my lord. All the creatures in Heaven and Earth have been

created in the same category as ourselves, and one is of no greater intrinsic value than another. It is only by reason of size, knowledge, or strength that some one of them gains the mastery, or that one preys upon another. None are produced in order to serve the needs of others. Man catches and eats those that are fit for food, yet can it be said that Heaven creates these expressly for man's use? Mosquitoes and gnats, moreover, bite his skin, and tigers and wolves devour his flesh, yet can it be said that Heaven creates man expressly for the benefit of mosquitoes and gnats, or to provide flesh for tigers and wolves?" (Section 8, Fung 1953, Vol. 2, pp. 190–4)

In this passage, the boy refutes the suggestion that a hierarchy amongst species exists as an inherent feature of the natural order. Indeed, the superimposition of a hierarchy on to nature is presented as being contrived, arbitrary, and misleading, as a mere product of human invention. In Daoist thought, indeed, the structuring and categorizing characteristic of human existence is projected as a symptom of improper interference and dogmatism, creating a hierarchy of modes of existence where, in the natural world, no such separation or hierarchy exists. The effects of such categorization and structuring are only negative, both for human beings and for all other forms of existence.

It is noteworthy that Chinese philosophers – in particular, those belonging to the Daoist tradition – during the classical period questioned not only the ethics of a separatist and hierarchical attitude to nature, but also attempted in some way to analyze the reasoning and rationale underlying such attitudes.

Qi (stuff)

"*Qi*" is a term used to connote some pervasive, basic stuff or energy. References to *qi* in pre-Qin (221–206 BCE) Chinese philosophy were sporadic. There is some mention of *qi* in *Zuozhuan, Lunyu, Mengzi,* and *Huainanzi,* though the use of the concept in these texts is not systematic. In the *Lunyu, qi* seems to refer to breath or vapor; in the *Zuozhuan* it refers sometimes to a primordial energy, and at others to personal states of emotion or attitudes (Schwartz 1985, pp. 179f). *Mengzi* discusses *qi* in the context of forging a (moral) connection between human nature and *tian* (section 2A: 2; see Legge (trans.) 1960) and the *Huainanzi* enlists *qi* as part of the cosmic evolutionary process, together with *tian* and *di, yin* and *yang,* and the principles of non-being (*wu*) and being (*yu*) (Fung 1947, pp. 113–15). Prior to the pre-Qin period, *qi* was often used to denote a normative standard for any thing or states of affairs. Thus, there are the *qi* of *yin* and of *yang* and of *tian* and *di,* of each of the *wuxing,* and of morality and social order (there is even a *qi* for negative features such as human greed) (ibid, pp. 119–23). It seems that the notion of *qi* as pervasive material stuff or energy is far less central in pre-Qin thought than the concept of a total cosmic and social order often referred to by *dao* (Schwartz 1985, p. 183).

There is, however, some reference to *qi* as the pervasive primordial material of all existence in the *Huainanzi* (Major 1993, p. 27), which seems to have pre-empted the Song (CE 960–1279) neo-Confucian usage of *qi* as the concrete manifestation of different species patterns. In the works of Zhang Zai (1020–77), Cheng Hao (1032–85), Cheng Yi (1033–1108), for example, *qi* is used in conjunction with *li* (ideal principle or pattern) to sketch a theory of existence: *qi* is the raw material in and through which *li* are actualized (Chan 1961, pp. 495–571). In the way the Song neo-Confucianists express the interplay between *li* and *qi*, it would appear that, while each is necessary for existence and non-reducible to the other, *qi* has lost the sense it previously had of normative significance, whereas *li* carries the definitive form or mode of existence.

Chinese Buddhism and the Buddhist view of nature

To date, the discussion has focused on Daoist and Confucian attitudes to nature. Buddhism was introduced into China from India as early as 2 BCE (Chan 1961, p. 336). Because it was a foreign philosophy, many Chinese Buddhist thinkers, anxious to promote Buddhism, attempted to explain Buddhist concepts via the "method of analogy" (*geyi*). During the Han and Wei periods, these thinkers were engaged in the matching of Buddhist concepts to existing Confucian and Daoist concepts (de Bary et al. 1960, Vol. 1, pp. 274–9; Fung 1953, Vol. 2, pp. 240–2).

Being strongly focused on metaphysical issues such as existence, causation, and reality, Buddhist thinkers found more affinity with Daoist than with Confucianist ideas. For instance, the Buddhist *kong* (empty; Sanskrit: *sunyata*) was likened to the Daoist notion of non-being (*wu*), as opposed to being (*yu*). Through the method of analogy, neo-Daoism was instrumental in the growth of the earliest Chinese Buddhist schools of thought.

On the other hand, Chinese Buddhism still managed to retain many basic features of its Indian form. This was partly because some Buddhist concepts and ideas were simply untranslatable into existing Daoist and Confucian concepts. For instance, Buddhism abhors the (Confucian) social and (Daoist) natural definitions of humanity, upholding a pneumatic, universal mind that transcends nature and even the cosmos (Lai 1997, p. 576).

> One of the fundamental and distinctive tenets of Buddhism is that [t]here has been no single act of divine creation that has produced the stream of existence. It simply is, and always has been, what it is. Even the gods in the Buddhist heavens are attached to the wheel of life and death and are not its creators ... [P]henomenal "existence," as commonly perceived by the senses, is illusory; it is not real inasmuch as, though it exists, its existence is not permanent or absolute. Nothing belonging to it has an enduring entity or "nature" of its own; everything is dependent upon a combination of fluctuating conditions and factors for its seeming "existence" at any given moment. This is the Buddhist theory of causation. (Fung 1953, Vol. 2, p. 237)

For two important reasons – a preoccupation with the adaptation of Buddhist concepts to existing frameworks of Chinese thought, and a focus on the topics of mind and consciousness transcending both the human and the natural worlds – there was relatively little discussion of the natural world and its processes during the classical period in Chinese philosophy in Buddhist thought. Instead, there was much discussion of the experience of transcendence, ideas of Buddhahood and existence, and, in many Buddhist schools, meditation as fundamental Buddhist practice.

At around the period of the Eastern Jin (CE 317–420), the concept of Buddha-nature was articulated by some Buddhist thinkers, such as Hui Yuan (CE 334–416) of the Pure Land sect (Day 1962, ch. 7 and 8) and Dao Sheng (CE 355–434), whose thoughts were esteemed by the later Chan Buddhists. A tenet associated with the Buddha-nature concept was that, given that Buddha was omnipresent (and not confined to bodily existence), it follows that Buddha-nature permeates all (sentient) beings (Lai 1997, pp. 578f; Fung 1953, Vol. 2, ch. 9). The theme of the universality of Buddha-nature was taken up at a later stage by the Chan Buddhists, a sect which appeared during the period of the South and North Dynasties (CE 420–589) (Lai 1997, p. 579). In some Chan Buddhist texts, there were references to the universal Buddha-nature as permeating all sentient (see SENTIENTISM), enlightened existence: "without enlightenment, a Buddha is no different from all living beings, and with enlightenment, all living beings are the same as a Buddha" (Platform Scripture of the Sixth Patriarch, Section 30, in de Bary et al. 1960, Vol. 1, p. 355).

In another Chan Buddhist text, there is reference to the universal Buddha-nature in all existence, sentient and non-sentient: "Question: What is the basic meaning of the Law of the Buddha? The Master said: Filling all streams and valleys" (Recorded Sayings of Ch'an Master Pen-Chi, no. 21, in de Bary et al. 1960, Vol. 1, p. 368).

In conclusion, while a number of Chinese Buddhist schools could accommodate the view of an all-encompassing and inclusive reality, there is little or no specific mention of the natural world and its processes in many of the schools. In other words, while inferences could be made from passages such as those just quoted that sentient and non-sentient beings are included in the enlightenment process and in the realization of the Buddha-mind, Buddha-nature, or some such ultimate reality, such inferences need to be made with caution because the Chinese Buddhist Scriptures and texts do not explicitly deal with this topic in a substantial manner (see also JAINISM and BUDDHISM).

References

Allan, Sarah (1991) The Shape of the Turtle: Myth, Art and Cosmos in Early China, USA: SUNY Press. [A scholarly and philosophical treatment of how religious and ritual practices during the Shang Dynasty were connected to ancient Chinese Cosmology.]

Ames, R. (1986) "Taoism and the nature of nature," Environmental Ethics 8, Winter. [A fresh approach to environmental ethics, drawing on Daoist ideas.]

Chan, W. T. (1961) A Source Book in Chinese Philosophy (Princeton: Princeton University Press). [A primer that introduces the classical Chinese schools of thought.]

Cheng, C. Y. (1997) "The origins of Chinese philosophy," Companion Encyclopedia of Asian Philosophy, ed. B. Carr and I. Mahalingam (London: Routledge), pp. 493–534. [This piece, though its aims are introductory, includes thoughtful consideration of the subject-matter.]

Day, C. B. (1962) The Philosophers of China (London: Peter Owen). [Introductory and interesting presentation of the Chinese world-view.]

De Bary, W. T., Chan, W. T., and Watson, B. (1960) Sources of Chinese Tradition, 2 vols. (New York and London: Columbia University Press). [A comprehensive source book which includes translations from sections of *Lushi Chunqiu* (Spring and Autumn of Mr Lu) and of the "Great Appendix" to the Book of Changes.]

Dubs, H. H. (1928) *The Works of Xunzi* (London: Probsthain). [Xunzi was a thinker belonging to the Confucian school.]

Forke, A. (1925) *The World-Conception of the Chinese: their Astronomical, Cosmological and Physico-Philosophical Speculations* (London: Probsthain). [A good introduction to the subject.]

Fung, Y. L. (1933) *Chuang Tzu, a New Selected Translation with an Exposition of the Philosophy of Kuo Hsiang* (Shanghai: Commercial Press). [Zhuangzi is a key figure in early Daoism, Fung's translation is often taken as authoritative.]

Fung, Y. L. (1947) *The Spirit of Chinese Philosophy*, trans. E. R. Hughes (London: Kegan Paul). [Fung examines and analyzes the assumptions behind Chinese thought.]

——(1951, 1953) *A History of Chinese Philosophy*, 2 vols, trans. Derk Bodde (Princeton: Princeton University Press). [A comprehensive work which focuses on the developments in Chinese intellectual history.]

Graham, A. C. (1986) "Yin-Yang and the nature of correlative thinking," *IEAP Occasional Paper and Monograph Series* 6 (Singapore: Institute of East Asian Philosophies). [A detailed, philosophical exploration of correlative thinking that does not skim over complexities.]

Lai, W. (1997) "Buddhism in Chinese philosophy," in *Companion Encyclopedia of Asian Philosophy*, ed. B. Carr and I. Mahalingam (London: Routledge). [A terse encyclopedia entry on Buddhism within Chinese thought.]

Legge, J. (trans.) (1960) *The Chinese Classics*, 5 vols. (Hong Kong: Hong Kong University Press; reprinted from the editions 1893–1895 of the Oxford University Press). [Legge has carried out extensive translations of classical Chinese texts, including Vol. 1: *Lunyu* (Confucian Analects), *Daxue* (Great Learning), and *Zhongyong* (Doctrine of the Mean); Vol. 2: *Mengzi* (Mencius); Vol. 3: *Shujing* (Book of Documents); Vol. 4: *Shijing* (Book of Poetry); Vol. 5: *Chunqiu* (Spring and Autumn Annals) and *Zuozhuan* (Commentary on the Spring and Autumn Annals).

Legge, J. (trans.) (1966) *Sacred Books of the East* (Delhi: Motilal Banarsidass; reprinted from Clarendon Press 1885 edition) [Vol. 3: *Shujing, Shijing* and *Xiaojing* (Book of Filial Piety); Vol. 16: *Yijing* (Book of Changes); Vols. 27 and 28: *Liji* (Book of Rites)].

Major, J. S. (1993) *Heaven and Earth in Early Han Thought* (Albany: State University of New York Press). [Includes excellent translation of and commentary on chapters 3, 4, and 5 of the *Huainanzi*.]

Schwartz, B. (1985) *The World of Thought in Ancient China* (Cambridge: Belknap Press). [A thoughtful, philosophical analysis of Chinese intellectual history.]

Further Reading

Special issues of two journals, *Philosophy East and West* 37, no. 2 (April 1987) and *Environmental Ethics* 8 (Winter 1986), contain collections of conference papers on environmental ethics and Asian and comparative philosophy.

There is an excellent collection of essays on environmental philosophy in Asian traditions, edited by J. B. Callicott and R. T. Ames, *Nature in Asian Traditions of Thought: Essays in Environmental Philosophy* (Albany: SUNY Press, 1989).

3

Classical India

O. P. DWIVEDI

Introduction

In the 1960s, when people started to recognize the gravity of environmental pollution, historian Lynn White Jr. (1967), wrote an article in *Science* on the historical roots of the ecological crisis. According to White, what people do to their environment depends upon how they see themselves in relation to nature. White asserted that the exploitative tendency that has generated much of the environmental crises, particularly in Europe and North America, is a result of the teachings of late medieval Latin CHRISTIANITY, which conceived of humankind as superior to the rest of God's creation and everything else as created for human use and enjoyment. He suggested that the only way to address the ecological crisis was to reject the view that nature has no reason to exist except to serve humanity. White's proposition impelled scientists, theologians, and environmentalists to debate the basis of his argument that religion could be blamed for the ecological crisis.

In the course of this debate, examples from other cultures were cited to support the view that, even in countries where there is religious respect for nature, exploitation of the environment has been ruthless. Countries where Hinduism, Buddhism, Taoism, and Shintoism have been practiced were cited to support the argument of Thomas Derr, among others, that "we are simply being gullible when we take at face value the advertisement of the ecological harmony of nonwestern cultures." Derr goes on to say:

> even if Christian doctrine had produced technological culture and its environmental troubles, one would be at a loss to understand the absence of the same result in equally Christian Eastern Europe. And conversely, if ecological disaster is a particularly Christian habit, how can one explain the disasters non-Christian cultures have visited upon their environments? Primitive cultures, Oriental cultures, classical cultures – all show examples of human dominance over nature which has led to ecological catastrophe. Overgrazing, deforestation and similar errors of sufficient magnitude to destroy civilizations have been committed by Egyptians, Assyrians, Romans, North Africans, Persians, Indians, Aztecs, and even Buddhists, who are foolishly supposed by some Western admirers to be immune from this sort of thing (Derr 1975, p. 43).

This chapter responds to Derr's challenge by explaining how the Hindus' attitude toward nature has been shaped by the religion's view of the cosmos and creation. Such an exposition is necessary to explain the traditional values and beliefs of Hindus and hence what role Hindu religion once played with respect to human treatment of the environment. At the same time, we need to know how it is that this religion, which taught harmony with and respect for nature, and which influenced other religions such as JAINISM AND BUDDHISM, has been in recent times unable to sustain a caring attitude toward nature. What are the features of the Hindu religion which strengthen human respect for God's creation, and how were these features repressed by the modern view of the natural environment and its resources?

The Vedic heritage

The relationship between human beings and nature attracted the seers of the Vedic period in a manner incomparable to any other religious and cultural traditions. The Vedic seers contemplated over the mysteries of the creation, the place of heaven and earth, and even beyond. (Concerning dates of the Vedic period, there is a difference of opinion among some Western Indologists and Indian scholars. For example, Griffith (1889) mentions the Vedic period being 1500–1400 BCE, while Indian scholars such as Tilak (1936) and Kane (1966) suggest about 5000–4000 BCE. Perhaps a more realistic date for Vedic literature would be about 2000 BCE (see Kak 1994).) Those Vedic seers would not accept as final what they saw around themselves; instead, they asked many penetrating questions, not only about life but more about death, because they were intrigued by what happens to the soul once it leaves the physical body. They were equally interested in the mystery of creation and the establishment of this universe. Through their deep thinking, guesses, conjectures and postulations, they came to acknowledge that the material causes of this creation happened to be the *Panch Mahabhutas* (Five Great Elements): traditionally, they are enumerated in the following order as earth/*Prithivi*, air/*Vayu*, space/*Akash*, waters/*Apah*, light-fire/*Agni*; the *Aitareya Upanishad* also names them: "There exist the five elements: earth, air, space, water, and light" (*Aitareya Upanishad*, chapter 3, verse 3. The *Upanishads* represent the profound thinking of early Indian seers to solve the problems of the origin, the nature, and the destiny of human beings and of the universe. The period of *Upanishads* is considered to be around 600 BCE. See Hume 1977, p. 6, and Deussen 1980.)

These five Mahabhutas are cosmic elements which create, nurture, and sustain all forms of life, and after death or decay they absorb what was created earlier; thus they play an important role in preserving and sustaining the environment (Dwivedi 1997). It should be noted that all these Mahabhutas have been deified in the Vedic and, later, in the Puranic literature (starting from 300 BCE to CE 900). Further, together they have been regarded as all-pervasive and omnipresent elements; they have the great creative potency; and, together, they constitute *Brahman*, who manifested the universe and whose manifestation goes on revolving forever. As mentioned in the *Shvetashvatara Upanishad*: "The Brahman by whom this entire universe is engulfed ...this creation is governed by Him as well as the five great elements: earth, air, space, water, and light" (*Shvetashvatara Upanishad*, chapter 6, verse 2). Some further description about these Mahabhutas is given below.

Prithivi (earth)   *Rig Veda* describes Prithivi as a divinity as well as one of the Mahabhutas. She is the mother and upholder of all (*Rig Veda*, book X, hymn 18, verse 10; and book I, hymn 155, verse 2). Prithivi is also identified with the goddess Aditi: a mother and protector of the holy cosmic law; she is also regarded as a divine ship, full of life-sustaining harvest. Along with the four other Mahabhutas, she sustains our universe. This relationship between earth and humans is superbly depicted by Rishi Atharva in *Prithivi Sukta* (Hymn to Mother Earth) of Atharva Veda. (*Sukta* is a short composition of verses which relate to a specific subject under discussion. Each Veda consists of several *Suktas*.)

Vayu (air)   In Vedic literature, Vayu is the bond and the thread which keeps the universe together. When Uddalaka asked Yagyavalkya: what is that thread which binds this world and the other world and all beings?, Rishi Yagyavalkya replied: "By air indeed, O Gautama, as thread, this world, the other world, and all beings are held together" (*Brahadaranyaka Upanishad*, Brahmanam, chapter 7, verse 2). Vayu is also likened to *Prana* (the life-sustaining breath). Vayu is the germ of the world and a transformer of seed. Without *Prana*, nothing survives.

Akash (space)   The word *Akash* denotes space rather than sky or ether as mentioned in some translated Vedic literature. It is not a material or physical element. This word has appeared more in the *Upanishads* than in *Rig Veda*, where synonyms such as *nabhas*, *kham*, *antarikchha*, or *dyaus* have appeared. In *Chhandogya Upanishad*, a discussion takes place between three Rishis. One of them, Shilak, asks: what is the foundation of this world? Pravaahana replies that it is the *Akash* because it is from the *Akash* (space) that all beings (their souls) come, and it is where they return after their death, and because the *Akash* is the final refuge of all beings (*Chhandogya Upanishad*, book I, part 9, verse 1).

Apah(water)   According to Vedas, water was the first of the cosmic elements. *Rig Veda* says that "in the beginning, all was water, and there was darkness which engulfed it" (*Rig Veda*, book X, hymn 129, verse 3); as a matter of fact, in *Rig Veda*, four hymns have been addressed to the waters (book VII, hymns 47 and 49; book X, hymns 9 and 30). Further, the *Rig Vedic* hymn 23 (book I, verses 16–21) considers water as the reservoir of all curative medicines and of nectar. Water is the mother of all beings and the foundation (*pratishtha*) of all in the universe (Lal 1995, p. 9). The genesis of the universe takes place in the primeval water. The following verse from *Atharva Veda* illustrates the place of water in our lives:

> May the waters from the snowy mountains bring health and peace to all people. May the spring waters bring calm to you. May the swift-current be pleasing to you; and may the rains be a source of tranquillity to all. May the waters of oasis in desert be sweet to you; and so be the waters of ponds and lakes. May the waters from wells dug by humans be good to them, and may the healing powers of water be available to all beings. (*Atharva Veda*, book XIX, hymn 2, verses 1 and 2)

Agni (light/fire)   *Agni* is considered in Vedas as the spring of our life because it creates life on earth. In later Vedic description, *Agni* is known as the sun and light. In the form of the sun, *Agni* is regarded as the soul, and also as the ruler and preserver of the world (*Maitrayana Upanishad*, chapter 6, verse 35). In *Rig Veda*, book X, a series of hymns (such as 1–8, 11–12, 16, 20–1, 37, 45–6, 51 etc.) are devoted to *Agni*; and its almighty primordial nature is depicted as both non-existent (*asat*), and existent (*sat*); that is, the first cause and the first effect of this creation (*Rig Veda*, book X, hymns 5 and 7).

The Prithivi Sukta

The *Atharva Veda* (about 2000 BCE) is perhaps the first of its kind of scripture in any spiritual tradition where the concept of respect to the earth has been propounded. An entire chapter consisting of 63 verses has been devoted in praise of Mother Earth. These verses integrate much of the thought of Hindu seers concerning our existence on earth. A series of verses follow, addressed to Devi Vasundhara, the Goddess Earth, evoking her benevolence (in Hindu tradition, a mother is also accorded the place of a goddess). Mother Earth is seen as the nourisher and provider of space for the entire family (*Kutumbakam*) of all beings – humans and others alike (Dwivedi 1998). In a prayer, verse 11 tells us:

> O Mother Earth! Sacred are thy hills, snowy mountains, and deep forests. Be kind to us and bestow upon us happiness. May you be fertile, arable, and nourisher of all. May you continue supporting people of all races and nations. May you protect us from your anger (natural disasters). And may no one exploit and subjugate your children. (*Atharva Veda*, book XII, hymn I, verse 11)

This prayer, which is based on the cosmic vision of our planet earth, and which also relates to our consciousness towards the environment, is based on the fundamental concept of *Vasudhaiv Kutumbakam*: every entity and organism is a part of one large extended family which is presided over by the eternal Mother Earth. It is She who supports us from her abundant endowments and riches; it is She who nourishes us; it is She who provides us with a sustainable environment; and it is She who, when angered by the misdeeds of her children, punishes them with disasters. As one ought not to insult, unduly exploit, and violate one's mother, but be kind and respectful to her, so, in the same way, one should behave toward Mother Earth. Through such exhortations and various writings, Hindu religion has provided a system of moral guidelines towards environmental preservation and conservation. From the perspective of Hindu culture (as well as from the Buddhist and Jain perspectives, see JAINISM AND BUDDHISM), abuse and exploitation of nature for selfish gain is unjust and sacrilegious.

The *Prithivi Sukta* also exemplifies the relevance of environmental sustenance, agriculture, and biodiversity to human beings. All three main segments of our physical environment – that is water, air and soil – are highlighted, and their usefulness is detailed in various verses (*Atharva Veda*, book XII, verses 3 and 4).

The *Prithivi Sukta* maintains that attributes of earth (such as its firmness, purity, and fertility) are for everyone, and that no one group or nation has special authority over them. That is why the welfare of all and hatred toward none is the core value for which people on this planet ought to strive (verse 18). For example, there is a prayer for the preservation of the original fragrance of earth (verses 23 and 25) so that its natural legacy is sustained for future generations. Further, there is a prayer which says that even when people dig the earth either for agricultural purposes or for extracting minerals, let it be so that her vitals are not hurt and that no serious damage is done to her body and appearance (verse 35) – that her natural resources and vegetation cover be conserved. Similarly, the importance of protecting medicinal herbs and other biodiversity are mentioned in the following verse: "O Mother Earth! you are the sustainer and preserver of all vegetation including medicinal plants as well as all living beings. May you the *Devi Vasundhara* nourish us as long as we live" (*Atharva Veda*, book XII, hymn I, verse 27). Furthermore, an importance given to plants and other vegetation is extolled by Lord Krishna in *Bhagavad Gita*, where the Lord says that, among all plants and trees, He is an Ashvatthah tree – a tree which grows anywhere, even on a very hard surface (*Bhagavad Gita*, chapter 10, verse 26). The *Prithivi Sukta* also mentions that urban centers (*Purah*) should be planned in such a way that the land remains a place of worthwhile living for all, with its natural beauty preserved (verse 43). The earth is considered, after the sun, as the main source of energy flowing through its vitals, such as plants, minerals, and other elements; the same energy is also present in all living beings because it is that energy which drives them to work for quenching their hunger and thirst. Verse 19 illustrates this:

> The Earth is full of energy, and the same energy flows through its herbs and other medicinal plants, the clouds carry energy in the form of thunder, also there is energy inside stones, and the same energy is prevalent among people and animals in the form of hunger. May that energy sustain us. (*Atharva Veda*, book XII, hymn I, verse 19)

Although human greed and exploitative tendencies have been the main cause of environmental destruction, inter-religious and inter-cultural conflicts and wars have also contributed to the environmental problems. The *Prithivi Sukta* urges there to be unity amongst all races and amongst all beliefs, with a prayer to Mother Earth to bestow prosperity upon all people living in all parts of the world:

> The Mother Earth where people belonging to different races, following separate faiths and religions, and speaking numerous languages cares for them in many ways. May that Mother Earth, like a Cosmic Cow, give us the thousand-fold prosperity without any hesitation without being outraged by our destructive actions. (*Atharva Veda*, book XII, hymn I, verse 45)

It is further mentioned that irrespective of the place of assembly, whether in public meetings, or in the woods, or even face-to-face on the field of battle, people should always remain respectful to Mother Earth. Verse 56 portrays this sentiment in the following manner: "Whether we are in rural area, in woods, in battleground or in public meetings (wherever we are), we should always speak graciously about the Mother Earth and be respectful to her" (*Atharva Veda*, book XII, hymn I, verse 56).

Those who defend and protect the environment are showered by blessings (verse 7). That is why, in verse 59, Mother Earth is implored to bless us with all kinds of nourishment and serenity so that we may live in peace and harmony: "May the Mother Earth who is the provider of milk and many nourishing things, grain and other agricultural produce, fragrance, bless us with peace, tranquillity and riches" (*Atharva Veda*, book XII, hymn I, verse 59).

In summary, it can be said that the *Prithivi Sukta*, whose entire set of 63 verses have been dedicated to Mother Earth, is the foremost ancient spiritual text from India which enjoins all human beings to protect, preserve, and care for the environment. This is beautifully illustrated in verse 16, which says that it is up to us as the progeny of Mother Earth to live in peace and harmony with all: "O Mother Earth! you are the world for us and we are your children; let us speak in one accord, let us come together so that we live in peace and harmony, and let us be cordial and gracious in our relationship with other human beings" (*Atharva Veda*, book XII, hymn I, verse 16). These sentiments denote the deep bond between the earth and human beings, and exemplify the true relationship between the earth and all living beings, as well as between humans and other forms of life. Such a comprehensive exposition of eco-spirituality is not found in any other religious tradition. The *Sukta* provides us with a guide to behave in an appropriate manner toward nature.

The Epics and Puranic heritage

According to Hindu scriptures, people must not demand or command dominion over other creatures. They are forbidden from exploiting nature; instead, they are advised to seek peace and live in harmony with nature (Dwivedi 1990). Further, the Hindu religion demands veneration, respect, and obedience to maintain and protect the natural harmonious unity of God and nature. This is demonstrated by a series of divine incarnations, as enunciated by Dr. Karan Singh in the Assisi Declaration:

> The evolution of life on this planet is symbolized by a series of divine incarnations beginning with fish, moving through amphibious forms and mammals, and then on into human incarnations. This view clearly holds that man did not spring fully formed to dominate the lesser life forms, but rather evolved out of these forms itself, and is therefore integrally linked to the whole of creation. (Singh 1986)

Hindu scriptures attest to the belief that the creation, maintenance, and annihilation of the cosmos is completely up to the Supreme Will. In the *Gita*, Lord Krishna says to Arjuna: "Of all that is material and all that is spiritual in this world, know for certain that I am both its origin and dissolution. And it is under Me. By My will it is manifested again and again and by My will, it is annihilated at the end" (*Gita*, 9:8). Further, the Lord says: "I am the origin, the end, existence, and the maintainer (of all)" (*Gita*, 9: 17–18). Thus, for Hindus, both God and nature (*Prakriti*) are one and the same. The most important aspect of Hindu theology pertaining to the treatment of animal life is the belief that the Supreme Being was himself incarnated in the form of various species. The Lord says: "This form is the source and indestructible seed of multifarious incarnations within the universe, and from the particle and portion of this form, different living entities, like demi-gods, animals, human beings and others, are created" (*Srimad-Bhagavata Mahapurana*, book I, discourse 3, verse 5).

The Hindu belief in the cycle of birth and rebirth, wherein a person may come back as an animal or a bird, gives these species not only respect, but also reverence. This provides a solid foundation for the doctrine of *ahimsa* – non-violence (or non-injury) against animals and human beings alike. Hindus have a deep faith in the doctrine of non-violence. It should be noted that the doctrine of *ahimsa* presupposes the doctrine of Karma and of rebirth (*punarjanma*). The soul continues to take birth in different life forms such as birds, fish, animals, and humans. Based on this belief, there is a profound opposition in the Hindu religion (as well as in Buddhist and Jain religions, see JAINISM AND BUDDHISM) to the institutionalized killing of animals, birds, and fish for human consumption. Almost all the Hindu scriptures place strong emphasis on the notion that God's grace can be received by not killing his creatures or harming his creation: "God, Kesava, is pleased with a person who does not harm or destroy other non-speaking creatures or animals" (*Vishnupurana*, book III, chapter 8, verse 15; Dwivedi and Tiwari 1987, p. 49). Further, the pain a human being causes other living beings to suffer will eventually be suffered by that person later, either in this life or in a later rebirth. It is through the transmigration of the soul that a link has been provided between the lowliest forms of life and human beings.

Concerning flora in the Hindu religion: as early as in the time of *Rig Veda*, tree worship was quite popular and universal. The tree symbolized the various attributes of God to the Rig Vedic seers. *Rig Veda* regarded plants as having divine powers, with one entire hymn devoted to their praise, chiefly with reference to their healing properties (*Rig Veda*, book X, hymn 97) Later, during the period of the great epics and *Puranas* (300 BCE to CE 900; see also Griffith 1889), the Hindu respect for flora was expanded further (Dwivedi and Tiwari 1987, pp. 57–71). Trees were considered as animate beings feeling happiness and sorrow. Green trees were likened to a living person.

The Hindu worship of trees and plants has been based partly on utility, but mostly because divinity is assigned to them. Hindu ancestors considered it their duty to save trees; and in order to do so they attached to every tree a religious sanctity. It is still popularly believed by Hindus that every tree has a *Vriksha-devata*, or "tree deity," who is worshipped with prayers and offerings of water, flowers, and sweets, and encircled by sacred threads. The following deities, for example, are considered to have made their abode in these trees/plants: Goddess Lakshmi in Tulasi (*ocinum sanctum*), Goddess Shitala in Neem, God Vishnu in Pipal/Bodhi (*ficus religiosa*), Lord Buddha in Ashoka, Lord Shiva in Bilva/Bela (*aegle marmelos*), and Lord Brahma and Lord Vishnu in Vata (*ficus indica*). Also, for Hindus, the planting of a tree is still a religious duty. Thus, sanctity has been attached to many trees and plants.

The sanctity-of-life principle

The principle of the sanctity of life is clearly ingrained in the Hindu religion. Only God has absolute sovereignty over all creatures; thus, human beings have no dominion over their own lives or non-human life. Consequently, humanity cannot act as a viceroy of God to oversee the planet, nor assign degrees of relative worth to other species. The idea of the Divine Being as the one underlying power of unity is beautifully expressed in the *Yajurveda*: "The loving sage beholds that Being, hidden in mystery, wherein the universe comes to have one home. Therein unites and there from emanates the whole; the Omnipresent One pervades souls and matter like warp and woof in created beings" (*Yajurveda*, chapter 32, verse 8). The sacredness of God's creation means no damage may be inflicted on other species without adequate justification. Therefore, all lives, human and non-human, are of equal value and all have the same right to existence. According to the *Atharva Veda*, the earth is not for human beings alone, but for other creatures as well: "Born of Thee, on Thee move mortal creatures; Thou bearest them, both quadruped and biped. Thine, O Earth, are these five races of humans, for whom the Sun as he rises spreads with his rays, the light that is immortal" (*Atharva Veda*, book XII, hymn 1, verse 15).

The following stanza from the *Isavasya Upanishad* is outstanding testimony to the best idealistic concept of ecological harmony in Hindu religion: "This universe is the creation of Supreme Power meant for the benefit of all; individual species must therefore learn to enjoy its benefits by forming a part of the system in close relationship with other species. Let not any one species encroach upon the other's right" (*Isavasya Upanishad*, chapter 1, verse 2). Hindus contemplate divinity as the one in many and the many in one. This conceptualization resembles both monotheism and polytheism. Monotheism is the belief in a single divine person. In monotheistic creeds that Person is God. Polytheism, on the other hand, believes in the many, and the concept of God is not monarchical. The Hindu concept of God resembles monotheism in that it portrays the divinity as one, and polytheism in that it contemplates the divinity as one in many. Although there are many gods, each one is the Supreme Being for the believer. We may call this attitude non-dualistic theism.

The earliest Sanskrit texts, the *Vedas* and *Upanishads*, teach about the non-dualism of the supreme power that existed before the creation. God as the efficient cause, and nature, *Prakriti*, as the material cause of the universe, are unconditionally accepted, as is their harmonious relationship. However, while these texts agree on the concept of non-dualistic theism, they appear to differ in their opinion about the creation of the universe (Dwivedi and Tiwari 1987, pp. 11–21). This important and intriguing question has been replied suitably in the *Rig Veda*:

He is one, but the sages call him by different names; such as Indra, Mitra, Varuna, Agni, Divya – one who pervaded all the luminous bodies, the source of light; Suparna – the protector and preserver of the universe; whose works are perfect; Matriswa – powerful like wind; and Garutman – mighty by nature. (*Rig Veda*, book I, hymn 164, verse 46)

Although separately stated in the *Vedas*, Sankhya philosophies, *Upanishads, Puranas*, and the two great Hindu epics *Ramayana* and *Mahabharata*, a single thought concerning the concept of creation flows between them. This unifying theory is well stated in the *Rig Veda*:

> The Vedas and the universal laws of nature which control the universe and govern the cycles of creation and dissolution were made manifest by the All-knowing One. By His great power were produced the clouds and the vapors. After the production of the vapors, there intervened a period of darkness after which the Great Lord and Controller of the universe arranged the motions which produce days, nights, and other durations of time. The Great One then produced the sun, the moon, the earth, and all other regions as He did in previous cycles of creation. (*Rig Veda*, book X, hymn 190, verses 1–3)

This concept is depicted later in the *Mahabharata* where it is stated:

> The Father of all creatures, Lord God, made the sky. From sky, He made water and from water made fire (*Agni*) and air (*Vayu*). From fire and air, the earth (*Prithivi*) came into existence. Actually, mountains are His bones, earth is the flesh, sea is the blood, and sky is His abdomen. The sun and moon are His eyes. The upper part of the sky is His head, the earth is His feet, and directions are His hands. (*Mahabharata*, Moksa-parva, chapter 182, verses 14–19)

Thus, for ancient Hindus, both God and nature were to be one and the same. While the *Prajapati* (as mentioned in *Rig Veda*) is the creator of sky, the earth, oceans, and all other species, He is also their protector and eventual destroyer. He is the only Lord of creation. Human beings have no special privilege or authority over other creatures; on the other hand, they have more obligations and duties.

The most important aspect of Hindu religion pertaining to the treatment of animal life is the belief that the Supreme Being was himself incarnated in the form of various species. The Lord says: "This form is the source and indestructible seed of multifarious incarnations within the universe, and from the particle and portion of this form, different living entities, like demi-gods, animals, human beings and others, are created" (*Srimad-Bhagavata Mahapurana*, book I, discourse 3, verse 5). Among the various incarnations of God (numbering from 10 to 24 depending upon the source of the text), He first incarnated Himself in the form of a fish, then a tortoise, then a boar, and then a dwarf. His fifth incarnation was as a man-lion. As Rama he was closely associated with monkeys, and as Krishna he was surrounded by cows. Thus, all species are accorded reverence.

Almost all the Hindu scriptures place a strong emphasis on the notion that one should not kill animals or harm other creatures. For example, in *Manusmriti* it is said that as meat can never be obtained without killing an animal or other living creatures, such killing is detrimental to the attainment of *moksha* (the heavenly bliss) (*Manusmriti*, book V, verse 48). It is further stated: "A person who kills an animal for meat will die of a violent death as many times as there are hairs of that killed animal" (*Manusmriti*, book V, verse 38). Similarly, *Yajnavalkya Smriti* warns of hell-fire (*Ghora Naraka*) to those who are killers of domesticated and protected animals: "The wicked person who kills animals which are protected has to live in hell-fire for the days equal to the number of hairs on the body of that animal" (*Yajnavalkya Smriti*, Acaradhyayah, verse 180). That is why *not* eating meat is considered both appropriate conduct and a duty.

By the end of the Vedic and Upanishadic period, JAINISM AND BUDDHISM came into existence, and the protection of animals, birds, and vegetation was further strengthened by the various kings practicing these religions. These religions, which arose in part as a protest against the orthodoxy and rituals of the Hindu religion, continued their precepts for environmental protection. The Buddhist emperor, Ashoka (273–236 BCE), promoted through public proclamations the planting and preservation of flora and fauna. Pillar Edicts, erected at various public places, expressed his concerns about the welfare of creatures, plants, and trees, and prescribed various punishments for the killing of animals, including ants, squirrels, and rats.

Pollution and its prevention in Hindu scriptures

Hindu scriptures reveal a clear conception of the ecosystem. On this basis, a discipline of environmental ethics developed which formulated codes of conduct (*Dharma*) and defined humanity's relationship to nature. An important code of conduct is the maintainance of proper sanitation. In the past, this was considered to be the duty of everyone and any default was a punishable offence. As Kautilya wrote:

> The punishment of one eighth of a pana should be awarded to those who throw dirt on the roads. For muddy water one-fourth pana, if both are thrown the punishment should be double. If latrine is thrown or caused near a temple, well, or pond, sacred place, or government building, then the punishment should increase gradually by one pana in each case. For urine the punishment should be only half. (*Kautilya's Arthasastra*, book II, chapter 36, verse 145)

Hindus considered the cremation of dead bodies and the sanitary maintenance of the human habitat as essential acts. When, in about 200 BCE, Charaka wrote about *Vikriti* (pollution) and diseases, caused by pollution of air and water, he said about air pollution:

> The polluted air is mixed with unhealthy elements. The air is uncharacteristic of the season, full of moisture, stormy, hard to breath, icy cool, hot and dry, harmful, roaring, coming at the same time from all directions, bad smelling, oily, full of dirt, sand, steam, creating diseases in the body and is considered polluted. (*Charaka Samhita*, Vimanastanam, chapter III, verse 6.1)

And about water pollution, he wrote: "Water is considered polluted when it is excessively smelly, unnatural in color, taste, and touch, slimy, not frequented by aquatic birds, aquatic life is reduced, and the appearance is unpleasing" (ibid, verse 6.2).

Hindus consider water to be a powerful medium for purification and also a source of energy. Sometimes, just by the sprinkling of pure water in religious ceremonies, it is believed purity is achieved. That is why, in *Rig Veda*, prayer is offered to the deity of water: "The waters in the sky, the waters of rivers, and water in the well whose source is the ocean, may all these sacred waters protect me" (*Rig Veda*, book VII, hymn 49, verse 2). The healing properties and medicinal value of water has been universally accepted – provided it is pure and free from all pollution. When polluted water and pure water were the point of discussion among ancient Indian thinkers, they were aware of the reasons for polluted water. That is why Manu advised: "One should not cause urine, stool, cough in the water. Anything which is mixed with these un-pious objects, blood and poison, should not be thrown into water" (*Man-usmriti*, book IV, verse 56).

Still today, many rivers are considered sacred. Among these, the river Ganga is considered by Hindus as the most sacred body of water. In *Pravascitta Tatva* (1.535), the disposal of human waste or other pollutants has been prohibited since time immemorial:

One should not perform these 14 acts near the holy waters of the river Ganga: i.e., remove excrement, brushing and gargling, removing cerumen from body, throwing hairs, dry garlands, playing in water, taking donations, performing sex, attachment with other sacred places, praising other holy places, washing clothes, throwing dirty clothes, thumping water and swimming. (Dwivedi and Tiwari 1987, p. 84)

On pollution in general, the Great Epic, *Mahabharata* states: "From pollution two types of diseases occur in human beings. The first which is related with body and the other with mind, and both are inter-connected. One follows the other and none exists without the other" (*Mahabharata*, Rajdharmanusasanparva, chapter 16, verses 8–9).

Eco-spirituality and environmental conservation

Eco-spirituality and eco-care require that the entire universe is seen as an extended family, with all living beings in this universe as members of the household. This concept, also known as *Vasudhaiv Kutumbakam* (*Vasudha* means earth; *Kutumba* means extended family), refers to all human beings as well as other creatures living on earth as members of the same extended family of *Devi Vasundhara*. Only by considering the entire universe as a part of our extended family, can we (individually and collectively) develop the necessary maturity and respect for all other living beings.

On this concept of *Vasudhaiv Kutumbakam*, Dr. Karan Singh says: "the planet we inhabit and of which we are all citizens – Planet Earth – is a single, living, pulsating entity; . . . the human race, in the final analysis is an interlocking, extended family – *Vasudhaiv Kutumbakam* as the Veda has it" (Singh 1991, p. 123). We also know that members of the extended family do not willfully endanger the lives and livelihood of others; instead, they first think in terms of caring for others before taking an action. That is why, in order to transmit this new global consciousness, it is essential that the concept of *Vasudhaiv Kutumbakam* is encouraged. For this, the world's great religions would have to cooperate with each other. The welfare and caring of all would be realized through the golden thread of spiritual understanding and cooperation at the global level. Sustainable development, from this perspective, ought to include the uplift (both spiritual and material) of all without exploitation and destruction of others. How to secure a development which creates conditions for environmental *Sarvodaya* and *Abhyudaya*, the welfare of all without harming others and destroying the environment, is a challenge for India – a nation endowed with a rich Vedic-Hindu heritage of eco-spirituality.

Hindu religion and culture, in ancient and medieval times, provided a system of moral guidelines regarding environmental preservation and conservation. Environmental ethics, as propounded by ancient Hindu scriptures and seers, was practiced not only by common persons, but even by rulers and kings. They observed these fundamentals, sometimes as religious duties, often as rules of administration or obligations for law and order, but always as principles properly knitted with the Hindu way of life. That way of life authorized Hindus, as well as other religious groups residing in India, to use natural resources, but not to have any divine power of control and dominion over nature and its elements.

If such has been the tradition, philosophy, and ideology of Hindu religion, what then are the reasons behind the present state of environmental crisis facing India and, more specifically, the seeming indifference about environmental conservation among Hindu people? As we have seen, ethical beliefs and religious values influence people's behavior toward others, including their relationship with all creatures and plant life. If, for some reasons, those noble values become displaced by other beliefs that are either thrust upon the society or transplanted from another culture through invasion, then the faith of the masses in the earlier cultural tradition is shaken. With about nine centuries of foreign cultural domination by Islamic and Christian traditions, including their languages and systems of governance, which penetrated all levels of Hindu society, and since appropriate answers and leadership were not forthcoming from religious leaders and priests, it was only natural for the masses to become more inward-looking. In addition, besides the influence of alien culture and values, what really influenced the Hindu view of life and consequently also damaged India's environment are the insidious forces of materialism, consumerism, individual and corporate greed, the blind race to industrialize the nation immediately after achieving independence, and the capriciousness as well as corruption among politicians, bureaucrats, and forest contractors. Under such circumstances, religious values that acted as sanctions against environmental destruction were sidelined as those insidious forces greatly inhibited the religion from continuing to transmit ancient values which encouraged respect and due regard for God's creation. Perhaps, this could be an answer to Thomas Derr's argument about why non-western cultures such as Hindus could not maintain ecological harmony.

Let us not forget that all religions and cultures will be judged by future generations by the depth of their response to the problems generated by our rape of the planet. Any religion or culture which refuses to respond to this challenge will be judged for its silence. Because, in the final analysis, the environmental crisis that we are facing today is not only a crisis of science and technology, nor a crisis of human values alone, but also a crisis of human spirit. Hindu religion and its cultural philosophy, in its own way, offers a unique set of moral values and norms to guide us in our relationship with nature. Not only the Hindu religion but all religions provide sanctions and other stiffer penalities, such as the threat of eternal damnation, for those who do not treat God's creation with respect. Of course, traditional religions such as Hindu religion have been unable to protect the environment from humanity's greed and exploitation, but neither have the secular institutions been very effective. Nature conservation and the protection of God's creation demand that secular and spiritual domains work together. Any framework for environmental conservation and sustainable development that ignores the role of spirituality and ethics in shaping our attitudes toward nature will remain imbalanced.

The Hindu heritage of eco-spirituality can lead us to control our base characteristics, such as greed, exploitation, abuse, mistreatment and defilement of nature. But before we can hope to change the exploitative tendencies, it is absolutely essential that we discipline our inner thoughts. It is here where the religious exhortations and injunctions may come into play for environmental stewardship. This eco-spirituality-oriented environmental stewardship can be a mechanism which strengthens respect for nature by enabling people to center their values upon the notion that there is a cosmic ordinance and a divine law which must be maintained. Further, environmental stewardship can provide new ways of valuing and caring. It can also influence and promote sustainable development. Eco-spirituality, if globally manifested, can also provide the values necessary for an environmentally caring world and will not advance a blind belief in economic growth at all costs, creating in its wake greed, poverty, inequality, and injustice as well as environmental destruction. Environmental stewardship, then, drawing upon the Vedic and Puranic precepts, may become a new universal consciousness around which the concept of global stewardship of the environment may develop; and in this way we may usher in new values in line with an environmentally caring world.

References

Atharvaveda (1982) translated by Devi Chand (New Delhi: Munsiram Manoharlal Publishers); see also *Atharva Veda: Prithivi Sukta* (1958) commentary by Pandit Shripad Damodar Satvalekar (Surat: Swadhyay Mandal). [One of the best commentaries available on *Atharvaveda* and its hymn *Prithivi Sukta*.]

Charaka-Samhita (repr. 1983) translated by Priyavrat Sharma (Varanasi: Chaukhambha Orientalia). [A Hindu treatise on science, medicine, and surgery, including a discussion on the impact of pollutants on humans and nature.]

Derr, Thomas S. (1975) "Religion's responsibility for the ecological crisis; an argument run amok," *World View* 18. [A defense of the Judeo-Christian tradition against White (1967) on the grounds that non-Christian nations also face environmental crisis.]

Deussen, Paul (1980) *Sixty Upanishads of the Veda*, 2 vols. Translated from German by V. M. Bedekar and G. B. Palsule (Delhi: Motilal Banarsidass). [Paul Deussen's original work in German, *Sechzig Upanisads Des Veda*, was first published in Leipzig in 1871. It is a standard text consisting of 60 selected Upanishads.]

Dwivedi, O. P. (1990) "Satyagraha for conservation: awakening the spirit of Hinduism," in *Ethics of Environment and Development: Global Challenges and International Response*, ed. J. Ronald Engel and Joan Gibbs Engel (London: Belhaven Press), pp. 201–12. [A much-quoted essay discussing the Hindu principle of the sanctity of life, duties to God's creation including flora and fauna, prevention of pollution in Hindu scriptures, modern movements in India to prevent deforestation (such as Chipko movement), and choices for the present generation.]

Dwivedi, O. P. (1997) "Vedic heritage for environmental stewardship," *World-views: Environment, Culture and Religion* 1, no. 1, pp. 25–36. [Traces the concept of environmental conservation and pollution prevention to the ancient Vedic era in India, and suggests ways for enhancing environmental stewardship.]

——(1998) *Vasudhaiv-Kutumbakam* (Jaipur, India: Institute for Research and Advanced Studies). [An ecological and sustainable development-oriented interpretation and commentary in Hindi language on the Atharvaveda's hymn *Prithivi Sukta*.]

Dwivedi, O. P. and Tiwari, B. N. (1987) *Environmental Crisis and Hindu Religion* (New Delhi: Gitanjali Publishing House). [Pioneering study of the Hindu view of the environment.]

Griffith, Ralph T. H. (1889) *The Hymns of the Rig Veda*, ed. J. L. Shastri, 1973 (Delhi: Motilal Banarsidass). [This is an excellent translation of *Rig Veda*, with an extensive commentary.]

Hume, Robert Ernest (1977) *The Thirteen Principal Upanishads* (New York: Oxford University Press). [Robert E. Hume selected 13 major Upanishads and translated them into English with an extensive commentary, bibliography, and exposition of the method of translation. The book was first published in 1921, and has been reprinted several times since then.]

Kautilya's Arthasastra (1967) translated and edited by R. Shamasastry (Mysore: Mysore Publishers). [Treatise written about 300 BCE on the duties of a king, managing state affairs, revenue and tax collection, crime and punishment, diplomacy and secret services, and conservation of lands and natural resources.]

Kak, S. (1994) "The evolution of writing in India," *Indian Journal of History of Science* 28, pp. 375–88. [This article examines the origin of Sanskrit writings in India and suggests that the Vedic period starts at about 2000 BCE.]

Kane, Panduranga Vaman (1963) *Dharmashastra Ka Itihas* (in Hindi) (Lucknow, India: Uttar Pradesh Hindi Sansathan). [Panduranga Kane wrote a five-volume history of Dharmashastras in which he examined the concept of Dharma, a commentary on all Dharmashastras, Samsakaras, pilgrimages to be taken by Hindus, fasting, Tantra-Mantras, pastoral duties, and various aspects of the Hindu code of conduct.]

Lal, S. K. (1995) "Pancamahabhutas: origin and myths in Vedic literature," in *Prakrti: An Integral Vision* (vol. 2), ed. Sampat Narayanan (New Delhi: Indira Gandhi National Center for the Arts), pp. 5–21. [An excellent exposition of the role of five Great Elements in Hindu Vedic literature, and their relevance to the modern concept of environmental conservation.]

Mahabharata (1988) Translated by M. N. Dutta, (Delhi: Parimal Publications). [An epic with more than 100,000 verses divided into 18 books, consisting of a mixture of history, mythology, and theology, woven around the story of a great war fought for 18 days between cousin princes.]

Manusmriti (The Laws of Manu) (1975) Translated by G. Buhler (Delhi: Motilal Banarsidass). [Hindu Code of Law given by Rishi Manu, includes a code of conduct for individuals, family life, sacrifices, property rights, the four stages of life, and guidance for Kings.]

Prithivi-Sukta (*Atharva Veda*) book XII (1958) (Surat: Swadhyay Mandal). Commentary by Pandit Shripad Damodar Satvalekar. [Depicts the Universal Mother and how she protects, nourishes, and takes care of all beings and organisms as a part of her extended family.]

Rig Veda (1974) Translated by Maharishi Dayandand Saraswati, 12 vols. (New Delhi: Sarvadeshik Arya Pratinidhi Sabha). [First of the four Vedic sacred books of Hindus, considered to be of divine origin and revealed to Hindu Rishis; consists of about 10,500 verses, a collection of various hymns and songs, including worship of natural elements.]

Srimad Bhagavata Mahapurana (1982) Translated by C. L. Goswami and M. A. Shastri (Gorakhpur: Gita Press). [One of the main Puranas, it narrates the glory and exploits of the god-incarnation, Lord Krishna as told by Rishi Vyasa.]

Singh, Dr. Karan (1986) "The Hindu declaration on Nature," *Declarations on Religion and Nature made at Assisi, Italy* (Gland, Switzerland: WWF). [A succinct document on the Hindu interpretation of the environment.]

——(1991). *Brief Sojourn* (Delhi: B. R. Publishing Corporation). [An autobiographical account of his tenure as India's Ambassador to the USA, including a discussion on ecology in the context of Hindu tradition.]

Tilak, Bal Gangadhar (1936) *Gita Rahasya* (Poona: Tilak Brothers). [An authoritative translation and commentary, with an extensive introduction about such concepts as Karma Yoga, *Sukhavada* (hedonism), happiness and misery, Atman, the origin of the cosmos, renunciation, and *Bhakti* (the path of devotion).]

White, Jr., Lynn. (1967). "The historical roots of our ecological crisis", *Science* 155, pp. 1203–7. [This is an oft-quoted essay by a historian who traces the roots of ecological crisis to the influence of Christianity (and the way it has been used) in western civilization to dominate and exploit the natural world.]

Yajurveda (1982) Translated by Devi Chand (New Delhi: Munsiram Manoharlal Publishers). [The second Hindu Vedic sacred book, consisting of about 2,000 verses, involving specific directions and codes of conduct to individuals and families, duties of the king, rituals, ceremonies, and respect for the natural world.]

4

Jainism and Buddhism

CHRISTOPHER KEY CHAPPLE

Introduction

Jainism and Buddhism arise from ancient India and share several basic features. Both emphasize asceticism and may be characterized as renouncer traditions. Unlike Hinduism, they do look to the Vedic texts as sources of religious inspiration, but owe their origins to human teachers (see CLASSICAL INDIA). Jainism is the older of the two traditions, looking to the teachings of 24 spiritual leaders known as Tirthankaras. It has been suggested that the 23rd of these teachers, Parsvanatha, lived in the eighth century BCE. His successor, Mahavira, the 24th Tirthankara, lived in northeast India during the time of the Buddha. Buddhism originated with the life and teachings of the Buddha (Siddhartha Gautama) who probably lived in the fifth or fourth century BCE.

Until the past decade, when thousands of Jainas migrated to Great Britain and North America, Jainism was found nearly exclusively in India. The largest concentrations of Jainas today reside in the northwest Indian states of Maharashtra, Gujarat, and Rajasthan. Buddhism spread from India throughout the rest of Asia. Theravada Buddhism (the Way of the Elders) continues to be the majority religion in Sri Lanka, Myanmar, Cambodia, Laos, and Thailand. Mahayana Buddhism (the Great Vehicle) is practiced in China, Korea, Japan, and Vietnam. Vajrayana Buddhism (Tantra) is prevalent within the Tibetan religious community. Information on Buddhism has been available to Europeans and Americans for nearly 150 years. For the past two decades sufficient numbers of Americans have practiced Buddhism of various types for an American form of Buddhism to emerge.

In this chapter, themes and texts from each tradition will be explored as possible indigenous Asian resources for coping with the issue of environmental degradation. Additionally, examples will be given of contemporary environmental action undertaken in Asia inspired by Jainism and Buddhism.

Jainism and environmental philosophy

According to the Jaina tradition, 24 great teachers (Tirthankaras) have urged their followers to cast off the shackles of karma in search of spiritual perfection (*kevala*). The *Kalpa Sutra*, a second or first century BCE text recognized by the Svetambara Jaina community of northwest India, recounts the lives of these great teachers, with particular emphasis on Rsibha, the legendary founder of Jainism, Parshva, the 23rd teacher (ca. 800 BCE), and Mahavira, the 24th and final great teacher.

The *Acaranga Sutra* (ca. fifth or fourth century BCE) outlines detailed practices for the observance of non-violence (*ahimsa*). By perfecting non-violent behavior, the Jaina practitioner cleanses one's life force or soul (*jiva*) and rids it of all traces of karma, which, for the Jainas, is considered to be a viscous, colorful, subtle substance. For laypersons, non-violence requires avoidance of professions that entail harm to any living being; for monks and nuns, this requires a life of utmost simplicity. Not only do monks and nuns avoid killing insects, by sweeping their path and covering their mouths, they also develop a conscious respect for the life force within the elements themselves, and hence eschew digging into the earth, wading in water, lighting or extinguishing flames, or speaking too forcefully into the air.

The Jainas developed a strict policy of vegetarianism in support of their quest for purification. In addition to the basic practice of *ahimsa*, four additional great vows (*mahavrata*) were observed: truthfulness (*satya*), not stealing (*asteya*), sexual restraint (*brahmacarya*), and non-possession (*aparigraha*). Mahavira observed this fifth vow by totally renouncing all possessions, even his clothes. Today, the most advanced monks of the Digambara school of Jainism likewise live without clothing.

Several aspects of the Jaina religion accord well with contemporary ecological theory. First, Jaina cosmology maintains that humans dwell in a universe suffused with life. Jainism values life in its particularity, as indicated by the many animal hospices it supports throughout India and its centuries-old advocacy of vegetarianism. Umasvati's *Tattvarthasutra* (ca. second or third century CE) outlines a continuity of life forms ranging from elemental and microbial forms to plants and animals to humans and gods. Depending upon how much karma a life accrues or disperses over the course of a lifetime, one will be reborn into a higher or lower life form. The highest birth is human birth, as humans are said to possess the presence of mind and will-power to practice non-violence effectively. The resultant vegetarian diet, the conscious decision to lead a non-violent lifestyle, and the concomitant minimal consumption of resources (particularly evident in the lives of monks and nuns) accord well with the basic tenets of DEEP ECOLOGY.

Throughout India's history, Jaina activists worked to convince the Hindu Brahmans to stop using ANIMALS in ritual sacrifice. Jaina advisors to the Mughal Court were also effective in persuading the Emperor Akbar to declare certain Jaina districts hunt-free. The Jaina layman Raychandbhai Mehta (1868–1901) profoundly influenced Mahatma Gandhi and helped shape his successful non-violent resistance campaign to throw off the shackles of British colonial rule. Today in India, the Jainas continue to work at integrating their philosophy of non-violence with daily life. Michael Tobias, commenting on encounters with Jaina "jurists, businessmen, professors, monks, children, industrialists, doctors, engineers" and others, remarked about the "stunning extent to which they are constantly talking about and attuned to [non-violence toward] nature" (Tucker and Grim 1994, p. 144).

The concern for integrating non-violent principles into daily life has been with Jainas since the beginning. Just as the development of consumer markets is wreaking havoc with traditional values in India today, Jainism arose during a period in Indian civilization of great urbanization. The rainforest that once covered the Indian peninsula largely disappeared during this phase of Indian history; India relied heavily upon timber for the construction and maintenance of cities. Feeling the pain involved with the destruction of the forest, Mahavira exhorted his followers to "change their minds" about things. Rather than seeing big trees as "fit for palaces, gates, houses, benches . . . boats, buckets, stools, trays, ploughs, machines, wheels, seats, beds, cars, and sheds," they should speak of them as "noble, high and round, with many branches, beautiful and magnificent" (Jacobi 1884: *Acaranga Sutra* II.4.2.11–12). This same advice may be applied to the modern consumer whose shopping habits may lead to the purchase of more than is needed to sustain one's well-being (see CONSUMPTION).

Acharya Tulsi (1910–97), a leader of the Terapanthi branch of Svetambara Jainas, initiated a non-violent campaign on March 1, 1949 called the Anuvrat Movement. He urged people throughout India to observe twelve vows, ranging from non-violence (*ahimsa*) to "I will do my best to avoid contributing to pollution." He has indicated that Jaina renunciation entails a profoundly ecological lifestyle (Chapple 1993, p. 61). Contemporary Jainas in India are involved with reforestation projects and a "re-greening" of Jaina temple areas in India. The Anuvrat Global Organization convened a conference on "Living in Harmony with Nature: Survival into the Third Millennium" in December, 1995 in Ladnun, Rajasthan. As part of the declaration generated by the conference, Acharya Mahapragya, head of the Terapanthi Svetambara Jainas, wrote: "A person responsible for polluting the environment is in fact endangering his own existence because he is an integral part of the ecological system. . . . Balanced development takes place only when there is a simultaneous development of human values and the environment is protected" (Gandhi 1996, p. 5). Environmental protection, according to the Ladnun declaration, depends on the cultivation of a lifestyle rooted in simplicity and non-attachment.

Overseas Jainas have been supportive of reinterpreting Jainism in light of ecological principles, as indicated in the *Jain Declaration On Nature* by L. M. Singhvi, India's High Commissioner to the United Kingdom. This fascinating document newly interprets Jaina principles in light of the perceived decline of the earth's ecosystems. It begins with a quote from Umasvati's *Tattvarthasutra*: "All life is bound together by mutual support and interdependence." It discusses the practice of non-violence as friendly towards all aspects of nature, emphasizing the principle of mutual dependence of life forms in an ecological idiom. The declaration explains the fundamentals of Jaina cosmology, including the hierarchic grouping of life forms according to the number of senses possessed by each (the elements, plants, and bacteria have only the sense of touch; worms have touch and taste; bugs have touch, taste, and smell; flying insects add the sense of sight; larger animals including humans add the sense of hearing and the thinking capacity). The declaration concludes with an ecological interpretation of Jaina conduct, emphasizing the primary five vows listed above, along with kindness to animals, vegetarianism, avoidance of waste, and charity. Jainas are urged to use any surplus wealth to help advance non-violent eco-friendly causes.

Though Jainas represent a tiny fraction of India's population, they have maintained their identity by adherence to a strict code of conduct and belief in a unique philosophical system. Their eagerness to adapt and reinterpret traditional Jaina teachings to accommodate the modern issue of ecosystem decline demonstrates the flexibility and the tenacity of this ancient tradition.

Buddhism and environmental philosophy

Buddhism emerged in northwest India during a time of economic growth which involved the expansion of both agriculture and trade. As noted by Lewis Lancaster, "it was a time when deforestation of the Ganges region was taking place, population growth was sizable, urban centers were the important hubs – urban islands in a sea of rain forests" (Tucker and Williams 1997, pp. 11–12). Siddhartha Gautama, later known as the Buddha or Awakened One, grew up in Kapilavastu, a city ruled by his father. At the age of 29 he left his home and family to wander throughout the villages of neighboring regions, begging for food, and learning philosophy and meditation first from two great teachers and then experimentally with a small group of fellow renouncers. After six years of wandering, while seated under the Bodhi Tree, he achieved his goal and entered into the state of *nirvana*, which he characterized as free from suffering, free from desire, a state of consciousness beyond all comparison. From the time of his first sermon in Sarnath, near modern-day Banaras, he was known as the Buddha.

Unlike his rival teacher Mahavira, the Buddha did not posit the existence of multiple souls. At variance with the sacrificial religion practiced by the Brahmans, he claimed that rituals do not serve to free one from karmic bondage. Furthermore, he also rejected the Upanisadic notion that the universe and one's self share the same fundamental identity or underlying reality. The Buddha preferred to avoid answering cosmological or even theological questions. He constantly invited his listeners to consider the source of their suffering (*duhkha*), and urged them to follow the precepts of non-injury, truth-telling, giving or not stealing, sexual abstinence, and avoidance of all intoxicants. Each of these helped his students to overcome the negative effects of past action and advanced their process of self-purification.

The goal of Buddhism, then as now, is to transcend all self-concept; by erasing personal attachment and identity, the Buddhist strives to overcome all constraints of past karma. The Buddha reminds his followers that they are not form, feeling, perception, conditioning, or consciousness, stating that "It is by the destruction of these, the not lusting for these, it is by the cessation of, the giving up of, the utter surrender of these things that the heart is called 'fully freed' " (Woodward 1925, p. 14). In other words, by not being attached to one's body or the bodies of others, by not craving feelings or sense perceptions, by not falling under the sway of past actions, and by not identifying oneself with the contents of one's awareness, liberation can be gained. Buddha states that one must regard all things, past, present, or future, as follows: "This is not mine; this am not I; this is not the Self of me" (Woodward 1925, pp. 67–8), thus indicating a total freedom from all attachment. Ultimately, during his lifetime, the Buddha declared 500 of his followers to have attained liberation, thereby being spared of any future rebirth into the realm of misery or *samsara*.

The Buddha taught for 45 years before passing into his final *parinirvana* at the age of 80. During this period he preached to virtually all the people of his day: merchants, politicians, women, kings, jewelers, and scoundrels, to name a few of the types of people listed in the many texts that document his teaching years. One primary vehicle used by the Buddha in addressing his diverse audience was the parable, couched in hundreds of stories (*Jataka*) that tell of past lives. In these stories, the Buddha and various people in the Buddhist community would assume the identities of animals and people who lived long ago. Some were rewarded for their virtue, while others were punished for their folly. Within these stories the Buddha conveys a sense of daily life, with reference to how the forests were being cut, how society was structured, and how the actions one undertakes determine future outcomes, either in this life or a future life.

One such story, the *Vyaddha Jataka*, tells of a dark jungle in which lived many ferocious lions and tigers. Tales of these beasts terrified the nearby villagers and they never entered the forest for fear of their lives. These particular lions and tigers were so skilled in the art of hunting that they slaughtered more creatures than they could possibly consume and left their offal on the forest floor to fester and decay. This created such a horrendous stench that one tree spirit decided to scare off the predators. Against the advice of another tree spirit which was later reborn as the Buddha, the tree spirit who despised the smell of rotting flesh assumed an awful shape, harassed the lions and tigers, and drove them out of the jungle. Several weeks passed and the villagers, having noticed that they no longer saw the tracks of lions or tigers, ventured into the woods, first to gather fallen firewood and then, when they realized they were safe, they chopped down the trees. Eventually, the entire forest was destroyed and the land was brought under cultivation (Chapple, in Tucker and Williams 1997, pp. 141–2). This fable warns against disturbing the natural order of things. To remove one piece of an ecosystem can have widespread deleterious results. This story also conveys a record of the process of deforestation mentioned above that swept through India during the time of the Buddha.

The core teachings of the Buddha on the efficacy of karma, the need for purification, and the non-substantiality of self do not in themselves constitute an environmental ethic. Nonetheless, the pervasive high ethical standards required by the Buddha provide an ample platform for developing such an ethic. For instance, India's great Emperor Asoka (ca. 269–232 BCE), who converted to Buddhism after a notorious spate of violent empire-building, used Buddhist ethics to urge people to grow medicinal trees along the roadways, protect animals, and generally abide by nonviolent principles. Buddhists and Jainas campaigned against the sacrifice of animals in religious ceremonies. Hindu kingdoms soon replaced Asoka's empire and throughout its nearly 1,500 years in India, Buddhism emphasized human salvation through monastic life. Long before its disappearance from India, Buddhism set down roots in Southeast Asia where it continues to flourish.

Environmental philosophy and Theravada Buddhism in Southeast Asia

Within several decades after the death of the Buddha, his teachings or dharma spread to Sri Lanka and the modern-day countries of Myanmar, Thailand, Cambodia, Laos, Malaysia, and Indonesia. Within the past five centuries Malaysia and Indonesia have become primarily Muslim countries. With the exception of Thailand (Siam) the entire region was subjected to European colonial domination for nearly three centuries, with most countries gaining their independence in the middle of the twentieth century. Since the 1970s, this region has been wracked with warfare, with most areas remaining largely agricultural. Theravada Buddhism, having survived the ravages of colonialism and war, remains an active presence in Sri Lanka, Myanmar, Thailand, Cambodia, and Laos.

Among the Buddhist countries of Southeast Asia, Thailand has experienced the largest degree of western-style development. Myanmar (formerly Burma) maintained an isolationist economic policy for several decades that has stunted the consumption of natural resources. Laos and Cambodia, devastated by the Vietnam War and its aftermath (including, for Cambodia, the terror of Pol Pot's reign), have experienced a period of slow rebuilding. Laos remains largely rural. Cambodia suffered a tremendous loss of human life and virtual destruction of its cities in the 1970s and 1980s, which are in the process of being rebuilt. These complex political factors result in an environmental situation quite unlike that experienced in the more developed nations of Western Europe, North America, and Japan.

In Thailand, on the other hand, the style and pace of economic growth in the last two decades of the twentieth century has paralleled that of industrial America in the years following the Second World War. Bangkok and other cities in Thailand have mushroomed. Forests have been clearcut both for internal use and for export. Several examples of local Buddhist response to environmental ravage can be found in Thailand, where "80 percent of the jungle... has disappeared in less than 25 years" (Batchelor and Brown 1992, p. 87). Both the formal monastic community and activist laypersons have been involved in environmental causes.

In addition to city-based monasteries that have exerted wide influence in areas of culture and politics throughout Thai history, the Buddhist community in Thailand has maintained a tradition of forest hermitages. These hermitages have nurtured an indigenous form of Buddhism that holds nature in high esteem. Buddhadasa Bhikkhu (1906–93) founded Wat Suan Mon, a forest retreat, in 1932. He wrote that "Trees, rocks, sand, even dirt and insects can speak... They help us understand what it means to cool down from the heat of our confusion, despair, anxiety, and suffering" (Swearer, in Tucker and Williams 1997, pp. 24–5). For several decades, Buddhadasa developed a biocentric spiritual view, equating oneness with nature and the practice of Buddhist *dharma*. Inspired by this interpretation of Buddhist teachings, many monastic and lay Buddhists in Thailand have become involved with environmental issues. Several monks have campaigned against the logging of teak and other precious woods, which threatens to destroy Thailand's rainforest. Phra Prajak and others have been arrested repeatedly for organizing protests against the development of commercial eucalyptus plantations on National Forest Reserve Lands. An association of monks interested in conservation has engaged in a variety of activities to stave off further environmental destruction. In the words of monk Ajahn Pongsak: "Dharma, the Buddhist word for truth and the teachings, is also the word for nature. When we destroy nature we destroy the truth and the teachings. When we protect nature, we protect the truth and the teachings" (Batchelor and Brown 1992, p. 99). One Thai Buddhist monk, Somneuk Natho, restored 40 acres of grasslands to forest at the Wat Plak Mai Lai monastery where he serves as abbot (Sponsel and Natadecha-Sponsel, in Tucker and Williams 1997, p. 54).

Lay intellectual Buddhists have been deeply involved with environmental con-sciousness-raising. Chatsumarn Kabilsingh, a professor of religion and philosophy at Thammasat University in Bangkok, has developed an environmental-awareness curriculum for children using Buddhist stories and examples. This work has been supported by the World Wild Fund for Nature. Sulak Sivaraksa has been coordinator of the Asian Cultural Forum on Development (ACFOD), a regional non-government organization founded in 1977 that has "consultative status with the Economic and Social Council of the United Nations, liaison status with the Food and Agriculture Organization of the United Nations, and is a partner to the World Council of Churches commission on Churches' Participation in Development" (Swearer, in Queen and King 1996, p. 201). Through ACFOD, Sulak Sivaraksa has worked to reduce the urban bias in Thailand's economic policies and to ensure greater harmony with the environment, emphasizing the conservation of resources rather than their exploita-tion and waste. He invokes the five precepts (*panca sila*) in his activism, with particular emphasis on the first precept, not taking life. He notes that:

> the use of chemical fertilizers and insecticides that deplete the soil of rich micro-organisms is also a form of taking life as is the destruction of forests, which has contributed to the loss of many animal species. Nuclear waste dumping and chemi-cal contamination are a clear violation of the first precept for they threaten to destroy the human race. (Swearer, in Queen and King 1996, p. 217)

Sulak Sivaraksa also writes passionately about vegetarianism. He notes that the consumption of meat by the wealthy deprives the less fortunate and violates the first Buddhist precept:

> For Buddhists, the first precept does not only mean to stop killing with weapons. It also means not to live luxuriously or consume wastefully while others are dying of starvation. Buddhists have traditionally expressed their respect for sentient life by opposing the slaughter of animals. Today, when the world faces recurring food crises, measures in meat-eating countries to discourage the breeding of animals for consumption would be doubly compassionate, not only toward the animals but also toward the humans who need the grains set aside for livestock. (Sulak Sivaraksa, in Kraft 1992, pp. 130–1)

Sulak Sivaraksa invokes the third precept, which repudiates improper sexuality, to address the problems of overpopulation and the abuse of women. Using both the precepts and the Buddhist theory of interdependence, he urges readers to seek physical, social, emotional, and intellectual freedom.

Another Asian Buddhist lay leader, Dr. A. T. Ariyaratne of Sri Lanka, has worked to integrate Buddhist values in the development of a viable, village-based society. Deeply influenced by the philosophy and accomplishments of Mahatma Gandhi, Dr. Ariyar-atne founded Sarvodaya, which means the "uplift of all," in 1958. As noted by George Bond, "Sarvodaya's ideal of an integrated development supported by spiritual values critiques the materialistic, capitalistic model of development dominant in Sri Lanka since the colonial period" (Bond, in Queen and King 1996, pp. 130–1). To the extent that Ariyaratne's system dignifies pre-industrial labor and yet works for an increase in education, sanitation, and general standard of living, it works to develop a network of village societies which, by their very nature, embrace and uphold ecological values. By 1985, Sarvodaya had reached 8,000 villages within Sri Lanka. Strife between Tamils and Buddhists on the island has since reversed some of Sarvodaya's work, particularly in the north. Furthermore, political difficulties with the Sri Lankan government and philosophical differences with external funding agencies present new challenges to Sarvodaya as it seeks to adhere to its Buddhist-inspired, environment-friendly local development strategies.

In summary, environmental philosophy in Theravada Buddhist countries has emerged depending upon the local situation. In Thailand, where clear-cutting, industrial pollution, and consumer waste proliferate, many monks and lay leaders have implemented a variety of environmental strategies from a Buddhist perspective. In Myanmar, Cambodia, and Laos, environmental activism appears to be less of a concern, due to internal economic and political difficulties that have precluded the western-style industrial, consumer-based development model found in Thailand. In rural Sri Lanka, Buddhist activists have pioneered a strategy for local development that avoids industrialization and consumerism, while still improving the life of village people.

Environmental philosophy and Mahayana Buddhism in East Asia

Buddhism began its spread throughout the northern and eastern reaches of Asia in the early centuries of the Common Era. By this time, Buddhism had developed a new philosophy, the Mahayana School, which emphasizes compassion for all sentient beings and applies a critique of ephemeral things as being empty. As Mahayana Buddhism entered first China and then Korea and Japan, it adapted itself to highly developed cultural forms which in some instances held nature and animals in high regard. Specifically, when Buddhism entered China early in the Common Era, its translators found great affinity with the Taoist tradition, which emphasizes the expansive beauty of nature and venerates the emptiness of the uncluttered sky. In China and also Japan, the metaphors to describe enlightenment arise from nature and pay homage to a life of non-interference with the present moment. (see CLASSICAL CHINA).

The first precept of Buddhism, reverence to life, resulted in the widespread observance of vegetarianism among the Buddhist community (with some ridicule on the part of Confucianists). It also led to the practice of releasing animals on special occasions known as *hojo-e*. This ceremony has been practiced for over a thousand years in China and Japan, where it originally entailed delivering animals to nature preserves. It eventually became associated with the demonstration of political power in medieval Japan, which, as Duncan Williams suggests, undermined its original purpose (Tucker and Willams 1997, pp. 154–7).

The Ch'an branch of Mahayana Buddhism was introduced to China from India by the Buddhist teacher Bodhidharma early in the sixth century. It took root in China, with a number of enlightened Chinese successors establishing a distinctive indigenous form of East Asian Mahayana. The Ch'an tradition, with its emphasis on direct perception and ample use of nature imagery in poetry and other artistic expressions, has been heralded by many as a good example of how Buddhism may be reconciled with environmentalist concerns. Many Ch'an monasteries were located in the mountains far from urban life, and afforded monks and visitors alike a retreat into nature.

When Ch'an Buddhism entered Japan, where it is known as Zen, it found new avenues of expression. William LaFleur has identified the poetry of Zen monk Saigyo (1118–90) with the Zen concept of becoming one with the present moment in nature. In a famous verse modeled after an earlier piece by Kukai (774–835), Saigyo writes:

> Cloud-free mountains
> Encircle the sea, which holds
> The reflected moon:
> A view of it here changes the islands
> Into holes of emptiness in a sea of ice.

LaFleur suggests that this poem works as a mandala in nature, and that through this perception of nature the poet comes to a vision of emptiness (*sunyata*) (LaFleur in Callicott and Ames 1989, pp. 202–3). He then points out this perception of emptiness does not require the negation of the natural world: "There is no necessity here of negating the physical and phenomenological world once it has served to point to something beyond itself ... the sky itself is both the symbol and the symbolized" (ibid, p. 203). Nature provides the vehicle for one's liberation; the direct perception of nature and hence unity with nature brings one into recognition of Buddha-nature.

Zen master Dogen (1200–53) similarly placed emphasis on the Buddha nature being found within mountains and rivers. As noted by Shaner, "Dogen believes the *dharma* permeates all sentient and nonsentient beings ... [he writes]: 'The ocean speaks and mountains have tongues – that is the everyday speech of Buddha ... If you can speak and hear such words you will be one who truly comprehends the entire universe'" (Shaner, in Callicott and Ames 1989, p. 173). This attitude toward the natural world could be interpreted as a reason to advocate for environmental protection.

D. T. Suzuki (1870–1966) often appeals to nature in his famous writings on Zen Buddhism, most notably in "Love of Nature," the final chapter of his classic book *Zen and Japanese Culture*. He writes:

> What is the most specific characteristic of Zen asceticism in connection with the Japanese love of nature? It consists in paying Nature the fullest respect it deserves. By this it is meant that we may treat Nature not as an object to conquer and turn wantonly to our service, but as a friend, as a fellow being, who is destined like ourselves for Buddhahood. Zen wants us to meet Nature as a friendly, well-meaning agent whose inner being is like our own, always ready to work in accord with our legitimate aspirations. Nature is never our enemy standing always against us in a threatening attitude; it is not a power which will crush us if we not crush it or bind it into our service. (Suzuki 1959, p. 351)

This attitude toward nature not only borders on reverence but emphasizes the non-separation of the human order from the natural order.

Various other schools of East Asian Buddhism similarly emphasize a continuity and identity within the human order and nature. Hua Yen Buddhism (known as Kegon in Japan) teaches a theory of organismic interrelatedness, characterized by Francis Cook as "cosmic ecology" (Cook, in Callicott and Ames 1989, 213–14). Pure Land and related schools of Buddhist thought in Japan also included teachings on the inseparability of the person from nature. Nichiren Daishonen (1222–82) developed a theory of *esho funi*, "the oneness of life and its environment" (Odin, in Tucker and Williams 1997, p. 96). In recent times, the Soka Gakkai movement in Japan, which considers Nichiren as its patron saint, has included environmental concerns in a variety of activities. It mounted a major exhibit displayed at the United Nations in 1989 that included such issues as "global warming, ozone depletion, acid rain, radioactive pollution, toxic wastes, deforestation, desertification, and extinction of species" (Metraux, in Queen and King 1996, p. 379). It convened a major environmental conference in London in 1992 and has been deeply involved with the struggle to protect the Brazilian rainforest.

As Japan industrialized and modernized during the Meiji Restoration (1867–1912), it developed a fascination with western modernity, including European intellectualism. Having closely studied the great western philosophers, scholars in Japan began to articulate Buddhist insight in a new idiom. The Kyoto School, beginning with Nishida Kitaro (1870–1945) developed the concept of *basho* or relational field which can be interpreted to include person, interpersonal relations, and one's place in nature. Watsuji Tetsuro (1880–1960) developed this notion of field into a theory of climate (*fudo*) which regards "living nature as the ultimate extension of embodied subjective space in which man dwells" (Odin, in Tucker and Williams 1997, p. 95). Although the environment was not an issue within the time of the development of the Kyoto School, contemporary representatives of the School, such as Masao Abe and Masatoshi Nagatomi, have introduced ecological themes into their later works.

In combination with other aspects of East Asian tradition, such as geomancy (*fengshui*) which emphasizes the role of placing architecture correctly within the environment, Buddhism would seem to be supportive of a world-view that would be inherently ecological in intent and application. This does not take into account, however, the decidedly anthropocentric orientation within the underlying ethos of East Asia. As noted by Ole Bruun, "The Chinese are known for their anthropocentrism in their philosophy and extreme sociocentrism in basic orientations – meaning that by far the greater part of the 'world that matters' is made up by humans and human society" (Bruun and Kalland 1995, p. 175). A contemporary scholar of Buddhism in Japan, Noriaki Hakamaya, has suggested that "Buddhism does not accept but negates nature" (in Schmithausen 1991, p. 53) and applies a hermeneutics of suspicion to the endeavor of cross-cultural environmental ethics. He questions whether Buddhist doctrines have room for developing an interest in ecological issues, noting that the Buddha relegated worldly to a secondary status, choosing always to emphasize human liberation from suffering.

The two most visible Asian Buddhist teachers, the Dalai Lama and Thich Nhat Hanh, include environmentalism as a topic within their frequent lectures. The Dalai Lama (b. 1935), leader of the Tibetan Buddhist tradition, addressing an interfaith conference at Middlebury College, stated that "All [beings] have a right to happiness, a right to freedom from suffering ... all beings seem beautiful to us ... Their presence gives us some kind of tranquillity, some kind of joy ... the forests, the plants, and the trees, all these natural things come together to make our surroundings pleasant ... our very existence is something heavily dependent on the environment" (in Rockefeller and Elder 1992, pp. 115–16). The Dalai Lama urges the development of love, kindness, and affection, coupled with individual initiative and involvement with advocacy organizations to address the planetary environmental crisis.

Thich Nhat Hanh (b. 1926), chair of the Vietnamese Buddhist peace delegation during the Vietnam War and nominated for a Nobel Prize by Martin Luther King, Jr., has written more than 60 books on Buddhism. In terms of environmental issues, he has written: "The excessive use of pesticides that kill all kinds of insects and upset the ecological balance is an example of our lack of wisdom in trying to control nature" (in Tobias and Cowan 1994, p. 128). He also uses poetry to inspire a visionary view of the place of self in the cosmos:

> Look deeply: I arrive every second
> to be a bud on a spring branch,
> to be a tiny bird, with wings still fragile,
>   learning to sing in my new nest,
> to be a caterpillar in the heart of flower,
> to be a jewel hiding itself in a stone.
> (from "Please Call Me By My True Names," quoted in Queen and King 1996, p. 238)

Thich Nhat Hanh emphasizes the Buddhist teaching of interpenetration, noting that mindfulness of this insight can "sustain the work of living and caring for the earth and for each other for a long time" (in Tobias and Cowan 1994, p. 136). Both the Dalai Lama, who resides in India, and Thich Nhat Hanh, who lives in France, have helped internationalize Buddhism.

Environmental philosophy in American Buddhism

America has long had an affection for the Buddhist religion, spanning several generations. The first Asian Buddhists settled in the American West to build railroads and mine for gold in the 1850s. Most of these Buddhists were Chinese and built several temples or Joss Houses, many of which still can be found in such towns as Mendocino, California. Women were not allowed to immigrate, with rare exceptions; most Chinese in America either eventually returned to Asia or died childless due to anti-miscegenation laws. Japanese immigrants, who tended to arrive in the later years of the nineteenth century and the early twentieth century, fared better. Japan was not subject to colonial rule and the Japanese government negotiated an immigration policy that allowed women as well as men to move to America. Hawaii and California were the most popular destinations. In order to maximize assimilation, the Buddhist churches of America developed a worship style similar to Protestant Christianity and, like many Christian churches, have developed written brochures on the importance of an ecological lifestyle.

The World Parliament of Religions in 1893 introduced many Americans of Western European ancestry to key Buddhist notions. D. T. Suzuki, who translated Soyen Shaku's address to the Parliament into English, first visited the United States in 1897, returning regularly until his death in 1966; historian Lynn G. White has stated that the "introduction of Suzuki's work to the West may one day be counted as important as the rediscovery of Aristotle" (in Fields 1992, p. 34). Buddhism received extensive attention during the years after World War II, when Alan Watts, Allen Ginsberg, and other writers helped popularize Zen terminology. Philip Kapleau, who trained for many years with Yasutani Roshi in Japan, established the Zen Center of Rochester, New York in 1967, from which many additional centers emerged. Maezumi Roshi established the Los Angeles Zendo (now the Zen Center of Los Angeles) in 1968.

Many of the Americans attracted to these and other Buddhist centers came of age during a time of great social conflict and cultural change. Resistance to the Vietnam War, gender issues, environmentalism, combined with Buddhist meditation, have resulted in a hybrid form of American Buddhism. Many American teachers have been initiated by Asian masters. Alternative governance structures along more democratic lines are being explored, at variance with Asian systems. Long-time American students of Buddhist disciplines such as Joanna Macy, Joan Halifax, Gary Snyder, Robert Aitken, and Jack Kornfield have emerged as leaders of this new form of Buddhism.

Advocates of what may be called Green Buddhism combine traditional Buddhist teachings on interdependence and interpenetration with modern psychological insights, contemporary science, and social outreach. In a volume titled *Dharma Gaia: A Harvest of Essays in Buddhism and Ecology*, a variety of Buddhist writers and teachers explore what Schumacher dubbed "Buddhist economics," and what Stephen Batchelor refers to as the "inherent ecological wisdom of Buddhism" (Badiner 1990, p. 180). For instance, Christopher Reed, a California American Zen teacher, has developed five "eco-precepts" in imitation of the traditional Buddhist precepts:

1. I vow to recycle everything I can. This includes glass, aluminum, tin, cardboard, plastic, paper, and motor oil.
2. I vow to be energy efficient. This includes lowering the thermostat on the water heater, fixing all leaks immediately, using rechargeable batteries and cloth diapers. Bring your own bag to the grocery, hang clothes up to dry, and take shorter showers. Put a water-filled plastic bottle in your toilet tank and turn off the lights when they are not needed. Reduce the amount of beef in your diet and try to eat low on the food chain.
3. I vow to be an active and informed voter. Learn how your representatives have voted on environmental issues. Let them know when you don't agree with them and when you do.
4. I vow to be car conscious. Drive a fuel efficient vehicle and keep it well tuned with tires properly inflated. Carpool whenever possible, and rediscover walking and biking.
5. I vow to exercise my purchasing power for the benefit of all sentient beings. Keep informed about boycotts against ecologically damaging products and corporate practices, like tropical hardwood, ivory, canned tuna, table grapes, and firms that make bombs. (Reed, in Badiner, p. 235)

This imaginative restructuring of Buddhist practice intertwines traditional ethics with applied environmentalism.

American Buddhists view the world in terms of relationality rather than through purely anthropocentric or egoistic categories. By applying traditional Buddhist ethical practices such as non-violence and frugality to the problems associated with the degradation of ecosystems, new paradigms are being developed. Green Buddhism asserts that individuals must be more fully attuned to the need for resource management and the protection of endangered ecosystems, and act accordingly.

Conclusion

Both Jainism and Buddhism seek to liberate their followers from the shackles of past compulsive action. Both emphasize processes of purification through ethical precepts. Jainism remained in India and helped shape the development of culture and politics on the subcontinent. Buddhism largely left India and made accommodations and adjustments to host cultures throughout Asia and, more recently, in the West. Jainism and Buddhism each can find textual and practical resources for grappling with the issues of environmental degradation. Jainism emphasizes the pervasiveness of life and the observance of non-violence toward all forms of life. Buddhism emphasizes the interdependence of all life forms, the fragile and fleeting nature of life, and the need to cultivate compassion toward all sentient beings.

Although the issues of environmental ravage and overconsumption of resources do not exactly match the issues that prompted the original teachings of Mahavira and the Buddha, each system is in the process of developing appropriate responses to this pressing contemporary issue. In India and in the diaspora community, Jainas are seeking to raise awareness of environmental harm and are advocating for the wider protection of living things. In Asia, Buddhist leaders are calling for a greater sensitivity to the ecosystem and warning against a wholesale embrace of western development models. In America, Green Buddhists strive to integrate Buddhist teachings on interbeing and relationality within the context of a fully developed consumer society. Jainism and Buddhism (in its Theravada, Mahayana, and "American" forms), like the other major religious traditions, are developing new philosophies and practices to address the pressing contemporary issue posed by ecological distress.

References

Badiner, Allan Hunt (1990) *Dharma Gaia: A Harvest of Essays in Buddhism and Ecology* (Berkeley, California: Parallax Press). [Varied collection of poetry and prose by Buddhist practitioners.]

Batchelor, Martine, and Brown, Kerry (1992) *Buddhism and Ecology* (London: Cassell Publishers). [Summary presentation of environmental themes in Buddhism.]

Bruun, Ole, and Kalland, Arne, eds. (1995) *Asian Perceptions of Nature: A Critical Approach* (Richmond, Surrey, UK: Curzon Press). [Critical analysis of nature in Asian thought and religion.]

Callicott, J. Baird, and Ames, Roger T., eds. (1989) *Nature in Asian Traditions of Thought: Essays in Environmental Philosophy* (Albany: State University of New York Press). [Pioneering collection from a cross-cultural perspective.]

Chapple, Christopher Key (1993) *Nonviolence to Animals, Earth, and Self in Asian Traditions* (Albany: State University of New York Press). [Historical, cultural, and theological analysis of non-violence in Asian traditions.]

Fields, Rick (1992) *How the Swans Came to the Lake: A Narrative History of Buddhism in America*, 3rd edn (Boston: Shambhala). [Comprehensive study of Buddhism in America.]

Gandhi, S. L., ed. (1996) *Ladnun Declaration for A Non-violent World and Ecological Harmony through Spiritual Transformation* (Jaipur: Anuvibha). [Proceedings of a conference in India on Jainism and ecology.]

Jacobi, Hermann, tr. (1884) *Jaina Sutras* (Oxford: Clarendon Press). [Translations of important primary sources.]

Kenneth Kraft, ed. (1992) *Inner Peace, World Peace: Essays on Buddhism and Nonviolence* (Albany: State University of New York Press). [Scholarly essays on Buddhism and current issues.]

Rockefeller, Steven C. and Elder, John C., eds. (1992) *Spirit and Nature: Why the Environment is a Religious Issue* (Boston: Beacon Press). [Selected excerpts from a conference at Middlebury College.]

Queen, Christopher S. and King, Sallie B., eds. (1996) *Engaged Buddhism: Buddhist Liberation Movements in Asia* (Albany: State University of New York Press). [Superb collection of scholarly essays on contemporary activist Buddhism in Asia.]

Schmithausen, Lambert (1991) *Buddhism and Nature* (Tokyo: The International Institute for Buddhist Studies). [Thoughtful and realistic presentation of Japanese Buddhist concepts of nature.]

Suzuki, Daisetz T. (1959) *Zen and Japanese Culture* (Princeton, New Jersey: Princeton University Press). [Classic early work on Zen Buddhism.]

Tobias, Michael and Cowan, Georgianne, eds. (1994) *The Soul of Nature: Celebrating the Spirit of the Earth* (New York: Continuum). [Collected essays on nature by scholars and activists.]

Tucker, Mary Evelyn and Grim, John, eds. (1994) *Worldviews and Ecology: Religion, Philosophy, and the Environment* (Maryknoll, New York: Orbis Books). [Pioneering scholarly collection of essays on world religions and environment.]

Tucker, Mary Evelyn and Williams, Duncan Ryuken, eds. (1997) *Buddhism and Ecology: The Interconnection of Dharma and Deeds* (Cambridge, Massachusetts: Harvard University Center for the Study of World Religions). [First in a series of books on ecology and religions based on conference proceedings.]

Woodward, F. L., tr. (1925) *The Book of Kindred Sayings (Sayutta Nikaya) or Grouped Suttas, Part III: The Khandha Book* (London: Luzac). [Primary source material for early Buddhism.]

Further reading

deSilva, Padmasiri (1998) *Environmental Philosophy and Ethics in Buddhism* (New York: St. Martin's Press). [Summary of western environmental philosophy with comparative reference to Buddhism.]

Martin, Julia (1997) *Ecological Responsibility: A Dialogue with Buddhism* (Delhi: Tibet House). [Collection of essays by scholars and activists on Buddhism and ecology based on a conference held in India.]

Singhvi, L. M. (1990) *The Jaina Declaration on Nature* (London: Jain Delegation of International Jain Community). [Pioneering document on developing an environmental interpretation of Jainism.]

Tatia, Nathmal, tr. (1994) *Tattvartha Sutra: That Which Is* (San Francisco: HarperCollins). [Philosophical compendium of Jainism.]

Tobias, Michael (1991) *Life Force: The World of Jainism* (Berkeley, California: Asian Humanities Press). [Contemporary reflections on Jaina life and practice.]

5

The classical Greek tradition

GABRIELA R. CARONE

In trying to find the roots of our contemporary environmental crisis, environmental philosophers have often looked at the ancient Greek thinkers, even though the assessment made of these philosophers has not always been fair. This chapter attempts to provide an outline of the attitude of some ancient Greek philosophers toward the environment, with an eye to emphasizing aspects in their theories which have been overlooked. One view that I will be showing prevailed in ancient Greek thought is that whatever stance we adopt toward nature and the universe is bound to affect the way we live. The answer to the question whether the universe should be conceived of as inert or alive, or as mechanistic or teleological, and whether such teleology in the latter case should be anthropocentric or not, had enormous bearing in determining our own role in the universe, with regard to plants, animals, other humans, and nature as a whole. In this chapter I deal mainly with the philosophies of Plato (through his master Socrates) and Aristotle around this main issue; though some attention will be paid, first, to some Presocratics and, finally, to some post-Aristotelian philosophers in whom many of those ideas may respectively be seen as anticipated or preserved.

Presocratics

Let us start with the Presocratics, and the first group of philosophers, called the Milesians (sixth century BCE). Little or nothing is preserved from them by way of direct evidence, but, from the scanty testimonies or fragments that we have, we can say that it would be incorrect to regard their views as crudely materialistic. The crudely materialistic interpretation often made of them is likely to be, in turn, a simplistic borrowing from Aristotle, who classifies such philosophers as those who first found an answer about the first principle of all things in the realm of matter. So, Thales is said to have found it in water, Anaximenes in air. Some people have thus spoken of the "Greek miracle": the moment when philosophy takes a scientific course of inquiry based on observation and breaks bonds with the religious Greek heritage. If such an interpretation were true, then we would have these Presocratics depict a universe of inert matter. However, this reading anachronistically imports into these ancient thinkers a dualism between matter and life which is not there. On the contrary, Thales is reported to have said not only that water is the material principle of all things (Ar., *Metaphysics* I 3, 983b6–27; see D&K 11A2 and 11A12) but also that the magnet has soul because it moves iron (Ar., *De Anima* [*On the Soul*] I 2, 405a19–21; see D&K 11A22) and that all things are full of gods (*De An.* I 5, 411a7–8; see D&K 11A22), which rather suggests a notion of matter as alive and even divine. Likewise, Anaximenes considers air to be a god, infinite and always in motion (D&K 13A10). So we have in these first philosophers what some have called a "hylozoistic" world-view, in which matter (*hulē*) and life (*zōē*) are inseparable. In Anaximenes, in addition, we have the assumption of a correspondence between the human and the natural world, when he argues, for example, that "as much as our life, being air, holds us together, so do breath and air embrace the whole cosmos" (D&K 13B2). The same correspondence is present in Anaximander, who sees the cosmos as a wider stage for the legality that the Greek city-states were starting to enjoy with Solon (cf. D&K 12B1 and 12A9). All this suggests that we are not isolated atoms, cut off from the world, but, rather, parts of a wider whole, which is governed by the same principles that should govern human life.

The same line of thought is followed by Heraclitus (sixth–fifth century BCE), who calls the first principle "fire" (D&K 22B30), "god" (D&K 22B67, cf. 22B32), and the "rational planning" (*logos*, cf. D&K 22B2, 72, 50) of the universe. Now, in Heraclitus we find explicitly the thought that the way the world is has an enormous bearing on the way one should behave toward it. To understand the harmonious opposition inherent in it (D&K 22B80) – that night must follow day (D&K 22B94) and death must follow life (D&K 22B88, 62) – is a lesson of sound-mindedness or moderation (*sōphrosunē*), as opposed to arrogance (*hubris*, D&K 22B43), for human beings. We have, basically, two choices, namely to act as people "asleep," that is, enclosed in our private thoughts and interests and unaware of our wider surroundings, or as people "awake," which means to bring our mind in tune with the operations of the universe, which is common to all (D&K 22B1, 2, 73, 89). Thus, "sound thinking is the supreme excellence, and true wisdom is to speak and act in accordance with nature [*phusis*], while paying attention [to it]" (D&K 22B112). In the orderly arrangement of the seasons, for example, or in the succession of days and nights, we have an example of cosmic harmony that we should try to preserve and imitate through our behavior. We have to use our reason (*logos*) and philosophical discourse (*logos*) to understand and unravel the rational workings of the universe, its *Logos*. We have to comprehend (as we could find hinted at in Anaximander) that "all laws are nourished by one law, the divine one" (D&K 22B114). To know oneself (D&K 22B116) is for Heraclitus tantamount to knowing what is our place in the universe: we are here at the antipodes of the Cartesian sort of introspection that separates us from the natural universe around us. On the contrary, "to know oneself" is "to think soundly" (D&K 22B116), and to think soundly is, as we have seen, to speak and act "in accordance with nature" (D&K 22B112). Thus, to introspect is to discover ourselves as part of a common world, and our reason (*logos*) as part of a wider *Logos*.

The Eleatic philosopher Parmenides (sixth–fifth century BCE) is often presented as the opposite of Heraclitus, and Parmenides' denial of change could be seen as a refusal to acknowledge the value of the world of becoming around us. Certainly, Parmenides does suggest that only "being" can be known by rational thinking, and that not-being is unthinkable and unknowable; so, given that change involves the problematic notion of non-being (e.g. something passing from being [Socrates] to not-being [Socrates]), then being is unchanging (D&K 28B8). However, Parmenides' argument can be seen, rather than as a deprecation of the world of change as such, as high-lighting (probably for the first time in the history of philosophy and science) the notion that the true object of infallible knowledge and rational thought must have the trait of stability. If we wish to find, as Parmenides suggests, unshakeable truth, we must take refuge in the realm of the unchanging. In any case, his emphasis on the "unity" of being as the reality over and above any scattered appearances brings him closer than one might initially expect to Heraclitus' notion of a superior *Logos* that realizes the unity of all opposites (D&K 22B50).

Socrates and Plato

Socrates (ca. 469–399 BCE) was mainly interested in ethics, as we can see from the early Platonic dialogues, which are usually taken to express Socratic thought. With Heraclitus, he is interested in self-knowledge (cf. *Apology* 21d–e, 23a–b; *Charmides* 164c ff), with an emphasis on an awareness of the scope of one's knowledge or ignorance, promoted by his philosophical method of interrogation (the *elenchos*). Such self-awareness is what his modest, human wisdom consists in, and furthers a state by which one's mind can get rid of false beliefs, thus attaining a harmonious state of non-contradiction (*Ap.* 29b–30d). This harmony, however, is not the object of a solipsistic quest, but a principle that will favor friendship with others in a harmonious society, and a principle also that pervades the whole of nature and the universe while holding everything together. So, in a way also reminiscent of Heraclitus, a remarkable passage in the *Gorgias* stresses that the one who does not have order in his soul

> could not be dear to another human or to god. For he is unable to have communion with the others, and for whom there is no communion, there could be no friendship. For the wise men say . . . that heaven and earth and gods and humans are held together by communion and friendship and orderliness and moderation and justice, and for these reasons they call this whole cosmos [= order] . . . not disorder or unrestraint. (*Gorg.* 507e–508a)

In the same dialogue, Socrates objects to a view of "nature" as representing the domain of unrestrained instinct and opposed to human civilization and law, as defended by his interlocutor Callicles. Rather, Socrates suggests ways to bring law-fulness in tune with nature (cf. *Gorg.* 488c–489b, 503d–504d).

But Socrates can also be seen to have shared with Parmenides an interest in getting to a state of certain knowledge. Even though Socrates does not claim to have that knowledge himself, at least he expects any pretender to knowledge to be able to provide a suitable definition of the subject in question (see e.g. *Euthyphro* 4e–5d). For this reason his interest is directed to universals rather than particulars (that is, e.g., to a universal definition of piety, rather than to a description of this or that other pious act), though not as an escape from particulars, but rather as a way to explain and understand them better (cf. *Euth.* 6d–e).

Both the Heraclitean and Parmenidean lines of thought are usually said to converge in Socrates' disciple Plato (ca. 427–348 BCE). Aristotle reports that Plato in his youth was acquainted with the Heraclitean views that all perceptible things are in flux and there is no strict knowledge of them; then he became a disciple of Socrates, who was interested in definitions. Plato agreed with Socrates, although, through his

Heraclitean beliefs, he took those definitions to apply not to perceptible but to other things, which he called "Ideas" or "Forms" (Ar. *Metaphy*. I 6, 987a29–b10). This view is usually presented as Plato's "metaphysical dualism," and can be found in his dialogues such as the *Phaedo* (74a–c), the *Republic* (V 476e–480a), and the *Symposium* (211). However, as I have pointed out elsewhere (Carone 1998), the relevant grounds for having postulated such dualism are mainly epistemological: the true philosopher has to resort to the Forms, which are unchanging, rather than to perceptible changing particulars, if he really wishes to attain a level of certain and stable knowledge and truth (cf. *Timaeus* 51b–e). The Forms, in addition, as Socrates had sought, explain particulars (cf. *Phaedo* 100b–101b) – which at most lend themselves to belief and opinion – by enabling us to provide a stable definition of the universal traits in which those particulars share. Even though Plato talks of the Forms as "what really is," as opposed to sensible particulars which "are and are not" (cf. *Rep.* V 476e–480a), what he seems to mean is not so much that the Forms exist more fully and that the perceptible world barely exists (or is an illusion), as the tradition has often taken it. Rather, he seems to be suggesting that each Form is really always stably the same, as opposed to particular things which, by being in a state of flux, are one thing (e.g. beautiful now, or beautiful to Rose) and are not that thing, but its opposite (e.g. ugly later, or to Peter; cf. *Rep.* V 478e7–479b9; *Symp.* 210e–211b). Forms and particulars are two kinds of real things (*ontōn*, *Phaedo* 79a). In addition, the reality of the natural surroundings is not only granted, but exalted, in passages such as *Phaedrus* 230b–c, where Plato has Socrates say of their meeting place:

> [It is] a beautiful spot, and this plane tree is very wide and tall, and the height and shade of the willow is wonderful. Since it is now in full bloom, it will make the place very fragrant. And the cold stream flowing by the plane is most charming... and how pleasing and sweet is the freshness of the air, with the summery and clear song of the cicadas!

Although Plato may attribute more value to Forms than to perishable sensible particulars, this is still compatible with some particulars being very valuable indeed. Let us then analyze in more detail Plato's attitude toward the natural environment, by considering what kind of value he attributed to animals, plants, the land, and the universe in general, and whether his view in this respect is anthropocentric or not.

Several passages in the Platonic dialogues speak of humans reincarnating into ANIMALS. Such views about reincarnation are often thought to have been influenced by the Pythagorean tradition, of whose beginnings, however, very little can be said with certainty. We have, for example, Xenophanes (ca. sixth century BCE) reporting that "once, when [Pythagoras, ca. sixth century BCE] walked past a place where a puppy was being beaten, it is said that he took pity and said these words: Stop, don't beat him, because it is the soul of a male friend: I recognized it when I heard the sound of its voice" (D&K 21B7); it seems also that, partly for those reasons, within the Pythagorean circle there were restrictions about meat-eating. Now, when it comes to Plato, some passages present reincarnation into animals as a "fall" from a supposedly higher human condition, so that not every soul reincarnates, but only those of humans who haven't lived up to the highest human standards of rationality (e.g.

Phaedo 81d–e, *Tim.* 90e–92c). Other passages, however (such as *Rep.* X 620a–d, 617a), speak of every soul reincarnating, and not only humans passing into animals, but animals passing into humans. It is also suggested that animals have the power of choice and responsibility to raise their status into humans (*Rep.* 620a–d, 617e; *Tim.* 90e, 92c), which suggests that reason is a possibility in animals even if it is not exercised. Thus, both animals and humans have the capacity to elevate themselves by choosing to let reason dominate over their passions, or to descend into less intelligent animals otherwise (cf. *Tim.* 42c, 91d–92b). This shows that animals and ordinary humans are not different in any relevant ways, but have equal possibilities of choice to fall or rise, and equal merit if they rise, or lack of merit if they don't. The distinction is not so much drawn here between humans and animals, but between humans who fully exercise reason on the one hand and humans who, on the other, do not, and in that respect do not differ from animals. So, on Plato's view, no one is intrinsically superior to animals merely by being human; it is reason that matters, and which thus presents itself as the goal of both human and animal striving.

If this is so, then it is no surprise that in the *Statesman* the division between humans and animals is rejected as unnatural and as based on anthropocentric relativism. For a crane could, on equally unobjective grounds, divide the whole of living beings into cranes and animals other than cranes, including humans (262a–c, 263c–e). Likewise, in the *Republic* (I 343a–345d) Socrates suggests that the art of the shepherd is concerned with nothing else than to provide what is best for his subjects, contrary to Thrasymachus' contention that shepherds tend their flocks in their own interest and not that of the flock. For Socrates, every form of rule, as such, only looks after the best for that which is ruled. The *Timaeus* too gives suggestions that are far from the idea that animals exist for the sake of humans. The purpose of animals in the universe is to make it complete (41b). This is an argument for the preservation of animal species, insofar as they contribute to the perfection and variegatedness of the universe.

It is not clear, however, that Plato should have any arguments for the preservation of the life of individual animals, even if it be granted that animals do not deserve substantially different treatment from humans in view of their kinship. For it is not sure that, for Plato, humans, as such, deserve the highest respect either (even if reason does), or that he had any clear notion of human rights. Some passages seem to allow for infanticide and the execution of humans for the sake of a larger rational purpose (such as communal or political well-being, cf. *Rep.* V 459d–461c; *State.* 293d–e, 297d–e), and so, by the same token, he could justify the killing of animals if it serves a further goal (e.g., religious practice: cf. *Phaedo* 118a on Socrates' expressing his duty to sacrifice a cock to Asclepius). Similarly, we can wonder whether Plato would have endorsed vegetarianism, and, if so, on what grounds.

A few passages suggest that in ideal human conditions no eating of animals would be involved. The "healthy state" of the *Republic* (II 369a–372d) just includes agriculture (and oxen for work) to satisfy the need for food. It is as a compromise with his interlocutors' demand for a more luxurious city that Socrates proposes a "fevered state" that includes the consumption of meat (373c), and this requires therefore the existence of more doctors (373c–d). It would seem, in this context, that it is mainly health reasons, rather than any special concern for individual animals, that make Plato prefer vegetarianism (after all, the killing of animals would seem to be involved even in the ideal city, in the obtaining of leather for shoes). However, if animals (or at least some animals) are reincarnated humans, it would also be understandable to prefer vegetarianism on the grounds that meat-eating would appear as a kind of cannibalism. In the "golden era" depicted in the myth of the *Statesman* we are told that no animal was wild, nor did they eat one another, and humans had abundant fruits from the earth (271e–272c); and in the *Timaeus* it is plants (and not animals) that serve the purpose in the cosmos to aid the body which is constantly wasting away (77a).

It is interesting to note that, in the *Timaeus*, even plants are given a faculty of sensitivity (*aisthēsis*), together with pleasure and pain; they are said to have a nature "akin to the human one" (77a). If one were to adopt the utilitarian perspective that takes the capacity to feel pleasure and pain as a criterion for intrinsic value, then one could think that it would be preferable to take fruits from plants rather than cut them (as suggested in *State.* 272a), if the latter involves plants suffering pain (see SENTIENT ISM). However, as we have seen, Plato does not seem to find anything wrong with feeling pain as long as it can serve a greater positive end. Typical examples are medical treatment for the individual or punishment for incurable criminals (cf. e.g. *Laws* IX 845b–e). This line of argument would pave the ground for the idea that inflicting pain on plants (or even animals) would be justified if it can be made to fit the overall teleological purpose. This purpose is not, we must however note, sheerly anthropocentric. For it is the whole (i.e. the universe) that has priority over its parts, including both humans and plants (cf. *Laws* X 903b–c). From this perspective, the treatment of each part of the universe – be it a rock, an animal, or a plant – has to be considered in relation to how such treatment would affect the entire system, and with an eye to the preservation of the whole, since "the whole does not exist for you, but you exist for the sake of the whole" (ibid). So, even if rationality ends up being valued higher, this is because it promotes not only the individual order but also that of the whole. This point brings us to consider more closely Plato's teleological cosmology and the role of humans within it.

It is particularly in the late dialogues (mainly the *Timaeus*, *Philebus*, *Statesman*, and *Laws*) where we see Plato's attempt to find some source of order and stability not only in the realm of Forms, but also within the sensible universe. The universe itself is, in those dialogues, endowed with life and a mind of its own, and this cosmic mind or soul appears as the main first cause of orderly changes within the system. In this respect, "nature" (*phusis*) can be seen not only as the result of a process of growth, but as the active process of generation itself, which is the source of all the beauties we see around us. And in the latter respect nature is the source of life and becomes a synonym of "soul" (cf. *Laws* X 891c, 892b–c, 896a–b). In the *Timaeus* such a soul is the element that brings excellence to the whole universe, which, by sharing in no irrationality, deserves to be called a god and indeed the greatest god (cf. 29a, 34a–c, 92c). Likewise, the heavenly bodies and the earth are said to possess a soul which is purely rational and are therefore called gods (cf. 40b–d). Unlike them, the human soul is complex and, through its share in irrationality, can result in effects other than orderly and harmonious. For this reason the rationality of the universe stands up as a model for human beings to follow. Thus, the *Philebus* presents the universe, composed of body and soul, as containing "the same elements as us, and yet in every way superior" (30a). In the *Timaeus* the earth is presented as "our nurse" and "the most venerable of the gods in heaven" (40b–c), and the *Laws* equally emphasizes that "the land [*chōra*] is our ancestral home, of which we must take greater care than children do of their mother, since it is a god and the mistress of mortal beings" (V 740a5–7). In this regard, the universe as a whole, and the earth in particular, possess, by being gods, a dignity in themselves that is superior to that of human beings and a paradigm for their aspiration.

More than one passage stresses the importance of our cooperation with god for the teleology of the good to be fulfilled in the world, in a way that leaves room for Plato's environmental concerns. Since human souls too are first causes of changes within the system (cf. *Laws* X 904c ff), we are encouraged not only to imitate but also to help sustain the universe's orderly structure. Thus, we are presented as the protagonists of a battle between good and evil taking place in the universe, and it is even suggested that human excess is the cause of natural disorders (cf. *Laws* X 906a–b; see Carone 1994 and 1998). In the *Critias* (111c–d) Plato shows awareness of environmental problems, such as the deforestation of Attica and the increasing non-absorption by the soil of rainfall there. But, far from showing indifference, he criticizes a society full of ships but devoid of virtue (cf. *Gorg.* 518e–519a). In the *Critias*, Plato contrasts the situation of his contemporary Athens with the ideal environmental conditions of a past Athens which also excelled in virtue (109c–112e).

In these ways, we have seen Plato taking up the leitmotif of the Milesians and Heraclitus about the divinity of the universe, and Heraclitus' ideas about a common rationality in which we should actively share. The Parmenidean search for stability in the objects of knowledge finds a foundation in the realm of Forms which grounds rather than annihilates the value of the perceptible universe. For, as we have seen, there is in the late dialogues a cosmic mind or reason that ensures most things' participation in the good. And this non-anthropocentric notion of teleology encourages rather than hinders human concern about the environment.

Aristotle

It is usually granted that Plato's successor, Aristotle (ca. 384–322 BCE), fixed his eyes on the perceptible, material universe, bringing the Forms down to earth, even though they will keep their explanatory role of particulars in philosophy and science: forms are, in the first place, expressed in the universal definition of each kind, or species, of thing (*Metaph.* VII 12, 1037b21–27 and 4, 1030b4–6; cf. V 11, 1013a24 ff and I 3, 983a26 ff). In Aristotle, "nature" appears as the intrinsic principle of motion or rest in things (as opposed to things whose change is induced by an external agent, cf. *Physics* II 1, 192b20–23, *Metaph.* XII 3, 1070a7–8). In this sense, things like rocks tending to move downwards, plants tending to reproduce, animals endowed with sense-perception, or humans sharing in rationality are called "natural," as opposed to the products of art or technology. Aristotle disagrees with Plato, however, that nature should be a synonym of soul: only higher natural things in the scale (such as plants, animals, and humans) have soul, even though many other things (such as tissues, organs, and fire) are natural (see e.g. *De An.* II 1). The nature of a thing is, for Aristotle, in one sense its matter, and in another sense its form, the compound of both existing "by nature" (cf. *Phys.* II 1, 193a28–b8). And the actual fulfillment of a thing's form acts as the goal of its whole process of generation (193b12–18). Aristotle disagrees also with any Pythagorean or Platonic views of reincarnation, on the grounds that the soul (i.e. the principle of life) exists mainly insofar as it is adapted to a suitable kind of matter, being, indeed, a function of that matter (cf. *De An.* I 3, 407b15–26).

The tradition has passed down the notion of an Aristotelian "scale of nature," by which things are classified in a hierarchy at the bottom of which we would find things such as rocks, which have no soul and even less rationality, going up to higher levels ending up with the domain of reason. Some evidence for this can be found in the Aristotelian treatise *De Anima*, which makes a distinction between living and lifeless substances (II 1, 412a13–16), and suggests that the lower levels of nature are preserved in the higher ones, but not vice versa. So, for example, the nutritive faculty pertaining to plants is an element presupposed by the animal kind of life, sharing in sense-perception – a faculty that plants lack in Aristotle, unlike in Plato – and the sense-perceptive faculty proper to animals is presupposed in the human kind of life, whose distinctive feature is rationality (cf. *De An.* II 3). Now, this, combined with a passage from Aristotle's *Politics* (I 3, 1256b15–22), has given rise to the view that the teleological arrangement of Aristotle's scale of nature is indeed anthropocentric, a view that has received strong support from David Sedley (1991). (Unlike the meaning that "anthropocentric" has received in contemporary environmental discussions, we speak here of teleology being "anthropocentric" in the sense that things in nature are arranged for the sake of humans.) The passage reads as follows:

> After birth, plants exist for the sake of animals, and the other animals for the sake of humans – domesticated animals for both usefulness and food, and most if not all wild animals for food and other assistance, as a source of clothing and other utilities. If, then, nature makes nothing incomplete or pointless, it is necessary that nature has made them all for the sake of humans. (Sedley's translation, slightly modified)

Now, one could certainly raise queries as to how decisively this passage conveys the notion of anthropocentric teleology in Aristotle. For, as Sedley anticipates, it could be objected that Aristotle in this context is not writing as a physicist and he could even be granting popular notions; in fact, Robert Wardy (1993) treats this passage as an aberration inconsistent with Aristotle's natural philosophy, which, Wardy argues, "shifts the balance of probability against cosmic anthropocentrism."

Now, all I wish to show here is that, together with some reasons that may make us think, with Sedley, and with a long tradition, that Aristotle's *scala naturae* and teleology are anthropocentric, things are more open than they seem when it comes to matters of interpretation. And a big question concerns whether the very admission that humans are the ultimate beneficiaries of (in terms of those who might need) the lower stages in the scale of nature constitutes by itself an argument for an anthropocentric notion of teleology in Aristotle. As Sedley himself also recognizes, a notion of teleology could be defined not necessarily, or at least not only, in terms of which entity is the ultimate beneficiary, but, instead, in terms of which entity is the final goal of aspiration. And if we wish to define teleology in terms of purposiveness, rather than in terms of benefit, there seems to be no doubt that God, and not humans, is the final goal. So, reproduction exists so that all living beings can participate in immortality (cf. *De An.* II 4, 415a25–b7), as represented by God, which is also the object of love of the heavenly bodies (*Metaph.* XII 7, 1072a26–30; b2–4), which are unequivocally above humans in the hierarchy. Such participation in immortality is in turn something human beings should strive for, and attain through the exercise of intellect, which makes them resemble God (cf. *Nicomachean Ethics* (*NE*) X 7, 1177b26–34). In this way, as suggested in *Metaph.* XII 10, 1075a19–25, God can be seen as the final end which guarantees the coordination of all, or at least most, individual goals in nature: different kinds of thing in the universe are not chaotically, but structurally, arranged, so that they can "exist in communion for the whole" ("*koinonei...eis to holon*," 1075a24–25).

Now, the traditional notion of a *scala naturae* could also be challenged from a different angle. Recent work, e.g. by Andrew Coles (1997), has queried the idea that there should be an essential gap between humans and ANIMALS in terms of rationality, despite the fact that the definition of human as a rational animal that the tradition has passed on as Aristotelian (probably based on *Pol.* I 1, 1253a9–10) would seem to suggest that reason is what we have as a specific difference, i.e. as something not shared by any other species. Coles distinguishes between, on the one hand, a "saltatory" view of the *scala naturae* in Aristotle (for which some people could find evidence also in *Nicomachean Ethics* I 7, whose famous "function argument" seems designed to establish that the function distinctive of humans, unlike animals or plants, is the use of reason or *logos*), and, on the other, a "gradual" view of the world, where things are more of a matter of more or less between the different stages than of discrete gaps. Purporting to stress such a gradual view, Coles draws our attention to numerous passages in the zoological works where we are told about a "continual change" (*metabasis sunechēs*) in nature (cf. *Parts of Animals* (*PA*) IV 5 681a12–15 and *History of Animals* (*HA*) VII [VIII] 1 588b4 ff) and about animals sharing in various degrees of intelligence, while arguing for a non-deflationary interpretation of such texts. It is noted, particularly, that, of the 50 or so chapters constituting *HA* VIII (IX), no fewer than 43 are devoted to animal intelligence. Thus, some sorts of animal at least are endowed with *nous* in the broad sense (cf. *HA* VIII (IX) 3, 610b22) and/or practical deliberation (*phronesis*, cf. e.g. *Generation of Animals* (*GA*) III 2 753a9 ff). For instance, in *HA* VIII (IX) 3, 610b24 ff, the sheep's lack of *nous* is illustrated by the animal's tendency to stray from shelter in stormy weather, as opposed to the deer which is held to be intelligent (*phronimos*) because, e.g., it gives birth along the roads, where the fear of humans prevents the approach of wild animals (5, 611a16 ff). Some passages in *HA* VIII (IX) even attribute second and third orders of intentionality and reflexive knowledge to animals about their own mental states, in a way that brings Aristotle "modestly close to attributing animals a status of quasi-personhood by modern philosophical standards": to cite only one example, the cuckoo manages its reproduction intelligently (*phronimōs*) because it is aware of its own cowardice (*dia gar to suneidenai autōi tēn deilian*) and inability to help its young, and it therefore makes its own chicks supposititious for their security (29, 618a26 ff). In opposition to the notion of discrete gaps rather than a continuum in the scale of nature, Coles shows, in addition, that the treatment of some animals in respect of intelligence does not differ from Aristotle's treatment of children (cf. *PA* IV 10, 686b23 ff, *HA* VII (VIII) 1,

588a21–b3), noting, again, that the picture of childhood development in *HA* VII (VIII) 1 is gradualist rather than saltatory. So, Coles concludes, it seems clear that in the zoology Aristotle was prepared to attribute to animals some level of *nous*, and, particularly, more-and-less degrees of practical intelligence or *phronēsis* (under which Aristotle seemed to have included the ability of each animal to take care of itself and of its own welfare) – even if he was not prepared to grant them every feature associated with the rational soul (as in *De An.* III 3) and the intellectual virtues discussed in *NE* VI.

If we go with Coles's line of argument, then we shall see elements in Aristotle's biological work pointing toward some sort of kinship, rather than a gulf, between humans and animals. And the very length of study that Aristotle devotes to such matters is a proof of his interest in, and even aesthetical appreciation of, the surrounding natural world, which, as he expresses in *PA* I 5, possesses its own "grace" (*charin*, 644b31). One must not leave out studying the nature of any animal however insignificant, since nature in that case provides "unimaginable pleasure" to those who love wisdom (645a4–10). There is, then, "something beautiful" in the study of every kind of animal, given that purposiveness in nature – as the study of their organs and functions evinces – is in the abode of the beautiful (645a21 ff).

To finish this section on Aristotle, let us pay some attention to a passage in the *Meteorologica*, which has been used to show indifference toward the environment, or even anti-environmental views, on the part of Aristotle by Hargrove (1989) and Attfield (1994). The passage occurs at *Meteorologica* I 14, where Aristotle is considering the fact that some parts of the earth become moist or dry at different times because of natural phenomena, in such a long period of time that can pass unnoticed to humans; and before this can be recorded whole peoples perish through war, illness, or famine (351a19–b14). So with Egypt, "it is manifest that the place is becoming drier and drier and the whole land is a deposit of the river Nile" (351b28–30). Aristotle criticizes those who think "that the sea is growing less by drying up," since more places appear to have experienced this now than formerly (352a19–21). The universe being eternal, one should think that dryness in one place compensates floods at another place (ibid, 17–31). All that Aristotle is arguing for here is that there is some cosmic balance that is kept on the earth even if we fail to notice the largeness of its scale; and these cyclical occurrences must be inscribed in some larger homeostatic regularity. Thus, "one must suppose that the cause of all these things is that, just as winter occurs in the yearly seasons, so in determined periods of time, in some big cycle, there comes a big winter and excess of rains" (ibid, 28–31), a contention that brings to us Heraclitean resonances about some cosmic, teleological balance prevailing in the world. A human could certainly complain that whole nations, as Aristotle says, are being destroyed by these cycles of nature, but Aristotle's neutrality in describing that does not make him, as such, hostile to the environment. For he is not saying in this context that humans should alter the workings of nature; rather, he can be seen as urging us to respect the latter and to insert them in a broader, holistic account of the world rather than assessing them according to mere anthropocentric interests. It is certainly true that Aristotle's world is eternal, and thus he could not have thought of the earth going out of existence as we may today; his world, as we have seen, is also teleological, i.e. in most cases arranged toward the best. But the very fact that he allows for cases where natural teleology can be frustrated (such as with monsters, *Phys.* II 8, 199a33–b4), together with his contention that human art can improve on nature (*Phys.* II 8, 199a15–16), and, above all, the very fact that he feels the need to establish a whole ethical system spelling out the goal for which humans should strive, leaves, undoubtedly, enough room for humans to better the state of the world as a whole in which they are parts. For one could think that, as much as the good of a city is superior to that of an individual by being greater (*NE* I 1, 1094b7–9; cf. *Pol.* I 1, 1253a19–20), so is the overall good of the world itself superior to the interests of people. "For the whole is necessarily prior to the parts": without the whole, the parts lose their proper function (*Pol.* I 1, 1253a20–22). After all, the virtues exalted in his ethics presuppose a life of moderation as opposed to excess in all levels, including a greed for sensual pleasures, power, or money that might end up, as we might think, in an abusive exploitation of the environment (cf. *NE* I5 and X 8, 1179a1–9). Quite the contrary, the highest life for humans is a life needing comparatively few external goods, namely, the life of abstract contemplation, which brings them close not only to the noetic activity of the divine Unmoved Mover of the heavens but also to the intellectual life of the divine heavens themselves (cf. *NE* X 7, 1177b26 ff, and *Metaph.* XII 7, 1072b14 ff), in a way that emphasizes the divine kinship between the highest in humans and the cosmos.

Post-Aristotelian philosophers

Let us finally say something about some post-Aristotelian philosophers, in whom the notion of "nature," variously understood, plays a vital role. Even though for Epicurus (ca. 341–271 BCE), the paradigmatic holder of hedonism, nature does not work teleologically, but mechanically, teleology becomes relevant in the ethical domain. Thus, pleasure as the goal is to be sought on the grounds that "as soon as every animal is born, it seeks after pleasure and rejoices in it as the greatest good, while it rejects pain as the greatest bad . . . ; and it does this when it is not yet corrupted, on the innocent and sound judgment of nature itself" (Cicero, *On Ends* I.29 ff; see L&S 21A(2); translations of Stoics and Epicureans are in L&S). But a life according to nature is preferred over a life of anti-natural sophistication, even when it comes to classifying pleasures (understood as the satisfaction of desire): we have desires that are natural and necessary (such as desire for food and a bed), natural and unnecessary (such as sex), and desires which are empty, or unnatural (such as the desire to dress fashionably, or have the nicest car; cf. Epicurus, *Letter to Menoeceus*, 127 ff; see L&S 21B(1)). And philosophy advises us to limit our desires to those that are natural as a means to attain happiness: "Everything natural is easily procured; but what is empty is hard to procure" (ibid, L&S 21B(4)). "Poverty, when measured by nature's end, is great wealth, but unlimited wealth is great poverty" (Epicurus, *Vatican Sayings* 25; see L&S 21F(3)). It is partly on these grounds, in addition, that Epicurus recommends vegetarianism:

> As for eating meat, it relieves neither any of our nature's stress nor a desire whose non-satisfaction would give rise to pain . . . What it contributes to is not life's maintenance but variation of pleasures, just like sex or the drinking of exotic wines, all of

which our nature is quite capable of doing without...Furthermore, meat is not conducive to health, but is rather an impediment to it. (Porphyry, *On Abstinence* I.51.6 ff; Usener 464, part; see L&S 21J)

A life in harmony with nature is in turn advocated by the Stoics (fourth century BCE to second century CE) as the goal for humans (see Stobaeus 2.77, 16–27, and 2.75, 11–76, 8; see L&S 63A and B). Borrowing from Heraclitus and from Plato, the Stoics believe in an overarching *Logos*, or cosmic reason, that orders and governs the material world, and nature evinces that order. So to live according to nature is for the Stoics to live in accordance with the rational element in us, which mirrors, and is a part of, the rational *Logos* that pervades the universe. A holistic, rather than an individualistic, perspective is in all cases advised as the means to obtain happiness: we shouldn't wish events to happen as *we* wish them, but rather wish them to happen as *they* happen (Epictetus, *Manual* 8). And even though their teleology is fatalistic, it is nonetheless pointed out that "many things cannot come about without our wanting them and applying the most intense determination and efforts over them; since it is together with this that they are fated to come about" (Diogenianus, apud Eusebius, *Evangelical Preparation* 6.8.25–9; see L&S 62F(5)). It is emphasized that "you are a citizen of the world and a part of it, not one of the underlings but one of the foremost constituents. For you are capable of attending to the divine government and of calculating its consequences" (Epictetus, *Discourses* 2.10.I–12; see L&S 59Q(3)). ANIMALS, however, are supposed to be devoid of reason and therefore inferior to humans and gods (cf. Seneca, *Letters* 124.13–14; see L&S 60H. 76.9–10; see L&S 63D). There is also the Aristotelian-sounding passage that animals exist for the sake of humans: So, even though they emphasize the idea of kinship between all human beings ("[the world] is as it were a city and state shared by men and gods", Cicero, *On Ends* 3.62–8; see L&S 57F(3)), they also "deny that any rights exist between men and animals. For Chrysippus excellently remarked that everything else was created for the sake of men and gods, but these for the sake of community and society; consequently men can make beasts serve their own needs without contravening rights" (ibid, L&S 57F(5)). There also seems to be a *scala naturae* in which the different realms of nature appear in a hierarchy: "The animal is superior to the non-animal in two respects, impression and impulse" (Philo, *Allegories of the Laws* I.30; see L&S 53 P(1)). Even though both humans and animals articulate sounds and receive impressions, humans differ from non-rational animals by internal speech and by impressions produced by inference and combination (Sextus Empiricus, *Against the Professors*, 8.275–6; see L&S 53T). However, one should not immediately conclude that Stoic teleology is straightforwardly anthropocentric: things happen for the best, but that best can often be beyond human understanding and the apparent immediate human interests, and the whole is again superior to the parts, even if there is a hierarchy between the species:

With the exception of the world everything else was made for the sake of other things: for example, the crops and fruits which the earth brings forth were made for the sake of animals, and the animals which it brings forth were made for the sake of men (the horse for transport, the ox for ploughing, the dog for hunting and guarding). Man himself has come to be in order to contemplate and imitate the world, being by no means perfect, but a tiny constituent of that which is perfect. But the world, since it embraces everything and there is nothing which is not included in it, is perfect from every point of view. (Cicero, *On the Nature of the Gods* 2.37–9; see L&S 54H(1))

Let us devote a last word to the revival and synthesis of many Platonic ideas in the philosophy of the Neoplatonist Plotinus (ca. CE 205–70) and his successor Porphyry (ca. CE 232–309). Plotinus encourages us to raise ourselves from the level of dispersion and multiplicity in which our several individual egos are buried, and discover a level of unity and communication with the whole of nature which promotes sympathy toward all of its aspects and creatures (cf. e.g. *Ennead* IV 9 3, 1–9). On that level, we are also made to share with the universal soul responsibility in the administration of the whole universe (cf. IV 8 2, 19–24; IV 8 4, 6–8). Higher levels of spiritual ascent will end up in embracing a One of suprametaphysical and ineffable nature, but for the purposes of the present chapter we can restrict our analysis to our first level of communion with the perceptible nature, the appreciation of which would in any case not so much be denied as enriched if we were to attain even higher levels of unification (see e.g. II 9 16). The most important thing still is to know oneself, but the true nature of the self turns out to go beyond the boundaries created by empirical individuality: as higher levels of self-awareness reveal, the self is not diminished, but increased (cf. VI 5 12, 24–25; IV 4 2, 22 ff) by attaining union and even identity with the whole of nature and the universe, the realm of Forms, and ultimately the One beyond all these.

Plotinus had a great impact on his disciple Porphyry, who describes his master as vegetarian (*Life of Plotinus* 2), and who produced the classic ancient text for vegetarianism and animal treatment. In his treatise *On Abstinence from Animal Food*, he recommends a vegetarian diet both as a purification and health-preserving condition of one's ascent to God (book 1) and because it is unjust to animals (book 3); he condemns animal sacrifice (book 2), and contends that justice requires us to spare animals, both because they are rational and because they experience (according to him, unlike plants) pain and terror (book 3; see Sorabji 1993). And in a way that directly goes back to Plato, Porphyry emphasizes that we should even treat earth as our mother and nurse (*Abstinence* 2.32).

In sum, we have seen elements in different ancient philosophers that might provide interesting suggestions for those wishing to integrate human life into the broader environment. Despite their different outlooks on many issues, it can be said that these ancient Greek and Hellenic philosophers tended not to dissociate their own lives from a wider world-view, notwithstanding what our contemporary perspective, so often centered on self-interest as opposed to other people's (and other beings') interests, might project on them. Even self-knowledge, as we have seen with various thinkers, is understood in terms of finding out what exactly our place in the larger world is. Much more could indeed be said about the topic expressed by the title of this essay, but I hope at least to have provided the reader with a different light by which to assess some main figures of the classical Greek tradition, and with an idea of what he or she might find if they dare dive into the fascinating world of their texts.

I wish to thank Richard Sorabji, Dale Jamieson, Andrew Coles, and Raphael Woolf for their comments on previous drafts of this chapter.

References

Primary sources

Translations of the ancient texts are my own unless otherwise stated.

Diels, H. and Kranz, W. (D&K) (1934–5) *Die Fragmente der Vorsokratiker*, vols. 1–3 (Berlin: Weidmann).

Bekker, E. (1960) *Aristotelis Opera*, vols. 1 and 2 (Berlin: Walter de Gruyter).

Burnet, J. (1900–7) *Platonis Opera* (Oxford: Oxford University Press).

Henry, P. and Schwyzer, H. R. ((1964–82) *Plotini Opera* (Oxford: Oxford University Press).

Long, A. and Sedley, D. (L&S) (1987) *The Hellenistic Philosophers* (Cambridge: Cambridge University Press).

De l'Abstinence, Bude edition with French translation, vols. 1 and 2, trans. J. Bouffartigue, M. Patillon, and A. Segonds (Paris: Les Belles Lettres, 1977–93).

Secondary Sources

Attfield, R. (1994) *Environmental Philosophy: Principles and Prospects* (Aldershot: Avebury). [His chapter 6 provides an assessment of ancient Greek philosophers.]

Carone, G. R. (1994) "Teleology and evil in *Laws* X," *Review of Metaphysics* 48, pp. 275–98. [An analysis of Plato's theory of the soul in *Laws* X, arguing that Plato there presents human souls as the source of all kind of evil, including natural.]

——(1998) "Plato and the environment," *Environmental Ethics* 20, pp. 115–33. [This article responds to various charges made against Plato by environmental philosophers, and presents elements in Plato of interest to modern environmental thought.]

Coles, A. (1997) "Animal and childhood cognition in Aristotle's Biology and the *scala naturae*," in *Aristotelische Biologie*, ed. W. Kullmann and S. Foellinger (Stuttgart: Franz Steiner Verlag), pp. 287–323. [This article presents Aristotle's scale of nature as a continuum where even animals are endowed with various degrees of rationality and quasi-personhood.]

Hargrove, E. (1989) *Foundations of Environmental Ethics* (Englewood Cliffs, NJ: Prentice-Hall). [This book contains some criticisms of the ancient Greeks addressed here and in Carone (1998).]

Sedley, D. (1991) "Is Aristotle's teleology anthropocentric?," *Phronesis* 36, pp. 179–96 [Here Sedley argues for humans being the ultimate beneficiaries of a global system of nature in Ar.]

Sorabji, R. (1993) *Animal Minds and Human Morals* (Ithaca NY: Cornell University Press). [This book explores the ancient debate on the philosophy of mind, both human and animal, and its ethical implications.]

Wardy, R. (1993) "Aristotelian rainfall or the lore of averages," *Phronesis* 38, pp. 18–30. [This article contains a critique of Sedley.]

6

Judaism

ERIC KATZ

Judaism has a rich and complex tradition regarding human interaction with the natural world. It would be a mistake to claim either that there is one distinct Jewish view of nature or that there is a consensus Jewish position in the elaboration of an environmental ethic. Judaism offers a wide variety of ideas that can contribute to the development of an environmental philosophy. To some extent, then, commentators are free to choose those themes and texts that are relevant to whatever issue is under discussion. As a general rule, Judaism eschews grand theoretical system-building; Jewish philosophy – and especially Jewish ethics – begins with the specific command-ments binding upon all practicing Jews. In Judaism, perhaps more than any other religion, philosophical meaning arises out of the procedures of concrete daily activity. As Robert Gordis writes, "The true genius of Judaism has always lain in specifics." Thus, Gordis continues, an understanding of Jewish teachings on the environmental crisis is "not to be sought in high-sounding phrases which obligate [Jews] to nothing concrete; rather [it] will be found in specific areas of Jewish law and practice" (Gordis 1990, p. 8).

This chapter will thus focus on specific laws and commandments in the Jewish tradition that concern human obligations to nature, the environment, and the non-human world. Four basic areas will be emphasized: the idea of stewardship, environ-mental regulations in the human community, obligations to animals, and the general injunction against wanton destruction (the principle of *bal tashchit*). This discussion will demonstrate that the multiplicity of Jewish traditions can contribute to recent debates in environmental philosophy concerning both practical environmental poli-cies and the theoretical justification of the moral consideration of the natural non-human world. The chapter will begin with two critical views that have influenced contemporary discussion: (1) the alienation of the Jewish people from the natural world, due to the urban character of modern Jewish life, the Jewish emphasis on the life of the mind, and the transcendence of God; and (2) the theme of the anthropo-centric domination of nature in Genesis 1: 28. A response to these critical themes is necessary before any positive Jewish position in environmental philosophy can be articulated.

The unnatural Jew: alienation and transcendence

One critical view of the Jewish relationship to the environment is based on the Jewish alienation from the natural world. In a controversial essay Steven Schwarzschild argued that the Jewish relationship to nature, as embodied in its religious teachings, philosophy, culture, and history, is one of alienation and confrontation (Schwarz-schild, 1984). CHRISTIANITY may be interpreted as permitting the fusion of God with the physical world, for Jesus entered the world and God became incarnate, but Judaism radically separates humanity (and God) from the natural or physical world. In Judaism, God is transcendent. Human life, characterized primarily by the life of reason and mind (and in this way similar to God), is distinct from the natural processes of the physical world. Nature – the physical world – can be used by God and humanity (created in His image) to serve His or our interests, but nature has no value in itself. Thus Judaism proposes a radical anthropocentrism in which nature is viewed merely as a resource for the satisfaction of human interests, wants, and needs.

Schwarzschild defends this view of the Jewish separation of humanity from nature by invoking Jewish literature, philosophy, and history: as an urban people living in the ghetto, the Jews of Europe have lacked a direct relationship with the natural world for 500 years. But their urban existence is also prescribed by Jewish law: "Well before the rise of towns and cities, Jews were not supposed to reside where there are no synagogues, physicians, artisans, toilets, water supplies, schoolteachers, scribes, organized charities, or courts" (Schwarzschild 1984, p. 362, citing Maimonides (1135–1204)). To be Jewish is to live in a human community, devoted to the establishment of human institutions, the study of the Torah, and the worship of God.

To believe that the natural world is in some way divine is to promulgate the great Jewish heresy of immanentism, for the idea that nature is sacred denies the absolute transcendence and separation of God from the physical world. CHRISTIANITY's belief in the incarnation of God is the most notable example of this heresy, but the secular philosophy of Spinoza (see EARLY MODERN PHILOSOPHY), the Hassidic traditions in Judaism, and the political ideology of Zionism, are also included. Schwarzschild here represents and defends a theme in Jewish thought that denies all value to the natural world. In support of his critical view he cites an important text from the Mishnah: "Rabbi Ya'akov says: One, who while walking along the way, reviewing his studies, breaks off from his study and says, 'How beautiful is that tree! How beautiful is that plowed field!' Scripture regards him as if he has forfeited his soul" (*Pirkei Avot*, "Ethics of the Fathers," 3: 7).

This passage is perhaps the most problematic text for any attempt to develop a specific Jewish environmental philosophy, for it suggests that any contemplation of the natural or physical world (the tree or the plowed field), if such contemplation interferes with the study of Torah, is to be condemned in the harshest terms. Thus this text presents proof that in the Jewish tradition the natural world is vastly inferior – indeed, worthless or even evil – compared to the life of the mind, the study of the Torah, the revealed word of God. The meaning of human life is to study the word of God, and if one interrupts this study to think about the beauty of the natural or physical world, then one abandons one's essential humanity. We humans must study the word of God, not His creation (the world). God is not in the natural world.

Jeremy Benstein (1995) has presented a detailed discussion of this passage. He attempts to reconcile its obvious criticism of a concern for the natural world with more broadly stated Jewish traditions regarding the environment (traditions that will be examined below). And although Schwarzschild and other environmental critics may cite the passage as a clear indication of Judaism's repudiation of nature, Benstein shows that the historical commentaries on the passage are divided, and that several differing interpretations can be proposed. Many commentators use the passage to show the complete lack of value in nature; but others merely argue that nature must be subordinated to the revealed word of the Torah. On this latter view, nature must be respected and praised as part of the divine creation – but one must be careful not to interrupt one's studies to offer the praise, for studying the Torah is more important than praising God's creation. A third interpretation, that of Rabbi Yosef Hayyim Caro (1800–95) gives full credit to the natural world as an expression of God's creation, but claims that the study of the natural world alone is an inadequate path to the truth of God. Our study of nature can be mistaken, while the study of the revealed word of God in the Torah is a surer path to the truth (Benstein 1995, pp. 153–7).

Benstein also reviews several Zionist interpretations of this passage (ibid, pp. 158–61), and here the main idea is that in the diaspora, alienated from their homeland, Jews learned to focus their attention exclusively on the word of God, the Torah. In the ghettos of Eastern Europe, exiled from their homeland in Palestine, it was unnecessary and wrong to contemplate the physical world. But in Israel this alienation has been overcome, for the Jewish people are in the process of rebuilding their traditional God-given homeland. Here, a concern for both physical creation and the word of God can co-exist.

Benstein's conclusion provides an answer both to Schwarzschild directly and to the common view that Judaism is alienated from the natural world. He argues that the real error is the dichotomizing of nature study and the Torah, for we need to do both. "Yes, if in order to relate to the natural environment you have to cease your learning, then your soul is in grave danger" (ibid, p. 163). The error here is the "radical rupture" between the revealed word and nature. We must effect a synthesis in our education so that we learn to mend the gap between the Torah and nature and appreciate both as the expression of the divine in the world. Alienation from nature is not an eternal state decreed by God – it is an ongoing process that must be overcome through a deeper understanding of both Jewish law and the laws of the natural universe.

Subdue the earth: domination, dominion, and stewardship

The second critical view of the Jewish tradition concerns the passage in Genesis in which God commands humanity to subdue the earth:

> And God blessed them [i.e., Adam and Eve]; and God said unto them: "Be fruitful and multiply, and replenish the earth, and subdue it; and have dominion over the fish of the sea, and over the fowl of the air, and over every living thing that moves upon the earth." (Genesis 1: 28)

This biblical passage appears in almost every discussion of the religious foundations of environmental attitudes and the environmental crisis. Most prominently, Lynn White, Jr. invokes the passage to demonstrate that the Judeo-Christian tradition is fundamentally biased toward the dominion – if not the actual domination – of the earth by humanity (White 1967). The text suggests that the earth and all non-human living beings in nature belong to the human race as mere means for the growth ("be fruitful and multiply") of humanity (see CHRISTIANITY).

As with the previous critical Mishnah passage, the anti-environmental interpretation of this biblical text needs to be answered if we are to understand the full complexity of the Jewish traditions regarding the natural environment. Fortunately, the idea of the stewardship of the natural world can provide a response to the argument that the Bible endorses the domination of nature for human ends. Judaism clearly limits the human dominion, ownership, and freedom of action within the natural world.

One limitation in human activity and dominion is obvious. Norman Lamm (1971, pp. 164) points out that the very next line in Genesis restricts humans to a vegetarian diet – a restriction that limits human control and ownership of the living creatures in nature: "And God said: 'Behold, I have given you every herb yielding seed, which is upon the earth, and every tree in which is the fruit of a tree yielding seed – to you shall it be for food'" (Genesis 1: 29). The Torah thus limits the human right to "subdue" and use nature. Genesis 1: 28 does not present earth's title to humanity; humanity is not free to dominate the planet.

Jewish scholars throughout history repeatedly disavow the idea that Genesis 1: 28 permits the unchecked use (or abuse) of nature by humanity. Gordis (1990, pp. 7–8) cites three examples. In one complicated piece of logic, a passage in the Talmud (*Yebemot* 65b) relates the phrase "subdue it" to the first part of the sentence, "be fruitful and multiply," and then, by connecting the act of "subduing" with warfare – a male activity – claims that the passage really means that the propagation of the human race is an obligation of the male. The medieval commentator Nachmanides (1194–1270) and the Italian commentator Obadiah Sforno (ca. 1470–ca. 1550) focus on the use of natural resources, not their destruction or misuse. Nachmanides sees the passage as granting permission to humanity to continue their activities of building, agriculture, and mining. Sforno's explanation is even more restrictive: "*And subdue it* – that you protect yourself with your reason and prevent the animals from entering within your boundaries and you rule over them." Here, humanity is limited to actions of self-defense and domestication. The power of humanity to use natural resources is thus recognized, but there are clearly limitations on human freedom regarding the natural world. Dominion does not mean unrestricted domination.

The limitations and restrictions are based on a fundamental Jewish tradition, that humanity is the steward of the natural world, not its owner. Genesis 2: 15 lends support to the idea of stewardship, as it declares: "And ... God ... put him into the garden of Eden to till it and to keep it." Stewardship means that there is a human role in the care and maintenance of the natural world. As David Ehrenfeld and Philip J. Bentley (1985) argue, stewardship is a middle position between the one extreme of exploitative domination and the other extreme of the sacred reverence and non-interference with nature – perhaps suggested by popular conceptions of Eastern religions such as JAINISM AND BUDDHISM. In the terminology of environmental philosophy, the Jewish concept of stewardship promotes neither the extreme of the destruction nor the extreme of the preservation of nature, but rather a compromise – its conservation and wise developmental use. The central idea of stewardship is that the steward exercises care for an entity that is in its power. The steward does not abuse or exploit the entity in its care.

Within Judaism, the idea of care implicit in the stewardship of the natural world is, however, based on a more fundamental concept: the proper ownership of the world. Stewardship is an expression of the limits to human power because humanity does not own the natural world. In Judaism the world belongs to God; Judiasm is a theocentric religion. God Himself, not human life and welfare, is the source of religious and moral obligation. The divine ownership of nature is most directly stated in Psalm 24: "The earth is the Lord's and the fullness thereof, the world and those who dwell therein." Humanity cannot have an unrestricted dominion over the natural world because the world belongs to God; humanity is merely the divinely appointed guardian of that which belongs to God.

The theocentrism of Judaism is the basis of many Jewish laws and rituals. Although humanity uses the physical world, God does not relinquish ownership. The laws concerning the sabbatical – and the jubilee – year clearly indicate that God is the owner of the earth: "And the land is not to be sold in perpetuity, for all land is Mine, because you are strangers and sojourners before Me" (Leviticus 25: 23). As Samuel Belkin writes, man possesses but a "temporary tenancy of God's creation" (1972, p. 253). In his discussion of the sabbatical year's prohibition on farming the land in the seventh year (see Leviticus 25: 3–4), Belkin argues that "the sages refuse to assign purely economic, agricultural or social motives to this law," for Rabbi Abahu cites the ownership of God as the primary reason for the existence of the sabbath and jubilee years (ibid, pp. 253–4, citing *Sanhedrin* 39a). Thus, these laws concerning the use of land are not to be understood as a primitive attempt at enlightened agricultural methods. Instead, the laws are meant to reinforce the centrality of God in Jewish practice and belief. For Belkin, "the entire structure of Judaism rests" on the principle "that creation belongs to the Creator." Without such a principle, humans would own the world and the entities within it; they would then be able to use those things without regard to any laws or principles other than their own will. But this is not the case: the moral code of the Torah, the ritual commands, and the laws of Judaism all strongly imply that the world belongs to God, and He has "instructed man concerning what he is permitted to do or prohibited from doing with His creation ... [God] alone dictates the terms of man's tenancy in this world" (Belkin 1972, p. 255).

The most obvious example of the way ritual action reinforces the notion of God's ownership is the commandment concerning the blessings over food. One contemporary commentator, Jonathan Helfand cites the *Tosefta: Berakhot* 4: 1: "Man may not taste anything until he has recited a blessing, as it is written 'The earth is the Lord's and the fullness thereof.' Anyone who derives benefit from this world without a [prior] blessing is guilty of misappropriating sacred property" (Helfand 1986, pp. 40–41). Because God owns the world we humans are required to ask permission before we ingest any item of food. All the objects of the material world are as sacred as the entities of Heaven, for they are all the creation of God, and belong to Him (Belkin 1972, p. 252).

The practical meaning of the theocentric ownership of the world by God is also expressed in the rituals concerning the weekly sabbath. Ehrenfeld and Bentley emphasize the meaning of the sabbath for contemporary environmentalists in relation to the idea of stewardship: "For Jews, it is the Sabbath and the idea of the Sabbath that introduces the necessary restraint into stewardship." Three elements of the observance of the sabbath are important: "we create nothing, we destroy nothing, and we enjoy the bounty of the Earth." The fact that nothing is created serves to remind us that we are not as supreme as God; the fact that nothing is destroyed emphasizes that the world does not belong to us, but to God; and our enjoyment of the earth's bounty reminds us that God is the source of nature's goodness (Ehrenfeld and Bentley 1985, pp. 309–10). Thus the concept of the sabbath itself – the absence of work and the appreciation of God – imposes a strict limit on human activity and achievement. Humanity in no way possesses dominion over the non-human world, since it does not even possess dominion over its own activities.

Observance of the sabbath is thus connected to the notion of stewardship, for without dominion, humanity is merely the steward of God's creation. Stewardship strongly implies a notion of responsibility, for the steward is responsible for the condition of the entities in his care. As an illustration, Ehrenfeld and Bentley recount a story told by the eleventh-century Spanish rabbi, Jonah ibn Janah: A man walks into a house in the midst of a deserted city; he finds a table with food and drink and begins to eat, thinking to himself, "I deserve all this, it is all mine, I will act as I please." Little does he know that the owners are watching him, and that he will have to pay for all that he consumes. Humanity, as merely the appointed steward of God's creation – the physical world – is responsible to God for its use (Ehrenfeld and Bentley 1985, pp. 306–7).

The second critical view of the Jewish tradition – the possible domination of nature implicit in Genesis 1: 28 – is thus answered by a serious commitment to the notion of stewardship as implied by Judaism's theocentrism. This then is the first of the four basic themes in the Jewish tradition that will be discussed in this chapter: in Judaism, humanity is the responsible steward of God's creation.

Environmental regulations: rituals and commandments

An abstract notion of responsibility for the guardianship of the physical world is not, however, an adequate summary of Judaism's environmental philosophy. As noted above, Judaism is concerned more with specific concrete commandments than with abstract ethical theories. Thus the second theme in an explication of Jewish environmental philosophy is the recognition that there are many practical commandments regarding human actions affecting the natural world. By following these commandments, the abstract notion of responsible stewardship becomes a living praxis binding on all observant Jews. An environmental philosophy of protection, preservation, and care is instilled as religious belief and a way of life.

Jewish law and ritual reveal specific commandments involving many different aspects of everyday Jewish life as related to the environment. Several commandments concern the general health and well-being of the human community as it is situated in the natural world. Deuteronomy 23: 13–15, for example, requires the burial of human sewage in wartime, with the command that the soldiers must possess a spade for that very purpose among their other weapons: "and it shall be when thou sittest down outside, thou shalt dig therewith, and shalt turn back and cover that which cometh from thee." The concern for anti-pollution and sanitation measures was deemed important enough that it could not be abrogated even in wartime.

A more general principle is *yishuv ha-aretz* ("the settling of the land"), which mandates restrictions both on the type of animals that can be raised and the type of trees that could be used for burning on the sacrificial altar. Goats and sheep were thought to be destructive to the land, and vine and olive trees were too valuable to be used in religious services. Helfand argues that *yishuv ha-aretz* is also the basis of the mandate to establish a *migrash*, an open space one thousand cubits wide around all cities in Israel, in which agriculture and building would be prohibited. The preservation of open and undeveloped space was considered an important amenity for the human community. "The operative principle . . . calls upon the Jew in his homeland to balance the economic, environmental, and even religious needs of society carefully to assure the proper development and settling of the land" (Helfand 1986, p. 46). Thus the general principle of *yishuv ha-aretz* and the specific commandment of establishing the *migrash* show that the laws regulating life in early Jewish cities are functionally equivalent to a fully realized notion of town planning. Open areas were preserved, and restrictions were placed on agriculture and other industries for the overall well-being of the human community situated in a specific environment.

In a comprehensive discussion, Aryeh Carmell (1976) examines many of the laws that restrict human activity in the community, laws that show the rabbinical concern for the quality of the environment in Jewish life. Maimonides, for example, explains that there are four classes of nuisance in which injury is always presumed: smoke, dust, noxious smells, and vibration. There is also a right to quietness. This leads to rabbinic regulations – a kind of ancient zoning ordinance – regarding the specific placement of certain industries within the town: threshing floors, cemeteries, tanneries, and slaughterhouses (Carmell 1976, p. 503, citing Maimonides *Hilchot Shechenim* ("Laws of Neighborly Relations") 11: 4–5). Tanneries, for example, were to be situated on the east side of town, so that the prevailing winds (in Israel) would blow the noxious fumes and smells away from human habitations. Carmell argues that the basis of the kinds of rabbinic regulation recorded by Maimonides was a limitation of individual property rights for the sake of the entire community (1976, p. 505). The fundamental theocentrism of Judaism again plays a key role here, for the limitations of individual property rights can be traced to the notion that all property belongs ultimately to God. The use of property by human individuals thus must be regulated by the laws of the Torah and the rabbinical interpretations of these laws.

Sanitation, zoning regulations, and the protection of undeveloped areas as amenities are all environmental regulations that benefit the human community. But another category of Jewish law concerns the human relation to the divine plan. Nature is conceived, in Judaism, as the result of a divine plan or intelligence. This plan is not to be altered by human activity. Thus, in Leviticus 19: 19 there is a prohibition against the hybridization of plants and animals, and even a restriction on wearing two types of cloth: "you shall not let your cattle mate with a different kind, you shall not sow your field with two kinds of seed, you shall not wear a garment of wool and linen." Although human activities must, by necessity, interfere with natural processes, there is a prohibition on activities that interfere too much.

Hybridization or the mingling of species violates natural law, the principles of God's creation. And so Nachmanides concludes in his discussion of Leviticus 19: 19: "He who mixes kinds denies and confounds the act of creation" (cited in Helfand 1986, p. 51). The divine plan for creation must be respected and maintained (see TECHNOLOGY).

The preservation of species is one aspect of the maintenance of the divine plan that has enormous ramifications for contemporary environmental issues. There are clearly Jewish traditions and commandments that aim, in modern terminology, to protect endangered species of animals. Two biblical passages prohibit the killing of both a mother and its offspring. In Leviticus 22: 28 there is a prohibition on slaughtering a cow (or ewe) and her calf (or lamb) on the same day. In Deuteronomy 22: 6–7 there is a prohibition against taking a mother bird with her young; rather, the young birds or eggs may be taken, but the mother is to be set free. Clearly, the survival of the mother in the latter case is meant to ensure the continuation of the bird species. Sustainability and the wise use of natural resources may be one of the motivations for this commandment, but there is mainly a concern for the preservation of the divine order of the universe. Again, the medieval commentator Nachmanides: "Scripture will not permit a destructive act that will cause the extinction of a species," and the thirteenth-century *Sefer Hahinukh* explains that it is God's desire to preserve each species according to divine providence (cited in Helfand 1986, p. 45; *Sefer Hahinukh* 294 and 545) (see BIODIVERSITY).

As these few examples demonstrate, there are many specific Jewish laws that codify and apply the general notion of responsibility and stewardship for the natural environment. These laws concern both the overall quality of the human environment and the maintenance and sustainability of natural entities and species as part of God's creation.

The treatment of non-human animals

The third major area of the Jewish tradition is the treatment of non-human ANIMALS. A comprehensive review of the Jewish concern for animal life would require a separate chapter; here, the discussion will be limited to those principles that have a direct bearing on environmental philosophy. In particular, Judaism can be seen as granting considerable moral weight to the interests of animal life. Although Judaism does not advocate a vegetarian lifestyle – the prohibition against eating meat implied in Genesis 1: 29 was rescinded by God after the flood in Genesis 9: 3 – there are definite restrictions on which animals can be killed for food and how they should be killed. The laws of kosher slaughtering were designed to minimize the pain of the animals being killed. And permission to eat meat is granted at the same time that a new prohibition on eating blood is introduced. "But flesh with the life thereof, which is the blood thereof, shall ye not eat" (Genesis 9: 4). Eating meat was clearly thought to be a necessity for human survival, but the Jewish tradition required a respect and reverence for life in all its forms.

Perhaps the most important principle concerning the human relationship with animals in Jewish thought is *tza'ar ba'alei chayim*, "the pain of living creatures." Although this principle does not directly concern the ethical treatment of the natural environment, it can be interpreted as the basis for the moral treatment of animals throughout Jewish life. *Tza'ar ba'alei chayim* requires a concern for the well-being of all living beings – an attitude of universal compassion. Judaism, however, is not a Schweitzerian ethic, not a full-scale sacred reverence for all life, for there is difference between domestic and wild animals. Humans have a specific covenant with domestic animals to protect them; the concern for wild nature is more mysterious, as it is based on the recognition of the divine presence in the entire world of creation. (This point will be expanded below – see Allen 1951, p. 103.) *Tza'ar ba'alei chayim* prescribes the sympathetic treatment of all animals within the human sphere of activity. Thus the fourth commandment concerning the sabbath requires rest for one's livestock as well as for humanity (Exodus 20: 10 and Deuteronomy 5: 14). There is also the law forbidding the yoking together of animals of unequal strength (Deuteronomy 22: 10), for this would cause pain to the weaker animal. And one is not permitted to muzzle an ox during the threshing of the grain (Deuteronomy 25: 4). All of these command-ments are based on the compassion for animal suffering, and thus demonstrate that Judaism extends the realm of moral consideration beyond the limits of the human community – an extension of moral consideration that has obvious implications for environmental philosophy.

In his discussion of *tza'ar ba'alei chayim*, Gordis (1990, p. 8) notes that one of the most unlikely textual affirmations of the principle is the conclusion of the book of Jonah, where Jonah complains to God about the destruction of a gourd, a plant that had been shielding Jonah from the sun as he awaited God's decision about the destruction of the city of Nineveh. Jonah is angry for two reasons: God has spared the city, thereby making Jonah's prophecy appear foolish or pointless; and God has caused the gourd that shaded him to wither and die. God's reply is this:

> "You pity the gourd, for which you did not labor, nor did you make it grow, which came into being in a night, and perished in a night. And should I not pity Nineveh, that great city, in which there are more than a hundred and twenty thousand persons who do not know their right hand from their left, and also much cattle?" (Jonah 4: 9–11)

This passage is significant first because it shows God's concern for both the human inhabitants and the cattle of Nineveh. Clearly God does not consider the potential loss of the cattle to be a minor point; the loss of the cattle with the human population is an event to pity, an event requiring divine compassion. Thus we have affirmation of *tza'ar ba'alei chayim*. But the passage also suggests that pity for the gourd – wild, undomesticated plant life – is not an absurdity. God's rebuke concerns a consideration of three different kinds of entity: the human inhabitants of Nineveh, the non-human domesticated animals that live in Nineveh, and the wild gourd – the plant life – outside the city. Jonah's mistake is not that he felt compassion for the gourd, but that his level of concern was too great. It is wrong to value the wild gourd more than God values the inhabitants of Nineveh. Compassion for all living beings is a moral obligation in Judaism, but the context will determine the appropriate level of response.

Bal tashchit: Do Not Destroy

The fourth general theme of the Jewish tradition concerning the natural environment is the fundamental principle *bal tashchit* – "do not destroy" – which is first outlined in Deuteronomy 20: 19–20:

> When you besiege a city for a long time . . . you shall not destroy its trees by wielding an ax against them. You may eat of them, but you may not cut them down. Are the trees in the field men that they should be besieged by you? Only the trees which you know are not trees for food you may destroy and cut down, that you may build siege-works against the city.

As with the commandment requiring the proper disposal of human waste by soldiers in the field, the principle of *bal tashchit* is introduced in the context of warfare to emphasize the seriousness of the restriction. The commandment "do not destroy" is so powerful that it cannot even be overridden for the sake of victory in war.

The precise meaning of *bal tashchit* is open to various interpretations. It is important to see that a distinction is made between fruit-bearing trees and non-fruit-bearing trees. Trees that are not useful for the human need for food may be cut down for other human purposes, such as the construction of equipment necessary for the war. The reason for this is stated by the commentator Ibn Ezra (1089–1164) as noted in a discussion by Eilon Schwartz: human life depends on the fruit of the tree. The human responsibility to preserve the tree is based on the preservation of human life (Schwartz 1997, pp. 358–9). Thus, the rabbinic analysis of the text has included the importance of economic considerations. In the *Talmud* (*Baba Kama* 91b–92a) there is an extended discussion on the permissibility of cutting down trees based on their economic worth: a fruit-bearing tree may be destroyed if the value of its crop is less than the value of the lumber the tree would produce; moreover, the tree may be destroyed if the land is needed for the construction of a house, or if there are more productive trees in the same area. These exceptions to *bal tashchit* are not permitted for purely aesthetic reasons, such as landscaping (Lamm 1971, p. 170; Schwartz 1997, p. 360). Thus Eric G. Freudenstein concludes: "the standards of bal tashchit are relative rather than absolute. The law is interpreted in the Talmud as limited to purposeless destruction and does not prohibit destruction for the sake of economic gain" (1970, p. 411). But Freudenstein supplements this conclusion with the point that what constitutes an appropriate economic value differs from generation to generation, and thus the correct use of *bal tashchit* at any time must be left to the authorities to decide. The keeping of goats and sheep was once banned because of the destructive impact on the environment, but it is now permitted (ibid, pp. 411–12). Thus the moral evaluation for the destruction of an object or natural entity will depend on the economic and social context of the act.

The key to understanding *bal tashchit* is that the principle prohibits wanton or useless destruction, but the meaning of "wanton" or useless will change throughout history. *Bal tashchit* is a general principle against vandalism, extended by rabbinical interpretation to include the destruction of both natural entities and human artifacts.

The idea of "wielding an ax" is extended to any means of destruction, even the diverting of a water supply (Gordis 1990, p. 9, cites *Sifre Shofetim*, section 203). Moreover, the principle is extended to all useful objects. In the *Sefer Hahinukh* (529) is written this comment on *bal tashchit*: "In addition [to the cutting down of trees] we include the negative commandment that we should not destroy anything, such as burning or tearing clothes, or breaking a utensil – without purpose." Lamm cites Maimonides, who includes the stopping of fountains, the wasting of food, or "wrecking that which is built" as violations of *bal tashchit* (1971, p. 169). Gordis concludes: "The principle of *bal tashchit* entered deep into Jewish consciousness, so that the aversion to vandalism became an almost psychological reflex and wanton destruction was viewed with loathing and horror by Jews for centuries" (1990, p. 9).

An additional economic issue is the relationship of *bal tashchit* to notions of private property. Both Lamm (1971, p. 171) and Gordis (1990, p. 9) claim that the principle is not tied in any way to our modern notion of private property; one is not permitted to destroy one's own property any more than one is permitted to destroy another's. *Bal tashchit* is concerned with "the waste of an economic value per se," i.e., the social utility of the object being destroyed. Lamm even cites the interpretation of the principle to include the idea that it is permissible to destroy a fruit tree if it is somehow damaging the property of others – thus the basis of the principle would be social concern. Nevertheless, Schwartz notes that the story of Rabbi Hanina (in *Talmud Baba Kama* 91b), whose son died supposedly after cutting down a fig tree while it was still producing fruit, is used as an argument not to cut down a tree even when it interferes with a neighbor's property (Schwartz 1997, pp. 360–1). The issues here are complex and not easily sorted through in any particular situation. But what is clear is that *bal tashchit* is a religious and moral law that requires a consideration of the social implications of actions that harm non-human entities. It concerns the proper human response to the non-human environment; it is not a law of financial and personal property.

Two discussions (Schwartz 1997 and Diamond 1998) have used the principle of *bal tashchit* to examine the environmental problem of the over-CONSUMPTION of resources. Judaism is not a religion that advocates asceticism; yet the misuse of resources, as when one poorly adjusts the energy flow in one's lamp, is considered a violation of *bal tashchit* (*Talmud Shabbat* 67b).

As a fundamental principle in a Jewish environmental philosophy, however, the true significance of *bal tashchit* does not appear in the mere consideration of social consequences. Questions of private property and social utility reintroduce the issue of the real ownership of the world. It was noted above that the fundamental basis of the idea of stewardship was the theocentric perspective of Judaism: the world belongs to God. The ultimate argument against the destruction of natural entities is thus a combination of *bal tashchit* and the Judaic theocentric world-view: such entities are the property of God and cannot be destroyed for insignificant human purposes. This argument avoids the economic or utilitarian justifications for *bal tashchit*. The principle is not designed to make life better for humanity; it is not meant to insure a healthy and productive environment for human beings. In the terminology of environmental philosophy, it is not an anthropocentric principle at all: its purpose is not to guarantee or promote human interests. The purpose of *bal tashchit* is to maintain respect for God's creation.

In this context, Gordis ties *bal tashchit* to the laws of the sabbatical and the jubilee years – the reaffirmation of God's ownership of the land (1990, p. 9). But the final sections of the Book of Job are even more compelling. Near the end of the story, Job is able to question God about the reasons for the misfortunes that have befallen him. God speaks to Job out of the whirlwind, but His answer is not a direct justification of the seemingly incomprehensible divine actions that have radically altered Job's life. Instead, God discusses aspects of the natural world – the wild domain outside of human control – and challenges Job to acknowledge the limits of human wisdom:

> Where wast thou when I laid the foundations of the earth? Declare, if thou hast the understanding. Who determined the measures thereof, if thou knowest? Or who stretched the line upon it? (Job 38: 4–5)

And God continues to paint a picture of a world that exists independent of human concerns, and free from human notions of rationality or cause and effect:

> Who hath cleft a channel for the waterflood, Or a way for the lightning of the thunder; To cause it to rain on a land where no man is, On the wilderness, wherein there is no man; To satisfy the desolate and waste ground, And to cause the bud of the tender herb to spring forth? (Job 38: 25–7)

And more than the useless rain on land where humans do not live, there are the ANIMALS, the great beasts "behemoth" and "leviathan," which do not exist for human purposes; they lie outside the sphere of human life (Job 40: 15ff).

God's speech to Job out of the whirlwind is a dramatic reaffirmation of the theocentrism of the universe, God's creation. Job, as well as any other human being, errs when he believes that the events of the world must have a rational explanation relevant to human life. The events of the world are ultimately explained only in reference to God. This theocentrism is the driving force of *bal tashchit*, for it gives meaning to the reasons behind a prohibition on wanton destruction. Destruction is not an evil because it harms human life – we humans should not believe that God sends the rain for us – it is an evil because it harms the realm of God and His creation.

One practical consequence of the restriction against destructive acts is the preservation of a natural diversity that may, in the long run, prove useful to humanity. Eliezer Diamond (1998) recounts the story told of David (from the *Alphabet of Ben Sira*) in which David asks God why he created such useless and bothersome animals as the wasp and the spider. God replies that David should not belittle God's creation, for the time will come when both these animals will be useful to him. Later, when David was fleeing Saul, he took refuge in a cave where a spider web shielded him from discovery; and later still, the sting of a wasp helped David escape from the clutches of Abner, Saul's general. Diamond concludes that the human evaluation of the value of natural entities is limited; only God has a full understanding of the value and meaning of

Creation. Thus environmental utility and theocentrism are mutually supportive (see BIODIVERSITY)

The theocentrism of the principle of *bal tashchit* is also useful in an analysis of a long-standing dispute in secular environmental philosophy: are anthropocentric (i.e., human-centered) or non-anthropocentric arguments the moral basis of environmental practices? Should policies of environmental preservation be pursued because such policies will benefit humanity, or because such policies are intrinsically beneficial to the natural world? Each position encounters ethical and policy-oriented problems. Anthropocentrism permits the use (and destruction) of natural entities for a correspondingly greater human benefit; but non-anthropocentrism, with its emphasis on intrinsic value, implies a policy of strict non-intervention in natural processes, an absolute sanctity of nature. One position may lead to the destruction of nature, and the other may lead to worshipful non-interference: thus the dilemma for environmental philosophy (see META-ETHICS).

The theocentrism of Judaism resolves this dilemma because it is functionally equivalent to a non-anthropocentric doctrine of the intrinsic value of nature without endorsing the sacredness of natural entities in themselves. Natural objects are valued, and cannot be destroyed, because they belong to God. They are sacred, not in themselves, but because of God's creative process. This conclusion may be derived from the Kabbalistic strand of Jewish thought, as is expressed by David S. Shapiro: "The quality of loving kindness is the basis of all creation. It is God's steadfast love that brought this world into being, and it is His steadfast love that maintains it" (1975, p. 25). Thus, "all creation is linked together in a bond of unity," which humans must act to preserve and not to destroy (ibid, p. 41). As Gordis concludes, "every natural object is an embodiment of the creative power of God and is therefore sacred" (1990, p. 10). Its sacredness and its integrity – its intrinsic value, perhaps – rests on its status as God's creation. Thus, it is the theocentric basis of *bal tashchit* that requires Jews to act with a practical respect for the value of all the entities in nature and in the world.

Conclusion

A survey of principles and commandments regarding nature and the environment does not lead easily into a unified Jewish position. As an intellectual discipline, Judaism appears to revel in the development of differing interpretations and arguments concerning the meaning of biblical and Talmudic texts. Nevertheless, we can conclude that in Judaism, nature has a value independent of human interests as an expression of the creative power of God. This divinely created value inspires respect and requires obedience on the part of humanity, the servants and stewards of God's creation.

As stewards of God's earth, humans serve as partners in the never-ending task of perfecting the universe. Gordis concludes that "Judaism ... insists that human beings have an obligation not only to conserve the world of nature, but to enhance it" as a "copartner with God in the work of creation" (1990, p. 10, citing *Talmud Shabbat* 10a). The universe is God's creation, and that is the undeniable and fundamental starting point of any Jewish environmental philosophy. Understanding the universe as an outgrowth of God's power is the most important aspect of the value of nature in the Jewish tradition. As God's creation, the natural world has a force, a presence, that cannot be ignored.

In the Jewish tradition nature is neither an abstraction nor an ideal, but rather one of the realms in which humans interact with God. E. L. Allen writes: "Nature is envisaged as one of the spheres in which God meets man personally and in which he is called upon to exercise responsibility" (1951, p. 100). But wild nature lies outside the human community, outside the rules and commandments dealing with domesticated animals and the quality of the human environment. A Jewish environmental philosophy must deal with the wild non-human world. In the Book of Job, in the speech out of the whirlwind, God sets forth the essence of the wild: a world beyond the control and understanding of humanity. But the lack of control does not breed disrespect; on the contrary, it creates a sense of awe, wonder, and responsibility, for we are in the presence of the divine. "The untamed world beyond the frontiers of human society is fraught with the numinous, it is a constant reminder that man is not master in the world but only a privileged and therefore responsible inhabitant of it" (Allen 1951, p. 103; see WILDERNESS).

I would like to thank Rabbi Steven Shaw of the Jewish Theological Seminary of America for his help in the preparation of this essay. Portions of this essay appeared in Eric Katz, "Judaism and the Ecological Crisis," in *Worldviews and Ecology*, ed. Mary Evelyn Tucker and John A. Grim (Lewisburg: Bucknell University Press, 1994; reprinted Maryknoll: Orbis Books, 1994); and in Eric Katz, *Nature as Subject: Human Obligation and Natural Community* (Lanham: Rowman and Littlefield, 1997).

References

Allen, E. L. (1951) "The Hebrew view of nature," *Journal of Jewish Studies*, 2, pp. 100–4. [Early classic essay that pre-dates contemporary awareness of environmental crisis, emphasizing the human interaction with the natural world.]

Belkin, S. (1972) "Man as temporary tenant," in *Judaism and Human Rights*, ed. M. R. Konvitz (New York: Norton), pp. 251–8. [From the large range of contemporary essays after the first Earth Day in 1970, Belkin considers the basic principle that in Judaism the earth belongs to God.]

Benstein, J. (1995) " 'One, walking and studying . . . ': Nature vs. Torah," *Judaism* 44, pp. 146–68. [Important recent essay examines significant obstacle to a Jewish environmental consciousness, the obligation to study Torah rather than the material world.]

Carmell, A. (1976) "Judaism and the quality of the environment," in *Challenge: Torah Views on Science and its Problems*, ed. A. Carmell and C. Domb (New York: Feldheim), pp. 500–25. [Another mid-1970s essay that emphasizes specific Jewish commandments regarding the treatment of nature, with an emphasis on the need to limit material consumption.]

Diamond, E. (1998) " 'The earth is the Lord's and the fulness thereof': Jewish perspectives on consumption," in *Ethics of Consumption*, ed. D. A. Crocker and T. Linden (Lanham: Rowman and Littlefield), pp. 391–402. [Good recent overview of basic principles noting the limits of human action.]

Ehrenfeld, D. and Bentley, P. J. (1985) "Judaism and the practice of stewardship," *Judaism* 34, pp. 301–11. [Interesting essay co-authored by a major pioneer in environmental philosophy

(Ehrenfeld) regarding the importance of the sabbath rituals as a restraint of human domination of nature.]

Freudenstein, E. G. (1970) "Ecology and the Jewish tradition," *Judaism* 19, pp. 406–14. [Another mid-1970s essay that emphasizes specific Jewish commandments regarding the treatment of nature, particularly the importance of *bal tashchit*, the prohibition on wanton destruction.]

Gordis, R. (1990) "Judaism and the environment," *Congress Monthly* 57, pp. 7–10. [A 1990 reprint of an essay originally appearing in 1971 by one of the most respected scholars of contemporary Judaism. Gordis emphasizes two basic principles, the care of animals and the obligation not to destroy.]

Helfand, J. L. (1986) "The earth is the Lord's: Judaism and environmental ethics," in *Religion and Environmental Crisis*, ed. E. C. Hargrove (Athens: University of Georgia Press), pp. 38–52. [Perhaps the best overall introductory essay on Jewish religious, philosophical, and legal principles concerning the use of nature.]

Lamm, N. (1971) "Ecology and Jewish law and theology," in *Faith and Doubt* (New York: KTAV), pp. 162–85. [Wide-ranging essay from the early 1970s that contains an important discussion of immanentism and transcendentalism in Jewish thought.]

Schwartz, E. (1997) "*Bal tashchit*: a Jewish environmental precept," *Environmental Ethics* 19, pp. 355–74. [Comprehensive recent discussion of the most basic Jewish environmental principle, the prohibition on wanton destruction.]

Schwarzschild, S. S. (1984) "The unnatural Jew," *Environmental Ethics* 6, pp. 347–62. [The most controversial essay written about Judaism and nature, arguing that Judaism is essentially an urban culture with no remaining ties to the natural world.]

Shapiro, D. (1975) "God, man and creation," *Tradition* 15, pp. 25–47. [A view of the human relationship with God and nature that is heavily influenced by a Kabbalistic metaphysics, emphasizing the holiness of the material world.]

White, Jr. L. (1967) "The historical roots of our ecologic crisis," *Science* 155, pp. 1203–7. [Classic essay concerning the opposition of the Judeo-Christian tradition toward the natural environment; served as an impetus to the development of the pro-environment scholarly analyses of the 1970s.]

7

Christianity

ROBIN ATTFIELD

Introduction

Christianity, despite well-publicized claims to the contrary, upholds the independent value of natural creatures, and is committed to an ethic of responsible care and stewardship of the natural world. These values were enshrined in the Old Testament, presupposed by Jesus Christ and assumed throughout the New Testament. They were sometimes forgotten or distorted, particularly in medieval and early modern times, but were never abandoned, and have continually been rediscovered, receiving renewed and widespread commitment in the late twentieth century.

Controversies surround the teaching, inherited from the Old Testament, that humanity has dominion or mastery over other creatures, and attach also to the desacralization of nature implicit in the adoption of the belief in nature as a creature of God, and not itself God. Yet dominion facilitates responsible stewardship and need not involve domination, recklessness, or ruthlessness; at the same time, belief in creation implies that the world does not belong to humanity but is God's world, full of God's glory, and need not involve objectionable varieties of metaphysical dualism such as other-worldliness or contempt of nature or non-human species. Central Christian teachings turn out to encourage ecological sensitivity, despite episodes (and whole periods) in history which seem to suggest the contrary.

Controversies, however, surround not only what Christianity can or should say in the present, but also what was said or implied in the Bible, the patristic (age of the church fathers) and medieval periods, and in subsequent periods. These periods, and their leading figures, will be considered in historical order in this chapter, which culminates in a brief discussion of modern debates.

Attitudes of Jesus and the Synoptic Gospels

To understand Jesus' teaching about nature, we have to bear in mind the Old Testament beliefs about creation and also the Jewish ethical and legal tradition which he and his hearers shared (see JUDAISM). The assumptions of Jesus and the New Testament about creation and thus about nature have been characterized by John Muddiman (in a public lecture given in 1995) as including the following beliefs: the one true God made everything in the universe; the world was created for God's glory, and not for the exclusive benefit or convenience of any one species; God orders everything with divine wisdom and providence; the world is God's world and shares, as creation, in the good gifts of its Creator, including the gift of freedom; and God bestows a little of the divine creativity upon human beings, who are made in God's image, and calls them to cooperate with the Creator's purposes as the responsible holders of dominion over nature. These are largely unspoken beliefs, surfacing just occasionally, but implicit throughout the New Testament, including the teaching of Jesus (although sometimes recessive in subsequent Christian history).

The related belief is also present that God has established a covenant with humanity, and (in some versions) with the animals too (Genesis 9: 8–11). Old Testament ethics and law express the human part in this covenant. Thus when Jesus appealed to recognized exceptions to the prohibition of work on the sabbath, exceptions concerning acts of compassion to relieve the suffering of domestic animals (Matthew 12: 11–12, Luke 13: 15–16 and Luke 14: 5), he assumed a responsibility for compassion toward domestic animals, and common practices embodying it. Such responsibility is commanded in passages such as Proverbs 12: 10 ("A right-minded person cares for his beast") and implicitly in several more detailed passages of law in Exodus, Leviticus, and Deuteronomy (Exodus 23: 19, 34: 26; Leviticus 22: 27ff; Deuteronomy 14: 21, 22: 10, 25: 4), passages which Jesus' near-contemporary, Philo of Alexandria, expressly interpreted as motivated by compassion for animals (Bauckham 1998). Far from focusing on animals, Jesus was arguing that relieving the suffering of human beings on the sabbath (such as his own hearings) must all the more be lawful; but shared beliefs about considerate treatment of animals comprised the indispensable background of this argument.

These passing references of Jesus to animals already show that, like the Old Testament, the New Testament cannot be interpreted as authorizing a despotic attitude according to which humans may treat nature as they please. This despotic interpretation is ascribed to the Bible as a whole by Lynn White (1967), and allowed as a possible interpretation of at least the New Testament by John Passmore (1974, pp. 3–40); but neither the teaching of Jesus nor the Old Testament beliefs which it presupposes can be interpreted in this way without distortion. Despotic interpretations have time and again been read into the Jewish and Christian scriptures, and have often suited those who find them there; but this does not make them any more deserving of credibility.

When Jesus' teaching explicitly focused on birds and plants, it again presupposed Old Testament teaching. "Your heavenly father feeds the birds and clothes the lilies," he reminds his hearers, echoing the creation theology of the Psalms; "are you not of greater value than they?" (Matthew 6: 29; Luke 12: 24). Jesus' point here is God's provision for humans; but his conclusion depends, as Richard Bauckham (1998) shows, on shared beliefs in birds being fellow-creatures, and in God's providential care for the birds. It also presupposes God's bestowal on humanity of dominion over nature; but not an authorization of despotic or tyrannical rule.

Further sayings of Jesus stress God's concern for individual sparrows, despite their cheapness in the human valuation of his day (Matthew 6: 26; 10: 29–31; Luke 12: 6–7; 12: 24), and for individual sheep (Matthew 12: 12). These passages, which also allude to Old Testament precedents, all argue that, because humans are of greater value, God is also concerned with each and every human. At the same time, they presuppose that individual animals too have intrinsic value in the eyes of God, albeit less than Jesus' individual human hearers; indeed, the saying about lilies implies the presence of such value in plant life as well (Matthew 6: 28–30).

Thus the New Testament (like the Old) is irreconcilable both with an anthropocentric ontology and with anthropocentric accounts of value, in which nothing but humans and their interests have independent value. Also, the presupposition about the intrinsic value of individual animals conflicts with the view of some medieval Jewish and Christian writers that God's providence extends not to individual animals, but only to species (Bauckham 1998). This later, species-related, view coheres with belief in the Great Chain of Being, often adopted by Christians influenced by Plato and Aristotle, but not with the New Testament (see THE CLASSICAL GREEK TRADITION). Yet it would be an artificial exercise to attempt to classify the Bible as biocentric, any more than anthropocentric or ecocentric, however much its value-theory may indicate such a label for its attitudes to creatures. For the Bible, all creatures derive their existence from God, and therewith the very possibility of having value in the actual world. If any "centrism" is found in the Bible, it is theocentrism, the belief that the world exists for God's glory.

As Bauckham adds, none of Jesus' teachings accept that animals have been created only to serve humans, an idea subsequently adopted by Rabbi Simeon ben Eleazar, but absent from Genesis, and inconsistent with Job 39 (and Psalm 104 too). As such, it is unlikely to be an assumption of Jesus or the New Testament writers. Such notions sometimes entered later Jewish and Christian thought from Aristotelian and Stoic sources, where it was often held that all non-human creatures exist for the sake of their usefulness to humanity (Bauckham 1998). Thus if the dominion over nature bestowed on humanity (according to Genesis 1 and Psalm 8) implies some kind of superiority for humans over animals, the context remains that humans and non-human animals are alike fellow-creatures, that animals are not to be regarded as merely of instrumental value, and that humans have responsibilities toward the animals that serve them.

This also clearly excludes the view of Augustine (354–430) that humans have no responsibilities toward animals. Augustine seems to have been influenced in an early work, *De Moribus Manichaeorum*, by the Stoic belief that humans are rational and animals irrational, and that therefore there can be no ties of justice in dealings with animals (Passmore 1975). But Jesus, who accepted human responsibilities toward domestic animals, would have rejected Augustine's view. Augustine was commenting on Jesus permitting the demons that he exorcized from the Gerasene demoniac to enter a herd of pigs, which then hurled themselves over a cliff. However, even if this narrative originated as an event (rather than as one of the parables which Jesus told), it does not show that he regarded pigs as valueless, unclean as they were held to be, but at most that he regarded a human being as of greater value than the pigs (Bauckham 1998).

Jesus' relation to animals and to nature figures more significantly in the prologue to Mark's gospel, which relates that after his baptism Jesus spent 40 days in the wilderness "with the wild beasts" (Mark 1: 13). The language used (in the wilderness Jesus is also tempted by Satan and ministered to by angels, and a heavenly voice had just proclaimed him "my beloved Son") presents him as the Messiah, inaugurating the kingdom of God. In the prophecy of Isaiah, an age is proclaimed of peace between wild animals and humans, in a context that makes it the age of the coming of the Messiah (Isaiah 11: 1–9). Against this background, Mark's phrase "he was with the wild animals" conveys that the Messianic age is dawning, in which relations of fear between humanity and wild nature will be overcome. However, the animals are not subdued or tamed (as in some contemporary Jewish portrayals of the restoration of paradise); Jesus' companionable presence with the animals affirmed their otherness and their independent value. As at other moments of his life and teaching, he thus enacted an anticipation of the forthcoming kingdom of God (a kingdom not confined to humanity), and of the relations that are to characterize it (Bauckham 1998).

Other New Testament attitudes

Paul, despite his emphasis on sin and corruption, retained the Old Testament belief that the world is God's world, holding that God's creation is to be clearly discerned from the material universe (Romans 1: 20). Here he was echoing a Jewish work of the recent past, the Wisdom of Solomon, which asserts that "the greatness and beauty of created things give us a corresponding idea of their creator" (Wisdom 13: 1–5); Paul's claim was to prove an important bulwark against both other-worldliness and critics of natural theology in centuries to come. Terrestrial bodies of different kinds (humans, beasts, fishes, birds), he taught, have their own glory, comparable with but different from the glory of celestial bodies (sun, moon, and stars) (1 Corinthians 15: 39–41). Indeed, everything visible and invisible was created by and for God's Son, and is to be reconciled through him to God (Colossians 1: 15–20).

Certainly, when discussing the Old Testament prohibition of muzzling the ox that treads the corn, Paul seems to forget these themes, and asks "Does God care for oxen?" (1 Corinthians 9: 9ff), implying that the answer is "no," and claiming that this text is to be interpreted as concerning human laborers. But when concentrating on non-human nature he represents the whole creation as groaning in travail in expectation of release from corruption and of participation in the liberty of the children of God (Romans 8: 19–22). For Paul, despite the effects of sin and of demonic influences, the entire created world forms part of God's redemptive plan and is destined to regain its proper glory.

The Johannine writings seek to counter tendencies (from within the Jewish and early Christian communities) to represent the world as a battleground between equal forces of good and evil, in which salvation requires rejection of the world of flesh (Gnosticism). John's prologue maintains that the bringer of salvation is also the *Logos*, God's agent in creation, who has also become flesh and dwelt amongst us (John 1: 1–14). Among other themes present here, the value of the created world is reaffirmed. In another of the Johannine writings, the Book of Revelation, John's vision symbolically concerns the restoration of Eden and the tree of life, the leaves of which "were for the healing of nations" (Revelation 22: 2).

Thus the cosmic visions of Paul and John cannot be regarded as instrumentalist or anthropocentric. Like Mark, and like the author of Hebrews (Hebrews 1: 2ff), these writers appealed to Old Testament beliefs concerning creation, and represented salvation as not confined to humanity, but as a cosmic fulfillment of the Creator's plan.

While the biblical writers do not use the metaphor of stewardship with regard to the role of humanity in relation to the natural world, and while their view of the roles of both humanity and nature extends beyond stewardship, the model of humanity as God's steward is, as Clarence J. Glacken writes (1967, p. 168), an appropriate one. It fits the injunctions to till and to keep the garden (Genesis 2: 15); the making of man and woman in the image of God (Genesis 1: 27); Jesus' presuppositions about the value of non-human creatures (see above); the Old Testament teaching that the land belongs not to humans but to God (Leviticus 25: 23, Psalm 24: 1), and is only held conditionally (Leviticus 25: 2–13); Jesus' parables about stewardship and account-ability for the use of resources (Matthew 21: 33–41; 24: 45–51; 25: 14–30; Mark 12: 1–9; Luke 12: 36–38; 19: 12–27; 20: 9–16); and the teachings about responsibilities for compassion and consideration to non-humans which (as we have seen) pervade the Old and New Testaments (see JUDAISM). It is noteworthy that the historian Keith Thomas (1983, p. 359) endorses, against John Passmore (1974, pp. 3–40), John Black's account (1970, pp. 44–57) of the biblical basis of belief in stewardship. While no anthropocentric interpretation is credible, and while stewardship has sometimes been charged, as by Clare Palmer (1992, pp. 69–82), with an anthropocentric tendency that treats nature as mere resources, an ethic of responsibility before God to work, cherish, and preserve the natural environment and respect the independent value (and the glory) of fellow-creatures, can fairly be recognized as immune from this charge, without ceasing to be one of stewardship.

Patristic and medieval attitudes

The fathers of the early church added an awareness of pagan attitudes to nature; while some sought to blend Greek philosophy with Christianity, others challenged and contested Gnosticism (see THE CLASSICAL GREEK TRADITION). Thus, Irenaeus, the second-century Bishop of Lyons, rejected the Gnostic belief that nature is evil, and maintained that nature is cared for by God as a home for humanity, and is to share in the fulfillment of the Creator's plan (Santmire 1985, p. 35). The role of humanity in completing creation, wrongly regarded by Passmore (1974, pp. 33–4) as a recessive view right from the times of the ancient Hermetic writings of the second century CE to the age of the German romantic writers of the nineteenth century, in fact became a recurrent theme among patristic writers of the third and fourth centuries, including Origen, Basil, and Ambrose, and also among modern writers such as John Ray (in the late seventeenth century), William Derham (in the early eighteenth century), and many others (Glacken, 1967; Santmire, 1985).

The Stoic view that irrational creatures have been made for the sake of rational ones became more explicit in the third century CE in Origen's reply to the contem-porary Epicurean philosopher Celsus' rejection of such teleology (Glacken 1967, p. 183). Origen, however, considered the diversity in the world the result of a decline from the unity and harmony of the original creation, and attributed it to a primeval fall, prior to the creation of humanity (ibid, p. 182), which would be rectified at the eventual restoration at the end of time. But this speculative view diverged so far from belief in the goodness of the non-human creation around us that it was rejected by most of Origen's successors, including Augustine, who cited in reply the significance of Genesis 1: 31 – "And God saw everything that he had made, and behold, it was very good" (ibid, p. 198).

Much more influential within Orthodox churches (and beyond) were the fourth-century Cappadocians Basil the Great, his brother Gregory of Nyssa, their sister Macrina, and their friend Gregory of Nazianzus. These writers respected classical Greek culture, and in particular Plato's *Timaeus* (see THE CLASSICAL GREEK TRADITION), but supplied Christian correctives to pagan accounts of creation, of ethics, and of the soul. While revering the Christian scholarship of Origen, they ascribed the diversity of nature to God's creation, and not to the wickedness of pre-human creatures. Thus, Macrina and Gregory of Nyssa held that it was impossible for "all created nature . . . to hold together . . . without the care and providence of God" (Pelikan 1993, p. 255), and that all things "are moving towards the goal" of "the transcendent good of the universe" (ibid, p. 325).

Developing a form of writing launched in Philo's meditation *On the Creation* (see JUDAISM), Basil composed a *Hexaemeron* or commentary in popular style on Genesis 1, a practice in which he was shortly to be imitated by Ambrose, an influential figure in the Latin West. The world is presented as a work of art, which is both beautiful and useful as a training-ground for human souls. However, at the original creation it was incomplete, and its completion is to be achieved in part by humanity: "for the proper and natural adornment of the earth is its completion: corn waving in the valleys, meadows green with grass and rich with many-colored flowers, fertile glades, and hilltops shaded by forests" (Glacken 1967, 192; Basil *Homilies*, 2, 3).

According to Basil, the grasses serve both animals and humanity (Glacken 1967, p. 193). That Basil's is not an entirely anthropocentric cosmology may also be learned from a prayer of his: "And for these also, o Lord, the humble beasts, who bear with us the heat and burden of the day, we beg thee to extend thy great kindness of heart, for thou hast promised to save both man and beast, and great is thy loving-kindness, o Master" (Passmore 1975, p. 198).

Overall, the Greek fathers certainly saw nature as a symbolic source of edification, expressed in many an allegory, and sometimes regarded it too as offering a retreat from contemporary civilization, with all its compromises. They were also careful to avoid the pantheism often implicit in pagan religion (see INDIGENOUS PERSPECTIVES), to avoid idolatry at all costs, and to distinguish sharply between the creature and the Creator, much as they relished arguing from the creation back to its source. But they also saw nature as created both for God's glory and as an invitation and challenge to human creativity and adornment; the impact of sin had not altogether deprived it of its perfectibility or humanity of the potential to complete God's work. All these themes have remained important in Orthodox theology down the centuries, and also strongly influenced western churches within the ecumenical movement throughout the twentieth century.

In the West, Ambrose, following Basil, popularized the conception of humanity as partner of God in improving the earth (Glacken 1967, p. 196). Augustine, a much more original thinker, developed another theme of eastern origins, that of nature as a book. Earlier, Athanasius had praised the book of creation which proclaims the divine master and creator of its harmony and order, and John Chrysostom had imparted how the book of nature was available to peoples who do not understand the language of the Bible (Glacken 1967, p. 203). Augustine now stressed how nature's book was open even to the most unlettered: "heaven and earth cry out to you: God made me!" (ibid, p. 204; Bauckham 1996, p. 120). In later centuries the nature-as-book analogy found new uses as a defense of the empirical methods of natural science.

Augustine also produced a new synthesis of themes from the Bible and from Aristotle and, more particularly, Plato (see THE CLASSICAL GREEK TRADITION), elaborating a Christian version of belief in the Great Chain of Being. All the rungs on the scale of possible being are occupied, sentient beings having greater value than non-sentient, intelligent beings greater value still, and immortal ones such as angels having greater value than mortal humans. The human body, however, has a beauty and dignity expressive of the glory and beauty of its Creator (Bauckham 1996, pp. 120–1). More generally, the world's phenomena glorify their divine artificer "not with respect to our convenience or discomfort, but with respect to their own nature." Aristotle's conception of the end of a species being internal to itself (Augustine, *City of God*, XII, 4; Glacken 1967, pp. 198–9) is blended here with the Pauline theme of the diverse glories of creatures, in a statement which excludes anthropocentrism, and is barely reconcilable with Augustine's despotic stance on relations with animals, noted earlier.

The works of humanity are also wonderful, but nothing in creation is to be compared to the Creator. However, the entire created world is now infected with the effects of human sin. While Origen's view of a pre-human fall is rejected, all evil is to be ascribed to humanity, which, since Adam's fall, is hopelessly depraved unless saved by God's grace in Christ (Glacken 1967, pp. 196–201). Augustine thus produces a remarkable combination of life-affirming and of ascetic themes. As Glacken acknowledges, summaries could be devised presenting his valuation of nature as a low one (ibid, p. 202), as subsequently Matthew Fox has done in *Original Blessing* (1983); but in Glacken's own summary, echoed by H. Paul Santmire, for Augustine, "The earth, life on earth, the beauties of nature, are also creations of God. Man, full of sin and prone to sinning, is nevertheless a glorious product of God's greatness" (Glacken 1967, p. 196; Santmire 1985, pp. 55–74). While his advocacy of an extreme doctrine of original sin has been influential and arguably detrimental, Fox is demonstrably mistaken to represent him as a despiser and distruster of creation; as Bauckham shows, Augustine's affirmative doctrine of nature and its glories actually supports an ecologically sensitive approach (Bauckham 1996, p. 120).

While the character of Augustine's influence remains open to debate, for many the teaching of Christianity about nature was mediated instead either by monasteries, for which sites of beauty were often sought, or by the church's liturgy. Monasteries now (in the sixth century) began to be founded in the West, in accordance with the Rule of Benedict. Work, as in gardens and fields, was regarded as prayer, and was conducted partly for its own sake and partly to enhance the land, its fertility, and thus its self-sufficiency (Glacken 1967, pp. 302–4), especially among the later Cistercian foundations, as described in the twelfth century by Bernard of Clairvaux (ibid, p. 214). Hildegard of Bingen, the eleventh-century founder of an abbey, also used to celebrate the beauty and glories of the natural world (Attfield 1991, p. 199).

Meanwhile, the medieval Roman liturgy incorporated prayers for sick animals and stables, as well as curses on vermin and pests (Attfield 1991, p. 37); like the well-known and much-loved story of Christ's nativity in a stable, such words cannot have presented a dispassionate or instrumentalist attitude to nature. The same is true of the "Benedicite" which has been used liturgically from earliest times to the present day.

Passmore claims that "Augustinian Christianity neither laid the task [of completing God's creation] on man's shoulders nor promised God's help if he should undertake it" (1974, p. 33). But Augustine held that humanity participates in God's work through the arts and the sciences, including agriculture (Glacken 1967, pp. 200, 299), and western monasteries, from Benedict to Bernard, bore this out in practice. (Glacken also (ibid, p. 300) finds explicit stewardship teaching in Cosmas Indicopleustes (of the sixth century), who compares the work of humanity on earth with decorating and furnishing a house.) The Augustinian belief that human wickedness was sufficient to infect nature with evil certainly smacks of arrogance, granted the technology of the time (ibid, p. 212). But the human effort invested over the next few centuries in the improvement of nature has recently generated White's opposing charge of a domineering attitude, specially prevalent in western attitudes (White, 1967), and embodied in medieval deep plowing, irrigation, and forest clearances. However, White is now widely recognized as guilty of over-generalization and exaggeration; the domineering attitude prevalent in nineteenth- and twentieth-century technology does not require western patristic attitudes for its explanation. Indeed, while the Benedictines accepted the inherited belief in the dominion of humanity over nature, René Dubos (1973) has aptly characterized their attitude of caring for and enhancing the land in their charge as one of stewardship, and therewith a paradigm of environmental responsibility.

Thomas Aquinas (1224–74) persistently defended the goodness of nature, in criticism of Albigensians and others who held that nature, including the human body, was evil. Each part of the universe, he argued, exists for its own particular end, and all are needed to comprise the hierarchy of being; despite Origen, nature is not a reflection of sin, and, on the contrary, everywhere reflects God's glory (Glacken 1967, p. 233).

However, the fall has reduced the obedience of other creatures to man; since the fall, domestication has been necessary to master the animals. This is in keeping with God's plan, whereby rational creatures rule over others; but this mastery depends on God, a fact that suggests the need for humility (Glacken 1967, p. 236). Here, Aquinas accepts Origen's view about the subordination of irrational creatures to rational ones, despite his beliefs about the distinct value of all creatures. Indeed, he sometimes comes close to the view that it is indifferent how humans behave to animals, but then adds that insofar as animals are sentient, pity at their sufferings is natural, and that this accounts for Proverbs 12: 10, the text about consideration for domestic animals. Though his text at once reverts to human needs, this point is prefaced with "besides," indicating that the previous point had some independent weight (Aquinas, *Summa Theologiae*, 2.1.102 a6 ad8). Yet Aquinas' eventually influential position still represents a narrowing of Christian teaching, and has sometimes been taken to deny any moral standing to non-human creatures.

A rival view was held by Francis of Assisi (1182–1226) and some of his followers. Francis, like Aquinas, accepted the goodness of creation in all its diversity, but he also praised God for all his creatures, not only as types but also as individuals, regarded them as brothers, and urged them to praise God too, as in Psalm 148. Francis actually preached to birds, fishes and flowers (Glacken 1967, pp. 214–16). While his stress on the individuality of living creatures exempts him from the charge of pantheism (the belief that identifies nature and God), and also from Lynn White's label of "panpsychism" (the belief that all creatures, animate and inanimate, are alike in having souls), his belief in God's immanence throughout creation makes him a panentheist (believing that God dwells in each and every creature). Thus, without rejecting the human dominion over nature, he interpreted it in a companionable and non-despotic manner.

Within the medieval period (when the days of printing and mass literacy lay in the future), ordinary believers were probably influenced less by the theologians than by the liturgy (see above) and by the lives of the saints. For St. Francis stood at the end of a thousand-year-long succession of saints, many of them famed for their fellowship with and compassion for animals, both wild and domestic, originating with St. Antony the Great (third century), founder of an ancient monastery in Sinai (Bratton 1988, pp. 31–53). Both in the East and the West, stories circulated widely of saints who resorted to wilderness for tranquillity and meditation, and in many cases (such as the seventh-century Cuthbert in Northumbria) sought to live in the spirit of Jesus' companionship with the beasts.

Attitudes of the subsequent period

The humanist writers of the Renaissance emphasized the supremacy of humanity over nature to the virtual exclusion of any ties with non-human creatures. Among them, the sense of creatureliness has disappeared, and an unlimited doctrine of human despotism has replaced traditional interpretations of belief in the dominion of humanity. Indeed, some of the attitudes that have contributed to the contemporary ecological crisis can be traced back to this source. Where the humanists abandoned belief in creatureliness and in creation, they also stepped outside Christianity, sometimes adopting a combination of Hermeticism and pantheism instead.

The Protestant Reformation re-emphasized dependence on the lordship and grace of God, Martin Luther (1483–1546) stressing God's immanence in every grain of creation (Santmire 1985, pp. 128–31). It also brought explicit discussion of stewardship on the part of Jean Calvin (1509–64), who wrote: "Let every one regard himself as the steward of God in all things which he possesses" (Welbourn 1975, p. 563), upholding a vocational view of all human activity. Like Aquinas and Luther (Santmire 1985, pp. 124–5), Calvin adhered to an anthropocentric stance; but he combined this with the belief that the beasts, though created for humanity, were to be treated with respect and not misused. Thus God "will not have us abuse the beasts beyond measure, but to nourish them and to have care of them." "If a man spare neither his horse nor his ox nor his ass, therein he betrayeth the wickedness of his nature. And if he say, 'Tush, I care not, for it is but a brute beast,' I answer again, 'Yea, but it is a creature of God' " (Thomas 1983, p. 154). Calvin's view was echoed in England in the next century by George Hughes; man's rule was "subordinate and stewardly, not absolutely to do what he list with God's creatures" (ibid, p. 155). Here, stewards are subordinates with creaturely duties concerning fellow-creatures, owed not to them but to God: an anthropocentric version of stewardship, comparable to Aquinas' view. Other Protestants of the sixteenth and seventeenth centuries, how-ever, adopted more biocentric views (ibid, p. 166).

Assuming an anthropocentric position, Francis Bacon (1561–1626) understood human dominion as the right and power to use nature for human benefit. The fall had a double impact, engendering both sin and ignorance about nature, but both falls can in part be repaired, the former by faith and the latter by intellectual labor. This latter restoration of the lost human dominion over nature was Bacon's central purpose (Attfield 1993, pp. 17–26). Unlike the Italian humanists, he recognizes that this will be a gradual, painstaking task, requiring the humility to observe and thus conform to and obey nature, to discern "the footsteps of the Creator imprinted on his creatures," and thus to discover (not dictate or remold) God's laws. For Bacon was strongly opposed to "domineering over nature" (Attfield 1993, p. 18), which he believed to be the main failing of previous (Greek and medieval) natural philosophy, and to be responsible for humanity's second fall.

While Bacon's motive was love of humanity, his project was the control of nature for human benefit, with no sense of nature's independent value, or even of its aesthetic or symbolic value. But it would be wrong to conclude that science became instrumentalist from this point. This view disregards the belief of most of its seven-teenth-century participants that the study of science was an expression of the duty to glorify God. Meanwhile, Bacon and his successors who founded the Royal Society presented theistic grounds for rejecting veneration of nature and the belief that scientific study and the application of that study were intrinsically impious; for (unlike pagan nature-worship) belief in creation implies that nature is neither sacred nor beyond investigation, while the biblical ethic suggests that effort is called for to relieve illness and hunger, and this presupposes that their causes can be discovered by humanity. Certainly, Bacon's language about putting nature to the test and extorting her secrets is exploitative, and lent support to the vogue for vivisection of the later decades of the century; but this approach was soon to be met with correctives within as well as outside the scientific community.

Bacon's contemporary René Descartes (1596–1650) proposed a different method for investigating nature, but on a markedly similar basis. Within his rationalist approach, non-human animals were regarded as machines, although the widespread view that he held that they lacked feelings is open to doubt. (The reality of animal suffering was vindicated against followers of his by contemporary followers of Aquinas (Attfield 1991, p. 38).) Despite his aim that we should "render ourselves the masters and possessors of nature," he, like Gassendi and Galileo, rejected the view that everything was made for humanity (Thomas 1983, p. 167). (See EARLY MODERN PHILOSOPHY.)

The language of stewardship was explicitly related to nature, the animals, and the earth for the first time by Sir Matthew Hale, a seventeenth-century Chief Justice of England, in 1677 in *The Primitive Origination of Mankind*. According to Hale, the purpose of "Man's Creation was that he should be the Viceroy" of God, "his Steward, Villicus, Bayliff, or Farmer of this goodly Farm of the lower World," man being "his Usufructuary of this inferior World to husband and order it, and enjoy the Fruits thereof with sobriety, moderation and thankfulness." "Man was invested with power, authority, right, dominion, trust and care," to limit the fiercer animals, protect the tame and useful ones, preserve vegetable species, to improve the species, to curtail unprofitable vegetation, and "to preserve the face of the Earth in beauty, usefulness, and fruitfulness" (Black 1970, pp. 56–7). Besides supplying here the classical expression of Christian teaching on stewardship of the Earth, Hale was seeking to ground theology not in revelation but in nature and the purposes that seem to underlie it (ibid, p. 57).

As Thomas points out, Hale's position was not exceptional; Thomas Tryon, for example, another seventeenth-century writer, stipulates that humanity's rule is not to be tyrannical, but to conduce to the glory of God, the benefit (but not the wantonness) of humanity, and also to the well-being of the beasts in accordance with their created natures (Thomas 1983, p. 155). With Tryon, a non-anthropocentric tendency is even clearer than in Hale.

Attitudes to animals were importantly affected in the eighteenth and nineteenth centuries by the humanitarian movement, which simultaneously changed public opinion and practice in Britain and America in matters of slavery, punishment, and working conditions. Thomas has shown the prevalence of blood sports in sixteenth-century England (Thomas 1983, pp. 17–50). But concern about animal suffering was also expressed at least from the time of the sixteenth-century Puritan Philip Stubbes onwards. Subsequent advocates of compassion included Christians such as John Locke, William Wollaston, John Balguy, and Francis Hutcheson, and generally Quakers, Methodists, and Evangelicals, as well as skeptics such as Montaigne, Shaftesbury, Voltaire, Hume, and Bentham (Attfield 1991, pp. 42–3, 50). During the nineteenth century the movement achieved a number of political reforms. With the introduction in the twentieth century of the practice of factory farming and with increasing experimentation on animals, humanitarianism is still far from victorious, but both Christian and secular ethics have long since accepted at the normative level the wrongness of treating non-human animals as simply means to human ends.

Negative attitudes to WILDERNESS were transmitted from England by early colonists to America, "America" being John Locke's term for "wilderness" in his second *Treatise on Civil Government* (1698). But by the early nineteenth century they began to be superseded by contrary valuations, based on interpretations of wild nature as creation, such as Ralph Waldo Emerson's *Nature* (1836) and Henry David Thoreau's *Walden* (1854) (Nash 1989, pp. 36–8), valuations more in line with those of the desert fathers, but appreciative also of the system of "Oeconomy of Nature" (Linnaeus' phrase), and the distinctive places of creatures within the meshes of its interlocking net. Subsequently, for the nineteenth-century environmentalist John Muir "the basis of respect for nature was to recognise it as part of the created community to which humans also belonged" (ibid, p. 37). Covertly a believer in the intrinsic value and rights of all creatures, Muir's entry into the politics of wilderness preservation led him (like many subsequent environmental campaigners) to adopt an anthropocentric public stance, laced with charges of sacrilege against destroyers of the temple of nature (ibid, pp. 40–1).

Charles Darwin's (1809–82) discovery of evolution by natural selection, presented in *The Origin of Species* in 1859, conveyed the continuity between humanity and other species. In *The Descent of Man* (1871), Darwin drew the implication that nature cannot be regarded as a hierarchy, with humanity as a special creation at its apex, and other species existing for humanity's sake (Nash 1989, pp. 42–5). Among Darwin's contemporaries, Christians such as Charles Kingsley and Asa Gray welcomed Darwin's discoveries, and, as Owen Chadwick has pointed out, the main Protestant denominations in Britain and USA had accepted Darwinism by 1900 (Chadwick 1973). Some twentieth-century self-styled "creationists" have attempted to retract this acceptance, but cannot claim that belief in creation requires rejection of Darwinism. (See NINETEENTH AND TWENTIETH-CENTURY PHILOSOPHY.)

In the twentieth century, Catholic Thomist theologians such as Maritain and Journet have proved willing to accept duties owed directly to animals (Passmore 1975, p. 206); while Anglican bishops have rediscovered the spirituality of eastern Orthodoxy and have been prominent in applying stewardship to environmental concern, some asserting that the sacraments of Christianity, with their focus on elements such as bread and wine, strengthen the Christian awareness of value in the material creation (Montefiore 1975). Certainly, the charge of other-worldliness and of disparagement of life on earth has no remaining credibility, in view of Catholic advocacy of social justice and of the social teaching of the Life and Work Division of the Protestant and Orthodox World Council of Churches. Some theologians even hail Darwinism for subverting the traditional static view of nature and introducing a more historical view, like that of the Bible (Berkhof 1968).

Overview

Besides the charges of other-worldliness and of disparagement of life on earth, the more widespread charges that Christianity teaches a despotic and anthropocentric attitude to nature turn out to be similarly misplaced, despite their relevance to some tracts of medieval and early modern history. Such charges are usually based on unreflective interpretations of the Judeo-Christian belief in human dominion over nature, which sounds as if it might support unqualified domination. But in view of the conditional and qualified understanding of all human authority in the Old Testament, and of explicit biblical teaching endorsing the independent value of natural creatures and recognizing the place of non-human nature in the scheme of salvation, such interpretations prove to have been no better than rationalizations of exploitative practices. Dominion over nature is rather to be construed as responsible stewardship, while, for Christians who are true to their scriptures, stewardship is best construed not anthropocentrically (as with Calvin), but as involving humble recognition of the intrinsic value of fellow-creatures.

Belief in stewardship is sometimes held to be actually inconsistent with belief in the independent value of natural creatures, or with God's immanent presence in creation, as it supposedly involves a managerial and instrumentalist attitude to the material order. But these claims of inconsistency are an illusion; for stewardship (as with Hale) need not involve an instrumentalist attitude, and need not be solely managerial (as even Calvin shows in teaching ethical limits to the treatment of animals). Further, belief in divine immanence in nature cannot preclude its use by humanity, or this belief would also have precluded using nature for food and shelter from earliest times.

Yet criticism of dualism continues, even after charges of other-worldliness and of arrogance and lack of humility have been discarded. Thus, Matthew Fox criticizes an ethic of care for the garden of creation as dualistic, since it distinguishes between God and the garden, instead of recognizing that God *is* the garden (Berry 1995). But if God *is* the garden, then the garden (and the rest of the material universe too) is not created, there is no Creator, there are no fellow-creatures to care for, and the world is not God's world. Short of some other basis, belief in the goodness of creation collapses too. Belief in the distinctness of God and creation is essential to theistic ethics, whether Christian, Jewish, or Islamic (see JUDAISM and ISLAM). If this is dualism, then dualism (of this kind) is essential to theistic ethics, and to positions such as the panentheism of St. Francis too. But this kind of dualism in no way implies either a dualism of body and spirit or the dualism of other-worldliness.

However, it is sometimes claimed that belief in stewardship itself implies dualism in the form of an unacceptable relation between humanity and other species. For it implies that humanity is empowered to remold much of the natural world, despite the ethical constraints that attach to this power. This, it is suggested, too greatly privileges humanity; instead, humans should see themselves as simply one species among others, and humanity as a plain citizen in ecological society.

Now if this just means that equal interests should be given equal consideration, whichever creature has these interests, it can be accepted. But it also seems to imply that there is nothing distinctive about human agency and human moral responsibility; for it seems to imply that no higher priority should be accorded to developing, preserving, and respecting capacities for freedom of choice than to the interests of creatures which lack these capacities. This, however, cannot be reconciled with a recognition of distinctive human moral responsibilities, which cannot be significantly exercised unless the corresponding capacities are fostered and respected. Once human moral responsibility is recognized, humanity cannot be seen as simply one species among others; and the distinctive role of humanity as empowered to shape considerable tracts of the natural world has to be recognized as well. This makes it all the more important to stress the ethical constraints on this power, as belief in stewardship does, rather than to pretend that this power does not or should not exist, as egalitarians in matters of species relations seem to do. Thus the distinctive role which belief in stewardship assumes for humanity is not fundamentally objectionable, or therefore incompatible with the aims of clear-thinking environmentalists.

Yet there is a danger that the exercise of human power will too greatly erode both wilderness and other species, and that well before all the mountains are mined, all the oceans are fished, and all the forests are felled, we should plan to halt human expansion, and devise sustainable means of survival which preserve most remaining creatures and habitats, together with the systems on which they and we depend. The Christian vision of companionship with the wild creatures supports such limits, as without them there will be no wild creatures to be companionable with, as opposed to domestic animals and parasite species. The claim that such limits should be endorsed is consistent with belief in stewardship, and can be argued to be mandated by that belief in the prevailing circumstances. Moreover, this claim is in any case supported by the biblical belief in the independent value of wild creatures. Hence, a range of Judaic and Christian teachings can be appealed to in its support.

Accordingly, despite ugly episodes and depressing periods in its history, Christianity turns out to encapsulate beliefs supportive of environmentally sensitive attitudes and policies, and can be appealed to as such. While this does not make Christian doctrines true, it means that no one need choose between Christianity and environmentalism, and that theistic belief in creation (whether Judaic, Islamic, or Christian) can inspire sustainable relations between humanity and the rest of the natural world.

Bibliography

Attfield, Robin (1991) *The Ethics of Environmental Concern*, 2nd edn (Athens, Georgia and London: University of Georgia Press). [Defense of stewardship as a mainstream Judeo-Christian tradition, and of a related environmental ethic.]

——(1993) *God and The Secular: A Philosophical Assessment of Secular Reasoning from Bacon to Kant*, 2nd edn (Aldershot: Gregg Revivals). [Welcomes Bacon's defense of science as dominion as against domineering.]

Bauckham, Richard (1996) "The new age theology of Matthew Fox: a Christian theological response," *Anvil* 13, pp. 115–26. [A critique of Fox's pantheism and neglect of historical Christian affirmations of the goodness of creation.]

——(1998) "What was Jesus' attitude to animals?," in *Animals on the Agenda: Questions about Animals for Theology and Ethics*, ed. A. Linzey (London: SCM Press). [Reinterprets Jesus in light of his cultural presuppositions and of his companionship with wilderness animals.]

Berkhof, Hendrikus (1968) "Science and the biblical world-view," in *Science and Religion*, ed. Ian G. Barbour (London: SCM), pp. 43–53. [A theological rejection of mechanical world-views and a welcome for Darwinism.]

Berry, R. J. (1995) "Creation and the environment," *Science and Christian Belief* 7 pp. 21–43. [Defense of stewardship from a leading Christian biologist and environmentalist.]

Black, John (1970) *Man's Dominion: The Search for Ecological Responsibility* (Edinburgh: Edinburgh University Press). [Pioneering historical and theological overview of attitudes to nature and future generations.]

Bratton, Susan Power (1988) "The original desert solitaire: early Christian monasticism and wilderness," *Environmental Ethics* 10, pp. 31–53. [Rediscovery of 1,000-year tradition of saintly predecessors of St. Francis; corrects Nash.]

Chadwick, Owen (1973) "Evolution and the churches," in *Science and Religious Belief*, ed. C. A. Russell (London: University of London Press), pp. 282–93. [Definitive history of acceptance of Darwinism among British Protestants of the late nineteenth century.]

Dubos, René (1973) "A theology of earth," in *Western Man and Environmental Ethics*, ed. Ian G. Barbour (Reading, Mass. and Don Mills, Ontario: Addison-Wesley), pp. 43–54. [Replies to White; presents St. Benedict as symbol of the human condition and patron saint of ecology, rather than St. Francis.]

Fox, Matthew (1983) *Original Blessing* (Santa Fe, New Mexico: Bear). [Critique of "dualistic" theology of creation and original sin; defends original goodness.]

Glacken, Clarence J. (1967) *Traces on the Rhodian Shore: Nature and Culture in Western Thought from Ancient Times to the End of the Eighteenth Century* (Berkeley: University of California Press). [Monumental treasury of intellectual history; presents stewardship account of the Bible and some Church fathers.]

Montefiore, Hugh, ed. (1975) *Man and Nature* (London: Collins). [Leading Anglicans endorse stewardship beliefs as rooted in tradition and ethically inescapable.]

Muddiman, John (1995; unpublished) "A New Testament basis for environmentalism?" Fourth Yvonne Workman Lecture, Mansfield College, Oxford (September). [The New Testament affirms the goodness of creation, and purposively resists its contemporary (Gnostic) detractors.]

Nash, Roderick (1989) *The Rights of Nature: A History of Environmental Ethics* (Madison, Wisconsin: University of Wisconsin Press). [Chronicles historical American naturalists, and recent theologians and philosophers of nature; not invariably accurate, as when praising Attfield on a misconceived basis.]

Palmer, Clare (1992) "Stewardship: a case study in environmental ethics," in *The Earth Beneath: A Critical Guide to Green Theology*, eds Ian Ball, Margaret Goodall, Clare Palmer, and John Reader (London: SPCK Books), pp. 67–86. [Controversial critique of the view of stewardship as biblical and ethical.]

Passmore, John (1974) *Man's Responsibility for Nature* (London: Duckworth). [Pioneering environmental philosophy monograph; finds resources for an environmental ethic in "seeds" within western traditions, including stewardship.]

——(1975) "The treatment of animals," *Journal of the History of Ideas* 36, pp. 195–218. [A brief and illuminating history of this subject; needs to be read alongside correctives such as Thomas 1983.]

Pelikan, Jaroslav (1993) *Christianity and Classical Culture: The Metamorphosis of Natural Theology in the Christian Encounter with Hellenism* (New Haven and London: Yale University Press). [Scholarly study of the Cappadocians, Basil, Gregory of Nyssa, their sister Macrina, and Gregory of Nazianzus.]

Santmire, H. Paul (1985) *The Travail of Nature: The Ambiguous Ecological Promise of Christian Theology* (Philadelphia: Fortress Press). [Thematic study of world-affirming and ascetic tendencies among great historical theologians.]

Thomas, Keith (1983) *Man and the Natural World: A History of the Modern Sensibility* (New York: Pantheon Books). [Authoritative study of attitudes to nature in England between 1500 and 1800; supplies a salutary corrective to Passmore 1974.]

Welbourn, F. B. (1975) "Man's dominion," *Theology* 78, pp. 561–8. [Defends stewardship interpretation of Judeo-Christian tradition, adducing historical and ethnographic evidence.]

White, Jr., Lynn (1967) "The historical roots of our ecological crisis," *Science* 155.37, pp. 1203–7. [The much-reprinted, controversial essay by a medieval historian, locating the roots of ecological problems in the western adoption of Christian doctrine, and commending the species-egalitarianism of St. Francis.]

8

Islam

S. NOMANUL HAQ

And there is no animal in the earth nor bird that flies with its two wings, but that they are communities like yourselves.

Qur'ān, 6: 38

Among the three grand monotheistic faiths, Islam has been spared the onus of explaining any scriptural imperatives for humanity to "subdue" the earth and seek to establish "dominion" over the natural environment – an onus that has exercised and troubled many a sage in the Jewish and Christian traditions. It has particularly embarrassed the latter, given the Aquinian position that nature is unredeemed (see JUDAISM; CHRISTIANITY), and given the arrogant seventeenth-century Latin western attitudes to the physical world – attitudes that were belligerently expressed, for example, in the enduringly influential works of the English philosopher Francis Bacon (1561–1626). Assuming the role of a spokesman for modern science, Bacon begot what is now considered the myth of the inductive method of science. He viewed science not as a historical phenomenon arising in a given cultural context, but as a supra-historical process of formal logical inferences that led to universal truths – and the purpose of this process was, indeed, to enlarge man's dominion and power over *all* else in the cosmos (see particularly his *Novum Organum Scientiarum*, 1620).(See EARLY MODERN PHILOSOPHY.)

To be sure, by virtue of its own declarations the Qur'ān does share the Abrahamic ethos of the Hebrew Scriptures. So here too human beings are spoken of and spoken to as God's supreme creation, higher even than angels who were all commanded by God to prostrate themselves before Adam (2: 34). Also, one may plausibly argue that, as in the Bible expressly, so too in the Qur'ān by implication, man is said to be created in God's image since He says – and, we must remember, the Qur'ān is believed to be God's *actual* speech revealed in history – that He breathed His own spirit into the human being after fashioning him from a form of earth (15: 29; 38: 72; also 32: 9). At the same time, there exist several elegant declarations in the Qur'ān which indicate in a brimful of evocative picturesqueness that the entire bounty of nature has been created for the sake of human beings – and that to them is subjected whatever is in the heavens and the earth (2: 22; 13: 17; 14: 32–3; 16: 5–16; 16: 80–1; 17: 70; 21: 31–2; 23: 18–22; 43: 10–12; 45: 12–13; 55: 1–78; 78: 6–16). And this holy book – which happens to be the only book commanding divine authority in Islam – says explicitly and solemnly at one place that humanity has, indeed, been created in the *best* of forms, or as one translator prefers, in the *fairest* stature (95: 1–4).

But this is to speak of things in isolation, without context. Viewed in its totality, the Qur'ānic notion of the world of phenomena and the natural environment is semantically and ontologically linked with the very concept of God on the one hand, and with the general principle of the creation of humanity on the other. In other words, there is no conceptual discontinuity in the Qur'ān between the realms of the divine, of nature, and of humanity. Speaking metaphysically, nature had a transcendental significance since it could not explain its own being, and thereby pointed to something beyond itself. It functioned as the means through which God communicated to humanity, the means through which, one may say, God made an entry into the flow of time. Indeed, natural entities were so many signs, or *āyāt* (singular *āya*), of God, like the multiplicity of the verses of the Qur'ān which, too, were *āyāt*. Thus, even though natural objects and Qur'ānic verses had different status, they were metaphysically on a par with each other.

Speaking morally, human beings were created by God as His vicegerents (*khalīfa*) in the physical world lying within the finite boundaries of time, and they were world-bound even *before* they committed their first transgression in the Garden. But the very principle of God's vicegerency also made them His servants (*'abd, 'ibād*) who were – by virtue of a Primordial Covenant (*mithāq*) they had affirmed, and a Trust (*amāna*) they had taken upon themselves in pre-eternity – the custodians of the entire natural world. Humanity was thus transcendentally charged not to violate the "due measure" (*qadr*) and balance (*mīzān*) that God had created in the larger cosmic whole.

Speaking naturalistically, the physical world existed to nourish, support, and sustain the process of life – in particular, human life. And the whole cosmos was an integral system, governed by unchanging natural laws (*amr*) which were God's immutable commands. These laws explained the regularity and uniformity in natural processes which cannot possibly be violated in the general run of things.

So we see that in the fullness of the Qur'ān, Adam's superiority over other creatures and his regency over nature arise in a context that is highly complex, with its interdigitating metaphysical, moral, and naturalistic dimensions; the conceptual setting here evidently being very different from that of the Old Testament and the Evangel. Indeed, with regard to the environment and humanity's relationship to it, the position of the Qur'ān can only be understood in a framework that is coherently constructed out of the range of notions that have been summarily referred to – the notions of *khilāfa* (vicegerency), *amāna* (trust), and *amr* (command) central among them.

When one examines Islam as a function, operating in the real contingencies of historical forces, one notes that it has bequeathed in its normative tradition a large body of principles governing both the ethico-legal and practical issues concerning the physical world and our encounter with it. Thus in the Hadīth – the authenticated corpus of Muhammad's (and sometimes his Companions') traditions which functions as a binding moral guide and, more formally, as one of the two material sources (*usūl*) of Islamic law (*fiqh*) – there are to be found numerous reports concerning the general status and meaning of nature, and concerning agriculture, livestock, water resources, birds, plants, animals, and so on. Quite remarkably, the Hadīth corpus also contains two fateful doctrines of land distribution and consecration, embodied in the principles of *hima* and *haram*. Further articulated by Muslim legists, these two related notions, both of which have the sense of a protected/forbidden place or a sanctuary, developed into legislative principles not only of land equity but also of environmental ethics, notions that were subsequently incorporated into the larger body of the Islamic legal code.

While we shall see that the principle of *hima* is particularly well developed in the Mālikī legal school – one of the four schools of law which are followed by the vast majority of Muslims – there are several other Hadīth- and Qur'ān-based environmental concepts that have been formally articulated in Islamic legal writings in general. One of them, for example, is the concept of *mawāt*, literally "waste land," a concept developed and discussed in great detail by some legists, appearing along with extensive discussions of rivers and other water resources, their distribution, maintenance, rights, and control. Likewise, Islamic legislative rules governing hunting and treatment of animals, including game, arise directly out of moral imperatives in the Qur'ān and Hadīth, these rules operating at once in a legal as well as an ethical framework. Given this, it is in principle possible to construct out of Islamic legal literature a fairly coherent and comprehensive system of Islamic environmental philosophy and ethics – both theoretical and practical. But this is something that will only be pointed to rather than carried out in this chapter, since in order to construct the system fully we shall have to cast a much wider net and ask much larger questions.

The Qur'ānic metaphysics of nature

One of the fundamental and most striking features of Qur'ānic metaphysics is the linkage it forges between the transcendental and the historical – that is, between that which exists in an intelligible world beyond space and time, and that which is bounded by and lies within the real spatio-temporal world with a finite beginning and an end. Expressed in religious terms, this means that the Qur'ān does not admit of a separation between the natural environment and the divine environment (see Seyyed Hossein Nasr 1991); indeed, nature in its Qur'ānic conception is *anchored in* the divine, both functionally and metaphysically. "It is of utmost significance," Nasr has pointed out, "that in the Qur'ān God is said to be All-Encompassing (*Muhīt*), as in the verse, 'But to God belong all things in the heavens and on the earth; And He it is who encompasseth (*Muhīt*) all things' (4: 126); and that the term *Muhīt* also means environment" (1991, p. 219). To be sure, the Qur'ān's concepts of God, nature, and humanity all have their roots in the transcendental realm and then issue forth into the moral-historical field.

When we read the dramatic story of the creation of Adam in the Qur'ānic chapter named after an animal, "The Cow," we note the striking fact that God announces to the angels His intention to "create a *khalīfa* (vicegerent) *on the earth*" (2: 30) – to this, angels make a protestation. That the earth was going to be Adam's abode seems, then, to be an integral component of the very concept of God's vicegerency that was to be bestowed upon humanity. By a legitimate rational extrapolation, we can say that even if Adam and "his pair" (*zauj*) had not been swayed by satanic beguiling and had resisted the temptation of going near the forbidden tree, they would still have ended up here on the earth – this was part of the divine plan throughout. The consequences here are far-reaching indeed. Thus, for example, there is no scope in the Qur'ānic context for thinking that human existence in historical time is a curse, or that the vast cosmic ocean of natural forces in which we are plunged is opposed to grace, or that salvation consists in a process of recovery of a lost glory whereby nature is to be humbled by the miraculous. The creation of Adam, one notes, is a transcendental phenomenon, but in its very conception it is linked to real life here on earth, linked to the historical, that is.

Humanity was not created merely for sport, the Qur'ān declares, it had a purpose – the purpose, namely, of creating a moral order in the real world. The human being was God's vicegerent, who in his very essence was a theomorphic being. Thus, operating on the transcendental plane, the Qur'ān speaks of the "Primordial Covenant" that God had elicited from humanity: "And when your Lord extracted from the children of Adam – from their spinal cord – their entire progeny and made them witness upon themselves, saying, Am I not your Lord? And they replied, No doubt You are, we bear witness!" (7: 172–3). The expression, "*Alastu bi-Rabbikum*" (Am I not your Lord?), rings loud until this day in the chambers of Islam, its mystical possibilities most creatively realized in Sufi thought and poetry. But what are the moral yields of this in the real world? Quite simply, it means, and so it has meant in Islam's normative tradition, that human beings cannot arrogate to themselves absolute power and capricious control over nature – they must submit to the commands of their Lord. And it is these commands that constitute God's *Sharī'a*, literally "path" or "way," which is given to humanity not as a fully articulated body of laws, one must note, but rather in the form of "indicators" (*adilla*) spread throughout God's *āyāt*. It is precisely the ferreting out of these indicators wherein lies the process of *fiqh*, or "understanding," a familiar term that is generally translated as "Islamic law." Indeed, the word "Islam" literally means submission – submission of the human will to the Divine Command, and this is the crux of humanity's regency over nature.

Thus, it is in a moral context – connecting the immediate to the ultimate – that the Qur'ān speaks about God making nature "subject to" humanity (*sakhkhara lakum*): it is made clear that this does not mean granting of unbridled exploitative powers, for human beings in their turn must remain subservient to God, and that it is His, not *our*, command that nature follows. So we read: "And He hath made subject to you whatsoever is in the heavens and whatsoever is in the earth – It is all from Him. Lo! herein indeed are portents for those who reflect" (45: 13). And again:

> It is God Who hath created the heavens and the earth, and sendeth down rain from the skies, and with it bringeth out fruit wherewith to feed you. It is He who hath made ships subject to you, that they may sail through the sea by His command (*amr*). And the rivers (too) hath he made subject to you. And He hath made subject to you the sun and the moon – both diligently pursuing their courses. And the night and the day hath he (also) made subject to you. And He giveth you of all that ye ask for. But if ye count the favors of God, never will ye be able to number them. Indeed, humanity is given up to injustice and ingratitude. (14: 32–4)

Likewise, speaking of sacrificial animals which were, let us note, symbols from God:

> The sacrificial animals We have made for you as among the symbols from God. In them is much good for you. Then pronounce the name of God over them. Eat ye thereof, and ... with due humility feed the beggar. Thus have We made animals

subject to you, that ye may be grateful . . . That ye may glorify God for His guidance
to you: And proclaim the Good News to all who do right! (22: 36–7)

To whom belongs the dominion over the creation? The answer is clear and explicit:
"Knowest thou not that to God belongeth the dominion of the heavens and the
earth?" (2: 107); "Yea, to God belongs the dominion of the heavens and the earth.
And to God is the final goal (of all)" (24: 42).

So we observe that while the creation of nature has its roots in the transcendental
realm, it manifests itself in historical time in the real world where humanity is
charged to establish a moral order – but, then, being an embodiment of God's symbols
or signs, nature ultimately recoils back into the transcendental. It is precisely these
metaphysical linkages between the immediate and the ultimate that constitute the
most characteristic feature of Qur'ān's entire philosophy of being. And this is what
that familiar Qur'ānic expression epitomizes which is so frequently heard all over the
Muslim world, echoing throughout its history: *Innā li'l-Lāhi wa innā ilayhi rāji 'ūn* –
"Surely, we are from God and to Him we return" (2: 156).

It is clear that in the Qur'ānic teaching humankind's superiority lies not in its
enjoying any higher powers or control among created beings – it lies rather in the fact
that human beings are accountable before God, like no other creature. This account-
ability arises out of the onus of global trusteeship that human beings, at their very
transcendental origin, had placed daringly upon their shoulders – a trusteeship that is
part of the very human essence. So we note that the Qur'ān speaks of the "Trust" (*al-
amāna*) that God had offered to the heavens and the earth and the mountains; they
refused to accept it, being frightened of the burden involved. But humankind accepted
it, and bore the Trust.

So enormous is the moral onus of this human undertaking, indeed, that the Qur'ān
recognizes it by way of what Rahman called (1989, p. 18) a "tender rebuke" to
humanity: "Surely, humankind is unfair to itself and foolhardy" (33: 72). It is an
interesting Qur'ānic paradox that human superiority in the created world turns out to
be an attribute that is exceedingly humbling – in fact, the Qur'ān at one place goes as
far as to say that the rest of the creation is a matter *greater than* the creation of people:
"Assuredly the creation of the heavens and the earth is (a matter) greater than the
creation of people: Yet most people understand not!" (40: 57).

It is important to note in this analysis that when the Qur'ān speaks about the *actual*
process of the creation of human beings, it operates utterly in a naturalistic context.
Thus, humankind is presented as a thoroughly natural creation, for Adam was fashioned out of baked clay (*salsāl*), from mud molded into shape (*hamā' masnūn*) (15: 26,
28, 33); from dust (*turāb*) (22: 5); from earth (*tīn*) (6: 2; 7: 12, etc.), which produced
through a confluence of natural processes an extract, *sulāla*, that functions as reproductive semen (Rahman 1989, p. 17). At one place we read a rather full account:

> Humankind We did create from a reproductive extract of clay. Then We placed him
> as a drop of sperm in a receptacle, secure. Then we made the sperm into a clot of
> congealed blood. Then of that clot We made a fetus lump. Then We made out of that
> lump bones and clothed the bones with flesh . . . So blessed be God, the Best of
> Creators! (23: 13–14)

Indeed, in the very first verse of what is generally believed to be chronologically the very first revelation in the Qur'ān (96), humankind is declared to have been created out of a clot of congealed blood ('alaq). There is to be found, most significantly, nothing supernatural in the Qur'ānic explanation of the real biological processes of the formation of the human animal.

To be sure, the Qur'ān is full of references to nature, natural forces, natural phenomena, and natural beings, and out of its 114 chapters some 31 are named after these. And in all cases, the physical world in its *real* operation is treated of in a naturalistic framework, in the framework of physical forces and processes that occur uniformly and with regularity – and this despite the fundamental fact that in the Qur'ānic metaphysics, as we have noted already, nature is anchored ultimately in the transcendental. Note that in the Qur'ānic methodology, the metaphysical–transcendental and the natural–historical interdigitate but do not mix *substantively*, nor do they enter into a combat. Therefore, at the operational level – or one may say, for immediate scientific and technological purposes – the natural world can legitimately be considered a fully organized system that is self-governing and practically autonomous.

So while humankind bears the burden of global trusteeship, the Trust, and functions as God's vicegerent here in the world, these are its transcendental attributes which must be linked to the real. In the actual world, then, as it exists in the immediate palpable reality, human beings are part of nature; they are a natural entity, subject fully to the laws of nature just like any other entity, participating as an integral element in the overall ecological balance (*mīzān*) that exists in the larger cosmic whole. And in the teachings of the Qur'ān this would mean that to damage, offend, or destroy the balance of the natural environment is to damage, offend, or destroy oneself. Any injury inflicted upon "the other" is self-injury (*zulm al-nafs*) – and this is a central principle of Qur'ānic ethics (on *zulm al-nafs* see Hourani 1985).

All this has a parallel in the Qur'ānic discourses on God, discourses to which it is coherently connected. Thus on the metaphysical–transcendental side, we have for example:

> Allah alone [is God], there is no God but He, the Alive the Sustainer; neither slumber nor sleep overtakes Him. To Him belong whatever is in the heavens and on the earth – Who can, then, intercede with Him except whom He permits? He knows what is before them and what is behind them, while they encompass none of his knowledge, except what He permits. His Throne envelopes the heavens and the earth and their preservation fatigues Him not – He is the High, the Great. (2: 255)

God's attributes, we note, are here specified in familiar terms but such as to transcend nature, and even human understanding. There are no naturalistic arguments here; rather the claim is that *all* is under divine control, and this is a metaphysical claim. The Qur'ān here reiterates metaphysically God's absolute centrality in the whole system of existence.

But then rises the current of a naturalistic discourse operating in the moral field, speaking of the heavens and the earth, rivers and water, mountains and oceans, orchards and vegetation, and other natural entities and phenomena. So, for example:

And who other than He created the heavens and the earth and sent down for you water from the sky, whereby We cause to grow lush orchards – for it is not up to you to cause their trees to grow! Is there, then, a god beside God? Yet these are the people who ascribe partners to Him! And who other than He made the earth a firm abode (for you), and set rivers traversing through it, and put firm mountains therein and sealed off one ocean from another? Is there, then, a god beside God? ... And who other than He responds to the distressed one when he calls Him and He relieves him of the distress and who had made you His vicegerent on earth? Is there, then, a god beside God? – little do you reflect. And who other than He guides you in the darkness of the land and the sea? And who sends forth winds heralding His mercy (sc. rain)? Is there, then, a god beside God? For exalted be He above what they associate with Him! And who other than He brings forth His creation and then re-creates it? And who gives you sustenance from the heaven and the earth? Is there, then, a god beside God? Say (O Prophet!): Bring your proof if you are right (in associating others with God). (27: 60–4)

God's lordship, stated elsewhere in metaphysical terms as we noted, is here being elucidated in terms of its expression in the naturalistic realm – and this is being done with rhetorical embellishment which adds a particular force and urgency to the message. Divine lordship, the Qur'ān is here pointing out, *manifests itself in* and is *expressed through* God's creation – that is, the entirety of nature. Again, note the linkage between the immediate and the ultimate, between the transcendental and the temporal.

Nature, then, serves as a means of God's *tanzīl* (sending down) of guidance to humanity. As we have observed already, the whole cosmos was but an embodiment of God's bountiful signs (*āyāt*) – these signs could not explain their own existence, thereby pointing to a creator beyond. And, again, all natural entities were contingent upon sustenance that must come from other than themselves; thus by virtue of their very being they all perpetually testified to God's glory – "The seven heavens and the earth and whatever is therein sing the glories of God" (17: 44; 57: 1; 59: 1; 61: 1; 13: 15; 16: 49; 22: 18; 55: 6; 7: 206; 21: 19). The significant thing to note here is the Qur'ānic doctrine that nature exists essentially in the temporal world, and follows God's *amr* – amr on the *operational level* is to be understood as the system of immutable and independent laws of nature. These laws were both uniform and knowable – and here one notes the corollary that the Qur'ān has opened up the possibility of scientific investigation of the cosmos.

Izzi Deen has pointed out (1990, p. 190) that one of the most outstanding jurists and philosophers of Islam, Ibn Taimiyya (1263–1328), commenting on the verses of the Qur'ān that speak about nature having being created for the sake of humankind, concludes: "In considering all these verses it must be remembered that God in His wisdom created these creatures for reasons other than serving human beings, for in these verses He only explains the [human] benefits of these" (quoted from *Majmū 'Fatāwā*; translation slightly emended). In the context of the first chapter of the Qur'ān, where God is referred to as "the Lord of the Worlds" ('*ālamīn*), Izzi Deen throws into perspective the fascinating position of an important fourteenth-century Qur'ān commentator Ibn Kathīr – a position which is not unshared in the classical Islamic tradition: "Ibn Kathīr, like so many Qur'ānic commentators, considers that the word 'worlds' means different kinds of creatures ... Muslims submit themselves to the Creator who made them and who made all other worlds." And then we learn that Ibn Kathīr adds: "Muslims also *submit themselves to the signs* of the existence of the Creator and his unity. This secondary meaning exists because 'worlds' (*ālamīn*) comes from the same root [out of which stems the word *alam* that also means 'sign']" (1990, p. 195; emphasis added).

But back to *amr*. This word, which literally means "command," denotes in the Qur'ānic context a universal operative principle whereby every created natural entity plays its assigned role and takes its assigned place as an integral element in the larger cosmic whole; and this according to the command it uniquely receives from God. Thus it was the *amr* of an acorn to grow into an oak tree; and that of an egg to hatch into a bird; and that of sperm to develop into an embryo; and that of the sun to rise from the far horizon. In other words, laws of nature express God's commands, commands that nature cannot possibly violate – and this explains why the entire world of phenomena is declared *muslim* by the Qur'ān: "Do they, then, seek an obedience other than that to God, while it is to Him that everyone (and everything) in the heavens and the earth submits [*aslama*]" (3: 83). From the divine act of the creation of the *āyāt* to the human act of belief or disbelief in God – we have here an integral conceptual system in which the transcendental is coherently linked to the naturalistic, the temporal (See Izutsu 1964, p. 38).

But on the other hand, and not in isolation from all this, there existed another aspect to the creation of nature. Nature was an embodiment of God's mercy. Indeed, it has been observed frequently that in the totality of the Qur'ānic teaching God's mercy and his omnipotence are inseparable: "These two perfections are the two poles of divine action, at the same time contrasted and complementary" (Gardet 1987, p. 30). God's creative action was a special expression of his mercy – for not only did he bestow being upon his creation, he also provided sustenance for that creation; and sent guidance for that creation; and made himself the very end (*al-Ākhir*) (57: 3) to which the entire created world was ordained by him to return finally.

The Qur'ān abounds in references to the bounty of nature as an unfalsifiable expression of God's mercy. Indeed, this is the very refrain of the collection of the verses that bears as its title God's exclusive Qur'ānic attribute, *al-Rahmān*, the Merciful. Speaking eloquently of nature's bounty and the naturalistic cosmic order as constituting divine favors and blessings, and asking rhetorically as to how they can possibly be denied, the Qur'ān says in a powerful sweep:

> The sun and the moon follow courses exactly computed. And the stars and the trees, both alike bow in adoration. And the Firmament – God has raised it high, and set the Balance ... It is He Who has spread out the earth for His creatures: Therein is fruit and date palms, with their clusters sheathed. Also corn, with its leaves and stalk for fodder, and sweet-smelling plants ...

And then emerges the resounding question which serves here as the refrain: "So, which of the favors of your Lord will you deny?" Again, referring back to the world in a naturalistic mode: "He created human beings from sounding clay, like the potter's ... He let free the two seas that meet together, between them is a barrier that they do not transgress . . . Out of them come pearls and coral." Then rises the finale of the matter at hand: "Of God seeks [its sustenance] every creature in the heavens and on the earth. Every day in a new splendor does He shine!" The intervening refrain goes on throughout: "So which of the favors of your Lord will you deny?" (55: 5–29).

Given that the natural world is an embodiment of God's signs (*āyāt*), and given that it is an expression of God's mercy (*rahma*), we have here a case of a unique meta-physical equivalence between nature and prophecy, and thereby between natural entities and Revelation. Through the created world God sent His guidance; but then, he also guided human beings directly in an articulated and clear language (*bayān*), speaking to them through His revealed word – and the Qur'ān, indeed, was this very speech (*kalām*) of God.

Just as natural entities exist in the form of real-historical objects, so God's Revela-tion is delivered by a real-historical Prophet, a human apostle who is no god and no supernatural being but is "from amongst yourselves" (9: 128). Just as nature is a guide, so is the Prophet a guide (*hādī*) (13: 7). Just as nature receives and follows God's *amr*, so does the Prophet receive "a spirit from [God's] *amr*" (45: 52) which the Prophet himself and the rest of the humanity ought to follow. Just as natural entities are called *āyāt*, so the verses of the Qur'ān are called *āyāt*. And just as natural entities, God's *āyāt*, express and manifest God's mercy, so Prophet Muhammad, the one chosen to receive God's speech, His *āyāt*, was "nothing but a mercy (*rahma*) to all beings" (21: 107).

Again, we note the characteristic parallelism between the natural field and the moral field, between the transcendental and the historical. And again we note the conceptual linkages between the divine, human, and natural realms, constituting a highly complex but coherent and integral system.

The normative tradition: Hadīth material

George Hourani once said that the Qur'ān uses the Arabic language with "semantic depth, where one meaning leads to another by a fertile fusion of associated ideas." He continued: "Such a use of language may set problems for analytical minds, but the Qur'ān must be understood not as a mere textbook of religious and ethical doctrines but more valuably as a rich and subtle stimulus to the religious imagination" (1985, p. 86). Hourani's learned observation explains a great deal about the development of Islamic normative tradition in the centuries after the death of the Prophet in 632 CE. No doubt the Qur'ān was the supreme guide to Muslim life in all its dimensions, but it was not a corpus of laws, or a catalogue of moral conduct, nor was it a schematic doctrinal treatise. Rather, it was a superbly rich literary document that contained broad and general principles, with all manner of poetic variations and rhetorical embellishments; its metaphors and its imagery highly evocative, its expressions providing enormous possibilities for the imagination.

So the Qur'ān did open up Muslim imagination. It was a creative but daunting task of *fiqh* to translate God's speech into a concrete program of action, and to develop a body of law and ethics out of the indicators (*adilla*) spread all over its *āyāt*. Indeed, it was a necessary task that had to remain ever-unfinished and ever-alive, for imagination has no finality. But how to go about it? Naturally, in the first place Muslims looked to their Prophet who was for them a model *par excellence*. Flawlessly interpretive of what the Qur'ān meant, and frequently supplementing and augmenting it, were the actual vicissitudes of the Prophet's life and his concrete public and private conduct. By the ninth century CE, with the impressive development of the legal science of *usūl al-fiqh*, this approach took on a formal character in Islam. Now, authentication and compilation of Hadīth reports – often referred to as Islam's Prophetic Traditions – had developed into a discipline proper, and along with the Qur'ān, Hadīth became the second material source of law. Note that a fully authenticated Hadīth was now legally binding.

Standard Hadīth collections are arranged according to the subject-matter of the reports, appearing as an extensive string of numerous books. The scope here is enormously wide, since it is aimed to comprehend universally *all* aspects of individual and community life. One of the most significant things from our point of view is the fact that issues pertaining to the natural environment appear throughout this large number of books in a single Hadīth collection. And this indicates that a concern for the physical world is fully integrated into the larger body of all kinds of other practical and moral concern. Environmental issues were not an isolated matter, it seems, and for this reason they are hardly treated separately in the collections.

Thus it is in the "Book of *Tayammum*" (ritual ablution performed with earth) of the Hadīth collection *Sahīh* (Correct) of al-Bukhārī (810–70), for example, that we find the famous and elegant saying of the Prophet, "The earth has been created for me as a mosque and as a means of purification" (Muhsin Khan (ed.) 1976, vol. 1, number 331). To declare the whole earth as being so pure in its essence that it functions as a place upon which one ceremonially prostrates before God, and to declare it so essentially clean in itself as to effect ritual cleansing upon humankind, is to give it a very high material and symbolic status. It would be legitimate to say that if this declaration is allowed freely to generate an attitude toward the earth, this attitude cannot possibly be that of arrogance. Note that what we have is an elaboration of a Qur'ānic principle (5: 9) which is here placed in an ethical, aesthetic, and fully humanized context.

Again, it is in the unlikely chapter, "On Protection from the Curse of the Oppressed" of the "Book of Generalities" (*al-Jāmi'*) in the famous Hadīth collection *al-Muwattā'* of Mālik ibn Anas (716–95), the Master of the Mālikī school of law, that we find a reference to the important principle of *himā* – protected pasture lands or sanctuaries (see below). This appears in a Hadīth of the Prophet's well-known companion and Islam's second Rightly Guided (*Rāshid*) caliph Umar ibn al-Khattāb (r. 634–44):

> Umar ibn al-Khattāb said to his freedman . . . whom he had placed in charge of *himā*, "Beware of the cry of the oppressed for it is answered. Do admit to *himā* the owners of small herds of camel and sheep . . . By God! this is their land for which they fought in pre-Islamic times and which was included in their terms when they became Muslims. They would certainly feel that I am an adversary [for having declared their land *himā*] – but, indeed, had it not been for the cattle to be used in the cause of God, I would never make a part of people's land *himā*." (Rahimuddin (tr.) 1985, number 1830)

Note here that while the public restricting and consecrating of a piece of fertile land appears to be an act *pro bono* that is meant for the protection and sustainable use of the natural environment, it is an act which in its very conception is essentially related to issues of social and economic justice. In another Hadīth collection considered authentic by the generality of Muslims, the *Mishkāt al-Masābīh* (Niche for Lamps) stemming from a compilation of Baghawī (d. ca. 1116), references to *himā* appear in the "Book of Business Transactions" (Robson (tr.) 1990, p. 592), a book that has to do with the ethics of trade and commercial dealings. This is true also of the *Sahīh* of Bukhārī (Muhsin Khan (ed.) 1979, vol. 3, number 267) – but here *himā* is mentioned additionally in the "Book of Distribution of Water" (vol. 3, number 558).

There is typically an entire "Book of Agriculture" in Bukhārī's *Sahīh*, a section rich in material concerning the environment. Thus, according to one report, the Prophet is quoted as saying, "There is none amongst the believers who plants a tree, or sows a seed, and then a bird, or a person, or an animal eats thereof, but is regarded as having given a charitable gift [for which there is great recompense]" (Mushin Khan (ed.) 1977, vol. 3, number 513). So noble in the perspective of Hadīth is the task of a *sustainable* cultivation of land that even in Paradise (*al-Janna*, which significantly means "the Garden"), existing beyond the physical world, it does not come to an end. So we read the Prophet telling his companions:

One of the inhabitants of Paradise will beseech God to allow him land cultivation. God will ask him, "But are you not in a state of being that you desired"? "Yes," he will say, "but I would still like to cultivate land" ... When the man will be granted God's leave for this task, he will sow seeds and plants will soon grow out of them, becoming ripe and mature, ready for reaping. They will become colossal as mountains. God will then say: "O Son of Adam, gather!" (Muhsin Khan (ed.) 1977, vol. 3, number 538)

In a similar vein we have the Hadīth quoting the Prophet as saying, "When doomsday comes if someone has a palm shoot in his hand he should plant it" (*Sunan al-Baihaqī al-Kubrā*, quoted in Izzi Deen 1990, p. 194). And this means that participating in the bounty of nature is a good *in itself*, even at Doom – a good beyond any immediate benefits that one may draw from it.

In Bukhārī's *Sahīh*, like other standard collections, there is also a section on the issues concerning the use, ownership, management, and distribution of water, even though these issues appear in other sections too. Playing on the word *fadl*, which means both "excess" and "grace," a Hadīth reports the Prophet's declaration:

[Among the] ... three types of people with whom God on the Day of Resurrection will exchange no words, nor will He look at them ... [is] the one who possesses an excess of water but withholds it from others. God will tell him, "Today I shall withhold from you my grace (*fazlī*) as you withheld from others the superfluity (*fazl*) of what you had not created yourself." (Muhsin Khan (ed.) 1977, vol 3, number 557)

Note that while the question of the ownership of wells and rivers, and other natural drinking and irrigation sources, is a complex one in Islamic law, it has been made abundantly clear on the moral plane in the Hadīth literature that water must be shared *equally* – so no living individual, and this includes animals, can be deprived of water if it is available; likewise no piece of cultivable land, irrespective of its ownership, can be left without irrigation if water resources have the capacity. This has far-reaching ecological consequences. Indeed, the "Book of Business Transactions" of the *Mishkāt* contains the Prophet's solemn declaration of the fundamental rule: "Muslims share alike in three things – water, herbage, and fire" (Robson (tr.) 1990, p. 640).

There seems to be no distinction between human beings and other animals with regard to the sharing of water. Thus, for example, in the "Book of Ablution" of the Bukhārī corpus, as well as in other corpora, there is to be found the account of a man

> who was walking along a road and felt thirsty. Finding a well, he lowered himself into it and drank. When he came out he found a dog panting from thirst and licking at the earth. He therefore went down again into the well and filled his shoe with water and gave it to the dog. For this act God Almighty forgave him his sins. The Prophet was then asked whether man had a reward through animals, and he replied: "In everything that lives there is reward." (Johnson-Davies 1994, p. x)

"In everything that lives there is a reward" must be considered a central broad principle of Islam's environmental ethics.

The Hadīth literature has, throughout, an abundance of traditions, admonitions, and rules concerning the treatment of animals. Contained in the "Book of Striving" (*Jihād*) of the *Muwatta'* is the resounding tradition about horses: "In the forehead of horses," the Prophet is quoted as saying, "are tied up welfare and bliss until the Day of Resurrection" (Rahimuddin (tr.) 1985, number 990). So much compassion and care for animals do there seem to be that in the same book there is an account that tells of the Prophet seen wiping the mouth of his horse with his personal cloth. Asked why, he replied: "Last night I was rebuked [by God] for not looking after my horse" (number 993). Again, in Bukārī's "Book of Water," we have this report:

> The one to whom horses are a source of reward is the one who keeps it in the path of God, and ties it by a long rope in a pasture or a garden. Such a person will get a reward equal to what the horse's long rope allows it to eat in the pasture or the garden. And if the horse breaks its rope and crosses one or two hills, then all marks of its hoofs and its dung will be counted as good deeds for its owner. And if it passes by a river and drinks from it, then that will also be regarded as a good deed on the part of its owner. (Muhsin Khan (ed.) 1977, vol. 3, number 559)

Appearing in the "Book of Jihād" in the *Mishkāt* is a set of rules that the Prophet pronounced concerning the treatment of camels. "When you travel in fertile country," he said, "give the camels their due from the ground, and when you travel in time of drought make them go quickly. When you encamp at night keep away from the roads, for they are where beasts pass and are the resort of insects at night" (Robson (tr.) 1990, p. 826). It is remarkable that a sensitive concern for animals does not disappear from the horizon even during military engagements. In the same book, there exists a particularly stern admonishment against animal abuse – "Do not treat the back of your animals as pulpits, for God the most high has made them subject to you only to convey you to a place which you could not otherwise reach without much difficulty" (p. 829; translation slightly emended). Likewise we have a fable from the Prophet in Bukhārī's "Book of Agriculture": "While a man was riding a cow, it turned toward him and said, 'I have not been created for this purpose [of riding]; I have been created for plowing'" (Mushin Khan (ed.) 1977, vol. 3, number 517). Here we have the Qur'ānic principles of *amr* and *qadr* (due cosmic proportion) translated into practical ethics. And again, in the "Book of Jihād" of another *Sahīh* (Correct) Hadīth collection, the *Sunan* of Abū Dā'ūd (817–88), one tradition clearly implies – and note that this implication is recognized by Muslim commentators – that each animal is to be considered as an individual, since the tradition speaks of animals being given proper names ("a donkey called 'Afīr") (al-Zaman (tr.) 1983, pp. 308–12). Quite remarkably, this individuation effectively admits a unique identity on the part of each and every member of a given animal species. One wonders, then, if Islam constitutes an exception to the "speciesism" of the classical world – this would indeed be a highly fruitful question to pursue.

Many Hadīth collections contain the story of a woman who was condemned to hellfire "because of a cat which she had imprisoned, and it died of starvation . . . God told her, 'You are condemned because you did not feed the cat, and did not give it water to drink, nor did you set it free so that it could eat of the creatures of the earth'" (Muhsin Khan (ed.) 1977, vol 3, number 553). This Hadīth story, which is rather widely known in the Islamic world, constitutes a basis of the *fiqh*-legislation that the owner of an animal is legally responsible for its well-being. If such owners are unable to provide for their animals, jurists further stipulate, then they should sell them, or let them go free in a way that they can find food and shelter, or slaughter them if eating their flesh is permissible. Given the requirement that animals should be allowed as far as possible to live out their lives in a natural manner, keeping birds in cages is deemed unlawful (Johnson-Davies, 1994, p. xii).

But large sections devoted exclusively to animals in general, and to hunting of animals and game, and animal sacrifice, are a standard feature of the Hadīth corpora. In these sections, or books, one finds quite detailed prophetic instructions and traditions concerning the treatment of animals, their rights, and their relationship to human beings. While all of this is treated with an ethical focus, underlying it is a particular conception of the natural environment that ultimately derives from the Qur'ān. At the same time, without making it explicit, this treatment generates both a philosophical as well as a moral attitude to the physical world that is uniquely Islamic. It is no surprise, then, that E. W. Lane, in his famous nineteenth-century work *Manners and Customs of the Modern Egyptians* would put this on record: "I was much pleased at observing their humanity to dumb animals." Noting that the Egyptians have subsequently become a little less sensitive to animals, Lane says, "I am inclined to think that the conduct of Europeans has greatly conduced to produce this effect, for I do not remember to have seen acts of cruelty to dumb animals except in places where Franks either reside or are frequent visitors" (quoted in Johnson-Davies 1994, p. xv, from the publication in 1836).

Indeed, we have in the *Mishkāt*, the saying of the prophet, "If anyone wrongfully kills [even] a sparrow, [let alone] anything greater, God will question him about it" (Robson (tr.) 1990, p. 874). There is in the same collection the story that the Prophet saw a donkey branded on the face; it upset him so much that he invoked God's curse: "God curse the one who branded it!" In fact it is explicitly stated here that "God's messenger forbade striking the face of an animal or branding on its face." Similarly, he is reported to have forbidden all forms of blood sports, and inciting living creatures to fight with one another, or using them as targets – "The Prophet cursed those who used a living creature as targets" (ibid, p. 872). One story in Abū Dā'ūd's *Sunan* has clear ecological dimensions: "Once a companion of the Prophet was seen crumbling up bread for some ants with the words, 'They are our neighbors and have rights over us'" (quoted in Johnson-Davies, 1994, p. xvii).

Killing of certain kinds of animals for food is permitted in Islam, but only if the animal is killed in a specified manner and – in order to prevent cruel and arrogant tendencies from developing – God's name is pronounced over it. There exist in the Hadīth corpora exceedingly detailed instructions concerning animal slaughtering. Again, a report in the *Mishkāt* has the Prophet saying, "God who is blessed and exalted has decreed that everything should be done in a good way, so when you kill use a good method, and when you cut an animal's throat you should use a good method, for each of you should sharpen his knife and give the animal as little pain as possible" (Robson (tr.) 1990, p. 872). It is declared reprehensible by the Prophet to let one animal witness the slaughtering of another, or to keep animals waiting to be slaughtered, or sharpening the knife in their presence – "Do you wish to slaughter the animal twice: once by sharpening your blade in front of it and another time by cutting its throat!" (quoted in Johnson-Davies 1994, p. ix).

Legal doctors of Islam have developed meticulously, and in the most minute of details, these prophetic principles formally into a structured body of law. Thus, in the *Hidāya* of the grand twelfth-century jurist al-Marginānī, considered to be the most authoritative single work of the Hanafī school of law which is followed by the majority of Muslims, we have an extensive treatment of these principles. In the chapter on *Dhabh*, or lawful killing of animals for food, the *Hidāya* says inter alia,

> IT is abominable first to throw the animal down on its side, and then to sharpen the knife; for it is related that the Prophet once observing a man who had done so, said to him, "How many deaths do you intend that this animal should die? Why did you not sharpen your knife before you threw it down?" IT is abominable to let the knife reach the spinal marrow, or to cut off the head of the animal. The reasons ... are, FIRST, because the Prophet has forbidden this; and, SECONDLY, because it unnecessarily augments the pain of the animal, which is prohibited in our LAW. – In short, everything which unnecessarily augments the pain of the animal is abominable ... IT is abominable to seize an animal destined for slaughter by the feet, and drag it ... IT is abominable to break the neck of the animal whilst it is in the struggle of death." (Hamilton (tr.) 1791, repr. 1957, vol. IV, p. 588)

The jurist Marginānī goes on. But let us survey the legal tradition a bit more closely.

The legal tradition: principles of *Himā*, *Haram*, and discourses on wastelands

It has already been remarked that *fiqh*, which literally means "understanding," and which is generally referred to by modern scholarship as "Islamic law," is a systematic search for God's *Sharī'a*, or Way, that has to be ferreted out from the *adilla* (indicators) spread all over God's *āyāt*. In more concrete terms, *fiqh* is a search for the legal status (*hukm*) of a particular public or private act, and this search is aimed to have a truly universal scope – that is, to comprehend the entire range of human acts (see Reinhart 1983). Thus *fiqh* is the structured articulation of the totality of Islam *as a function* (Rahman 1979, pp. 68–84). By the middle of the ninth century CE, the formal structure of *fiqh* had been fully developed, its procedural rules and methodological framework solemnly established. Several sources (*usūl*) of *fiqh*-legislation were admitted, but there were to be only two material sources – the Qur'ān and the *Sunna* (custom), which was now embodied in authenticated corpora of Hadīth collections.

We have noted that the Qur'ān is not a textbook of laws or procedures; and Hadīth collections, though classified according to the subject-matter, do not have a formal structure either – these collections are a body of stories, accounts, reports, and anecdotes, and have all kinds of variations in reliability and factual contents. It is only in *fiqh* writings that we find a formal, structured, and systematic legal discourse on issues. Of course, an isolated concern for the environment as such was not on the horizon of the normative tradition of classical Islam; it is a contemporary concern of our present-day world. But it is possible to find diffused all over the body of Islamic legal literature matters directly related to issues of the environment. Indeed, it would be an enormous task to glean these fully integrated environment-related materials from *fiqh* writings, and this is where future research must lie, if our interest in Islam's environmental philosophy is more than rhetorical. The task of the contemporary scholars of Islam is doubly heavy: first, they will have to carry out a *fiqh* of *Fiqh*, that is, to reconstruct from legal writings an environmental philosophical system; and, secondly, they will have to do what medieval Muslim legists did – carry out a *fiqh* of the two material sources afresh in an environmental perspective.

But in *fiqh* writings, some principles directly related to issues of the environment have already been developed in their own terms. One of them that has been referred to already is the principle of *himā*. The word literally means "protected, forbidden place," and it names an institution that has pre-Islamic origins. So *himā* was a piece of land, not totally infertile, which is declared forbidden by some powerful figure who has taken possession of it. This was a means of usurping an expanse of ground, and arrogating to oneself or to one's tribe all grazing and watering rights within the area the ground covered. Islam abrogated this practice, and transformed the institution of *himā*. Thus we read in the Qur'ān, "O my people, this is the camel of God, which is for you a sign (*āya*). Leave it to graze on the land of God" (11: 64). And in Bukhārī we have the Hadīth, "Nobody has the right to declare a place *himā* except God and His Messenger" (Muhsin Khan (ed.) 1977, vol. 3, number 558). Gradually, *himā* took the status close to that of *haram* (see below), in that it became a sanctuary, with its flora and fauna receiving special protection (see Chelhod 1971, p. 393). It is reported in the Hadīth that the Prophet declared as *himā* a place in Medina called al-Naqī' (Muhsin Khan (ed.) 1977, vol. 3, number 558).

The environmental dimensions of the institution of *himā* make themselves readily apparent, and the Mālikī school of law has developed it particularly. The conditions to be met for a piece of land to qualify as a possible *himā* are systematically specified: (1) It should be governed by people's general need to maintain a restricted area, not by the whim or greed of some powerful individual or group. (2) The area to be declared as *himā* should not be too large, and this is to avoid general inconvenience. (3) The protected area should not be built upon, or cultivated for financial gain. (4) The aim of *himā* should be the welfare and benefit of people (al-Zuhaili, 1984, vol. 5, pp. 523–4, 571–5; quoted in Izzi Deen 1990, p. 196). What we have here is the outline of a concrete environmental policy concerning restricted areas.

Another similar institution articulated by legists is that of *haram* (or *harīm*) – sacred territory, inviolable zone, sanctuary. Mecca was a *haram* by the decree of God Himself (Qur'ān, 17: 91). Here, for example, no animal of the game species is ever put to death. By extension, Medina too enjoyed the same privileges as the Meccan *haram*. By further extension it became an environmental institution and is often discussed in the section devoted to waste land in legal works. Izzi Deen writes:

"The *Harīm* is usually found in association with wells, natural springs, underground water channels, rivers and trees planted on barren lands or *mawāt* [waste land]. There is [in some parts of the Islamic world] a careful administration of the *Harīm* zones based on the practice of the Prophet Muhammad and the precedent of his companions as recorded in the sources of Islamic law" (1990, p. 190).

One also finds in legal writings detailed discourses on wasteland (*mawāt*); and, in this connection, systematic discussions on water rights, resources, and their maintenance. Thus, in the *Hidāya*, we have a "Book on the Cultivation of Waste Lands" with sections on the definition of *mawāt*, rights of cultivating them, treatment of adjacent territories, status of adjacent territories, water courses in *mawāt*, matters related to aqueducts running through the *mawāt*, and so on. There is a large section here on waters, including issues of control and direction of flow, a large section on digging canals, on rivers, their kinds, their cleaning, and rules with respect to drains and water courses. There is furthermore a whole section on water rights, which discusses the right to alter or obstruct water courses, dams, digging of trenches, construction of water engines or bridges, water vents – the minutiae here are astounding (Hamilton (tr.) 1791, repr. 1957, vol. IV, pp. 609–18). All this must be studied to move toward reconstructing a coherent body of Islamic environmental philosophy.

The fundamental counter-Baconian principle is clear – the world is not in existence solely for one generation of human beings. Once again, the Qur'ān: "And there is no animal in the earth nor bird that flies with its two wings, but that they are communities like yourselves" (6: 38).

References

Classical Islamic Sources

Translations of the Qur'ān

The Holy Qur'ān, translated by A. Y. Ali (Brentwood, MD: Amana Corporation 1989). [Somewhat old-fashioned translation, includes translator's notes and conventional explanations.]

The Koran Interpreted translated by A. J. Arberry (New York: Macmillan Publishing Company, 1955). [A rather free translation, with a deliberate poetic quality. Verse numbering imprecise.]

Qur'ān Commentaries

Ibn Kathr, *Tafsīr*, ed. M. A. al-Sabuni, *Mukhtasar Tafsīr ibn Kathīr* (Beirut: Dar al-Qur'ān al-Karīm, 1981). [Abridgment of a classical Qur'ān commentary by a fourteenth-century scholar who is held in high esteem in the Islamic tradition.]

Hadīth Collections

Mishkāt al-Masābīh, translated by J. Robson (Lahore: Sh. Muhammad Ashraf, 1990). [Regarded as one of the most respectable Hadīth compilations, originating from a work of al-Baghawī who died around 1116].

Muwattā' of Mālik ibn Anas, translated by M. Rahimuddin (Lahore: Sh. Muhammad Ashraf, 1985). [Well-known Hadīth collection of the eighth-century Master of the Mālikī school of law.]

Sahīh al-Bukhārī, translated and edited by M. Muhsin Khan (Chicago: Kazi Publications, 1976–79). [By far the most authentic ("Correct") corpus of Hadīth in Sunnī Islam; its status practically just second to none other than the Qur'ān itself. Translation of a poor quality.]

Sunan Abū Dā'ūd, translated by Wahid al-Zaman (Urdu) (Lahore: Islami Academy, 1983). [Considered by Sunnī Muslims to be one of the six authentic ("Correct") corpora of Hadīth.]

Legal Works

Hidāya of al-Marghinānī, translated by C. Hamilton (London: T. Bensley, 1791). Reprinted from the second edition of 1870 (Lahore: Premier Book House, 1957). [The grand work of a twelfth-century jurist, considered to be the most authoritative single work of the Hanafī school of law.]

Modern Primary Sources

al-Zuhaili, Wahba (1984) *al-Fiqh al-Islamī wa Adillatuhu* (Islamic Law and Its Material Foundations) (Damascus: Dar al-Fikr). [A modern compilation of the Mālikī school of law.]

Western Works and Secondary Sources

Bacon, Francis (1863 [1620]) *Novum Organum Scientiarum* in *The Works of Francis Bacon*, ed. James Spedding, R. L. Ellis, and D. D. Heath (Boston: Houghton, Mifflin, and Company). [Aggressive analysis of the western scientific enterprise by a seventeenth-century English philosopher who speaks of establishing and enlarging human power over all else in nature.]

Chelhod, J. (1971) "Himā," in *Encyclopaedia of Islam*, new edition, ed. H. A. R. Gibb and H. Kramers et al. vol. 3 (Leiden: E. J. Brill). [A very brief but learned exposition of what developed into an ethico-legal principle of Islam's environmental thinking.]

Gardet, L. (1987) "God in Islam," in *Encyclopedia of Religion*, ed. M. Eliade (New York: Macmillan). [An inspired and rigorous study of the concept of God in Islam.]

Hourani, George F. (1985) *Reason and Tradition in Islamic Ethics* (Cambridge: Cambridge University Press). [A collection of essays on the ethical concerns of Islam by an important scholar of the "Orientalist" tradition.]

Izutsu, Toshihiko (1964) *God and Man in the Koran* (Tokyo: The Keio Institute of Cultural and Linguistic Studies). [As the full title of this book announces, this is a semantic study of the Qur'ānic *Weltanschauung*, a thorough and interesting work of a Japanese Islamicist.]

Izzi Deen (Samarri), M. Y. (1990) "Islamic Environmental Ethics," in *Ethics of Environment and Development*, ed. J. Ronald Engel and Joan G. Engel (Tucson: University of Arizona Press), pp. 189–98. [A statement on Islam's environmental ethics by a contemporary Muslim thinker.]

Johnson-Davies, D. (1994) *The Island of Animals, Adapted from an Arabic Fable* (Austin: University of Texas Press). [An elegant adaptation of a fable that appears in the *Epistles* of the tenth-century Islamic philosophical fraternity, "The Brethren of Purity."]

Lane, E. W. (1836) *Manners and Customs of the Modern Egyptians* (London: John Murray). [A sympathetic and highly literate classic account by a major Arabist of modern times.]

Nasr, Seyyed H. (1991) "Islam and the Environmental Crisis," *The Islamic Quarterly* 34, no. 4, pp. 217–34. [A pioneering doctrinal statement by a major scholar and spokesman of Islam's environmental philosophy.]

Rahman, F. (1989) *Major Themes of the Qur'ān* (Minneapolis: Bibliotheca Islamica). [Highly learned excursus on Qur'ānic themes by one of the finest modern scholars of our times.]

Rahman, F. (1979) *Islam* (Chicago: The University of Chicago Press). [A sophisticated, and very scholarly introduction to Islam.]

Reinhart, A. Kevin (1983) "Islamic Law as Islamic Ethics," *The Journal of Religious Ethics* 11, no. 2, pp. 186–202. [Very apt, lucid, and compact but comprehensive examination of what is generally referred to as Islamic law.]

Further reading

Baljon, J. M. S. (1958) "The 'Amr of God' in the Koran," *Acta Orientalia* (Copenhagen), 23, nos. 1–2 (1958), pp. 7–18. [A highly scholarly study of the Qur'ānic notion of *amr* (literally, "command").]

Khalid, Fazlun and O'Brian, Joanne, eds. (1992) *Islam and Ecology* (London: Cassell). [A useful collection of essays on the Islamic approach to ecology.]

Llewellyn, Othman (1982) "Desert Reclamation and Conservation in Islamic Law," *The Muslim Scientist* 11, no. 9, pp. 9–29. [A modern issue treated in the normative perspective of classical Islamic law.]

Manzoor, S. Parvez (1984) "Environment and Values: the Islamic Perspective," in *The Touch of Midas*, ed. Z. Sardar (Manchester: Manchester University Press), pp. 150–69. [A comprehensive, comparative, and creative examination of Islamic environmental ethics.]

Nasr, Seyyed H. (1978) *The Encounter of Man and Nature* (London: Allen and Unwin). [A classic, seminal work on the metaphysics of human–environment relationship.]

Peirone, Federico (1982) "Islam and Ecology in the Mediterranean *Kulturkreise*," *Hamdard Islamicus* 5, no. 2 (Summer), pp. 19–31. [Explains, among other things, nature's devotional relationship to God in Islamic thinking.]

Spring, David and Spring, Eileen, eds. (1974) *Ecology and Religion in History* (New York: Harper and Row). [One of the earliest contemporary volumes on the religious perspectives on ecology.]

Timm, Roger E. (1997) "The Ecological Fallout of Islamic Creation Theology," in *Worldviews and Ecology*, ed. Mary Evelyn Tucker and John A. Grim (Maryknoll, NY: Orbis Books), pp. 83–95. [A balanced, but somewhat limited study of the Qur'ānic position on nature.]

9

Early modern philosophy

CHARLES TALIAFERRO

The beginning of modern philosophy in Europe was prompted, in part, by the rise of modern science in the seventeenth century. Modern scientists advanced a heliocentric or sun-centered view of the cosmos in place of a geocentric or earth-centered understanding of our planetary system. Observation and experimentation were given pride of place in the investigation of nature over divine revelation in Scripture. Aristotle and other ancient authorities were challenged, and a premium was placed on mechanistic or naturalistic explanations of nature. This scientific and intellectual revolution helped generate unprecedented philosophical experimentation and fierce debate. Other contributing factors to this complex emergence of modern philosophy were the invention of the printing press, the Reformation, and the breakdown of feudalism. Modern philosophy began with an array of competing theories of nature, God, and civil society. This vibrant period in the history of ideas and culture is often referred to as "The Enlightenment."

This chapter on early modern conceptions of nature will cover the first stage of modern philosophy, chiefly the seventeenth and eighteenth centuries. The philosophies of nature that were advanced at that time had important ethical and social implications and they remain vital for us to address today, both for the sake of understanding European history and the histories of parts of the world affected by Europe. It is also vital in a thoroughgoing assessment of the resources available for developing and assessing our own philosophies of nature. Many contemporary theories in environmental ethics are articulated with explicit reference to Enlightenment figures. To fully engage these projects requires taking stock of the emergence of modern philosophy.

In order to appreciate the distinctive character of modern philosophy, it is desirable to consider, if only briefly, some of the salient features of the medieval world from which modern philosophy emerged.

The medieval background

The term "medieval" (from the Latin for "middle") refers to Europe between ancient and classical Greco-Roman culture on the one end and the Renaissance and modern era on the other. The medieval era was depicted by Petrarch and others as the "Dark Ages," a wasteland of superstition, plague, famine, fractious feudal politics, and war, all of which came about after the collapse of the Roman Empire in the West. The medieval period – customarily charted from the fourth to the fifteenth century – did indeed have a dark side. There were crusades, widespread oppression, military strife, and the Black Death (bubonic and pneumonic infections) in the fourteenth century in which a quarter of the population (25 million people) of Europe perished. And yet not everything was abominable. There were periods of peace and tolerance, important developments in art, literature, architecture, agriculture (for example, the cultivation of beans in the tenth century was so successful it has been called "the century of beans"), and important philosophical and theological work was undertaken by Jewish, Christian, and Islamic thinkers. (See JUDAISM, CHRISTIANITY, and ISLAM)

A brief summary of "the medieval world-view" is doomed because of the rich variety of this era. Even so, some broad generalizations are worth noting. What follows covers a significant body of the medieval landscape with some privileging of the work of Thomas Aquinas (1225–1274). By the lights of many prominent scholars, medieval philosophy reached its zenith with Aquinas (Gilson 1940).

On the whole, the medieval conception of nature is theistic. Nature is a good realm made up of earth, plants, animals, humans, heavenly bodies, and supernatural beings that are created and sustained by an all-good, all-powerful, all-knowing God. Nature is not itself divine, nor is it, as the Stoics thought, a soul or animal. Nature is diverse but not self-explaining, for the very existence and all the powers of the natural world are derived from God's good power. The philosophy of God in common with Jews, Muslims, and Christians at the time is that God necessarily exists. God is not a contingent entity, for God's existence does not depend on any created being; there is no law of nature or force behind God that created God. God exists *a se* (in Godself) as a spiritual, immaterial, omnipresent being, eternal, imperishable, incorruptible, and without origin or end. In this theological-philosophical system, the creation is recognized as real and a fitting object of care and pleasure, but God is recognized as the most real being (*ens realissimum*), the most perfect and therefore the most worthy of worship and obedience. Augustine taught that nature should be prized for the love of God who made it.

The flourishing of each kind of being that constitutes nature is willed eternally by God. Etienne Gilson summarizes the medieval picture of nature: "The very physical world, created as it is for God's glory, tends with a kind of blind love towards its Author; and each being, each operation of each being, depends momentarily, for existence and efficacy, on an omnipotent conserving will" (1940, p. 364). Our malleable world's history unfolds underneath the heavens which signify and testify to the God behind and around nature who providentially wills its fecundity or flourishing. While nature was understood to be a diverse realm of goods, it was also seen as less perfect than God, subject not only to temporal passage, but to decay, corruption, and perishing. Historically, nature suffers from human wickedness, beginning with an aboriginal turning away from God which has poisoned human endeavors (Genesis). Because nature was understood to be fundamentally good, evil was thought of as something unnatural or against nature. In a sense, health was thought of as conceptually prior to disease; it would not do to analyze health as simply the absence of disease, whereas one could say that someone with a disease was someone who is not healthy. On this view, according to which illness and wickedness are an abuse of something that can be properly used and enjoyed, evil was considered *privatio boni*, or the absence of good.

In the medieval world-view, correcting ills involves the establishment of one's God-given purpose, discovering right reason and appropriate appetites in a God-centered life, and a right order of love (what Augustine called the *ordo amoris*). For human beings this meant realizing that persons are made in the image of God and are called into God's likeness. This was interpreted as appreciating that human beings had certain powers such as agency, reason, and love, that reflect God, who is unsurpassable in power, agency, reason, and love. One of the reasons why evil was viewed with profound abhorrence at this time was that it was believed to involve the contorting of something divine. Christian philosophers and theologians held further that for humans to be released from evil (or sin) they must accept God as revealed in the life of Jesus Christ. Christians held that God became incarnate (from the Latin for "infleshed") as a human being to manifest divine love and mercy, and to point the way to a reconciliation with God that involved fulfillment in this life and the next. Medieval Christians were not just apprised of the allure of deeper fulfillment; there is also evidence of a fear of failing to realize a merciful reconciliation with God. The art, literature, and architecture of the period provide evidence of both a longing for heaven and a fear of hell.

As a world of diverse goods, many of the medievalists posited rightful relations among the different orders or ranks of good. In this, Aquinas followed Aristotle in ranking plants as lower than non-human animals and non-human animals as lower than humans. Human beings were considered of greater perfection among corporeal, created beings, for humans have mass (like earth), life (like plants), movement and senses (like non-human animals), and also reason. As a being of higher rank on what amounts to a Great Chain of Being, Aquinas thought this order made hunting and meat eating permissible: "As the plants make use of the earth for their nourishment, and animals make use of plants, and man makes use of both plants and animals" (*Summa Theologica*, Part 1, LXXV).

Medieval astronomy was largely a refinement of the work of Ptolemy (second century CE), according to which the earth is the center of the universe. While it is popular to cast medieval science as pure superstition (hypothesizing about demons and witches), it was more sophisticated than is often credited. For example, there is a widespread impression that medievalists thought the earth is flat. But this is false. As C. S. Lewis correctly observes: "Physically considered, the earth is a globe, all the authors of the high Middle Ages are agreed on this" (Lewis 1964, pp. 140–1; see also Russell 1991).

By Aquinas's lights, civil society was a natural human development and essential part of our nature. We are completed partly in relation to one another. As he rooted ethics in nature, Aquinas distinguished between the eternal law which may be abstractly formulated as "Do good and avoid evil," whereas more specific moral truths are grounded in the nature of the person or beings at issue. Thus, it is because of our biological nature that nourishment counts as a good for human beings. To use an extreme example, by contrast, if human beings were profoundly different and had bodies that were non-flammable, then putting one's own hand in a furnace would not count as an ill act and thus not something evil or wrong. For Aquinas, good and evil are not *ad hoc* features of the world but grounded in nature, including the divine nature. On his view, God's will essentially reflects goodness; God cannot will something intrinsically evil for its own sake.

The above summary is meant as no more than a high altitude overview of medieval philosophy and tradition. There is much diversity and conflict. Consider only one cross-current. Some medieval sources may be used to develop a higher view of animals than Aquinas and many medievalists countenanced. The fact that Aquinas and others saw animals as making up natural kinds whose goodness consisted in their flourishing provides an inroad to recognizing them as possessing intrinsic value. Moreover, there are some medieval precedents for treating animals as partners in creation, as is evident in contemporary narratives of St. Francis of Assisi and St. Anthony of Padua, Celtic tradition, pious stories of the Desert Fathers, and primitive tradition about Jesus' disciples – according to some early sources, Matthew, Peter, and James refrained from meat-eating (see Linzey and Regan 1988; see also CHRISTIANITY).

The emergence of modern science

Modern science did not begin in complete antithesis with the medieval world. The stress on experience, observation, and testing that defined early science was at least anticipated by Aquinas, who taught that there was nothing in the intellect unless it was first in the senses (*Nihil in intellectu nisi prius in sensu*). And before Aquinas, Roger Bacon (1214–94) stressed experience and experimentation. Bacon thought of mathematics as "the alphabet of philosophy," a dictum that would later be applied to nature as modern scientists sought to discover the structure of the created world. Each of the prominent early modern scientists were self-described theists who saw themselves as using God's gifts of reason and inquiry in the investigation of nature, and in overturning what they took to be mistaken pictures of the world inherited from the ancients.

The leading figures in early modern science include Copernicus (1473–1543), Kepler (1571–1630), and Galileo (1564–1642). Copernicus's challenge to geocentricity was seen as a direct attack on the medieval bulwark, and Kepler's further defense of a sun-centered planetary system was an additional blow. Modern scientists put enormous weight on mathematics and geometry in observation. Each of the early scientists construed this as using divine gifts. Kepler thought our geometrical powers were implanted in us as part of our being made in God's image. Like Kepler, Galileo also advanced a geometric view of nature.

> Philosophy is written in this grand book, the universe, which stands continually open to our gaze. But the book cannot be understood unless one first learns to comprehend the language and read the letters in which it is composed. It is written in the language of mathematics, and its characters are triangles, circles, and other geometric figures without which it is humanly impossible to understand a single word of it. (1957, pp. 237–8)

As a mathematician, physicist and astronomer, Galileo's life and teaching were perhaps the most dramatic in terms of the collision between modern science and reigning medieval authority. His articulation and justification of heliocentricity in *Dialogue Concerning the Two Chief World Systems* (1632) and elsewhere pitted him against the teaching office of the Roman Catholic Church. The Church had adopted the reigning medieval picture of the universe inherited from Ptolemy; there was nothing biblical or essential to medieval philosophical teaching in faith and morals requiring belief in geocentricity. But the Church had set its case on that front, and placed its authority behind it. Galileo's endorsement of Copernicanism led to his being condemned in the Inquisition and held in house arrest.

In Galileo's work we encounter a problem that will run through all of modern philosophy, the problem of integrating the mental and physical. Galileo conceived of material objects as being defined by shape, size, and location.

> Now I say that whenever I conceive any material or corporeal substance, I imme-diately feel the need to think of it as bounded, and as having this or that shape; as being large or small in relation to other things, and in some specific place at any given time; as being in motion or at rest; as touching or not touching some other body; and as being one in number, or few, or many. (1957, p. 274)

These quantifiable, geometric properties of material objects were primary, and differed from secondary qualities such as color, taste, sound, and feel.

> But that it [any material or corporeal substance] must be white or red, bitter or sweet, noisy or silent, and of sweet or foul odor, my mind does not feel compelled to bring in as necessary accompaniments...Hence, I think that tastes, odors, colors, and so on are no more than names so far as the object in which we place them is concerned, and that they reside only in the consciousness. Hence if the living creature were removed, all these qualities would be wiped away and annihilated. (Ibid)

A split is thereby introduced between the world that is disclosed to our sensory perception, and the material objects themselves which, in their sheer, colorless, odorless, tasteless geometry, seem alien.

Galileo did not see himself as providing any difficulties for theism, nor of under-mining the conviction that human beings are in the image of God. Still, he helped facilitate an important shift from medieval conceptions of God and nature which, by contrast, were more organic and holistic, than Galileo's geometric atomism. Accord-ing to atomism, all of the material world is composed of simple, non-compound objects. "Atom" is from the Greek for "not" (*a*) and "cut" (*tomos*); an atom is a simple, indivisible entity. Atomism led some of Galileo's followers to believe that mathematical and empirical investigation can offer a reductive analysis of the world, disclosing the very building blocks of nature. Robert Boyle (1627–92) intro-duced the term "mechanical philosophy" to refer to this new, scientifically based atomism. Boyle thought of nature itself as a colossal machine and compared it to a huge clock. Just as clocks have a maker, so does the cosmos.

Materialism and dualism

Two philosophical visions of nature and God were at the fore in the wake of the scientific revolution: materialism and dualism. The English philosopher Thomas

Hobbes (1588–1679) is representative of materialism, and the French philosopher René Descartes (1596–1650) of dualism.

Hobbes was thoroughgoing in his enthusiasm for the new science and the advent of a materialist conception of human beings as part of nature.

> The world . . . is corporeal, that is, the whole mass of all things that are, is corporeal, that is to say, body, and hath the dimensions of magnitude, namely, length, breadth, and depth: also every part of body, is likewise body, and hath the like dimensions; and consequently every part of the universe, is body, and that which is not body, is no part of the universe: and because the universe is all, that which is no part of it, is nothing; and consequently *no where*. (Hobbes 1962, p. 483)

Hobbes's understanding of human life and behavior was atomistic and determinist. By his lights, God is a material reality, "a most pure, simple, invisible spirit corporeal."

Hobbes's materialist analysis of human sense, appetite, and passion had important ethical implications. He was at complete odds with Aquinas's notion that persons are somehow ingrained by nature with a social instinct. Rather, Hobbes held that persons are constitutionally driven first and foremost by self-interest. Without external checks on human endeavors, we are in profound conflict. The natural state of human life is not peace, but war.

> Hereby it is manifest, that during the time men live without a common power to keep them all in awe, they are in that condition which is called war; and such a war, as is of every man, against every man. For War, consisteth not in battle only, or the act of fighting; but in a tract of time, wherein the will to contend by battle is sufficiently known: and therefore the notion of *time*, is to be considered in the nature of war; as it is in the nature of weather. For as the nature of foul weather, lieth not in a shower or two of rain; but in an inclination thereto of many days together: so the nature of war, consisteth not in actual fighting; but in the known disposition thereto, during all the time there is no assurance to the contrary. All other time is Peace. (Ibid, p. 100)

This state of war was depicted succinctly in one of the most often quoted line from Hobbes's work, "the life of man is nasty, solitary, brutish and short" (ibid). In the midst of such perilous conditions, our only hope is for each of us to agree to curtail our self-serving desires and to hold ourselves accountable to a sovereign civil power. Civil government is thus a rational prudential outcome of perceived self-interest.

Hobbes's philosophy is an extraordinary synthesis of philosophy and the new science. He met with Galileo in 1636 and set out to do for philosophy and politics what Galileo did for the natural sciences. One of the strongest reasons behind Hobbes's project is his appeal to a unified picture of human life, nature, and God. Because he resisted positing non-material realities, he was not faced with explaining how the material and spiritual interact. He is one of the first modern advocates of the unity of science and philosophy.

Descartes and his followers, who are called Cartesians (from the Latinized form of "Descartes"), were, like Hobbes, impressed by modern science and the geometrization of nature. Descartes developed analytical geometry, and advanced what may be considered a geometrical method in philosophy. He sought to identify sure and indubitable foundational beliefs upon which to structure and justify all other beliefs about nature and God.

Descartes's work stands out for his bold skeptical query at the center of his philosophy. In his *Discourse on Method* and *Meditations on First Philosophy* he unleashed a thought experiment of extraordinary power. Descartes entertains the possibility that all his ostensible perceptions of the world are the outcome of an arch, all-powerful, evil force. This is the equivalent of considering whether it is possible that instead of believing you are reading this book just now, you are actually being subject to a massive, systematic, interwoven hallucination; you are in some "virtual reality" as opposed to the world as depicted by common sense. In the wake of such a comprehensive hypothesis, Descartes came to conclude that however powerful the demonic, deceptive force, he could not be mistaken in his belief that he exists. His very doubting of everything presupposed that he exists. Descartes then locked his certitude in his own existence with an argument for God's existence to bolster his further conclusion that, due to the goodness of God, he could trust his sensory perception, memory, et al. In a sense, Descartes sought to bracket nature, to hold it all open to doubt, and then to welcome it back as now properly perceived with justification as opposed to blind faith.

Descartes's critics are legion. One substantial objection is that his skeptical method and proposed solution foisted on the world an unprecedented preoccupation with the self. Another criticism is that his solution is profoundly unsatisfactory; once one entertains the evil demon hypothesis, one can never recover. In brief, if you leave nature as Descartes did, you will never return. By way of a modest point in Descartes's defense, his appeal to God in his argument for the trustworthiness of perception admits of a plausible analogue. After all, in child-rearing it seems essential that the child's care-givers do not subject the child to systematic delusions. Language-acquisition, for example, appears to require trustworthiness. Imagine a child who is never given reliable, consistent definitions of terms, nor a consistent grammar. So, Descartes's invoking of God, a God whom Descartes believes has implanted an idea of God within each of us, suggests that Descartes's world-view is not quite as "nasty, solitary, brutish and short" as one finds described in standard introductory textbooks. Contrary to some popular caricatures of his thought, Descartes did not propound an incurable isolationist philosophy. (For a contemporary defense of a related theistic account of reason and perception, see Plantinga 1993.)

Unlike Hobbes, Descartes was not a materialist. He was impressed by the natural scientific analysis of the natural world; indeed, his book *The World* upheld a great confidence in the uniformity of matter and mechanistic explanations. Descartes was also impressed by the profound unity of the person as an embodied being. Nonetheless, he was convinced that the person is not exclusively material. Strictly speaking, a person (or mind) is a non-physical concrete being that is materially embodied. His chief reason for this was his belief that he can conceive of himself existing without thereby conceiving of his body or any physical body whatsoever. A sympathetic reconstruction of his argument is that it is based on a principle called the indiscernibility of identicals which may be formalized as: if A is B, then whatever is true of A is true of B. For example, if the morning star is the evening star, then whatever is true of the morning star is true of the evening star. In this case, it seems to work, for both terms refer to the planet Venus and thus there is nothing true about what is referred to as the evening star which is not also true of the morning star. To see the morning star is to see the same thing as the evening star: Venus. In the case of persons, though, Cartesians argue that it is possible for persons to exist without their bodies, and possible, too, for their bodies to exist without them (e.g. after you die your body may still exist as a corpse). If these represent genuine possibilities – and Descartes thought he could clearly and distinctly conceive of himself without material body – then it appears that the person (or mind) is not identical with her or his body.

Descartes's position amounts to a form of dualism. Today, dualism is considered public enemy number one by many environmentalists. Arguably, a dualism of person and body seems to introduce a damaging breach between human beings and the rest of nature. Four observations may be mustered in reply. First, to posit a distinction between the person and body is not to suggest that persons are now somehow disembodied. One can be a dualist and believe that, under natural conditions, the person functions as a unified embodied being. Second, dualism by itself implies no denigration of the body; there is no need for a dualist to regard the body as a prison or shell or container. Dualists are free to depict material embodiment as a great good. Third, it is not obvious that the science of Descartes's day or ours has disproven dualism. Much of the most advanced work on the brain establishes an integral relation between the mental and physical, but these results may be read as securing a correlation of the mental and physical, not identity. Fourth, one can be a dualist and believe that non-human animals also consist of both minds and bodies. Famously, Descartes did not take this view, however, and it is to this matter that we must now turn.

Descartes is well known for his conviction that non-human animals lack consciousness. Descartes delimited various grades of awareness. In his view, non-human animals only met the first grade.

> To the first (grade) belongs the immediate affection of the bodily organ by external objects; and this can be nothing more than the motion of the sensory organs and the change of figure and position due to that motion. The second (grade) comprises the immediate mental results, due to the mind's union with the corporeal organ affected; such are the perceptions of pain, of pleasurable stimulation, of thirst, of hunger, of colours, of sound, savour, cold, heat, and the like . . . Finally the third (grade) contains all those judgments which, on the occasion of motions occurring in the corporeal organ, we have from our earliest years been accustomed to pass about things external to us. (1911, p. 436)

Descartes's argument against non-human consciousness took two forms. One was an appeal to parsimony. If you do not need to posit grades two and three to describe and explain non-human constitution and behavior, then do not do so. This appeared to Descartes to be good science and philosophy. His second argument rested on his supposition that non-human animals lack language.

> For it is quite remarkable that there are no men so dull-witted or stupid – and this includes even madmen – that they are incapable of arranging various words

together and forming an utterance from them in order to make their thoughts understood; whereas there is no other animal, however perfect and well-endowed it may be, that can do the like. This does not happen because they lack the necessary organs, for we see that magpies and parrots can utter words as we do, and yet they cannot speak as we do: that is, they cannot show that they are thinking what they are saying. On the other hand, men born deaf and dumb, and thus deprived of speech-organs as much as the beasts or even more so, normally invent their own signs to make themselves understood by those who, being regularly in their company, have the time to learn their language. This shows not merely that the beasts have less reason than men, but that they have no reason at all. (1985, p. 140)

In light of these considerations, Descartes countenanced vivisection. Of course both arguments have been roundly criticized, and both also have defenders today.

Let us now consider two of the major movements in modern philosophy, empiricism and rationalism.

Empirical philosophies of nature

Empiricism is from the Greek *empeiria* for "experience in." Hobbes was an early empiricist. John Locke (1632–1704) was Hobbes's successor and, at key places, his critic. In general, those classified as empiricists privilege experience as a source of knowledge and distrust the role of reason as an independent faculty that permits us to expand our knowledge of reality. There is also a tendency among empiricists to dispense with the belief in innate ideas. Locke was famous at this point for his insisting that at birth the human mind is a blank slate, a *tabula rasa*.

Locke located human beings squarely in nature. Like Descartes he was a dualist, but he opened the door to thinking otherwise. In *An Essay Concerning Human Understanding* he suggests that it is possible for God to grant matter the power to think. Locke thought of animals as possessing sensory powers and faculties at a much higher level than Descartes posited, but he still thought animals lacked our abilities of abstraction and moral powers.

Locke continued Galileo's distinction between primary and secondary properties. The nature of matter perplexed him, however, and he characterized matter as a "something we know not what" underneath the primary qualities. In Locke's work we can see the ongoing modern problem of integrating the mental and physical. Because we cannot picture matter in itself without all the accompanying characteristics of color (which we bring to our view of the world), matter became a mysterious substratum, that which stands underneath observable qualities.

Locke resisted the appeal to the divine right of kings, and supported democracy, with a limited role given to a monarch. Unlike Hobbes, and in closer alliance with medieval forebears such as Aquinas, Locke held that we are by nature social, and oriented to civil ties.

Locke's conception of property was pre-eminent and has had an important role in the subsequent philosophy of nature and society. As a theist, Locke believed that God owns the whole cosmos. Putting this differently, and toning down the economic imagery, he held that the cosmos belongs to God. In creating human persons God confers on persons a limited self-ownership. In *The Second Treatise of Government* Locke writes: "Every man has a property in his own person; this nobody has any right to but himself" (1980, p. 19). This construes property as something that is pre-conventional and societal. That is, property rights inhere in a person naturally; they are not the creation of some government. Construing oneself as one's own property may seem to treat oneself as a commodity, but it may be argued that Locke was simply securing here a high view of an individual's right to self-determination. Because each person has such self-possession, each one owns or is entitled to their agency of labor. The ownership of things outside oneself then comes about owing to one's exercise of labor. "The labor of his body and the work of his hands, we may say, are properly his. Whatsoever then he removes out of the state that nature has provided and left it in, he has mixed his labor with it, and joined to it something that is his own, and thereby makes it his property" (ibid). So, while Locke held that the whole world made up a commons, it was common in the sense that no individual could claim by divine right ownership of it all and yet any individual could acquire parts of it under certain conditions. "As much land as a man tills, plants, improves, cultivates, and can use the product of, so much is his property" (ibid, p. 21).

Locke's labor-centered concept of property was enormously influential in North American views of wilderness. He deemed uncultivated land as waste and of profoundly less value than land that has "benefited" from labor. Locke is often critiqued as an arch-individualist who encouraged ecologically reckless exploitation of nature. Some of these charges are difficult to dismiss. But it should be underscored that he held that private property acquisition was countenanced only when there was enough to go round, and his theistic religious convictions led him to insist on the importance of generosity and care for others. An ample conservationist ethic can be forged in Lockean terms.

George Berkeley (1685–1753) is an empiricist whose work should be of interest to those who hold that nature is itself largely a construct of society and culture. Berkeley was a great idealist who argued against Locke's concept of matter. By his lights, Locke's substratum was too mysterious; it made more sense simply to deny the mind-independent character of this "something" no one can directly grasp. Instead, Berkeley held that the whole cosmos is constituted by minds and perception; "to be is to be perceived" (*Esse est percipi*) is his famous dictum. In *A Treatise Concerning the Principles of Human Knowledge*, he launched the following objection to those who suppose they can picture things that are mind-independent.

But say you, surely there is nothing easier than to imagine trees, for instance, in a park, or books existing in a closet, and no body by to perceive them. I answer, you may so, there is no difficulty in it: but what is all this, I beseech you, more than framing in your mind certain ideas which you call *books* and *trees*, and at the same time omitting to frame the idea of any one that may perceive them? But do not you your self perceive or think of them all the while? This therefore is nothing to the purpose: it only shows you have the power of imagining or forming ideas in your mind; but it doth not shew that you can conceive it possible, the objects of your thought may exist without the mind: to make out this, it is necessary that you conceive them existing unconceived or unthought of, which is a manifest repugnancy. (1982, p. 32)

A version of this puzzle is sometimes advanced by those who claim that all our concepts of nature are indeed reflections of our own categories. Berkeley's belief in God allowed him to believe in objects not perceived by humans. Because God is all-perceiving, nature and its laws are sustained.

David Hume (1711–76) was a great champion of empiricism, a skeptic about the power of reason to establish truths about the natural world, and yet a strong advocate of a scientific approach to nature, including human nature. In *A Treatise of Human Nature*, Hume writes:

There is no question of importance, whose decision is not compriz'd in the science of man; and there is none, which can be decided with any certainty, before we become acquainted with that science. In pretending therefore to explain the principles of human nature, we in effect propose a complete system of the sciences, built on a foundation almost entirely new, and the only one upon which they can stand with any security. (1978, p. xvi)

Hume's scientific inquiry led him to believe the self is not a concrete, substantial individual existing over time, but a bundle of mental properties and ideas. He was also led to see human life as firmly placed in the natural world. We are not radically displaced from nature, but part of the bundle of nature that includes us. His work on religion placed theistic belief and practice in natural history. Unlike medieval Christianity, Hume resisted a supernaturalist view of God in which God miraculously affects human history.

While Hume was a skeptic about the capacity of reason to establish an ethic, he instead looked to sympathy as a more suitable foundation. He held that sympathy with others was a natural, fundamental human trait and that when this was refined by knowledge of the relevant circumstances and impartiality, sympathy could ground an ethic of virtues and a body of moral rules. This understanding of values may appear to some critics as too unstable, but Hume sought to secure a rich view of the sustained (and sustainable) power of sympathy and the other emotions behind moral judgments. Hume's ethical theory was refined by Adam Smith (1723–90) and later by advocates of what is known as the Ideal Observer theory.

Because reason was not the benchmark for ethics, Hume thought virtues were rife within the natural world among creatures not capable of abstract reasoning.

'Tis plain that almost in every species of creatures, but especially the nobler kind, there are many evident marks of pride and humility. The very port and gait of a swan, or turkey, or peacock show the high idea he has entertain'd of himself, and his contempt of all others ... All these are evident proofs, that pride and humility are not merely human passions, but extend themselves over the whole animal creation (Ibid, p. 326).

This is radically different from Descartes's assessment of animal life.

Rationalist philosophy of nature

Rationalism diverges from empiricism in its assessment of the power of reason. Benedict Spinoza (1632–1677) was a rationalist philosopher of the first order. His view of nature was at the heart of his philosophy; indeed he held that the only thing that exists as a substantive thing is what he refers to as *Deus sive Natura* (God or nature). He did not thereby deny variation in nature. Rather, he thought there were indefinitely many attributes or aspects of *Deus sive Natura* which may be distinguished and identified individually. So, he allowed that there is a kind of mental–physical dualism in the sense that one can think of the mental and physical as different ways of conceiving something. Still, in the end, everything is a reflection of a vast divine, natural unity: "Mind and body are one and the same individual which is conceived now under the attribute of thought, and now under the attribute of extension" (Spinoza 1909, vol. 2, p. 102). Spinoza's integrated, holist concept of nature laid some of the groundwork for late twentieth-century, DEEP ECOLOGY as found in Arne Naess's philosophy of nature. Naess's high valuation of the symbiotic complexity of life can be thought of as extending Spinoza's vision of nature.

Spinoza was a firm determinist. He captured this in terms of the expression *natura naturans*, or nature naturing. "By *natura naturans* I understand whatever follows from the necessity of God's nature" (ibid, p. 68). His rationalism is displayed in his proof of God's or nature's existence and in his ethics. While these arguments are too elaborate to reproduce here, it is worth noting how his understanding of reason and liberty was folded into a liberal understanding of society.

> The ultimate aim of Government is not to rule or restrain by fear, not to exact obedience, but on the contrary, to free every man from fear, that he may live in all possible security; in other words to strengthen his natural right to exist and work without injury to himself and others. The object of government is not to change men from rational beings into puppets, but to enable them to develop their minds and bodies in security, and to employ their reason unshackled.... The true aim of Government is liberty. (Ibid, vol. 1, p. 258–9)

This may seem a paradoxical claim for a determinist, but for Spinoza liberty involved the right use of reason and freedom from external constraints, which may be secured even though we reflect the necessary features of God or Nature.

Gottfried Wilhelm Leibniz (1646–1716) was a German rationalist as well as a mathematician. He is probably most popularly known today for claiming that our cosmos is the best possible world, a claim that is lampooned in Voltaire's *Candide*. His view may be defended by placing it in the broader context of his theory of values and philosophy of God, but in this context it will be more important to look at another area of his thought.

Leibniz contended that the atomism of the new science resulted in profound philosophical problems. If the world were indefinitely divisible there would be no way in which extant physical objects could be forged. That is, a world of atoms that take up no space whatever are not able to be the building blocks of the material world.

If I am asked in particular what I say about the sun, the earthly globe, the moon, trees, and other similar bodies, and even about beasts, I cannot be absolutely certain whether they are animated, or even whether they are substances, or, indeed, whether they are simply machines or aggregates of several substances. But at least I can say that if there are no corporeal substances such as I claim, it follows that bodies would only be true phenomena, like the rainbow. For the continuum is not merely divisible to infinity, but every part of matter is actually divided into other parts as different among themselves as the two aforementioned diamonds. And since we can always go on this way, we would never reach anything about which we could say, here is truly a being, unless we found unity independent of the external union arising from contact. And if there were none, it then follows that, with the exception of man, there is nothing substantial in the visible world. (1989, p. 80)

We are secured because, by his lights, we are souls or simple substances he called "Monads." By analogy with ourselves he proposed that the cosmos itself is made up of monads, centers of force that are alive in some fashion. This is a version of "panpsychism" (literally, "everything is alive"). These monads are attributed with appetite, perception, and feeling.

Like Spinoza, Leibniz's rationalism led him to prize a world order informed by wisdom and just balance.

Everything is regulated in all things once for all with as much order and agreement as possible, since supreme wisdom and goodness cannot act without perfect harmony: the present is big with the future, what is to come could be read in the past, what is distant expressed in what is near. The beauty of the Universe could be learnt in each soul, could one unravel all its folds which develop perceptibly only with time. (1951, p. 28)

Regardless of the credibility of Leibniz's monadology as a metaphysic, there is an appreciable attraction to his comprehensive understanding of a harmonized universe.

Empires, naturism, and fideism

In closing, consider three additional features of modernity.

With the end of the medieval period and the advent of modern science, we also see the development of new technology for war. The so-called Enlightenment had its own dark side. Nation-states became increasingly ambitious at empire-building, as European Great Powers expanded to the Americas, Africa, Near and Far East. The expansion was sometimes justified on the grounds that "primitive persons" were not really persons, not fully rational, akin to non-human animals; they failed to exercise proper labor and thus failed to have legitimate property rights, they were religiously and morally depraved. This adventurism was critiqued by some. From the medieval period, Aquinas's ethics was employed and refined by Francisco de Vitoria (1486–1546) to critique the treatment of Native Americans by Spanish Conquistadors. Francisco sought to secure natural rights across ethnic, cultural and religious boundaries. Hugo Grotius (1583–1645) also argued for a theistic treatment of natural law to contain expansionist wars. Throughout early modern philosophy, there were recurrent efforts to check what was perceived as the wrongful use of industry and technology, from Erasmus and More to Hume and to Kant's republican cosmopolitanism. Despite the case for tolerance advanced by both empiricists and rationalists, Europe built its empires. And some prominent figures in the Enlightenment shared in the racism of the period. Hume, for example, characterized "negroes" as inherently inferior to whites. Locke countenanced slavery in his contribution to the Carolina proprietors in the American colonies.

A second important feature of the age may be called "naturism." The eighteenth century fostered various forms of romanticism, among which one finds Jean-Jacques Rousseau (1712–78) and his high view of the goodness of nature. In his book on education, *Emile*, Rousseau proclaims the goodness of nature over the malady of ill-conceived human interference:

> Everything is good as it leaves the hands of the AUTHOR of things; everything degenerates in the hands of man. He forces one soil to nourish the products of another, one tree to bear the fruit of another. He mixes and confuses the climates, the elements, the seasons. He mutilates his dog, his horse, his slave. He turns everything upside down; he disfigures everything; he loves deformity, monsters. He wants nothing as nature made it, not even man; for him, man must be trained like a school horse; man must be fashioned in keeping with his fancy like a tree in his garden. (1979, p. 31)

The root of evil comes about through socially conceived entitlements and conventions, especially the advent of property.

> The first man, who, having enclosed a piece of land, thought of saying "This is mine" and found people simple enough to believe him, was the true founder of civil society. How many crimes, wars, murders; how much misery and horror the human race would have been spared if someone had pulled up the stakes and filled in the ditch and cried out to his fellow men: "Beware of listening to this impostor. You are lost if you forget that the fruits of the earth belong to everyone and that the earth itself belongs to no one!" (1984, p. 109)

Rousseau praised vegetarianism:

> One of the proofs that the taste for meat is not natural to man is the indifference that children have for that kind of food and the preference they all give to vegetable foods, such as dairy products, pastry, fruits, etc. It is, above all, important not to denature this primitive taste and make children carnivorous. If this is not for their health, it is for their character; for, however one explains the experience, it is certain that great eaters of meat are in general more cruel and ferocious than other men. This is observed in all places and all times. (1979, p. 153)

Finally, I note that this age of modernism had its share of skeptics about reason and experience. Michel de Montaigne (1533–92), Blaise Pascal (1623–62), and Pierre Bayle (1647–1706) all took issue with what they saw as the pretensions of their day, philosophical, religious, and political. All were theists but their faith was tempered by an appreciation of opposing viewpoints, and they were more guarded still about whether modern science and the modern philosophies of nature that were fueled by them contained all the answers to our deepest needs. Isaac Newton (1642–1727) may have secured a comprehensive, scientific portrait of the physical world for early moderns. And yet skeptical questions were also very much alive as to whether any system of mechanics or philosophy could be devised that would secure a sustained, beneficent enlightenment.

References

Berkeley, George (1982) *A Treatise Concerning the Principles of Human Knowledge* (Indianapolis: Hackett Publishing Co.). [Along with *Three Dialogues Between Hylas and Philonus*, these are accessible, classic, idealist works.]

Descartes, René (1911) *Philosophical Works of Descartes*, ed E. Haldane and G. Ross. London: Cambridge University Press, 1911.

[Descartes' *Meditations* provides the best in-road to his highly influential philosophy.]

——(1970) *Philosophical Letters*, trans. A. Kenny (Minneapolis: University of Minnesota Press).

——(1985) "Discourse on the Method," in *The Philosophical Writings of Descartes Vol. 1*, trans. John Cottingham, Robert Stoothoff, and Dugald Murdoch (New York: Cambridge University Press).

Galileo (1957 [1623]) "The Assayer," in *Discoveries and Opinions of Galileo*, trans. Stillman Drake (New York: Doubleday Anchor Books). [This is a useful, accessible introduction to Galileo's work.]

Gilson, Etienne (1940) *The Spirit of Medieval Philosophy* (New York: Charles Scribner's Sons). [A superb, unsurpassed overview.]

Hobbes, Thomas (1962) *Leviathan*, ed. M. Oakeshott (New York: Macmillan). [Essential reading for political philosophy.]

Hume, David (1978) *A Treatise of Human Nature* (Oxford: Clarendon Press). [Along with *An Enquiry Concerning Human Understanding* and *An Enquiry Concerning the Principles of Morals*, key Enlightenment texts.]

Leibniz, G. W. (1951) "Principles of Nature and Grace," in *Philosophical Writings* (London: J. M. Dent and Sons Ltd). [Leibniz's work is forbidding in its complexity but will reward careful reflection.]

——(1989) *Philosophical Essays* (Indianapolis: Hackett Publishing Co.).

Lewis, C. S. (1964) *The Discarded Image* (Cambridge: Cambridge University Press). [An elegantly written overview of medieval thought and culture.]

Linzey, Andrew and Regan, Tom, eds. (1988) *Animals and Christianity* (New York: Crossroad). [A text that opens up debate on the standing of animals in the Christian tradition.]

Locke, John (1980) *The Second Treatise of Government* (Indianapolis: Hackett Publishing Co.). [Essential reading for environmentalist theories of property.]

Plantinga, A. (1993) *Warrant*, 2 vols. (Oxford: Oxford University Press). [An account of cognition that is linked to the goodness of nature and God.]

Rousseau, Jean-Jacques (1979 [1762]) *Emile or on Education*, Translated by Allan Bloom (New York: Basic Books). [An extensive treatment of education in light of the goodness of nature.]

——(1984) *A Discourse on Inequality*, trans. M. Cranston (Middlesex: Penguin Books). [Flamboyant, engaging text in praise of nature.]

Russell, Jeffrey Burton (1991) *Inventing the Flat Earth* (New York: Praeger). [Blasts some misconceptions of the medieval period.]

Spinoza, Benedict (1909) *Spinoza's Works*, vols. I and II (London: George Bell and Sons). [Spinoza's *Ethics* (available in several translations) is highly recommended, especially Parts IV and V.]

Further reading

Taliaferro, Charles (1994) *Consciousness and the Mind of God* (Cambridge: Cambridge University Press). [An effort to redress the conflict between materialism and dualism, a conflict that defines much of modern philosophy.]

10

Nineteenth- and twentieth-century philosophy

ANDREW BRENNAN

The eighteenth-century legacy

Two figures dominated the nature philosophies of the late eighteenth century – the German philosopher Immanuel Kant (1704–84) and the Swiss thinker Jean-Jacques Rousseau (1712–78). Both capture the fascination of Romanticism with wild nature, and with the dignity and freedom of the individual. In his aesthetics of the sublime, Kant draws attention to the way that nature can be awe-inspiring and fearsome. His *Critique of Judgment*, argued that the fear engendered by the power of nature, say an erupting volcano, challenges our powers of reason to master the fear. This is one kind of "sublime" experience; another occurs when our imagination is unable to comprehend the vastness of the Milky Way or a towering mountain. The spine-tingling sense of the sublime arises, so Kant thought, from the combination of displeasure we feel that our imagination is unable to comprehend the absolutely great, and pleasure in our pure capacity of thinking which gives us the ability to comprehend the limitations of our imagination.

Kant believed that contemplation of nature could result in experiences of sublime beauty only if it was disinterested, and free from all taint of desire or concern with practical situations. Such experience makes us aware of a relationship we have with the world which is in part mystical, for it lies beyond the scope of our everyday empirical knowledge which is subject to two things: the categories of the understanding and the forms of sense perception. Experiences of the sublime somehow enable us to transcend the everyday so that beauty can become, as Kant put it, "the symbol of the good."

It would be in keeping with Kant's conception of aesthetic experience to regard nature rather than the art gallery as a good place for getting in touch with beauty. The gallery is, after all, a place of everyday distractions, while in wild nature, by contrast, the lonely aesthete can be free from such diversions. It seems appropriate that the final work of the eighteenth century's most prominent nature philosopher, Rousseau, should be the *Reveries* (1776) of a solitary walker. Driven to solitude he walked "alone in the world, with no brother, neighbor or friend, not any company left me but my own." Going beyond Kant's focus on human experience, the *Reveries* depict nature itself as valuable in its own right:

> No one imagines that the structure of plants could deserve any attention in its own right...Linger in some meadow studying one by one all the flowers that adorn it,

and people will take you for a herbalist and ask you for something to cure the itch in children, scab in men, or glanders in horses . . . These medicinal associations . . . tarnish the color of the meadows and the brilliance of the flowers, they drain the woods of all freshness and make the green leaves and shade seem dull and disagreeable. . . . It is no use seeking garlands for shepherdesses among the ingredients of an enema. (Rousseau 1979, p. 110)

Rousseau used botanical images and the smells of flowers to transport him back to his past, so that he was able to interpret and reinterpret events from his life. In this way the *Reveries* anticipate not only present-day demands for treating nature as of value in its own right, but also contemporary philosophies of place.

Rousseau speculated that what really distinguishes humans from the animals is our "perfectibility." If we considered a group of animals at one time, and then studied a similar group five hundred years later we would find no change in their patterns of behavior. By contrast, humans are born free, able to make choices, and hence able to create a history and culture for themselves. This gives us possibilities of progress and improvement, or of regress and impairment. By nature, he argued, we are much more like animals than was allowed by other philosophers, such as the English political philosopher Thomas Hobbes (1588–1679). Hobbes depicted the natural state for humans as one of war of each against all, one in which the life of man is "solitary, poor, nasty, brutish and short." Civilization rescued us from this state of barbarism. Anticipating modern ethology, Rousseau regarded Hobbes as completely misguided on this. Primitive humans, Rousseau argued, would share with the apes two significant features – first, the desire to preserve their own lives; second, compassion for the suffering of others. In Rousseau's view, then, the state of nature would be one in which we looked out for ourselves, while caring also for others. Hobbes's war of all against all, he thought, is only possible once moral depravity has been established by our choices. This state would not be a state of nature, but a result of becoming civilized. It is the vices of civilization – vanity and selfishness – which oust our natural compassion for others.

Despite many insightful discussions, Rousseau nowhere articulates an ethic as explicit as the one hinted at a century earlier by the Renaissance essayist Michel de Montaigne (1533–92): "there is a kind of respect and a duty in man as a genus which link us not merely to the beasts, which have life and feelings, but even to trees and plants" ("On Cruelty," Montaigne 1991 [1588], p. 488). Rousseau's ethological and botanical work is exemplary for its time, however, and far better than Montaigne's. In the absence of an articulated ethic, it can be argued that implicit in Rousseau's writings is an approach to nature that emphasizes the continuities between humans and animals, a celebration of nature's intrinsic value and a respect for other forms of life for their own sake. His conception of nature as a domain of cooperation rather than purely one of struggle of each against all was revived late in the nineteenth century, when it served as an antidote to Darwinian, and social Darwinist, depictions of nature as ruthlessly competitive (see EARLY MODERN PHILOSOPHY).

Philosophy in the late eighteenth century reflected and encouraged the emergence of Romanticism in the arts. The increasing interest in nature as a source of artistic inspiration, and as the location for wild and romantic adventures (see, for example, the novels of Sir Walter Scott (1771–1832)), was endorsed and legitimated by the philosophies of Kant and Rousseau. As the eighteenth century drew to a close, it is perhaps not surprising that two poets gave voice to a form of environmental ethic. The first, Robert Burns (1756–96), a farmer and plowman from Ayrshire, found common cause with the mouse whose nest he turned over while at work:

> I'm truly sorry man's dominion
> Has broken nature's social union
> An' justifies that ill opinion
>   Which makes thee startle
> At me, thy poor earth-born companion,
>   An' fellow-mortal!
> ("To a Mouse", 1785)

The reference to "man's dominion" and to "nature's social union" picks up two strands of thought that are grounded in Christian attitudes to the natural world. Dominion over the fish of the sea, the fowl of the air, and all other living things is said to be the lot of humanity according to the book of Genesis. The same Christian tradition has resources for two other conceptions of our relations to nature. Burns's plowman himself represents one of them: a respectful attitude of stewardship toward plants and animals. The farmer's reflections on the damage done by the necessary tilling of the fields shows his sensitive recognition that both he and the mouse are fellow-citizens of a world which neither of them has created. Many of Burns's other poems show compassion for animals, including insects, drawing often poignant comparisons between their lives and the human condition.

There is a further suggestion in the Burns poem. This is that human dominion has supplanted an earlier "social union" in which both plowman and mouse were in some sense "equal" citizens of the natural world. According to this, more radical, version of Christian environmentalism, celebrated in the myth of Eden, Adam and Eve were originally members of a biological community within which they lived lives of comfort and plenty. After tasting the forbidden fruit, however, they developed the capacity to judge for themselves what is right and wrong, good and bad. The fall into sin is, on this interpretation, the result of usurping God's role as the judge of right and wrong (see CHRISTIANITY, and the discussion in Callicott 1994, pp. 14–21). The myth of a golden age of ecological innocence followed by a fall from grace as a result of adopting agriculture, industrialism, or capitalism is a recurrent theme of subsequent reformist writers, from the socialism of Pierre-Joseph Proudhon (1809–65) right up to contemporary radical ecologists.

The English poet Samuel Taylor Coleridge (1772–1834) was a pantheist for a time before giving up this "living atheism." Nonetheless he retained a belief in the healing power of nature and held that a youth spent wandering "like a breeze / By lakes and sandy shores" was educationally preferable to anything on offer in the great city schools. His most famous ballad, *The Rime of the Ancient Mariner*, has a powerful conservationist message. Of special interest is the way the curse is lifted from the Ancient Mariner. About to die, surrounded by the corpses of his fellow-sailors, he blesses, of all things, the sea-snakes around his ship. Instead of being repelled by the mats of poisonous snakes, the condemned mariner is struck by their beauty:

> Beyond the shadow of the ship,
>   I watched the water-snakes:
> They moved in tracks of shining white,
>   And when they reared, the elfish light
>   Fell off in hoary flakes.
>
> Within the shadow of the ship
>   I watched their rich attire:
> Blue, glossy green, and velvet black,
>   They coiled and swam; and every track
>   Was a flash of golden fire.
>
> O happy living things! no tongue
>   Their beauty might declare:
> A spring of love gushed from my heart,
>   And I blessed them unaware:
> Sure my kind saint took pity on me,
>   And I blessed them unaware.
>
> The self same moment I could pray;
>   And from my neck so free
> The Albatross fell off, and sank
>   Like lead into the sea.
>   (*The Rime of the Ancient Mariner*, 1798)

On the interpretation that humans have unlimited dominion over the earth and over every creeping thing upon it, there would be no grounds for criticizing the mariner for having shot the albatross. On a stewardship interpretation, however, his action was irresponsible. Finally, on the radical account of the state of nature as a social union, the mariner's action continued our alienation from the earlier innocent state. By taking on a power that is properly God's – the right of deciding what is good and what is evil – humans set themselves apart from the rest of creation, thus calling forth the primordial curses of painful childbirth and having to toil to produce food. The Ancient Mariner likewise carried a curse for the rest of his life. While blessing the sea-snakes led to immediate improvement in the situation and the miraculous awakening of his shipmates, he was fated to wander the world telling his cautionary tale to others. Coleridge's poem resonates with fundamental chords of the Judeo-Christian tradition. His work, like Burns's, might be seen as evoking, in the dying years of the eighteenth century, a new environmental sensitivity which called for valuing and respecting nature beyond its usefulness to human purposes. The call was not to be answered for some time (see LITERATURE).

Idealism and nature philosophy

The philosophical agenda of the nineteenth century was not set by Kant's aesthetic of the sublime nor by Rousseau's dreams. No ethic of the environment was articulated to capture the feelings evoked by Burns and Coleridge. Instead, philosophy in the new century became entangled in working through a different legacy also bequeathed by Kant – idealism. In his theory of knowledge, Kant had emphasized the contribution made by subjects to what they know. For example, we see things around us as being in spatial relations to each other, but the space is *in us*, a form of sensibility that we impose on what we sense. Likewise, the understanding imposes fundamental conceptual structures on what we know. Kant called these the categories of the understanding. For Kant, all our knowledge of ourselves and the world ultimately depends on sense perception and understanding. He was forced, then, to the conclusion that things as they are in themselves are not only unknown to us but forever unknowable. The logical conclusion to Kant's speculations was that we do have knowledge, but only of the world as we structure it.

For many early nineteenth-century thinkers there seemed to be only one way to go in the face of Kant's findings. If all our knowledge of things in the world was likely to be skewed by our own forms of representation, then the world only appears on the scene – so to speak – given the existence of a human mind equipped with its own forms of knowledge. To try to say what there is independent of our knowledge would be to attempt to say the unsayable.

The nature philosophy of the German thinker Friedrich Schelling (1775–1854) involved just this recognition of the limits to what can be said. For Schelling, the whole sequence of things that happen in the "outer world" had to be deduced from ideas that arise in the mind as an activity of the mind. The objective world was no more than a determining result of the mind. Unlike his teacher Johann Fichte (1762–1814), Schelling saw the human mind and the natural world as two aspects of one supra-individual thing: a self-creating cosmos, which might be called "God." The two aspects meet in the synthesis of art which unites nature and history. Art, Schelling claimed, is nature made conscious. When an Australian radical ecologist declared not long ago that he was the rainforest become conscious, his remark was pure Schelling.

Georg Hegel (1770–1831), frustrated by Schelling's obscurity, complained that his intellectualized pantheism was like the "depth of night in which all cows are black." Despite this, Schelling's philosophy had influences outside the subject. His ideas were taken up enthusiastically by the Swiss biologist Jean Louis Aggassiz (1807–73) who became the chief opponent of Charles Darwin's (1809–82) theory of evolution by natural selection. Heavily influenced by Schelling's later work, Aggassiz argued that nature was a storehouse of divine thoughts expressed in living realities. Once the presence of divinity in nature was admitted, this gave grounds for urging the protection and preservation of nature.

There are odd echoes of Schelling and Hegel later in the century in the crudely materialist thought of Ernst Haeckel (1834–1919), the German naturalist who first coined the term "ecosystem." Haeckel tried to merge pantheism with Darwinian naturalism by insisting, first, that humans and the rest of the universe are all simply physical things, and, second, that even at the most elementary levels material stuff is combined with spirit (*Geist*) or force (*Kraft*). Since all of reality is pervaded by this living spirit, a certain reverence for the world as a whole – regarded as a naturalized version of the God of Christianity – is mandated. The term *Geist* was a key term in Hegel's philosophy where it represented the common intelligence in which all human beings participate. This general mind – according to Hegel – is spread through all of reality including nature, and has developed through history. In a superficial way, Haeckel's nature philosophy appears like a materialist reinterpretation of the earlier idealists. Although some writers have been tempted to depict him as providing a metaphysical foundation for a "land ethic," Haeckel's arguments are too crude and simple-minded to be taken as a serious contribution to any form of metaphysics.

Mud and gold

By the middle of the nineteenth century, pantheism and the hopes of the romantics were challenged by the claim that humans were both the measure and the makers of beauty. This idea finds expression in an arresting remark by the French poet Charles Baudelaire (1821–67): "God gave me mud and I made gold of it." While the romantics found the divine in nature, Baudelaire seemed to think it was only the infusion of the artist's personal and human vision which gave nature any aesthetic value at all. In a century which saw an unparalleled expansion of industrialism, it was perhaps not surprising that modern visions came to focus on the human as the inspired creator of gold from mud.

By the mid-century there was already a clear tension between those who saw nature only as the mud, and those who would respect and cherish the soil. This opposition was to reach its clearest theoretical expression in the opposition between Karl Marx (1818–85) and Pierre-Joseph Proudhon (1809–65). Although there are hints of a care for nature in Marx's early theories of estrangement or alienation, in his mature work he depicts nature as mechanical and inorganic, providing resources which are given value only by human labor. For all its evils, capitalism has at least civilized humans by enabling them to escape from the worship of nature's "all-powerful and unassailable force."

Proudhon's complaint that property is theft and that humans no longer love the soil resonated with some of Marx's early remarks on the alienation of humans from nature, but thereafter the two thinkers divided. Proudhon championed mutualism and decentralization, trusting that small groups would be best equipped for managing their own affairs, and that these district-level communities would form networks of communication and trade with each other so that the tyranny of large-scale centralized government could be avoided. Contemporary bioregionalists espouse similar hopes nowadays, purged of Proudhon's unfortunate anti-feminist commitments. For them and Proudhon, the land is to be cherished, respected, and preserved, not "tortured, violated, and exhausted" in the impatient desire for profits at all costs.

In the second part of the nineteenth century there is a movement represented by Antoni Gaudi (1852–1926) in Spain, and by William Morris (1834–96) and John Ruskin (1819–1900) in Britain. This movement was at odds with mass-production, emphasizing instead the uniqueness of place and the importance of local skills. For Ruskin and Morris, industrialism meant further degradation of the poor, a lifetime of being tied to repetitive and unfulfilling work. Deploring the poor standards of design and craftsmanship of the new industrial age, Morris exploded: "It is a shoddy age. Shoddy is king. From the statesman to the shoemaker, all is shoddy." As an antidote, his *News From Nowhere* (1890) described an ecotopian vision of worthwhile voluntary labor in scattered rural workshops in a society where everyone has plenty of space and abundant produce to enjoy, while crime, marriage, money, and private property have all been abolished.

By the turn of the nineteenth and twentieth centuries, the well-to-do would be familiar with telephones and cameras, they would have sampled food and other goods from all over the world, and could have confidence that medical interventions would have some significant chance of success in healing their ailments. Labor was mobile too, and at the disposal of ever more mechanized industry geared to mass-production at the lowest unit cost. Against the march of business, industrial, and scientific progress, Ruskin, Gaudi, and Morris seemed to be out of step with their times. Yet, surprisingly, there was still no general philosophical or ethical ground for their position. The articulation of an appropriate ethic and metaphysical world-view had to await the twentieth century. Before that could happen, other influences outside academic philosophy had to make themselves felt. Two of particular importance stand out. First, there was the revolution in nineteenth-century biology represented by the theory of evolution. Second was the establishment of sociology and the associated conception of organicism.

Evolution and naturalism

Early in the century, the English writer Thomas Malthus (1766–1834) had already achieved fame through the publication of two essays on the "Principle of Population" (published in 1798 and 1803). Charles Darwin (1809–82) cited Malthus as a major influence on his thinking about natural selection through the "struggle for existence" and Malthus is still quoted nowadays either approvingly by those who see him as the pioneer of population studies, or disapprovingly by those who regard him as the advocate of loathsome policies against the poor. Early in his career, Malthus had been much impressed with the possibility of thinking about human population on analogy with Newton's first law of motion. This states, roughly, that a freely accelerating body will continue forever in a uniform motion along a straight line unless checked or diverted by some other force. Malthus deemed there to be a similar "law" of population which meant that population would tend to increase exponentially unless checked by other forces. These forces themselves were the natural checks such as disease and famine. Any intervention to alleviate poverty, Malthus argued, would simply defer the day of reckoning. It followed that poverty itself was not so much a social evil as the result of the inevitable operation of natural laws.

Despite his appeal to laws of nature, Malthus inconsistently added to his second essay on population the claim that "moral restraint" can itself be a factor in limiting population growth. This had been prompted by an attack on the earlier essay in which the anarchist William Godwin (1756–1836) had argued that careful husbandry would surely increase the earth's fecundity while moral restraint would lead to a harmonious leveling of population. In taking Godwin's criticism on board, Malthus fell into a trap which has snared many subsequent writers on culture and nature. On the one hand, a naturalistic approach to human life depicts us as subject to causal laws. On the other, humans seem to have some scope for moral freedom. Malthus seemed to want to have it both ways.

The Puritan in Malthus was revealed when he considered why God should have made things so that the eaters' power of reproduction should so outstrip the means of the planet to feed their offspring. His answer was that we are not meant patiently to submit to the inevitable calamity. Rather, God's intention is that we work, work from which emerges progress and civilization. Malthus saw himself as providing a hard-headed and much-needed antidote to the utopians of the day who argued that the "natural" state of humans was one of comfort and enjoyment. It is the savage who has the life of ease (or "sloth"). As more acres are subdued by the plow, and humans struggle to feed their swelling numbers, so the waste and wild places of the earth will be tamed and brought to order, and human progress is maintained.

The problem of nature and its relation to culture had been deepened, but by no means resolved, by the publication in 1859 of Charles Darwin's *Origin of Species*. From the point of view of the history of ecology, Darwin is a more significant figure than Haeckel, and the *Origin* is rich in carefully reported ecological studies. However, in the absence of additional premises, the theory of evolution through natural selection does not give rise to any ethic, ecological or otherwise. Darwin himself went in one direction ethically; the co-discoverer of the theory of evolution, Alfred Russel Wallace (1823–1913), went another.

Darwin argued that his theory could not be restricted only to the development and change in the physical characteristics of animals. Consider, for example that one kind of bird has a long narrow beak adapted to exploring crevices, while on a nearby island a related population (belonging to the same species) has short strong beaks adapted to cracking seeds. Darwin reasoned that there must be other, invisible differences between the birds that accompany these morphological peculiarities. It is no use having a beak suitable for exploring crevices if the animal has no instinct to explore crevices. The conclusion was obvious. Not only morphology, but also instincts and characteristic behaviors, must have been produced by the steady working of natural selection.

What then of human beings? Our moral faculties, Darwin proposed, were a sophisticated development of more primitive behaviors found among the social animals (*The Descent of Man*, 1871). To reach the conclusion that human morality was a product of evolutionary processes, Darwin had to make the untestable assumption that similar effects are always the product of similar causes. Put crudely, the reasoning was this: moral behavior, such as friendliness, generosity, loyalty, compassion for others, and so on, seems superficially similar to some naturally evolved behaviors among the social animals; hence moral behavior is a product of natural selection. Darwin himself was nowhere so explicit in stating this argument. He was careful to leave some space for specifically human reasoning about ethics by insisting that only humans have (self-)consciousness, and that without consciousness there is no scope for reasoning about conduct and behavior.

Wallace had no doubt that the theory of evolution through natural selection was right. However, he was unwilling to endorse Darwin's conclusion that human ethics is "founded upon" the same social instincts that can be observed in several of the higher mammal species. In *Darwinism* (1890), Wallace used a simple analogy, appropriate given the important role that geology had played in the development of the theory of evolution. Consider, he asked, the various forces that have played a part in shaping the earth, especially those of erosion, the weather, volcanoes, and earth-quakes. We might think that any change to the earth was due only to these causes. However, with the discovery of glaciation, an entirely different kind of cause was encountered. Spelling out the point, Wallace wrote: "Because man's physical structure has been developed from an animal form by natural selection, it does not necessarily follow that his mental nature . . . has been developed by the same causes only." Nearly a century later, biologists and philosophers of biology are still recapitulating the Darwin–Wallace debate.

A potent aspect of the nineteenth-century revolution in biology was the appreciation of interconnections among living things. Darwin himself had emphasized that competition was at its fiercest within species and between closely related species which were struggling to use the same resources. Things apparently remote from each other on nature's scale were often linked in unexpected ways, so that interference with one plant or animal population could produce rapid and surprising changes among other populations in the same area. As he put it: "plants and animals remote in the scale of nature, are bound together by a web of complex relations." It did not take long before this scientific endorsement seemed to give credence to notions such as holism or "organicism" and even to the vitalism of Henri Bergson (1859–1941).

It has often been remarked that the nineteenth century has been the source of the twentieth century's most contested problems and puzzles. Certainly, there seems no more agreement nowadays than there was at the close of the nineteenth century on the matter of nature and culture. To what extent humans are distinct from nature, to what extent culture is non-natural, remains as puzzling as ever. A new school of anti-naturalism was born in the twilight of the nineteenth century, inspired by the *Logical Investigations* of Edmund Husserl (1859–1938). The resulting phenomenological movement, as it came to be called, produced further work on nature, including Max Scheler's (1874–1928) treatise, *Man's Place in Nature*. Its most significant influence on environmental philosophy, however, is found in the work of Husserl's student Martin Heidegger (1889–1976), who emerged as the most significant philosopher of nature in the first half of the twentieth century. Heidegger rejected the Cartesian conception of the world as lifeless machinery, a conception that left nature open to abuse, exploitation, and destruction.

Sociology, organicism, and anarchism

Perhaps the pre-eminent figure outside the natural sciences in the late nineteenth century was Herbert Spencer (1820–1903), the thinker who supplied Darwin with the phrase "survival of the fittest." Whereas Darwin often treated evolution as the changing distribution of characteristics in a population through time, Spencer thought of it as the unfolding of some pre-existing plan. The direction of evolution, he claimed, was always from the simple, and less differentiated to the complex. Complexity was defined by two complementary features: differentiation of the parts of the evolving system, on the one hand, and their mutual interdependence (or integration) on the other. As the more complex and integrated systems appear, they displace, so the theory went, the less complex ones.

Bold though his theory was, Spencer's account of evolution did not fit natural systems: simple structures sometimes have great survival value and do not always yield to the complex in the struggle for existence. However, the principle of the "survival of the fittest" seems to work for some kinds of social organization, if fitness is defined in terms of organizational complexity. A large nation-state, for example, is unlikely to be defeated in any struggle for existence with a smaller, less organized state. If war drives social evolution, then the history of human societies ought to provide many examples of the complex – more socially evolved – defeating the less complex in the struggle for existence. Spencer's theories on language, the family, religion, and art, summarized in his *Principles of Sociology* (1876–96), are built on this conception of progressive evolution and had enormous influence on the development of both sociology and anthropology.

From organicism combined with Spencer's evolutionism arose social Darwinism, the view that those who triumphed in political and commercial competition with their rivals must be the fittest. The link between fitness and moral justification is of course not a necessary one. It only follows once some other assumptions are made. One of these is that the universal evolutionary trend from simple to complex is good. It follows, so the social Darwinists thought, that those who are winners in the struggle for existence are promoting the greater good, hence deserve moral praise. Spencer himself held back from the extremist social Darwinist position, emphasizing that the social organism required cooperation as well as competitiveness among its parts.

Social Darwinism fell prey to its own conceptual problems. Those who embraced the new mechanism, materialism, and naturalism were comfortable with the idea that novel values could be brought to bear on human activity. Selfishness and greed were no longer vices, but perhaps naturally present in all of us. Colonialism was no more than the progress of evolution by which the strong subdued and even elimi-nated the weak in the struggle for existence. The extreme versions of social Darwin-ism were happy to combine ideals of natural progress through social evolution, with a loathing for the primitive and fallen state of some parts of nature and humanity.

Clearly, maintaining both faith in – and disgust with – nature at the same time was not a stable position. For those who, like Haeckel, insisted on taking nature as a guide to truth, the main thing was to learn how to organize society on the basis of models provided by observation of nature. Philosophically, John Stuart Mill (1806–73) provided a compelling response to this. His essay, *Nature*, supplied a powerful attack on those who tried to deduce morality from nature. If all that humans do is "natural," Mill pointed out, then the claim that we should follow nature is morally empty, for we can do no other. By contrast, if we have a choice over whether to follow our "natural" inclinations or the dictates of reason and morality, then the claim that we should follow nature is odious and morally repellent.

Spencer's organicism paved the way for process philosophy and the organicism of Alfred North Whitehead (1861–1947), as well as for the holism defended by Jan Smuts (1870–1950). These thinkers maintained that the relation of part to whole in complex systems means that the whole system is more than merely the sum of its parts. Recognizing the interactions of part and whole means that we can begin to give some account of the apparently creative aspects of evolution, and that we can explain the benefits of collective association, as of trees in a forest. "In nature," Whitehead writes, "the normal way in which trees flourish is by their association in a forest. Each tree may lose something of its individual perfection of growth, but they mutually assist each other in preserving the conditions for survival" (1925, p. 244). Whitehead's application of his view to human societies, however, has the drawback that individuality and justice may have to be sacrificed for the greater good of the whole (see Palmer 1998).

Mutual assistance was also a key idea in the thought of Peter Kropotkin (1842–1921), Russian prince, geographer, and revolutionary anarchist, who expressed what he called "serious doubts" about Darwin's idea of inter-specific competition in the struggle for existence. Kropotkin argued that although such competition did exist, it paled into relative insignificance beside the terrible challenges posed by snowfalls, droughts, flooding, and the other natural hazards of existence. His speculation was that where animal life was in abundance "mutual aid and mutual support [was] carried on to an extent which made me suspect in it a feature of the greatest importance for the maintenance of life, the preservation of each species and its further evolution."

Kropotkin's observations convinced him that mutual aid was the basis on which sustainable human societies could be built. These would be decentralized, self-regulating networks of communes, with only the occasional large industrial concentrations which are "better placed at certain spots indicated by Nature." Trusting to future technological advances, he also believed that the towns and factories of the future would be able to combine the benefits of both rural and urban life. Underlying this utopia would be a revived and transformed medievalism, for Kropotkin regarded the medieval cities with their craft guilds, religious communities, and other focal groups as approximating to the ideal anarchist state. Also important was the creative spirit of the masses, supported by the tradition of mutual aid. Note again that the existence of cooperation in nature does not, without extra argument, lend moral weight to Kropotkin's view that anarchism is the best form for a polity. Kropotkin's arguments have been a major source in shaping the doctrines of contemporary eco-anarchists, especially Ivan Illich (1926–) and Murray Bookchin (1921–). In the case of the latter theorist (as noted in Keulartz 1999), there is also a striking similarity between parts of his theory and the holism of Jan Smuts.

Behind the optimism of Kropotkin lurk connections to two other trends. First, his conception of factories opening to fields is a reminder that the garden city movement, championed by Ebenezer Howard (1850–1928), flourished briefly early in the twentieth century and left a mark on subsequent architecture and planning. Second is the question of the city. The suspicion of cities is not as pronounced in Kropotkin as the loathing shown by Ruskin and Morris, or in Frank Lloyd Wright's (1867–1959) later description of the city as a kind of cancer. The nineteenth-century city was, however, widely seen to be a problem. A major issue for theorists early in the twentieth century was to decide on an appropriate form for, and attitude to, the city. Was it a blot on the landscape, a place of depravity and human degradation? Or was it a place of love, discovery, liberation, and joy? It was perhaps inevitable that the urban environment should attract the attention of geographers and biologists alike, calling forth the special attention of the eccentric Scottish biologist Patrick Geddes (1854–1932) and his disciple Lewis Mumford (1895–1988).

The city and the country

A huge migration from country to town in the rapidly industrializing parts of Europe (replicated some time later in the United States) changed the shape and styles of cities with stupendous rapidity. Patrick Geddes, a Glaswegian who came under the influence of Darwin's follower T. H. Huxley while studying biology in London, theorized that the body and the city developed along parallel lines. To take this view, he had to depart from Huxley's conception of a bloodthirsty and competitive nature. Instead, he followed Spencer's conception of society as an organism.

In his *Evolution of Sex* (1889), Geddes theorized that the two sexes exemplify two different "rhythms," manifested even in the different behavior of sperm and ovum. The one was outgoing, characterized by bouts of energy, exploration, and conquest. The other was passive, emotional, nurturing, altruistic, sociable. The two kinds of trait were called katabolic and anabolic, respectively. In his new version of the yang and the yin, Geddes maintained that a healthy society, and a healthy city, required both sets of trait to be exemplified, and to be in balance with each other.

Like Kropotkin, Geddes admired the medieval city, with its spacious market areas and healthy mix of distinct communities. Too rapid an expansion of the city into its surrounding country, he claimed, upsets the balance, as the katabolic qualities of industrial expansion become expressed and the anabolic ones are quashed. Howard's proposal for garden cities was seen by Geddes as a useful device for developing the expression of anabolic traits. In addition to his generalized sociobiological arguments, Geddes was also quick to point out that economic calculations were not a good measure of physical efficiency. Like Gifford Pinchot (1865–1946) whom he admired (he called him America's "national forester"), Geddes pointed out the physical inefficiency and wastefulness associated with the impact of unplanned and speculative railway building and property development. Never a great stylist, or very clear writer, it was left to his disciple Lewis Mumford to popularize Geddes's theories and continue the quest to raise consciousness over the meaning and planning of the city environment. The city can be an "organ of love", according to Mumford, but only if its maternal, life-nurturing functions are restored and a healthy balance regained between anabolism and katabolism.

Wilderness and the loss of Being

The establishment of national parks and reserves in the nineteenth century testified to an early recognition that untrammeled industrialism and colonial expansion threatened to destroy valuable landscapes, species, and systems. In the United States the Scot John Muir (1838–1914), spending his first summer in California's Sierra Nevada in 1869, found himself full of admiration for its natural splendors. All around him he saw the beauties of God's creation, spoilt only by intrusions of human origin:

> with her choicest treasures, spending plant beauty as she spends sunshine, pouring it forth into land and seas, garden and desert. And so the beauty of the lilies falls on angels and men, bears and squirrels, wolves and sheep, birds and bees, but, as far as

I have seen, man alone, and the animals he tames, destroy these gardens. (Muir 1911, p. 56)

The value of wild nature seemed for Muir to consist in two features: one was its beauty and the other was that, from his perspective as a theist, to experience it was a way of experiencing the divine (as argued by Schelling). Muir's energetic and enthusiastic defense of WILDERNESS established two strands in contemporary environmental thinking. First, human intervention in natural systems is liable to degrade them, and therefore, if we care for the beauty, richness, diversity, and creativity of nature, we will want to keep some parts of it wild and free from interference. A second, and morally less agreeable strand in Muir is his misanthropy and apparent indifference to slavery and other suffering of humans. A similar misanthropy pervades some of the recent literature in environmental ethics and conservation biology.

In the development of modern conservation-consciousness in the United States, Muir's life and thought can be contrasted with Gifford Pinchot's. Pinchot was a major figure in the development of the US forest service, and – like Muir – cared about nature, especially forests. However, Pinchot insisted that natural features contain resources for humans and are thus of instrumental value. However, he deplored what he described as "the gigantic and gigantically wasteful lumbering of the great Sequoias, many of whose trunks were so huge they had to be blown apart before they could be handled." He wrote: "I resented then, and I still resent, the practice of making vine stakes hardly bigger than walking sticks out of these greatest of all living things" (Pinchot 1947, pp. 102–3).

The ethics and politics of Pinchot did not involve any direct concern for trees and landscapes, any more than Geddes valued cities for themselves. They constituted a human-centered environmental ethic driven by concern for distributional equity, quality of human life, and meeting the needs of future generations. Pinchot's interest in intergenerational fairness was influenced by the writings of W. J. McGee (1853–1912), a self-taught scientist described by Pinchot as the "scientific brains" of the American conservation movement. By contrast, in Muir's early writings the beauty in nature was portrayed as being of value independent of any use to which natural things can be put. This conception of independent aesthetic value gives sense to the following moral position: that it is wrong to destroy natural things unnecessarily, or – more positively – that it is right to set aside some wild areas that will be free from human meddling. There seemed to be two paradigms here: Pinchot and McGee with a philosophy of wise use, Muir with the idea that nature had value in itself independent of human purposes. (See META-ETHICS.)

Some commentators (see Norton 1991) have argued that the opposition between the two positions does not run very deep. Perhaps a synthesis can be found in Aldo Leopold's land ethic. Ethics had to be extended to the land, he argued:

> When god-like Odysseus returned from the wars in Troy, he hanged all on one rope a dozen slave-girls of his household whom he suspected of misbehavior during his absence. This hanging involved no question of propriety; the girls were property.... There is as yet no ethic dealing with man's relation to land and to the animals and plants which grow upon it. Land, like Odysseus' slave-girls, is still

property.... The extension of ethics to this... element in human environment is... an evolutionary possibility and an ecological necessity. (Leopold 1949, pp. 201–3)

The final sentence echoes the sociobiological approach of Geddes and Kropotkin. Like Muir, Leopold was concerned with wilderness and the values to be found in it – hardly surprising given his lifelong interest in hunting and love of treks into the wild. Like Pinchot, he recognized that nature was a source of food, fiber, minerals, and sport for human beings. But Leopold urged farmers and foresters to avoid merely utility-based ways of thinking about the land. His land ethic, despite its somewhat simplistic and totalitarian character – "a thing is right when it tends to promote the integrity, beauty and stability of the land; it is wrong when it tends otherwise" – was a down-to-earth crystallization of many of the trends of the previous century (see THE LAND ETHIC).

By contrast, the more explicitly philosophical treatment in Heidegger focuses on a metaphysics of Being in general. The features of nature delimit a stage which admits our actions; but our actions in turn can help disclose these natural features. Archi-tecture and engineering are means of bringing a landscape into being: "The bridge gathers the earth as landscape around the stream.... It does not just connect banks that are already there. The banks emerge as banks only as the bridge crosses the stream." The contribution of the individual to the greater totality is to protect and articulate the place he or she has been given to take care of: "mortals dwell inasmuch as they save the earth." "To save really means to set something free into its own presencing.... Saving the earth does not master the earth and does not subjugate it, which is merely one step from spoilation." The essays (Heidegger 1971) from which these remarks are taken set a project for humans, a project in which they can let Being (das Sein) disclose itself. In particular, good building lets specific places stand forth, and allows humans to dwell poetically on the earth.

While Leopold's land ethic was firmly focused on the special significance of wild nature, Heidegger's more general approach to humans in relation to Being permitted the generation of both urban and wilderness ethics. Between them, and quite inde-pendently, a forester and a metaphysician had set the stage for the emergence of a new subdiscipline of philosophy.

References

Heidegger, Martin (1971) *Poetry, Language, Thought*, trans. A. Hofstadter (New York: Harper and Row). [A sample of Heidegger's later philosophy and poetry (1935–54).]

Keulartz, Josef (1995) *Strijd om de natuur: Kritiek van de radicale ecologie* (Amsterdam: Boom); English translation: *Struggle for Nature* (London: Routledge, 1999). [A detailed historical treatment of environmental ideas, with a critical focus on radical ecology and with a useful and careful account of the work of Geddes and Mumford.]

Leopold, Aldo (1949) *A Sand County Almanac* (New York: Oxford University Press). [The standard inspirational text for contemporary wilderness preservation movements.]

Montaigne, Michel de (1991 [1588]) *The Complete Essays*, trans. M. A. Screech (Harmonds-worth: Penguin). [In several passages, Montaigne anticipates contemporary sympathy for animals and concern for nature.]

Muir, John (1911 [1869]) *My First Summer in the Sierra* (Houghton Mifflin; new edition: Edinburgh: Cannongate Publishing, 1988). [Muir's ecstatic romancing of the Californian Sierra reveals his religious orientation and his sharp eye for the details of nature.]

Norton, Bryan (1991) *Toward Unity Among Environmentalists* (New York: Oxford University Press). [Norton provides a useful account of Muir's and Pinchot's differing orientations, suggesting that they reflect two different aspects of conservation awareness.]

Palmer, Clare (1998) "Identity, Community and the Natural Environment: Some Perspectives from Process Thinking," *Worldviews: Environment, Culture, Religion* 2 (1998), pp. 257–68. [Cautions against the political and ethical implications of process thinking, and organicism, which give little scope for anchoring liberal theories of justice.]

Pinchot, Gifford (1987 [1947]) *Breaking New Ground* (Island Press). [Pinchot's autobiography.]

Rousseau, Jean-Jacques (1979) *The Reveries of a Solitary Walker* (Harmondsworth: Penguin). [The "walks" are a combination of recollection with fictionalizing, containing some resources for environmental ethics, but combined with an overall sombreness of tone which suggests that human life can never guarantee contentment.]

Whitehead, Alfred North (1925) *Science and the Modern World* (Cambridge: Cambridge University Press). [This work outlines the fundamentals of Whitehead's process metaphysics, a theory in which things – including human subjects – are composed of events and processes, the latter being the fundamental categories of existence.]

Further reading

Callicott, J. Baird (1994) *Earth's Insights* (Berkeley: University of California Press). [A tour of various environmental philosophies, comparing them with the Leopold land ethic.]

Jamieson, Dale (1984) "The City Around Us," in Tom Regan *Earthbound: New Introductory Essays in Environmental Ethics*, ed. (Philadelphia: Temple University Press). [One of the few writers to deal with urban environmental ethics in the 1980s, Jamieson argued that we should trust the judgment of ordinary citizens in matters of town planning and design.]

Marshall, Peter (1992) *Nature's Web: An Exploration of Ecological Thinking* (London: Simon and Schuster). [Provides general overview and brief histories of major nineteenth- and twentieth-century figures in environmental thinking.]

Nordberg-Schulz, Christian (1988) "Heidegger's Thinking on Architecture," in *Architecture, Meaning and Place* (New York: Electa/Rizzoli), pp. 39–48. [Nordberg-Schulz purges Heidegger's work of some of its toxic associations, and uses it as a basis for a philosophy of architecture.]

Worster, Donald (1985 [1977]) *Nature's Economy: A History of Ecological Ideas* (originally published by Sierra Club Books; Cambridge: Cambridge University Press). [One of several histories of ecology which contains material that bears on the present chapter.]

PART II

CONTEMPORARY ENVIRONMENTAL ETHICS

11

Meta-ethics

JOHN O'NEILL

Meta-ethics and normative ethics

Meta-ethics is concerned with the status and nature of the ethical claims we make. As such, meta-ethics deals not with substantive questions *in* ethics but with questions *about* ethics – for example, whether or not ethical claims can be true or false, whether there is an ethical reality, whether ethical claims are open to rational justification. Substantive questions in ethics are the matter of NORMATIVE ETHICS. Normative ethics deals with particular ethical claims, including those at the center of environmental ethics concerning environmental change and its effects on human and non-human beings. Normative ethics often involves an attempt to offer systematic theoretical frameworks for the justification and articulation of such claims: Kantian, contractarian, utilitarian, and deep ecological theories provide standard examples of normative theories (see DEEP ECOLOGY).

A central question in meta-ethics is whether ethical utterances are assertions that can be true or false. The ethical realist holds that ethical statements are descriptions of states of the world and, in virtue of being so, they are like other fact-stating assertions, true or false independently of the beliefs of the speaker. On this view, it is the job of ethical judgments to track properties in the world, to get something right about the way the world is. Against ethical realism stand a variety of views. One is the error theory, according to which ethical statements are descriptions of the world, but they are all false – we project values on to a world and then talk as if they had independent existence (Mackie 1977). Another is expressivism, the view that ethical statements are not descriptions of the world at all; rather, they serve to express the attitudes of the speaker toward the world. On this view, if we sometimes say things like "it is true that destroying rain forests is wrong," the phrase "it is true that" serves only to give emphasis to the force of the attitude expressed. It should not be understood, as the realist supposes, as indicating that we are asserting something about states of the world that hold independently of the beliefs of the ethical agent. What of the way we use specific ethical concepts, such as "cruel," "kind," "cowardly," "brave," to both describe and appraise states of the world? Isn't it the case that to say that a farming practice is cruel is to state facts – that it involves the intentional infliction of pain? The expressivist answers that the descriptive component of specific concepts such as "cruel" can be prised apart from an evaluative component. We can analyze the concepts as a conjunction of a descriptive component that does the describing and an evaluative component expressing an attitude toward the act – a preference or feeling against it. To say an act is cruel is to say something like it causes intentional suffering and I disapprove of it. Someone might accept the factual component – that factory farming causes suffering – but reject the use of the concept "cruel" because they reject the attitude expressed about the practice.

The choice between realism and non-realist positions carries implications for a number of other meta-ethical questions about the status of ethical utterances. Are ethical judgments open to rational justification? Could we expect all rational agents to converge in their moral judgments? How are ethical judgments connected with actions? If one accepts a moral judgment is one necessarily motivated to act upon it? What is the relationship between general ethical concepts – good, bad, right, and wrong – and particular concepts – courageous, cowardly, kind, cruel, just, unjust, and the like?

Discussions in environmental ethics are enmeshed in meta-ethical controversies. If environmental ethics is primarily concerned with substantive issues, why should this be so? What relevance do such meta-ethical disputes have for environmental ethics? The answer is that where the relationship of humans to a non-human world is concerned, the pull of some form of realism about values has seemed to be particularly strong. Is the pull toward realism in environmental ethics a temptation to be resisted or one to which we should yield? To answer one way or another is to take a position on a general issue about the relation of meta-ethics and substantive issues in norma-ive ethics. There is a long-standing view that the two spheres of philosophical discussion should be kept separate (Mackie 1977, p. 16). Given that environmental ethics concerns substantive ethical issues, on this view, the excursion into meta-ethics is indicative of logical confusions in the literature. Alternatively, such excursions might give additional reasons for skepticism that meta-ethical and normative ethics can be kept separate (von Wright 1963, ch. 1).

Intrinsic value

One of the main sources of the realist pull in environmental ethics has been the claim that to hold an environmental ethic is to hold that beings and states of affair in the non-human world have "intrinsic value." This claim is taken to distinguish "deep" biocentric ethical theory from the more traditional "shallow" and anthropocentric counterparts. The term "intrinsic value," however, has a variety of senses, and many arguments on environmental ethics suffer from conflating them.

Intrinsic value is often used as a synonym for non-instrumental value. Objects, activities, and states of affair have instrumental value insofar as they are a means to some other end. They have intrinsic value if they are ends in themselves. It is a well-rehearsed point that, under pain of an infinite regress, not everything can have only instrumental value. There must be some objects, activities, and states that have intrinsic value. However, this concept of non-instrumental value is itself complex. It is sometimes predicated of objects, states, and activities that an agent pursues or aims at. Of activities, one might say a person climbs mountains or studies the behavior of birds for its own sake; the person might also be said to value mountains or birds for their own sake; or that he admires states of these for their own sake, the beauty of mountains, or the complexity of the bird's behavior. These activities, objects, and states are said to be ends in themselves for the person.

The use of non-instrumental value in this first sense is distinct from that employed, for example, by the eighteenth-century philosopher Immanuel Kant, when he claims that persons are ends in themselves. To assert a being is an end in itself in this Kantian sense is to assert that it has ethical standing. A central move in much environmental ethics has been to extend ethical standing beyond persons. To say that elephants, wolves, plants matter in the sense that their good must be considered in making choices is to assign standing to them. To say one values climbing mountains, the beauty of mountains, or mountains themselves for their own sake need not involve the ascription of any such standing. However, while the notions are distinct, there is a plausible claim to be made about the relation between them – that if y is of value to x, and x has ethical standing, then there is a prima facie ethical duty for ethical agents not to deprive x of y.

Intrinsic value is also used in a third sense, in a contrast with "extrinsic value," to refer to the value an object has solely in virtue of its intrinsic properties, that is, its non-relational properties. The concept is thus employed by G. E. Moore: "To say a kind of value is 'intrinsic' means merely that the question whether a thing possesses it, and in what degree it possesses it, depends solely on the intrinsic nature of the thing in question" (1922, p. 260).

Finally, intrinsic value is also used as a synonym for "objective value," i.e. value that an object possesses independently of the valuations of valuers (Mackie 1977, p. 15). If intrinsic value is used in this sense, to claim that non-human beings have intrinsic value is not to make an ethical but rather a meta-ethical claim. It is to assert a form of realism about values.

If a "deep" environmental ethic is taken to be a substantive ethical position, according to which some non-human beings have intrinsic value, then "intrinsic value" is being used in one of the first two senses: it is to hold that non-human beings are not simply of value as a means to human ends, but are ends in themselves, either in the sense of being valued for their own sake or more strongly of having ethical standing: "The well-being of non-human life on Earth has value in itself. This value is independent of any instrumental usefulness for limited human purposes" (Naess 1973, p. 266). However, it might be that to hold a defensible ethical position about the environment, one needs to be committed to the view that they also have intrinsic value in the third and fourth senses.

Is the rejection of meta-ethical realism compatible with an environmental ethic?

In much of the literature on environmental ethics the different senses of "intrinsic value" are used interchangeably. In particular, intrinsic value as non-instrumental value and as ethical standing is often conflated with intrinsic value as objective value. There is a widespread assumption that a rejection of a realist meta-ethics entails that non-humans can have only instrumental value. The assumption is made not just by defenders of an environmental ethic but also by some critics who reject it on meta-ethical grounds thus: to claim that items in the non-human world have intrinsic values commits one to a realist view of values; a realist view of values is indefensible; hence, the non-human world contains nothing of intrinsic value.

The claim that an environmental ethic is incompatible with the rejection of a realist meta-ethic is mistaken. A rejection of a realist meta-ethic does not commit one to the view that non-humans have only instrumental value. The apparent plausibility of the assumption that it does is founded on a confusion of claims about the source of values with claims about their object (Callicott 1989, ch. 8). An expressivist can be said to claim that the only source of value is the evaluative attitudes of humans. But this does not entail that the only ultimate objects of value are the states of human beings. Likewise, to hold a realist view of the source of value, according to which the value of an entity does not depend on the attitudes of valuers, is compatible with a thoroughly anthropocentric view of the object of value – that the only things which do in fact have value are humans and their states.

To expand, consider the expressivist meta-ethic. Evaluative utterances express a speaker's attitudes. They state no facts. Within the expressivist tradition Stevenson (1944) provides a clear account of intrinsic value. Intrinsic value is defined as non-instrumental value: "intrinsically good" is roughly synonymous with "good for its own sake, as an end, as distinct from good as a means to something else." Stevenson then offers the following account of what it is to say something has intrinsic value: "X is intrinsically good" asserts that the speaker approves of X intrinsically, and acts emotively to make the hearer or hearers likewise approve of X intrinsically (1944, p. 178). There are no reasons why the expressivist should not fill the X place by entities and states of the non-human world. There is nothing in the expressivist's meta-ethical position that precludes her holding basic attitudes that are biocentric. She can hold that non-humans have ethical standing. There is no reason why the expressivist must assume that either egoism or humanism is true, that is, that she must assign non-instrumental value only to her own or other humans' states.

It might be objected, however, that there are other difficulties in holding an expressivist meta-ethic and an environmental ethic. In making humans the source of all value, the expressivist is committed to the view that a world without humans contains nothing of value. Hence, while nothing logically precludes the expressivist assigning non-instrumental value to objects in a world which contains humans, it undermines some of the considerations that have led to the belief in the need to assign such value. For example, it is not compatible with the last man argument (Routley and Routley 1980, pp. 121–3). The argument runs thus: if non-humans only have instrumental value, then the last man whose last act was to destroy a forest would have done no wrong; the last man does do wrong; hence it is false that non-humans only have instrumental value. However, given an expressivist account of value the last man does no wrong, since a world without humans is without value. This objection, however, still confuses the source and object of value. There is nothing in expressivism that forces the expressivist to confine the objects of her attitudes to those that exist at the time at which she expresses them. Her moral utterances might express attitudes toward events and states of affairs over periods in which she no longer exists – she might express her preference that her great-grandchildren live in a world without poverty; over periods in which humans no longer exist – she might express her preference that rainforests exist after the extinction of the human species and hence deplore the vandalism of the last man; and over different possible worlds – she might concur with Leibniz (1646–1716) that this world is the best of all possible worlds, or, in her despair at the destructiveness of humans, express the attitude that it would have been better had humans never existed and hence a preference for a possible world in which humans never came into existence. That humans are the source of value is compatible with their expressing normative attitudes about worlds which they do not inhabit.

While the rejection of realism does not rule out non-humans having non-instrumental value, realist positions do not rule it in. To claim that moral utterances have a truth value is not to specify which utterances are true. The realist can hold that the moral facts are such that only the states of humans possess value in themselves: everything else has only instrumental value. Indeed, a common view of ethical realists earlier this century was that only states of conscious beings have intrinsic value, on the ground that any world without a mind would contain nothing good in itself.

What is the relation of the use of intrinsic value in the sense of non-instrumental value and objective value to the third Moorean-sense of intrinsic value – to the value an object has that "depends solely on the intrinsic nature of the thing in question" (Moore 1922, p. 260)? The intrinsic properties of an object are its non-relational properties. Many of the properties that are central to environmental valuation – rarity, species richness, biodiversity – are non-intrinsic in this Moorean sense. For example, rarity is an irreducibly relational property that cannot be characterized without reference to other objects. In practical concern about the environment a special status is often ascribed to rare entities. The preservation of endangered species of flora and fauna and of threatened habitats and ecological systems is a major practical environmental problem. It has been argued that such value can have no place in an environmental ethic which holds that non-humans have intrinsic value. However, such arguments rely upon an equivocation between "intrinsic value" in its Moorean sense and "intrinsic value" used as a synonym for non-instrumental value. Thus, while it may be true that if an object has only instrumental value it cannot have intrinsic value in the Moorean sense, for instrumental value is necessarily value predicated on a relational property of an object, it is false that an object of non-instrumental value is necessarily also of intrinsic value in the Moorean sense. We might value an object in virtue of its relational properties, for example its rarity, without thereby seeing it as having only instrumental value for human satisfactions.

Is it the case that if there is value that "depends solely on the intrinsic nature of the thing in question" then any denial of realism about values should be rejected? If an object has value only in virtue of its intrinsic nature, does it follow that it has value independent of human valuations? The answer depends on the interpretation given to the phrases "depends solely on" and "only in virtue of." If these are interpreted to exclude human evaluation and desires, as Moore intended, then the answer to both questions is immediately "yes" – to have intrinsic value would be to have objective value. However, there is a natural non-realist reading to the phrases. The non-realist can talk of the valuing agent assigning value to objects solely in virtue of their intrinsic natures. Given a liberal interpretation of the phrases, a non-realist can hold that some objects have intrinsic value in the Moorean sense.

The upshot of the discussion of this section is a traditional one – that meta-ethical commitments are logically independent of ethical ones. However, in the realm of environmental ethics it is one that needs to be reaffirmed. No meta-ethical position is required by an environmental ethic. In particular, one can hold such an ethic and deny realism. However, this is not to say that there might not be other reasons for holding a realist account of ethics and that some of these reasons might appear particularly pertinent when considering evaluative statements about non-humans. The realist pull might still be a rational one.

Objective value and the flourishing of living things

I have argued that the claim that nature has intrinsic value in the sense of non-instrumental value does not commit one to a realist meta-ethics. However, I left open the question as to whether there might be other reasons particularly pertinent in the field of environmental ethics that would lead us to hold a realist account of value. Is there anything about evaluations of the environment that make the case for realism especially compelling? Part of the pull for strong realism in the environmental sphere lies in a broadly Aristotelian observation that there is a sense in which we can talk of what it is for natural entities to flourish and what is good and bad for them without this being dependent upon human interests (Attfield 1987; Taylor 1986; Rolston 1988, ch. 3). Consider the gardener's use of the phrase "x is good for greenfly." The term "good for" can be understood in two distinct ways. It might refer to what is conducive to the destruction of greenfly, as in "detergent sprays are good for greenfly," or it can used to describe what causes greenfly to flourish, as in "mild winters are good for greenfly." The term "good for" in the first use describes what is instrumentally good for the gardener: given the ordinary gardener's interest in the flourishing of her rosebushes, detergent sprays satisfy that interest. The second use describes what is instrumentally good for the greenfly, quite independently of the gardener's interests. This instrumental goodness is possible in virtue of the fact that greenflies are the sorts of things that can flourish or be injured (von Wright 1963, ch. 3). In consequence, they have their own goods that are independent of both human interests and any tendency they might have to produce in human observers feelings of approval or disapproval. A living thing can be said to flourish if it develops those characteristics which are normal to the species to which it belongs in the normal conditions for that species. Correspondingly, the truth of statements about what is good for a living thing, what is conducive to its flourishing, depends on no essential reference to human observers. The use of the evaluative terms in the biological context does then provide good reasons for holding that some evaluative properties are real properties. Their use does tell for some kind of realism about the use of the term "good" and "goods."

What is the class of entities that can be said to possess such goods? In an influential passage von Wright identifies it with the class of living things: "The question 'What kinds or species of being have a good?' is therefore broadly identical with the question 'What kinds or species of being have a life'" (von Wright 1963, p. 50; cf. Taylor 1986, pp. 60–71). In doing so, he rejects the claim that social units such as families and political associations have their own good in any literal sense. In any literal sense their good is reducible to that of their members (von Wright 1963, pp. 50–1.). Whether this is correct is central to environmental questions, for it touches on the question of whether it makes sense to talk of the goods of collective biological entities – colonies, ecosystems, and so on – in a way that is irreducible to that of its members (see O'Neill 1993, pp. 20–2; see also SENTIENTISM).

If it is the case that individual living things and/or the collective entities of which they are members can be said, then, to have their own goods, there is ground for some kind of realism about some uses of the term "good." However, it leaves open whether the existence of such goods entails any human obligations and whether it gives any reason for realism about specifically ethical goods. It is standard in much environmental literature to argue that possession of goods does entail moral considerability: "moral standing or considerability belongs to whatever has a good of its own" (Attfield 1987, p. 21; cf. Rolston 1988, and Taylor 1986). However, this claim demands an argument. It is possible to talk in an objective sense of what constitutes the goods of entities, without making any claims that these ought to be realized. Our gardener knows what it is for greenfly to flourish, recognizes they have their own goods, and has a practical knowledge of what is good for them. No moral injunction follows. "Y is a good of X" does not immediately entail "Y ought to be realized" (Taylor 1986, pp. 71–2). This gap clearly raises problems for environmental ethics. The existence of objective goods was promising precisely because it appeared to show that items in the non-human world were objects of proper moral concern. Can the gap be bridged?

One influential argument runs roughly thus: since for any living being x there are objects and states of affairs $y_1 \ldots y_n$ that are of value to x, it follows that x values $y_1 \ldots y_n$. By consistency, if we value ourselves in virtue of being valuing agents then we have to extend this to all living things (Rolston 1988). The argument contains a number of errors. First, the inference from "y is of value to x" to "x values y" is invalid. There is a difference in the logical properties of the two types of sentence: "y is of value to a" is extensional, i.e. if y is of value to a, and $y = z$, then z is of value to a; "a values y" is intensional, i.e. it is not the case that if a values y and $y = z$ then a values z. "Joseph is of great value to Martha" – unbeknownst to her he has assisted her through her education. Since Joseph is the local priest, it follows that "the local priest is of great value to Martha." But "Martha values the unknown benefactor who has assisted her through her education" does not entail "Martha values Joseph" or "Martha values the local priest." She may despise Joseph and loathe the clergy. Whether or not something is of value to someone depends on the nature of the object, its capacities to contribute to the flourishing of a being however that is defined. Whether an object is valued by someone depends upon the nature of the person's beliefs about the object. Valuing requires certain cognitive capacities. Non-rational nature does not display those capacities.

There are also more general problems with the appeal to consistency that is employed in the argument. The use of some form of consistency argument of the kind found in both Kantian and utilitarian ethical traditions has become the standard move in the environmental literature. The Kantian version runs something like this: since we regard ourselves as of ethical standing in virtue of being beings that pursue our own good, then consistency demands that we extend standing to any being that similarly pursues its own good; since all living things have a good of their own, we must extend moral considerability to them. A similar appeal to consistency runs through utilitarian-based positions: ethics demands impartiality, that we give equal consideration to the interests of all affected by an action; hence, we must extend moral standing to any being that has its own interests; since all living things have their own good, they have interests; hence, consistency demands that we must extend moral standing to all living things (Attfield 1987).

However, these appeals to consistency look unconvincing. Take again the gardener. There is nothing irrational or inconsistent in her attitudes. She can accept that greenfly have their own good and quite consistently believe they ought to be done harm. We can know what is "good for X" and what constitutes "flourishing for X" and yet believe that X, under that description, is the sort of thing that ought not to exist and hence that the flourishing of X is just the sort of thing we ought to inhibit. One can state what it is to be a good tyrant, what it is for tyrants to flourish, and the conditions in which they will (Aristotle *Metaphysics*, 1021b 15ff), but believe that tyrants, qua tyrants, have no claims upon us. That Y is a good of, or good for, X does not entail that Y should be realized unless we have a prior reason for believing that X is the sort of thing whose good ought to be promoted. Thus, just as, against hedonistic utilitarianism, there are pleasures that simply should not count, but rather should be the direct object of appraisal, e.g. those of the sadist, so there are interests we can quite properly refuse to count. There are some entities whose flourishing simply should not enter into any calculations – the flourishing of tyrants and some viruses for example. Correspondingly, it is implausible to suggest that human beings ascribe ethical standing to themselves simply in virtue of having goods or interests of our own. While it might be the case that if a being has ethical standing then we have a prima facie obligation to promote its good, it is not the case that if a being has a good or interests then it has ethical standing.

How then can we show that the goods of non-humans ought to count in our moral considerations? Another possible solution is the more traditional Aristotelian one. Human beings, like other entities, have goods constitutive of their flourishing, and correspondingly other goods instrumental to that flourishing. The flourishing of many other living things ought to be promoted because they are constitutive of our own flourishing. While the approach might seem narrowly anthropocentric, it need not be in any objectionable sense. Friendship requires that we care for others for their own sake and not merely for the pleasures or profits they might bring. This is compatible with friendship being constitutive of a flourishing life. Given the kind of beings we are, a person without friends is leading an unhappy existence. On similar lines it might be argued that for a large number, although not all, of individual living things and biological collectives, we should recognize and promote their flourishing as an end itself. Such care for the natural world is constitutive of a flourishing human life. The best human life is one that includes an awareness of and practical concern with the goods of entities in the non-human world. I believe something like this view is correct (O'Neill 1993) and I will return to it in the final section. However, whatever account we offer, it needs to be one that offers some account of how the goods of non-human beings make a call upon human ethical sensibilities. In the following section I consider the more general question of how this relation might be characterized.

Human sensibilities and environmental values

The ethical realist holds that the evaluative properties of objects are real properties of objects: our ethical judgments are taken to track those properties. What is meant by a "real property" here? What contrast is being drawn with "unreal" properties? The term "real property" can have strong or weak interpretations. On the strong interpretation, a real property is taken to be one that can be characterized without reference to the experiences or responses of observers. That strong interpretation is associated with an "absolute" conception of reality, that identifies what is real with what is accessible from any point of view (McNaughton 1988). We can identify what is real by stripping away any property that cannot be characterized without referring to particular human sensibilities and experiences. The view is often associated with physicalist or scientistic views, where what is real is identified with that which the true physical theory describes. But there is a weaker interpretation of "real property": a real property is one that exists in the absence of the experiences and responses of observers, which our experiences and judgments track, and about which the judgments of rational inquirers can be expected to converge. However, there is no requirement that they be such that they can be characterized without reference to the responses of observers, that they be accessible from any point of view.

The realist turn in environmental philosophy is normally one that claims that there are "intrinsic values" out in nature independent of human sensibilities in a strong sense. They are real properties in the sense of properties that can be characterized without reference to human responses. Indeed, that is sometimes what "intrinsic" in this context is taken to mean – a property that can be characterized without mentioning any relationship with a human observer. The terms "good" and "goods" of non-humans in the biological context look promising because they appear to offer candidates for properties that can be characterized without referring to particular human sensibilities and experiences. The problem with that position is that having thus characterized "intrinsic values," it is difficult to see why they should be of concern to us at all. Hence the problem raised in the last section. Why should they matter ethically to us? Given the absence of any tie to a notion of appropriate human responses, the appeal to objective values looks ethically idle. One response for the realist might be to move to a more modest form of realism that employs a weaker account of a "real" property. The point can be approached from consideration of possible analogies between values and secondary qualities.

The distinction between primary and secondary qualities is one that is associated with the possibility of an absolute conception of reality. Primary qualities are those, like mass and position, that can be characterized without any reference to the experiences and responses of an observer. Secondary qualities are those, like color and sound, which require some reference to such experiences and responses. Thus we can only characterize colors with reference to human observers. So, for example, an object is green if and only if its nature is such that it would appear green to a perceptually ideal observer in perceptually ideal conditions. Given an absolute conception of reality, secondary qualities do not belong to the domain of what is real, for they are properties of objects that cannot be characterized without reference to the responses of observers. Hence, while light waves of particular length might belong to reality, colors do not. Given that view, any analogy between values and secondary qualities would show that values, like secondary qualities, are not real properties of objects. "Vice and virtue...may be compared to sounds, heat and cold, which, according to modern philosophy, are not qualities in objects, but perceptions in the mind" (Hume 1972, Book III, §1, p. 203) For the Humean, both secondary qualities and evaluative properties are not real properties of objects, but, rather, illustrate the mind's "propensity to spread itself on external objects": as Mackie puts it, moral qualities are the "projection or objectification of moral attitudes" (Mackie 1977, p. 42).

What response might be made to this kind of argument? One popular move in environmental philosophy has been to argue against this position on the basis of developments in physics. The argument runs that the Copenhagen interpretation of quantum mechanics shows the distinction between primary qualities and secondary qualities to have broken down – all properties of objects are observer-dependent. Hence, the evaluative properties of objects are as real as their primary qualities (Callicott 1989, ch. 9). This argument is flawed. The Copenhagen interpretation of quantum theory is but one amongst many and is not, in any case, committed to the ontological extravagance that all properties of objects are observer-dependent. Moreover, the argument shares the scientistic premises exhibited in the absolute conception of reality. Why should it be thought that developments in physics determine what is to count as real or not, and in particular the status of values?

A second response to the Humean position is to question the assumption that what is real is given only by a true physical theory that captures properties that can be characterized without any reference to human responses, attitudes, and interests. The issues around the truth or falsity of an absolute conception of reality are large ones on which more extended discussion is required than is possible here. However, given a rejection of that conception of what is real, then the assumption that either values or secondary qualities are mere "projections" of the human mind to be contrasted with the world as it is really is described in a purely physicalist language looks less plausible. While it may be that to characterize secondary qualities we need to refer to the responses of human observers, they can be said to be unreal only if one assumes a strong interpretation of the criteria for something being real – that we can characterize the properties without reference to the responses or attitudes of observers. Secondary qualities are real dispositional properties of objects, passive powers, to appear in a certain way to ideal observers in ideal conditions. It does not follow that they are "projections" of the human mind. It is consistent with this characterization of secondary qualities that an object possesses that quality even though it may never actually be perceived by an observer. They persist in the absence of observers. In the kingdom of the blind the grass is still green. Moreover, in developing perceptual powers the agent is developing her capacities to discern these properties. Our perceptions and judgments track the qualities and not vice versa. Hence, the Humean analogy between secondary and evaluative qualities might be taken in the opposite direction (McDowell 1985). Like the secondary qualities, evaluative qualities are real properties of objects. An object's evaluative properties are similarly dispositional properties that are tied to certain attitudes and reactions in specified observers in specified conditions. Thus, we might tentatively characterize goodness thus: x is good if and only if x merits feelings of moral approval in an ideal observer in ideal conditions. If the analogy is taken in this direction then the realist is not open to objection that real evaluative properties would be torn from any notion of an appropriate response. The appropriate responses would be conceptually tied to the concepts.

However, while the position has attractions, there are clear problems with any close analogy between secondary qualities and values. The anti-realist can respond by pointing out that the analogy between secondary and evaluative properties is imperfect. The notion of the "ideal observer" in the case of color is different from that in the case of values. In the case of color it means something like a statistical normality, in the case of moral judgments it has no such meaning. Moral judgments do not answer to democracy in that way: the environmentalist might want to say that destroying an ancient forest for a Disneyland theme park is wrong even where he lives in a society in which the statistical norm is to see a forest as a mere nuisance, standing in the way of some good fun. Correspondingly, any plausible account of values talks of their "meriting" a response rather than their having the power to induce such a response. These objections do undermine any straightforward parallels between judgments about secondary qualities and judgments of value.

However, what remains powerful after the specific disanalogies are accepted is the rejection of an absolute conception of reality upon which many of the arguments for moral anti-realism are predicated. The analogy does point to the possibility that evaluative properties can be both dependent upon human sensibilities and responses, in the sense that they can only be characterized with reference to our responses, but also real, with conditions of correctness independent of individual responses. The realist only requires the evaluative properties to be real in the weak and not the strong sense. Can a meta-ethic of this kind be developed and defended?

Environmental ethics through thick and thin

A promising line of argument for a meta-ethic of this kind would be one that focused upon "thick" normative concepts. Thick normative concepts are specific reason-giving concepts, concepts such as cruel, kind, just, and unjust. They contrast with "thin" concepts, general normative concepts such as right, wrong, good, or bad, or the favorites of environmental philosophy, "has value" or "lacks value" (Williams 1985). A feature of thick concepts is that they are both descriptive and evaluative: to say that a farming practice is cruel is to both characterize and appraise the practice. As I noted in the opening section, the non-realist responds to this apparent feature of thick concepts by prising apart the evaluative and descriptive components. We can analyze them as a conjunction of a factual component that does the describing and an evaluative component which is captured by the thin concept. So to say "a practice is cruel" is to say something like: "the practice involves the intentional infliction of suffering and the practice is bad." The evaluative component is then given a non-realist reading – it serves to express attitudes or preferences. Now the realist might respond to this argument by accepting that thick concepts can be reduced to thin concepts in this way, but give a realist rather than expressivist account of the thin concept. However, another response might be to deny that thick concepts can be reduced to thin. The attempt to prise apart descriptive and evaluative components of thick concepts is not possible, since the descriptive content of the concept, its extension, is in part determined by the evaluative content. Only someone who understood the evaluative point of calling an act cruel or a mountain beautiful would know how to continue to use the concepts in new cases.

This response opens up grounds for a particular form of realism which does not rely on an absolute conception of reality. It might be argued that properties such as "cruelty" are real properties: our judgments track the properties; we can make mistakes; claims that acts are cruel or not are true or false. However, at the same time, they cannot be adequately characterized without reference to particular kinds of human evaluative responses to the world. Hence the feature of thick concepts noted earlier, that they are both action-guiding and descriptive of states of the world. To characterize particular human acts as acts of cruelty is both to make a claim about the nature of those acts which are true or false, and to appraise them and offer reasons to oppose them. There does appear then to be grounds for a form of realism that stays at the level of thick ethical concepts but rejects an absolute conception of reality.

There is also much to be said for that position in terms of its implications for environmental ethics. A feature of a great deal of theorizing in environmental ethics of which the search for "intrinsic value" is typical is that it loses sight of what moves environmental concern. There is a stark contrast between the richness in the normative vocabulary that informs our appraisal of the environments with which we live and the austerity of the vocabulary that environmental philosophers employ to theorize about it. Our appraisals of non-human nature call upon a range of normative vocabularies. For example, we can talk of cruelty inflicted on fellow creatures, of the vandalism involved in the wanton destruction of places rich in wildlife and beauty, of the pride and hubris exhibited in the belief that the world can be mastered and humanized, of our lack of a sense of humility in the midst of a natural world that came before and will continue beyond us. We possess a rich aesthetic vocabulary to talk of the tones, forms, sounds, and textures of the natural world, the evocativeness of landscapes, the moods of nature (see AESTHETICS). From the biological and ecological sciences come concepts that have normative significance, such as BIODIVERSITY, species richness, integrity, and fragility. What, it might be asked, has all this rich vocabulary to do with what is claimed to be at the heart of environmental ethics, namely that "nature has intrinsic value"? References to intrinsic value only have power insofar as they call upon more specific reason-giving concepts and corresponding claims about the ways in which natural objects are a source of wonder, the sense of proportion they invoke in us of our place within a wider history, the care we feel called upon to give as we develop our understanding of the lives of fellow creatures, the diversity of forms of life to which we respond, and so on. Robbed of that more specific content, one is left with concepts adrift that lend themselves to the kind of abstract metaphysics of value often to be found in environmental philosophy.

Is a realism of thick concepts defensible? There are strong objections to giving priority to thick ethical concepts. One worry is that specific reason-giving concepts are culturally local – the intelligibility of the concepts relies on the particular practices of particular cultures. Hence, the objection goes, there is no possibility of a universal ethical language that is thick. That this is the case also militates against realism about ethical utterances, for one mark of truth for the realist is that it is that upon which reasoned judgments converge: if thick concepts are local, we cannot assume the possibility of convergence (Williams 1985). This meta-ethical point has an additional significance for environmental problems, for it might be argued that these are global and hence require an ethical language that crosses cultures. Any such language, the argument goes, is necessarily thin. Hence, the appeal to thin cosmopolitan concepts that is the feature of environmental philosophy is to be welcomed. Moreover, it might be argued that such cosmopolitanism in philosophy is part of the nature of its enterprise. It relies on the possibility of standing outside our own ethical practices and formulating skeptical questions about them – and for this it might be added we need a thin language to formulate criticism. We must be able to ask questions of the form "but is x good?," for example, "but is humility before nature good?"

These arguments assume that specific reason-giving concepts must be tied to culturally local contexts. However, there is no reason to assume that this is true. In particular, there is no reason to assume in advance that thick ethical concepts cannot be universally shared, but open to local specifications. These might include concepts that characterize our relations to nature. That possibility is characteristic of an Aristotelian account of ethics, that there are features we share as human beings that define what it is to lead a flourishing human life, and that characterization of a good life will employ thick concepts, most notably the virtue concepts. Neither is it the case that the use of thick concepts rules out theoretical reflection and general principles in ethics. However, there is no reason to assume that critical theoretical reflection on our practices must be or even can be adequately undertaken in the thin ethical concepts in which much recent environmental ethics has been articulated. To ask "Is humility before nature good?" is not to ask whether it has some property of goodness, but to raise questions about the relationship of such humility to other evaluative claims we might make – for example, about its compatibility with other admirable human accomplishments. The form of realism outlined here requires elaboration and defense. However, it is more promising than the more popular realist position in environmental ethics which looks for values that exist independent of all human responses to the world.

References

Attfield, R. (1987) *A Theory of Value and Obligation* (London: Croom Helm). [Defends a consequentialist approach to ethics which includes the goods of all living things in its account of maximizing value.]

Callicott, J. B. (1989) *In Defense of the Land Ethic* (Albany: SUNY Press). [Contains some influential papers on meta-ethics and environmental values.]

Darwall, S., Gibbard, A., and Railton, P. (1992) "Towards *fin de siècle* ethics: some trends," *Philosophical Review* 101, pp. 115–89. [An excellent overview of recent work in meta-ethics.]

Hume, D. (1972 [1739]) *A Treatise of Human Nature* (London: Fontana). [Hume's position is still the starting point for most modern non-realist accounts of ethics.]

Mackie, J. (1977) *Ethics* (Harmondsworth: Penguin). [An enormously influential and accessible text on meta-ethics which defends an "error theory."]

McDowell, J. (1985) "Values and secondary qualities," in *Morality and Objectivity*, ed. T. Honderich (London: Routledge). [A realist use of the analogy between secondary and primary qualities.]

McNaughton, D. (1988) *Moral Vision* (Oxford: Blackwell). [An excellent overview of recent work in meta-ethics which defends a version of realism.]

Moore, G. E. (1922) "The conception of intrinsic value," in *Philosophical Studies* (London, Routledge and Kegan Paul). [Moore's fullest account of the concept of intrinsic value.]

Naess, A. (1973) "The shallow and the deep, long range ecology movement," *Inquiry* 16, pp. 95–100. [The opening statement of the deep ecological position that made the concept of the intrinsic value of nature one of its defining features.]

O'Neill, J. (1993) *Ecology, Policy and Politics: Human Well-Being and the Natural World* (London: Routledge). [A defense of an Aristotelian approach to environmental ethics.]

Rolston, H. (1988) *Environmental Ethics* (Philadelphia: Temple University Press). [An extended defense of the claim that nature has intrinsic value in the sense of objective value.]

Routley, R. and Routley, V. (1980) "Human chauvinism and environmental ethics," in *Environmental Philosophy*, ed. D. Mannison, M. McRobbie, and R. Routley (Canberra: Australian National University). [An early and deservedly influential case for the claim that non-human nature has intrinsic value.]

Stevenson, C. L. (1944) *Ethics and Language* (New Haven: Yale University Press). [A classic statement of an expressivist meta-ethic.]

Taylor, P. (1986) *Respect for Nature* (Princeton, Princeton University Press). [A broadly Kantian defense of a "biocentric" approach in environmental ethics.]

von Wright, G. H. (1963) *The Varieties of Goodness* (London: Routledge and Kegan Paul). [An influential account of the variety of the uses of "good," including the application of "good" to living entities which has had a deserved influence in environmental ethics.]

Williams, B. (1985) *Ethics and the Limits of Philosophy* (London: Collins). [An argument for the limits of theory in ethics.]

12

Normative ethics

ROBERT ELLIOT

The human assault on the terrestrial environment shows no signs of abating and some signs of spilling over into non-terrestrial environments. Deforestation continues, soil is eroded, water and air are poisoned, species are extinguished, human POPULATION and resource use are burgeoning, CLIMATE change caused by human activity threatens island states with inundation and fertile areas with protracted drought, and human activity generally leaves its unhappy mark on every part of the biosphere, prompting some commentators to proclaim the death of nature (see BIODIVERSITY, LAND AND WATER.) Many are appalled by this destruction, much of it insidious and temporarily hidden, because of what it implies for themselves, their children, their friends, other creatures, the biomass, and the planet we inhabit. This response is in many instances an ethical response. People judge that what is occurring is not merely irritating, inconvenient, disappointing, or unfortunate, but immoral, bad, wrong, or evil.

It is easy to connect with this kind of response and it is worth taking some time unpacking it and working out exactly why the destruction and despoliation of natural systems engenders it. This involves the application of ethical categories to domains in which they have historically not been applied. Ethical categories and ethical systems have for too long had primarily a human focus, with limited application outside the human domain. The recent development of normative environmental ethics has necessitated reviewing these categories and their application. In this chapter, various approaches to normative environmental ethics, that is, to the principles and values in terms of which human impacts on the natural environment might be morally evaluated, are discussed. This is done in two stages. The first discusses the varying scope or content of normative environmental ethics and aims to provide an overview of the kinds of concern that have motivated the development of normative environmental ethics, especially those that are not assimilable to human-centered concerns. The second discusses several important approaches to normative ethics, namely consequentialism, deontology (including Kantianism), and virtue theory, and indicates their ability to accommodate the shifting and expanding concerns identified in the first step.

Human-centered environmental ethics

Much of the ethical response to environmental destruction is undeniably human-centered and so does not compel a re-examination of ethical concerns and structures. In principle at least, this part, and for some theorists it will be the whole, of normative environmental ethics is simply the application of principles and values that are thoroughly human-centered. Of course the development of adequate policy responses will still be complex, difficult, and fraught. Moreover, the fact that so many environmental issues can be compellingly argued in terms of human-centered concerns massively increases the constituency of environmentalism by appealing to the many who will be, unfortunately, unresponsive to broader concerns. In any case, much environmental concern quite rightly focuses on harm to humans, with some commentators warning that human civilization as such is threatened. Others warn of adverse impacts on human health and well-being and lament the destruction of natural resources which have important economic, scientific, medical, recreational, and aesthetic uses (see AESTHETICS, ECONOMICS).

There are human-centered environmental ethics which do not emphasize harm to humans. For instance, there are perfectionist ethics which concern themselves not so much with the well-being of particular humans but rather with human accomplishments in general, such as the development of knowledge, the refinement of culture, and the creation of new forms of aesthetic expression. No doubt such accomplishments contribute to the well-being of individual humans, and so are instrumentally valued, however they may be valued intrinsically, that is to say for their own sakes or in their own right, as well. The realization of such perfectionist ideals depends on the preservation of nature and the maintenance of biospheric health, for example as a source of inspiration, as an object of contemplation, or simply as a material precondition for civilized life.

Virtue ethics, which are a kind of perfectionist ethic in that they focus on ideals of human character, might also assist us in understanding the ethical response to environmental destruction. The key idea of virtue ethics is that certain kinds of action, insofar as they manifest particular traits of character, may be ethically laudable – that is to say, virtuous – or ethically dubious – that is to say, vicious. The virtuousness or viciousness of actions is not, according to such ethics, straightforwardly reducible to a consideration of their consequences, although it is difficult to believe that there is no connection between the consequences of actions, or types of action, and the evaluation of the underlying motivational and affective structures as virtuous or vicious. Nor do assessments in terms of virtues and vices reduce to the intrinsic wrongness or rightness of the actions themselves, as deontological ethics, which are discussed below, might suggest. Thus, environmental despoliation is sometimes represented as the exemplification of a vicious, or less than virtuous, character and condemned for that reason. Furthermore, the condemnation of the action implies a condemnation of the character of the person whose action it is. And, plausibly, virtue ethics may be deployed beyond the level of particular individuals, commenting as well on the character of institutions, governments, and even economic systems. This extension is important, since many of the policies and practices that assault the environment result not so much from the personal decisions of particular individuals but from the structures and momentum of the social and economic institutions within which individuals act. This is not to say that individuals are not ultimately responsible; it is, rather, an acknowledgment of the institutional impediments to individuals doing the right thing.

It is important to avoid viewing these human-centered ethics as mutually exclusive. It is helpful instead to think of them as possibly overlapping ways in which we might articulate the basis for our environmental concern. There may be instances in which the pertinent normative principles conflict – for instance considerations to do with well-being might sometimes conflict with virtue considerations or other perfectionist considerations. We are no strangers, though, to situations in which there are good reasons for each of several conflicting actions, and we are usually able to achieve a satisfactory ordering of the reasons so that we might, perhaps with some discomfort, choose a course of action. The same point applies when environmental ethics other than human-centered ones are considered. The principles and values that emerge from them may be added to the plurality of things that ethically matter.

Beyond human-centered environmental ethics

A human-centered environmental ethic may go quite a way toward articulating the moral responses many have to environmental damage and destruction. But not everyone who endorses environmentalist policies is moved merely by human-centered considerations. Indeed, some might regard them as comparatively insignificant and others would regard them as no more significant than considerations that extend beyond the interests of our own species. The first step outside the circle of human interests is to include the interests of other ANIMALS in our ethical deliberations. An immediate issue, though, is how we define the scope of "non-human animals." Presumably it would include all other primates and indeed all other mammals. And very likely it would include all sentient creatures, that is all creatures having sufficient neurophysiological complexity to sustain conscious experience (Singer 1979; see also SENTIENTISM). While for the vast majority of sentient creatures it may be difficult for us to represent to ourselves the way they might experience the environments they inhabit, it requires no excessive acts of imagination to understand that they have a point of view from which they experience the world. There are also broad commonalities, such as pleasure, pain, satisfaction, and dissatisfaction, that characterize, across species, experience of environments. Within the class of animals and even within the class of sentient animals there is scope for drawing boundaries that might be alleged to be normatively relevant. The challenge, however, is to show that the boundaries suggested are more than merely arbitrary, that they do not merely reflect uncritical habits and prejudices, and that they do signal non-trivial difference between creatures whose interests ethically count and those whose interests do not ethically count. It should be acknowledged, though, that non-arbitrary boundaries will not always provide precise and clear differentiations: often the distinction between the ethically privileged and non-privileged items will be blurred at the edges.

While extensions of moral consideration to non-human animals do challenge human chauvinism, some normative environmental ethics hold that it constitutes another unjustifiable chauvinism and that further extensions are required. Thus it has been claimed that all living things are morally considerable (Goodpaster 1978). Here, the moral significance of, for instance, uprooting a bush is not exhausted by the relationship of the act to humans and other animals. The suggestion is that the bush itself has a direct claim to moral consideration. Drawing a boundary that omits some living things fails, so it is argued, to take proper account of what it is to harm a thing or to act contrary to a thing's interests. Limiting the extension to, say, sentient creatures assumes that harm and interests presuppose a capacity for experience, whereas all that is required, or so the argument continues, is some loosely specifiable set of biological goals or states in terms of which a thing could be characterized as flourishing or not flourishing to some degree (Feinberg 1974). Thus there could be a normative environmental ethic based on a principle of respect for the biologically goal-directed activity of natural entities (Taylor 1986). Such an ethic would take biological organization, including biologically-based tendencies and dispositions to behave or act in certain ways, as the defining characteristic of living things. It would urge that these tendencies and dispositions, which define what it is for a living thing to flourish according to its kind, be respected, perhaps equally, in every living thing.

The extension of moral consideration to all living things highlights a problem that is, perhaps, somewhat less obvious where the extension is only to sentient animals. The problem is simply that the flourishing of many living things is inevitably at the expense of the flourishing of others, giving rise to multitudinous cases of conflicting interests. The problem threatens to render the relevant ethic vacuous or at least computationally intractable. It may be possible to ameliorate the problem by introducing, and justifying, principles that establish ethical hierarchies, permitting, for instance, trade-offs between the interests of plants and the interests of humans. Or again the problem might be addressed by extending some but not all moral categories across the whole range of living things. Thus it might be argued that while moral value attaches to the flourishing of plants as much as it does to the flourishing of humans, there is nevertheless no extension of the rights that protect human flourishing to the whole domain of living things. It is also possible to appeal to gradations of value, arguing that the flourishing of a human has more value than the flourishing of a non-human sentient creature which has more value than the flourishing of a non-sentient living thing. While these mechanisms might render normative evaluation more tractable, we are still left with a situation that seems overwhelmingly messy and resistant to clear-cut moral judgments.

Matters become more complicated when we note that important foci of normative environmental judgment are yet to be included. Thus there is an extension even beyond living things that some have suggested, according to which all natural entities are morally considerable, irrespective of whether or not they are living things. Here moral considerability is extended to significant natural entities such as rocks, fossils, mountains, rivers, waterfalls, stalactites, cliffs, glaciers, dunes, asteroids, moons, and ecosystems (Rolston 1988). Some of these entities are hosts to living things, and some, such as ecosystems, crucially involve them, but this mooted extension would give them direct moral standing independently of that extended to the living things they contain. Extensionism carried to this extreme will strike many as implausible, but at least some of these critics might think that the putative inclusion of such items in the domain of the morally considerable points to something important. When some of us worry about the despoliation of the natural world, our focus is clearly on the inert natural structures that gave rise to, and support, living things, as much as on those living things themselves. This kind of concern needs somehow to be inserted into the normative framework.

One response is to say that extensionism is hopelessly atomistic and individualistic. The thought is that it tries to develop an acceptable environmental normative ethic through the application of ideas at home in the human domain to the whole gamut of natural items. In so doing, it arguably fails to recognize, and is in tension with, the compelling claims of a holistic environmental ethic (Callicott 1989). What is supposedly required is a more general alteration in the form of ethical theories to reflect the moral significance of wholes, such as specific ecosystems, sets of ecosystems, bioregions, or the biosphere itself. Extensionism, it is argued, distorts our view of nature, inclining us to see it as an aggregation of individuals as opposed to an integrated, organic, dynamic whole. Some who offer this line of criticism take the view that the value of individuals is purely instrumental and that intrinsic value is exemplified only by certain systemic properties such as the integrity of, and diversity within, ecosystems. It is possible, however, to combine the holistic view with individualistic considerations, taking each into account in evaluating policy (Elliot 1997). Further, an important aspect of the development of normative environmental ethics has been the move from human-centered to non-human-centered concerns. Some of the flavor of this has been provided above. But a normative ethic strives to fit our ethical concerns into a systematic structure that generates principles of action. This takes us to our second stage, namely the investigation of how amenable various styles of normative ethics are to the content constituted by our environmental concerns.

Consequentialist environmental ethics

The dominant ethical framework in philosophical ethics in the recent past is consequentialism, although it is not widely endorsed by environmental ethicists. Consequentialism defines the obligatory as a function over intrinsic value. In other words, considerations to do with intrinsic value, the value that something has in itself or for its own sake, are taken to exhaust the normative content of consequentialist principles of obligation. These considerations define what, in consequentialist terms, is permissible, obligatory, and impermissible. Other moral concepts, such as duty, will, on the consequentialist view, be similarly defined via the concepts of the permissible, the obligatory, and the impermissible. Consequentialism enjoins examination of the consequences of actions in determining whether they ought to be performed, ought not to be performed, are right, wrong, obligatory, permissible, etc. Specifically, it requires examining the intrinsic values and disvalues attaching to those consequences and to the actions themselves. The most common form of consequentialism directs us to maximize intrinsic value. Another form worth discussing directs us to increase intrinsic value and another directs us to maintain intrinsic value. These variants express obligation generally as a non-maximizing function over value: inserting the relevant values specifies particular obligations.

Consider, first, maximizing consequentialism. It tells us that an action is obligatory if, compared to the other actions that it is open to an agent to perform, it maximizes the expected quantity of intrinsic value, and, further, that only those actions that maximize expected intrinsic value are permissible. The obligatory and the permissible coincide. Utilitarianism is perhaps the best known maximizing consequentialism, recognizing only pleasure or happiness as intrinsic values. It obliges us to maximize expected pleasure or happiness, other actions being impermissible (Singer 1979).

Utilitarianism is only one possible kind of maximizing consequentialism. Other versions are identified by the different intrinsic values they specify. The practical outcome of applying these principles of obligation is determined by these intrinsic values. And according to some theorists there are distinctively natural intrinsic values that are exemplified by nature in its relatively unspoiled states (Elliot 1997; Rolston 1988; Sylvan and Bennett 1994). According to maximizing consequentialisms, if failure to preserve wild nature delivers a less than maximal increase in intrinsic value, then there is an obligation to preserve it. Similarly, if restoring a natural area that has been degraded maximizes expected intrinsic value, then there is an obligation to restore it. With all serious variants of consequentialism, the support for environmentalist policies is strongest where nature itself is taken to have intrinsic value. The support will be exceptionally strong where natural values are the only intrinsic values recognized, although a normative environmental ethic that counts only natural values as intrinsic values would be immensely controversial. Support will also be very strong where, even though other values are recognized, natural values are taken to be the most important values.

A further aspect of consequentialisms should be particularly stressed; namely that they permit trade-offs between quantities of the same intrinsic value and also between different intrinsic values. For example, if pleasure is the only intrinsic value, then a maximizing consequentialist would say that it is obligatory to reduce one person's pleasure, or even to inflict pain, in order to maximize pleasure overall. A consequentialist who accepts that there is a plurality of intrinsic values, including natural values, is faced with a very difficult task, having to make comparative judgments not only about different quantities of the same value but also about different quantities of different values. For example, the consequentialist who thinks both pleasure and the acquisition of knowledge are distinct values, has the problem of deciding just how much pleasure should be sacrificed in order to advance some particular area of knowledge and vice versa. Because of the possibility of trade-offs, it is useful to say that if some natural item has intrinsic value it is prima facie obligatory not to destroy it, rather than obligatory all things considered. Noting that something is of intrinsic value puts us on a warning not to destroy it or degrade it unless it really is, and can be shown to be, the case that such an action maximizes value. It is, moreover, always necessary to ensure that there are no alternative actions that might be performed that would increase value to a greater extent. Furthermore, consequentialism takes a global and long-term perspective in delivering its normative assessments. Establishing that some action is permissible, all things considered, requires a serious attempt to assess its impact far from its geographical location and also into the further future. This is especially pertinent where natural ecosystems and processes, upon which all life and well-being depend, are involved.

Still, when relevant consequences, values, and alternative courses of action are assessed and compared, we might discover that the loss of intrinsic value through environmental despoliation could, in principle, be compensated for by increases of intrinsic values that are human-centered. For instance, environmentalist policies are often countered with the claim that the development of some natural area will result in substantially increased benefits for humans, such as employment opportunities and increased material wealth. The implication is that environmentalists have their value priorities wrong or that they are illegitimately discounting the substantial benefits for humans that flow from environmental pillage. The possibility of this style of argument is one reason that many environmental ethicists have been cool toward consequentialism, looking elsewhere for a framework for their normative beliefs (Sylvan and Bennett 1994). Consequentialism, provided it recognizes natural values, nevertheless is in a strong position to defeat this style of argument. This is because such arguments typically exaggerate benefits for humans, underestimate deleterious environmental impacts, ignore alternative means of benefiting humans, do not investigate alternative social and economic arrangements, underestimate the costs of environmental despoliation and degradation to present and future humans and non-humans, and fail to interrogate the connections between quality of life and material wealth. And of course if the consequentialism in question recognized only natural value, although that would constitute an extremely controversial value theory, or gave natural values special significance or intensity within a plurality of intrinsic values, then the concern that consequentialism is an inadequate normative environmental ethic should be allayed.

A feature of maximizing consequentialism, noted earlier, is that it does not allow any deep distinction between the obligatory and the permissible. This is sometimes thought to be a weakness of maximizing consequentialism in that, allegedly, the theory asks more of people than a normative ethic could reasonably ask. Some variants of consequentialism, however, do allow that actions that are permissible need not be obligatory. Assume, for example, that there are natural values, and consider improving consequentialism, which says that it is obligatory to act so as to increase, although not necessarily maximize, intrinsic value. Such a view is not, if we think about it, all that odd. It reflects the plausible maxim that we should leave the world better than we found it. This variant of consequentialism is, it seems, less onerous than the maximizing variant, requiring less of agents than a total, all-out effort to maximize value. But environmentalists who were concerned by the trade-offs implicit in maximizing consequentialism will be concerned here too. In particular, there are cases where some environmental despoliation may lead to an increase in value, but in which some alternative action, not involving environmental destruction, would increase value to a greater extent. Improving consequentialism seems to leave open the possibility that the former action is permissible and the latter not obligatory. There are three reasons, though, for thinking that the implications of adopting an improving consequentialism are not, from an environmentalist perspective, quite so worrying.

First, improving consequentialism does not require us to do the best we can, requiring us only to improve matters to some degree. If, however, a person is willing to make a specific degree of effort to improve things, we might reasonably require that she or he use that degree of effort to produce the best result possible. Improving consequentialism might reasonably be taken to have an efficiency requirement built into it. The upshot would be an obligation not merely to ensure that an action improves value, but also to ensure that no alternative action involving the same degree of effort improves value more. An improving consequentialism that recognized intrinsic natural values and took them to be intense would thus strongly favor environmentalist policies. Second, improving consequentialism also takes a global and long-term perspective, requiring agents to take pains to ensure that their actions are improving from that perspective. Relatedly, improving consequentialism must engage in an honest appraisal of the actual consequences of those actions embarked on in order to improve value. Third, in improving consequentialism there is considerable looseness involved because improvements may be very large or very small. Serious advocates of improving consequentialism might think their position is trivialized if acceptable improvements need only minimally increase value. Instead they might insist, still with a degree of looseness, that significant improvements are required.

Another, still less onerous, variant of consequentialism makes it obligatory to act so as to maintain, although not necessarily increase, let alone maximize, intrinsic value. Maintaining consequentialism might be thought to provide little support for environmentalist policies but initial impressions might here be misleading, especially where natural values are taken to be intensely significant. Thus it is not difficult to imagine the maintaining consequentialist trying to maintain intrinsic natural value in the face of extensive and recurring acts of environmental destruction. Actions, including those which impact directly on wild nature, will, all too frequently, depress intrinsic value. Acting to promote environmentalist policies will be a clear and obvious way to fulfill the requirement to maintain intrinsic value. Ironically, an onerousness objection might be pressed even against maintaining consequentialism, since in a world in which the loss of intrinsic natural value proceeds apace, the requirements of even maintaining consequentialism may be exceptionally demanding.

The three variants of consequentialism considered involve differing relationships between value and obligation, although they have in common the view that figuring out our obligations is nothing more than a matter of calculating values and plugging them into some function, such as a maximizing, improving, or a maintaining one. Each provides a framework for a normative environmental ethic and their adequacy in this regard is crucially dependent on the specific values that are recognized and the comparative primacy given to natural values. Nor should we lose sight of the range of possible values, including those that reflect the interests of humans and other sentient creatures. The assault on the natural environment massively threatens these interests and a consequentialism that recognizes them would certainly compel serious environmentalist policies.

Deontological environmental ethics

Let us turn now to another major ethical tradition that is constituted by deontological normative ethics. Deontological ethics are often characterized as ethics of principle rather than ethics focused on promoting intrinsic value. Unlike consequentialist theories, they offer principles of obligation or duty that do not reduce to functions over value, allowing the judgment that actions are obligatory for reasons in addition to the value of their consequences. Deontological theories claim that certain kinds of action are obligatory, permissible, impermissible, and so on, in virtue of specific, nonconsequential properties of that action. They do not, however, necessarily exclude such axiological or value assessments, and complete deontological assessments may require some prior axiological assessments.

Thus it might be claimed that, since some natural object has intrinsic value, it is obligatory not to destroy it. The property of being destructive of a thing with intrinsic value would, according to this ethic, be a wrong-making property; the relevant maxim or principle being "do not destroy things which have intrinsic value." While this maxim has about it the flavor of a consequentialist principle, the normative assessment is not carried out by calculating the loss of intrinsic value associated with the destruction of the object and figuring it into some principle of obligation, such as those variants of consequentialism earlier considered – that is, a function over value. Instead, the wrongness of the act can be established without having to look beyond the fact that it involves destroying something of intrinsic value. There is, then, no suggestion that one need look to the consequences of such acts or that one ought to act in accordance with some function of the intrinsic value of the consequences of the act and that of its alternatives. There is, moreover, no suggestion that it is permissible to destroy something of lesser value in order to protect or create something of greater value, which is one reason some environmentalists have felt less unease about deontology than consequentialism. The difference is akin to the difference between a principle that enjoins us to minimize pain, which is consequentialist, and a principle that forbids us to cause pain, which is not consequentialist. Indeed it may be impermissible to act in ways that maximize, improve, or even maintain intrinsic value – for instance, in situations where the only means of doing one of these things involves the destruction of something of intrinsic value contrary to the prohibition on destroying such. There is, then, a deontological structure that would sustain a distinctively environmental normative ethic, the scope of which extends beyond human interests and concerns. Thus destroying or degrading the natural environment could be wrong because, among other things, it is an act of destroying things which possess natural intrinsic value. But the wrongness does not result from the reduction of value as such: the wrongness results from an independent non-consequentialist principle.

There are other ways of fitting a distinctively environmental ethic into a deontological structure. Theories of rights, for example, are often presented as deontological theories because they imply the proscription and prescription of acts independently of the consequences of those acts. Thus, someone's right to life might be said to result in an absolute proscription on taking that person's life, except perhaps in self-defense or in a judicial context, irrespective of the consequences. The fact that value is increased as a consequence is not, it is often claimed, an acceptable justification for violating the right. Much environmental ethics might be cast in terms of rights. Most obviously it makes sense to invoke the rights of non-human animals in objecting to the destruction of natural habitat. But some have wanted to extend the concept of rights beyond the set of sentient creatures, suggesting that, in addition, plants have rights, that species have rights, or that ecosystems have rights. This proliferation of rights generates problems. In the first place there is the issue of whether the extension of rights in these ways is conceptually sound (Feinberg 1974). Does it, for example, make sense to attribute rights to entities that do not even have desires, that are not even conscious? And do we even want to suggest that non-living natural items, such as rocks or glaciers or rivers, could have rights?

Equally important is the practical problem of how to process and adjudicate the barrage of rights claims that would be generated by such profligate deontological ethics. The problem would be ameliorated if we could be sure that the rights in question would not conflict, but that is not at all clear even where we are focusing only on the rights of humans. In the context of extended rights theories, conflicting rights seem inevitable, with attendant problems of weighing up, balancing, and adjudicating countless apparently competing rights claims. Furthermore, the problem seems more acute for a deontological theory than a consequentialist theory because the former eschews trade-offs based on consequences. How exactly do we respect the rights of every organism? Is there a hierarchy of rights? Is there a hierarchy of rights-bearing individuals, such that, for example, the rights of humans have priority over the rights of sentient non-humans which have priority over the rights of other living things? The answer, even in theory, is not clear and the ethic that suggests the principle might therefore be thought vacuous. The prospect of vacuousness is brought out if we consider the claim, often associated with the Norwegian philosopher Arne Naess's (1986) DEEP ECOLOGY view, that every living thing has an equal right to flourish. Life on earth is such, though, that particular organisms can flourish only if others do not. Taking the right literally seems to leave no room for action.

Some are tempted to say that the problem just sketched is the general one that affects ethical extensionism as the method for generating an environmental ethic, namely that things go awry when we focus on individual entities at too fine-grained a level. Such theorists might suggest that we should be focusing on macro-entities such as whole ecosystems or the biosphere as the pertinent rights bearers. This move might stem the proliferation of rights but it still leaves the problem of how to make sense of the claim that entities that lack consciousness or desires could have rights. Of course there is no parallel problem in the suggestion that they have intrinsic value, and so no problem in a deontological theory that prohibits the destruction of what has intrinsic value. It is odd, however, to suggest that they have rights in the sense that humans and sentient non-humans have rights. For one thing, unless an entity is conscious there seems no content to the suggestion that from its point of view things are going well or badly. And the point of rights theories seems to be to create a set of entitlements on the part of individuals that allow things to go well from an individual's point of view.

In any case, there would still be a residual ranking problem in working out the respective priorities of the rights of sentient creatures, ecosystems, and the biosphere. A simple solution would be to give absolute priority to biospheric rights. This solution would be unpalatable to many because it would demote human rights to little more than an afterthought, making human interests subservient to those of the biosphere. Perhaps, though, this is an idea that we could get used to if we are convinced of the intense ethical significance of the natural environment. While there are limits to the capacity of a deontological theory based on rights to support the moral sentiments expressed by many environmentalists, such a theory can accommodate many. Certainly, acts of environmental destruction and degradation will be wrong for human-centered and animal-centered reasons that a deontologist would likely find compelling. For example, such damage would wrongfully injure and kill non-humans and wrongfully impose costs and burdens on humans, including future humans. The attendant ethical concerns can be powerfully and coherently expressed in the language of rights.

There is a deontological theory, Kantianism, deriving from the views of the eighteenth-century German philosopher Immanuel Kant (see NINETEENTH- AND TWENTIETH-CENTURY PHILOSOPHY), that is similar in structure to the rights-based theories and which deserves some comment. The central tenet of Kantianism is that each person is an end in herself or himself, having a capacity for rational autonomy and therefore requiring respect as a person. The idea of respect for persons indeed might be thought to be the basis of theories of rights that, among other things, articulate and elaborate the idea of respect for persons. At first sight, Kantianism, emphasizing as it does respect for persons, might not seem to provide an amenable structure for anything much more than a human-centered environmental ethic. At least one prominent theorist, the American philosopher Paul Taylor, has, however, elaborated a normative environmental ethic with a Kantian flavor. Taylor (1986) asks us to see all living things as autonomous, in that, at the very least, they have biologically based goals that are definitive of the kinds of organism they are and that define for them what counts as flourishing. He suggests that just as Kantianism enjoins us to respect the rational autonomy of persons, so too a naturalized Kantianism enjoins us to respect the natural autonomy of all living things. The force of Taylor's position derives from whatever success he might have in convincing us that there is a useful analogy between rational autonomy and natural autonomy, and, of course, our views about the significance of rational autonomy. And Taylor, by the way, does not seem to want natural autonomy to swallow up rational autonomy, seeking instead to maintain a moral distinction, with hierarchical implications, between persons and other living things.

The conceptual and proliferation problems that affected rights-based deontological theories are present in Taylor's theory. The analogy between rational autonomy and natural autonomy might well founder on the fact that so much of the latter involves no consciousness of preferences or desires. Although we might well see the point of allowing that non-sentient living things have a kind of autonomy, we might think the conceptual distance between the autonomy of, say, an orchid and that of a primate is too great to sustain the mooted ethical extension. Moreover, the theory runs into problems of ranking claims based on natural autonomy. How, for instance, do we adjudicate situations in which human welfare is promoted, or rational autonomy protected, at the cost of destroying entities, such as plants or microbes, that have natural autonomy? One response to these problems is to try to render Taylor's insights in a non-Kantian form. Thus we might accept that there is something ethically significant about natural autonomy but suggest that its significance is best articulated through the concept of intrinsic value. We can say that natural autonomy is a basis of intrinsic value and either plug that into a consequentialist framework or into a non-Kantian, non-rights-based deontological framework.

There is a final problem that should be sketched. Taken literally, deontological ethics apparently render impermissible actions that do not seem impermissible and that may even be obligatory. For instance, the degradation of some small area of the natural environment in order to create a firebreak may be necessary to ensure the protection of an extensive area. If what we value is wild nature, then surely it is permissible to make the firebreak even though it involves the destruction of items of value. Thus a strict deontology is likely to deliver normative conclusions that are difficult to accept. One response, not unproblematic, is to suggest a mixed ethic, containing both consequentialist and deontological components. If enough of value is at stake, then it may be judged permissible to act in a way that a strict deontology would proscribe. By the same token, the deontological component would act as a brake on consequentialist justifications of environmental degradation (Sylvan and Bennett 1994).

Virtue-based environmental ethics

Virtue ethics, which has its roots in the views of the Greek philosopher Aristotle (384–322 BCE), is enjoying a reviving popularity (see THE CLASSICAL GREEK TRADITION). The basic idea is that there are kinds of behavior that should be cultivated by humans and others that should be avoided, virtues and vices respectively. For example, it might be urged that generosity is a virtue, a kind of action that should be cultivated, and that it is to be encouraged not merely because it is true that the greater the number of generous people there are, then the less human misery there will be. The alleged ethical significance of virtuous action supposedly outruns the good consequences that such actions on balance produce, including those that accrue to the generous person through the admiration and reciprocity of others as well as the enjoyment of the act. Apart from the issue of which kinds of action are virtuous and which are not, there is the more theoretical issue of whether ethical judgments couched in terms of virtue can be reduced to judgments couched in terms of values, such as the value of happiness, or indeed couched in deontological terms, for example involving rights or duties. Proponents of a virtue approach to environmental ethics believe that it provides a way of expressing deeply felt moral sentiments concerning the natural environment within the framework of a human-centered ethic that is focused on the appraisal of human character exemplified through action (Hill 1983). Thus the alleged obligation to preserve natural value is turned into an injunction to virtuous action and the pursuit of ideals of human excellence. A suggested benefit of this approach is that it avoids controversial and contested concepts such as intrinsic value.

It is helpful to focus on a particular issue, so let us ask what virtue ethics might say about the kind of environmental research that we might think ethically dubious. We need to look for vice under which we can subsume at least some kinds of environmental research. Perhaps some such research is susceptible to a negative evaluation because it is frivolous, because it exemplifies hubris or arrogance, because it exemplifies a disposition to dominate, because it is vandalistic, or because it is voyeuristic. Of course, in categorizing actions in these various ways we need to delve beyond the superficial properties of the action and inquire into the motives, attitudes, and goals of the action. For example, in categorizing an action as frivolous we are judging it to be performed with a particular attitude and to be devoid of serious goals. So actions that, from an external perspective, look to be of the same kind, might, when relevant internal factors are taken into account, turn out not to be, even where the consequences of the actions are the same.

Consider a case in which two people are conducting the same environmental research with the same goal in mind and giving rise to the same consequences. Assume the goal is to add to the sum of knowledge about a particular ecosystem in order to make a case against its disruption. The two researchers go through the same kinds of activity, use the same methods, and the like. Moreover, their research contributes similarly to the same result. One of the researchers, however, has a serious attitude toward their research, which is not to say they take no pleasure in it. The other researcher has a very different attitude. They understand the point of the research but have a frivolous, even sneering, attitude to what they are doing. They take no direct pleasure in exercising their research skills, they certainly take no pleasure in the knowledge to which they are contributing and they are not engaged by the general goal of the project. Even though, from an external perspective, these two researchers are doing the same kind of thing, their actions can be differentiated when we examine underlying attitudes and motives. We might say that the first has a virtuous approach to the research that is not exemplified by the second. We might even say that the second researcher's approach amounts to a vice. It is a separate matter, though, whether we would want to prevent that person doing research in that way. The exemplification of some vices might not pose any threat to others. So, we might think that the second researcher is acting in a way that is ethically defective but judge that it is not a defect warranting intervention, although we might attempt to get them to see their mode of conduct in the way that we see it. Or imagine a researcher pursuing their research with a cold curiosity, eager to understand the workings of the natural environment and to contribute to the sum of human knowledge, who also regards nature purely as an object for examination, something to be poked, used as an object to satisfy particular intellectual interests, and something that is dominated by the inquiring activity of the researcher. This is arguably not virtuous action. It is worth mentioning here that some variants of ECOFEMINISM can be understood as appealing to virtue ethics, in that they imply that certain modes of behavior toward the natural environment reveal a stymied capacity for caring, a stunted aesthetic sensitivity, a limited affective capacity, and a disposition to dominate, all of which are defects of character displaying masculine modes of being and relating (Plumwood 1993).

Let us remind ourselves of the issue here. It is whether there is a mode of ethical evaluation that focuses on attitudes, traits of character, and motives, and that does not turn on some weighing up of the consequences, on the application of rights considerations or some other deontological element. In any case, the examples of the environmental researchers give some credence to the suggestion that there is such a mode of ethical evaluation and that it might provide a structure for a normative environmental ethic. In the end, however, it is doubtful that the suggestion can be sustained. It is helpful to consider a view, put by Hill (1983), which says that those who damage the environment exemplify a defect of character that can be condemned in terms of standards of human excellence. Hill suggests that the indifference to the natural world that might dispose someone toward such acts, while not itself a vice, reflects traits that are vices, such as ignorance, self-importance, lack of self-acceptance, lack of appropriate humility, lack of an aesthetic sense, and lack of gratitude. Hill attempts to link the preservation of nature with living a virtuous life, suggesting that we should minimize our impact on it as an appropriate expression of gratitude to, and love for, that to which we owe our existence and our happiness. Hill seeks thus to provide arguments against environmental degradation and for the protection and preservation of the natural environment without attributing to it intrinsic value and without invoking deontological theories, focusing instead on what virtue would require.

The problem with Hill's enterprise is how to give content to the claim that exhibiting hubris, ingratitude, philistinism, vandalism, or the like is ethically deficient, without also accepting that nature in itself is of intrinsic value and without invoking some deontological principle that puts nature in the ethical framework as a direct player. Without this foundation Hill's argument amounts to not much more than the observation, admittedly important, that people who behave this way are a danger to have around. The assessment in terms of virtuous or vicious character seems plausible only if we already accept, for example, that there are natural values that are reduced by the vicious act or that there are harms that flow from it. Certainly, it is difficult to see what lever we might have for preventing or discouraging such behavior unless we are able to indicate another, non-virtue based, ethical consideration. Consider an argument that Passmore (1975) uses to defend a claim about philistinism with respect to nature. Passmore points to the extension of the notion of cruelty, a vicious kind of action, to evaluations of our treatment of non-human animals. The idea is that a moral notion, which has its central use in the context of relationships between humans, quite naturally extends to human relationships with non-human animals. This extension, however, depends on the belief that there are certain psychological states that a non-human animal may be in which have negative value, such as pain or distress. This is what makes the extension of the notion of cruelty to non-humans so natural. The reason, in other words, that one ought not to be cruel has to do directly with the disvalue that cruel acts bring about. And the reason that cruelty is a vice, a moral defect of character, is that those disposed to cruelty are unmoved by the knowledge of the impact of their actions. Because this element is missing in the case Passmore is chiefly interested in, his argument, like Hill's, does not succeed. The prospects of a virtue-based environmental ethic seem dim (see META-ETHICS).

References

Callicott, J. (1989) *In Defense of the Land Ethic* (Albany: State University of New York Press). [A collection of essays developing a holistic environmental ethics and also providing arguments for the ascription of biotic rights.]

Elliot, R. (1997) *Faking Nature: the Ethics of Environmental Restoration* (London: Routledge). [Provides an extended discussion of the links between natural values and obligation, taking an approach that mixes consequentialist and deontological theories.]

Feinberg, J. (1974) "The rights of animals and unborn generations," in *Philosophy and Environmental Crisis*, ed. W. Blackstone (Athens, Ga.: University of Georgia Press). [Landmark discussion of the conceptual boundaries of rights.]

Goodpaster, K. (1978) "On being morally considerable," *Journal of Philosophy* 75, pp. 308–25. [Landmark discussion of the conceptual requirements for moral considerability.]

Hill, Jr., T. (1983) "Ideals of human excellence and preserving the natural environment," *Environmental Ethics* 5, pp. 211–24. [Attempts a justification of environmentalism in terms of a virtue-based ethic.]

Naess, A. (1986) "The deep ecological movement: some philosophical aspects," *Philosophical Inquiry* 8. [Representative of the normative views associated with the deep ecology movement.]

O'Neill, J. (1993) *Ecology, Policy and Politics: Human Well-being and the Natural World* (London: Routledge). [A good elaboration and defense of a human-centered environmental ethic.]

Passmore, J. (1975) "Attitudes to nature," in *Nature and Conduct*, ed. R. S. Peters (London, Macmillan), pp. 251–64. [A discussion of aspects of historical attitudes to nature that are relevant to normative environmental ethics.]

Plumwood, V. (1993) *Feminism and the Mastery of Nature* (London: Routledge). [Interesting development of an ecofeminist view with discussion of normative implications.]

Rolston III, H. (1988) *Environmental Ethics: Duties to and Values in the Natural World* (Philadelphia: Temple University Press). [Landmark work developing a comprehensive environmental ethic.]

Singer, P. (1979) "Not for humans only," in *Ethics and Problems of the 21st Century* (Notre Dame, University of Notre Dame Press), pp. 191–206. [Good elaboration of an environmental ethic based on the view that only sentient creatures are morally considerable.]

Sylvan, R. and Bennett, D. (1994) *The Greening of Ethics: from Human Chauvinism to Deep-Green Theory* (Cambridge: Whitehorse Press). [Excellent discussion and critique of recent normative environmental ethics and development of a comprehensive ethic with consequentialist, deontological and virtue-based elements.]

Taylor, P. (1986) *Respect for Nature* (Princeton: Princeton University Press). [Careful development of an environmental ethics based on respect for nature with a Kantian approach.]

Further reading

Brennan, A. (1988) *Thinking about Nature* (London: Routledge). [Explores the relationship between ecology and normative environmental ethics.]

Goodin, R (1992) *Green Political Theory* (Oxford: Polity Press, 1992). [Good discussion of the basis of natural values, resultant obligations and implications for political action.]

Regan, T. (1992) "Does environmental ethics rest on a mistake?," *Monist* 75, pp. 161–83. [Interesting critique of normative environmental ethics that are based on the claim that nature has intrinsic value.]

13

Sentientism

GARY VARNER

In contemporary writings about ethics, saying that an entity is "sentient" generally means that it is conscious of pleasure and/or pain. Etymologically, however, the term "sentient" refers more broadly to consciousness of something or other, rather than to consciousness of pleasure and pain specifically, and this is reflected in the work of the most prominent contemporary proponents of sentientist ethics. While Peter Singer (1990) [1975]) uses the term to refer to consciousness of pleasure and pain, Joel Feinberg (1974) and Tom Regan (1983) defend sentientist ethics but make animals' moral standing depend on their consciously striving for things in the future, a capacity which may be less widespread in the animal kingdom than is bare consciousness of pain. John Rodman (1977) appears to have first used the term "sentientism" to refer to ethics which restrict moral standing to conscious entities.

This chapter surveys the sentientist ethics of Singer, Regan, and Feinberg, and then critically examines the notion of an "adequate" environmental ethic. One of the few points of consensus to emerge among environmental ethicists during the field's first two decades was the claim that an adequate environmental ethic cannot be sentientist. Because holistic entities such as species and ecosystems are among the primary objects of environmentalists' concern, most environmental ethicists concluded that an adequate environmental ethic must be some version of holism – it must attribute moral standing or intrinsic value to species and ecosystems, neither of which are plausible candidates for sentience. Although not a sentientist myself (see Varner 1998), I think the inadequacy of sentientist environmental ethics has been more assumed than adequately demonstrated, as explained below.

Contemporary sentientist ethics

Although the classical utilitarians who shaped much of philosophical debate about ethics in the nineteenth century were sentientists, they did not spend much time discussing the implications of taking animals' moral standing seriously. The most widely discussed contemporary version of sentientism does. Peter Singer's *Animal Liberation* has become "the Bible" of the animal rights movement, and for this reason the term "animal liberation" has become closely associated with Singer's views, even though Singer is not, strictly speaking, a rights theorist.

In *Animal Liberation*, Singer avoided specific commitments in NORMATIVE ETHICS, preferring to base his criticisms of widely accepted practices on the more basic notion of equal consideration of interests. Nevertheless, he follows the classical utilitarians in holding that the capacity to experience pleasure and/or pain (broadly construed) is both necessary and sufficient for having morally considerable interests:

> The capacity for suffering and enjoyment is *a prerequisite for having interests at all*, a condition that must be satisfied before we can speak of interests in a meaningful way. It would be nonsense to say that it was not in the interests of a stone to be kicked along the road by a schoolboy. A stone does not have interests because it cannot suffer. Nothing that we can do to it could possibly make any difference to its welfare. A mouse, on the other hand, does have an interest in not being kicked along the road, because it will suffer if it is. (1990 [1975], pp. 7–8)

And in his professional philosophical work Singer is a thoroughgoing utilitarian. Indeed, in *Practical Ethics* he claims that "The universal aspect of ethics ... provide[s] a persuasive, although not conclusive, reason for taking a broadly utilitarian position" (1993 [1973], p. 12). The basic idea is that "taking the moral point of view" consists of taking the same attitude toward others' well-being as you would take toward your own well-being when thinking prudentially. So just as it would be flawed prudential thinking for you to count tonight's drinking pleasure while ignoring tomorrow's hangover, it would be flawed ethical thinking for anyone to count some individual's benefits while ignoring others' harms. What Singer calls "speciesism" is the related ethical mistake of taking harms and benefits to humans into account while ignoring (or differentially weighting) similar harms and benefits to animals.

In *Animal Liberation* Singer argued that standard defenses of diverse practices in animal agriculture, medical research, etc. are speciesist, and in *Practical Ethics* he shows how this is so from a specifically utilitarian perspective. Thus "animal liberation" has become associated in philosophical circles with a specifically utilitarian approach to thinking about the ethics of our interactions with animals.

What is most important for present purposes is that since utilitarianism is commonly defined as the view that right actions and institutions maximize aggregate happiness, utilitarianism is not a form of holism. The reason is that for an entity to have moral standing according to a utilitarian, it must literally be capable of being made happy or unhappy, and literal attributions of (un)happiness require that the entity be sentient. Although many animals are sentient, the species and ecosystems of which they are members are not themselves sentient. A utilitarian thinks in terms of aggregate happiness, but unless the aggregate itself can be happy or unhappy, the whole does not have a welfare that matters from the utilitarian perspective; for a utilitarian, the "welfare of the whole" is reducible to or a function of the welfare of all the individuals who make it up.

In the quotation above, Singer claims that the capacity for consciousness of pain would, all by itself, suffice to give an animal moral standing. A potentially more stringent sentientist criterion was proposed in an influential essay by moral and political philosopher Joel Feinberg. Feinberg contributed an essay titled "The rights of animals and unborn generations" to one of the first anthologies on environmental ethics (*Philosophy and Environmental Crisis*, 1974). In it, he argued that while it makes sense to attribute rights to some non-human animals and to future generations of humans, neither plants, species, nor ecosystems are plausible candidates for rights. The reason, Feinberg argued, is that rights function somehow to protect interests, and

> an interest, however the concept is finally to be analyzed, presupposes at least rudimentary cognitive equipment. Interests are compounded somehow out of *desires* and *aims* – both of which presuppose something like beliefs, or cognitive awareness.... Mere brute longings unmediated by beliefs – longings for one knows not what – might be a primitive form of consciousness... but they are altogether different from the sort of thing we mean by "desire," especially when we speak of human beings. (1974 pp. 52–3)

So on Feinberg's view, in order to have rights, an entity must be capable of consciously aiming at – thinking about – things in its future.

Feinberg's 1974 paper attracted a great deal of attention during the 1970s and 1980s, because it expressed a classic conception of the relationship between rights and interests and it clearly showed why this classic conception is sentientist. One reaction to this insight was to explore how the classic conception could be modified to make rights applicable to non-sentient entities such as species and ecosystems. Christopher D. Stone's *Should Trees Have Standing?* (1974) can be read as an example of this, although Stone was writing his essay at the same time as Feinberg. However, many environmental ethicists responded by saying that Feinberg's analysis showed how rights views are just as ill-suited to environmental ethics as Singer's utilitarianism (see, e.g., Rodman 1977 and Goodpaster 1979).

A third widely discussed proponent of sentientism, Tom Regan, effectively reached the same conclusion. In an early article in the journal *Environmental Ethics*, Regan characterized a truly environmental ethic as one in which "all conscious beings and some non-conscious beings [are] held to have moral standing" (1981, p. 20). In that article, Regan offered a brief rejoinder to the argument that having a good of one's own (which rights might function to protect) requires sentience, but he subsequently rejected that argument and embraced a sentientist rights view, labeling Aldo Leopold's environmental holism "environmental fascism" (Regan 1983, pp. 361–2; for more on Regan's rejoinder and his subsequent dismissal of it, see Varner 1998, ch. 3; also see THE LAND ETHIC and Leopold 1949).

Regan's *The Case for Animal Rights* (1983) is a rigorous exploration of the implications of extending a common conception of moral rights from humans to animals which have the kind of cognitive capacities that Feinberg took to be necessary for having interests. Regan's account of the tie between interests and rights can be paraphrased this way: If an entity A "has moral rights," then it would be wrong to harm A in any significant way on purely utilitarian grounds – it would be wrong to set back significant interests of A unless a certain kind of non-utilitarian justification for doing so was available. Although appeals to rights in day-to-day speech are significantly more nuanced than this simple account, it does capture a core meaning of rights claims as used in daily arguments about ethics. For instance, when opponents of abortion invoke a fetus's right to life, they are in effect saying that the costs of carrying it to term cannot suffice to justify aborting it – that only by invoking a similar right to life on the mother's side could abortion be justified.

It is important to note that, for Regan, "having moral rights" is an all-or-nothing thing; to "have rights" at all is to have a blanket right not to be significantly harmed in any way (at least not for the sake of purely utilitarian goals). In daily talk about rights, by contrast, we typically invoke various specific rights not to be harmed in fairly specific ways. For instance, to have a right to free speech is to have the right not to be harmed in the specific way we would be harmed by having our speech limited, to have a right to a public education is to have the right not to be harmed in the way we would be harmed by not being provided with an education, etc.

Regan's argument for extending to animals a blanket right not to be harmed has two parts. First, he argues that recognizing this blanket right in humans is the essence of respecting them as individuals. To think that aggregate benefits to others can suffice to justify us in harming an individual is to think of that individual as a mere "utility receptacle." Regan claims that the classic objections to utilitarianism – that it could justify punishing the innocent, slavery, etc., if only the aggregate benefits are large enough to outweigh the costs to the harmed individuals – arise because utilitarianism fails to respect individuals in this way.

Second, Regan argues that any non-speciesist explanation of why very nearly all human beings deserve to be treated with this kind of individual respect will imply that many animals deserve the same. In particular, Regan argues that what he calls the "subject of a life criterion" best explains the scope of moral rights among humans and implies that at least all normal adult mammals, and probably all normal adult birds, deserve similar respect. To be a subject of a life in Regan's sense is (roughly) to have a conscious well-being which is tied to having one's conscious desires for one's future satisfied (for a more exact characterization, see Regan 1983, p. 243). On this criterion, a permanently comatose human no longer has moral rights, because he no longer has any conscious desires for his future in terms of which we can conceive of him as being harmed in the relevant sense; but even very profoundly retarded humans would, and so too animals with at least rudimentary conscious desires for their future.

So Regan's view, like Feinberg's, may be even more restrictive than Singer's. For Singer, the bare capacity to feel pleasure or pain gives an entity moral standing. According to Regan and Feinberg, however, something more is required: the capacity to consciously desire things in one's future – it is in terms of one's desires for the future, rather than bare consciousness of pain, that Feinberg and Regan unpack the notion of harm. But evolution may have produced consciousness of pain in some organisms without coupling it with the ability to consciously plan for the future. Pain combines vital information about tissue damage in the present with strong negative affect, and these might aid organisms in simple conditioned learning where thinking about how to achieve things in the future is unnecessary. (For more on the scope of pain and desire in the animal kingdom, see Varner 1998, ch. 2.)

In none of the sentientist views surveyed here, however, are entities such as species or ecosystems (as opposed to some of their individual members) plausible candidates for moral standing, and this basic feature of sentientist views has played a major role in their rejection by many prominent environmental ethicists.

Is sentientism an "adequate" environmental ethic?

Many prominent authors in the field think of "environmental ethics" as departing from traditional western ethics by abandoning individualist views such as sentientism and anthropocentrism and embracing some form of holism. These include Aldo Leopold (see THE LAND ETHIC), but also Callicott (1980), Goodpaster (1979), Rodman (1977), Routley (1973), and Routley and Routley (1980). Even Tom Regan assumed something like this when he distinguished between "an ethic *for the use* of the environment" and "an ethic *of* the environment" (1981, p. 20, emphasis altered).

Of course, if the term were *defined* so that a necessary condition for something's being an "environmental ethic" is that it attribute moral standing to non-conscious entities, then it would be an analytic truth that no form of sentientism could be an environmental ethic. But the authors listed above do not simply define sentientism out of the game from the start. For as Richard Routley noted in the first essay on environmental ethics ever published in a professional philosophy journal, "It is not of course that old and prevailing ethics do not deal with man's relation to nature." Routley also noted that "it is none too clear what is going to count as a new ethic," since the traditional approaches can be modified extensively in a variety of ways and there are a variety of minority traditions (1973, pp. 205–6 – indeed, as Callicott (1980) points out, Plato's ethics had a holistic dimension).

Rather, the authors listed above all claim that no version of sentientism would be "adequate" as an environmental ethic. They give three kinds of reason for this conclusion.

The first is that for a broad range of policy goals which environmentalists favor – things such as preserving the health or integrity of ecosystems in which we live, preserving wilderness and endangered species, etc. – sentientist ethics cannot support these goals, or at least do not support them as fully as a holistic ethic could. The second is that in certain hypothetical situations (the best-known being so-called "last man" cases) sentientist ethics conflict with the intuitions of environmentalists, either by yielding a different answer or by seeing them as raising no ethical question at all. The third is that because environmentalists are directly concerned with preserving holistic entities such as species and ecosystems, the conceptual machinery of traditional ethical theory, which was developed to deal with conflicts among individual humans, is ill-suited to capturing the general value framework environmentalists think with.

The most widely discussed example of the first kind of argument is J. Baird Callicott's 1980 paper "Animal liberation: a triangular affair." Aside from Leopold's essay "The land ethic" (in Leopold 1949), this essay has probably been reprinted more often than any other on environmental ethics, contributing to the widespread impression among students of the field that sentientist ethics must be an inadequate basis for an environmental ethic.

Below are several contrasts Callicott draws between the implications of sentientist ethics and the land ethic on practical issues. (Note: in this essay, Callicott uses the term "animal liberation" to refer to animal welfare and animal rights views in general, including but not limited to Singer's utilitarianism and Regan's rights view

(Callicott 1980, p. 312, note 2); but assuming that only animals are sentient, "animal rights/welfare views" and "sentientism" are co-referential expressions, so in what follows I will use these terms interchangeably.)

1. Callicott says that the land ethic would permit or even require hunting of animals like white-tailed deer "to protect the local environment" (1980, p. 320), implying that animal liberationists should oppose hunting even in such situations.
2. He says that the two kinds of ethic differ in the value they attach to predators and to members of endangered species versus rare species. Whereas the land ethic sees large feline predators as "critically important members of the biotic community," Callicott says that animal liberationists should condemn them as "merciless, wanton, and incorrigible murderers"; and Callicott says that "humane herdspersons" might allow sheep to graze freely on plants that are "overwhelmingly important to the stability, integrity, and beauty of biotic communities" (ibid).
3. Animal liberationists advocate vegetarianism, but Callicott argues that because it is more efficient than an omnivorous diet, universal vegetarianism *"probably"* would produce an environmentally "catastrophic" human population increase (ibid, p. 335).
4. And Callicott imagines the consequences of literally liberating domesticated animals; either they would fail to survive, "becom[ing] abruptly extinct"; they would become hardier but, like feral horses, harm their environments; or their human keepers would have to stop slaughtering them while continuing to house and feed them, dramatically increasing our society's ecological footprint. Alternatively, he sees "some irony" in the option of simply ceasing to breed future generations of these animals (ibid, p. 331).

Callicott (1989) subsequently regretted some of the more fulminatory rhetoric of this famous piece and even tried to bring animal liberation and environmental ethics "back together again" by showing how Leopold's land ethic could accommodate some of the concerns of animal welfarists (especially with regard to domesticated animals). Yet it is easy to understand why he drew the contrast between animal rights views and environmental ethics in the very stark terms he chose. First, self-styled "animal liberationists" have quite literally liberated animals from research facilities and from fur farms – with some rather ironic results in the latter case. Second, the exigencies of political combat generally preclude animal activists from doing the kind of theorizing and careful casuistry which might show that they can agree with environmentalists more than is initially apparent. And finally, even Tom Regan, in his academic work on animal rights, claims that his own view implies that *all* hunting is wrong – even to prevent overpopulation (1983, pp. 355–7), and it is he who labels the Leopold land ethic "environmental fascism" (ibid, pp. 361–2).

Nevertheless, a sentientist ethic need not reach any of the practical conclusions listed above. Obviously point #3 (about vegetarianism) is armchair speculation which totally discounts human forethought, and, as Edward Johnson pointed out in an article published shortly after Callicott's, "the catastrophic scenarios imagined by Callicott [in point 4 above] are not to the point." First, because any actual liberation of domesticated animals "would almost certainly happen gradually." Second, any actual liberation would almost certainly take the final form Callicott mentions (that is, via decisions not to breed future generations of the animals), and there is no real "irony" in this, "since it is not the species that is being liberated, but individual members of the species." On a sentientist view, a species as such cannot be "liberated from cruel and pointless suffering and exploitation" (Johnson 1981, p. 267).

The real force of Callicott's argument against animal rights views is in his first two points, but an ecologically enlightened sentientist can avoid those anti-environmental implications as well. Regarding hunting of species which, like deer, routinely over-shoot the carrying capacities of their ranges, it is important to keep in mind that environmentalists are themselves of two minds with regard to sport hunting. The only hunting that environmentalists uniformly support is that which prevents damage to ecosystems or threatened species. Although Regan explicitly denies that his rights view can countenance hunting even in such cases, this is, arguably, false. Assuming that more deaths would occur if we allowed nature to take its course and/ or the deaths which do occur would involve more suffering than if we hunted and killed the same number of animals, why would not equal respect for individual rights require us to see to it that the smaller number of deaths occurs? In dealing with humans, numerous auxiliary concerns arise, including the possible effectiveness of persuasion and obligations created by a social contract, but neither of these seem relevant when dealing with wild animals.

Regan's response might be that although more deaths occur when we knowingly allow nature to take its course, nature does not violate anyone's rights as we would were we to actively kill some individuals in order to save others or to make the deaths that do occur more humane. Additionally, Regan probably would respond that the suggested justification for hunting in such cases treats individuals with rights as if they were mere "utility receptacles."

However, it should be clear that *some* form of an animal rights view *could* endorse hunting, at least in those situations where environmentalists feel compelled to support it on ecological grounds, as could a utilitarian view such as Singer's. The deep reason animal rightists oppose hunting is not so much that it is inherently unjustifiable from such an ethical perspective, but rather that other means to the same end are now, or at least could soon be made, available. However, once alternative means to the end of wildlife population control are affordable and effective, there is no longer any ecological necessity in hunting – if ecosystem health or integrity can be achieved just as well by non-lethal means, then environmentalists will not uniformly support hunting as the means, anymore than they now uniformly support sport hunting. (The case for, as I call it, "therapeutic hunting of obligatory management species" is developed in much greater detail in Varner 1998, ch. 5.)

The greatest difficulties reconciling environmentalists' intuitions with sentientist ethics arise in regard to Callicott's point #2. Variations on Callicott's "humane herdspersons" example seem genuinely troubling. For if the only way to argue for preserving a certain species of plant was in terms of its preservation's effect on present or future generations of humans or other sentient creatures, then it really is hard to see how one could justify inflicting death, or significant suffering, or bodily pain on one, let alone a large number, of sentient animals. However, this way of describing the challenge to sentientism misstates the issue in a subtle but important way, and if we are to see how a sentientist could hope to build an adequate reply to the concerns raised in Callicott's #2 above, we must understand how.

Consider, first, Callicott's specific language in the "humane herdspersons" case. He describes the plants in question as "overwhelmingly important to the stability... of the biotic community" (1980, p. 320). If this were the case, then on a purely anthropocentric stance, defending them would be pre-eminently important, because background ecological stability is crucially important to long-term human flourishing. But so too from an animal rights or animal welfare perspective. If a plant species' survival is crucial to the stability of the ecosystem on which future generations of sentient animals depend, then surely sentientist considerations could drive whatever practical choices are necessary to secure the species' survival. That is, if a sentientist ethic can be used to justify hunting to prevent ecosystem damage through over-population, then it can be used to justify hunting to prevent ecosystem destabilization caused by the extinction of a plant.

Here I am skipping over important philosophical problems about the interests of potential versus actual beings, but these problems are at least not unique to environmental issues (see POPULATION, FUTURE GENERATIONS). More apposite is the problem that by the time a species becomes critically endangered, it almost never plays a crucial role in its ecosystem. (An exception would be when a keystone species becomes critically endangered over a short period of time relative to how fast its ecosystem evolves, so that, if restored promptly, it could resume whatever crucial functions it formerly played.) So endangered species are almost never "overwhelmingly important to the stability... of the biotic community," and this derails the kind of anthropocentric and sentientist arguments sketched in the foregoing paragraph.

So why worry about endangered species? One answer, an anthropocentric one, is: because overall BIODIVERSITY is important, and although no species taken by itself is crucial to the stability and fecundity of the ecosystems on which we depend, we must stop the *general trend* toward simplification in order to avoid significant harms to future generations of humans. To what extent this rationale applies to non-human animals is uncertain. Modern humans exploit biodiversity in their environment in ways no previous organism has (e.g. via medical applications, genetic engineering, etc.), and so modern humans may depend on background biodiversity in a unique way. But even if this general argument applied only to humans, it would be relevant to a generally sentientist ethic insofar as sentientists usually acknowledge that only humans have certain pre-eminently important interests. Regan (1983, in his treatment of the "worse-off" principle) and Singer (1990, pp. 18–19), for instance, both do. Yet if a sentientist acknowledges that certain human interests are preeminently important, and if preserving biodiversity is necessary to protect those interests, then preserving biodiversity is itself pre-eminently important.

This general approach to the biodiversity issue is consistent with a sentientist stance. Admittedly, it does not justify preserving every species, in every situation, at whatever cost, and on a sentientist view the costs include suffering and death to sentient animals who must be removed from a plant species' habitat in order to save it. However, by the 1990s many environmentalists were calling for a more

ecosystem-based approach to the preservation of biodiversity, in contrast to the spe-
cies-by-species approach of the US Endangered Species Act of 1973, and that new
approach does not call for the preservation of every species in every situation either.

This approach to the biodiversity question also gives us a handle on how a
sentientist could respond to the other issues raised in Callicott's #2 above. Callicott
says that sentientists must see large predators as "merciless, wanton, and incorrigible
murderers" (1980, p. 320). This is, of course, hyperbole insofar as no non-human
predators are moral agents, and hence when they kill they do not commit murder. Yet
some sentientists have argued that the elimination of predators really would be a good
thing *if it were possible to do so without causing damage to the ecosystems involved*
(Sapontzis 1987, ch. 13). The italicized "if" clause points the way out, however. To
the extent that it is factually correct that prey species "need" their predators to
stabilize the ecosystem on which they depend, even predator reintroduction can
look good from a sentientist perspective.

The foregoing account of how a sentientist ethic need not have the implications
Callicott alleges relies upon certain empirical assumptions, which *could* turn out to be
false. For instance, the importance of biodiversity to long-term human interests could
have been exaggerated above, or it could be false that removing predators from an
ecosystem harms its prey species in any way. However, these sorts of claim are
commonly endorsed by environmentalists (including Aldo Leopold 1949) and therefore the foregoing considerations show how, on factual assumptions which environmentalists themselves commonly make, a sentientist ethic can avoid the kinds of
implication Callicott charges them with having. (Some of the preceding considerations regarding BIODIVERSITY and predators are elaborated in greater detail in Varner
1998, ch. 6.)

So sentientism is not inadequate as an environmental ethic because it necessarily
has anti-environmental implications. In conclusion, I turn to the other sorts of reason
given for thinking that sentientism is environmentally inadequate. One is that in
certain hypothetical situations, sentientist ethics conflict with the intuitions of environmentalists, either by yielding a different answer or by seeing them as raising no
ethical question at all.

The best-known examples of this sort of claim are so-called "last man" cases.
Australian philosopher Richard Routley (who subsequently changed his last name
to Sylvan) first used such examples in "Is there a need for a new, an environmental
ethic?" (1973). Routley later co-authored a greatly expanded version of this paper
with Val Routley (who subsequently changed her name to Plumwood), entitled
"Human chauvinism and environmental ethics" (1980). The latter paper is not as
readily available, but it is much more detailed and philosophically rich. In particular,
it makes explicit how the last man argument applies to both sentientism and anthropocentrism.

The Routleys argue that both are environmentally inadequate, because neither
would have anything negative to say about cases where the last man destroys an
insentient organism, species, or ecosystem. For, assuming that the actions of the last
man do not adversely affect him and cannot adversely affect other humans, an
anthropocentrist has no grounds for saying that any morally significant harm has
been done. So although an environmentalist would (they assume) condemn such

pointless destruction, an anthropocentrist would either reach the opposite conclusion and say that the last man's mere whim suffices to justify it, or deny that there is any moral issue at all, since no other humans' interests are at stake. And a sentientist would have to give the same analysis of a case in which the last man destroys an organism, species, or ecosystem without affecting any sentient beings.

I do not see any way for sentientists to respond directly to this objection, but I do not think this should worry them. To see why, we must first consider the final sort of reason which is commonly given for thinking that no version of sentientism can be an adequate environmental ethic: because environmentalists are directly concerned with preserving holistic entities such as species and ecosystems, the conceptual machinery of traditional ethical theory, which was developed to deal with conflicts among individual humans, is ill-suited to capturing the general value framework environmentalists think with.

In his quizzically titled essay "The liberation of nature?" John Rodman (1977) used a lengthy review of Singer's and Stone's books to press this point regarding both utilitarian and rights-based approaches to ethics. Both, he argued, developed as ways of dealing with conflicting claims of humans, and although each approach can be extended to cover more and more of the non-human world, this is itself a kind of humanizing of nature. Rodman asserts that it is the domestication of nature in general that environmentalists oppose, and he concludes that forcing environmentalists to think about our treatment of nature in terms of these traditional ethical theories necessarily distorts the environmentalist position.

It is important to consider a second variation on this charge because of the way I have chosen to characterize various kinds of environmental ethic in this chapter. Throughout, I have spoken in terms of which entities have "moral standing" according to various views. But even using this terminology could be claimed to subtly stack the deck against holism. To see why, let me be more specific about the meanings of the terms "moral standing" and "intrinsic value." As I use them, to say that something has intrinsic value is to say that its existence or flourishing is a (morally) good thing, independently of its relation to anything else; and to say that an entity has moral standing is to say that it has desires and/or needs the fulfillment of which creates intrinsic value. So defined, the range of things that have "intrinsic value" could be much broader than those that have moral standing, and to insist on characterizing different types of environmental ethic in terms of which things have moral standing might subtly bias us against holism. For neither species nor ecosystems literally have desires, and neither has needs in the same familiar and uncontroversial sense that conscious organisms do. Thus, if environmentalists tend to think like holists, then forcing them to articulate their position in terms of species and ecosystems having moral standing would distort their position in a subtle way.

If it is indeed a fact that environmentalists tend to think like holists, then I can see the propriety of insisting that "a truly environmental ethic" would necessarily have a holistic component. However, to think of doing environmental ethics as simply attempting to accurately describe environmentalists' values would be philosophically misguided. For philosophical ethics is ultimately concerned with how people ought to think about ethics rather than merely descriptive of how they do think. The fundamental philosophical question about environmental ethics should not be "Do environmentalists *in fact* think that holistic entities have intrinsic value?" but rather "*Should* one think that?"

In light of what was said above about Callicott's 1980 paper, it will not do to respond to the latter question by simply dismissing sentientist ethics as thoroughly inconsistent with sound environmental policy. But then what kind of reason are we left with for insisting that an "adequate" environmental ethic must be holistic? The third kind of reason (that environmentalists in fact think like holists) reduces environmental ethics to a kind of moral anthropology. But we can now see why the second kind of reason ("last man" type cases) effectively begs the question against sentientist ethics. For if sentientist ethics are not inconsistent with sound environmental policy as long as the interests of humans and other sentient animals are involved, what reason can be given for thinking that it does matter what the last man does?

In his reply to Callicott's 1980 paper, Edward Johnson pressed this point in the form of a dilemma for the environmental holist:

> To treat the Whole as sentient would fail to challenge the doctrine of sentientism. But, if the Whole is not sentient, then a number of questions arise: how can it have a good? If it can have a good, how can we, as individual moral agents... know what that good is? If we can know what the good of the Whole is, why should we care? (1981, p. 269)

Holists must either show how species and ecosystems have interests in some traditional sense, or give a convincing argument for attributing intrinsic value to them on some other basis. But since holists almost universally reject the first option, the burden of proof is on the holist to explain why such entities have intrinsic value and just how significant that value is. This is all the more true if, as argued above in response to Callicott, the range of cases in which the implications of sentientist ethics conflict with the intuitions of environmentalists is much narrower than is often assumed (see META-ETHICS).

References

Callicott, J. Baird (1980) "Animal liberation: a triangular affair," *Environmental Ethics* 2, pp. 311–38. [The classic statement of why environmental ethics and animal rights views are incompatible.]

——(1989) "Animal liberation and environmental ethics: back together again," in *In Defense of the Land Ethic*, J. Baird Callicott (Albany: State University of New York Press), pp. 49–59. [Attempts to show how some of the concerns of animal welfarists can be accommodated by Leopold's land ethic.]

Feinberg, Joel (1974) "The rights of animals and unborn generations," in *Philosophy and Environmental Crisis*, ed. William Blackstone, Jr. (Athens: University of Georgia Press), pp. 43–68. [A classic analysis of the relationship between rights and conscious desires.]

Goodpaster, Kenneth (1979) "From egoism to environmentalism," in *Ethics and Problems of the 21st Century*, ed. Kenneth Goodpaster and Kenneth Sayre (Notre Dame: University of Notre Dame Press), pp. 21–35. [Questions the adequacy of any environmental ethic which merely extends traditional conceptions of moral standing based on characteristics which make our own conscious lives seem valuable to us.]

Johnson, Edward (1981) "Animal liberation versus the land ethic," *Environmental Ethics* 3, pp. 265–73. [An early rejoinder to Callicott's widely discussed 1980 essay, which raises most of the problems others saw in it.]

Leopold, Aldo (1949) *A Sand County Almanac, and Sketches Here and There*, illustrated by Charles W. Schwartz (New York: Oxford University Press). [A landmark work in environmental philosophy, written from a non-sentientist perspective.]

Regan, Tom (1981) "The nature and possibility of an environmental ethic," *Environmental Ethics* 3, pp. 19–34. [Here Regan defined a truly environmental ethic in terms of extending moral standing to non-conscious entities and sounded more sanguine about the prospects for developing one than he does in his 1983 book.]

——(1983) *The Case for Animal Rights* (Berkeley: University of California Press). [A rigorous analysis of the logic of rights claims and the consequences of extending moral rights to animals.]

Rodman, John (1977) "The liberation of nature?" *Inquiry* 20, pp. 83–145. [A review of Singer 1975 and Stone 1974, which draws parallels between the two and questions whether extending traditional accounts of moral standing and rights is the way to develop an adequate environmental ethic.]

Routley, Richard (1973) "Is there a need for a new, an environmental ethic?" *Proceedings of the XV World Congress of Philosophy*, pp. 205–10. [The first essay on environmental ethics by a professional philosopher, this paper popularized the use of "last man" cases.]

Routley, Richard and Routley, Val (1980) "Human chauvinism and environmental ethics," in *Environmental Philosophy*, ed. Don Mannison, Michael McRobbie, and Richard Routley (Canberra: Australian National University), pp. 96–189. [This essay has never been reprinted in whole apart from in this relatively obscure anthology, but it provides a much more thorough working-out of themes touched on in Routley 1973.]

Sapontzis, Steve F. (1987) *Morals, Reason, and Animals* (Philadelphia: Temple University Press). [A comprehensive treatment of "animal rights" as an extension of common-sense thinking about ethics; chapter 13 argues that although predator elimination would indeed be a good thing, it is not practicable.]

Singer, Peter (1990 [1975]) *Animal Liberation: A New Ethics for Our Treatment of Animals* (New York: Avon Books). [The most widely read book in the animal rights literature.]

——(1993 [1979]) *Practical Ethics* (Cambridge: Cambridge University Press). [A more philosophically sophisticated treatment of the issues in Singer 1990 (1975).]

Stone, Christopher D. (1974) *Should Trees Have Standing? Toward Legal Rights for Natural Objects* (Los Altos, California: William Kaufmann). [An attempt to extend the individualistic rights paradigm to holistic natural entities; originally published in the *University of Southern California Law Review* 45 (1972), pp. 450–501.]

Varner, Gary E. (1998) *In Nature's Interests? Interests, Animal Rights and Environmental Ethics* (New York: Oxford University Press). [Defends a non-sentientist account of interests, but also attacks the claim that anthropocentric and sentientist ethics are both antithetical to sound environmental policy.]

14

The land ethic

J. BAIRD CALLICOTT

The Darwinian roots of the land ethic

Of all the environmental ethics so far devised, the land ethic, first sketched by Aldo Leopold (1887–1948), is most popular among professional conservationists and least popular among professional philosophers. Conservationists are preoccupied with such things as the anthropogenic pollution of air and water by industrial and municipal wastes, the anthropogenic reduction in numbers of species populations, the outright anthropogenic extinction of species, and the invasive anthropogenic introduction of other species into places not their places of evolutionary origin (see LAND AND WATER and BIODIVERSITY). Conservationists as such are not concerned about the injury, pain, or death of non-human specimens – that is, of individual animals and plants – except in those rare cases in which a species' populations are so reduced in number that the conservation of every specimen is vital to the conservation of the species. On the other hand, professional philosophers, most of them schooled in and intellectually committed to the modern classical theories of ethics, are ill-prepared to comprehend morally such "holistic" concerns. Professional philosophers are inclined to dismiss holistic concerns as non-moral or to reduce them to concerns about either human welfare or the welfare of non-human organisms severally (see NORMATIVE ETHICS). And they are mystified by the land ethic, unable to grasp its philosophical foundations and pedigree.

Without a grasp of its philosophical foundations and pedigree, however, it is difficult to know how the land ethic might be related to the more familiar moral concerns that loom large in the modern era (roughly the seventeenth through the twentieth centuries) – such as human happiness, human dignity, and human rights – and how it might be applied to and illuminate cases other than those Leopold himself considers in his brief sketch of it in *A Sand County Almanac* (1949). In this chapter, I outline the philosophical foundations and pedigree of the land ethic and indicate how it might be related to more familiar modern moral concerns and how it might be applied to a range of novel environmental concerns, some of which Leopold himself does not consider. In addition, I also address some of the theoretical and practical challenges to the land ethic raised by professional philosophers.

To discover its philosophical foundations and pedigree, we may begin by looking for clues in the text of Leopold's "The land ethic," the capstone essay of his *A Sand County Almanac*. Leopold provides the most important clue in the second section of the essay, entitled "The ethical sequence." Having observed that ethics have grown considerably in scope and complexity during the 3,000 years of recorded history in western civilization, Leopold writes:

> This extension of ethics, so far studied only by philosophers [and, Leopold's insinuation is clear, therefore not very revealingly studied] is actually a process in ecological evolution. An ethic, ecologically, is a limitation on freedom of action in the struggle for existence. An ethic, philosophically, is a differentiation of social from anti-social conduct. These are two definitions of one thing. The thing has its origin in the tendency of interdependent individuals or groups to evolve modes of co-operation. (1949, p. 202)

Leopold, I should hasten to point out, was no better a student of philosophy than most professional philosophers are of conservation and its concerns. Hence his characterization of an ethic, "philosophically," is, put most charitably, incomplete. In any case, what he hints at, rather insistently and unmistakably, is some sort of evolutionary interpretation of ethics. Leopold's use here of such words and phrases as "evolution," "struggle for existence," "origin," "evolve," "social and anti-social conduct" evokes not only a general evolutionary context in which to locate an understanding of ethics, it alludes, more particularly, to the classical evolutionary account of ethics in *The Descent of Man* (1871) by Charles Darwin (1809–82), the fourth chapter of which is devoted to "the moral sense." Doubtless, therefore, Darwin's account of "the thing"'s origin and development is what mainly informed Leopold's thinking about ethics.

The evolutionary origin of ethics

The existence of ethics presents a problem for Darwin's attempt to show how all things human can be understood as gradually evolved by natural (and sexual) selection, from traits possessed by closely related species, his project in *The Descent of Man*. Ethics demands that moral agents selflessly consider other interests in addition to their own. The theory of evolution would seem to predict, however, that the selfish would out-compete the selfless in the "struggle for existence," and thus survive and reproduce in greater numbers. Therefore greater and greater selfishness, not selflessness, would seem to be nature's choice in any population of organisms, including those ancestral to *Homo sapiens*. But history indicates the opposite: that our remote human ancestors were more callous, brutal, and ruthless than are we. At least so it seemed to a refined English gentleman who, while serving as naturalist on the round-the-world voyage of the HMS *Beagle*, had observed first hand what he and his contemporaries regarded as states of savagery and barbarism similar to those from which European and Asian civilizations were believed to have emerged.

In the absence of a convincing evolutionary explanation of its existence and progressive development, Darwin's pious opponents might point to ethics among human beings as a clear signature by the hand of Providence on the human soul.

To the conundrum presented him by the existence and putatively progressive development of ethics, Darwin's resolution is straightforward and elegant. For many kinds of animals, and especially for *Homo sapiens*, life's struggle is more efficiently prosecuted collectively and cooperatively than singly and competitively. Poorly armed by nature, as solitaries hominids would fall easy prey to their natural enemies or starve for lack of the wherewithal to obtain food. Together our primate ancestors might stand some chance of fending off predators and attacking prey larger than themselves. Like many other similarly situated species, evolving human beings thus formed primitive societies; or, put more precisely, those hominids that formed primitive societies evolved. But without some rudimentary ethics, human societies cannot stay integrated. As Darwin puts it: "No tribe could hold together if murder, robbery, treachery, &c., were common; consequently such crimes within the limits of the same tribe 'are branded with everlasting infamy'; but excite no such sentiment beyond these limits" (1871, p. 93).

Darwin's speculative reconstruction of the evolutionary pathway to ethics begins with altruistic "parental and filial affections" which motivate parents (perhaps only the female parent in many species) to care for their offspring and their offspring to desire the company of their parents. Such affectionally bonded nuclear families are small and often ephemeral societies, lasting, as in the case of bears, only until the next reproductive cycle. But the survival advantage to the young of being reared in such social units is obvious. Should the parental and filial affections chance to spill beyond the parental–filial relationship to that between siblings, cousins, and other close kin, such plurally bonded animals might stick together in more stable and permanent groups and defend themselves and forage communally and cooperatively. In which case there might also accrue additional advantages to the members of such groups in the struggle for life. Thus do mammalian societies originate in Darwin's account.

By themselves, the social impulses and sentiments are not ethics. An ethic is a set of behavioral rules, or a set of principles or precepts for governing behavior. The moral sentiments are, rather, the foundations of ethics, as David Hume (1711–76) and Adam Smith (1723–90) argued, a century or so before Darwin considered the matter. In addition to the social sentiments and instincts, *Homo sapiens* evolved a high degree of intelligence and imagination and uniquely possesses a symbolic language. Hence we human beings are capable of generally representing those kinds of behavior which are destructive of society ("murder, robbery, treachery, &c.") and articulating prohibitions of them in emotionally colored formulae – commandments – which today we call moral rules (see META-ETHICS and EARLY MODERN PHILOSOPHY).

The development of ethics correlative to the development of society

So much then for the origin of ethics; Darwin goes on to account for the development of ethics. As human social groups competed with one another for resources, the larger and better organized out-competed the smaller and less well organized. Hence clans, firstly, merged into tribes; tribes, next, into nations; and nations, eventually, into republics. The emergence of each of these levels of social organization was attended by a corresponding extension of ethics. Darwin sums up this parallel growth of ethics and society as follows:

As man advances in civilisation, and small tribes are united into larger communities, the simplest reason would tell each individual that he ought to extend his social instincts and sympathies to all the members of the same nation, though personally unknown to him. This point being once reached there is only an artificial barrier to prevent his sympathies extending to the men of all nations and races. (1871, pp. 100–1)

Quite remarkably, the influence of Hume, who lived long before evolutionary thinking was habitual, can be found even in Darwin's speculations about the development of ethics correlative to that of society. Compare the passage quoted from Darwin in the previous paragraph with this one from Hume:

But suppose the conjunction of the sexes to be established in nature, a family immediately arises; and particular rules being found requisite for its subsistence, these are immediately embraced; though without comprehending the rest of mankind within their prescriptions. Suppose that several families unite together into one society, which is totally disjoined from all others, the rules which preserve peace and order, enlarge themselves to the utmost extent of that society.... But again suppose that several distinct societies maintain a kind of intercourse for mutual convenience and advantage, the boundaries of justice still grow larger in proportion to the largeness of men's views and the force of their mutual connexions. History, experience, reason sufficiently instruct us in this natural progress of human sentiments, and in the gradual enlargement of [them]. (1957 [1751], p. 23)

Further, with the emergence of each new level in the social hierarchy – the clan, the tribe, the nation, the republic, the global village – the content of the moral code changed or was supplemented to reflect and facilitate the novel structure of each newly emerged level. At the tribal level of society, "when the question is put...is it worse to kill a girl of a foreign tribe, or to marry a girl of one's own, an answer just opposite to ours would be given," Darwin (1871, p. 91) observes. Since Darwin's day, matrimonial ethics have developed further still. In contemporary post-patriarchal society, we would still answer that it is certainly wrong to *kill* a girl of any ethnic group, but we would add that neither is it right to marry a *girl* of one's own ethnic group or, for that matter, any other. Among ourselves, mature men are allowed to marry only women some four to six years beyond menarche – otherwise they would be guilty of "statutory rape" – and it is, though lawful, "inappropriate" for men to marry or sexually consort with women much younger than themselves.

The land ethic as the next step in the Darwinian society-ethics pas de deux

During Darwin's lifetime, as during Hume's, a universal ethic of human rights was only dimly visible on the horizon. By the mid-twentieth century, when Leopold was gestating the land ethic, a universal human rights ethic may have seemed more nearly attainable. In any case, Leopold, often called a prophet, looked farther ahead than did Darwin himself, indeed farther ahead than Darwin could have looked in the absence of a well-developed ecological world-view. Leopold (1949, p. 203) summarizes Darwin's natural history of ethics with characteristic compression: "All ethics so far evolved rest upon a single premise: that the individual is a member of a community of interdependent parts." Then he adds an ecological element, the community model of the biota espoused most notably by Charles Elton (1900–91): ecology "simply enlarges the boundaries of the community to include soils, waters, plants, and animals, or collectively: the land" (ibid, p. 204). When we all learn to "see land as a community to which we belong" not as "a commodity belonging to us" (ibid, p. viii), that same "simplest reason," of which Darwin speaks, might kick in. And, when it does, what results will be a land ethic that "changes the role of *Homo sapiens* from conqueror of the land community to plain member and citizen of it" (ibid, p. 204).

So, now the philosophical foundations and pedigree of the land ethic should be manifest. Basically, what Leopold did to cook up the land ethic was to take over Darwin's recipe for the origin and development of ethics, and add an ecological ingredient, the Eltonian "community concept." Darwin in turn had taken over a sentiment-based theory of ethics from Hume and Smith. Leopold may never have studied Hume's or Smith's moral philosophies; certainly he never cites them; indeed he may have known of Hume only as a historian and Smith only as an economist. But because he surely did read Darwin and allude in "The Land Ethic" to Darwin's account of the origin and development of ethics, the philosophical foundations and pedigree of his land ethic are traceable through Darwin to the sentiment-based ethical theories of Hume and Smith.

The holism of the land ethic and its antecedents

According to Leopold, "a land ethic implies respect for . . . fellow-members *and also for the community as such*" (1949, p. 204, emphasis added). The land ethic, in other words, has a holistic dimension to it that is completely foreign to the mainstream modern moral theories going back to Hobbes. The holistic dimension of the land ethic – respect for the community as such, in addition to respect for its members severally – is, however, not in the least foreign to the Darwinian and Humean theories of ethics upon which it is built. Darwin could hardly be more specific or emphatic on this point:

> Actions are regarded by savages and were probably so regarded by primeval man, as good or bad, solely as they obviously affect the welfare of the tribe, – not that of the species, nor that of an individual member of the tribe. This conclusion agrees well with the belief that the so-called moral sense is aboriginally derived from the social instincts, for both relate at first exclusively to the community. (1871, p. 96–7)

Gary Varner states flatly that "concern for communities as such has no historical antecedent in David Hume" (1991, p. 179). But it does. Demonstrably. Hume insists, evidently against Hobbes and other social contract theorists, that "we must renounce the theory which accounts for every moral sentiment by the principle of self-love. We must adopt a more publick affection, and allow that the interests of society are not, even on their own account, entirely indifferent to us" (1957 [1751], p. 47). Nor is this an isolated remark. Over and over we read in Hume's ethical works such statements as this: "It appears that a tendency to publick good, and to the promoting of peace, harmony, and order in society, does always by affecting the benevolent principles of our frame engage us on the side of the social virtues" (ibid, p. 56). And this: "Everything that promotes the interests of society must communicate pleasure, and what is pernicious, give uneasiness" (ibid, p. 58).

That is not to say that in Hume, certainly, and even in Darwin there is no theoretical provision for a lively concern for the individual members of society, as well as for society per se. The sentiment of sympathy being so central to it, I should expressly acknowledge that in the moral philosophy of Adam Smith one finds little ethical holism. Sympathy means "with-feeling." And that "all important-important emotion of sympathy," as Darwin (1871, p. 81) styles it, can hardly extend to a transorganismic entity, such as society per se, which has no feelings per se. Hume and Darwin, however, recognized other moral sentiments than sympathy, some of which – patriotism, for example – relate as exclusively and specifically to society as sympathy does to sentient individuals. In Leopold's "The land ethic," in any event, the holistic aspect eventually eclipses the individualistic aspect. Toward the beginning of his essay, Leopold, as noted, declares that a land ethic "implies respect for fellow-members" of the biotic community, as well as "for the community as such." Toward the middle of the essay he speaks of a "biotic right" to "continue" but such a right accrues, as the context indicates, to species, not to specimens (1949, p. 210). Toward the end of the essay, Leopold writes a summary moral maxim, a golden rule, for the land ethic: "A thing is right when it tends to preserve the integrity, stability, and beauty of the biotic community. It is wrong when it tends otherwise" (ibid, pp. 224–5). In it, there is no reference at all to "fellow-members." They have gradually dropped out of account as "The Land Ethic" proceeds to its climax.

Why? One reason has already been noted. Conservationists, among whom Leopold counted himself, are professionally concerned about biological and ecological wholes – populations, species, communities, ecosystems – not their individual constituents. And the land ethic is tailored to suit conservation concerns, which are often confounded by concerns for individual specimens. For example, the conservation of endangered plant species is often most directly and efficiently effected by the deliberate eradication of the feral animals that threaten them. Preserving the integrity of a biotic community often requires reducing the populations of some component species, be they native or non-native, wild or feral. Another reason is that ECOLOGY is about metaorganismic entities – biotic communities and ecosystems – not individuals, and the land ethic is expressly informed by ecology and reflects an ecological world-view. Its holism is precisely what makes the land ethic the environmental ethic of choice among conservationists and ecologists. In short, its holism is the land ethic's principal asset.

Whether by the end of the essay he forgets it or not, Leopold does say in "The Land Ethic" that "fellow-members" of the "land community" deserve "respect." How can we pretend to respect them if, in the interest of the integrity, stability, and beauty of the biotic community, we chop some down, gun others down, set fire to still others, and so on. Such brutalities are often involved in what conservationists call "wildlife management." Here again, to resolve this conundrum, we may consult Darwin, who indicates that ethics originated among *Homo sapiens* in the first place to serve the welfare of the community. Certainly, among the things that threaten to dissolve a human community are "murder, robbery, treachery, &c." However, as ethics evolve correlatively to social evolution, not only do they widen their scope, they change in content, such that what is wrong correlative to one stage of social development, may not be wrong correlative to the next. In a tribal society, as Darwin observes, exogamy is a cardinal precept. It is not in a republic. Nevertheless, in all human communities – from the savage clan to the family of man – the "infamy" of murder, robbery, treachery, etc. remains "everlasting." But the multispecies biotic community is so different from all our human communities that we cannot assume that what is wrong for one human being to do to another, even at every level of social organization, is wrong for one fellow-member of the biotic community to do to another.

The currency of the economy of nature, we must remember, is energy. And it passes from one member to another, not from hand to hand like money in the human economy, but from stomach to stomach. As Leopold observes of the biotic community, "The only truth is that its members must suck hard, live fast, and die often" (1949, p. 107). In the biotic community there are producers and consumers, predators and prey. One might say that the integrity and stability of the biotic community depends upon death as well as life; indeed, one might say further, that the life of one member is premised squarely on the death of another. So one could hardly argue that our killing of fellow-members of the biotic community is, prima facie, land-ethically wrong. It depends on who is killed, for what reasons, under what circumstances, and how. The filling in of these blanks would provide, in each case, an answer to the question about respect. Models of respectful, but often violent and lethal use of fellow-members of the biotic community are provided by traditional American Indian peoples (Callicott and Overholt 1993).

The holism of the land ethic and the problem of eco-fascism

Its holism is the land ethic's principal strength, but also its principal liability. Remember that, according to Leopold, evolutionary and ecological biology reveal that "land [is] a community to which we belong" not "a commodity belonging to us" and that from the point of view of a land ethic, we are but "plain members and citizens of the biotic community." Then it would seem that the summary moral maxim of the land ethic applies to *Homo sapiens* no less than to the other members and citizens of the biotic community, plain or otherwise. A human population of more than six billion individuals is a dire threat to the integrity, stability, and beauty of the biotic community. Thus the existence of such a large human population is land-ethically wrong. To right that wrong should we not do what we do when a population of white-tailed deer or some other species irrupts and threatens the integrity, stability, and beauty of the biotic community? We immediately and summarily reduce it, by whatever means necessary, usually by randomly and indiscriminately shooting the members of such a population to death – respectfully, of course – until its numbers are optimized. It did not take the land ethic's critics long to draw out the vitiating – but, as I shall go on to argue directly, only apparent – implication of the land ethic. According to William Aiken, from the point of view of the land ethic, "massive human diebacks would be good. It is our duty to cause them. It is our species' duty, relative to the whole, to eliminate 90 per cent of our numbers" (1984, p. 269). Its requirement that individual organisms, apparently also including individual human organisms, be sacrificed for the good of the whole, makes the land ethic, according to Tom Regan, a kind of "environmental fascism" (1983, p. 262). Frederick Ferré echoes and amplifies Aiken's and Regan's indictment of the land ethic:

> Anything we could do to exterminate excess people . . . would be morally "right"! To refrain from such extermination would be "wrong"! . . . Taken as a guide for human culture, the land ethic – despite the best intentions of its supporters – would lead toward classical fascism, the submergence of the individual person in the glorification of the collectivity, race, tribe, or nation. (1996, p. 18)

Finally, Kristin Shrader-Frechette adds her voice to those expressing moral outrage at the land "ethic": "In subordinating the welfare of all creatures to the integrity, stability, and beauty, of the biotic community, then one subordinates individual human welfare, in all cases, to the welfare of the biotic community" (1996, p. 63).

If the land ethic implies what Aiken, Regan, Ferré, and Shrader-Frechette allege that it does, it must be rejected as monstrous. Happily, it does not. To think that it does, one must assume that Leopold proffered the land ethic as a substitute for, not an addition to, our venerable and familiar human ethics. But he did not. Leopold refers to the various stages of ethical development – from tribal mores to universal human rights and, finally, to the land ethic – as "accretions." "Accretion" means an "increase by external addition or accumulation." The land ethic is an accretion – that is, an addition – to our several accumulated social ethics, not something that is supposed to replace them. If, as I here explain, Leopold is building the land ethic on theoretical foundations that he finds in Darwin, then it is obvious that with the advent of each new stage in the accreting development of ethics, the old stages are not erased or replaced, but added to. I, for example, am a citizen of a republic, but I also remain a member of an extended family, and a resident of a municipality. And it is quite evident to us all, from our own moral experience, that the duties attendant on citizenship in a republic (to pay taxes, to serve in the armed forces or in the Peace Corps, for example) do not cancel or replace the duties attendant on membership in a family (to honor parents, to love and educate children, for example) or residence in a municipality (to support public schools, to attend town meetings). Similarly, it is equally evident – at least to Leopold and his exponents, if not to his critics – that the duties attendant upon citizenship in the biotic community (to preserve its integrity, stability, and beauty) do not cancel or replace the duties attendant on membership in the human global village (to respect human rights).

Prioritizing the duties generated by membership in multiple communities

The land ethic involves a limited pluralism (multiple moral maxims, multiple sets of duties, or multiple principles and precepts) not a thoroughgoing pluralism of moral philosophies *sensu* Stone (1987) – Aristotelian ethics for this quandary, Kantian ethics for that, utilitarianism here, social-contract theory there. Thus, as Shrader-Frechette points out, the land ethic must provide "second-order ethical principles and a priority ranking system that specifies the respective conditions under which [first-order] holistic and individualistic ethical principles ought to be recognized" (1996, p. 63). Leopold provides no such second-order principles for prioritizing among first-order principles, but they can be easily derived from the communitarian foundations of the land ethic. By combining two second-order principles we can achieve a priority ranking among first-order principles, when, in a given quandary, they conflict. The first second-order principle (SOP-1) is that obligations generated by membership in more venerable and intimate communities take precedence over those generated in more recently emerged and impersonal communities. I think that most of us, for example, feel that our family duties (to care for aged parents, say, to educate minor children) take precedence over our civic duties (to contribute to United Way charities, say, to vote for higher municipal taxes to better support more indigent persons on the dole), when, because of limited means, we are unable to perform both family and civic duties. The second second-order principle (SOP-2) is that stronger interests (for lack of a better word) generate duties that take precedence over duties generated by weaker interests. For example, while duties to one's own children, all things being equal, properly take precedence over duties toward unrelated children in one's municipality, one would be remiss to shower one's own children with luxuries while unrelated children in one's municipality lacked the bare necessities (food, shelter, clothing, education) for a decent life. Having the bare necessities for a decent life is a stronger interest than is the enjoyment of luxuries, and our duties to help supply proximate unrelated children with the former take precedence over our duties to supply our own children with the latter.

These second-order principles apply as well in quandaries in which duties to individuals conflict with duties to communities per se. In a case made famous by Jean-Paul Sartre (1905–80) in *L'Existentialisme est un Humanisme* (1960), a young man is caught in the dilemma of leaving his mother and going off to join the French Free Forces in England, during the Nazi occupation of France in World War II. Sartre, of course, is interested in the existential choice that this forces on the young man and in pursuing the thesis that his decision in some way makes a moral principle, not that it should be algorithmically determined by the application of various moral principles. But the second-order principles here set out apply to the young man's dilemma quite directly and, one might argue, decisively – existential freedom notwithstanding. SOP-1 requires the young man to give priority to the first-order principle, "Honor Thy Father and Thy Mother", over the other first-order principle at play, "Serve Thy Country." But SOP-2 reverses the priority dictated by SOP-1. The very existence of France as a transorganismic entity is threatened. The young man's mother has a weaker interest at stake, for, as Sartre reports, his going off – and maybe getting killed – would plunge her into "despair." His mother being plunged into despair would be terrible, but not nearly as terrible as the destruction of France would be if not enough young men fought on her behalf. So the resolution of this young man's dilemma is clear; he should give priority to the first-order principle, "Serve Thy Country." Had the young man been an American and had the time been the early 1970s and had the dilemma been stay home with his mother or join the Peace Corps and go to Africa, then he should give priority to the first-order principle "Honor Thy Father and Thy Mother" and stay home. Had the young man been the same person as Sartre constructs, but had his mother been a Jew whom the Nazis would have sent to a horrible death in a concentration camp if her son does not stay home and help her hide, then again, he should give priority to the first-order principle, "Honor Thy Father and Thy Mother" and stay home.

The priority (second-order) principles applied to the old-growth forest quandary

Let me consider now those kinds of quandaries in which our duties to human beings conflict with our duties to *biotic* communities as such. Varner supplies a case in point:

> Suppose that an environmentalist enamored with the Leopold land ethic is consider-ing how to vote on a national referendum to preserve the spotted owl by restricting logging in Northwest forests.... He or she would be required to vote, not according to the land ethic, but according to whatever ethic governs closer ties to a human family and/or larger human community. Therefore, if a relative is one of 10,000 loggers who will lose jobs if the referendum passes, the environmentalist is obligated to vote against it. Even if none of the loggers is a family member, the voter is still obligated to vote against the referendum. (1991, p. 176)

The flaw in Varner's reasoning is that he applies only SOP-1 – that obligations generated by membership in more venerable and intimate communities take preced-ence over those generated in more recently emerged and impersonal communities. If that were the only second-order communitarian principle then he would be right. But SOP-2 – that stronger interests generate duties that take precedence over duties generated by weaker interests – reverses the priority determined by applying SOP-1, in this case. The spotted owl is threatened with preventable anthropogenic extinction – threatened with biocide, in a word – and the old growth forest biotic communities of the Pacific Northwest are threatened with destruction. These threats are the environ-mental-ethical equivalent of genocide and holocaust. The loggers, on the other hand, are threatened with economic losses, for which they can be compensated dollar for dollar. More important to the loggers, I am told, their lifestyle is threatened. But livelihood and lifestyle, for both of which adequate substitutes can be found, is a lesser interest than life itself. If we faced the choice of cutting down millions of 400-year-old trees or cutting down thousands of 40-year-old loggers, our duties to the loggers would take precedence by SOP-1, nor would SOP-1 be countermanded by SOP-2. But that is not the choice we face. The choice is between cutting down 400-year-old trees, rendering the spotted owl extinct, and destroying the old growth forest biotic com-munity, on the one hand, and displacing forest workers in an economy which is already displacing them through automation and raw-log exports to Japan and other foreign markets. And the old growth logging lifestyle is doomed, in any case, to self-destruct, for it will come to an end with the "final solution" to the old growth forest question, if the jack-booted timber barons (who disingenuously blame the spotted owl for the economic insecurity of loggers and other workers in the timber industry) continue to have their way. With SOP-2 supplementing SOP-1, the indication of the land ethic is crystal clear in the exemplary quandary posed by Varner, and it is opposite to the one Varner, applying only SOP-1, claims it indicates.

The land ethic in the time of a shifting science of ecology

Leopold penned the land ethic at mid-century. ECOLOGY then represented nature as tending toward a static equilibrium, and portrayed disturbance and perturbation, especially those caused by *Homo sapiens*, to be abnormal and destructive. In view of the shift in contemporary ecology to a more dynamic paradigm (Botkin 1990), and in recognition of the incorporation of natural disturbance to patch- and landscape-scale ecological dynamics (Pickett and Ostfeld, 1995), we might wonder whether the land ethic has become obsolete. Has the paradigm shift from "the balance of nature" to the "flux of nature" in ecology invalidated the land ethic? I think not, but recent developments in ecology may require revising the land ethic.

Leopold was aware of and sensitive to natural change. He knew that conservation must aim at a moving target. How can we conserve a biota that is dynamic, ever changing, when the very words "conserve" and "preserve" – especially when linked to "integrity" and "stability" – connote arresting change? The key to solving that conundrum is the concept of scale. Scale is a general ecological concept that includes rate as well as scope; that is, the concept of scale is both temporal and spatial. And a review of Leopold's "The Land Ethic" reveals that he had the key, though he may not have been aware of just how multiscalar change in nature actually is.

Leopold writes: "Evolutionary changes ... are usually slow and local. Man's invention of tools has enabled him to make changes of unprecedented violence, rapidity, and scope" (1949, p. 217). As noted, Leopold was keenly aware that nature is dynamic, but, under the sway of mid-century equilibrium ecology, he conceived of natural change primarily in evolutionary, not in ecological terms. Nevertheless, scale is equally normative when ecological change is added to evolutionary change, that is, when normal climatic oscillations and patch dynamics are added to normal rates of extinction, hybridization, and speciation.

Homo sapiens is, in Leopold's opinion, a part of nature, "a plain member and citizen" of the "land-community." Hence, anthropogenic changes imposed on nature are no less natural than any other. Nevertheless, because *Homo sapiens* is a moral species, capable of ethical deliberation and conscientious choice, and evolutionary kinship and biotic community membership add a land ethic to our familiar social ethics, anthropogenic changes may be land-ethically evaluated. But by what norm? The norm of appropriate scale.

Let me first, as a model, recount Leopold's use of the temporal scale of evolutionary change as a norm for evaluating anthropogenic change. Consider the current episode of abrupt, anthropogenic, mass species extinction, which many people, I included, intuitively regard as the most morally reprehensible environmental thing going on today. Episodes of mass extinction have occurred in the past, though none of those has been attributed to a biological agent. Such events are, however, abnormal. Normally, speciation out-paces extinction – which is the reason why biological diversity has increased over time. So, what is land-ethically wrong with current anthropogenic species extinction? Species extinction is not unnatural. On the contrary, species extinction – anthropogenic or otherwise – is perfectly natural. But the current *rate* of extinction is wildly abnormal. Does being the first biological agent of a geologically significant mass extinction event in the 3.5-billion-year tenure of life on planet earth morally become us *Homo sapiens?* Doesn't that make a mockery of the self-congratulatory species epithet: the sapient, the wise species of the genus *Homo?*

Now let us apply this model to a quandary that Leopold himself never considered. Earth's CLIMATE has warmed up and cooled off in the past. So, what's land-ethically wrong with the present episode of anthropogenic global warming? We are a part of nature, so our recent habit of recycling sequestered carbon may be biologically unique, but it is not unnatural. A land-ethical evaluation of the current episode of anthropogenic climate change can, however, be made on the basis of temporal scale and magnitude. We may be causing a big increase of temperature at an unprecedented rate. That's what's land-ethically wrong with anthropogenic global warming.

Temporal and spatial scale in combination are key to the evaluation of direct human ecological impact. Long before *Homo sapiens* evolved, violent disturbances regularly occurred in nature. And they still occur, quite independently of human agency. Volcanoes bury the biota of whole mountains with lava and ash. Tornadoes rip through forests, leveling trees. Hurricanes erode beaches. Lightning-set fires sweep through forests and savannas. Rivers drown flood plains. Droughts dry up lakes and streams. Why, therefore, are analogous anthropogenic disturbances – clear cuts, beach developments, hydroelectric impoundments, and the like – environmentally unethical? As such, they are not. Once again, it's a question of scale. In general, frequent, intense disturbances, such as tornadoes, occur at small, widely distributed spatial scales, while spatially more extensive disturbances, such as droughts, occur less frequently. And most disturbances at whatever level of intensity and scale are stochastic (random) and chaotic (unpredictable). The problem with anthropogenic disturbances – such as industrial forestry and agriculture, exurban development, drift net fishing – is that they are far more frequent, widespread, and regularly occurring than are non-anthropogenic disturbances; they are well out of the spatial and temporal range of disturbances experienced by ecosystems over evolutionary time.

Proponents of the new "flux of nature" paradigm in ecology agree that appropriate scale is the operative norm for ethically appraising anthropogenic ecological perturbations. For example, Pickett and Ostfeld note that

> the flux of nature is a dangerous metaphor. The metaphor and the underlying ecological paradigm may suggest to the thoughtless and greedy that since flux is a fundamental part of the natural world, any human-caused flux is justifiable. Such an inference is wrong because the flux in the natural world has severe limits. . . . Two characteristics of human-induced flux would suggest that it would be excessive: fast rate and large spatial extent. (1995, p. 273)

Among the abnormally frequent and widespread anthropogenic perturbations that Leopold himself censures in "The Land Ethic" are the continent-wide elimination of large predators from biotic communities in North America; the ubiquitous substitution of domestic species for wild ones; the ecological homogenization of the planet resulting from the anthropogenic "world-wide pooling of faunas and floras"; the ubiquitous "polluting of waters or obstructing them with dams" (1949, p. 217).

The summary moral maxim of the land ethic, however, must be dynamized in light of developments in ecology over the past quarter-century. Leopold acknowledges the existence and land-ethical significance of natural environmental change, but seems to have thought of it primarily on a very slow evolutionary temporal scale. Even so, he thereby incorporates the concept of inherent environmental change and the crucial norm of scale into the land ethic. In light of more recent developments in ecology, we can add norms of scale to the land ethic for both climatic and ecological dynamics in land-ethically evaluating anthropogenic changes in nature. One hesitates to edit Leopold's elegant prose, but as a stab at formulating a dynamized summary moral maxim for the land ethic, I will hazard the following: A thing is right when it tends to disturb the biotic community only at normal spatial and temporal scales. It is wrong when it tends otherwise.

References

Aiken, W. (1984) "Ethical issues in agriculture," in *Earthbound: New Introductory Essays in Environmental Ethics*, ed. T. Regan (York: Random House), pp. 274–88. [An overview of ethical issues in agriculture including anthropocentric, animal liberation, and ecocentric perspectives.]

Botkin, D. (1990) *Discordant Harmonies: A New Ecology for the Twenty-first Century* (New York: Oxford University Press). [A popularization of the shift from a static, equilibrium model of nature in ecology to a more dynamic, non-equilibrium model.]

Callicott, J. B. and Overholt, T. W. (1993) "American Indian attitudes toward nature," in *Philosophy from Africa to Zen: An Invitation to World Philosophy*, ed. R. C. Solomon and K. M. Higgins (Lanham, MD: Rowman and Littlefield). [A characterization of American Indian environmental ethics based on various traditional and contemporary sources.]

Darwin, C. R. (1871) *The Descent of Man and Selection in Relation to Sex*, 2 vols. Vol. 1 (London: John Murray). [The extension of the theory of evolution to human psychological character-istics, including such phenomena as ethics and religion, as well as to human physical traits.]

Ferré, F. (1996) "Persons in nature: toward an applicable and unified environmental ethics," *Ethics and the Environment* 1, pp. 15–25. [A critique of the approaches to environmental ethics by Holmes Rolston III and J. Baird Callicott in favor of a Whiteheadian alternative.]

Hume, D. (1957 [1751]) *An Inquiry Concerning the Principles of Morals*, ed. C. W. Hendel (New York: The Liberal Arts Press). [The work that Hume regarded as his best in which he develops his ethical philosophy based on a theory of moral sentiments.]

Leopold, A. (1949) *A Sand County Almanac with Sketches Here and There* (New York: Oxford University Press). [A slim, posthumously published volume of essays conveying an ecological and evolutionary world-view and its moral implications.]

Pickett, S. T. A. and Ostfeld, R. S. (1995) "The shifting paradigm in ecology," in *A New Century for Natural Resource Management*, ed. R. L. Knight and S. F. Bates (Washington: Island Press), pp. 261–77. [A comparison of the classic balance-of-nature paradigm in ecology with the new flux-of-nature paradigm with attention to the environmental ethics implications of both.]

Regan, T. (1983) *The Case for Animal Rights* (Berkeley: University of California Press). [A magisterial analysis of rights and an argument for according rights to a narrow set of animals – mature mammals.]

Shrader-Frechette, K. S. (1996) "Individualism, holism, and environmental ethics," *Ethics and the Environment* 1, pp. 55–69. [A critique of economistic individualism and ecological holism as approaches to environmental ethics in favor of hierarchical holism in which strong human rights have priority over environmental obligations, while the latter have priority over weak human interests.]

Stone, C. D. (1987) *The Case for Moral Pluralism* (New York: Harper and Row). [An argument for selecting off the rack from among a suite of traditional and contemporary ethical theories, depending on the moral quandary one faces, instead of working to develop a comprehensive ethical theory that might adequately address all moral quandaries.]

Varner, G. E. (1991) "No holism without pluralism," *Environmental Ethics* 19, pp. 175–9. [A reiteration of Stone's claim that a single moral theory cannot adequately address the full range of human, humane, and environmental concerns.]

Further reading

Callicott, J. B. (1989) *In Defense of the Land Ethic: Essays in Environmental Philosophy* (Albany: State University of New York Press). [A miscellaneous collection of essays most of which elaborate on the Aldo Leopold land ethic.]

15

Deep ecology

FREYA MATHEWS

The term "deep ecology" was introduced to the world in a short article in a fairly obscure academic journal in the early 1970s (Naess 1973a). The author, Arne Naess, was a Norwegian philosophy professor, who was well known in Norway for his social activism, but virtually unknown, outside narrow academic circles, elsewhere. Yet "deep ecology" is now a term which enjoys wide currency and considerable charisma in the international environment movement. What is the story behind this term and its journey into prominence?

It is not possible simply to explain deep ecology in a definitive way, partly on account of successive revisions of its meaning undertaken by its original exponents, and in part because unintended meanings have attached to it as it has permeated popular culture. This protean quality of deep ecology has in fact contributed to its popular appeal. However, any exposition must start with the formulation offered by Naess in the 1973 article. In that first statement, Naess contrasted a "shallow" but powerful ecology movement with a "deep" but less influential one. He characterized shallow ecology summarily as involving an exclusive concern with issues of pollution and resource conservation insofar as these impacted on the interests of people in developed countries. The deep ecology movement was more fully elaborated by him in terms of seven principles. These were: (i) a metaphysic of inter-relatedness, (ii) an ethos of biospherical egalitarianism, (iii) the values of diversity and symbiosis, (iv) an anti-class posture, (v) opposition to pollution and resource depletion, (vi) the value of complexity, and (vii) an emphasis on local autonomy and decentralization.

In his explanatory comments on these principles, Naess sketched the (barest) out-lines of what amounted to an ecological world-view. According to the first principle, the identity of each individual, at whatever ontological level, is not logically independent of the rest of reality, but is a function of the relations of the individual in question with other individuals. Reality is thus viewed as fundamentally relational (ecological), rather than as aggregative, in its structure. To this metaphysic of inter-relatedness is then added an ethic of interrelatedness, according to which all forms of life are equally entitled to live and blossom. In other words, human beings are not morally privileged in any way in this ecological scheme of things – other life forms are just as morally considerable as we are. The ecological principles of diversity and symbiosis are then invoked in the service of the egalitarian ethic, since by sustaining the basis of natural selection and thereby promoting the project of life on earth, these principles enhance the opportunities for all beings to live and blossom. The value of diversity is then qualified by the fourth principle, which adds that certain (non-ecological) forms of difference are not to be encouraged, namely those differences which arise as a result not of mutuality but of the exploitation and suppression of one group by another – where class differences fall into this category. The fight against pollution and resource depletion is then included, as part of the deep, as well as the shallow, ecology movement, but on the proviso that the other principles should not be subordinated to this one – pollution should not be combated in ways that would exacerbate class differences, for instance. The appeal to complexity is, in effect, a further appeal to ecological thinking – a plea for recognition of the ontological interrelatedness adverted to under the first principle. Recognition of the multivariant interdependence of the elements comprising natural systems entails recognition of the unpredictability of the effects of our large-scale interventions in these systems. Finally, the principle of decentralization is invoked on the grounds that, in ecologically stable systems, particular life forms are primarily vulnerable to influences from outside the system, and the further outside these influences originate, the more destructive they are likely to be. In the interests of promoting the integrity of both individuals and systems, then, local autonomy is to be protected.

Although the principles in terms of which Naess defines the deep ecology approach, in this early article, are presented in a highly abbreviated and ad hoc way, they do point toward a cohesive ecological world-view, and to some of the ethical and political implications of such a world-view. "Deep ecology" could thus be read as signifying that our world was ecological, or relational, to its ontological depths, and that our relationship with nature had to be reinterpreted in the light of this. When "deep ecology" is read this way, it converges with an interdisciplinary stream of thought that was developing throughout the 1980s, and was sometimes described as constituting a "new paradigm."

The new paradigm was generally defined in contrast to the "dominant paradigm," which was basically the paradigm of the European Enlightenment. The Enlightenment was built on the classical scientific view of nature, and the liberal view of society. From this perspective, the physical world was to be understood in mechanistic terms, as consisting of an inert realm of autonomous material particles set in motion by blind laws of physics, while society was understood as an aggregate of autonomous rational individuals driven together by the "blind" law of self-interest (Mathews 1991). Fundamental to the Enlightenment world-view was a principle of division. Matter was divided up into logically independent parcels, and society into logically independent individuals. In a world of logical units, attributes were localized in specific particulars, rather than diffused throughout reality. Morally significant attributes – such as mind – could be dualistically separated out from morally insignificant attributes – such as materiality – and particulars endowed with mind ranked above particulars not so endowed, thereby creating hierarchies of moral worth. In this way, human beings, as repositories of mind, could be set apart from and above the rest of nature. Nature, as sheer materiality, could properly be subordinated to human purposes, and, devoid of its own intelligence, rendered transparent to human science, a fit object for both exploitation and investigation. From a presupposition that things are in their fundamental nature divided and separate, then, we are quickly led to a world of oppositions and hierarchies, in which some groups see themselves as justified in taking control of other groups, and where humanity, in particular, sees itself as justified in, and capable of, taking charge of nature (See EARLY MODERN PHILOSOPHY).

This paradigm, based on a principle of the division of reality into independent parts or units, was contrasted in the 1980s by thinkers across a range of disciplines from physics to systems theory with a paradigm which was relational and hence more holistic in its import. Although thinkers in different disciplines elaborated this latter paradigm in different ways, physical reality was generally represented by them in dynamic, indivisible, field-like, or systemic terms, with individuals taking their (merely relative) identity from the wider systems within which they were embedded, and out of which they had crystallized. It follows that in such a world the attributes of any given individual would be a function of the wider system or field to which it belonged. Privileged attributes, such as mind, could thus not be regarded as the exclusive province of particular individuals, such as human beings, but must rather be seen as suffusing nature at large. In this way, by making the system itself the locus of all attributes, the justification for ranking some individuals over others, on account of their "higher" attributes, is eliminated within the relational paradigm. Relationality is thus an antidote both to a dualistic organization of attributes such as mentality and materiality, and to the construction of moral hierarchies – hierarchies of "higher" and "lower" orders of being. (The same relational model could be applied to society, with society itself, as a field of linguistic and cultural practices and discourses, having ontological primacy, and individuals achieving definition according to their position within this field. Privileged personal attributes, such as "genius," would, from this point of view, be considered a function of particular societies rather than the exclusive preserve of the individuals who manifested them.)

The first of Naess's principles of deep ecology, his "rejection of the man-in-environment image in favor of the relational, total-field image" (Naess 1973a) was thus an early heralding of an idea which was to become, in the 1980s, a transdisciplinary frontier, a "paradigm shift" in western thought, toward forms of knowledge organized around principles of relationality rather than division, forms of knowledge which already entailed a broad commitment to ontological "egalitarianism," as Naess made explicit in the second of his deep ecology principles, viz the principle of "biocentric egalitarianism." The other five principles followed more or less naturally from these twin premises.

It was as a new "ecological" world-view, a part of this paradigm shift, that "deep ecology" was understood by some of its early interpreters and followers (Fox 1984, Devall and Sessions 1985). It was agreed that although Naess had developed his own particular version of such a world-view, the core relational principles could be elaborated in a great variety of ways, and with a variety of cultural and conceptual tools, from the mathematical and scientific to the religious, poetic, and mythological. Naess himself drew on a number of his long-time philosophical influences, including Spinoza, Gandhi, and a certain form of phenomenology or gestalt ontology, in developing his own "ecosophy," as he designated such personalized versions of the ecological world-view. But he made it clear that each individual would need to find their own personal and cultural pathway to this "new" wisdom which was also at the core of many old, premodern spiritual traditions.

The ecosophy developed by Naess – labeled by him "ecosophy T," in honor of his own spiritual home and source of ecological inspiration, a cabin named Tvergastein, situated high above the snowline in the mountains of Norway – revolved around a notion of ecological selfhood understood as an ideal of human self-realization (Naess 1987, 1989a). Starting from the premise that reality is fundamentally relational in structure, and that individual identity is accordingly not a metaphysical datum in this system, Naess postulates a notion of selfhood that is based on active identification with wider and wider circles of being. Such identification is possible because, for Naess, the self is not identical with the body, nor with the mind, nor with a mere conjunction of body and mind. The self is not a fixed entity at all, but a cultivated one – it encompasses everything with which a person identifies. Naess understands maturity generally as consisting in a widening of our circles of identification, and self-realization is nothing but the final stage of maturity, where we achieve the widest possible circle of identification. That is, we identify not merely with our family, our community, our culture, or with humanity as a whole, but also with our immediate environment, the place where we were born or to which we belong, our land, our earth. In this way Naess envisages self-realization as involving the transition not only from ego to social self, but from social self to ecological self.

When we are identified with nature at large in this way, our innate self-love expands in proportion to our new sense of self, and our self-interest becomes convergent with the interests of the rest of life. Defense of nature becomes a matter of self-defense. Naess points out that this process of self-realization has affinities with Gandhi's notion of enlightenment. From Gandhi's basically Hindu point of view, the enlightened being is he or she who sees "the same" – the oversoul or self – in everything, and is hence not alienated from anything.

In answer to the question *why* one should aspire to the kind of "cosmic" or ecological self-realization that he recommends, Naess replies that it is in our own deepest interests to do so, because self-realization in this sense represents the actualization of our greatest potentiality for being. Our self is richer to the extent that it encompasses more reality, and if we take the basic impulse of the self to be to preserve and enrich its own being, then self-realization represents the fulfillment of the impulse at the core of the self.

Although Naess is careful not to equate self-realization with happiness, in any personal sense thereof, he promises that the joy and meaningfulness of life are increased through increasing self-realization. The conditions under which the self is widened are, he says, experienced as positive and basically joyful; such expansion is akin to "falling in love outward." Naess consciously and strategically focuses on the rewards rather than the costs of ecological self-realization because he thinks that our environmental conscience will be sounder and more reliable if it arises out of self-interest rather than resting on moral reason or a sense of duty. He invokes the Kantian distinction between moral acts and beautiful acts. An act qualifies as moral, according to Kant, if it is both right and undertaken out of a sense of duty, and against the natural inclination of the agent (i.e. if it springs from reason rather than sentiment or inclination), while an act is said to be merely beautiful if it is right but is performed spontaneously, without deliberation, out of the natural inclination of the agent. Kant preferred moral acts, but Naess, unimpressed with the record of morality in bringing about right conduct, thinks that the natural world will be better served if the environment movement is grounded in inclination rather than a sense of moral duty. The process of ecological self-realization fosters the inclination to act on behalf of nature, because this process involves perceiving the interests of nature as the interests of one's own wider self.

From Naess's point of view, then, ecological self-realization is in the truest and deepest interests of the human self, while at the same time it provides the firmest foundation for the protection of the natural environment. Self-realization is thus a path to both personal fulfillment and ecological wisdom and virtue. In this way Naess makes "seeking one's own good" rather than "saving the world" a central tenet of deep ecology.

Naess's ecosophy of ecological self-realization had informed his original (1973a) version of the principles of deep ecology, notably via the notion of relational identity and the metaphysical egalitarianism that this implied. However, a new set of principles was drawn up by Naess and George Sessions in 1984, and published in a book entitled *Deep Ecology: Living as if Nature Mattered*, co-authored by Sessions and Bill Devall. In this new set of principles – now described as the platform of the deep ecology movement – all reference to a metaphysic of interconnectedness and to an ethos of biocentric egalitarianism was dropped, and these original philosophical premises of deep ecology were replaced with a statement of the "intrinsic value" of the non-human world. The first principle of the new platform read: "The well-being and flourishing of human and non-human Life on Earth have value in themselves (synonyms: intrinsic value, inherent value). These values are independent of the usefulness of the non-human world for human purposes" (Devall and Sessions 1985, p 70). Via this notion of intrinsic value, Naess and Sessions formulated the crucial contrast between an anthropocentric and a non-anthropocentric attitude to the natural world. According to the anthropocentric, or human-centered, attitude, the natural world is of instrumental value only – it is valued only to the extent that it serves as a resource for us. From a non-anthropocentric point of view, the natural world is valuable in its own right, as an end in itself, independently of its utility value for us. With the new platform, the principle of the intrinsic value of nature became the philosophical premise of deep ecology.

The remaining principles supervene in various ways on this philosophical premise. These principles were spelt out as follows:

2. Richness and diversity of life forms contribute to the realization of these values [i.e. the well-being and flourishing of human and non-human Life on Earth], and are also values in themselves.
3. Humans have no right to reduce this richness and diversity except to satisfy vital needs.
4. The flourishing of human life and cultures is compatible with a substantial decrease of the human population. The flourishing of non-human life requires such a decrease.
5. Present human interference with the non-human world is excessive, and the situation is rapidly worsening.
6. Policies must therefore be changed. These policies affect basic economic, technological and ideological structures. The resulting state of affairs will be deeply different from the present.
7. The ideological change is mainly that of appreciating life quality (dwelling in situations of inherent value) rather than adhering to an increasingly higher

standard of living. There will be a profound awareness of the difference between big and great.

8. Those who subscribe to the foregoing points have an obligation directly or indirectly to try to implement the necessary changes. (ibid)

The basic thrust of the platform is to advocate, on the strength of the intrinsic value of non-human life, the minimization of human interference with the natural world. Humans are entitled to take from the biosphere whatever they truly need for a culturally rich, materially simple life, but no more. This applies to humanity as a species as well: we are not entitled to multiply ourselves beyond the numbers needed for us to sustain meaningful cultures. The message is that humanity should, as far as possible, leave nature alone. This means allowing WILDERNESS areas to expand beyond their present limits. In the comment to principle (5), Naess and Sessions say:

> The fight to preserve and extend areas of wilderness or near-wilderness should continue and should focus on the general ecological functions of these areas (one such function: large wilderness areas are required in the biosphere to allow for continued evolutionary speciation of animals and plants). Most present designated wilderness areas and game preserves are not large enough to allow for such speciation. (Drengson and Inoue 1995, p. 52)

The ideal of non-interference in nature thus finds expression in the affirmation of wilderness. The idea of deep ecology as constituting an ecological world-view, or alternative metaphysical paradigm, has thus given way to the more general idea of it as a non-anthropocentric, let-nature-be approach to the environment.

This shift, from deep ecology as a world-view to deep ecology merely as a non-anthropocentric stance, was accompanied by a new emphasis on deep ecology as an activist movement. A sharp distinction was now drawn between the "platform" and the ecosophies, or philosophical and religious world-views, which underpinned it. Naess formulated his painstaking "apron diagram" showing the derivational structure of deep ecology. According to this diagram, four levels of deep ecology could be distinguished: (i) the ecosophical level, consisting of "verbalized fundamental philosophical and religious ideas and intuitions," (ii) the platform, (iii) "more or less general consequences derived from the platform – lifestyles and general policies of every kind," (iv) "concrete situations and practical decisions made in them" (Naess 1995, pp. 11–12). The main effect of this differentiation of levels was to focus attention on the platform as the core of deep ecology, and to emphasize that, in order to identify as a deep ecologist, it was necessary only that one commit to this platform, and in particular to the principle of intrinsic value, or the non-anthropocentric stance. One was not required to commit to any particular world-view – ecological or otherwise. One might subscribe to Buddhist, Hindu, indigenous, pantheistic, Heideggerian, or Christian metaphysics, and still uphold the principle of intrinsic value. Indeed, even a fundamentalist anti-Darwinian Christian might eschew anthropocentrism – on the grounds that nature is intrinsically good insofar as it is the creation of God – and so qualify as a deep ecologist.

The rationale for this shift – from philosophical paradigm to activist movement premised on the principle of intrinsic value but otherwise agnostic with respect to philosophical foundations – was presumably undertaken in order to broaden the support base of deep ecology. All those who valued the natural world for its own sake, and not merely as a resource for humankind, could now be counted deep ecologists, whatever their underlying belief systems. However, such an attempt to maximize support was not without cost to the cohesiveness of the position. For one might justifiably ask whether the new position could properly any longer be described as "deep," on the one hand, since it was no longer metaphysically prescriptive, or even as "ecological," on the other, since it no longer involved a commitment to relationality. In answer to the query about depth, Naess pointed out that he had intended the word "deep" in deep ecology to signify depth of questioning.

> The essence of deep ecology – as compared with the science of ecology, and with what I call the shallow ecological movement – is to ask deeper questions. The adjective "deep" stresses that we ask why and how, where others do not. For instance, ecology as a science does not ask what kind of a society would be the best for maintaining a particular ecosystem. (Bodian 1982)

But deep ecology does ask such questions. So depth was preserved as depth of questioning, which now figured as a kind of meta-principle of deep ecology. However, while deep ecology might unquestionably remain deep, under its new aspect, the extent to which it could still be regarded as ecological was more open to question. With all reference to ecological principles deleted from the platform, and relegated at most to the ecosophical level, where they were in any case optional, the appeal to ecology seems unfounded. The new position might perhaps be more accurately described as nature-inclusive rather than as ecocentric.

It might also be asked whether grouping people on the grounds of their rejection of anthropocentric attitudes to nature, independently of their reasons for such rejection, is in fact coherent. People with vastly different primary allegiances, and hence wide areas of disagreement, might nevertheless concur in valuing the natural world for its own sake. This does not mean that they would want to identify with a movement whose major mouthpieces did not share their respective primary allegiances. So, for instance, many feminists, socialists, and Christians who respect the natural world for its own sake might nevertheless not want to count themselves members of a movement which was neither feminist, socialist, nor Christian in its essentials. They might prefer to call themselves ecofeminists, ecosocialists, or green Christians (see CHRISTIANITY, ECOFEMINISM). For deep ecologists simply to co-opt such people to their position, on the grounds that they satisfy the criterion of what it is to be a deep ecologist, is politically insensitive, to say the least. An appropriate procedure, in this connection, might rather be to invite people with different political identities but a nature-inclusive ethic, into a strategic coalition of groups, rather than attempting to melt them all down into a single movement.

This suggests that deep ecology cannot in fact be fully understood merely in terms of its 1984 platform, with its unspecified philosophical underpinnings. Those who are most happy to be identified as deep ecologists are those who not only reject anthropocentric attitudes to nature, but put the cause of nature first, ahead of causes relating to gender, race, social justice in general, or institutionalized religion. (The main activist organization which has explicitly taken deep ecology as its ideology is Earth First! in the USA. The name "Earth First!" clearly signals not just a non-anthropocentric stance, but the political prioritizing of such a stance.) The fact that the primary allegiance of such people is to nature does not imply that they are not also concerned with other causes, any more than the fact that some people's primary allegiance is to feminism or anticolonialism or socialism or Christianity means that they are not also sensitive to the interests of nature. There are many important causes in the contemporary world, and most people have to choose to make a primary commitment to one of them, in accordance with their particular positioning in society. Rather than trying to capture all who concede the intrinsic value of nature, deep ecology might achieve greater cohesion and force by reserving itself for those for whom the cause of nature is paramount, and providing philosophical articulations and rationalizations for such a position – where this is, of course, what Naess was attempting to do in his earlier ecosophical work.

It was largely due to the efforts of Devall and Sessions that deep ecology started to gain currency in the English-speaking world in the mid-1980s. Although their book, *Deep Ecology*, included the new platform, it was also a catch-all of readings, from the nature writers of nineteenth-century America to Zen Buddhism to Spinoza. This eclecticism actually encouraged people to develop their own interpretations of the mysterious and rather numinous term, "deep ecology." In the public mind, or to the extent that it penetrates the public mind, "deep ecology" still carries some of its earlier metaphysical connotations in addition to its clear challenge to anthropocentrism. It is understood as indeed being a deeply ecological view of the world – a position which, unlike other green positions, such as ecofeminism and ecosocialism, construes our human identity and purpose essentially in terms of our relationship with the natural world, and, ultimately, with the cosmos, rather than in terms of our gender or class, for instance. It has thus in practice been much trickier than Naess and his followers anticipated to sustain the sharp distinction between ecosophies and the deep ecology platform, and deep ecologists themselves in fact tend to slip between wider and narrower construals of their position.

Critiques of deep ecology have generally been addressed to aspects of ecosophy rather than merely to the deep ecology platform, and few commentators have tried to keep the two levels distinct. However, most critiques have focused on features of the deep ecology literature which, though not crystallized into principles of the platform, have been shared presuppositions or themes of several key authors. Many such critiques have been forthcoming, from ecofeminists, postmodernists, postcolonialists, and social ecologists (eco-anarchists), amongst others. Although too many to detail here, some of the major objections have included the following.

1.   Deep ecologists had from the start recognized that the anthropocentrism of the western tradition rested on a conceptual division between humankind and nature: humanity was seen as set apart from, and above, the rest of nature by virtue of its faculty of rational thought. As a "higher" order of being, humanity was, according to this view, entitled to use the rest of nature as it saw fit. Deep ecologists sought to heal this conceptual divide between humankind and nature by revisioning the latter as

having meaning and value of its own: when nature was reconceptualized in this way, it would presumably no longer be possible for humankind to justify its unqualified instrumentalization of non-human life.

Ecofeminists challenged this assumption. They argued that deep ecologists did not understand the political roots of the human/nature divide. This divide is, according to ecofeminists, part of a wider framework of dualistic thinking that serves to naturalize and legitimate political oppression generally: the domination of nature is ideologically inextricable from the domination of human by human, particularly of women by men. In feminist analyses of dualistic thinking, a core dichotomy, such as that of reason/nature, is identified (Plumwood 1993). This core is defined by, and in turn helps to define, a wider, continually expanding system of interrelated dichotomies. Such dichotomies include the following: mind/body, spirit/matter, subject/object, human/nature, culture/nature, reason/emotion, science/superstition, civilized/primitive, colonizer/colonized, mental/manual, production/reproduction (in Marxism), public/private (in liberalism). These pairs of terms are dualistic insofar as they are construed as logically disjunctive, or non-overlapping, and insofar as the term on the left-hand side is systematically ranked above the term on the right: the term on the right stands in an instrumental relation to that on the left.

Ecofeminists point out that this entire conceptual system is gendered, in the sense that the terms on the left are associated, in western thought, with masculinity or masculine ideals, and the terms on the right with femininity or feminine ideals. Although this led earlier ecofeminists to see patriarchy as the prototypal form of political oppression, more recent accounts of dualism, such as that provided by Val Plumwood, have shown that the dualistic system as a whole constructs a master identity which can in certain circumstances be assumed by women. So, for instance, although in a European context reason and mind are likely to be associated with men, and emotion and body with women, in a colonial context, reason and mind are likely to be associated with the colonizer, and hence with being white and civilized, regardless of gender, while emotion and body are likely to be associated with the colonized, and hence with being black and "primitive," also regardless of gender. Similarly, a woman engaged in mental work may assume the master identity in relation to a male manual worker. This is not to say that mental work is not masculine-coded, and manual work feminine-coded, within the dualistic terms of reference, but only that masculinity and femininity cannot here be correlated in simple one-to-one fashion with men and women respectively. Dualism serves to legitimate domination along lines of race and class as well as along lines of gender. The upshot of this kind of analysis is that since the ideology which justifies the domination of nature by humankind is only a subset of a much more comprehensive ideology of domination, the latter ideology must be dismantled before anthropocentric thinking can be eliminated. According to ecofeminists, then, the task of changing the thinking that underlies the environmental crisis turns out to be far greater and more complex than deep ecologists envisaged: it entails overturning the entire ideology of domination that pervades the political life of contemporary western civilization (see ECOFEMINISM).

In reaction to this objection, deep ecologists such as Warwick Fox (1989) have attempted to represent the domination of nature by humankind as the prototypal form of domination, on which further political forms of domination rest. Thus in patriarchies, Fox argues, the domination of women will be justified by their association with nature, and in colonial regimes, indigenous peoples will be assimilated to nature while the colonizers will be taken to exemplify human-ness. And so on. From the viewpoint of this argument, the liberation of nature, though a precondition for all other forms of liberation, can be accomplished in isolation from them. But arguments attempting to prioritize the domination of nature are ultimately no more persuasive than earlier ecofeminist arguments prioritizing the domination of women. Ultimately there is no way of deciding, either historically or logically, which was the prototypal form of domination. Plumwood's analysis of dualism as a comprehensive and holistic ideology of domination sidesteps the reductionist issue, while still making the political point that all systems of domination have to be dismantled simultaneously if any are to be dismantled.

2.   Like ecofeminists, social ecologists hold that the human domination of the natural world is an extension of habits of domination within society. If the psychology of domination which underpins current regimes of environmental exploitation is to be rooted out, all forms of social hierarchy will have to be eliminated. These include not only economic hierarchies, but hierarchies based on other social variables, such as gender, age, race, birth, and expertise: the roles of dominator and dominated are learned in the family and the workplace as well as via the political operations of the state. In envisaging a society in which domination is eliminated at every level of life, private as well as public, social ecologists appeal to anarchist principles of social organization, emphasizing human scale, decentralization, and face-to-face interaction between citizens. In such small-scale communities, consensual and participatory decision-making procedures foster the autonomy and self-directedness of individuals, thereby breaking cycles of domination and subordination. When societies are no longer predicated on the dualistic ideologies of "higher" and "lower" that legitimate political hierarchies, they will no longer construct the human as "higher" than the non-human, nor hence regard humankind as the rightful ruler and possessor of nature.

Murray Bookchin, the originator of social ecology as a distinctive branch of green political theory, explains in greater depth why a non-hierarchical society will, in his view, necessarily be an ecological one. Political hierarchies obstruct the self-realization of individuals – we cannot realize our true human potential when we are in thrall to the will of others. But our true human potential is, according to Bookchin, a function of our place in nature. Bookchin does not agree with deep ecologists that human beings are simply part and parcel of nature – "plain members of the biotic community," as Aldo Leopold put it – nor does he view humans in anthropocentric terms as essentially apart from and above nature. From Bookchin's perspective, humanity has evolved out of, and remains inextricably continuous with, the non-human world, but is no longer part of it in just the same way that other species are. In this connection Bookchin distinguishes between "first nature" – the non-human component of nature – and "second nature" – the human component. In the framework of his evolutionary eco-cosmology, in which the incipient subjectivity of matter achieves its potential for self-awareness and self-directedness through an ever-unfolding process of ecological differentiation, humanity represents a significant new evolutionary departure: through our rationality, nature comes closer to realizing its own immanent telos. By actualizing this potential to become the self-awareness of nature, with both the sensitivity to the ecological interests of nature and the appreciation of our own specialness that this implies, we achieve our essential human-ness. Societies which afford their members the freedom to realize their true human potential will accordingly be profoundly ecologically sympathetic societies (Bookchin 1982).

For social ecologists, then, an ecological way of life involves not turning away from society, back to the regenerative wild, as it tends to do for deep ecologists, but rather a deeper participation in society. By participating more deeply in society, we win back our capacity for self-determination and self-realization. Freed from external control, we become attuned again to our essential vocation, which is to facilitate the unfolding of the evolutionary telos of the universe at large through our specifically human rationality. Our rationality fulfills itself not by working for ourselves-as-set-apart, but for ourselves-as-vehicle-of-nature. Civilization as the school for such evolutionary reason is thus not the obstacle to ecology that it is for deep ecologists, but rather its instrument.

3.   The emphasis that is placed on WILDERNESS in deep ecology may be criticized from various perspectives, including those of feminism and postcolonialism. Concern for wilderness preservation is, as we have seen, indirectly written into the 1984 deep ecology platform, via the comment to principle (5), stating that existing wilderness areas should be expanded. However, the issue of wilderness is far more emotionally and ideologically loaded in the wider deep ecology literature than this comment implies. Sessions goes so far as to say that "Thoreau's 1851 statement 'In wildness is the preservation of the world' provides the basis for modern ecocentric environmentalism" (1995, p. 165). According to Sessions, this remark, together with Thoreau's other famous dictum, "all good things are wild and free," suggests that "the modernist project of domesticating and destroying the wild, along with the corollary process of further domesticating human life and making it increasingly artificial and out of touch with the wild, is resulting in disaster" (ibid, p. 325). Clearly, wilderness and wildness are valued in deep ecology not only as sources of biodiversity, but as sources of authentic experience, the kind of experience that will enable us to achieve ecological selfhood, in Naess's sense.

From a postcolonial point of view, this valorization of wilderness can be problematic. Wilderness-oriented deep ecologists often point to hunter-gatherer cultures as exemplars of the deep ecology ideal of non-interference in nature, on the assumption that these "first peoples" took their living directly from the natural world, without disturbing the ecology of their environment in any more significant ways than non-human species do. However, this assumption has been challenged and rejected by many of the first peoples themselves. It is now clear that native Australians, for instance, managed their lands in an unquestionably interventionist way by use of fire regimes, and that to suggest that the land was in a "state of nature" at the time of European invasion is to perpetuate the pernicious colonial assumption that Australia was "*terra nullius*" – a true wilderness. Captain Cook wrote in his journal concerning Australia: "We see this country in a pure state of Nature. The Industry of man has nothing to do with any part of it and yet we find all such things as Nature hath bestowed upon it in a flourishing state." The Aborigines, he noted, seemed to have "no fix'd habitation but move about from place to place like wild Beasts in search of food, and depend wholy [sic] upon the success of the present day for their subsistence" (quoted in Wright 1991, p. 143). In "idealizing" indigenous peoples as simply part of nature, deep ecologists are in fact perpetuating racist misunderstandings. Aboriginal people today demand recognition that the land under their custodianship was a "managed estate" (Wright 1991). Yet this managed estate was ecologically intact at the time of colonization. If the homelands of human cultures have in fact never been wildernesses, and if neither wilderness nor wildness is a necessary condition for ecological viability, with what justification can deep ecologists perpetuate the cult of wilderness? (See INDIGENOUS PERSPECTIVES.)

This cult of wilderness is also questionable from a feminist point of view. Feminists might ask why deep ecologists do not regard the subsistence traditions of settled horticultural communities as furnishing experiential sources of ecological selfhood. To work with nature via the domestic activities of growing food and husbanding animals is to enter into a relationship with nature arguably as profound as that of the hunter-gatherer. For the farmer or gardener becomes a nurturer of non-human life, as well as a consumer of it, and is likely to develop a profound identification with the plants and animals that she has tended. She is also likely to become deeply invested in the land she cultivates, especially since she embodies it by virtue of the fact that she consumes its produce. In light of this, we might wonder whether the valorization of the wild at the expense of the domestic in deep ecology (Sessions 1995, p. 6) simply reflects a masculine urge to escape from society, particularly from the domestic sphere, with its confining feminine associations. The fact that subsistence practices throughout prehistory and the less-developed world today are predominantly the province of women tends to support the case that in excluding these practices as a source of ecological selfhood, male deep ecologists (where most deep ecologists, whether self-appointed or appointed by those who take it upon themselves to make such appointments, *are* male) are privileging their own masculine experience and the lifestyle ideals to which it gives rise.

Turning for ecological inspiration to subsistence gardening cultures rather than to atavistic and politically dubious notions of wilderness would help deep ecology over-come a further objection from the postcolonialist quarter. For in the non-industria-lized regions of the world in which subsistence traditions still hold sway, and in which poverty places all land under intense economic pressure, wilderness is perceived as a luxury which the West is presumptuous to insist upon or even suggest (Guha 1989; Taylor 1995). To promote subsistence as an ecological ideal avoids the political confrontation that the demand for wilderness entails. It also accords recognition and respect to subsistence cultures for their ecological wisdom, overturning the modernist perception of their traditions as "primitive" ("unscientific"), and support-ing them in their struggle to preserve these traditions against overwhelming tides of modernization and development (Taylor 1995).

Finally, in advocating a subsistence ethos rather than a wilderness ethos, deep ecology would not only be joining forces with other resistance movements, such as feminism and postcolonialism; it would also be providing its supporters with a praxis for living in the contemporary world. To date, deep ecology has really functioned only as a posture of resistance to this world. It has enjoined its supporters to awaken to the value illuminating non-human creatures, and it has called them out into the last remaining strongholds of wildness – into the forests and swamps and mountainous wastes – to make their stand. It has offered idyllic images of how to live with spiritual attunement in a world consisting only of wild things – a world of undisturbed nature. It envisions how, in such an ecologically pristine world, people could return to the estate of natives, occupying their intended place in the scheme of things. But it has not yet shown its supporters how, in the world-as-it-is, the "disturbed" world of rampant urbanism and industrialism, to which one returns after one's stints of eco-warriorship, one might live in attunement with the inner principle of things. In this respect deep ecology is arguably, even on its own terms, incomplete. It has invited its followers to resist the machines of modernity in defense of nature, but at the same time it has left most of them still helplessly hooked up to modern technologies and industries and modes of production in their everyday lives.

The principle of subsistence, articulated for the West in the theories of permaculture and bioregionalism, for instance, offers a solution to this. It suggests ways in which we can indeed gradually begin the process of becoming native again, reinhabiting our homeplaces, even when they lie in the degraded hearts of cities. By growing food where we live, by turning material wastes into resources, by honoring places whatever their ecological status, we find a new intimacy with nature, different from the kind of (touristic?) relationship which is forged in wilderness, but appropriate to our present condition. By deepening our connection with nature through such subsistence practices, we shall call life back into our urban midst. This is important. We can no longer afford to entertain a notion of nature which is exclusively "out there" – in the wilderness beyond the walls of civilization. In the course of the twenty-first century, most of the planet will be brought within those walls. If we cannot reverse the process of the human colonization of nature, and allow nature to begin to infiltrate the city, the prospects of environmentalism are dim. The city is the great ecological frontier of the new millennium (Mathews 1999). Deep ecology, if it is to be effective, must adjust to this reality. In doing so, it might also begin to revise the stark and in fact dualistic disjunction it poses between anthropocentric and ecocentric approaches to nature: we might discover that we, like the subsistence peoples of the world, can at the same time thoroughly inhabit nature and yet honor its integrity and appreciate that it is immeasurably greater than we are (Taylor 1995; Mies and Shiva 1993 pp. 297–324).

However deep ecology unfolds in the future, one cornerstone of Naess's ecosophy that is likely to continue to uplift eco-philosophers and eco-activists, of whatever stripe, indefinitely, is his notion of joy. Naess encourages environmentalists not to succumb to grief in the face of ecological holocaust, but to be of good cheer. Following Spinoza, he promises that joy will result from our very activeness in addressing crisis:

> The remedy (or psychotherapy) against sadness caused by the world's misery is to do something about it . . . It is very common to find those who constantly deal with extreme misery to be more than usually cheerful. According to Spinoza, the power of the individual is infinitely small compared with that of the entire universe, so we

must not expect to save the whole world. The main point...is that of activeness. (Naess 1973b)

Our power to act may be finite, but it is truly our own; when we realize this power through engaging with the world, we experience joy. By making grave demands on us, the ecological crisis offers us extraordinary opportunities to rise above the trivial dimension of life, and extend ourselves to the full. In doing so, we discover unlooked-for joy-of-life in the midst of environmental sorrow.

References

Bodian, Stephan (1982) "Simple in means, rich in ends: an interview with Arne Naess," in *The Ten Directions* (Los Angeles Zen Center); reprinted in Sessions 1995.

Bookchin, Murray (1982) *The Ecology of Freedom* (Palo Alto, California: Cheshire). [A *locus classicus* for Bookchin's metaphysics of nature and its implications for social and political organization.]

Devall, Bill and Sessions, George (1985) *Deep Ecology: Living as if Nature Mattered* (Salt Lake City, Utah: Peregrine Smith Books). [The first book-length exposition of deep ecology for an English-speaking readership, containing an eclectic range of inspiring ideas from a variety of nature traditions.]

Drengson, Alan and Inoue, Yuichi, eds. (1995) *The Deep Ecology Movement* (Berkeley, CA: North Atlantic Books). [A useful collection of Naess's definitive articulations of deep ecology together with a selection of sympathetic elaborations and explorations by other authors.]

Fox, Warwick (1984) "Deep ecology: a new philosophy for our times?," *The Ecologist* 14, no. 5/6, pp. 194–200. [An early clarion call to deep ecology by one of its principal interpreters.]

——(1989) "The deep ecology–ecofeminism debate and its parallels," *Environmental Ethics* 11, no. 1 (Spring). [A defense of deep ecology against the ecofeminist charge that it is "andro-centric."]

Guha, Ramachandra (1989) "Radical American environmentalism and wilderness preservation: a third world critique," *Environmental Ethics* 11 (Spring), pp. 71–83. [The title is self-explanatory: a classic postcolonial critique of the wilderness ethos.]

Mathews, Freya (1991), *The Ecological Self* (London: Routledge). [An exploration of the metaphysical assumptions that underlie modern western attitudes to nature and a detailed articulation of an alternative, more ecological metaphysic.]

——(1999) "Letting the world grow old: an ethos of countermodernity," *Worldviews* 3, no. 2. [A reinterpretation of environmentalism in custodial terms that apply to urban as well as ecological contexts.]

Mies, Maria and Shiva, Vandana (1993) *Ecofeminism* (Melbourne: Spinifex). [The final chapter offers a suggestive outline of a "subsistence perspective" that can be realized in western as well as third world societies.]

Naess, Arne (1973a), "The shallow and the deep, long-range ecology movement," *Inquiry* 16; reprinted in Drengson and Inoue 1995.

——(1973b) "The place of joy in a world of fact," *The North American Review* 258, no. 2; reprinted in Sessions 1995.

——(1987) "Self-realization: an ecological approach to being in the world," *The Trumpeter* 4, no. 3, pp 35–42; reprinted in Sessions 1995.

——(1989a) *Ecology, Community and Lifestyle* (Cambridge: Cambridge University Press). [A source book for Naess's more discursive treatment of deep ecology themes.]

——(1995) "The apron diagram," in Drengson and Inoue 1995.

Naess, Arne and Sessions, George (1985) "platform principles of the deep ecology movement," in Devall and Sessions 1985; reprinted in Drengson and Inoue 1995.

Plumwood, Val (1993) *Feminism and the Mastery of Nature* (London: Routledge). [A comprehensive analysis of the systematic ways in which different forms of social and political domination are linked with the domination of nature.]

Sessions, George, ed. (1995) *Deep Ecology for the Twenty-first Century* (Boston: Shambhala). [A voluminous anthology of deep ecology writings by Naess and others which attempts to convey and enlarge the sweep of deep ecology as a movement for the twenty-first century.]

Taylor, Bron ed. (1995) *Ecological Resistance Movements* (Albany: State University of New York Press). [A collection of accounts of radical ecology from the different cultural perspectives of movements in first world and third world countries.]

Wright, Judith (1991) *Born of the Conquerors* (Canberra: Aboriginal Studies Press). [A collection of essays on colonialism and environmentalism from this foremost Australian poet.]

Further reading

Fox, Warwick (1990) *Towards a Transpersonal Ecology* (Boston: Shambhala). [An influential systematization, exposition, and further development of the deep ecology approach to environmentalism.]

Katz, Eric, Light, Andrew, and Rothenberg, David, eds. (2000) *Beneath the Surface: Critical Essays in the Philosophy of Deep Ecology* (Cambridge, Mass.: MIT Press). [The first collection of essays which engages critically with deep ecology from points of view that lie outside those of the "rival" eco-philosophies.]

16

Ecofeminism

VICTORIA DAVION

In this essay I shall present several influential ecological feminist positions, discuss some common criticisms of ecological feminist views, and situate ecological feminism with respect to some other approaches to environmental philosophy. Although the focus of this volume is on environmental ethics as an academic discipline, a central commitment of ecofeminist theorists, including Noel Sturgeon and Greta Gaard, has been to link theory with political activism. Although ecological feminist scholarship is extremely rich and varied, someone else could have approached this topic very differently. Although what follows is not meant to be comprehensive, I do hope to provide readers with an appreciation for the kinds of concerns and questions commonly taken up in ecological feminist literature.

"Ecological feminism," or "ecofeminism," refers to a series of theoretical and practical positions bringing feminist insight to environmental philosophy. Feminist theorists began formulating theories explicitly addressing similarities and connections between sexism and abuses of nature in the early 1970s. Anthologies specifically devoted to the topic, such as *Healing the Wounds: The Promise of Ecological Feminism* (Plant 1989) and *Reweaving the World: The Emergence of Ecofeminism* (Diamond and Orenstein 1990), began to appear in the late 1980s. Although there is a variety of ecofeminist positions, ecofeminists agree there is a link between dominations of women and dominations of nature, and that an understanding of one is crucial to the understanding of the other. Ecofeminists argue that an environmental philosophy that fails to attend to these important links will be theoretically and practically deficient. The kinds of connection commonly made by ecological feminists between feminism and the environment include the historical, conceptual, empirical, epistemological, ethical, theoretical, and political. I shall present examples of arguments for these connections from prominent ecological feminist work.

Historical connections

Many ecological feminists argue that a historical look at the ways in which women and other oppressed groups have been associated with the "natural" and the ways in which nature has been associated with the "womanly" or the "feminine" in western contexts reveals important connections. Prominent examples can be found in Griffin (1978) and Merchant (1983). Merchant examines the emergence of modern science in Europe in the fifteenth to seventeenth centuries. She argues that the shift in worldviews from the organic to the mechanistic was a major vehicle for the devaluation of both women and nature.

Merchant maintains that the shift from the earth-centered to the sun-centered world-view was a significant factor. In the earth-centered view, characteristic of Renaissance and pre-Renaissance thought, earth was associated with two aspects of womanliness: nurturing mother and uncontrollable female who could be violent and chaotic. Shifting to a sun-centered view meant replacing a woman-centered universe with a male-centered one, as the sun was traditionally associated with manliness. In addition, the Aristotelian association of activity with masculinity and passivity with femininity was revived in the sixteenth century, as is shown by the following quote from Copernicus: "the earth conceives by the sun and becomes pregnant with annual offspring" (1983, p. 7). Merchant argues that the idea that change could occur not only on earth but everywhere, which was associated with the sun-centered view, caused fear that nature's order could break down. This resulted in the desire to control nature. Hence, the part of womanliness that became the dominant conception of nature was the wild, violent side. The other association of nature as a nurturing mother that was part of the organic approach became less prevalent. Merchant quotes Machiavelli:

> Fortune is a woman and it is necessary, if you wish to master her to conquer her by force; and it can be seen that she lets herself be overcome by the bold rather than by those who proceed coldly, and therefore like a woman, she is always a friend to the young because they are less cautious, fiercer, and master her with greater audacity. (ibid, p. 130)

Other disruptions in the social order, including the breakdown of the feudal system, brought fear of chaos. Merchant suggests that women's increased visibility in social life, such as the Protestant reform movements in northern Europe, and the long reign of Elizabeth I, was threatening to the social order. At any rate, fear of women by the men in control reached a peak in the European witch hunts.

Merchant's discussion of Francis Bacon (supposedly the father of modern science) is often discussed by ecological feminists as a particularly clear example of how the association of women and nature has been dangerous for both. Bacon's justification of the scientific method involved likening nature to a woman being tried for witchcraft. His mentor, James I of England, was a strong supporter of the trials. In an attempt to "sell" James on the scientific method Bacon stated:

> For you have but to follow and hound nature and as it were hound nature in her wanderings, and you will be able when you like to lead and drive her afterward to the same place again.... Neither ought a man to make a scruple of entering and penetrating those holes and corners, when the inquisition of truth is his whole object – as your majesty has shown in his own example. (ibid, p. 168)

Ecofeminists such as Merchant have been a major source for reminding feminists, environmentalists, and others how the twin dominations of women and nature have been intertwined historically and conceptually (see EARLY MODERN PHILOSOPHY).

Value dualisms and the logic of domination

Analysis of value dualisms plays a major role in ecological feminist critiques of western patriarchal cultures. Val Plumwood (1993) offers one of the most comprehensive discussions of dualisms and dualistic thinking. A value dualism is a disjunctive pair in which the disjuncts are seen as oppositional and exclusive, and which places higher value on one disjunct than the other. Many ecological feminists argue that a reason/nature dualism underlies the conceptual framework of western patriarchal cultures. This dualism is thought to form the basis for a series of related dualisms in which whatever is associated with reason is viewed as fundamentally different and superior to whatever is associated with nature.

Examples of such dualized pairs involve not only reason/nature and masculine/feminine, but also mental/manual, civilized/primitive, and human/nature. These pairs function to legitimate a number of oppressions, including sex, race, and class oppression, which can all be seen in terms of the central dualism underlying the system, that of reason/nature.

It is crucial to realize that not all differences are dualisms, and deconstructing value dualisms does not mean denying all differences between dualized pairs. The problem with value dualisms lies in the construction of dualized pairs as absolutely different in morally relevant ways, which leads to the construction and justification of moral hierarchies.

The construction of dualized identities involves five features, according to Plumwood. These are (i) backgrounding, the oppressors' creation of a dependency on the oppressed while simultaneously denying that dependency; (ii) radical exclusion, constructing supposed differences between oppressors and the oppressed in terms of radical difference in order to justify subordination of the oppressed; (iii) incorporation, the construction of the devalued side of a dualized pair as lacking morally relevant features associated with the other side; (iv) instrumentalism, the construction of groups seen as morally inferior, lacking any morally important independent interests; (v) homogenization, the denial of differences between those on the underside of dualized pairs (seeing all women or all slaves as the same).

Another influential critique of dualistic thinking places it in a larger oppressive framework said to underlie all the "-isms" of domination. Karen J. Warren (1990) explores major conceptual connections between the domination of women by men and the domination of nature by humans. She argues that both depend on the "logic of domination." This logic uses premises about differences between entities, asserts that such differences constitute the moral superiority of one group, and that being superior entitles members of the superior group to subordinate members of the inferior group. A typical form of such arguments is as follows:

(A1) Humans do, plants do not, have the capacity to consciously change the community in which they live.
(A2) Whatever has this capacity is morally superior to whatever doesn't have it.
(A3) Humans are morally superior to plants and rocks.

(A4) For any X and Y, if X is morally superior to Y, then X is morally justified in subordinating Y.
(A5) Humans are morally justified in subordinating plants and rocks. (Warren 1990, p. 129)

Warren maintains that the same logic allows for the sexist domination of women under patriarchy by way of the association of women with nature. She articulates this argument as follows:

(B1) Women are identified with nature and the realm of the physical; men are identified with the "human" and the realm of the mental.
(B2) Whatever is identified with nature and the realm of the physical is inferior to ("below") whatever is identified with the "human" and the realm of the mental;
(B3) Thus, women are inferior to men.
(B4) For any X and Y, if X is superior to Y, then X is justified in subordinating Y.
(B5) Men are justified in subordinating women. (ibid, p. 130)

The fact that the domination of nature by humans, and the sexist domination of women by men, rely on the same general framework, and the fact that the devaluation of women depends upon the prior devaluation of nature, means projects to end sexism and the exploitation of nature are conceptually linked. According to Warren, this important insight means that environmentalists and feminists should be allies, and makes explicit what it is we must work against. It represents a very important ecofeminist contribution to both movements. If one grants conceptual links between the domination of nature and the domination of women, it follows that a movement that is not feminist will yield at best a superficial understanding of the domination of nature. Those fighting to save the environment should, as a matter of consistency, be working to overthrow patriarchy, and those working to overthrow patriarchy should be fighting to save the environment. At a conceptual level, these fights are one. Warren maintains that the logic of domination underlies not only sexism and naturism, but racism and all other "-isms" as well, and thus movements to end all of these "-isms" are conceptually linked.

Ecofeminism and animals

A long tradition in feminist theory addresses links between the domination of ANIMALS and the domination of people of color and white women. In "Am I Blue?" (1988) Alice Walker gives a moving analysis of the similarities between racism and the mistreatment of animals. She compares the way in which children are encouraged to forget that humans can have deep and meaningful communication with animals to the ways that white children raised by "mammies" were encouraged to forget that their first all-accepting love came from black women. She also compares the use of animals for breeding without regard for their feelings to the way slaves were used for breeding purposes.

Although not all ecological feminists deal explicitly with animals, there has been a clear commitment to animals evident in ecofeminist literature. Leading anthologies on ecological feminism include articles on animals and discussions of hunting. Theorists such as Greta Gaard, Lori Gruen, Dean Curtin, and Carol J. Adams argue that vegetarianism should be a component of an ecofeminist praxis.

Adams argues that concern about animals is part of the ecological feminist project not only because acknowledging their value is part of dismantling the logic of domination, but also because the domination of the earth more generally is part of animal agriculture. In addition, Adams ties the domination of animals in with the domination and exploitation of black women, who as "lung gunners" in US poultry processing plants must scrape the lungs out of 5,000 chickens' chest cavities per hour. According to Adams: "Both women workers and the chickens themselves are the means to the end of consumption, but because consumption has been disembodied, their oppressions as worker and consumable body are invisible" (1991, p. 131).

The strategy of looking for connections between various types of oppression, domination, and exploitation is evident in other ecofeminist discussions of animals. Chris Cuomo's examination of chicken processing includes the cruel treatment of chickens, discusses how 33 percent of the Perdue workers hired to slaughter chickens end up with a crippling condition of the hands and wrists caused by having to slaughter up to 75 chickens per minute, and that the huge majority of these workers are women of color (1998, p. 103). She writes about how the dairy industry mistreats cows, and also discusses farms as sites of human oppression. Her examples include that 80–90 percent of hired farm workers are Latino, followed by African-Americans, Caribbeans, Puerto Ricans, Filipinos, Vietnamese, Koreans, and Jamaicans; that it is estimated that as many as 313,000 farm workers contract pesticide-related illnesses per year; that Hispanic women show higher levels of pesticides in their milk than white women; and that the miscarriage rate for female farm workers is seven times the national average (ibid, p. 36).

Adams uses the ecological feminist critique of dualistic thinking to argue against the current split between maintenance and production. This split allows people to maintain diets based on animal flesh without thinking about the ethically problematic aspect of meat production. An ethic that linked maintenance with production would identify not only the exploitation of animals and workers as part of the costs of meat production, but would count the loss of topsoil, water, and the demands on fossil fuels that meat production requires (see LAND AND WATER). However, government aid to the dairy and beef industry prevents the price of animal-eating from being reflected in the commodity of meat. For example, hamburger would be $35 per pound and beefsteak would be $89 per pound (1991, p. 131). Another way in which production processes are hidden from consumers is by concealing the true lives of both animals and workers from the majority of consumers. Thus, the fact that those of us who eat meat interact with animals daily is hidden from many meat eaters because the animal disappears when we interact with a form of food named meat. While Adams views all meat-eating as morally problematic, others such as Gaard, Gruen, and Curtin have argued for a contextual vegetarianism, granting that in certain contexts meat-eating may be acceptable, while in others it is not.

Environmental racism

The strategy of looking for connections between oppressions is also evident in ecofeminist discussions of environmental racism. Environmental racism is demonstrated by figures such as these: two-thirds of all Blacks and Latinos in the United States reside in areas with one or more unregulated toxic-waste site, and race is the most significant factor which differentiates between communities with such sites and communities without them (Cuomo 1998, pp. 65–6). As Cuomo points out, ecological feminist analysis is helpful in raising questions such as how ethical, economic, and aesthetic discourses justify racist, toxic politics, how disempowerment and alienation make it particularly difficult for communities to fight back, how racist conceptions of people and cities as unclean and hopeless justify mistreatment, and how in male-dominated contexts women may be disproportionately affected by toxins. In addition, ecological feminism reminds us that toxic dumping is not only a problem concerning human well-being, but it affects non-humans as well. Ecological feminism helps reveal how various oppressions are linked, and can ensure that strategies for change which might actually replicate oppression are not pursued (see ENVIRONMENTAL JUSTICE).

Ecofeminism and critiques of development

Another key direction in ecological feminist thought analyzes how first-world development of third-world countries imports problematic patriarchal ideals, causing special problems for women in the countries that are "developed." Vandana Shiva's book *Staying Alive* (1989) is a classic. Shiva claims that development, which she terms "maldevelopment," has been highly problematic for those who have been developed, and that while both sexes are affected by development, it is often women who have the most to lose. Her book is a theoretical analysis of the development process, using India as an example.

According to Shiva, western development was supposed to be a postcolonial project, giving "underdeveloped" countries the choice to accept the western model of progress, without having to undergo the subjugation and exploitation involved in being colonized. This assumed that western-style progress was possible and desirable for all. However, Shiva argues that western-style progress and the economic model that it involves creates poverty as it creates wealth, and this is endemic to western models of progress.

Shiva maintains that this kind of development destroys sustainable lifestyles and creates true material poverty for those who are developed. Resources needed for the purpose of sustenance are diverted for use in the production of cash crops and other commodities to be sold on the market. This robs those who suffer development of the resources they had been using to survive. Shiva distinguishes between two types of poverty: "culturally perceived poverty" and real material poverty. According to western models, people living in subsistence economies are seen as poor because they do not produce surplus to be bought and sold on the global market. In reality, people living in subsistence economies might indeed have their survival needs met quite well, and the quality of their lives can be even better than those living according to western models of progress. By standards of western development, these people are poor by definition, as poverty is defined as not participating in the global economy. One of Shiva's central points is that attempts to remove culturally perceived poverty often create real material poverty, the absence of things needed for survival. The quality of life of those who are "developed" is often higher before "maldevelopment" occurs.

Shiva refers to the western model as western patriarchy. Drawing on work by Merchant and others, she argues that the devaluation of women and nature typical of western-style patriarchy is imported in development projects. The result is that while men and women are negatively affected by development projects, the patriarchal nature of the values which are part of the western model means development is often worse for women than it is for men. Just as in the West, women's knowledge is discredited as unscientific, useless, and perhaps even dangerous. Real "scientific" knowledge, mainly controlled by men, is said to be the only true knowledge. As these new "scientific methods" are employed, women, as the primary producers of food, water, and fuel, are displaced, and their practices are undermined. However, because new methods paid little or no attention to nature's cycles, and to the ways that natural processes are interconnected, the results are often unsustainable. In chapters on food, water, and forests Shiva documents in impressive detail how modern scientific techniques are largely unsuccessful, destroying previously sustainable lifestyles. She also documents how women have become organizational leaders against development in India.

Charges of essentialism

A large number of ecological feminists argue that to solve the "ecological crisis," we need to celebrate values which have been devalued in western patriarchal contexts. Hence, there have been calls to celebrate such things as "femininity" and "feminine values" within the literature. I've discussed the following examples in "Is Ecofeminism Feminist?" (Davion 1994). Ariel Kay Salleh says the following:

> if women's lived experience were recognized as meaningful and were given legitimation in our culture, it would provide an immediate "living" social basis for alternative consciousness which the deep ecologist is trying to formulate and introduce as an abstract ethical construct. Women already, to borrow Devall's turn of phrase, "flow with the system of nature." (1984, p. 340)

According to Salleh, we do not need abstract ethical constructs to help create a consciousness of our connection with the rest of nature; women already have it. We need to recognize the value of women's experiences, something which patriarchal societies fail to do.

Brian Swimme says the following in praise of women's intuition:

> Starhawk intuits effortlessly what remained beyond the group of the scientists. Our universe is quite clearly a great swelling and birthing event, but why was this

hidden from the very discoverers of the primeval birth? The further truth of the universe was closed to them because central regions of the mind were closed...this sentience is awake in Starhawk because of her life as a woman, as one who has the power to give birth herself, and because of her work as a scholar.... Women are beings who know from the inside out what it is like to weave the earth into a new human being. Given that experience and the congruent sensitivities seething within body and mind, it would be utterly shocking if ecofeminists did not bring forth meanings to the scientific data that were hidden from the scientists themselves. (1990, p. 19)

Swimme claims there is some truth to the idea that the earth is a birthing process, but this truth can only be seen, in fact, effortlessly intuited by women. Swimme seems unsure whether this epistemic privilege is the result of biology, socialization, or both. He refers both to Starhawk's life as a woman, and to the fact that she is a being who can give birth.

Vandana Shiva also adopts an uncritical standpoint epistemology:

In contemporary times, Third World Women, whose minds have not yet been dispossessed or colonised, are in a privileged position to make visible the invisible oppositional categories that they are the custodians of.... Third World women and those tribals and peasants who have been left out of the process of maldevelopment, are today acting as the intellectual gene pools of ecological categories of thought and action. Marginalization has thus become a source for healing the diseased mainstream of patriarchal development. (1990, p. 46)

Certainly the voices of those suffering, whoever they are, must be central to any ecological feminist ethic. Warren (1990) and Plumwood (1993) make this point as well. However, we need to be careful about saying that suffering oppression makes one a source for healing the diseased mainstream. It is a key feminist position that oppression is wrong, and one of the reasons it is wrong is that it is damaging to those who suffer it. While the voices and experiences of the oppressed will be central to any liberatory movement, uncritical glorification is dangerous. It fails to acknowledge the complexity of oppression. Questions of the merits of standpoint epistemology are central to the development of ecological feminism.

Finally, Shiva's discussion appears to glorify or romanticize supposedly pre-patriarchal times. She implies that sexism came along with western development. However, in her discussion of the dowry system, she argues that development caused women's work to be seen as less valuable, thus it increased the amounts of money families needed to come up with in order to marry off women. Development may have made the situation worse, but the dowry system was in place prior to western attempts at development. And this seems like an important factor in understanding sexism in India. A tendency to glorify and romanticize certain groups as having been "pure" before contact with what is now being called western patriarchy is clearly present here and in other ecofeminist work.

I have argued (1994) that positions such as these are problematic in that they appear to accept in a wholesale manner gender roles as constructed under patriarchy.

Yet, a feminist analysis must pay attention to the ways that patriarchy is damaging to women, rather than simply celebrating what has been devalued.

Positions such as those discussed above have been among the reasons for one of the most common criticisms of ecological feminism from feminists and others – the charge of essentialism. The basic criticism is that ecological feminists tend to refer to "woman" and "nature" as if they are metaphysically real categories with essential qualities. Thus, in discussing the category "woman," it is assumed that individual women of different racial, class, and cultural identities fit into the category unproblematically, and, therefore, that they share some essential attribute. The category "nature" is also dealt with as if it is static, real, metaphysically given, and unproblematic. Clearly, many ecological feminist positions seem to use essentialist notions of "woman" and "nature." Some critics, such as Janet Biehl (1991), dismiss ecological feminism altogether because of such charges. This is unfortunate for several reasons. First, it simply is not the case that all ecological feminist positions are guilty of essentialism, and second, even in cases when there is some basis to the charges of essentialism, we can learn more by examining in greater depth what is wrong with such positions rather than refusing to engage with them altogether.

Warren (1990) states that ecological feminists agree that women are identified with nature, and that whatever is identified with nature is seen as inferior to whatever is identified with the "human" in western patriarchal contexts. Yet she correctly points out that ecological feminists differ with respect to the truth of the identification of women and nature. Because many ecological feminists are anxious to deny any ahistorical identification of women with nature, they deny the claim that women are identified with nature as anything more than a historical claim about assumptions within patriarchal culture.

In addition, even when it is claimed that women are closer to nature, this is rarely a claim about women's immutable essence. It is more often a claim about their socialization within patriarchy. When this is the case, the problem is about making false generalizations about all women, generalizations which are insensitive to racial, class, cultural, ethnic, sexual preference, and other differences between women. This is certainly problematic, but it is not the same as attributing ahistorical essences.

Some anti-essentialist critics seem to think merely referring to the categories of "woman" and "nature" is problematic, because nothing fits into these categories unproblematically, and to refer to such categories is to promote the idea of such unproblematic fits. If this were the case, ecological feminism would indeed be a dead end. One cannot examine links between oppressions of women and nature if one cannot even refer to these categories. However, Cuomo argues that simply ceasing to refer to the categories of "woman" and "nature" is not the correct remedy for false generalization and essentialism: "In fact, these relationships are most compelling when they are understood as providing clues about the ways concepts like "woman", "nature", and "body" get written and interwoven, and the ways cultural constructions, practices, and biological matter are formed and reformed" (1998, p. 206). And it will be impossible to look at how being associated with the natural affects the lives of people who are poor, of color, women, without referring to the discursive categories of "woman" and "nature."

Thus, while some ecological feminists are guilty of essentialism, and perhaps even more are guilty of false generalization, these are certainly not essential or necessary characteristics of ecological feminist analysis. And to claim that they are is to commit essentialism or false generalization. An ecological feminism that examines who gets labeled in certain ways, and how those labels affect one's prospects for a decent life, is certainly possible, and at least some ecological feminists are attempting it.

I shall conclude by attempting to situate ecological feminism in relation to other traditional and radical approaches to environmental ethics.

Mainstream approaches

Mainstream approaches to environmental philosophy can be divided into two basic categories, those that argue for environmental protection based on the instrumental value of the environment, and those that seek to extend intrinsic moral value to at least some non-human entities (see NORMATIVE ETHICS, META-ETHICS). Well-known examples of environmentalists arguing for environmental protection based on its instrumental value to human beings include people such as John Muir (1838–1914). These works attempt to demonstrate the importance of environmental health and integrity for human flourishing. Ecological feminists criticize these approaches for such things as their replication of nature/culture dualisms, and the failure to question anthropocentrism, including its androcentric elements. An example of an influential mainstream approach attempting to extend moral consideration to non-human animals is offered by Peter Singer (1975), who argues that certain non-human animals should be accorded moral value using a utilitarian approach, claiming that any being who can suffer deserves moral consideration (see SENTIENTISM). Theories such as Singer's can be characterized as extensionist, attempting to extend traditional ethical theories to non-human beings. Extensionist-type theories have been criticized by ecological feminists and others for failing to question liberal conceptions of the human self as fundamentally an atomistic individual whose personal experiences and freedom are the key ethical considerations. Liberal conceptions of the self start with the idea that atomistic human individuals are the paradigm example of beings with moral value and then argue that at least some animals possess the qualities which account for individual human moral value. While ecological feminists argue for the extension of moral value to include non-humans, ecological feminists insist that an adequate environmental ethic must include a reconception of what it means to be a human being, and of what criteria are necessary for the recognition of moral value to begin with.

Another common criticism of mainstream approaches is that they tend to separate issues of environmental ethics from questions of inter-human ethics which makes impossible discussions such as the one about the ethics of poultry processing. For example, Cuomo is critical of Singer's opening statement in *Animal Liberation*. Singer states: "Discrimination on the basis of sex, was said to be the last form of discrimination that is universally accepted and practiced without pretense, even in those liberal circles which have long prided themselves on their freedom from prejudice against racial minorities" (quoted in Cuomo 1998, p. 170). Singer, of course, argues that while these other discriminations are no longer seen as tolerable, discrimination against non-human animals is. However, not only is Singer wrong in stating that racism and sexism are intolerable in today's America, his assumption that they have disappeared makes it impossible for him to construct a social critique, such as Adams's, which shows how racism and sexism are linked with animal exploitation.

Social ecology and deep ecology

More so-called "radical" approaches such as deep ecology and social ecology join ecological feminists in their charge that mainstream views accept problematic assumptions about what it is to be human. Some ecological feminists also identify themselves as deep ecologists or social ecologists, seeing these as consistent approaches. Social ecology combines anarchist critiques of social hierarchies with an ethic that calls for recognition of the interdependence between humans and other parts of nature. Those ecological feminists identifying themselves as social ecological feminists do so in order to indicate their commitment to the anarchist critiques found in social ecology. For example, Ynestra King did some of her earliest ecofeminist work at the Institute for Social Ecology, founded by one of the leading social ecologists, Murray Bookchin. However, some ecological feminists have been critical of Bookchin's work in particular, because it seems to hold that humans are superior to the rest of nature because of our rationality. Plumwood (1993), for instance, is disturbed by Bookchin's acceptance of enlightenment notions of rationality.

DEEP ECOLOGY, a movement founded by Norwegian philosopher Arne Naess (1973), is based on the principles of biocentric egalitarianism and self-realization. Biocentric equality is the principle that all things in nature have equal value, and is thus supposed to be radically non-anthropocentric. Self-realization, seeing oneself as part of a larger whole as opposed to a radically separate and egoistic being, is said to challenge dualistic thinking and our deepest assumptions of what it is to be human. According to Naess, we can reach higher levels of being through a process of deep questioning, a kind of spiritual journey ending in an ecologically conscious self. Both social ecologists and ecological feminists have criticized deep ecology for its abstract approaches and for its failure to offer any in-depth critique of how problematic social hierarchies within human society are part of environmental problems.

Some deep ecologists, such as Warwick Fox and Michael E. Zimmerman, have argued that the two basic principles of deep ecology, biocentric egalitarianism and self-realization, can subsume the concerns of ecological feminism (Slicer 1995). These two principles together are said to make the theoretical framework of deep ecology anti-hierarchical, which includes anti-sexist, anti-racist, anti-classist, and anti-speciesist. However, many ecological feminists resist this, arguing that deep ecology fails to pay adequate attention to inter-human oppression, domination, and exploitation. Thus, some ecofeminists argue that deep ecology's non-anthropocentrism is superficial, and that the notion of self-realization is both vague and masculinist. Finally, some ecological feminists object to the lack of attention to ecological feminism by deep ecologists, by inaccurate and overly broad characterizations of ecological feminism, and that deep ecologists have tended to refer to men writing about ecological feminism when most of the writings on the topic are by women. In referring to an essay by Fox on the debate between ecological feminism and deep ecology, Deborah Slicer says, "I have this sort of experience each time I read the essay by Fox, who is having a conversation with Zimmerman and [Jim] Cheney while the women stand gagged in the footnotes" (1995, p. 153). I shall now examine the claim that deep ecology can subsume ecological feminism, and some ecological feminist responses.

Warwick Fox writes, "In accordance with this extremely broad ecocentric egalitarianism, supporters of deep ecology hold that their concerns ... well and truly subsume the concerns of those movements that have restricted their focus to the attainment of a more egalitarian human society" (quoted in Slicer 1995, p. 53). However, as Slicer, among others, notes, ecological feminists argue that the gender-neutral analysis provided by deep ecologists overlooks that androcentrism embedded in the western notion of "human." Fox maintains that the central disagreement between deep ecology and ecological feminism involves whether androcentrism or anthropocentrism should be given logical, historical, or political priority. But this reveals a lack of attention to a large body of ecological feminist writings which argue that androcentrism is part of anthropocentrism and vice versa.

Posing the question as one of priority, as an either/or question, as Fox so clearly does, misses the point altogether. An accurate understanding of ecological feminist concerns over the intersections of various types of oppression notices that the "anthropocentrism," which is supposedly the pillar of a system giving human beings moral priority over everything else, is in reality not only sexist, but racist, classist, and homophobic, protecting the moral rights of what tends to be a privileged class of usually white, usually middle-class to wealthy, usually heterosexual, usually men.

Ecological feminists also have been concerned with the concept of self-realization that deep ecologists offer as the solution to dualistic thinking which constructs the human self as radically different and in opposition to the rest of nature. Ecological feminists, including Cheney and Plumwood, argue that the ideal of self-realization offered by deep ecology is problematic.

Plumwood (1993) argues that deep ecological solutions to the discontinuity problem are themselves problematic. The discontinuity problem is that in western contexts humans tend to see themselves as discontinuous with the rest of nature. Deep ecologists offer the notion of self-realization as a solution. However, Plumwood maintains that the notion of self-in-self is vague, and deep ecologists slide between at least three different meanings – the indistinguishable self, the expanded self, and the transcended self. She believes not only that sliding between these makes accounts imprecise, but also that all three are basically masculinist.

The indistinguishability account of self obliterates the self/other dichotomy. According to Plumwood, John Seed accurately expresses this idea as follows: "I am protecting the rain forest" becomes "I am part of the rain forest protecting myself. I am that part of the rain forest recently emerged into thinking" (in Plumwood, 1993, p. 177). Plumwood is critical of self-merger theories, and holds that such obliteration fails to recognize and respect differences. Failure to see oneself as distinct from others means an inability to separate the well-being of others from one's own well-being. This can easily lead to a failure to pay attention to the needs of others, and a failure to care about those needs. The expanded conception of self has similar difficulties according to Plumwood. In this version, identification becomes not identity, but something more like empathy. Plumwood uses Naess's articulation of this version: "The self is as comprehensive as the totality of our identifications ... Our self is that with which we identify" (Plumwood 1993, p. 179). Plumwood points out that the expanded self is not a critique of egoism, it is simply another expression of it. Rather than questioning the structures of possessive egoism and self-interest, it tries to expand the notion of self-interest to include more interests. Thus, we end up with an atomistic non-relational self, just a bigger one. The transcended self account suggests that we detach from the particular concerns of the self. On this account we are to strive for impartial identification with all particulars, the cosmos, and disregard our identifications with our own particular concerns, emotions, and attachments. Plumwood argues that this account again devalues particular attachments, and subsumes the "emotional" to the "rational" in ways that are common in western ethical frameworks, and thus promotes the problematic reason/emotion dualism.

Hence, many ecological feminists not only argue that the account of anthropocentrism offered by deep ecologists is shallow, they argue that deep ecologists incorporate androcentric elements into their suggestions for change. Therefore, many ecological feminists argue that not only does deep ecology fail to address androcentrism, it ends up promoting it.

In my opinion, the lack of explicit attention to issues such as sexism and racism in deep ecology means that even if it turns out to be true that on some highly abstract level the principles of biocentric equality and self-realization could subsume ecological feminist concerns, ecological feminists have good reasons to resist this when deep ecologists include sexism on a long list of things they are against, but never get around to dealing with in any detail. Instead of debating whether deep ecology can theoretically address sexism, a better approach would be for deep ecologists actually to address it.

Some future hopes for ecofeminism

This brings me to my final point. Shamara Shantu Riley calls for a strong Afrocentric ecowomanism to link issues of environmental exploitation and issues of gender, race, and class in the United States and in Africa. Her analysis includes a critique of what she calls Eurocentric masculinist ideology, including dualistic thinking. She states: "Because nature–culture dualism conceives of nature as an other that (male) human undertakings transcend and conquer, women, non-human nature, and men of color become symbolically linked in Eurocentric masculinist ideology" (1993, p. 195). This may sound a lot like ecological feminist analysis. However, Riley quite specifically rejects the label ecological feminist.

> There are several differences between ecofeminism and Afrocentric ecowomanism. While Afrocentric ecowomanism also articulates the links between male supremacy and environmental degradation, it lays far more stress on other distinctive features, such as race and class, that leave an impression markedly different from many ecofeminist theories.
>
> Many ecofeminists when analyzing links between human relations and ecological degradation, give primacy to gender and thus fail to thoroughly incorporate (as opposed to mere tokenism) the historical links between classism, white supremacy, and environmental degradation in their perspectives. For instance, they often don't

address the fact that in nations where such variables as ethnicity and class are a central organizing principle of society, many women are not only viewed in opposition to men under dualism, but also to other women. (ibid, p. 197)

One possible ecological feminist response (which to my knowledge has not been made) could be that ecological feminism can subsume Afrocentric ecowomanism because being opposed to logics of domination implies a conceptual commitment to address issues of race and class. However, this would be an awful response. My hope is that we never see a debate over whether ecological feminism can subsume Afrocentric ecowomanism. A more appropriate response would be for those identifying as ecological feminists to pay attention to Afrocentric ecowomanism to see what can be learned. Opening a dialogue means opening up possibilities for coalition-building and doing activist work. A common theme in ecological feminist scholarship is the desire to combine ecofeminist theory with strong ecofeminist activism. Arguing over whether one theory can, at an abstract level, subsume another, diverts energy away from this task. Therefore, it is counterproductive to ecofeminism's commitment to activism. Riley does not argue that it is somehow theoretically impossible for ecological feminism to attend to issues of race and class. She states that she does not see this actually being done. In my opinion, some of the latest work in ecological feminism pays closer attention to these issues, a trend that will, I hope, continue, and do so without making any attempt to subsume other approaches.

References

Adams, Carol J. (1991) "Ecofeminism and the eating of animals," *Hypatia: A Special Issue, Ecological Feminism* 6, no. 1 (Spring), pp. 125–45. [An article discussing the connections between ecological feminism and vegetarianism.]

Biehl, Janet (1991) *Rethinking Ecofeminist Politics* (Boston: South End Press). [A critical analysis of ecological feminism.]

Bookchin, Murray (1996) *The Philosophy of Social Ecology: Essays on Dialectical Naturalism* (London: Black Rose Books). [An analysis of social ecology.]

Cuomo, Chris J. (1998) *Feminism and Ecological Communities: An Ethic of Flourishing* (London: Routledge). [The concept of flourishing is used to ground an ecological feminist ethic.]

Curtin, Deane. W. and Heldke, Lisa W., eds. (1992) *Cooking, Eating, Thinking: Transformative Philosophies Of Food* (Bloomington: Indiana University Press). [Essays on philosophy and food.]

Davion, Victoria (1994) "Is ecofeminism feminist?" in *Ecological Feminism*, ed. Karen J. Warren (London: Routledge). [Arguments against the uncritical glorification of femininity are offered.]

Diamond, Irene and Orenstein, Gloria Feman, eds. (1990) *Reweaving the World: The Emergence of Ecofeminism* (San Francisco: Sierra Club Books). [A collection of essays exploring different aspects of ecological feminism.]

Gaard, Greta, ed. (1993) *Ecofeminism: Women, Animals, Nature* (Philadelphia: Temple University Press). [A discussion of the relationship between ecological feminism and the green movement.]

Griffin, Susan (1978) *Woman and Nature: The Roaring Inside Her* (New York: Harper and Row). [Written in a poetic style, this book documents the twin dominations of women and nature throughout the history of western patriarchy.]

Gruen, Lori (1993) "Dismantling oppression: an analysis of the connection between women and animals," in *Ecofeminism: Women, Animals, Nature,* ed. Greta Gaard (Philadelphia: Temple University Press). [A critical analysis of conceptual connections between women and animals.]

King, Ynestra (1989) "The ecology of feminism and the feminism of ecology," in *Healing the Wounds: The Promise of Ecofeminism,* ed. Judith Plant (Philadelphia: New Society Publishers). [A conceptual analysis of connections between issues in feminism and environmental ethics.]

Merchant, Carolyn (1983) *The Death of Nature: Women, Ecology, and the Scientific Revolution* (New York: Harper and Row). [A historical grounding of the relationships between conceptions of women and conceptions of nature in western science.]

Naess, Arne (1973) "The shallow and the deep, long-range ecology movements: a summary," *Inquiry* 16, pp. 95–100. [A discussion of why dealing with environmental issues requires changes in underlying values.]

Plant, Judith, ed. (1989) *Healing the Wounds: The Promise of Ecofeminism* (Philadelphia: New Society Publishers). [A collection of essays on ecological feminism.]

Plumwood, Val (1993) *Feminism and the Mastery of Nature* (London: Routledge). [An analysis of the logic of dualistic thinking within western patriarchies and some suggested alternatives.]

Riley, Shamara Shantu (1993) "Ecology is a sistah's issue too: the politics of emergent Afrocentric ecowomanism," in *Ecofeminism and the Sacred,* ed. Carol J. Adams (New York: Continuum). [A discussion of why ecology is important for African and African-American women.]

Salleh, Ariel Kay (1984) "Deeper than deep ecology: the ecofeminist connection," in *Environmental Ethics* 6, no. 1. [A discussion of masculine and feminine approaches to environmental ethics.]

Shiva, Vandana (1989) *Staying Alive: Women, Ecology and Development* (London: Zed Books). [A discussion of the negative impact of patriarchal style western development in India.]

——(1990) "Development as a new project of western patriarchy," in *Reweaving the World: The Emergence of Ecofeminism,* ed. Irene Diamond and Gloria Feman Orenstein (San Francisco: Sierra Club Books). [A discussion of the feminine principle and development.]

Singer, Peter (1975) *Animal Liberation.* (New York: Avon Books). [A call for the ethical treatment of animals based on utilitarianism.]

Slicer, Deborah (1995) "Is there an ecofeminism–deep ecology debate?" *Environmental Ethics* 17, no. 2 (Summer), pp. 151–69. [A discussion of why deep ecology fails to capture androcentrism in its presentations of anthropocentrism.]

Sturgeon, Noel (1997) *Ecofeminist Natures: Gender, Feminist Theory, and Political Action* (New York: Routledge). [A critical analysis of ecological feminist approaches and suggestions for some new directions.]

Swimme, Brian (1990) "How to cure a frontal lobotomy," in *Reweaving the World: The Emergence of Ecofeminism,* ed. Irene Diamond and Gloria Feman Orenstein (San Francisco: Sierra Club Books). [An analysis of how modern science is fragmented.]

Walker, Alice (1988) *Living by the Word: Selected Writings 1973–1987* (New York: Harcourt Brace Jovanovich). [A collection of writings including "Am I Blue," comparing treatment of African-American women and breeding animals.]

Warren, Karen J. (1990) "The power and promise of ecological feminism," *Environmental Ethics* 12, no. 2 (Summer), 125–46. [A discussion of the conceptual connections between environmentalism and feminism.]

PART III

ENVIRONMENTAL PHILOSOPHY AND ITS NEIGHBORS

17

Literature

SCOTT SLOVIC

Art and Community

When David W. Orr published *Ecological Literacy: Education and the Transition to a Postmodern World* in 1992, he made a strong case for the importance of the "liberal arts" – such as history and philosophy – in helping humanity to respond to the current "crisis of sustainability" (p. 83), as he describes the condition of human society at the end of the twentieth century. The primary aims of the liberal arts, according to Orr, are as follows: (i) to "develop balanced, whole persons, [integrating] the analytic mind with feelings, the intellect with manual competence"; (ii) to overcome the "cacophony" of academic subjects that are not synthesized into a meaningful pattern; (iii) to "provide a sober view of the world, but without inducing despair"; and (iv) to "equip a person to live well in a place" (ibid, pp. 100–2). It is striking, however, to find that literature, music, and the visual arts receive almost no attention in *Ecological Literacy*, despite the fact that these are some of the central modes of contemporary ecological thinking and are ideal ways of realizing the above-stated aims of the liberal arts.

During the second half of the twentieth century, and particularly since the late 1960s, literary artists have been among the leaders in exploring the relationship between human culture and the natural world, articulating the principles of scientific ECOLOGY and the personal experience of contact with non-human nature, and putting into words the almost indefinable processes by which our attitudes and ethical systems are formulated and undergo constant adjustments and reality checks. In the United States, especially, the stories and images of the genre known as "environmental literature," defined broadly to include not only non-fiction essays, but also poetry, fiction, and drama that scrutinize the relationship between humans and the natural environment, have become prominent facets of environmental studies. There are many prominent examples of international environmental writers, ranging from Homero Aridjis in Mexico (the president of PEN International from 1997 to 2000, the founder of the environmental organization known as the Group of 100, and a distinguished poet and novelist) to Michiko Ishimure in Japan (a novelist who writes about the Kyushu villages affected by Minamata Disease in the 1960s as a result of industrial pollution). However, nowhere else in the world is there the concentration of first-rate literary artists working on environmental topics that exists presently in the United States, and for this reason I will emphasize contemporary American environmental literature in this chapter. Readers interested in international writing may wish to consult two anthologies: *Family of Earth and Sky: Indigenous Tales of Nature from Around the World*, edited by John Elder and Hertha D. Wong (Boston: Beacon Press, 1994); and *Encompassing Nature: A Sourcebook*, edited by Robert M. Torrance (Washington, DC: Counterpoint, 1997). International scholars and writers may also wish to know about *Literature of Nature: An International Sourcebook*, edited by Patrick D. Murphy (Chicago, IL, and London, UK: Fitzroy Dearborn, 1998).

Literature and the other arts are ideal media for exploring and communicating systems of values – ethical frameworks – within specific communities and between one culture and another. This is not a particularly novel idea, but it flies in the face of postmodern critical theory, which is frequently noted for its indeterminacy, its devotion to textual (and meta-textual) problematics, and its indifference to real social problems. Many literary scholars in recent years have forgotten the traditional social function of the arts. Increasingly, however, critics are now coming to question this asocial, valueless perspective. For instance, James S. Hans writes:

> A good number of our current novelists and poets ... have quite clear commitments to the concerns that developed out of the environmental movement, and yet it is hard to find serious discussions of these concerns in academic journals. We confine ourselves to their words, not to the implications of them, and we have come to think that there is no place in "serious scholarship" to evaluate these "outside" concerns. Our business is with words, nothing more, nothing less, or so it all too often seems. (1990, p. 2)

However, Hans continues,

> If we assume that literature does have an ethical component to it, we must then broaden the ways in which criticism deals with particular texts and with the tradition as a whole. ... [L]iterature does not exist in its own discrete space, so to limit our discussion of it to its "literariness" is to denude it of its crucial links to the other systems that combine to articulate our sense of values. (ibid, p. 15)

This consciousness of the "ethical component" of literature is an important tenet of the new ecological literary criticism, or "ecocriticism," which Cheryll Glotfelty has broadly defined as "the study of the relationship between literature and the physical environment" (Glotfelty and Fromm 1996, p. xviii). One of the central repositories for environmentally oriented literary scholarship is the journal *ISLE: Interdisciplinary Studies in Literature and Environment* (available from the Association for the Study of Literature and Environment; website: <http://www.asle.umn.edu/>).

One of the most succinct statements about the role of literature in formulating environmental values, in the particular context of the American West, is William Kittredge's essay "Owning It All." "A mythology can be understood," he writes, "as a story that contains a set of implicit instructions from a society to its members, telling them what is valuable and how to conduct themselves if they are to preserve the things they value" (1987, p. 62). He continues this line of thought a few pages later:

> In the American West we are struggling to revise our dominant mythology, and to find a new story to inhabit. Laws control our lives, and they are designed to preserve a model of society based on values learned from mythology. Only after re-imagining

our myths can we coherently remodel our laws, and hope to keep our society in a realistic relationship to what is actual. (ibid, p. 64)

Writers, and artists in general, are trying to craft and communicate such a new story, or multiple new stories, at this moment. In many cases, the "new story" requires the recycling of old, sometimes very old, stories. In fact, one of the reasons nature writing has become and continues to emerge as such a powerful force in contemporary literature is that writers such as Kittredge – as well as Barry Lopez, Terry Tempest Williams, Rick Bass, Robert Michael Pyle, Scott Russell Sanders, Wendell Berry, Gary Snyder, and dozens of other environmental writers – understand their work as the effort to achieve not only aesthetic brilliance, but an understanding of human society's "realistic relationship" to the actualities of the planet.

Barry Lopez, who received the National Book Award in 1986 for *Arctic Dreams*, commented explicitly about the social dimension of the arts in a 1990 catalogue essay that he wrote for an exhibit of collages by the Maine artist Alan Magee. Confessing that his own expertise is in the literary arts rather than the visual, Lopez nonetheless raises a series of issues that are fundamental to the linkage of art and environmental awareness:

> What is the meaning of this work . . . to a *community* of people? Is it rich in allusion and metaphorically striking, more in other words than just an announcement of the artist's presence in the world? Does it disturb complacency or stimulate wonder? Does it awaken anger or compassion?
>
> These questions, I think, are more social than aesthetic. They proceed . . . from a feeling that if art is merely decorative or entertaining, or even just aesthetically brilliant, if it does not elicit hope or a sense of the sacred, if it does not speak to our fear and confusion, or to the capacities for memory and passion that imbue us with our humanity, then the artist has only sent us a letter that requires no answer. (1990, p. 1)

This concept of the social responsibilities of art requires a basic paradigm shift for most viewers, listeners, and readers, a shift that broadens the attention from mere "aesthetic brillian[ce]" to the moral dimension of the work or works in question. Such a perspective is not unique to Lopez or to environmental writers. In fact, there is considerable activity today in environmental film, music, theater, and the visual arts. For instance, the Spring/Summer 1994 issue of the journal *Theater* is devoted specifically to "Theater and Ecology." More recently, the art critic Suzi Gablik commented on the social and ecological concerns of contemporary visual artists:

> In Western art today, we have an aesthetic framework for those who believe the world is composed of discrete objects, and who are fascinated with the individual self, but we do not yet have a process-oriented framework for those for whom the world consists of dynamic interactions and interrelational processes. Such a framework would entail a transformation of aesthetic traditions based on individual autonomy and technical mastery into artistic practices based on the interdependent, ecological, and process character of the world, and implies a different level of interaction and permeability with the audience. (1995, p. 44)

In other words, the development of a truly ecological aesthetic in the visual arts and other media (including literature) will require nothing short of a revolution in our notion of what art is. Preceding this revolution, though, must come a rethinking of the purposes of art. Literary artists, in many cases, have never forgotten that values are at the heart of their work. Literary scholars cannot afford to shy away from the issue of human values and attitudes – this is the proper domain of literary studies (and such fields as philosophy, religious studies, and art history), and it is one of the reasons why the arts and humanities are gradually becoming central components of university programs in environmental studies (see AESTHETICS).

Henry David Thoreau seemed to anticipate the social function of literature when he commented, in the "Higher laws" chapter of *Walden*, on the difficulty of expressing complex and subtle ideas. "The greatest gains and values are farthest from being appreciated," he wrote.

> We easily come to doubt if they exist. We soon forget them. They are the highest reality. Perhaps the facts most astounding and most real are never communicated from man to man. The true harvest of my daily life is somewhat as intangible and indescribable as the tints of morning or evening. It is a little stardust caught, a segment of the rainbow which I have clutched. (1971 [1854], p. 145)

Likewise, the lessons of modern environmental science – including the work of ecologists, environmental historians, and environmental anthropologists – are often extremely abstract and difficult for the public to believe, difficult even to decipher. What is an "ecosystem" and why is it so delicate (see ECOLOGY)? Does the "ozone layer" that protects the earth from the sun's ultraviolet rays really have a hole in it? How do we know that hundreds and hundreds of animal and plant species are disappearing each year, becoming extinct (see BIODIVERSITY)? Why does this matter, especially if extinction itself is a natural process? It's easy for people in urban, industrialized countries, such as the United States and Japan, simply to live from day to day, to satisfy our immediate needs and trust that there will always be a tomorrow for our species. The challenging task of the people I refer to as "nature writers" or "environmental writers" is both to create an interest in nature among their readers and to impress these readers with the necessity of living with discipline and a long-term vision of our relationship to the rest of the planet. It's the job of these writers to communicate the subtleties of this relationship that are often, as Thoreau puts it, "farthest from being appreciated."

The rhetoric of environmental literature

Many environmental writers see their work as combining ingenuous exploration of personal experience and the workings of the natural world and more didactic responses to particular environmental problems or issues. A clear way of understanding these important modes of expression is to identify the categories of "epistemological" writing and "political" writing, realizing that in actual literary texts one seldom encounters either form in isolation from the other. "Epistemology," in this context, suggests the attempt to illuminate the natural world and the relationship between the human and the non-human. "Political," on the other hand, implies the effort to persuade an audience to develop a new set of attitudes toward the environment. Nature writers have traditionally viewed their work as a combination of epistemological exploration and political persuasion. I would like to offer an ecocritical reading of two brief examples of contemporary environmental writing, one that is predominantly epistemological and another that is overtly hortatory, or political. Both examples illustrate some of environmental literature's most important traits: attentiveness to the physical world beyond human beings and stimulus for ethical reformation.

My first example comes from Gary Snyder's *No Nature: New and Selected Poems*, a collection that was nominated for the National Book Award in 1992. The final poem in the collection, entitled "Ripples on the surface," operates mainly in the epistemological mode and uses a rhapsodic, or celebratory, style. It reads as follows:

> "Ripples on the surface of the water –
> were silver salmon passing under – different
> from the ripples caused by breezes"
>
> A scudding plume on the wave –
> a humpback whale is
> breaking out in air up
> gulping herring
>   – Nature is not a book, but a *performance*, a
> high old culture
>
> Ever-fresh events
> scraped out, rubbed out, and used, used, again –
> the braided channels of the rivers
> hidden under fields of grass –
>
> The vast wild
>   the house, alone.
> The little house in the wild,
>   the wild in the house.
> Both forgotten.
>
>   No nature
>
> Both together, one big empty house.
>   (1992, p. 381; reprinted with permission)

Close reading of this text will draw the audience initially into an apparent passage from the poet's journal, an entry devoted to detailed observation of an ocean scene. We follow the poet's mental processes in discerning one set of water ripples ("silver salmon") from another ("caused by breezes"). Our attention is next directed toward the "scudding plume" of a surfacing whale, which leads to the realization that "Nature is not a book, but a *performance*." Nature, in other words, is movement, patterns, physical material, something other than the staticity and abstractness of a written text. The following stanza confirms the idea of nature as active and changeable: "Ever-fresh events / scraped out, rubbed out, and used, used, again." Where does such a revelation lead? To the poet's concluding dissolution of the classic western distinction between "domestic" and "wild," "culture" and "nature." Although the poem opens with the human mind noticing subtle differences between superficial things, it moves toward the profound conclusion that everything – culture ("little house") and nature ("wild") – belongs "together," that the universe is "one big empty house." The inclusively defined "house" (as in the Greek root, "oikos," for the word "ecology") of the poem's final line implies habitat for the "performance" of active phenomena, human and non-human. This "house" is "empty" of distinctions, free from such ideas as culture and nature; it is a realm of "No nature" (and implicitly a realm of "No culture," except the "high old culture" of physical performance). The repetition of the word "both" in two of the final three lines reinforces the idea of connection rather than separation.

The point of walking through a close reading of Snyder's "Ripples on the surface" is to demonstrate, in brief, the experience of interpreting a work of environmental literature that enacts what the author may consider an exemplary mental process (careful perception of the world) and then pursues the subtle didactic strategy of imagining a world-view from which such polarized concepts as culture and nature have been abolished. Such an interpretative procedure, whether conducted in writing or in a lecture, does not mandate that the critic's audience agree with the interpretation or even sympathize with the apparent perspective of the literary text. Rather, literary analysis is a process of exploration and reflection, and anyone who participates thoughtfully in this process is likely to end up having worked through a set of ideas that will lead to an enriched consciousness of language, mind, and world.

Another example of contemporary environmental literature comes from the well-known Utah author Terry Tempest Williams, whose 1991 book *Refuge: An Unnatural History of Family and Place* helped to galvanize public attention to the condition of populations living "downwind" from the nuclear weapons testing site in southern Nevada. A short piece of non-fiction prose concludes Williams's 1994 book *An Unspoken Hunger: Stories from the Field*. This essay, entitled "Redemption," directly engages one of the major environmental debates of the rural American West: the presumed conflict between wild predators and domestic livestock. Unlike Snyder's stance of wonderment and reflectiveness in "Ripples on the surface," Williams uses in much of her piece a more aggressively persuasive style of writing, opting for the "jeremiadic" language of warning and critique as a way of capturing her readers' attention. Her entire short essay reads as follows:

> Driving toward Malheur Lake in the Great Basin of southeastern Oregon, I saw a coyote. I stopped the car, opened the door, and walked toward him.
>
> It was another crucifixion in the West, a hide hung on a barbed-wire fence with a wrangler's prayer: Cows are sacred. Sheep, too. No trespassing allowed. The furred skin was torn with ragged edges, evidence that it had been pulled away from the dog-body by an angry hand and a dull knife.
>
> Standing in the middle of the High Desert, cumulus clouds pulled my gaze upward. I thought about Coyote Butte, a few miles south, how a person can sit on top between two sage-covered ears and watch a steady stream of western tanagers fly through during spring migration; yellow bodies, black wings, red heads.

And how a few miles west near Foster Flats, one can witness dancing grouse on their ancestral leks, even in rain, crazy with desire, their booming breasts mimicking the sound of water.

Down the road, I watched a small herd of pronghorn on the other side of the fence, anxiously running back and forth parallel to the barbed wire, unable to jump. Steens Mountain shimmered above the sage flats like a ghost.

My eyes returned to Jesus Coyote, stiff on his cross, savior of our American rangelands. We can try and kill all that is native, string it up by its hind legs for all to see, but spirit howls and wildness endures.

Anticipate resurrection. (1994, pp. 143–4; reprinted with permission)

This essay, obviously, is laden with Christian symbolism and terminology: the title "Redemption" and the final word "resurrection"; the repeated references to "crucifixion"; and the startling phrase "Jesus Coyote" in the emotionally intensified conclusion. Even the essay's dedication – "For Wendell Berry" – signals that the principal audience for this work is likely to be rural, Christian readers, people who work the land like Berry, but who are probably less enthusiastic about wildness than the distinguished Kentucky nature writer.

Williams's prose style in this text is clipped, imagistic, and symbolic. She uses few words to sum up an entire environmental and social issue. Unlike the Snyder poem, which aims mostly to grapple with physical observation of the world and with the philosophical and psychological issue of how humans conceptualize nature, Williams is primarily intent upon expressing her own emotional and aesthetic response to wild creatures in the Great Basin Desert and her revulsion toward the anti-nature animosity of some of her neighbors in the rural West. She offers no analysis of the conflict between grazing practices and territory for wild predators, no explanation of *why* she expects wildness – embodied in coyotes and, presumably, other wild animals such as wolves and mountain lions and grizzly bears – to be resurrected in this region. Her particular persuasive technique is to sweep up readers in the narrative scene through a series of "deictic" maneuvers ("pulled my gaze upward," "a few miles to the west," "down the road," "my eyes returned") and emotionally intensified verbs ("booming," "anxiously running," "shimmered"), hoping that by the end of the story our vicarious experience of this beautiful place will draw us into sympathy with her critique of coyote poaching.

It is common for specific works of environmental literature to use a combination of epistemological reflection and political argument, celebratory reverie and sober warning. This brings to mind David Orr's contention that one of the goals of the liberal arts in environmental education should be to create a mood of sobriety without despair. He writes:

> This is a time of danger, anomie, suffering, crack on the streets, changing climate, war, hunger, homelessness, spreading toxics, garbage barges plying the seven seas, desertification, poverty, and the permanent threat of Armageddon.... The often-cited indifference and apathy of students is, I think, a reflection of the prior failure of educators and educational institutions to stand for anything beyond larger and larger endowments and an orderly campus. The result is a growing gap between the real world and the academy, and between the attitudes and aptitudes of students and the needs of their time. (1992, p. 102)

Environmental literature, and the ecocriticism that provides commentary and con-textualization for this literature, offers an opportunity to overcome this perceived gap between world and classroom, between the vivid experience of beauty and ugliness and the abstractions presented by textbook and newspaper accounts of nature and environmental crisis. By keeping these basic rhetorical modes in mind, it is possible to appreciate the goals and strategies of environmental literature more deeply.

Ethical wholeness and living in place

There are many examples in contemporary environmental literature of writers strug-gling to come to terms with "otherness" and with the experience of "place." In fact, two of the main contributions of environmental literature to the discussion of envir-onmental ethics may be the various ways writers have explored the implications of expanding ethical consideration to non-human species and the myriad literary stu-dies of what it means to live a responsible and engaged life in place. Recall that David Orr, in his seminal discussion of the role of the liberal arts in offering sustainable education, emphasizes "wholeness" and "equip[ing] a person to live well in a place" as key goals of the humanistic disciplines.

Environmental literature, since its earliest emergence on the American continent, has emphasized the phenomenon of the individual human mind engaging with physical landscape, with plants and animals, and with new cultures. Although many readers think of Henry David Thoreau in the mid-nineteenth century as the progenitor of American environmental writing, the tradition is much older than that: as far back as Cabeza de Vaca, who spent the years 1527–37 exploring what later became Florida, Texas, and New Mexico (and described his experiences in a volume published in 1542, later translated as *Adventures in the Unknown Interior of America*), we find an American literature rooted in engagement with "otherness." The same is true of colonial American literature, from William Bradford's *Of Plymouth Plantation: 1620–1647* (pub. 1856) to Anne Bradstreet's *The Tenth Muse, Lately Sprung Up in America* (1650), and later exploration narratives and nationalistic landscape appre-ciations such as Hector St. John de Crevecoeur's *Letters from an American Farmer* (1782), Thomas Jefferson's *Notes on the State of Virginia* (1787), and William Bar-tram's *Travels through North & South Carolina, Georgia, East & West Florida* (1791).

The tradition of American environmental literature did not begin with Thoreau, but Thoreau nevertheless crystallized and articulated some of the traits that have since been recognized as hallmarks of this tradition. One of these is the idea of kinship to the non-human world. An important statement about this subject appears in the chapter "Solitude" from *Walden*:

> I experienced sometimes that the most sweet and tender, the most innocent and encouraging society may be found in any natural object, even for the poor misan-thrope and most melancholy man....I have never felt lonesome, or in the least oppressed by a sense of solitude, but once, and that was a few weeks after I came to the woods, when, for an hour, I doubted if the near neighborhood of man was not essential to a serene and healthy life. To be alone was something unpleasant. But I was at the same time conscious of a slight insanity in my mood, and seemed to

foresee my recovery. In the midst of a gentle rain while these thoughts prevailed, I was suddenly sensible of such sweet and beneficent society in Nature, in the very pattering of the drops, and in every sound and sight around my house, an infinite and unaccountable friendliness all at once like an atmosphere sustaining me, as made the fancied advantages of human neighborhood insignificant, and I have never thought of them since. Every little pine needle expanded and swelled with sympathy and befriended me. I was so distinctly made aware of the presence of something kindred to me, even in scenes which we are accustomed to call wild and dreary. (1971 [1854], pp. 131–2)

This famous passage from *Walden* emphasizes not the misanthropy that is sometimes ascribed to Thoreau, but rather the positive sense of kinship with extra-human nature that may well make this one of the ur-texts of the contemporary movement to expand ethical and legal consideration to animals and other natural phenomena. Literary scholars have commonly recognized in such Thoreauvian statements as the one just quoted antecedents to the "inhumanist" perspective in some twentieth-century writers, such as Robinson Jeffers, Loren Eiseley, and Edward Abbey. In poem after poem published between the 1920s and the 1960s, from "Hurt hawks" to "Oh, lovely rock," to "The answer" (from which the line "Love that, not man apart from that" comes), Jeffers developed an ethos of respect for the intrinsic value of non-human nature that had nothing to do with nature's economic or even aesthetic benefit to humanity. In his own jaunty and irascible style, we see a rearticulation of this inhumanist perspective in the various novels and essay collections of Edward Abbey that appeared from the 1960s to the 1980s; in fact, Abbey's *Desert Solitaire* (1968), taken by some as the cornerstone text of the modern American renaissance of environmental writing, has a distinctly Jeffers-esque cast in such passages as "I prefer not to kill animals. I'm a humanist; I'd rather kill a *man* than a snake" (1985 [1968] p. 20; cf. Jeffers's line "I'd sooner, except the penalties, kill a man than a hawk" from "Hurt Hawks," *Selected Poetry* (1937), p. 198).

The inhumanist stance toward the natural world has come to permeate much of the environmental literature of the late twentieth century, although not always as overtly as in the works of Jeffers, Eiseley, and Abbey. Generally, the notion of nature's intrinsic value, as articulated in this literature, is not directly linked to particular legal contexts or to formal ethical principles. However, there are some notable exceptions to this. For instance, in April of 1989, the distinguished Alaskan anthropologist and nature writer Richard K. Nelson (whose *The Island Within* won the John Burroughs Medal for natural history writing that same year) published an eloquent editorial in the *Los Angeles Times*, responding to the recent oil spill in Prince William Sound. "Oil and ethics: adrift on troubled waters" is, mostly, a jeremiad that warns of the broader cultural implications of the Exxon Valdez disaster. But rather than simply complaining about the oil spill and pointing fingers at the corporation that was directly responsible for the accident, Nelson takes a more subtle and meaningful approach to the cost of modern civilization and the issue of responsibility. In addition to more abstract philosophical and political reflections, the essay makes crucial use of concrete, experiential information from Nelson's memories of a similar oil spill off the coast of Santa Barbara, California, twenty years earlier. "I have forgotten how many barrels of oil went into the Santa Barbara Channel," writes Nelson, how much it cost to clean up the spill, how those who suffered damages were compensated, how blame was decided, how punishment was administered, how many animals were calculated to have died and how many were saved. But one memory is lodged forever in my mind – that dying bird [mentioned in the previous paragraph], her feathers matted and shining with oil, her wings drooped, her body quivering. (1993, p. 676)

This is a particularly interesting section because it demonstrates implicitly the power of literary representations of nature in guiding public attitudes and opinions. For better or worse, images are more impressive than statistics – they have an immediate emotional impact on an audience and they stick in readers' minds. Nelson's short editorial on the Exxon Valdez disaster, written for the vast readership of the *Los Angeles Times*, shows how nature writing often achieves impressive eloquence (lasting literary quality), even when seeking, primarily, to draw the attention of the general public to contemporary environmental issues. In the remaining paragraphs of this essay, Nelson weaves together his account of what it's like to witness an oil spill with his reflections on the moral implications of this phenomenon, concluding that "we must now recognize the need for a further growth of moral conscience, to encompass the whole community of life – the environment that nurtures, uplifts our senses and sustains our existence" (ibid, p. 677). "Oil and ethics" is an example of the hybrid form of epistemological and political nature writing that aims to make readers sit up and pay closer attention to important environmental problems. It represents an intriguing extension of the Thoreauvian tradition of inhumanist writing by showing the implications of an expanded ethical scheme for contemporary economic and industrial behavior. Moreover, Nelson's essay offers a lesson in how we, as human beings, process ecological, political, economic, and aesthetic information – and this experience of holistic, multidisciplinary thinking, as David Orr implies, is a crucial contribution to the process of environmental education.

Another major part of Henry David Thoreau's legacy to more recent environmental literature is his appreciation of immediate and local places rather than the distant and exotic. For some writers, such as Wendell Berry, this idea has become a crucial rallying point. In June 1989, Berry gave a speech to a group of graduating students at the College of the Atlantic in which he explained that "the question that *must* be addressed . . . is not how to care for the planet but how to care for each of the planet's millions of human and natural neighborhoods, each of its millions of small pieces and parcels of land, each one of which is in some precious way different from all the others" (in 1990, p. 200). The ability to evoke the subtle mysteries of specific "neighborhoods" is one of the great contributions of nature writing to American culture, and when this nature writing is exported to other cultures, I believe its proper function is not simply to attract tourists to Edward Abbey's Arches National Park or Rick Bass's Yaak Valley or even to Walden Pond, but rather to offer models for the process of noticing – and caring about – the world wherever readers might live. There are many good examples of place writing in American environmental literature, from Henry Beston's *The Outermost House* (1928) set on Cape Cod to Aldo Leopold's *A Sand County Almanac* (1949) which takes place largely in rural Wisconsin, from Gary Paul Nabhan's *The Desert Smells Like Rain* (1982) about the Tohono O'odham people of southern Arizona to Scott Russell Sanders's meditation on nature and community in the Ohio River Valley in his book *Staying Put: Making a Home in a Restless World* (1993).

Wendell Berry himself offers one of the best examples of a nature writer who eloquently explores what it means to live meaningfully and constructively – rootedly – in a specific place on earth. Many writers are now working to articulate the experience of urban places (see Sandra Cisneros's 1989 volume of fictional vignettes set in inner-city Chicago, *The House on Mango Street*; John Edgar Wideman's 1992 short story collection *All Stories Are True*, set in urban Pittsburgh; and Robert Michael Pyle's 1993 book of non-fiction about Denver, *The Thunder Tree: Lessons from an Urban Wildland*) or of suburbia (for instance, Annie Dillard's essays such as "Living like weasels" in the 1982 collection *Teaching a Stone to Talk* and Michael Pollan's 1991 book, *Second Nature: A Gardener's Education*, set in Long Island, New York, and the commuter towns of Connecticut). But Berry has always been steadfastly a writer of rural American experience; in fact, much of his work laments the ever-increasing urbanization of the country. Some of Berry's writing is overtly a form of social critique, chastening his readers for participating in a culture that has lost touch with the moral and psychological and economic benefits of conscientious living in rural places; an important example of this work is the 1980 essay "The making of a marginal farm," which concludes, "the land is heavily taxed to subsidize an 'affluence' that consists, in reality, of health and goods stolen from the unborn" (in 1981, p. 340). Other writings by Berry, including novels such as *The Memory of Old Jack* (1976) and essays such as "A country of edges" (1971), explore not the political and moral implications of degrading and neglecting place, but the more fundamental processes by which we come to attach ourselves to place. In "A country of edges," Berry uses physical descriptions of water, analysis of the natural phenomenon of erosion, and a story about an excursion into the Red River Gorge of Kentucky to develop a sense of water, land, and the attentive human mind coming together:

> We pass through carefully, no longer paddling as we wish but as we must, following the main current as it bends through the rocks and the grassy shoals. And then we enter the quiet water of the pool below. Ahead of us a leaf falls from high up in a long gentle fall. In the water its reflection rises perfectly to meet it. (ibid, p. 229)

In his evocation of the political complexities and the daily experience of "living in place," Wendell Berry may be the best exemplar of what Wallace Stegner, in an essay called "The sense of place," praises as "the placed person" (1992, p. 200). Yet there is increasing dissension among environmental writers over the value of rootedness versus the value – indeed the common necessity – of migratoriness in industrialized societies. Such authors as John Daniel (in his 1992 book *The Trail Home: Nature, Imagination, and the American West* and his more recent essay "A Word in Favor of Rootlessness") and Alison Hawthorne Deming (in her 1994 book *Temporary Homelands: Essays on Nature, Spirit and Place*) aim to understand what it means to live in a modern, industrialized society that often requires mobility for economic and social reasons. The purpose of such explorations of place in contemporary environmental literature is not to advance a single perspective on how people should conceptualize and experience place, but to provide a vocabulary for readers to use in formulating their own relationships to the cities and landscapes where they happen to dwell, even if they are only passing through.

It would be presumptuous to guess precisely the future trajectory of ecocriticism and environmental literature in the United States and other countries, such as Japan and the UK, where this is a rapidly growing field. Unlike other forms of environmental scholarship that tend to respond to specific problems in specific geographical locations, "literary ecology" (to use the phrase of Cheryll Glotfelty and Harold Fromm 1996) typically plays an indirect, long-term role in social evolution, challenging readers to consider deeply – and to work gradually toward – just and sustainable relationships between their human communities and the planet.

References

Abbey, E. (1985 [1968]) *Desert Solitaire: A Season in the Wilderness* (New York: Ballantine Books). [One of the classic works of the contemporary renaissance of American nature writing, emphasizing the author's experience at Arches National Monument in southern Utah.]

Berry, W. (1981) *Recollected Essays: 1965–1980* (San Francisco: North Point Press). [A retrospective collection of non-fiction writings by the eminent farmer and author from Kentucky.]

——(1990) *Word and Flesh. What are People for?* (San Francisco: North Point Press). [A more recent collection of essays by the Kentucky author.]

Gablik, S. (1995) "Arts and the earth: making art as if the world mattered," *Orion*, pp. 44–53. [A discussion of the social implications of contemporary environmental work in the visual arts.]

Glotfelty, C., and Fromm, H., eds. (1996) *The Ecocriticism Reader: Landmarks in Literary Ecology* (Athens: University of Georgia Press). [The seminal introduction to literary studies from an environmental perspective.]

Hans, J. S. (1990) *The Value(s) of Literature* (Albany: State University of New York Press). [A polemical work that calls for renewed attentiveness to values in literary studies.]

Jeffers, R. (1937) *The Selected Poetry of Robinson Jeffers* (New York: Random House). [A major collection by one of the great American nature poets of the twentieth century.]

Kittredge, W. (1987) "Owning it all," in *Owning it all* (Minneapolis, MN: Graywolf Press). [A collection of essays, some political and others experiential, about recent changes in the rural American West.]

Lopez, B. (1990) *Alan Magee: Inlets* (The Joan Whitney Payson Gallery of Art, Westbrook College, Portland, Maine). [A catalogue essay on visual artist Alan Magee by the major nature writer, Barry Lopez.]

Nelson, R. K. (1993) "Oil and ethics: adrift on troubled waters," in *Being in the World: An Environmental Reader for Writers*, ed. Scott H. Slovic and Terrell F. Dixon (New York: Macmillan). [This essay was originally written as an editorial for the *Los Angeles Times* in response to the Exxon Valdez oil spill in 1989.]

Orr, D. W. (1992) *Ecological Literacy: Education and the Transition to a Postmodern World* (Albany: SUNY Press). [An important argument for educational reform to reflect the planet's changing environment.]

Snyder, G. (1992) *No Nature: New and Selected Poems* (New York: Pantheon). [A comprehensive collection of poetry by one of the great American environmental writers.]

Stegner, W. (1992) *The Sense of Place. Where the Bluebird Sings to the Lemonade Springs: Living and Writing in the West* (New York: Random House). [The final collection of essays by one of the central figures in the late twentieth-century renaissance of American environmental writing.]

Thoreau, H. D. (1971 [1854]) *Walden* (Princeton: Princeton University Press). [The work sometimes singled out as the starting point of the American tradition of environmental literature.]

Williams, T. T. (1994) *An Unspoken Hunger: Stories from the Field* (New York: Pantheon). [A collection of lyrical essays by one of the major contemporary American women nature writers.]

18

Aesthetics

JOHN ANDREW FISHER

Aesthetic preservationism

Between 1908 and 1913 William Mulholland supervised construction of a vast aqueduct 223 miles long diverting the Owens River on the eastern slopes of the Sierra Nevada Mountains to Los Angeles. This enabled that city to expand into a giant metropolis and incidentally transformed lush Owens Valley into a semi-arid land. So great was Mulholland's desire for even more water for Los Angeles that twelve years later he met with the superintendent of Yosemite National Park and proposed damming up the famous and scenic valley of Yosemite, making an enormous reservoir out of it. As he explained, "I'd go in there and build a dam from one side of the valley to the other and *stop the goddamned waste!*" (Reisner 1986, p. 92). Mulholland looked at Bridalveil Fall and saw not an awesomely tall, beautiful spidery mist but, rather, an extremely useful source of water for urban households and San Fernando valley farmers; he looked at the powerful glacier-carved shapes of the mountains forming the valley and he saw a natural reservoir to hold the water for those households and farmers.

Mulholland concentrated on the instrumental uses to which Yosemite valley and its rivers could be put. Typical of those who developed the frontier regions of the world, he did not concern himself with the effects on nature of such grand public works projects. He did not consider the damage that such a project would do to the plants and animals or, indeed, to the whole Yosemite ecosystem. His proposal also failed to give any weight to what is perhaps the most obvious effect of all: the erasure of an arrestingly beautiful environment. As horrifying as Mulholland's threat to dam Yosemite Valley might seem to early twenty-first-century readers, it was far from idle. In the 1960s the Glen Canyon of the Colorado River was dammed to form Lake Powell. In contrast to earlier dam projects, however, this one caused a public battle that largely turned on the extraordinary beauty of Glen Canyon and its hundred side canyons, slender, steep and fantastically colored and shaped. (Although the aesthetic considerations have been less central, similar struggles over dams have occurred in Australia, India, and China.) Surely it was the public's concern for the aesthetic value of nature that finally won out in stopping the next project on the Colorado: to dam the river at a lower point and turn the Grand Canyon into a reservoir.

These days the aesthetic qualities of nature are commonly invoked to justify preservation of nature areas. Consider, for example, on-going proposals to clear-cut wilderness areas of Tongass National Forest in southeastern Alaska. Environmentalists offer many reasons why these largest remaining stands of old-growth trees in the

United States should be protected from clear-cutting: to preserve a wild ecosystem for its own sake; to preserve habitat for bears, salmon, bald eagles, and other rare species; to protect the recreational values of fishing, camping, hiking, boating. But prominent among common reasons given is this: to preserve the extraordinary beauty of hundreds of miles of majestic mountains, islands, sparkling glaciers, and fjords.

Although aesthetic considerations have always carried practical weight in the environmental movement, they have often been ignored by theorists of environmental ethics. But many environmental theorists now believe that attempts to justify preservation based solely on the instrumental value of nature need to be supplemented by some notion of nature's intrinsic value. Merely appealing to the ways that humans are dependent on nature will not provide sufficient reason to preserve nature in an undeveloped state. This dependence might convince us to conserve water, to restrain the use of toxic pesticides, to not drive fish species to extinction, and to limit excessive air pollution. But all of this falls far short of preserving nature as WILDERNESS or returning her to a pristine state. The damming up of rivers in the American West illustrates this point: merely on the basis of instrumental values, the conversion of wild rivers to reservoirs may make irresistible sense. This has led thinkers, such as Sagoff (1991), to argue that we need to regard nature as having intrinsic moral and aesthetic value if we want to motivate comprehensive preservation of nature (see NORMATIVE ETHICS, META-ETHICS).

We might call those who think that the aesthetic values inherent in nature provide a significant if defeasible reason for its preservation, "aesthetic preservationists." (Aesthetic preservationists will typically be pluralists who grant there are also other sorts of reason for preservation.) Sagoff outlines such a position by suggesting that appreciation of aesthetic value, in conjunction with a moral love of nature in and for itself, can be used to justify projects of preservation and restoration. Can aesthetic value by itself provide sufficient justification for preservation? Thompson (1995) argues that it can. She holds that aesthetic value by itself can be used to argue validly that some parts of nature have an aesthetic worth that merits respect and thus preservation. Just as we have an obligation to preserve beautiful artworks, we have obligations to preserve beautiful nature areas. Hargrove (1989) develops a similar argument appealing to G. E. Moore's (1873–1958) notion that we have a duty to promote and preserve good. Hargrove contends that natural beauty constitutes an aesthetic good. This makes up a part of the general good that exists and ought to exist. The loss of a given example of natural beauty simply represents a loss of the total good in the world. (Indeed, Hargrove holds that the loss of natural beauty amounts to a greater loss of good than the loss of artworks and that, therefore, we have an even greater obligation to preserve natural beauty.)

Although appeals to aesthetic values to justify preservation of nature have great intuitive appeal, they also raise several basic questions. First, what accounts for the aesthetic value of elements of nature, of landscapes, and of ecosystems? Second, how is aesthetic value to be determined? Third, how much weight does aesthetic value have? Does it equal or trump instrumental values that nature can be exploited to generate?

Sober (1986), who argues that the aesthetic may be the only intrinsic value that works to support preservation, nonetheless thinks it is trumped by basic human needs for the essentials of life. For nature, if not for art, we genuinely have a version of the "Baby or Botticelli" conundrum occasionally addressed in art theory: if we had to choose between saving a baby or a Botticelli painting, which should we choose? Such a puzzle can be rejected for artworks as absurdly artificial. But in our relations to nature, these choices will appear frequently. In India, for instance, we may well have to choose between babies and the wolves and tigers that can hunt near the villages and occasionally kill vulnerable young humans. In the American West there is a conflict between the natural beauties of western river canyons and the need to provide more water for the growth of cities. The need to find out how much weight we ought to give to aesthetic value is much more pressing in our interactions with nature than it is in our interactions with artworks, which have few if any instrumental uses that would conflict with their preservation.

There is a fourth question, less obvious than the others, but equally important for aesthetic preservationism: Why is the aesthetic value of wild nature preferable to the aesthetic value of either altered nature or human-made environments? Even if we grant significant weight to the aesthetic values of environments, preservationists typically hold that the aesthetic value of undeveloped nature is greater than the aesthetic value of the same land developed in some way. Almost everyone will agree that clear-cut forests are ugly scars. But what if the forest is cut to make room for an architecturally interesting city (Brasilia) or an attractive golf course? What if beautiful canyons are flooded in order to create a beautiful lake (Lake Powell)?

Few people question the enormous beauty of areas and elements of nature. But to use that beauty effectively to counter the many instrumental uses to which nature can be put, a complete aesthetic preservationist account will have to suggest at least rough answers for these four questions.

Aesthetic value

We have seen that one central problem for aesthetic preservationism is to provide an account of what underlies and determines the aesthetic value of nature. It is natural to hold that our aesthetic responses to nature are key to answering this question. Not only is the aesthetic value of items in nature estimated through acts of appreciation, but to ascribe positive aesthetic value to objects is perhaps no more than to say that the results of our acts of appreciation are positive. These relations are expressed in the general account of aesthetic value due to Monroe Beardsley. Beardsley ties aesthetic value directly to response when he defines the aesthetic value of an object as "the value it possesses in virtue of its capacity to provide aesthetic gratification" (1982, p. 21). Aesthetic gratification follows on or is part of an aesthetic response to elements of nature.

Beardsley's perceiver-dependent account of aesthetic value is fully within the spirit of modern aesthetics. Since the eighteenth century the western aesthetics tradition has tended to assume that a metaphysical realist view of beauty and other aesthetic qualities is not plausible. Among realist views we can distinguish a Platonic view, that Beauty, like Justice, is a self-subsistent form that objects in the world participate in, from a more modest realist view that some of the properties that objects have in the world are beautiful and necessarily so, independent of any human perception or taste.

Even this more modest view conflicts with the apparent viewer-dependency of aesthetic qualities such as beauty. As Hutcheson, one of the originators of the modern view, asserts: "by absolute or original beauty is not understood any quality supposed to be in the object [which] should of itself be beautiful, without relation of a mind that perceives it" (1725, sec. I, 17). Hutcheson noted specifically that when we speak of beauty we mean "that such objects are agreeable to the sense of men" (1725, sec. II, 1).

The biophilia hypothesis

If, as the modern position has it, aesthetic value is a function of aesthetic response, we are immediately led to a central question for nature aesthetics: what is an aesthetic response to nature? How does it differ from other modes of response to nature, many of which can also yield gratification?

In the environmental literature it is common to mention "aesthetics" without much attention to what is genuinely aesthetic. This can be illustrated by considering the biophilia hypothesis due to E. O. Wilson. Although quite speculative at present, this hypothesis has been proposed as giving a biological grounding for the fact that we find nature aesthetically valuable. As Wilson formulates it, the hypothesis is founded on the claim that there is an "innately emotional affiliation of human beings to other living organisms" (Kellert and Wilson 1993, p. 31). This innate tendency is invoked to explain what attracts us to zoos, to nature and to "dwellings on prominences above water amidst parkland" (ibid, p. 32). According to the hypothesis, this innate tendency, imparted by the evolutionary history of our interaction with many other organisms, leads to a need to relate to living organisms and, consequently, to all sorts of emotional responses to nature, "from attraction to aversion, from awe to indifference, from peacefulness to fear-driven anxiety" (ibid, p. 31).

The biophilia hypothesis is attractive to preservationists because by postulating a biological basis for our responses to nature it imputes to us an innate need to experience a variety of nature settings. The satisfaction of these emotional needs would give us a strong self-interested (as opposed to altruistic) reason to protect nature and to promote biodiversity. Proponents of biophilia, for example, point to the psychological benefits, such as tension release, relaxation, and peace of mind, that studies have shown accrue to those who recreate in nature. But however desirable stress reduction may be, it does not seem to be an aesthetic response. Kellert's suggestion that "the adaptational value of the aesthetic experience of nature could further be associated with derivative feelings of tranquillity, peace of mind, and a related sense of psychological well-being and self-confidence" (ibid, p. 50) grants that the valuable derivative feelings associated with our experience of nature are not themselves aesthetic. Is there any reason to think, however, that the state from which these desirable states derive ought to be regarded as an aesthetic response to nature? Why not more simply suppose they are caused by satisfying a simple need to interact with organisms and nature settings?

In fact, there is a general problem for attempts to give biological explanations of our aesthetic responses. Insofar as our favorable reactions to nature are explained by supposing they are keyed to particular types of animals and settings in which humans have prospered over evolutionary time, some of our stronger aesthetic reactions become inexplicable. What we in fact appreciate in nature appears to diverge from what we should have been selected to appreciate. Among common aesthetic responses to nature are these: finding high, rugged mountain peaks beautiful, finding Arctic ice-flows and ice-sheets and violent seas sublime, and so on. Such beautiful and sublime objects don't seem to correspond to environments in which humans have prospered.

A significant problem from a preservationist point of view is that biophilia seems indifferent to the fourth issue (see above) to be settled by any adequate preservationist position. Logically, it implies no preference for undeveloped over developed nature. As long as a development does not significantly reduce the number of organisms or reduce the chance to interact with them and to interact with nature settings, there seems no basis for an objection on behalf of our alleged biophilia. A themepark could even be preferable to a wilderness area if it were to contain more charismatic species than did the same area unaltered.

What is an aesthetic response to nature?

Some theorists think that our mode of appreciation of nature should contrast with the disembodied and artificially focused ways we appreciate artworks. These thinkers propose that appreciation of nature should be holistic and interactive: lying on the tundra, turning to feel the sun on one's skin, smelling the flowers and earth, hearing the bubbling brook, climbing a tree, etc.; in short, an experience that integrates all of our sensory modalities and that acknowledges that the perceiving subject is a part of the natural context rather than a god-like observer (Carlson 1979). The argument of Carlson and others is that the nature of what we are responding to – in the case of nature, a setting that entirely surrounds us and which has developed without human interference – dictates a mode of appreciation different from that appropriate to artworks intentionally made to be individually appreciated in isolation on the walls of museums or heard in silence in a concert hall.

Some philosophers, noting the great differences between art and nature, draw an opposite conclusion. They deny that the concept of aesthetic appreciation can even be applied appropriately to nature. The fundamental reason is that nature is standardly contrasted with what humans have made or altered. However, the absence of human intentionality in undomesticated nature may remove the feature that is responsible for making criticism and appreciation in the arts possible at all. Mannison claims, for example, that "only *artifacts* which have been fashioned with the *intention* of being, at least, in part, objects of aesthetic judgment can be objects of aesthetic judgment" (Thompson 1995, p. 293). Why should this be? Mannison argues that artistry is an essential component of aesthetic judgments, and obviously non-artifactual nature cannot be judged for its artistry or lack thereof. However, many aesthetic judgments appear to be ascriptions of aesthetic properties, for instance, the property of being beautiful. So it is not surprising that the claim that aesthetic appreciation only applies to artworks and other intentionally made objects goes against the main tradition in aesthetics.

The account of aesthetic judgment that helped launch aesthetics as a field and which is still in many ways canonical, is Immanuel Kant's, given in the *Critique of*

Judgment, published in 1790. For a judgment of an object to be a pure aesthetic judgment, a judgment for Kant that something is beautiful, first it has to be based on a feeling of pleasure resulting from a particular experience of the object, and second, it cannot result from a previous desire for the object. Such a desire for the existence of the object would bias the judgment and remove it from the realm of an objective aesthetic judgment. Kant also argues that pure aesthetic judgments are not based on the application of concepts of perfection, concepts of what the object should be like. There is little room, then, on Kant's account of aesthetic judgments, for consideration of what authors and artifact makers are trying to achieve by creating an object. Instead, on Kant's view, an aesthetic judgment arises from the pleasure consequent upon the "free play" of the cognitive faculties in experiencing the object. A particular rose is beautiful for Kant, not because it conforms to some ideal of a rose, but, rather, its beauty results from its appearance as a unique item and not because of the particular concepts or antecedent values we might bring to an experience of it. Kant's theory of aesthetic judgment, if anything, applies to nature much more naturally than to artifacts.

Mannison and others imply that when we appreciate nature and ascribe aesthetic qualities to nature we are extending concepts to nature that have their paradigm or proper application in our responses to the arts. Not only does Kant's aesthetics argue against this idea, it is not very plausible anyway. Sibley's influential general account of aesthetic qualities, for instance, argues that many aesthetic concepts are first learned by applying them to prominent things in nature: sunsets, woods in autumn, roses and mountains: "it is in these circumstances that we find ourselves introducing general aesthetic words to [children], like 'lovely,' 'pretty,' and 'ugly' " (1995 [1959], p. 330). Carlson too notes that such instances of natural beauty are paradigms of aesthetic appreciation: "ones in terms of which we acquire and understand the concept of the aesthetic" (1984, p. 12).

Sibley's account of aesthetic qualities highlights the relevance of taste. Aesthetic qualities are qualities we ascribe to objects on the basis of other (non-aesthetic) properties of the objects. However, according to Sibley, aesthetic qualities must be ascribed through an exercise of taste or perceptiveness. For Sibley, there are no necessary or sufficient conditions in terms of non-aesthetic qualities that imply that an aesthetic quality must be true of an object – for example, that an object is graceful because it is tall, curved, has a slender support, etc. Someone must perceive the object and, on the basis of the total set of particular non-aesthetic qualities that this object has, see that it is graceful. Sibley thinks that all humans are able to exercise this taste or discernment, but that this capacity is variable across humans. Particular aesthetic concepts – serene, dynamic, powerful, delicate, and so on – must be learned, and the capacity to make judgments applying them is presupposed in such instruction.

Perceiving nature as nature

Are there further requirements for an appropriate aesthetics of nature? Budd (1996) argues that it is a mistake to regard every aesthetic response to nature as an appreciation of nature. It may be that when we respond positively to something in nature we are doing so without regard for whether it is a natural item. We may be delighted by the iridescent colors of a hummingbird's wings, but not because they are the colors of a bird's wings. If it doesn't matter to our appreciation of a natural item whether it is artificial (an artifact) or natural, then we are not appreciating that item as nature.

Budd also notes that the character of our experience is determined by how we conceptualize what we are experiencing. It makes a difference if we experience particular sounds as produced by a living bird, particular lights in the sky as northern lights, particular colors in the sky as a thundercloud. Under this account of perception, the requirement that we respond to nature as nature becomes a requirement that we experience objects under appropriate natural descriptions.

What is it to perceive something as natural or a part of nature? It is surprisingly difficult to provide a satisfactory account of this. There is a temptation to require the perceiver to be informed by a correct scientific theory – that surely would be to experience the item as a part of nature as it really is. Carlson (1981) argues for such an account of the proper way to appreciate nature. He wants to understand aesthetic judgments of nature in such a way as to show that there can be correct and incorrect aesthetic judgments of nature. He agrees with Budd that our notion of the proper response to nature should be guided by the true nature of what we are experiencing. To achieve that end, Carlson seeks a way to conceptualize items in nature that is analogous to the fact that artworks are appropriately experienced only under their correct categories as artworks: painting (versus sculpture), cubist painting (versus impressionist painting), and so on. Like Budd, he holds that these categories make an enormous difference to our psychological experience of objects, in this case, artworks. Moreover, aesthetic judgments in art are only correct if they are based on perceiving the artwork in its correct category. Analogously, as we have seen, there are different ways of experiencing nature and these make a large difference to the qualities of our experience – consider perceiving a whale as a fish or as a mammal. Finally, there really are, Carlson thinks, correct categories to apply to things in nature, and these are the categories of natural history and natural science.

Unfortunately, these categories change over time. To require that the categories suitable for nature perception be the correct descriptions of nature may set the standard too high. Scientific theories are in constant flux, and it may not be plausible to suppose that our current conceptions of astronomy, biology, geology, etc., are actually correct. Besides, if people in the nineteenth century experienced a land formation (say, the Alps) under the influence of now outdated uniformitarian conceptions of geology, did they not experience nature as nature? If not, then it is possible that we, under the influence of current geological theory, may also not be experiencing nature as nature. On the other hand, if we set the standard lower, so that all that is required is perception under common-sense perceptual concepts, such as "bird," "star," and so on – will that be adequate? When we look at the night sky, for example, what is the minimum set of concepts that makes our experience an experience of nature? If the Greeks thought of the stars as made of ether turning eternally around the unmoving earth on a transparent sphere only a few thousand miles away, does that count? One is tempted to say "yes," but does that mean that any concept will do no matter how misguided it may have been? Clearly it will not be easy to find the right criteria to apply to the concepts under which we might experience the natural world if we want to specify a general account of what it is to truly experience nature as nature.

A way to sidestep the demand that appreciation of nature be based on fully adequate conceptions is suggested by Rolston, who holds that some aesthetic responses to nature are better than others. Although he is tempted by the view that "nature is a smorgasbord that humans can do with as they please. No one aesthetic response is more or less correct than any other" (1995, p. 376), he argues that there are two themes to be emphasized in an aesthetics of nature. One is that aesthetic experience of nature must be participatory, and the other is that it should be faithful to the objective reality of what nature is. The physical and biological sciences tell us what nature really is and how it got that way. They cannot but help make our experience richer, whereas "mistaken interpretive frameworks do blind us so that we cannot see what is there, they create illusions of what is not there, they leave us ignorant of what is really going on; and here science greatly educates us to what is really taking place" (ibid, p. 383). So while traditional peoples of the world did have aesthetic experiences of their environments, science-based experience can provide a deeper understanding of a much wider range of environments, including "wilder, fiercer landscapes" (ibid) than we might otherwise be disposed to appreciate.

Positive aesthetics

One of the most intriguing ideas about nature is that it is all beautiful in its own way. This idea has been extensively developed by Carlson (1984) and others into a position called "positive aesthetics." Nineteenth-century social critic William Morris states the underlying intuition clearly: "surely there is no mile of earth's inhabitable surface that is not beautiful in its own way" (in Carlson 1984, p. 7). Such intuitions about the aesthetic value of nature are in sharp contrast to our common view of the aesthetic value of artworks. Artworks may be good or bad; they may be mediocre, awkward, unresolved, or even ugly and repulsive. But many thinkers have urged that nature is never properly subject to such criticism; it is always aesthetically good. John Ruskin, for example, held that certainty of beauty was to be found only in nature. Why should this be so? Ruskin tellingly points to our experience of clouds: "the clouds, not being liable to man's interference, are always beautifully arranged" (in Carlson 1984, p. 6).

There are several different theses that fall under the umbrella of "positive aesthetics" ((1)–(4) are quoted from Carlson, 1984):

1. All the natural world is beautiful.
2. All virgin nature is essentially aesthetically good.
3. The natural environment, in so far as it is untouched by man, has mainly positive aesthetic qualities; it is, for example, graceful, delicate, intense, unified, and orderly, rather than bland, dull, insipid, incoherent, and chaotic.
4. Being natural is essentially connected with positive aesthetic qualities.
5. Any part of nature is aesthetically more valuable if it is unaffected by human activities than if it is.

These positions have different implications. Numbers (4) and (5), for example, do not necessarily imply the stronger claims of (1) and (2). There could be aesthetic features of natural items that were not a part of "being natural" that outweigh the positive aesthetic qualities they have in virtue of being natural. For instance, the blandness of a calm gray ocean and sky might outweigh the attractions of their color. Thus, taken as a whole, the overall aesthetic result might not be positive, and we would have room for a variety of aesthetic judgments both positive and negative. Thesis (5) is even weaker than (4). It may not amount to a genuine positive aesthetics position, for it is clearly consistent with a whole range of negative evaluations of natural settings. Its only commitment is to the idea that humans cannot improve the aesthetic qualities of nature. Yet, when looking for arguments that might establish such strong claims as (3), (2), and (1), it is easy for proponents to appeal to the aesthetic inferiority to nature of human constructions. There remains, however, a significant logical gap between (5) and the stronger claims.

A difficult problem for positive aesthetics is whether to hold that all parts of nature are equally beautiful or whether there are gradations of aesthetic value, even if all positive. There is a strong motive to hold that all of nature is equally beautiful. To say otherwise might seem to compromise the position, to open the door to discriminations of value, and to say that some parts of nature have greater aesthetic value than other parts. If A is more valuable than B, then B is less valuable than A. But where could one find a basis for such comparative claims in the theory of positive aesthetics? After all, the property of being natural applies equally to all of nature.

Is it plausible to claim that all parts of nature are equally aesthetically valuable? Wouldn't many people regard the following as instances of ugly or repulsive items in nature: deformities of animals, rotting carcasses, animal waste, worms, larvae, fly embryos, the mudskipper fish (a paradigm of homeliness), etc.? Are there not also boring, bland, or aesthetically neutral items in nature: stretches of the sea (out of sight of land) with no clouds and not much wind, stretches of the steppes of Russia, etc.? It seems that such things have positive aesthetic values or even beauty only in the sense that one might make the radical claim that all things, including the unsightly and repulsive things that humans do and make – trash heaps, parking lots, dirty industrial cities, chemical spills – have their own beauty. But that cannot be the view of positive aesthetics, which finds an essential difference between the aesthetic values of nature and the aesthetic values of artifacts.

Advocates of positive aesthetics grant that their position is counter-intuitive. Most counter-intuitive is the egalitarian view that all parts and elements of nature have equal (positive) aesthetic value. This view diverges sharply from conventional opinion: a sparrow as attractive as a bird of paradise, a stretch of the shore of Lake Erie as attractive as a section of the spectacular Oregon coast, an ant as attractive as a butterfly, a gray overcast sky as attractive as a unique and complex cloud formation at sunset, etc.?

The egalitarian version of positive aesthetics is also problematic as a basis for preservation. Not only does a successful aesthetic preservationist position need to be able to argue that wild nature is aesthetically preferable to domesticated nature, but, arguably, it also needs to be able to say that some bits of wild nature are more beautiful than other bits. The latter is crucial, according to Thompson (1995), because those parts of nature that are of greater aesthetic value will impose on us greater duties to care for them. If, however, we adopt the version of positive aesthetics that holds that all of undomesticated nature, from the plainest and most common to the most spectacular and unique, has exactly the same aesthetic value, it might seem that all of it is reduced to an average aesthetic value. It is doubtful that such a position could provide a realistic motivation for preservation: aesthetic value must drop out of any equation concerning which parts to choose to preserve. Moreover, the average person's intuitions about aesthetic value – which include such commonplaces as that the Grand Canyon is more stunningly beautiful than any stretch of the Minnesota river – become irrelevant to motivating preservation.

Mixed and influenced environments

Many people accept the minimal claim of positive aesthetics that undeveloped nature has a higher aesthetic value than developed or altered nature. However, if we hold that human influence necessarily degrades the aesthetic value of nature, how are we to understand the appreciation of environments that have been affected by human activity? These environments cannot be ignored, since there is little completely unaffected nature left anywhere in the world. Although this would appear to be an important question for nature aesthetics, it has not received the attention it merits. The main reason for this is that theorizing about the aesthetics of nature has often been done under the influence of environmentalism. This has meant that nature aesthetics has focused attention on wild nature and in general has adopted a conception of nature as the antipode of human products and processes.

We should distinguish two ways an environment can be affected by humans: it may be mixed or it may be influenced. Most environments, even wild nature areas, have been influenced, that is, causally affected, by human activities and by-products: water and air pollution, the introduction of exotic species, hunting and fishing, and climate effects are all examples. Such causal influences rarely have no significant effect on an environment. This human causal influence, by appearing to undermine the purity of nature, generates at least a prima facie problem for those views that claim that aesthetic appreciation of nature and its aesthetic value are different in kind from the appreciation and value of human products.

Positive aesthetics obviously presupposes such a categorical distinction. Making a distinction between the natural and the artificial is also necessary for those thinkers who believe that wild nature is valuable to us just because in experiencing it we comprehend its "autonomy" and "otherness" (Elliot 1997, p. 59). If such second-order properties as wildness and autonomy from human influence are falsified by human causal influences, and if experiencing nature under the influence of attribution of these properties is what makes the aesthetics of nature distinctive (and positive), then our appreciation of nature would be flawed in many cases. To avoid this result it is necessary to find a way to make a distinction between nature that is influenced but still natural (e.g., an over-abundant elk herd in a national park) and nature as artifact (e.g., artificial reservoirs). Such a distinction seems intuitively plausible, but it is not obvious how to make it in a convincing way.

The second way that environments can be affected by human activities and products is for artifactual elements – highways, power lines, smoke from distant power plants, jets roaring overhead, and so on – to impinge on a natural setting. I will call environments of this sort "mixed environments."

Just as influenced environments can be awkward for aesthetic preservationists, so can mixed environments, at least if one holds the position that pure natural environments are aesthetically valuable and impure environments are not aesthetically valuable in the same way. Such a view is tempting because otherwise the intrusion of human elements into wild nature might not undermine to any great extent its aesthetic value. The fact that even wild environments are often mixed to some extent, however, makes it difficult for preservationists to argue that we cannot appreciate any mixed environments as natural. Can we not appreciate the Grand Canyon even though we can see roads, buildings, airplanes, trails, and many other signs of human activity?

Can we draw a line beyond which an environment has too many artifactual elements to have natural aesthetic value? This may be difficult. Consider an environment that has been cultivated for thousands of years: Italy's Cinque Terre. It has many beautiful natural features: breathtaking cliffs, verdant green slopes, beautiful sea vistas, even the occasional wild boar. Yet human signs are everywhere, not just the paths between the five villages, but the villages themselves; not just the vineyards, but the fences, paths, and occasional mechanical devices to move grape harvesters up and down the precipitous slopes. They do not, however, seem to prevent us from appreciating the undomesticated, even wild, elements of the environment as natural. Yet, if we can generally appreciate the natural items within human-made environments, it would seem that we cannot rule out less favored mixed environments as having no natural aesthetic value.

Mixed environments raise a further question about nature appreciation. How are we to understand the appreciation of nature in mixed environments? Why not say that we simply appreciate what we are perceiving as if it were wilderness, while at the same time pretending or imagining that the human elements are eliminated? While this may be possible in some cases, it does propose a surprising use of imagination in the appreciation of nature. Budd, well aware that most encounters with nature are in mixed environments, proposes a doctrine of the possibility of aesthetic abstraction. He notes: "At a zoo you cannot appreciate an animal in its natural environment. But it does not follow that your appreciation must be of a caged animal. Rather, you can ignore its surroundings and appreciate the animal itself (within the limits of its captive state)" (1996, p. 210). In fact, the zoo is both a mixed and influenced environment. The suggestion that the perceiver abstract from both sorts of element is difficult to make concrete. Since the animal is caged and in artificial surroundings, its behavior will not be fully natural. Even its appearance may not be fully natural because the zoo keepers and veterinarians with their food and care influence to some extent how the animals look.

The zoo is an extreme case. Yet, even in more favorable cases, the proposed model of appreciation raises questions. Budd holds that "the aesthetic appreciation of nature, if it is to be *pure*, must abstract from any design imposed on nature, especially a design imposed for artistic or aesthetic effect" (ibid, p. 210). It is not clear whether we can make sense of doing this in particular cases. How do we appreciate the fields of Central Park, abstracting from the fact that the grass and trees would not naturally be there if they had not been planted? Although the large boulder is natural, it used to be located in upstate New York. If, still, one can appreciate the boulder and grass as natural, abstracting as best one can from the human influence on their properties both inherent and relational, then wouldn't every situation have natural aspects to be appreciated?

Budd seems to embrace such a radical position: "In looking at a fountain, you are not looking at a natural state of affairs. Nevertheless, you can appreciate some of the perceptible properties of water, a natural substance, in particular its liquidity, mobility and the way in which it catches the light" (ibid, p. 210). But by parity of reasoning it would seem that you can also admire a sculpture in a Venetian glass-blower's shop as natural, appreciating the properties of glass (the fusion of sand, potash, and lime) for its liquidity, plasticity, and the way it catches the light. Very little is so artifactual that it involves no natural substances or processes. But to appreciate everything for its natural origins, properties, and processes takes us very far from nature as forest, sea, and sky.

Although the abstraction thesis has problems, it is not yet easy to see what the alternative to it might be. It would seem desirable to have an account that involved appreciating nature within and related to artifactual elements and frames. In any case, some sort of account of mixed environments seems necessary.

Conclusion

Although nature's aesthetic qualities provide a strong intuitive reason for cherishing and preserving wild nature, there remain two overarching theoretical issues that will need to be resolved before aesthetic preservationism can elicit wide agreement. First, preservationism needs to articulate an account of nature's aesthetic values that shows such values to be a significant counterweight to instrumental uses of nature. Among questions to be answered are how to determine and how to weigh such aesthetic values.

Second, there is a need to sort out the many competing views about nature appreciation in order to arrive at a plausible account of the aesthetic appreciation of nature. To be successful, such an account must retain a credible connection to aesthetic theory – else it is not an account of the *aesthetic* dimension of nature – and yet it must also address what is special about the appreciation of nature in comparison to the appreciation of art. In explaining why undeveloped nature is aesthetically superior to developed nature, however, such an account should not make the appreciation of nature in mixed and influenced environments inexplicable. Steering between these many reefs and shoals is a daunting task. Given the obvious beauty of nature, however, there is every reason to believe that the task can be accomplished.

References

Beardsley, M. (1982) "The aesthetic point of view," reprinted in *The Aesthetic Point of View: Selected Essays*, ed. Michael J. Wreen and Donald M. Callen (Ithaca: Cornell University Press), pp. 15–34. [Defines aesthetic point of view and aesthetic value.]

Budd, M. (1996) "The aesthetic appreciation of nature," *British Journal of Aesthetics* 36, pp. 207–22. [Exploration of requirements of aesthetic appreciation of nature.]

Carlson, A. (1979) "Appreciation and the natural environment," *The Journal of Aesthetics and Art Criticism* 37, pp. 267–75. [Refutes traditional approaches to the appreciation of nature.]

——(1981) "Nature, aesthetic judgment, and objectivity," *The Journal of Aesthetics and Art Criticism* 40, pp. 15–27. [Argues that adequate appreciation of nature requires regarding nature under scientific categories.]

——(1984) "Nature and positive aesthetics," *Environmental Ethics* 6, pp. 5–34. [Defense of the position of positive aesthetics.]

Elliot, R. (1997) *Faking Nature: The Ethics of Environmental Restoration* (London: Routledge). [Examination of restoration ecology and the value of naturalness.]

Hargrove, E. C. (1989) *Foundations of Environmental Ethics* (Englewood Cliffs, NJ: Prentice-Hall). [Systematic treatment of environmental ethics, with emphasis on importance of natural beauty.]

Hutcheson, F. (1725) *An Inquiry into the Original of our Ideas of Beauty and Virtue* (London). [Early theory of beauty.]

Kellert, S. and Wilson, E., eds. (1993) *The Biophilia Hypothesis* (Washington, DC: Island Press). [Collection of articles exploring biophilia.]

Reisner, M. (1986) *Cadillac Desert: The American West and Its Disappearing Water* (Penguin: London). [History of the exploitation of water in the American West.]

Rolston III, H. (1995) "Does aesthetic appreciation of landscapes need to be science-based?," *British Journal of Aesthetics* 35, pp. 374–86. [An account of appreciation of nature.]

Sagoff, M. (1991) "Zuckerman's Dilemma: a plea for environmental ethics," *Hastings Center Report* 21, pp. 32–40. [Argument that instrumental value of nature cannot justify preservation.]

Sibley, F. (1959) "Aesthetic concepts," *Philosophical Review* 68, reprinted in Neill, A. and Ridley, A. eds., *The Philosophy of Art: Readings Ancient and Modern* (New York: McGraw-Hill, 1995), pp. 312–31. [Classic account of the nature of aesthetic terms.]

Sober, E. (1994) "Philosophical problems for environmentalism," in *Reflecting on Nature*, ed. L. Gruen and D. Jamieson (Oxford, Oxford University Press), pp. 345–62. [Claims that aesthetic considerations are the only ones that can justify nature preservation.]

Thompson, J. (1995). "Aesthetics and the value of nature," *Environmental Ethics* 17 (1995), pp. 291–305. [Defense of an environmental preservationist position.]

19

Economics

A. MYRICK FREEMAN III

Introduction

Economics is about how societies organize themselves to produce the goods and services that sustain human well-being. Throughout most of the past 200 years, economics as a field of inquiry has focused primarily on the activities of production and exchange within the economy and to a lesser extent on the role of land in producing food. But the past 30–40 years have seen the emergence of environmental economics as a specialized field of study in which the analytical tools of economics are applied to understand and make policy recommendations about the role of the environment and natural resources in economic activity.

In this chapter, I will first explain some basic economic concepts, including efficiency, market failures, and externalities. I will then discuss the role of benefit-cost analysis in making decisions about government intervention in the economy. I will next turn to three central issues in environmental economics: the valuation of environmental resources and services, the discounting of future benefits and costs, and the role of economic incentives in controlling pollution. I will conclude with a brief description of the emerging field of ecological economics and comment on its relationship to environmental economics.

Some basic economics

Economists base their analysis on the premises that the purpose of economic activity is to increase the well-being of the individuals who make up the society and that each individual is the best judge of how well off he or she is in a given situation. To give the second premise some operational content, we assume that each individual has preferences over alternative bundles of economic goods and services. The contents of these bundles include not only those things that can be bought in markets but also those that are provided by governments and that flow from the environment, for example, health, visual amenities, and opportunities for outdoor recreation.

The term "preferences" refers to a person's ordering or ranking of alternatives. Preferences are assumed to be the basis for the choices that people make. We assume that individuals choose the most preferred (by them) of all of the available bundles, given the constraints imposed by prices and income. Preferences are revealed by these choices. Finally, if something happens so that a person is able to choose a more preferred bundle, this represents an increase in that person's well-being.

Saying that a person has preferences is equivalent to saying that he or she has a utility function that assigns utility numbers to all possible consumption bundles with more preferred bundles receiving higher utility numbers. And to say that a person chooses the most preferred bundle is equivalent to saying he or she chooses the bundle that conveys the most utility. However, none of the results of what is called neoclassical welfare economics requires interpersonal comparisons of utility measures or the adding up of different people's utilities.

Individuals' preferences are assumed to have the property of substitutability among the components of bundles of goods and services. By "substitutability" economists mean that if the quantity of one good in a person's bundle is reduced, it is possible to increase the quantity of some other good so as to leave the person no worse off because of the change. In other words, an increase in the quantity of the second good can substitute or compensate for the decrease in the first good. The property of substitutability is at the core of the economist's concept of value because substitutability establishes trade-off ratios between pairs of goods that matter to people.

Much of economic theory is concerned with understanding how individuals with given preferences interact as they seek to attain the highest possible level of satisfaction. Many societies have developed systems of markets for guiding this interaction; and the bulk of economists' efforts have gone to the study of market systems. In part, this can be explained by the historic fact that economics as a separate discipline emerged during a period of rapid industrialization, economic change, and growth in the extent of the market system. But it is also true that as early as Adam Smith's time (1723–90), it was recognized that a freely functioning market system had significant advantages over alternative means of organizing and coordinating economic activity. Even in simpler societies, markets facilitate exchanges by which individuals can make themselves better off by giving up less preferred goods in exchange for more preferred goods. And in more developed economies, markets also facilitate the specialization of productive activities and the realization of economies of scale in production. They also channel economic resources into their most productive uses and provide incentives for innovation and technological change.

A market system can be said to have advantages only in terms of some criterion and in comparison with some alternative set of economic institutions. It is time now to make the criterion explicit. The criterion is economic efficiency or Pareto Optimality. An economy has reached a state of economic efficiency or Pareto Optimality if it is not possible to rearrange production and consumption activities so as to make at least one person better off except by making one or more other individuals worse off. Alternatively, an economy is in an inefficient position if it is possible to raise at least one individual to a more preferred consumption bundle while hurting no one. If an economy is in an inefficient position, it is possible to achieve a sort of "free lunch" in the form of an improvement for at least one individual at no cost to anyone else.

One of the fundamental conclusions of economics is that, given certain conditions, a market system will always reach a Pareto Optimum. The conditions are that: (a) all goods that matter to individuals (that is, all goods about which individuals have preferences) must be capable of being bought and sold in markets; and (b) all such markets must be perfectly competitive in the sense that there are large numbers of both buyers and sellers, no one of which has any influence over market price. The extensiveness and competitiveness of markets are sufficient to assure that economic efficiency in the allocation of resources will be achieved. This conclusion provides much of the intellectual rationale for laissez-faire capitalism as well as the justification for many forms of government intervention in the market, for example, anti-monopoly policies, the regulation of the prices charged by monopolies, and, as we shall see, the control of pollution.

The ideal of perfect competition and economic efficiency is a powerful one. But it is not without its limitations. Perhaps the most important of these is that there is no single, unique Pareto Optimum position. Rather there is an infinite number of alternative Pareto Optimums, each different from the others in the way in which it distributes economic well-being among the members of the society. A society in which one individual owned all of the capital, land, and resources could achieve a Pareto Optimum position. It would be one in which all but one of the individuals lived in relative poverty. But it would not be possible to make any of the workers better off without making the rich person worse off. This Pareto Optimum position would be quite different from the Pareto Optimum which would be achieved if each individual owned equal shares of the land, capital, and so forth.

Which Pareto Optimum position is attained by an economy depends upon the initial distribution of the entitlements to receive income from the ownership of factor inputs such as land and capital. Each distribution of rights of ownership has associated with it a different Pareto Optimum. And each Pareto Optimum position represents the best that can be done for the members of society *conditioned* on acceptance of the initial distribution of entitlements. The ranking of different Pareto Optimums requires the comparison of alternative distributions of well-being. Some economists have proposed ranking alternatives by using a *social welfare function* that weights the well-being of different individuals according to their position in the distribution of income. A concern for equity would be reflected in higher weights for the well-beings of the least well off. How a society would choose a social welfare function is inherently an ethical question.

While the perfectly competitive market economy represents an ideal in the Pareto sense, real world economic systems fall short of this standard. They are beset by a variety of what are called "market failures." Market failures are pervasive in the realm of the environment and natural resources. To better understand the role of market failures in the economic analysis of the environment, it will be useful to consider the environment as an economically valuable resource.

The environment yields a variety of valuable services to people in their roles as consumers and producers. These services include basic life support and flows of food, fiber, and other materials. The environment can be used for a variety of recreational activities and as a source of amenities and aesthetic pleasures. And it can be used as a place to deposit the wastes from production and consumption activities.

When viewed as a resource, we can see that the environment is characterized by scarcity. This means that it cannot provide all of the desired quantities of all of its services at the same time. Greater use of one type of service usually means that less of some other type of service is available. For example, greater use of the waste absorption services of the environment results in poorer health (less life support) and reduced amenities. The use of the environment involves trade-offs among different types of service. To increase the contribution that the environment makes to individuals' well-being, we must manage the environment as an economic resource. But unlike other resources such as land, labor, and capital, the market does not perform well in allocating environmental resources to their highest valued uses.

If a firm wants to use one hour of labor time in production, it must find someone who is willing to provide an hour of labor and it must pay that person an amount at least equal to the value to the individual of that time in some other use. This voluntary exchange of labor for money (or other goods and services) makes both parties better off.

But if a firm wishes to dump a ton of soot in the atmosphere, it does not have to determine whose health would be damaged and to obtain their voluntary agreement through an exchange of money. At least in the absence of laws governing pollution, firms do not need to take into account the costs imposed on others by their use of the environment. Because the costs are external to the decision-making of firms, situations like this are called "externalities." Where there are externalities, the decentralized decision-making of individuals and firms will result in a misallocation of environmental resources. The market economy fails to achieve a Pareto Optimum.

A similar form of market failure can arise where there are no established rights of ownership to economically valuable resources. Examples include the fishery resources of the ocean, flowing water in rivers, groundwater aquifers, and common grazing lands. One person's exploitation of the resource leaves less available for others and imposes costs on all users. But since most of these costs of use are borne by others, the result is over-exploitation or what Garrett Hardin (1968) called the "tragedy of the commons."

Economists have suggested two kinds of remedy for these types of market failure. The first is to establish markets in these services by creating legally transferable property rights, just as establishing property rights in land can solve the problem of overgrazing on the commons. If property rights can be established and enforced, then markets can assume their proper role in achieving an efficient allocation of environmental services. But because of the indivisible nature of many aspects of the environment and the problems of enforcing private property rights, there is limited scope for this solution.

The second remedy is government intervention. This means using the visible hand of regulation and control where the invisible hand of the market cannot function. Forms of government intervention include setting ambient air and water quality standards, placing limits on discharges from individual polluters, and imposing taxes on pollution. The objective of such intervention is to create incentives which replicate the incentives that a properly functioning market system would produce.

When governments intervene to correct market failure, there are two important economic questions. The first is how to determine whether a proposed intervention or policy will result in an improvement in human well-being. I will describe the economists' answer in the next two sections where I discuss benefit-cost analysis (BCA) and the underlying principles for defining and measuring benefits and costs. The second question is what form that intervention should take. There are two broad alternatives. The first is often referred to as command and control or direct regulation. The second is incentive-based approaches such as taxes on pollution. I will show why incentive-based approaches are usually preferable because of their ability to achieve pollution-control targets at lower total costs than command and control.

Benefit-cost analysis and environmental policy

If society is to make the most of its scarce resources, it should compare what it receives from pollution control and environmental protection activities with what it gives up by taking resources from other uses. It should measure the values of what it gains (the benefits) and what it loses (the costs) in terms of the preferences of those who experience these gains and losses. Society should undertake environmental protection and pollution control only if the results are worth more in terms of individuals' well-being than what is given up by diverting resources from other uses. This is the underlying principle of the economic approach to environmental policy.

BCA is a set of analytical tools designed to measure the net contribution of a public policy to the economic well-being of the members of society. It seeks to determine if the aggregate of the gains that accrue to those made better off is greater than the aggregate of losses to those made worse off by the policy. The gains and losses are both measured in dollars and are usually defined as the sums of what each person would have to give up or to receive to be restored to their original level of well-being in the absence of the project. If the gains exceed the losses, the policy will yield an increase in economic efficiency, that is, it will move the economy closer to a Pareto Optimum position.

Economists justify the acceptance of policies where the aggregate benefits outweigh the aggregate costs on the grounds that the gainers could fully compensate the losers with monetary payments and still themselves be better off with the policy. Thus, if the compensation were actually made, there would be no losers, only gainers. This is referred to as the "potential compensation criterion." The logic of BCA does not require that those who benefit pay for those benefits or that those who ultimately bear the cost of meeting a standard be compensated for those costs. Whether compensation should be paid is considered to be a question of equity. BCA is concerned exclusively with economic efficiency as represented by the aggregate of benefits and costs.

If society decides that compensation should always be paid, then policies that pass a benefit-cost test should generate no opposition, since there would be no losers from such policies. If society decides that compensation should never be paid, then BCA becomes a modern form of utilitarianism in which the sum of the money values of goods and services consumed by all individuals represents the aggregate of utilities (see NORMATIVE ETHICS). Finally, society might decide that whether compensation is paid or not depends on the relative deservingness of the gainers and losers. In this case, society must adopt some basis for determining relative deservingness, that is, a social welfare function.

The simple summing of individuals' values to calculate net benefits is not without its problems. One is that the economic values of individuals reflect not only their preferences but also their economic circumstances, especially their wealth or income. In general we expect people of higher income to express higher economic values, other things being equal. In effect, rich people's preferences are given greater weight because of their higher incomes. One who judges the present distribution to be inequitable has reason to reject the economic values that emerge from that distribution as a basis for making public policy decisions.

For reasons such as this, many writers advocate using aggregate net benefits as only one input into the process of making decisions about public policy and allowing consideration of other factors such as distributional equity as well (Arrow et al. 1996).

Valuing environmental resources

If BCA is to be used in environmental policy-making, we need to be able to estimate the economic values of environmental changes, that is, the changes in economic well-being or welfare brought about by these policies. Since the focus is on changes in the welfare of people, economic values are anthropocentric and instrumental (see META-ETHICS). Economic values can be placed in one of three categories: direct use value, indirect use value, and non-use or existence value. Examples of direct use values include the value of improved health associated with reduced air pollution and the value of improved recreation opportunities. Indirect use value refers to the value of ecosystem functions such as photosynthesis and nutrient recycling that are not directly used by people but that indirectly support economic well-being. Non-use or existence value stems from the satisfaction that people might get from knowing that an ecosystem or a species is preserved even though they will never use it. For example, people have expressed a willingness to pay money to assure that endangered species such as bald eagles and grizzly bears survive even though they never expect to see one.

The theory of welfare measurement for changes in the environment has been developed and applied extensively over the past 25 years. If the quantity of an environmental good, say air quality, is increased, each person who experiences the improvement is made better off. The economic value of the improvement to a person can be measured by the amount of money that can be taken away from the person without making him or her any worse off, that is, by the reduction in other goods which can be bought with the money that exactly offsets the original gain.

The methods for estimating these values are of two types. Revealed preference or indirect methods are based on the actual behavior and choices of individuals. Hypothetical methods draw data from people's responses to hypothetical questions.

In the case of revealed preference methods, values must be inferred by applying some model of the relationship between market goods and the environmental service. Revealed preference methods involve a kind of detective work, piecing together the clues about the values individuals place on environmental services from the evidence that they leave behind as they respond to prices and other economic signals.

Most of these models are based on the assumption of some kind of substitute or complementary relationship between the environmental good and marketed goods and services or the identification of an implicit price or opportunity cost that constrains choices. An example of a substitute relationship is that between expenditures on cleaning and repairs on the one hand and the absence of an air pollutant that causes soiling or materials damage on the other. The cost of traveling to a recreation site is a form of implicit price. Travel cost models use data on the relationship between the travel cost an individual must incur to visit a specific site and the number of visits made to estimate the value of the site and changes in that value as environmental attributes of the site change. The premium that the housing market places on houses in cleaner areas is another form of implicit price.

A number of studies have shown that jobs with higher risks of fatal accidents have higher wages, other things held equal (Viscusi 1993). The wage/risk trade-off is another form of implicit price that can be used to infer the average worker's willingness to pay for a small reduction in the risk of death. Estimates of this willingness to pay can be used to value public policies that reduce the risk of death by, for example, reducing pollution levels.

For example, suppose that each of 10,000 people has revealed a willingness to pay $100 for a reduction in the risk of death in the coming year from .0004 to .0003. The aggregate willingness to pay of the group is therefore $1 million. If a policy is implemented that reduces risk by this amount, there will be one less death in the group. We can never know which of the survivors' death was avoided. But we can say that the value of saving on average one life is $1 million. This is referred to as the "value of a statistical life."

There are some issues that arise concerning the use of estimates of the value of statistical life from labor market studies of the wage/risk trade-off to calculate the benefits of controlling pollution. One is that there is not perfect agreement among studies as to what the value of statistical life is. The most credible estimates fall in the range of $3–7 million (Viscusi 1993). Another difficulty is that there may be differences between the group at risk from pollution and the group of workers for whom willingness to pay was estimated. In most of the wage/risk trade-off studies the average age of the workers was around 40, while the evidence from studies of air pollution and health suggests that the population at highest risk of death from air pollution is much older. Third, willingness to pay for reduced risk of death may depend on the cause of the potential death. For example, people's willingness to pay to reduce risk of death from cancer may be higher than for accidental death.

Hypothetical methods use data from responses to hypothetical questions rather than from observations of real world choices. In some cases people are asked what choices they would make or how they would change some activity (e.g., visiting a park) in some hypothetical setting. But the most common hypothetical question is some variation of "How much would you be willing to pay?" for some environmental change. Studies based on hypothetical responses are most commonly referred to as "contingent valuation" studies because the values obtained are contingent on the hypothetical situation created by the researcher.

Hypothetical or contingent valuation methods have become very controversial in the USA, in large part because of the leading role they have played in the estimation of damages to natural resources from releases of chemicals into the environment and from oil spills such as the Exxon Valdez spill of 1989 in Alaska. These natural resource damage assessments are used to establish the amounts claimed in suits filed by the federal government against the potentially responsible parties. The chief issues are whether people can formulate meaningful responses about the values of environmental changes that they have no direct experience with, and whether the responses to hypothetical questions will mirror the responses people would make in similar real choice situations.

One of the challenging areas for economic valuation is ecological systems and the functions and services they perform. The functions of ecological systems include photosynthesis, decomposition, nutrient recycling, and so forth. The services of ecological systems are the materials and other services that they provide that enhance human welfare and are therefore valued directly by people. Examples of service flows include wood and fiber from forests, and amenities such as scenic vistas and wildlife observation (see ECOLOGY).

The functions of ecological systems may have intrinsic worth or value in the eyes of some. But they do not have economic value unless they help to support service flows to people. If they do support a valuable service flow, the contribution made by these functions is an indirect use value. The indirect use value of a function can be derived from the change in the value of the service flow that it supports. For example, if an increase in the rate of photosynthesis in an ecological system results in an increase in the flow of economically valuable food or fiber, the economic value of the increase in photosynthesis is the increase in the value of the food or fiber it supports. What is required to measure this indirect use value is knowledge of the link between the function of the ecological system and the economically valuable service that it supports.

Sometimes the connection between a function of an ecological system and an economically valuable service flow may be quite direct, as in the case of photosynthesis producing useful plant material. But, the connection can be indirect and quite subtle. For example, photosynthesis by wild flowers may help to support a population of wild bees that also pollinate commercially valuable fruits. The basic point is that, in principle, the economic values of changes in the functions of ecological systems that affect the well-being of individuals only indirectly can be estimated, provided that the links between functions and services are known.

Some people may be distrustful of economists' efforts to extend economic measurements to such things as human health and safety, ecology, and AESTHETICS, and to reduce as many variables as possible to commensurate monetary measures. Some skepticism about the economist's penchant for monetary measurement is no doubt healthy, but it should not be overdone. The real world often presents us with situations where trade-offs between such things as deaths avoided and some other things of value cannot be avoided. Choices must be made. The real questions are how the problem of making choices about such trade-offs is to be approached and what information can be gathered to help in the problem of choice. Are the choices to be made after consideration of the consequences of each choice, that is, the gains and losses associated with each of the alternatives? And how are gains and losses to be defined? The economic approach to valuation and decision-making is based on the assumption that the answer to the first question is "yes," and that the answer to the second question is that the relevant gains and losses involve changes in human well-being. Rational decisions about these trade-offs require commensurate measures of gains and losses in well-being; and money is the most convenient unit of measure.

Aggregation over time: discounting

Most environmental policies generate benefits and costs that accrue at different points in time. Equal monetary gains or losses occurring at different points in time will be valued differently by people. For example, given a choice of receiving $1 now or one year from now, most people would choose to receive the payment now. This might be because they prefer present consumption over future consumption (positive time preference) or because they know that the $1 invested now will make it possible to consume more than $1 next year because of the interest received.

Since BCA involves the aggregation of all benefits and costs, it is necessary to take the time value of money into account through discounting. This means applying weights to the benefits and costs accruing at different times before adding them up, where the weights are lower for gains and losses accruing in the more distant future. What discount rate should be used, or how rapidly should the weights decrease over time? Most economists would agree that the discount rate should reflect individuals' own preferences for present over future consumption.

I do not think that there is much controversy over the appropriateness of discounting future benefits and costs when the people who experience them are alive today, that is, for effects that occur within the present generation. Where discounting becomes problematic is where the effects are spread out across two or more generations. The problem is that at any reasonable non-zero discount rate, large benefits or costs to FUTURE GENERATIONS appear to be trivially small when discounted to the present. For example with a discount rate of 5 percent, a cost of $100 imposed on someone 100 years from now is valued at only $0.76 today. Whether to discount future benefits and costs and if so at what rate are central issues in the analysis of several key environmental problems, e.g., greenhouse gasses and global CLIMATE change, and the depletion of non-renewable resources.

In this section I present three alternative positions on discounting across generations. The first is an argument for discounting based on the potential compensation criterion of standard benefit-cost analysis. The second position also favors discounting on the grounds that, with continued economic growth, future generations will be better off than we are. The third position rejects discounting across generations on equity and related grounds.

Consider the case where this generation wishes to do something which will yield benefits today worth $B but will also set in motion some physical process which will cause $D of damages 100,000 years from now. Assume for the sake of argument that the events are certain and that the values of benefits and damages based on individual preferences can be accurately measured.

At any reasonable non-zero discount rate, r, the present value of damages

$$\$P = \frac{\$D}{(1 + r)^{100,000}}$$

will be trivial and almost certainly will be outweighed by present benefits. The implication of discounting is that we care virtually nothing about damages that we inflict on future generations provided that they are postponed sufficiently far into the future. Alternatively, a zero discount rate would give equal weight to the benefits and costs accruing to present and future generations.

The potential compensation test asks how much money would the present generation have to set aside today in order to fully compensate the future generation for its damages of $D, taking account of the interest to be earned over the interval. If the trivial sum of $P is set aside now at interest, in 100,000 years it will grow to

$$(1 + r)^{100,000} \cdot \$P$$

This of course is the same as $D and therefore by definition would just compensate the future generation for the damages our actions will have imposed on them. If actual compensation is provided for, no one, present or future, will be made worse off, and some will benefit.

The second position on intergenerational discounting is based on the assumption that future generations will be better off than us because of continued technological innovation and capital accumulation. Given that assumption, the discount rate should be the sum of individuals' pure rate of time preference, which could be positive, zero, or negative, and a factor reflecting the anticipated rate of growth of future per capita consumption and the rate at which the marginal utility of consumption diminishes. The argument is that if a future generation has higher per capita income than we do, the law of diminishing marginal utility means that they will place a lower value on an extra dollar than we would, and this should be taken into account through discounting.

Of course, one who is pessimistic about the possibility of long-run economic progress and SUSTAINABILITY would use this reasoning to argue for a negative discount rate that would give greater rather than less weight to future benefits and costs compared to those in the present. The problem with implementing this position is that we do not know what the future rate of change (growth or decline?) of consumption will be.

The argument for discounting based on potential compensation also provides some insight into why one might choose not to make discounting calculations across generations. Recall that what is being discounted is individuals' values, either positive or negative. The ethical justification for making these welfare calculations is their use in applying the compensation test to determine whether it is possible to compensate the losers so that no one is made worse off. When the gainers and losers are part of the same generation, actual compensation is feasible, and in any event both groups can participate in the decision. If a proposed policy would impose costs on a future generation, it is hard to imagine mechanisms for assuring that the compensation would be paid if it were thought desirable or necessary to obtain the consent of future generations. And the future generation has no voice in present decisions. The real problem with discounting across generations is not that it results in very small numbers for the present values of future effects. Rather, it is hard to imagine a meaningful role for measures of compensation in the context of intergenerational resource reallocations.

Using economic incentives for controlling pollution

In an unregulated market economy pollution arises because of the way individuals and firms respond to market forces and incentives. Firms find that safe and non-polluting methods of disposing of wastes are usually more costly than dumping them into the environment, even though the latter harms others. Because polluters are generally not required to compensate those who are harmed, they have no incentive to alter their waste-disposal practices.

Economists have long argued for an approach to pollution-control policy that is based on the creation of strong positive incentives for firms to control pollution. One form that the incentive could take is a charge or tax on each unit of pollution discharged. The tax would be equal to the monetary value of the damage that pollution caused to others. Each discharger wishing to minimize its total cost (clean-up cost plus tax bill) would compare the tax cost of discharging a unit of pollution with the cost of controlling or preventing the discharge. As long as the cost of control was lower than the tax or charge, the firm would want to prevent the discharge. In fact, it would reduce pollution to the point where its marginal cost of control was just equal to the tax and, indirectly, equal to the marginal damage caused by the pollution. The properly set tax would cause the firm to undertake on its own accord the amount of pollution control that was justified by the damages avoided relative to the marginal cost of avoiding them.

The pollution tax or charge strategy has long appealed to economists because it provides a sure and graduated incentive to firms by making pollution itself a cost of production. And it provides an incentive for innovation and technological change in pollution control. Also, since the polluters are not likely to reduce their discharges to zero, the government would collect revenues which could be used to finance government programs, reduce the deficit, or to cut other taxes that themselves reduce economic efficiency.

A system of marketable or tradable discharge permits (TDPs) has essentially the same incentive effects as a tax on pollution. The government would issue a limited number of pollution permits or "tickets." Each ticket would entitle its owner to discharge one unit of pollution during a specific time period. The government could either distribute the tickets free of charge to polluters or auction them off to the highest bidders. Dischargers could also buy and sell permits among themselves. The cost of purchasing a ticket or of forgoing the revenue from selling the ticket to someone else has the same incentive effects as a tax on pollution of the same amount.

Polluters can respond to the higher cost of pollution that a tax or TDP system imposes in a variety of ways. Polluters could install some form of conventional treatment system if the cost of treatment were less than the tax or permit price. Polluters can also change to processes that are inherently less polluting. They can recover and recycle materials that otherwise would remain in the waste stream. They can change to inputs that produce less pollution. For example, a paper mill's response to a tax on dioxin in its effluent might be to stop using chlorine as a bleaching agent. Finally, since the firm would have to pay for whatever pollution it did not bring under control, this cost would result in higher prices for its products and fewer units of its products being purchased by consumers. The effects of higher prices and lower quantities demanded would be to reduce the production level of the firm and, other things being equal, to further reduce the amount of pollution being generated.

A system of pollution taxes or TDPs can make a major contribution to reducing the cost of pollution control relative to command and control regulations. If several sources are discharging into the environment, they will be induced to minimize the total cost of achieving any given reduction in pollution. This is because each discharger will control discharges up to the point where its marginal or incremental cost of control is equated to the tax or permit price. If all dischargers face the same tax or price, their marginal costs of pollution control will be equal. This is the condition for minimizing the cost of achieving any given target or objective. Low-cost sources will control relatively more than high-cost sources; and there will be no reallocation of responsibilities for reducing discharges that will achieve the same total reduction at a lower total cost.

A marketable permit program is a key component of the US program to reduce acid deposition resulting from emissions of sulfur dioxide. The Clean Air Act Amendments of 1990 called for a reduction of sulfur dioxide emissions of 10 million tons per year (to about 50 percent of 1980 levels) by the year 2000. Starting in 1995, major sources of these emissions (primarily coal-burning electric power plants) were given permits for emissions (called allowances) equal to a percentage of their historic emissions levels. The numbers of permits were reduced in two steps to the target level of emissions for the year 2000. The cost savings relative to direct regulation are expected to be several billion dollars per year.

There is much controversy about the possible role of an emissions trading system for carbon dioxide emissions. The United States has insisted on allowing trading of carbon dioxide emissions rights among nations because of the great potential to reduce the cost burden faced by the industrialized nations to meet the emissions reduction targets agreed to under the Kyoto Protocol of 1997. But other nations have opposed an emissions trading system on the grounds that it would enable the USA to avoid having to reduce its own carbon dioxide emissions if it can find other nations willing to reduce emissions for it. Economists would point out that the USA would have to pay for the emissions reductions achieved elsewhere and, from an environmental point of view, it is irrelevant which nations actually undertake the reductions, as long as the total of all emissions is reduced (see CLIMATE).

Ecological economics: an alternative paradigm?

So far, I have been describing environmental economics from a conventional or neoclassical perspective. Over the past 10–15 years, this neoclassical perspective has come under criticism from a number of scholars who are working in what some of them have called "the transdisciplinary field of ecological economics" (Costanza et al. 1997, p. xi). These scholars, mostly from the disciplines of economics and ecology, are raising questions about both the positive analysis and the normative stance of the neoclassical perspective on environmental economics.

The primary normative focus of neoclassical economic analysis is on economic efficiency. This is not to say that neoclassical economists are unconcerned about equity in economic outcomes. Many are; and some use the tools of economic analysis to attempt to explain the distributions of income and wealth. But they have not found any basis within the neoclassical paradigm for determining what equity goals society should strive for.

In contrast, most ecological economists make the quest for equity, especially equity among generations, a central part of their analysis (see FUTURE GENERATIONS). In particular, they have adopted the goal of sustainable development as the primary basis for making decisions about the use of natural resources and the environment. Most have adopted the Brundtland Commission's definition of sustainable development as "development that meets the needs of the present without compromising the ability of future generations to meet their own needs" (WCED 1987, p. 43; see also SUSTAINABILITY). Ecological economists point to population growth, environmental degradation, and depletion of non-renewable resources as the major threats to sustainable development. Neoclassical economists have also examined these issues. But in general, they have tended to be more optimistic about the ability of capital accumulation and technological change to continue to raise standards of living in most parts of the world.

At the level of positive analysis, ecological economists have made a major contribution to environmental economics by emphasizing the role of ecosystem services in sustaining a productive economy. For example, they have said that stocks of renewable and non-renewable resources should be considered to be natural capital and that the services of natural capital are essential inputs into production processes. Until recently, standard models of the economics of production posited only labor and manufactured capital (and sometimes energy) as inputs.

The standard models also are based on an assumption that different types of inputs are substitutes for one another, for example as fiberglass insulation is a substitute for energy in maintaining a given comfort level in a building. The assumption of substitutability between natural capital and manufactured capital is denied by ecological economists (Costanza et al. 1997, pp. 85–6, 100–7). They point out that natural capital in the form of materials is a necessary ingredient in manufactured capital. But if the necessary materials are abundant (e.g., silica) this complementarity between natural capital and manufactured capital may not prove to be a serious constraint on production.

Is ecological economics a new paradigm? Or is it simply raising questions that can be dealt with within a suitably modified and evolving neoclassical paradigm? The cautious answer is that it is too soon to tell. But since I put this section at the end of the chapter rather than at the beginning, the reader can guess where I would place my bet.

References

Arrow, K. J., et al. (1996) "Is there a role for benefit-cost analysis in environmental, health, and safety regulation?" *Science* 272, pp. 221–2. [A statement on the role of benefit-cost analysis in public policy-making by a group of prominent economists.]

Costanza, R., Cumberland, John, Daly, Herman, Goodland, Robert and Norgaard, Richard (1997) *An Introduction to Ecological Economics* (Boca Raton, Florida: St. Lucie Press). [A statement of the principles of ecological economics and its main policy goals.]

Hardin, G. (1968) "The tragedy of the commons," *Science* 162, pp. 1243–8. [A classic treatment of the economic problems of open access resources, written by an ecologist.]

Viscusi, W. K. (1993) "The value of risks to life and health," *Journal of Economic Literature* 31, pp. 1912–46. [A review of conceptual and empirical issues in valuing policies that reduce the risk of death.]

WCED (World Commission on Environment and Development) (1987) *Our Common Future* (Oxford: Oxford University Press). [The report of an international commission charged with defining sustainability and assessing how it can be achieved with special attention to the issues of population, food security, ecosystems, and energy.]

Further Reading

Boadway, R. and Bruce, N. (1984) *Welfare Economics* (Oxford, England: Basil Blackwell). [A comprehensive treatment of neoclassical welfare economics, including social welfare functions, discounting, Pareto Optimality, and the potential compensation criterion.]

Coase, R. H. (1960) "The problem of social cost," *Journal of Law and Economics* 3, pp. 1–44. [A pioneering treatment of externalities, market failure, and property rights.]

Cropper, M. L. and Oates, W. E. (1992) "Environmental economics: a survey," *Journal of Economic Literature* 30, pp. 675–740. [A good overview of the neoclassical perspective on environmental economics.]

Goulder, L. H. and Kennedy, D. (1997) "Valuing ecosystem services: philosophical bases and empirical methods," in *Nature's Services: Societal Dependence on Natural Ecosystems*, ed. G. C. Daily (Washington, DC: Island Press), pp. 23–47. [An overview of some of the issues and problems in valuing ecosystem services.]

Solow, R. M. (1993) "Sustainability: an economist's perspective," *Economics of the Environment: Selected Readings*, 3rd edn, ed. R. Dorfman and N. S. Dorfman (New York: W. W. Norton), pp. 179–87. [A clear statement of the neoclassical perspective on sustainable development; to be contrasted with Costanza et al. 1997.]

20

History

IAN SIMMONS

Ten thousand years of change

If we consider the last 10,000 years (10 KY) of the history of this planet and its biophysical systems, then we chronicle also a time when humans have been inescapable members of most of those systems. Both nature and human societies have acted as colonists in the epoch which has followed the last major withdrawal of ice-sheets from temperate latitudes (see COLONIZATION). These millennia are the era of humans-in-society which connects the Upper Paleolithic to our own day. During these 10 KY, humans have gained access to many material resources and built around them a series of complex cultures. Some have been devoted more or less entirely to survival, whereas others have produced resource surpluses that were invested in art, architecture, or conspicuous CONSUMPTION. Even a small amount of surplus allowed the development of a commentary whose function was to describe and explain the past and present of the immediate cultural group, to symbolize and represent it, and indeed to manipulate the symbols so as to foretell the future: the shaman and the think-tank have that much in common.

There is one additional stage. Humans now not only build mental constructs of their world, they know that they are doing so. Reflexivity cannot be ignored since we know what we are doing and we know that we know (we think). So the tracing of relations between material history and the history of ideas is always open to the chill of irony. And yet – are there connections between the ecological-economic complexes which have dominated societies these last 10 KY and their ideational development, or is the latter totally free-floating and a product only of the world of symbols?

Environmental history: a realist narrative

Many constructions of the history of the last 10 KY deal with the impact of the human species upon a natural world. The chronicle is difficult to periodize since world history has no agreed schema of cultural-historical divisions which do not reflect a rather blatant Eurocentrism: to speak of "medieval China" seems a Procrustean distortion. Happily for our present purposes, an economic classification can be regarded as universal, for all of humanity were once hunter-gatherers, most became solar-based agriculturalists, and some have remained so, though all have felt the outer ripples if not the tsunami of fossil-fuel-based industrialism. We can add a final stage of change: that of the electronics-based information-rich society, generally labeled "post-industrial." The key material element in all of them is that of energy, for it flows through both natural and human communities (and their hybrids), and access to it facilitates various kinds of cultural and technological development. For each of these energy-related periods, it is possible to describe the essential character-istics of the material ecology in terms of resources gained and environments altered (Simmons 1996). There are limits: energy use clearly does not determine the aspira-tions and activities of human societies in any detail. It may however serve for economic analysis if not for cultural valuation: wastes, for example, may be high in embodied energy but low in social valuation. Energy considerations may be of little use, too, in explaining the collapse of complex societies, but there is a hint of its non-material connections when we consider that in an early stage of development, every recent energy source has been seen as a problem-free source of unbounded magni-tude: coal in the nineteenth century and then both electric power and nuclear power in the twentieth century have carried on a Promethean tradition.

In 10,000 BCE, all the members of the human species were hunter-gatherers; now, perhaps 0.001 percent or less live that way. Their early success is attested by the very wide range of environments in which they survived: literally from tundra to tropic forest. This was made possible by a low population density brought about by having to live off relatively dilute solar energy and so the average hunter-gatherer needed access to ca. 26 km^2 of terrain for food. Having to move seasonally encouraged a family size in which there was never more than one child that had to be carried.

Many examples exist of the power of hunter-gatherer groups to change their environments permanently. Lasting landscape changes were produced by repeated management practices – for example the use of fire – to the point where fauna, flora, and soils may all be said to be adapted to such techniques. The control of fire at landscape scale is a key tool in many groups' environmental relations. Although an apparently robust and sustainable way of life, most such societies quickly adapted to cultivation when it became available; most of our knowledge of these people comes from times when they had had prolonged contact with agricultural or indeed indus-trial economies. The ecology of the agriculture fully developed after 7000 BCE depends upon the concentration of food energy by bringing the plants and animals in, rather than going out for them. The field and the herd are high concentrations of energy compared with the wild systems that preceded them. Agriculturalists produced the first totally humanized landscapes outside actual dwelling places, as land clearing, irrigation, and the use of domesticated plants occupied intensely cultivated fields and gardens. With the development of political empires, transmission of land use patterns and of technology was facilitated. Most land uses ever known were implanted during this phase, including metal-based industry. Quite large cities, with complex social stratifications, were made possible by agricultural surpluses. There was, however, always a likelihood that population growth would exceed agricultural production, especially when a degree of immunity to major trans-continental infectious diseases had been acquired.

In the case of industrialism (1750 CE onwards), the access to energy from recently dead biomass is now subsidized by immense amounts of stored solar energy as fossil fuels. Of these, coal was the first to be developed on a large scale. Oil was added to the repertoire in the late nineteenth century, followed by natural gas. The application of energy through technology has made environmental alteration much more thorough and widespread. Steam power meant the more rapid transport of materials and ideas over larger distances and, indeed, consolidated empires whose purpose was to supply home countries with materials. Thus a periphery of less-developed countries experienced the transformation of subsistence agriculture or pastoralism into commercial plantations. For the first time, some of the consequences of human activity have become truly global rather than simply worldwide at discrete points. "Greenhouse gases" are the obvious example. After 1950 we can recognize a post-industrial phase: cheap electricity has made instant electronic communication available virtually everywhere via satellites. This technology is paralleled by the ability to accomplish the genetic manipulation of organisms with predictable biological if not ecological results. It is a world of considerable unevenness of access to resources, as shown for example by the differences in per capita energy use during recent years. But low income or low access to technology does not necessarily mean low environmental impact, as poor people are forced into marginal environments by the pressures of population growth or landlords' use of land for cash-crop production.

The outcome of 10,000 years of resource use has been a humanizing of the earth. Very little is now in the kind of pristine condition which maps of "biomes" or "world vegetation" in atlases might suggest. There is still a large area of dry land which shows only minimal human effects, most of which is desert, tundra, or ice: the rest has been transformed by the human hand and its mechanical extensions. Some 45 percent of the land surface has undergone such change. In terms of global biological productivity, an estimated 39 percent of the terrestrial biomass is appropriated by humans. Current concerns often focus on the future of the plenty and riches and the identity of those who will enjoy them. Is it a just world, for instance, in which the world's richest 20 percent of nations absorbed 70 percent of global income in 1960 but increased that share to 83 percent by 1989, and in the same period diminished the share of the poorest 20 percent from 2.3 percent to 1.4 percent?

The idealist narrative

Each age has spawned its environmental thought. Like all history, however, our record is highly selective. It is strongly biased in favor of literate societies and those with a large European or Euro-American element. The thought may, too, be embodied in myth or in records compiled for diverse purposes: only after the nineteenth century can we be sure of historical material written with a quasi-modern conception of "environmental science" in mind. Some practitioners of "psycho-history" have given us examples of how the environmental connections of societies through history can be related to ways of thinking. Paul Shepard, for example, asks questions about whether the hunter-gatherer phase of human history (which must account for about 95 per cent of the species' evolutionary time) had any permanent psychological effects, comparable to the ecological ones. The cosmic world-view of hunter-gatherers suggests a yearly renewal of the earth, to which is added many worlds of being and meaning (i.e. religion is polytheistic) in which all life can participate. There is a contrast between hunter-gatherers and early irrigated agriculture. The dissimilarity between the river valleys and the semi-arid surroundings must have been very great. Whereas the hunter moves through the land, the farmer is centered in it and can overview it as a whole. All important things are human-created and all else is other. History became linear and so might lead to a predetermined end. An infusion of Zoroastrian duality transformed ambiguity into polar opposites. An added measure of Christian Gnosticism provided the Manichean expression of an unresolved tension and division of the world. Mainstream CHRISTIANITY kept up the idea of the fall to explain undesirable places and events. This faith was implicated in the rise of Renaissance humanism and then of science, which promised the recovery of a prelapsarian state and, eventually, the perfection of mankind. Monotheism and utopianism led to authoritarian, imperialistic thinking informed by philosophies which were unambiguous, dichotomous, and unmetaphorical. This stage of world economic history also highlighted the need for manpower in agrarian societies (for labor and defense), leading to a propensity to conflict as well as a Malthusian relationship with the productive environment.

Whatever priority we accord within the pairing of society and technology, the great change of the industrial phase is completely to enclose humans within a technologized world. Science and technology are interrogated first (and, often, solely) for the answer to short-term problems, whether of resource shortages or environmental pathologies. They were also the crucial factor in the success of European imperialism during the nineteenth century. That this movement also spun off ideas that we would now label environmentalist, has been documented by Grove (1995). Mauritius, for instance, was the scene of early experiments in systematic forest conservation, pollution control, and fisheries protection. Back in the industrialized world, Shepard's (1982) account of the nineteenth–twentieth-century city proposes that such places favor knowledge of physics and perhaps chemistry but not of biology. Urban growth certainly sanctions a machine paradigm of the world, since to the city child nature is much less coherent than the constructions of humanity. Then, to the adult, the city looks more organized than a wilderness. Transience is a feature, as is a detached sense of the value of things like work or soil, which appear unrelated to the money markets of London, Tokyo, and New York, for instance. Indeed, single-shot activities and specialization are rational acts in a way which would not have been legitimized in hunter-gatherer societies and perhaps less so in agrarian times. Interestingly, the late nineteenth to mid-twentieth century seems to have been a period when less attention has been paid by major philosophers to the consideration of what their predecessors would have called the relationships of man and nature (see NINETEENTH- AND TWENTIETH-CENTURY PHILOSOPHY).

The tendency to globalization, seen especially in the ubiquity of electronic communication, is subject to countervailing forces which emphasize the virtue of the local and regional (witness the upsurge of nationalism in Europe in the early 1990s), so that small ethno-cultural groups assert their independence of the nation-states to which earlier mores bound them. Yet there are some signs of a growth of a world consciousness that encompasses the non-human world at a level of intrinsic value rather than simply as materials for human use. But there is also the opposite case of increased demand for production of all kinds. This may result in the occurrence of unpredictable instabilities in major biogeochemical cycles and increased reliance on science and technology to produce solutions to any consequential problems. At the same time has come the realization that the findings of science are neither empirically nor epistemologically always reliable. This could bring the nihilistic realization that humanity might not be destined for a very long evolutionary tenure on earth: the metaphor of an eternally rising escalator might be replaced by that of a candle being burned at both ends.

Connected ideas

Commentary on the combination of ecology and economy that seeks to inform both with meaning for the long-term well-being and indeed survival of the human species has only been possible since the great compilations of accurate knowledge of the world. These perhaps start with Alexander von Humboldt (1769–1859) and his highly ambitious notion to depict in a single work the entire material universe that led to his *Cosmos* of 1845–62. Although not attempting to be either systematic or universal, Charles Darwin (1809–82) was also prolific and he too had experienced humans living in fundamentally different economies, being especially impressed with the pre-agricultural communities of Tierra del Fuego. His open-ended evolutionary hypotheses, founded upon empirical observation, are without equal after the nineteenth century in influencing western ideas about organic nature.

In the present context, their main avenue of persuasion is through Karl Marx (1818–83). The environmental aspects of Marx are implicit rather than explicit and urban-industrial rather than global-historical. Nevertheless, he viewed the integrated development of a political economy as a humanizing, socializing, and indeed internalizing of natural substances and forces in the environment. So one interpreter, H. C. Parsons (1977, p. 23), is able to say that for Marx all human values, whether economically-linked, such as food, or "higher" values like music, have their ultimate origin in non-human nature. The focus of the thought is, however, the separating, fragmenting, and alienating effects of industrialization. A more refined working-out comes in the materialist view of history espoused by Karl Kautsky (1854–1938). He attempted (1988 [1929]) an isomerism between the processes of nature and those of human history: for both, environmental change was the motor of all change. The human environment was human-created in many aspects and therefore evolution was social but it had material connections, since for him every social innovation originated in the last analysis from a new technology. Thus, for Kautsky, TECHNOLOGY is a mediating influence between the natural environment and human societies. The whole system is seen by its author as a *widerspruchloser Gesamtzusammenhang*.

A more recent restatement of some of these notions has come from Max Oelschlager, from whom there are assertions such as "once the agricultural turn was made, philosophy and theology sprung forth with a vengeance. ... the crucial interaction between existential and conceptual materials – lying at the heart of cultural process and the ecological transition – increased in both frequency and pervasiveness ... ideological reconstruction was inevitable" (1991, pp. 29–30), and "The idea of nature as a machine was deeply rooted in the experience of the Industrial Revolution and the pervasive influence of machines on life" (ibid, p. 77). The first of these statements traces its connections in part at least to the surpluses created by irrigated agriculture: philosophy may bake no bread, but an assured supply of bread enables philosophers to live. The second reinforces the Kautsky directive that technology is a key mediator between humans and all else. The development of fossil fuels has clearly allowed profound transformations of social structures to take place (Adams 1988). New work groupings and new social groupings with specialized interests are examples, though it would be generally agreed that energy and technology are principal factors but not *the* principal factor.

The classic extension of material change to economic life (and by extension to the social consequences therefrom) is in the development during the inter-war period of business cycles in the West, which can be interpreted to show an unmistakable correlation between new energy sources and innovative prime movers on the one hand, and accelerated investment on the other. The upswing of 1787–1814 is related to the development of coal and the stationary steam engine, that of 1843–69 to moving steam engines in the forms of the steamship and the railroad, together with improvements in iron smelting, that of 1898–1924 to the introduction of commercial electricity in the form of electric motors in factories, that period centered around 1937 to the gas turbine, fluorescent light, and the discoveries in nuclear physics, and the phase that was ended in 1973 by OPEC to cheap oil, the extensive use of the motor vehicle, and nuclear fission power. The ideational effects of these surges are difficult to trace directly, but there can be little doubt that each of them helped to strengthen the Promethean aspects of the western world-view. The height of industrialization in the West (say 1880–1950) was also a period when the "professional" philosophers of the relations of "man and nature" were largely silent; it was left to the creative writers and the painters in particular to articulate both the positive and negative aspects of these transformations.

The connections between the development of technology and the evaluation of nature have nowhere been more evident than in the control of water. The construction of large dams during the late nineteenth and in the twentieth centuries made possible the generation of electricity on a large scale, the control of floods, and the promulgation of large-scale irrigation in nations like the USA and the Soviet Union, and led to the use of phrases such as "the conquest of nature." The large dam has been seen in many low-income countries as symbolic of modernity: it is perceived as not only conferring material benefits but as a symbol of development. This can be seen even today in India's plans for the Narmada and in the Three Gorges developments in China. But what is perhaps equally interesting is that the large-scale impoundment has acted also as a focus for countervailing thought. From early resistance in the Sierra Nevada of California, and the Glen Canyon controversy, through Cow Green in northern England, to recent fights over dams on the Danube, and most of all the deep divisions at all levels over the Narmada project, the environmental transformations wrought by large-scale diversions of the hydrological cycle have often acted as foci for the emergence or strengthening of environmentalist movements. Though the issues may have been cast largely in local and regional terms, the bodies of thought invoked by the antagonists have without doubt linked them to contrasting world-views.

Free-floating thought

One result of ranging across 10,000 years of change is the provision of examples to suit almost any taste in narrative. Rather like the collected works of Marx, or the

Bible, something can be found to bolster any point of view. Collectively, the materials deployed above do show a range of connectivities, from the obviously direct to the three-stages-removed types of barely apparent causality. It is scarcely surprising then to be able to find examples of environmental thought which bear no perceptible relationship to the material circumstances of their origins and development.

To take one example: if we accept the magnitude of the classical Greek achievements in both chronicling their own past as well as in thought about humanity and nature, then it is difficult to tie much of this to the agricultural economies of the time. Those economies had been in largely the same condition for centuries before the unique efflorescence of thought that we associate with the golden age of Greek philosophy and history. There is one possible exception to this: in the soil erosion of Attica, the Epicureans found evidence for their view that the earth was senile, over-populated and generally on its way to perdition. This is one position within today's environmentalist spectrum, and so if indeed it can be traced to the combination of fire and pastoralism prevalent on the mountains of Attica, there is a powerful link. Even so, the actual course and intensity of the soil erosion has been disputed and its general role may have been exaggerated. But a false report is not necessarily any less influential than a true one, as any media-person will confirm (see THE CLASSICAL GREEK TRADITION).

A rather similar ambiguity can be seen for the Renaissance period in Europe. Again, it is possible to interpret this as a flowering of a particular culture which bears no relation to major changes in production from the land. It is true that nature is relevant, as can be seen in the loving depictions of landscape which now become a part of so many paintings (usually of the background, but in the case of Giorgione's influential *La Tempesta* of 1505–10, being the dominant element in the frame), yet once more, no obvious connection with regional economic change is apparent. The contextual factor to be considered, perhaps, is that of increasing wealth and security made possible by trade and technology. Medieval Europe may not have been static technologically (though indeed less developed than China), for it is possible to suggest that advances in technology during the medieval centuries enabled societies to flourish in which the developments of thought, art, and consumption which could be later constituted as "The Renaissance," were cultivated. But the really revolutionary ideas of the period and its aftermath, such as the new cosmologies of Copernicus (1473–1543) and Galileo (1564–1642) where, as John Donne (1572–1631) put it,

> ...new philosophy calls all in doubt,
> The element of fire is quite put out;
> The sun is lost, and th'earth, and no man's wit
> Can well direct him where to look for it.

are certainly little related to energy efficiency, climatic change, or soil type.

Later centuries show some similarities. Sir Keith Thomas's (1983) book on the revaluation of nature in England in the years 1500–1800 argues that in many ways the men and women of those years developed a willingness to be more tender toward the living but non-human components of their world. But nowhere does he hold that these are strongly related to material change: he associates a new kindness to ANIMALS with the oncoming of industrialization (both in Britain and elsewhere in Europe) but thinks that the conditions for it were in place by 1700, rather before any strong manifestations of the new order. Yet, as he says, if the prerequisites were latent in the Judeo-Christian tradition, why did they emerge at a particular time, if it were not for changes in social and economic conditions? The point of nexus for him is the greater use of working animals in the sight of well-to-do townsmen or the clergy, though he embeds this in a wider context of cultural and social practices, mostly of a pre-industrial type. Possibly the growth of city living is more important than the primary economic type.

In her account of western ideas from the hunter-gatherers of the Americas through to sustainability, Carolyn Merchant (1995) constructs an inclusive history in which the story of western civilization since the seventeenth century can be conceptualized as a grand narrative of fall and recovery. The story is carried by the three subplots of religion, modern science, and capitalism. None of these, we may notice, enforces a particular economy, though capitalism and industrialization seem to be umbilically linked outside the former Communist nations. Individual values therefore are attached to this narrative as a whole rather than major changes in material circumstances. The same might possibly apply to other metanarratives: in a different interpretation of western ideas, Arran Gare (1993) details the withdrawal of philosophy from any attempt at the totalizing of knowledge: it no longer deals with the whole world's interactions of nature, history, and society. In large measure, this is caused by a drift down the centuries toward the dominance of nihilism. Its current end-point is a highly individualistic society which involves an extreme detachment from, and instrumentalization of, the world, whether that world be of nature or of other people. People in particular are not participants in the stream of life and in the becoming of the world, but transcendent consciousnesses in a world of things which are only externally related to each other. The watchwords are reason, foresight, and efficiency. The connections to material conditions are at most secondary. This last point seems to emerge from many studies of the possibility of technological determinism, where a considerable body of opinion avers that technology constrains but does not determine. Even highly coupled technological explanations of socio-economic change cannot account for all the variance in the historical picture. It is becoming increasingly clear that the gender relations of a society will be important in these kinds of connections.

In any summary of world-views, therefore, the self-image of the human being is intimately bound up with what can be technologically achieved but which then feeds back in a reflexive view of him/herself that cannot but affect human-environment relations but at a remove. The "economic man" (*sic*) of the post-Enlightenment period who is individualistic, materialistic, and utilitarian; the competitive individual beloved of the social Darwinists, the person successful because they could deal with the base instincts revealed by Freud; the reductionist product beloved of psychologists who think (and perhaps hope) that behavior will all be explicable at the molecular level, and indeed the notion that humans are essentially "spirit" in a contingent animal case – none of these is closely coupled to the evolution of different types of economy. None, however, could be said to be irrelevant to the construction of the western world-view which is now so dominant in all its aspects, including those of environmental thought. Uncertainty seems to be the only reasonable judgment upon the apparent free-floaters: like a kite in unskilled hands, there is a lot of swooping about even if the strings are finite in length.

Coherence and fragmentation

For John Donne, the world of the seventeenth century's new philosophy was a fallen place, for "'Tis all in pieces, all coherence gone; / All just supply, and all relation" and a history of environmental change can in some sense be seen to be a story of fragmentation parallel to the history of the splintering of many human activities and relationships. The hunter-gatherer can be envisaged as living in a close engagement with the land, as can the farmer, but a successful agricultural society creates surpluses off which people live who are separated from the flows of nature. The idea of individuals acting upon external objects was reinforced in medieval Europe when the pronoun "I" (and its equivalents in other languages) becomes compulsory, especially in combination with "shall" and "will." These verb forms make life appear as a constant series of willed and directed activities. As Arran Gare puts it, "this [outside] world is not spoken of as a world of momentary objective events of which people are part, but as a world of objects which is the substratum of will and duty, of planning and doing" (1993, p. 98).

This is exacerbated in industrial societies, which often have a large urban population and whose planning focus seems often to vanish in the pluralities of social dissolution. After the celebration of the city by Claude Monet (1840–1926) comes the retreat to the garden; after Impressionism, the apartness of cubism. Isomeric creations of the inter-war period include Webern's short sharp pieces, T. S. Eliot's *The Waste Land*, and the linguistic collage of James Joyce's *Finnegan's Wake*. A pre-industrial fragmentation comes along with the division of the land and its allocation as private property: the distribution of the land in medieval Europe became a reflection of the power to till the soil using the deep plow, just as the power of the water-mill became emblematic in all kinds of ways. The face of the land can be seen mirrored in the increasing privatization of the individual: the lord and his family sequester themselves into the solar, the corridor introduces a separateness into the large house. Each development of housing as a society gets more wealthy increases the apartness of people; housing with walled enclosures is echoed by the bubble of the personal stereo; the cinema is threatened by the VCR and TV, the concert-hall (itself an eighteenth-century development) by the CD player. Many features of environment thus reflect the specialization of human lifeways. The landscape becomes increasingly fragmented as land-use systems which were interdependent lose those qualities and both ownership and purpose become more specialized. Thus there is land for intensive production, land for recreation, and land for conservation, but all are fenced and are managed with a single purpose in mind. This has been a dominant trend of the twentieth century and one which is not easily encompassed within the dominant metaphor of the machine, and so has, to a great extent, escaped notice by the environmental thinkers of the century. As POPULATION has grown and as CONSUMPTION has increased in what can now be talked of as a "full world" the parceling of the environment has become more intensive: as if the less per head there were, the more obviously it had to be owned and devoted to an obvious purpose. This is encouraged by conservatives who argue that resource management is the more effective if the resources are "owned"; it is, they say, common property resources which are over-used. The UN Law of the Sea conventions setting up Exclusive Economic Zones (EEZs) were a practical expression of this, as are permits to trade pollution.

It would be too much to expect some neat parallel to occur in the history of environmental thought or in philosophy more narrowly defined. Nevertheless we may point to Jürgen Habermas's plaint that "Philosophy can no longer refer to the whole of the world, of nature, of history, of society, in the sense of a totalizing knowledge...philosophical thought has withdrawn self-critically behind itself" (1984, p. 1).

So there are theoretical, practical, and aesthetic discourses, but they are separate. Such a set of world-views finds its currently strongest mode of expression in the type of thought labeled "postmodernist." For such thinkers, each discourse is at best a set of epistemologically equivalent language games, and science is included in the lack of privilege. There are no grand narratives of authentication of anything: neither theology, nor science, nor indeed the search for justice on anything but a local, relativized scale. The clearest exposition of this in the context of environment comes in Niklas Luhmann's (1989) assertion that, first of all, humans cannot communicate directly with nature (to which many twentieth-century rationalists will assent, though not all the Aquarians and New Age believers) but, secondly, that in talking to ourselves about it, we are incapable of formulating a realistic representation because our discourses are split into distinct channels. Given the history of western culture, each channel's discourse (which may be thought of as a resonance) tends toward one of two conditions: dualisms are writ large. Examples, include legal/illegal, economic/uneconomic, employed/unemployed, religious/heathen, immanent/trans-cendent, reason/non-reason, and, eventually, good/evil. Small wonder that the digital computer, which is either 1 or 0, has found such a welcome reception. One analogy might be the pipe-organ: in each pipe there is a resonance and in the world of the Baroque and of Modernity there is a score, to which all the soundings are referred. In the postmodern world, the music is aleatory: the sense even of improvising on a theme is being rapidly lost and replaced by snatches of inter-pipe resonances which temporarily have meaning or make a nice sound or are sufficiently discordant to make people move away.

So life and history could be just one damned thing after another. The moral equivalence granted by postmodern deconstruction is a source of concern to many. For some, the granting of equal cultural standing to Disneyland *and* Yosemite, to graffiti *and* Giotto is so much a nonsense that it is dangerous (Worster 1995). For others, the transpersonal and transcultural arguments on the nature of things is a kind of intersubjective truth which validates some of the findings of science, for example, and so prevents every last transnational corporation (TNC) from eviscerat-ing the world with impunity.

Perhaps not all that is solid is melting into air; or at least it is recrystallizing in a new form. Though the phenomena known as globalization constitute a re-arrange-ment of many practices and priorities, they nevertheless use the same materials as their predecessor processes. Since both the phenomena and their interpretations are ongoing, statements have to be more than usually provisional, but it appears that certain forms of coalescence are characteristic. The global simultaneity of electronic communications, for example, allows the transfer of capital in nanoseconds, just as it can show the internet freak an updated view from an Antarctic base every 30 seconds. Such networks were anticipated by the TNCs, which are structured so as to allow the polyfocal creation of profit, switching operations as advantage becomes apparent, in a kind of pinstripe version of shifting agriculture. Even before the TNCs, the industrial world was creating a global coalescence of enhanced levels of carbon dioxide in the upper atmosphere. All these are consequences of the emergence of a central civilization depending upon its connectedness for separating it from its ancestors, something which has only happened in the industrial and post-industrial phases of human history.

It would be convenient to point to isomeric trends in currently emerging environmental thought. It seems to be the case that some at least of the new environmental philosophy celebrates a unity of all entities in their time-lines as they "become" together (Mathews 1991). On the other hand, just as there are countervailing trends within the global scene that advocate for instance bioregionalism as an environmentally tender life-structure, there are philosophies that crucially depend upon local negotiations: the "politics of the rhizome." This scale accords well with the view of the world currently held by those scientists and philosophers who think in terms of self-organizing systems of matter, energy, and ideas, of radical contingency, and of responses which avoid concepts of utopia in favor of fudge and well-meaning shuffle.

Crooked timber

Isaiah Berlin's use of this metaphor might remind us that it takes very odd-shaped pieces of wood to build ships: trees were planted and managed so as to produce the futtocks and the strakes as well as the masts. So let there be no surprise that what is constructed in these pages is not a simple hollowed-out log in which the human response (in both material and ideational terms) fits neatly into the cavity provided by scientifically produced information. Rather, both science and the humanities share a boat which has continually to be rebuilt, member by member, while they stay afloat in it. So the vessel is constantly changing shape according to what new pieces of wood are available and what re-use can be made of the existing pieces. From time to time, the boat conforms to the picture in the mind of the shipwrights; at other times, the sheer necessity of using only whatever is to hand shapes the craft. So the connection between material relations and their representations in the symbols of languages (whether these be of European *parole*, mathematics, or oil painting, for example) is rarely direct. Equally, it seems foolish to assert that there have never been any connections of a traceable nature. Further, it seems unhelpful to suggest that any of this history has predictive value. The contingent nature of material change has continually produced conditions which would now be described as unsustainable: the virtual disappearance of hunting/gathering in the face of agriculture and the transformation of solar-powered economies by both core and periphery of industrialization are examples. The non-linear nature of the world's systems seems to be common ground for many discourses and in them, as in daily life, it will continue to provide hope and despair, though not always in equal amounts.

It is, of course, possible that we are living in an interglacial period. There is no evidence that the glacial–interglacial sequences of the Pleistocene have finished for ever. In another few thousand years, ice-sheets may again visit the course of the River Thames and surround Cairo, Illinois. Time then once again to remember John Donne, listening for the sound of tolling bells.

References

Adams, R. N. (1988) *The Eighth Day. Social Evolution as the Self-Organization of Energy* (Austin: University of Texas Press). [A materialist interpretation of human history much influenced by the physics of energy transformations.]

Gare, A. (1993) *Nihilism Incorporated. European Civilization and Environmental Destruction* (Bungendore, NSW: Eco-Logical Press). [The trend from classical Greece to present times is toward a form of applied nihilism which emphasizes divisions of all kinds rather than living unities.]

Grove, R. H. (1995) *Green Imperialism. Colonial Expansion, Tropical Island Edens and the Origins of Environmentalism 1600–1860* (Cambridge: Cambridge University Press). [Argues that the roots of much of today's green thinking can be found in the ideas and work of far-sighted colonial administrators from a number of European nations.]

Habermas, J. (1984) *The Theory of Communicative Action* (Boston: Beacon Press). [One of the classic statements of twentieth-century social thinking.]

Kautsky, K. (1929) *Die materialistische Geschichtsauffassung*, 2 vols. (Berlin: Dietz); ed. J. H. Kautsky, trans. R. Meyer, *The Materialist Conception of History* (New Haven and London: Yale University Press, 1988). [A selection and translation of Kautsky's major work previously available only in German; Kautsky is much influenced by Marx but has a finer division of the types of human economy.]

Luhmann, N. (1989) *Ecological Communication* (Cambridge: Polity Press). [A major rationalist statement making the major point that humans cannot communicate directly with the environment, but communicate with each other about it.]

Mathews, F. (1991) *The Ecological Self* (London and New York: Routledge). [A good example of today's environmental philosophy: an exploration of the resources of the seventeenth-century writer Spinoza and how his ideas might be developed.]

Merchant, C. (1995) "Reinventing Eden: western culture as recovery narrative," in *Uncommon Ground. Toward Reinventing Nature*, ed. W. Cronon (New York and London: W. W. Norton), pp. 132–59. [The latest in a series of attempts to draw out major themes in human–environment relations which link the material world and that of ideas, especially those of European origin.]

Oelschlager, M. (1991) *The Idea of Wilderness* (New Haven and London: Yale University Press). [Much focused on the North American view of wilderness and on writers from the USA, but some interesting material on the origins of their thinking.]

Parsons, H. L., ed. (1977) *Marx and Engels on Ecology* (Westport and London: Greenwood Press). [Parsons has edited, compiled, and translated several extracts from the work of both authors and provided a commentary of their contemporary context as well as relevance for today.]

Shepard, P. (1982) *Nature and Madness* (San Francisco: Sierra Club). [A piece of psycho-history for whole lifeways in the history of humankind from hunter-gatherers to today and reminding us of the importance of childrens' cognition of environment in forming world-views.]

Simmons, I. G. (1996 [1989]) *Changing the Face of the Earth*, 2nd edn (Oxford: Blackwell). [A materialist chronicle of human-induced manipulation of nature from the first control of fire to today's microelectronics.]

Thomas, K. (1983) *Man and the Natural World. Changing Attitudes in England 1500–1800* (London: Allen Lane). [A classic ordering of many sources to provide a coherent picture of changes in peoples' outlooks, especially toward animals.]

Worster, D. (1995) "Nature and the disorder of history," in *Reinventing Nature? Responses to Postmodern Deconstruction*, ed. M. E. Soulé and G. Lease (Washington DC and Covelo: Island Press), pp. 65–85. [Worster uses his ability to combine historical knowledge with modern thinking to consider the problem of relativism in its environmental context.]

21

Ecology

KRISTIN SHRADER-FRECHETTE

As Buckminster Fuller observed, the most striking fact about planet earth is that no instruction book came with it. Yet most people believe that ecology ought to play a central role in helping to formulate and justify environmental philosophy (see McIntosh 1985, pp. 289–323). To what degree has ecology succeeded in grounding environmental philosophy, especially environmental ethics? To answer this question, this chapter, first, provides an overview of the science of ecology, including its two main methodological branches (quantitative and deductive, or "hard" ecology, and qualitative or "soft" ecology); it argues for a middle path between the two (practical ecology). The chapter, secondly, surveys the degree to which ecology can ground environmental philosophy and, thirdly, argues that philosophical appeals to ecological concepts such as "balance" or "stability" fail because the concepts are vague and not fully empirical. The chapter also shows that scientific appeals to holistic ecological concepts or theories err because they typically are not precisely definable or testable. Although it explains that ecology cannot provide precise, fundamental, testable, scientific laws, the chapter shows how ecology can ground environmental philosophy through case studies.

The science of ecology

Ecology is "the study of patterns in nature, of how those patterns came to be, how they change in space and time, why some are more fragile than others" (Kingsland 1995, p. 1). These patterns deal both with relationships among biotic or living things (e.g., their competition for food), as well as between living things and their abiotic or non-living environment (e.g., the increase in numbers of species as a function of increasing air or water temperatures). Abiotic factors include soil, climate, air, water, temperature, and light. Because ecology deals with the relationships among living beings and their environment, it is arguably "the most important and all-embracing of the sciences" (Peters 1991, pp. xi, 2). Yet because its subject-matter includes everything, ecology also is one of the most controversial and difficult sciences in which to achieve unifying and successful laws and predictions. At the simplest level of controversy, ecology can be divided into two main methodological camps (which we call "hard ecology" and "soft ecology").

On the one hand, if people want to develop an environmental philosophy that is mainly a system of ideals to guide attitudes toward the biosphere, then soft ecology (which is general and qualitative) will be able to provide scientific principles, such as "desert plants have large fleshy stems." Soft ecology typically is inspirational or interesting to backpackers and birders, ecologists and scuba divers. Soft ecology, however, has little practical use in helping to resolve environmental controversies because it often lacks precision and predictive power. It tends to focus on ecological processes and functions (like fixing nitrogen or purifying water), to be holistic or "top-down" in its scientific explanations, and to emphasize ecosystem approaches.

On the other hand, if people want a type of ecology that gives a precise foundation for answering courtroom challenges involving wetlands protection or development rights, then the general, qualitative scientific principles of soft ecology – despite their motivational and educational value – will not work. Instead, the underlying science must be predictive and explanatory; in other words, "hard ecology" is necessary. The principles of hard ecology, such as "species number on islands tends to remain constant," tend to focus on ecological structures (like communities or populations); to emphasize more individualistic, statistical, or bottom-up approaches to scientific explanation; and to provide complex, rationally defended principles that are capable of clear, specific, practical applications.

Although ecologists use both general (soft) and specific (hard) approaches, too many people think that the former is sufficient, not merely necessary, for solving environmental problems. The argument here is that the ecology necessary to undergird sound environmental philosophy requires that people avoid the extremes of using either soft or hard ecology alone and instead use a "practical ecology" based primarily on case studies, natural history, and rules of thumb.

Peters and "hard ecology": underdetermined theories

In an analysis that is both tough-minded and controversial, Peters (1991, p. 11; see Shrader-Frechette 1995) argues that ecology is a "weak science." He claims that the primary way to correct this weakness is to judge every ecological theory "on the basis of its ability to predict" (1991, p. 290). Peters's argument is somewhat correct in at least two senses. First, prediction often is needed for applying ecology to environmental problemsolving; second, if scientists did not seek prediction, at least in some cases, they likely would foreclose the possibility of ever having any predictive scientific theories. Nevertheless, Peters's argument is misguided in several ways (Shrader-Frechette and McCoy 1993, pp. 106–11). First, he is wrong to use prediction as a *criterion for*, rather than a *goal of*, ecological theorizing, because not all sciences are equally predictive. Many geological phenomena – such as whether a given rock formation will be intact in 100,000 years – are not susceptible to precise, long-term prediction. In overemphasizing the importance of prediction in ecology and science generally, Peters has erred in underemphasizing the role of explanation. Second, as critics of the positivist paradigm have argued, science is likely based more on retroduction and good reasons than on deduction and testing through prediction. No sciences can be perfectly deductive in method because they depend on methodological value judgments (for example, about whether certain data are sufficient, about whether a given model fits the data, about whether non-testable predictions are reliable). Because such value judgments render strict deduction impossible, falsification and confirmation of hypotheses – on the basis of prediction – are always somewhat questionable. A major source of value judgments in ecology is the fact that the island-biogeographical theory underlying a major ecology paradigm has rarely been tested and is dependent primarily on ornithological data, on correlations rather than causal explanations, on assumptions about homogeneous habitats, and on unsubstantiated turnover rates and extinction rates. As a result, ecologists who use island biogeography must make a number of value judgments about the representativeness and importance of their particular data (Margules, Higgs, and Rafe 1982, pp. 115–28).

Because of the empirical and conceptual underdetermination illustrated by theories like island biogeography, the methodological value judgments (essential to the theory's use) make a purely deductive, predictive ecology impossible. Of course, there are rough generalizations that can aid problem-solving in specific ecological situations (see Orians 1986). Nevertheless, precise, predictive ecological laws are unlikely because fundamental ecological terms (such as "community," "stability," or "species") are imprecise and vague, and therefore unable to support precise empirical laws (Shrader-Frechette and McCoy 1993). As a result, although the "hard ecology" of Peters may be an important ideal, it demands too much of current ecology and overestimates its potential for certainty.

Regier and soft ecology: untestable theories

At the other extreme of the proposed ecological foundations for environmental philosophy, concepts such as "integrity" demand too little of ecology because they are qualitative, unclear, and vague. To illustrate the difficulties with "soft ecology," consider some of the problems associated with the scientific foundations of the theory surrounding ecosystemic integrity. As late as 1992, one of the leading experts on integrity, Henry Regier, noted that the theory has been explicated in a variety of ways: to refer to open-system thermodynamics, to networks, to Bertalanffian general systems, to trophic systems, to hierarchical organizations, to harmonic communities, and so on (Regier 1992, pp. 25–37). Obviously, a clear, operational scientific theory cannot be explicable in a multiplicity of ways, some of which are mutually incompatible, if one expects a theory to be useful in doing field ecology and in resolving environmental controversies. Often the best account of ecosystem integrity that scientists can provide is necessary conditions, such as "indicator species." For example, the 1987 Protocol to the 1978 Great Lakes Water Quality Agreement formally specified lake trout as an indicator of a desired state of oligotrophy (Regier 1992, pp. 25–37). Nevertheless, tracking the presence or absence of an indicator species is imprecise and inadequately quantitative. Also, the presence or absence of an indicator species, alone, presumably is not sufficient to characterize everything that might be meant by "integrity." Otherwise, people would not speak of "ecosystem integrity" but merely of "ecosystem presence of lake trout."

Integrity theory also is methodologically suspect because the Index of Biological Integrity (IBI)

> does not relate directly to anything that is observable by the nonexpert, nor to any encompassing theoretical or empirical synthesis. As a conceptual mixture put together according to judgment of knowledgeable observers, it is not

"understandable" in a theoretical sense. It is conceptually opaque in that it provides only a number on a scale; this number is then interpreted as bad or good according to practical considerations. (Regier 1992)

The whole theory surrounding ecosystem integrity seems to be conceptually opaque and vague, because even integrity proponents admit that general, qualitative judgments of experts provide the basis for understanding the theory. Also, because only experts can recognize integrity, and because "integrity" is not tied to any publicly recognizable, testable criteria, the whole theory seems "soft" – incapable of uncontroversial operationalization.

Problems with balance and stability

One reason for the underdetermination of the theories of hard ecology and the untestability of the theories of soft ecology is that they rely, respectively, on concepts that are vague or incoherent, such as "balance of nature," "equilibrium," and "stability." Perhaps the greatest problem with appealing to balance or stability is that there is no precise, confirmed sense in which one can claim that natural ecosystems proceed toward homeostasis, stability, or some "balance" (see Taylor 1986, p. 299, and Shrader-Frechette and McCoy 1993). Admittedly, the concept of a balanced or stable ecosystem has great heuristic power, and there appears to be some general sense in which nature is balanced or stable. Nevertheless, in the specific case of the ecosystemic view of the balance of nature, there is no consensus among ecologists. Instead, scientists have called for pluralistic theoretical treatments (Cooper 1990).

Nor is there support for the diversity-stability view held by MacArthur, Hutchinson, and Commoner (Sagoff 1985). The reasons for the disfavor attributed to the view of MacArthur et al. are both empirical and mathematical. Salt marshes and the rocky intertidal provide only two of many classical counterexamples to the diversity-stability view. Salt marshes are simple in species composition, but they are stable, and they are not diverse ecosystems. On the other hand, the rocky intertidal is one of the most species-rich and diverse natural systems, yet it is highly unstable, since it may be perturbed by a single change in its species composition. Empirically based counterexamples of this sort have multiplied over the last fifteen years, and May, Levins, Connell, and others have seriously challenged the diversity-stability hypothesis on both mathematical and field-based grounds (McIntosh 1985, pp. 187–8). Diversity, for example, can be defined to suit almost any conclusion. Yet, numerous policy-makers continue to cite the diversity-stability hypothesis, the most famous version of the balance of nature, as grounds for supporting many tenets of environmental ethics and law, such as the Endangered Species Act. Most ecologists, however, have either repudiated the thesis or cast serious doubt on it. They say it cannot be defined, at least at present (see Shrader-Frechette and McCoy 1993).

Their doubts have arisen in part because we cannot say, in all cases, what it would be to hinder the balance of nature. Ecosystems regularly change, and they regularly eliminate species. How would one use an ethic based on some balance of nature to argue that humans ought not modify ecosystems or even wipe out species, for example, when nature does this herself, through natural disasters such as volcanic eruptions and climate changes like those that destroyed the dinosaurs? Nature doesn't appear merely to extirpate species, or cause them to move elsewhere because their niches are gone. But if not, then one cannot obviously use science, alone, to claim that it is always wrong on ecological grounds for humans to do what nature does: wipe out species. However, given a number of ecocentric or biocentric ethics based on notions such as teleology, inherent worth, or intrinsic value – all non-scientific notions – it is possible to argue against species extinctions (see BIODIVERSITY, NORMA- TIVE ETHICS). Likewise, there are obvious anthropocentric grounds for saying it is wrong to cause extinction because it is wrong for humans to cause unnecessary suffering or to destroy something in a wanton or selfish manner. But if one's only basis for condemning such actions is anthropocentric, because there are no adequate and universal theories of ecological "balance," then it is not clear how ecological theory (as apposed to philosophical notions) can support purely ecocentric environ- mental philosophy (see Taylor 1986, pp. 4ff, 81–5, 174–6). Moreover, the criterion for justifiable species extinction, for those who appeal to the balance presupposition, cannot be that what happens naturally is good, while what happens through human intervention is bad. Using this criterion would saddle scientific and empirical meaning with a purely stipulative and ad hoc definition. Nor can the difference be merely that humans do quickly (e.g., cause lake eutrophication) what nature does slowly. One must have some arguments to show that accelerating ecosystemic changes is bad, even if the changes themselves (e.g., wiping out species) are natural.

In several ways, medical science (if it is a science) also faces problems of defining what is "balanced" or "healthy," problems that are similar to those of ecological science. Both disciplines need to specify criteria for health or for "balance" in order to evaluate the success of their scientific practice. With medical science, however, it is relatively easy to do so because one's goal is always the well-being of the *individual* patient or organism. Environmental and land-use problems, however, almost never focus on the health of one organism or species at the expense of thousands of communities, species, or individuals. Maintaining the health or balance of the *entire system* is a far more difficult enterprise than specifying the health of one individual within some system. Because it is so difficult, it is not clear how one could specify an ecological "balance" without knowing precisely how to define the system that is allegedly balanced.

Problems with appeals to holism

To specify this ecological "system," many soft ecologists appeal to some kind of holism. Purely scientific versions of holism are problematic because there are com- munities of different species, as well as interactions and interdependencies among the abiotic and biotic elements of the environment. As a result, there is no precise, empirically confirmed ecological whole. Most well-known ecologists have either remained agnostic or rejected the Gaia hypothesis (i.e. the idea that the earth is a living organism), the basis of many accounts of holism. They regard it as possibly correct, but at present only unproved speculation. Of course, they admit the ecological fact of interconnectedness and co-evolution on a small scale. Moreover, an ecosystem, as the same collection of individuals, species, and relationships, certainly does not persist through time. Hence any notion of the "dynamic stability" of an ecosystemic whole is somewhat imprecise and unclear (Shrader-Frechette and McCoy 1993; see Norton 1987). Also, the selection of the "ecosystem" as the unit which is or ought to be maximized is peculiar. Why not choose, as the unit, the community, or the association, or the trophic level? The early twentieth-century American ecologist, Frederic Clements, said that the community is an organism (McIntosh 1985, pp. 228, 252–6). If so, then why is the ecosystem also an organism? Which is it, and what are the criteria for a holistic organism? Or, if one is a holist, why not choose the collection of ecosystems, the biosphere, as that which is maximized in nature and which we are morally enjoined to optimize? Once one abandons an individualistic ethic, from a scientific point of view, how does one choose among alternative non-individual units to be maximized? Such questions suggest that scientific holism – organicism – despite its apparent heuristic power, is an arbitrary and imprecise notion.

As an empirical notion in ecological science, holism is further undercut by the current reductionist dispute in ecology among individualists and holists. Admittedly, various ecological conclusions are valid within particular spatial and temporal scales. Nevertheless, a given ecological conclusion (regarding balance) typically holds for some (but not other) "wholes" (e.g., populations, species, communities). For example, there may be some sort of stability or balance for a given species within a certain spatial scale, but not for other species, or not within another such scale. Ecologists cannot optimize the well-being of all these different wholes (having different spatial and temporal scales) at the same time. Because they cannot, there is no general level at which ecological problem-solving takes place, and no general temporal or spatial scale within which a stable "whole" is exhibited. Likewise, because there is, as yet, no general, predictive, and universal ecological theory, ecologists must work on a case-by-case basis. They recognize that there is no universal level (across species, populations, or communities) at which some balanced or stable whole exists. In part this is because numerous alleged "wholes" (e.g., populations) exhibit density vagueness rather than density dependence, while other "wholes" do not (Strong 1986). As a result, there is no universal level at which a balanced or stable whole is evident, and there is no clear, precise, universal sense of biological or scientific holism to which environmental ethicists can appeal, despite its apparent heuristic value.

Another scientific problem with the presupposition (that ecosystems are holistic units engaged in maximizing their well-being) is that ecosystems are not agents in any meaningful sense. Moreover, it is scientifically wrong to suggest that ecosystems, rather than populations, adapt. Although species may evolve in a way that benefits a given ecosystem, there is no selection at the level of the ecosystem. Adaptation is restricted to heritable characteristics; no alleged knowledge of the past operates in natural selection, and the individual that is better adapted to the present environment is the one that leaves more offspring and hence transmits its traits. Given neo-Darwinian theory, Dobzhansky, Goodpaster, Lovelock, Mayr, Rolston, Wright, and other holistic philosophers and ecologists are fundamentally wrong when they suggest either that natural selection operates to produce organs of a given kind because their presence gives rise to certain effects, or that ecosystemic processes operate in certain ways because they maximize ecosystemic excellence. Moreover, although it is possible to claim that adaptation maximizes individual survival, in the sense already discussed, it is not clear what a community or an ecosystem maximizes. Traits advantageous to the individual are not always advantageous to the species or the ecosystem, as in the case of traits such as an individual's "taking all the food." And what is advantageous to the species or to the ecosystem is not always advantageous to the individual, as in the case of dying young to hasten the cycling of nutrients.

Finally, despite their heuristic power, many ecosystemic or holistic explanations are neither falsifiable nor even testable. There is a clear definition neither of what it is to maximize some pattern of excellence (e.g., based on interspecific competition) nor of the ecosystem that is the subject of this alleged excellence. Theorists simply do not agree on the underlying processes that structure communities and ecosystems (Shrader-Frechette and McCoy 1993).

Why ecology has limits

Obviously, both hard ecology and soft ecology have serious epistemological shortcomings. Consider the practical effects of such limitations. In the United States's longest legal conflict over environmental policy, for example, general ecological theory was of little help. The controversy began in 1964 and was between the US Environmental Protection Agency (EPA) and five New York utility companies. The basic problem was that the disputants disagreed over the effect of water withdrawals by the utilities on the Hudson River striped-bass population. After spending tens of millions of dollars, scientists could still not estimate the precise ecological effects of the water withdrawals. In other words, they knew, at the level of a first-order ethical principle, that they wished to avoid serious harm to the striped-bass population. Because of the inadequacy of ecological theory, however, they were unable to specify some second-order principle for adjudicating the dispute between those attempting to protect the utility and those attempting to protect the bass (Barnthouse 1984). This controversy (between the utility and the EPA) suggests a number of reasons why it is difficult for ecologists to get a hold on fundamental ecological processes.

1. Because many important ecological problems, such as the causes and consequences of global CO_2 or acid rain, involve many parameters and a high degree of complexity and uncertainty, there is too much "going on" to be captured by any model.
2. Because of inadequate data bases in ecology, different ecologists often claim evidential support for inconsistent hypotheses (see Peters 1991).
3. Ecologists are encumbered with masses of untested, untestable, often tautological, hypotheses (McIntosh 1985, pp. 249, 269–70, 273, 284; Simberloff 1983).
4. Ecologists often advocate overly simple (almost always wrong) theories about ecosystem response because empirical data are hard to obtain.
5. Ecologists are forced to examine and understand ecosystems that are constantly changing, and changing in ways that are not always predictable or uniform.

6. Virtually every ecological situation is so unique that there are no obvious "state variables," few similarities across cases, and (as yet) no general theoretical laws in ecology (see Shrader-Frechette and McCoy 1993).

7. Often, scientists cannot make ecological measurements, e.g., for r (the intrinsic rate of natural increase of a population), as closely as the legitimate use of proposed equations might require.

8. Ecologists often must know how to optimize a situation involving many individual entities, species, communities, and populations, and yet this optimization always relies on troublesome value judgments.

Although the eight reasons just listed mean that ecology often cannot provide fundamental, predictive, theoretical laws capable of informing particular environmental decisions, they suggest both some useful methodological rules and some insights regarding what ecology can tell us. It can tell us very general things (as the soft ecologists do), such as: "behave as if everything is connected to everything else," or "do not exceed the carrying capacity of the area or the planet." But none of these generalizations is very helpful in doing the precise, practical, hard ecology that environmental decision-makers want.

What ecology can do

Nevertheless, ecology can help us if it steers a middle course between the under-determined theories of hard ecology and the untestable theories of soft ecology. To avoid problems with underdetermination, this "middle path" ought to rely on much more *empirical* generalizations. To prevent difficulties with untestability, this middle path needs to depend on *narrow and precise* local hypotheses. In other words, this middle path – practical ecology – can tell us how to solve very specific problems whose solutions may be subjected to short-term empirical testing. Ecologists often can tell us, for example, what interventions in ecosystems are likely to reduce species diversity. *If* we define "balance" in terms of species diversity, *then* indeed ecologists can give us some help in environmental ethics and policy-making. That is, given the *end* of maximizing species diversity, ecology can tell us about the *means* of attaining it. Ecologists, however, cannot provide us with a general definition of an end or goal of ecosystemic activity, but they can often reveal the best means of attaining some goal, once it is specified. This is in part because, as a recent US National Academy of Sciences report (Orians 1986) noted, there is typically no general, predictive, ecological "theory" that can be applied to solve environmental and land-use problems, even though particular ecological facts, gained from specific cases, have often been useful in environmental policy-making. In other words, ecologists can rarely tell us how to protect entire ecosystems or how to define such protection, although they can often help us manage particular species so as to benefit human interests.

Where does all this leave us? Ecology can't tell us that more diverse ecosystems are more stable, that tropical rainforests contribute net oxygen to the atmosphere, that there is a testable balance of nature, or that organochloride pesticides magnify along food chains. McIntosh (1985, p. 321) puts the point well: all the schools of ecology have failed to provide it with a general ecological theory having predictive power. Nevertheless, ecology has great heuristic, if not always predictive, power. Until ecology is able to give us precise and predictive theoretical explanations, as a basis for environmental ethics and land-use policy, we have several interim suggestions. First, we ought to avoid defending our views by means of controversial ecological hypotheses like diversity-stability, or the ethical and scientific versions of the holism and balance presuppositions (Norton 1987). Second, following the example of the famous Hudson River controversy over the striped-bass population, we ought to conceive of environmental and land-use policy, not as justified by appeals to questionable ecological hypotheses, but as established on the basis of a negotiated settlement for mitigating impacts (Barnthouse 1984). Third, just as we ought to avoid untestable grand theories in ecology as a basis for environmental and land-use policy, so also we ought to avoid assuming, as Sagoff (1985) does, that ecology can never become anything more than natural history. Environmental philosophy and policy, like good science, must remain open to new discoveries.

Despite the fact that hard ecology is often too narrow, and soft ecology is often too broad and vague to undergird environmental philosophy, there are important ways in which ecology can support environmental philosophy. The main point of this chapter is to show that this ecological foundation is not as simple as many persons currently suppose. As a recent US National Academy of Sciences report on ecology noted: "the point of discussing the many obstacles to making accurate predictions is not to argue the futility of trying, but to show that the process of prediction must be viewed as complex and probabilistic" (Orians 1986, pp. 91–2).

A middle path: practical ecology

Given widespread controversy over environmental philosophy, soft ecology is able to provide little more than stipulative definition, just as hard ecology is able to provide little more than untestable hypothetico-deductive theories. Because both types of ecology are uncertain, anyone who does environmental philosophy needs both a procedure for making ethical decisions under conditions of ecological uncertainty, and a method for using ecology, in a practical sense, to direct environmental philosophy and policy. One procedure for dealing with ecological uncertainty is to minimize type II, rather than type I, statistical errors when both cannot be avoided (i.e., avoid "false negatives" rather than "false positives"). Contrary to current scientific norms, this rule of thumb does not place the burden of proof on anyone who posits a damaging environmental effect, but, instead, on anyone who argues that there will be no damaging effect from a particular environmental action. One can defend this rule, despite its reversal of the norms of statistical practice, on straightforward grounds of protecting welfare (Shrader-Frechette and McCoy 1993).

Another means of avoiding the scientific uncertainty of both soft and hard ecology is to develop the more reliable middle path, "practical ecology." Based neither on stipulatively defined concepts nor on general theories lacking precise predictive power, practical ecology is grounded on rules of thumb (like the norm regarding types I and II error), on rough generalizations, and on case studies about individual organisms. A recent National Academy of Sciences committee illustrated how case-specific, empirical, ecological *knowledge*, rather than an uncertain general ecological *theory* or *model*, might be used in environmental problem-solving (Orians 1986). According to the committee, ecology's greatest predictive successes occur in cases that involve only one or two species, perhaps because ecological generalizations are most fully developed for relatively simple systems. This is why, for example, ecological management of game and fish populations through regulation of hunting and fishing can often be successful (ibid, p. 8). Applying this insight to our discussion, ecology might be most helpful in undergirding environmental ethics and policy-making when it does not try to predict complex interactions among many species, but instead avoids the uncertainties of both soft and hard ecology and attempts to predict what will happen for only one or two taxa in a particular case. Predictions for one or two taxa often are successful because, despite the problems with general ecological theory, there are numerous lower-level theories in ecology that provide reliable predictions. Application of lower-level theory about the evolution of cooperative breeding, for example, has provided many successes in managing red-cockaded woodpeckers. In this case, successful management and predictions appear to have come from natural history information, such as data about the presence of cavities in trees that serve as habitat.

Examples like that of the woodpecker suggest that, if the case studies used in the National Academy committee report are representative, then some of the most successful ecological applications arise when (and because) scientists have a great deal of knowledge about the natural history of the specific organisms investigated in a particular case study. As the authors of the report put it, "the success of the cases described ... depended on such [natural history] information" (ibid, p. 16). The vampire-bat case study, for instance, is an excellent example of the value of specific natural history information when ecologists are interested in practical environmental problem-solving (ibid, p. 28). The goal in the bat study was to find a control agent that affected only the "pest" species of concern, the vampire bat. The specific natural history information that was useful in finding and using a control, diphenadione, included the facts that the bats are much more susceptible than cattle to the action of anticoagulants; that they roost extremely closely to each other; that they groom each other; that their rate of reproduction is low; that they do not migrate; and that they forage only in the absence of moonlight (ibid). Using this natural history information, ecologists were able to provide a firm foundation for policy about controlling vampire bats and for the ethics of doing so. Rather than attempting to apply some general ecological theory, "top down," they scrutinized a particular case, "bottom up," in order to gain explanatory insights. Their explanation was local or "bottom up" in the sense that it showed how particular occurrences come about. It explained particular phenomena in terms of collections of causal processes and interactions (Shrader-Frechette and McCoy 1993). Their explanations do not mean, however, that general laws play no role in ecological explanations, because the mechanisms discussed in the vampire-bat study operate in accord with general laws of nature. Nor do they mean that all explanations are of particular occurrences, because we can often provide causal accounts of regularities. Rather, their explanations, like the accounts of practical ecology that we wish to emphasize, are more inductive or "bottom-up" in that they appeal to the underlying microstructure of the phenomena being explained.

They avoid both the hard ecology of more deductive or "top-down" explanation, that appeals to the construction of a coherent world picture and to fitting particular facts into a unified picture, as well as the soft ecology based on stipulative definition.

Conclusion

The success of the National Academy of Sciences case study, with its "bottom-up" or practical approach to scientific explanation, suggests that – whenever policy-makers need ecology to ground environmental philosophy and policy – ecological method needs to avoid soft ecology's uncertain, grand concepts such as integrity and stability. It also needs to avoid the equally uncertain grand theories of hard ecology. Reliable environmental actions seem to require case studies, natural history knowledge, autecology, and humans making value judgments about the merits of their actions. Practical ecology is particularly needed in unique situations, like most of those in community ecology, where we cannot replicate singular events. If we can use the vampire-bat study as a model for future ecological research, and if the National Academy Committee is correct, then both suggest that accounts of ecological method might do well to focus on practical applications and on unavoidably human judgments about environmental management (see Shrader-Frechette and McCoy 1993).

We also need the insights from fields such as conservation biology, a new synthetic discipline that arose in the early 1980s and specifically focused on addressing the alarming loss of biological diversity throughout the world. Likewise, we need the advocacy of biological scientists to address environmental problems that threaten all living things. Just as medical doctors ought not be so scientific that they neglect advocacy for their patients, so also ecologists ought not be so scientific that they neglect advocacy for the planet. Besides, in the presence of uncertain, underdetermined, untestable ecological science, ethical advocacy (for all that ecology studies) is the only way to preserve the very things we wish to study.

References

Barnthouse, L. W. et al. (1984) "Population biology in the courtroom: the Hudson River controversy," *BioScience* 34, no. 1 (January) pp. 17–18. [A good example of how ecology affects policy.]

Cooper, G. (1990) "The explanatory tools of theoretical population biology," in *PSA 1990*, vol. 1, ed. A. Fine, M. Forbes, and L. Wessels (East Lansing, Mich.: Philosophy of Science Association), pp. 165–78. [A classic article by a top philosopher of ecology.]

Kingsland, Sharon (1995) *Modelling Nature* (Chicago: University of Chicago Press). [One of the two best books on the history of ecology.]

Margules, C., Higgs, A., and Rafe, R. (1982) "Modern biogeographic theory: are there any lessons for nature reserve design?," *Biological Conservation* 24, pp. 115–28. [A classic article on island biogeography.]

McIntosh, R. P. (1985) *The Background of Ecology: Concept and Theory* (Cambridge: Cambridge University Press). [One of the two best books on the history of ecology.]

Norton, B. G. (1987) *The Spice of Life: Why Save Natural Variety?* (Princeton, NJ: Princeton University Press). [The classic philosophical text on diversity.]

Orians, G. H. (1986) (Chair, Committee on the Applications of Ecological Theory to Environmental Problems) *Ecological Knowledge and Environmental Problem Solving* (Washington, DC: National Academy Press). [The best National Academy volume on ecological method.]

Peters, Robert Henry (1991) *A Critique for Ecology* (Cambridge: Cambridge University Press). [One of the best critiques of ecological method.]

Regier, H. (1992) "Ecosystem integrity in the Great Lakes basin," *Journal of Aquatic Ecosystem Health* 25, pp. 25–37. [Classic article on integrity.]

Sagoff, M. (1985) "Fact and value in ecological science," *Environmental Ethics* 7 (Summer) pp. 99–116. [A classic article by an environmental philosopher and policy analyst.]

Shrader-Frechette, Kristin (1995) "Practical ecology and foundations for environmental ethics," *Journal of Philosophy* XCII, no. 12 (December), pp. 621–35. [A criticism of two basic ecological methods.]

Shrader-Frechette, K. and McCoy, E. D. (1993) *Method in Ecology: Strategies for Conservation* (Cambridge: Cambridge University Press). [The first book on philosophy of ecological method.]

Simberloff, D. S. (1983) "Competition theory, hypothesis testing, and other community ecological buzzwords," *American Naturalist* 122, pp. 626–35. [A classic article on island biogeography.]

Strong, D. (1986) "Density vagueness: abiding the variance in the demography of real populations," in *Community Ecology*, ed. J. Diamond and T. Case, (New York: Harper and Row). [A classic ecological article on ecological structure.]

Taylor, P. W. (1986) *Respect for Nature* (Princeton, NJ: Princeton University Press). [Classic book on environmental ethics.]

22

Politics

ROBYN ECKERSLEY

Characterizing green political thought

The question as to whether green political thought represents a distinctive political ideology, worthy of a place in the pantheon of political ideologies such as liberalism, conservatism, socialism, and so on, is a matter of ongoing debate. Part of this debate arises from disagreement over the precise contours of green political thought, and over the theoretical linkages between different ideas in the ensemble of green ideas. At least two reasons for this disagreement may be singled out.

First, green political thought has no clear beginning, no towering prophets, and no master discourse. There is no overarching theorist (such as a Karl Marx), and no influential philosophical touchstone such as *The Wealth of Nations* or *Das Kapital*. As a body of ideas, it has numerous antecedents in western thought that can be traced back to Greek and Christian sources, eighteenth- and nineteenth-century romanticism, American transcendentalism, the emergence of the science of ECOLOGY, and to many nineteenth-century political philosophies that were critical of the dehumanizing and destructive effects of the industrial revolution – most notably utopian socialism and communal anarchism (see PART I). In its contemporary manifestation, green political thought is nothing if not eclectic, building a wide variety of philosophical links between radical ecological thought and a selection of critical political philosophies (e.g., feminism, democratic socialism, anarchism), indigenous traditions and eastern and western religions (e.g., Buddhism, Creation Spirituality) – to name just a few. This eclecticism is itself a sign that green political thought is still in the process of formation, providing support for the claim that it is not (yet?) capable of standing alone as a political ideology.

Second, the term "green" is regularly used in a variety of different contexts to designate not only different ecological and political ideas, but also different agents or political "carriers" of those ideas. For example, the phrase "green movement" is sometimes used to describe (i) simply the ecology or environment movement, or (ii) a new progressive political grouping of new social movements (typically the ecology, peace, women's, social justice, overseas aid, and indigenous rights movements), with the ecology movement playing a pivotal role in providing an overarching theoretical matrix for the "new politics," thereby giving a special primacy to ecological concerns. While the second designation is the more common manifestation of green party politics, the question as to which is "correct" can only be answered in the specific context of different states, regions, jurisdictions, and communities. For example, the political opportunity structure in particular states and regions (which includes whether the electoral system favors the emergence of minority parties and the extent to which existing political parties have absorbed environmental concerns) may militate against the formation of a new green party or coalition of parties, in which case particular segments of the environment movement or indeed other radical political alliances may take on the burden of defending the broader green agenda by other means.

Despite the significant eclecticism in green ideas, and the different political manifestations of those ideas, it is nonetheless possible to identify and draw together a cluster of core features of green political thought, based on a generic encapsulation of the main recurring features of the existing political platforms and programs of green parties, and green political movements in general. Whether these features ultimately serve to define green political thought as a new political ideology remains a moot point, as we shall see below. For the moment we are concerned to provide a general delineation of green political thought so that we may then position it against other political traditions in general, and liberalism in particular. The core features comprise:

- a concern and preoccupation with the ecological crisis;
- an ethic of respect for the ecological integrity of the earth and its myriad species;
- a relational ontology – i.e., an acknowledgment of social and ecological interdependence (see DEEP ECOLOGY);
- acceptance of the idea that there are ecological limits to growth;
- a corresponding support for an ecologically sustainable society which respects ecological limits;
- political support for radical social, technological, and economic changes to achieve an ecologically sustainable society;
- intergenerational and intragenerational equity (see FUTURE GENERATIONS);
- a commitment to participatory democracy and the decentralization of power to the lowest practical level.

While the broad green political agenda goes well beyond environmental protection, it is the overriding preoccupation with the ecological crisis and the quest to achieve an ecologically sustainable world which arguably gives green political thought its distinctive character vis-à-vis other political philosophies. To be sure, the goal of SUSTAINABILITY has now been embraced by the United Nations and political parties and organizations of many hues. However, the green movement and green parties can rightly claim to have been the initiators and political champions of the more radical, cutting edge of this popular (and rather flexible) concept. Of course, the meaning of sustainability remains contested within green circles, just as it remains amenable to different interpretations in broader political discourse. Nonetheless, the green debate on sustainability tends to take place in much more challenging terms than the mainstream political debate in addressing the fundamental questions as to what is to be sustained, for whom, and how. In response to these questions, greens overwhelmingly favor an ecological rather than economic understanding of sustainability.

From an ecology-centered (or ecocentric) perspective, the fundamental thing to be sustained is the ecological integrity of the earth and the flourishing of its myriad species. This is a basic ethic of green political thought. The most distinctive aspect of this green normative argument is that it is not enough to look after nature simply because it looks after us (although this prudential argument is an important reason in and of itself). Rather, we should look after nature for its own sake, because it has its own inherent value, dignity, and/or beauty. According to this argument, a purely instrumental posture toward other beings and communities – whether human or non-human – may not only give rise to unwelcome and unforeseen ecological and social repercussions, but is also morally repugnant insofar as it diminishes the moral standing of both people and non-human nature (see META-ETHICS and NORMATIVE ETHICS).

The green ethic of respect for the earth is intimately connected with an ontology which acknowledges the interrelatedness of all life. According to this understanding of the world, not only are we are all constituted by our biological and social relations but also everything we do has social and ecological repercussions. This ontology supports the practical green ethic of acting in the world with both empathy and caution (Eckersley 1992, p. 28), that is, with a greater sense of concern and respect for the fate of others, and a keener appreciation that our activities generate consequences for ourselves and others (both human and non-human). The green ontology and ethic together give rise to a cautious approach to risk assessment, including environmental and technology impact assessment, and a rejection of the Promethean notion that humans are capable of fully controlling all their interventions in the natural world. It is frequently pointed out that ecosystems behave in unpredictable ways and may even be more complex than we can ever know.

The green call for an ecologically sustainable society flows from the related argument that there are ecological limits to growth. The view that we should respect ecological limits to economic and population growth rests on the idea that the earth has a limited ecological carrying capacity. (That this should be a matter of concern flows from the core green ethic of respecting and protecting the ecological integrity and biological diversity of the earth.) Infringement of those limits gives rise to ecological problems – such as pollution build-up, loss of natural resources, reduction of biological diversity – which can have potentially dire consequences for both human and non-human life by jeopardizing both well-being and survival. Indeed, it was the so-called "limits to growth" debate of the early 1970s which prompted the formation of the world's first green parties (in Australia in the island state of Tasmania in 1972, New Zealand in 1972, and in Britain in 1973, in response to the publication of *A Blueprint for Survival 1972*). While the key publication of this period – *The Limits to Growth* (Meadows et al. 1972) – has been shown to be flawed, and while the idea of fixed "natural limits" has given way to a more flexible idea of ecological limits as thresholds that are determined not just by crude numbers of people or the amount of energy and resources consumed but also by social organization, culture, and available technology, the basic idea of ecological limits to growth has endured.

The political and economic implications of moving toward an ecologically sustainable world are potentially far-reaching. Strictly applied, ecological SUSTAINABILITY requires that natural resources must not be used beyond their regenerative capacity, waste production must not exceed the absorption capacity of ecosystems or otherwise threaten or compromise biological diversity and ecosystem integrity, and human

POPULATION must not exceed the carrying capacity of ecosystems (this latter requirement remains a matter of some contention within and beyond green circles). Moving
toward this goal requires changes in social and legal relations, technology, energy
and resource use, modes of production, CONSUMPTION patterns, patterns of human
settlement and movement, and lifestyles generally. In the early days of the movement
(notably in the early 1970s), the "limits to growth" analysis provided a basis for the
green critique of economic growth and gave rise to calls for "zero growth" or steady-
state growth. Nowadays, the critique is more typically couched in terms of a critique
of indiscriminate economic growth and a concomitant call for qualitative, or ecologically sustainable growth, measured in terms of a meaningful quality of life index
rather than in terms of indiscriminate Gross National Product figures (which is the
measure usually relied upon by politicians to measure their nation's progress).

   Despite the ideological differences within the green movement, it is generally
agreed that both unbridled capitalism and centrally planned state socialism cannot
deliver the democratic control of social and economic life that is required if genuine
sustainability is to be achieved. More generally, the green critique of economic growth
has exposed western capitalism and Soviet-style communism as essentially two
different versions of the same "super-ideology" of industrialism (Dobson 1995, p.
33), despite their important differences about the respective roles of the market and
the state. The green critique of industrialism is part of a broader re-examination of
taken-for-granted ideas about the virtues of progress (understood in technological,
economic, and material terms) inherited from the Enlightenment. Both liberalism and
orthodox Marxism developed on cornucopian premises. They assumed that unbridled
economic growth was both possible and desirable. They were also optimistic about
the benefits of science and TECHNOLOGY, and either explicitly or implicitly accepted the
idea of the human manipulation and domination of nature for human advancement.
By critically calling into question humanity's relationship with nature, the green
movement has sought to widen the political debate about who controls and receives
the benefits of the "economic pie" (who gets what, when, and how) to include who
bears the ecological costs associated with its production. This widening of the debate
has not eclipsed the politics of "left versus right" (although some greens ingenuously
claim that green politics is "beyond left and right"), but it has certainly placed it in a
broader and more challenging context. Hitherto, both liberals and orthodox socialists
have assumed that freedom could be sought and found in material plenitude, in new
labour-saving technologies, and a rising stock of manufactured wealth. The alternative green argument is a sobering one: as we approach ecological limits to growth,
we are likely to witness a growing gap between rich and poor, the undermining of life-
support services, and a diminishment in the overall quality of life for everyone.

   While the ecological crisis has served as the primary rallying point for the green
movement and green theorists, most self-styled green politicians, party activists, and
green political theorists are concerned with a much broader political agenda than
simply environmental protection. That is, although solving the ecological crisis may
be seen as the *raison d'être* of the green movement, its concerns range well beyond
those of single-issue environment campaigns. Included in this broader agenda are the
political goals of achieving greater social and environmental equity (including a more
equitable distribution of environmental "goods" and "bads"), a "greening" of the

economy, greater democratic control of social and economic life, greater decentralization of political power, and a greater focus on the qualitative rather than quantitative aspects of individual and community development. For example, most green parties have organized around a broad, shared platform, originally developed by the German Green party, based upon the so-called "four pillars" of green politics: ecology, social responsibility (or ENVIRONMENTAL JUSTICE), grassroots democracy, and non-violence. Many new parties have added to this list, but the core principles have served as an important touchstone in the development of green political theory and practice throughout the world.

While the principle of "social responsibility" or environmental justice may not appear at first blush to necessarily flow from a strict, ecological understanding of sustainability, green political theorists and activists have nonetheless pointed out how justice and sustainability are inextricably linked together in a number of important ways. Indeed, the notion of intergenerational equity has always been central to the sustainability debates, both within and beyond the green movement. That is, the very idea that we should maintain a healthy environment over time presupposes some future class of beneficiaries who will inherit that healthy environment. At the very minimum, those beneficiaries will be FUTURE GENERATIONS of people, although we have seen that an ecocentric ethic is concerned to extend the class of beneficiaries to include non-human species as well. However, this does not require present generations to sacrifice all of their needs in order to provide for the future – this would be self-defeating. Rather, it requires that present generations meet their needs in a way which enables future generations to meet their own needs. This is the now classic formula for sustainable development defended by the Brundtland Commission (WCED 1987). However, green political theorists argue that if the needs of the present generation are to be met in a sustainable manner, then intragenerational equity is also essential. This entails, at the very minimum, the notion of an equal entitlement of all people to the basic necessities of life, along with the idea that the rich should not pass on their ecological costs to the poor or consume more than their fair share. This argument is an especially important feature of the green intervention in the international development debates, particularly in relation to the problem of uneven development between the developed and the developing countries.

While each of the different sub-schools of green political thought have their own particular spin on this complex debate, it is possible to identify three interrelated propositions running through all of the green literature. The first is that ecological SUSTAINABILITY and ENVIRONMENTAL JUSTICE are interdependent phenomena and therefore cannot be dealt with in isolation but rather must be addressed simultaneously. The second is that both extreme wealth and extreme poverty are implicated in environmental destruction (albeit in very different ways), either because of "overconsumption" of resources on the part of the rich (relative to the poor) or because of a lack of alternative options (due to lack of means, education and/or power) on the part of the poor. The third is that the satisfaction of basic human needs and the avoidance of extreme wealth differentials within and between nations are required for both ecological sustainability and environmental justice. Indeed, it is frequently argued that the most radical changes must occur in the affluent societies, and that the rich countries should scale down and adjust their patterns of CONSUMPTION and waste production to levels that can be reasonably sustained by all the peoples of the world. A related argument flowing from these insights is that the rich countries should not only set an example to the rest of the world (because they have the means to do so), but must also assist the less-developed countries to move toward sustainability through debt relief, technology transfer, various forms of aid, and more equitable trading relations. All of these arguments have played a key role in the international sustainable development debates, most notably in the recent round of negotiations on CLIMATE change.

Many contemporary green theorists (particularly ecofeminists, but also ecosocialists and other environmental justice theorists) have pointed to many of the conceptual (as well as practical) links between the exploitation of nature and the exploitation of women and other marginalized social groups. That is, environmental destruction is less often a matter of the domination of nature by a blanket "humanity" and more often the upshot of the domination of some humans (the poor and/or disenfranchised) by others (the more economically powerful) in relation to development projects which serve the privileged few at the expense of the many. According to this analysis, ecologically sustainable development requires much greater democratic control over development decisions. Moreover, associating certain groups (e.g., women, indigenous peoples) with a devalued nature serves to legitimate their exploitation. In particular, less powerful social groups or cultures are sometimes devalued and marginalized because they are deemed to lack something that is possessed by the dominant group or culture to be the measure of human worth (such as reason, "civilization," Christianity). In this marginalization process, women or indigenous cultures have historically been placed on the lower rungs of a hierarchy of being (i.e., typically God, Man, Women/Heathen, Nature) and therefore seen to be less human, less worthy, and "closer to nature" than those privileged groups which possess power to define worthiness. According to this green critique, avoiding such invidious and self-serving comparisons requires the cultural celebration of ecological and cultural diversity (see ECOFEMINISM) along with a rejection of any notion of a hierarchy of being (within both human society and within the biological world).

From the beginning, the green movement and new green parties sought to stand for not only new values and new issues – and new issues linkages – but also a new style of politics, manifested in more participatory and decentralized organizational structures. From the point of view of most greens, questions of political analysis, values, and goals cannot be separated from the question of political means. Accordingly, greens have placed considerable emphasis on the importance of maintaining consistency between ends and means. For example, the green support for a democratic and non-violent society requires that they must necessarily rule out the use of undemocratic and/or violent means to achieve their goals.

Although participatory democracy and decentralization have been defended as basic principles of green politics, many critics have questioned whether either of these means of social organization is necessarily connected with, or conducive to, ecological sustainability. For example, there is a controversial strain of eco-authoritarian literature within the broader eco-political literature (e.g., Heilbroner 1974; Ophuls 1977), which maintains that perhaps only an authoritarian government is capable of ushering in the sorts of radical changes that are required to place society on an ecologically sustainable footing. Other critics have suggested that a sustainable society may be just as easily attained by a fascist government as a democratic one, or that ecological ideas lend themselves to fascist politics insofar as they celebrate the "blood and soil" of particular "home-grown" communities. In rejecting these claims on moral grounds, green political theorists have also argued that the weight of evidence suggests that eco-fascist and eco-authoritarian regimes are much less capable of achieving lasting ecological sustainability than democratic governments. This is because the success of ecologically sustainable development policies is dependent on an informed citizenry which understands and supports the need for such policies, and freely cooperates with a government which the majority accepts as legitimate. This presupposes at the very least a free flow of information between government and citizenry, along with other basic civil and political rights. In advancing the case for democracy, green theorists (such as Paehlke 1988 and Parkin 1991) have shown how the argument has also worked in reverse: that the flourishing of the environmental movement and the broader green movement has served to extend and deepen democracy in both the East and the West. At the very least, then, the green case for democracy has been defended as not merely an incidental or desirable "add-on" to the green case but rather an essential requirement to the achievement of green goals. Indeed, green theorists have generally been critical of "actually existing" liberal democracy as "too thin" and incomplete to enable the type of informed, discursive dialogue that is considered necessary to protect public goods such as the environment. According to this argument, the partisan, competitive bargaining that is characteristic of liberal democratic dialogue usually enables the more powerful, well-resourced and better organized private sector interests to prevail over the weaker, countervailing power of the public interest. If green goals are to be achieved, what is needed are more participatory or deliberative forms of dialogue which enable a free and rational evaluation of common or generalizable interests, where decisions are reached by the force of the better argument rather than on the basis of a truncated, politically managed, and lopsided debate which generally favors the interests of the powerful (Dryzek 1987).

The green case for decentralization is linked to the case for participatory democracy, but it is also defended on separate social and ecological grounds. Indeed, the popular green slogans "small is beautiful" and "think globally, act locally" seek to encapsulate an interrelated set of green arguments concerning the importance of human-scaled institutions, democratic self-management and local ecological responsibility. Together, these ideas are often presented as the "third way," that is, the green alternative to the hierarchical and exploitative institutions of western capitalist democracy and state socialism. In terms of the link with participatory democracy, it is typically argued that smaller, human-scaled institutions and communities are more conducive to face-to-face, participatory democracy than mass consumer societies. From a social perspective, local communities are more likely to engender a sense of belonging, and a corresponding sense of personal responsibility for the fate of community and its environment. From an ecological perspective, the ideal is that local communities live within the means of their local ecosystems so that energy and transport costs would be reduced, natural resources would be utilized sustainably, wastes would be recycled, and there would be no externalization of ecological costs onto other communities and regions. One distinctive offshoot of this green perspective is bioregionalism, an essentially eco-anarchist strand of green political thought which maintains that political borders should be determined according to ecological criteria (such as watershed boundaries) rather than on the basis of arbitrary political or historical factors. Local communities living within particular bioregions should form a loose confederal government with their bioregional neighbors. Moreover, each local community would practice "reinhabitation," or learning to live-in-place, which entails cultivating a detailed knowledge of the local ecosystem, respecting its processes, and repairing any damage from past exploitation (Berg and Dasmann 1978, pp. 217–18).

While the green defense of decentralization has much to commend it, not least from an environmental educational perspective, many variants of this argument have nonetheless come under heavy criticism and are often contradicted by the day-to-day lobbying strategies and policies promoted by some of the more cosmopolitan manifestations of the environment movement and broader green movement. Part of this apparent contradiction stems from ambiguity in the core term "decentralization." In particular, it is not always clear exactly what ought to be decentralized (political power, economic power, environmental management, or all of the foregoing) and what this might mean for the nation-state. Eco-anarchists (many of whom are also bioregionalists) tend to defend decentralization in all of these terms, and either reject or seek to bypass the nation-state. Ecosocialists, on the other hand, accept the principle of democratic self-management in terms of worker democracy, and local government and community planning, but also strongly defend the state as playing an essential role in raising and spending revenue at the national level to maintain basic standards across different regions within the country (whether in terms of welfare, education or environmental quality) (Frankel 1987).

One of the problems with the green case for decentralization is that it is typically advanced in optimistic and visionary terms, and does not adequately grapple with the realities of economic and political power in an increasingly interdependent world. Doubtless, if every local community were relatively stable, democratically organized, and socially homogeneous enough to share the kind of ecological consciousness required to practice bioregional living, then there would no longer be an ecological crisis. However, simply ceding political and economic control (including environmental management powers) to existing local communities does not in itself provide any guarantees that those communities will exercise their powers in an ecologically responsible manner. Indeed, many development conflicts have seen local and national environmental organizations lobby national or indeed international institutions in an effort to override the development decisions of local elites. Moreover, the more extreme case for local autarchy or local self-sufficiency defended by some eco-anarchists cannot be reconciled with the green ontology of interdependence and the broader cosmopolitan goals of global ecological integrity and environmental justice. The case for autarchy naively fails to acknowledge that not all regions are equally endowed with the conditions for human flourishing (in terms of climate, natural resources, and appropriate technologies), and that resource transfers between communities are essential if environmental justice and sustainability are to be maintained. In light of this realization, greens more typically defend the concept of "self-reliance" rather than self-sufficiency in the development debates. The former concept accepts trade and resource transfers between regions, but insists that such exchanges be democratically managed to avoid the subjugation of local people and their environment to the external dictates of the market.

Green political thought: a distinctive political ideology?

Now it might be generally argued that while the green movement does constitute a new political force in contemporary politics, which challenges so-called conventional political parties, there is nonetheless nothing *politically* distinctive about green political thought in terms of the history of political ideas, since it merely represents a critical ecological reinterpretation and reworking of a select range of otherwise familiar political themes and strategies (such as the critique of capitalism, patriarchy, bureaucratic domination, and instrumental reason, the dehumanizing effects of certain technologies, and support for participatory democracy and decentralization). According to this argument, green theorists must admit to having borrowed these various political themes and arguments from other political traditions.

It might be further argued that many existing political traditions (ranging from left to right) are capable of incorporating ecological ideas, including the notion of sustainability, into their political analyses and agendas. Proponents of this view might point to the emergence of a range of new eco-political hybrids such as eco-anarchism, eco-Marxism, ecosocialism, ecofeminism, and "free market environmentalism," all of which take on board ecological problems, and support various versions of sustainability. According to this argument, it is possible to point to an environmental wing in virtually all of the existing political traditions, but none of these wings can be said to constitute a new *political* ideology, capable of standing alone in the line-up of political traditions. Rather, each must be seen as merely a further accretion to, or development of, existing political traditions.

In response, it might be argued that novelty can be found in hybridization, and that although some of the political elements in the green mix may be familiar, their reworking and re-arrangement into a new, ecologically oriented constellation of ideas serves to transform their ideological character and potential political impact. According to this view, green political thought does represent a distinctive political ideology, despite the fact that many of its branches may have strong affinities with some well-established traditions of political philosophy (such as anarchism, democratic socialism, and feminism) and arguably weak or negligible affinities with others (such as orthodox Marxism, liberalism, conservatism, and fascism). Political philosophies are distinguishable by, among other things, the core problems they identify and the core values they defend in response to those problems. If liberalism's core values – liberty and respect for the individual person – arose from its preoccupation with the problem of tyranny, then green political philosophy's core values – ecological sustainability and respect for nature – have arisen in response to the ecological crisis.

Andrew Dobson (1995) has called the political philosophy of the green movement "ecologism" to distinguish it from environmentalism, which he characterizes as a reformist and largely managerial response to the environmental crisis which does not fundamentally challenge dominant values and current patterns of production and consumption. Unlike reformist environmentalism, ecologism "holds that a sustainable and fulfilling existence presupposes radical changes in our relationship with the non-human world, and in our mode of social and political life" (1995, p. 1). Dobson goes on to defend ecologism as a distinctive political ideology. It is an ideology because it encompasses an analytical description of society (which includes an explanation of the ecological crisis and associated social ills), a vision of an alternative society and an associated program of political action. And it is distinctive because ecologism cannot be hybridized with any political ideology in the way that environmentalism can. That is, ecologism is philosophically at odds with some political ideologies and sympathetic with (but not identical to) others.

Dobson's characterization of ecologism does not command universal agreement within green circles. It has nonetheless served as an influential benchmark in the ongoing debate about the characterization of green political thought. It is consistent with the more common manifestation of the green movement identified above (that of a political alliance of new social movements, organized under the uniting banner of ecology). It is also consistent with the broad bipartite distinction in the environmental philosophy literature between anthropocentric versus non-anthropocentric, or ecocentric versus technocentric (O'Riordan 1981) approaches to understanding and addressing the ecological crisis, while also going to greater lengths to draw out and articulate the explicit social and political dimension of the radical end of this spectrum. For Dobson, then, ecocentrism serves as a core value of ecologism (1995, p. 5).

From an analytical perspective, Dobson's characterization makes the task of distinguishing green political thought from other political traditions quite straightforward. That is, if one supports an ecocentric perspective then one would also be expected to subscribe to the idea of ecological interdependence, limits to growth, and support radical moves toward an ecologically sustainable society, all of which are encapsulated in his rendering of ecologism. In this sense, ecocentrism serves not only as the moral bedrock of green political thought but also as the value which most distinguishes green political thought from other political ideologies, all of which place people, the community, the social collectivity or "the person", rather than nature writ large (comprising both the human and non-human worlds), at the center of their respective moral and political universes.

Nonetheless, against Dobson, it might be argued that while it may be the case that ecocentrism is perhaps the most distinctive and philosophically radical aspect of green political thought, to insist that this serve as the defining feature may be to define green political thought in unduly circumscribed terms. An alternative and more ecumenical approach to characterizing green political thought might be to understand ecocentrism as representing the philosophically radical wing of green political thought, without serving as the defining feature. That is, it might be argued that the defining feature of green political thought is support for the idea that human societies should respect ecological limits by practicing ecologically sustainable living. On this broader and more catholic view, green political thought may be said to rest on the general norm that we should respect and protect the ecological integrity of the earth and its myriad organisms, but this norm may be supported by anthropocentric and/or ecocentric ethical arguments, or for spiritual or aesthetic reasons. In other words, people may divide in the reasons they give for supporting "strong sustainability" (with "light greens" supporting anthropocentric and prudential arguments and "dark greens" enlisting intrinsic value arguments as well, and with different cultures in the North and the South drawing on their own philosophical and religious traditions) but it is the support for strong sustainability which makes them green, not their particular philosophical or religious leanings. Many theorists have defended this interpretation as the most politically desirable one insofar as it avoids unnecessary and divisive eco-philosophical hairsplitting and is likely to win the broadest number of political supporters.

While these arguments might be granted, it can nonetheless be noted that the more ecumenical characterization also potentially threatens the unique identity of green political thought, reducing it to a broad arena of environmental debate around recurrent themes, issues, values, and strategies concerning sustainability, rather than a tight and analytically coherent body of political ideas that is distinguishable from other political philosophies. Indeed, the broader and more popular the green political agenda is defined, the more likely it is to be co-opted by other left-libertarian political movements and parties, thereby stripping green political thought of any remaining identity. Such a development would give weight to the argument advanced earlier, that green political theory cannot stand alone, and that each branch of green political thought, such as eco-socialism, ecofeminism, and eco-anarchism, must be seen as further developments of socialism, feminism, and anarchism respectively, rather than sub-schools of green political thought.

Yet there is no reason why each of these sub-branches cannot be seen as part of an ongoing dialogue within both traditional political theory and green political theory circles. Green politics began as "a practice in search of a theory" (Eckersley 1988) and we have already noted the eclecticism of green political thought, and the fact that it does not (yet?) have a settled identity. However, the fact that green political thought cannot boast a clear and distinct philosophical lineage, a united voice, and a settled identity should not alone disqualify it as a distinct political philosophy. It is, after all, not appreciably different from other political philosophies, such as anarchism, conservatism, liberalism, socialism, and feminism, all of which have uneven intellectual histories, inconsistencies, overlaps with other traditions, internal differences and factions. Yet all of these bodies of political thought are still recognized as more or less distinctive "families" or political traditions. That liberalism may be seen to comprise a right wing and a left wing does not mean that the left wing properly belongs to the family of socialist thought, rather than a branch of liberal thought. Provided the more left-leaning variant otherwise possesses the family resemblances of liberalism, then it may be considered part of the liberal family. By parity of reasoning, so long as any socialist, anarchist, or feminist variant of green political thought otherwise possesses the family resemblances of green political thought (i.e. the core features identified above), then it may be classified as properly belonging to green political thought – irrespective of what else it might be classified under.

Green political thought and liberalism

One way of bringing green political thought into sharper relief is to set it against one of the more influential and enduring of the western political traditions, namely, liberalism. We have already noted that green political thought does not have an especially close affinity with liberalism. However, this incompatibility does not extend equally to every feature and/or sub-school of the broad and diverse family of liberal thought. Indeed, it is important to acknowledge those parts of liberalism which are accepted by greens as having enduring value. These include the basic idea that government power should not be absolute or arbitrary but rather must be limited and exercised according to law; that government should take place with the consent of the governed; that basic civil and political rights be upheld; that each person should enjoy equal political liberty (a basic requirement of democracy); and that support be given to the principle of toleration and respect for diversity. All of these liberal ideas are essentially assumed and carried forward by green political theorists. Indeed, some nineteenth-century liberal theorists (notably J. S. Mill and T. H. Green) are arguably proto-green theorists in their support for the flourishing of individual and biological diversity and/or their support for a stationary state economy.

What has come under critical scrutiny by green theorists, however, is the meaning and context of the basic liberal value of freedom of the individual, and the associated liberal ideas of property rights and market freedom. It is important to emphasize that this critique is largely an immanent critique. That is, green theorists do not reject the idea of freedom of the individual, nor the related idea of the equal inherent value and dignity of each and every individual. Rather, they seek to recontextualize freedom in a new ecological and social context by arguing that human freedom should not be purchased at the expense of ecosystem integrity, biological diversity, or social justice. Building upon and extending the socialist, feminist, and communitarian critiques of liberal freedom, green political theorists have rejected the atomistic ontology of liberal theory, and the related liberal conception of the person as a free (i.e., isolated, asocial, unencumbered) agent making rational choices in the world, as if there were no social ties or responsibilities. They have also joined socialist, feminist, and communitarian critics of liberalism in pointing out that the liberal notion of freedom is unrealizable for everyone and undesirable in the form in which it has been theorized, because it is based upon a denial of social interdependence and a selfish or egoistic conception of the individual. This is especially marked in the libertarian conception of freedom as "negative liberty," which is understood as the right to be unencumbered by external restraint of any kind. According to this libertarian model, the state is a necessary evil and any restraints imposed upon the individual should be kept to an absolute minimum. Helping others is a matter of individual charity, not individual or social responsibility.

It is frequently pointed out that liberal values were born in a frontier setting, which assumed an expanding resource base and a continually rising stock of wealth. We have already noted that liberalism, along with its great rival Marxism, fully absorbed the Enlightenment idea of progress, assuming that scientific progress and the technological domination of nature would provide plenty for all. (For example, John

Locke's (1632–1704) quaint defense of private property, outlined in his *Second Treatise on Civil Government*, argued that property rights grew out of individuals mixing their labor with nature – in a world where it was conveniently assumed that there was plenty of unappropriated land and no one around to object (see EARLY MODERN PHILOSOPHY).) Green political theorists, as we have seen, have argued that as we approach limits to growth, the realization of freedom in liberal terms becomes untenable for the majority of people, and sometimes even for the very rich (who cannot insulate themselves from global problems such as CLIMATE change). Instead, we are likely to witness an increasing gap between rich and poor, growing social unrest, and an escalating ecological crisis. Drawing on the arguments of ecological economists, green political theorists generally maintain that if we are to move toward an ecologically sustainable society, then macro-limits (set by the local community, the state, and the international community) on market freedom are essential (see ECONOMICS). Left to its own devices, the economic rationality of the market actor (especially the abstract entity known as the corporation) is one that knows no ecological limits or social bonds. Its primary concerns are economic efficiency, growth, and profit maximization, not social justice or sustainability. From the perspective of market actors, it is more rational to privatize gains and socialize costs. From an ecological and social perspective, however, it is more "rational" to cultivate ecological citizenship and, if necessary, impose legal sanctions to protect public goods such as the environment by laying down sustainability parameters to ensure that economic activity does not encroach upon ecosystem integrity or biodiversity. While green political theorists acknowledge the proactive role that green consumers might play in greening the market, the important task of laying down sustainability parameters is one that should primarily belong to people acting publicly and democratically as citizens, not privately and individually as consumers (Jacobs 1991). Not surprisingly, green political theorists are generally skeptical of new eco-libertarian ideas such as "free market environmentalism," which assert that the solution to the "tragedy of the commons" is the privatization of the commons. Any management regime which seeks to relinquish public control of environmental quality can no longer provide for democratic dialogue over environmental management nor provide any security against private interests prevailing over the public interest in environmental protection. We have also seen that green theorists have generally been critical of "actually existing" liberal democracy as "too thin" and incomplete to enable the type of informed, deliberative, and public-spirited dialogue that is necessary to develop strategies for ecologically sustainable development.

To the extent that a green model of freedom is discernible, it has much in common with socialist, communitarian, and republican interpretations, which posit individual freedom not as something that exists prior to civil society or the state (which can then be encroached upon by society or the state), but rather something that is constituted by social relations and the state. On this understanding, ecological freedom for all can only be fully realized in a social setting which enables and, where necessary, enforces ecological responsibility. Ultimately, as we have seen, this requires that the rich should scale down their resource consumption to a level that is compatible with global justice, while also providing the necessary resource transfers to the poor to ensure that ecological sustainability can be achieved on a worldwide scale.

In light of the foregoing analysis, there is room to conclude that green political thought represents simultaneously a new environmental ethic, a new political ideology, and a new meta-ideology, signaling a broad cultural shift beyond humanism.

References

Berg, P. and Dasmann, R. F. (1978) "Reinhabiting California," *Reinhabiting a Separate Country: A Bioregional Anthology of Northern California* ed. Peter Berg (San Francisco: Planet Drum Foundation). [This article, and the broader anthology in which it appears, is one of the foundational texts on bioregionalism.]

Dobson, A. (1995) *Green Political Thought*, 2nd edn (London: Routledge). [One of the classic introductory texts on green political thought.]

Dryzek, J. (1987) *Rational Ecology: Environment and Political Economy* (Oxford: Blackwell). [A pioneering assessment of the "ecological rationality" of different social choice mechanisms.]

Eckersley, R. (1988) "Green politics: a practice in search of a theory?" *Alternatives: Perspectives on Society, Technology and Environment* 15, no. 4, pp. 52–61. [An early assessment of the underdeveloped character of green political theory.]

——(1992) *Environmentalism and Political Theory: Toward an Ecocentric Approach* (London: University College of London Press). [A broad overview of "emancipatory" green political thought from an ecocentric perspective.]

Frankel, B. (1987) *The Post-Industrial Utopians* (Cambridge: Polity). [A critical assessment of the work of Andre Gorz, Alvin Toffler, and Barry Jones from an ecosocialist perspective.]

Heilbroner, R. (1974) *An Inquiry into the Human Prospect* (New York: Norton). [A very pessimistic inquiry into the prospects of managing the ecological crisis in a sane and democratic manner.]

Jacobs, M. (1991) *The Green Economy: Environment, Sustainable Development and the Politics of the Future* (London: Pluto Press). [One of the most accessible and robust introductions to green economics.]

Meadows, D., Randers, J., and Behrens III, W. W. (1972) *The Limits to Growth: A Report to the Club of Rome's Project on the Predicament of Mankind* (New York: Universe). [One of the landmark "survivalist" publications of the "limits-to-growth" debate of the early 1970s.]

Ophuls, W. (1977) *Ecology and the Politics of Scarcity: A Prologue to a Political Theory of the Steady State* (San Francisco: Freeman). [An influential and somewhat pessimistic analysis of the political implications of responding to the ecological crisis.]

O'Riordan, T. (1981) *Environmentalism*, 2nd edn (London: Pion). [A pioneering discussion of environmentalism, introducing the ecocentric/technocentric divide.]

Paehlke, R. (1988) "Democracy, bureaucracy and environmentalism," *Environmental Ethics* 10, pp. 291–308. [A much cited article which explains the ways in which environmental protest has strengthened democracy.]

Parkin, S., ed. (1991) *Green Light on Europe* (London: Heretic Books). [A wide-ranging anthology on green politics in Europe, both East and West.]

WCED (World Commission on Environment and Development) (1987) *Our Common Future: The Report of the World Commission on Environment and Development* (Oxford: Oxford University Press). [A landmark publication in the international sustainable development debate.]

Further reading

Goldsmith, E., Allen, R., Allaby, M., Daroll, J., and Lawrence, S. (1972) *A Blueprint for Survival* (Boston: Houghton Mifflin). [One of the landmark "survivalist" publications of the "limits-to-growth" debate of the early 1970s.]

23

Law

SHEILA JASANOFF

The codification of environmental law around the world during the last three decades of the twentieth century can justly be seen as an achievement of humankind's enhanced capacity to reflect upon its place in nature. With this body of legislation, the governments of virtually all the nations of the earth announced their intention to safeguard the environment through systematic regulatory action, and to subordinate the desires and appetites of their citizens to the needs of other species and biological systems on the planet.

Yet, the development of environmental law over a generation ran counter to many conventional assumptions about learning and progress (Andrews 1999; Vig and Kraft 2000). Increasing scientific knowledge about the environment did not, in all cases, bring more clarity or certainty about what the law should seek to accomplish. A legislative process that began in the late 1960s with fairly straightforward attempts to regulate the harmful consequences of industrial activity found itself considerably less sure by the late 1990s about the ends as well as the means of policy. Environmental impacts displayed an unsuspected fluidity, crossing media as well as geopolitical boundaries in ways that confounded state-centered regulatory action. Policy instruments, such as risk assessment, that were once thought to be largely technical gradually revealed themselves as irreducibly political. Arguments among experts precluded consensus-based action on significant environmental problems and helped shift power from state agencies to less predictable and less publicly accountable non-governmental organizations. Throughout the period, moreover, there was a sense of impending crisis, as people recognized that failing to protect the environment might have consequences more dire than once imagined – that the stakes were no less than the sustainability of meaningful human life on a threatened and resource-constrained planet.

The progressive dimension of environmental law consists, then, not in its increasing control over well-defined hazards, but in its capacity to adapt to growing knowledge of the limits of prediction and management (Paehlke 1989). Contemporary environmental law began, as noted, with a fundamental commitment to preventing harm rather than merely mitigating damage that had already occurred. But prevention seemed very often to require a leap of faith, as governments had to choose between competing probabilistic scenarios on the basis of inadequate knowledge. Among the shifts in understanding that complicated the law's development, the following were especially significant: recognition of long-term, cross-media, cross-species, and transboundary effects; awareness of inextricable links between human development and environmental quality; sensitivity to the complexity of environmental processes, and hence to the limitations of models; and, not least, acknowledgment of the imperfection of legal rules and standards as instruments for enforcing deep-seated changes in human behavior. These factors affected legal decisions concerning what should be protected, what counts as adequate protection, who should take protective action, what instruments should be used in effectuating environmental goals, and what procedures are appropriate for implementing legal mandates.

Environmental impacts and health effects

A convenient point from which to trace the development of modern environmental law is the passage of the US National Environmental Policy Act (NEPA) in 1969. Responding to domestic political pressure, the US Congress enacted this law to ensure that federal agencies would behave in a more proactive, environmentally responsible manner. For this purpose, NEPA required all agencies to prepare an environmental impact statement (EIS) before undertaking any major action "significantly affecting the quality of the environment." Actions falling under this mandate included both projects directly promoted by federal agencies, such as dam construction by the US Army Corps of Engineers, and those licensed or approved by the government, such as construction and operation of nuclear power plants or the release of genetically modified organisms into the environment. Among the earliest laws to require such precautionary assessment, NEPA served as a model for other industrial nations concerned with environmental degradation.

NEPA's injunction to federal agencies to exercise greater environmental foresight proved to be complicated in practice. The law gave rise to a series of legal challenges, many of which questioned the adequacy of EISs carried out with respect to particular technological initiatives. Early court decisions construed agency obligations broadly, requiring, for instance, that attention be given to long-term and cumulative environmental impacts as well as more immediate ones, and esthetic or recreational effects as well as biological ones. Secondary effects, such as increased road building along new sewer lines or changes in demographic patterns around housing projects, were required to be considered along with the project's primary effects on the environment. Later decisions interpreted the law more narrowly. In *Metropolitan Edison* v. *People Against Nuclear Energy* (1983), the US Supreme Court ruled that possible psychological effects associated with reopening the Three Mile Island power plant, site of America's most serious nuclear accident, did not count as an "environmental" impact and therefore did not have to be considered under NEPA.

More than changing judicial attitudes, scientific controversies about the severity of environmental impacts proved to be the factor that most often frustrated NEPA's orderly implementation. Although techniques of environmental assessment gradually became more routine and sophisticated, the law forced scientists onto territory where predictions could no longer be validated through accepted methods of experiment or observation. There were no readily available models for assessing such potential impacts as the long-term effects of cooling tower discharges on riverine fish populations, the vulnerability to earthquake or water seepage of deep salt beds used to store high-level radioactive wastes, or the ecological consequences of planting insecticide-resistant crop plants on commercial scales. Without scientific consensus on such issues, agency decisions for or against particular projects were often bitterly contested, and courts were thrown into the unfamiliar – and unwanted – role of acting as final assessors of the government's technical arguments. During the 1980s, courts largely retreated from this thankless task, deferring in most cases to the government's superior technical expertise (Vig and Kraft 1994). NEPA retained bite mostly in those rare cases in which an agency failed to carry out a patently necessary EIS.

Another early piece of US environmental legislation that fell victim to scientific controversy and changing values was the Endangered Species Act of 1973, which gave effect domestically to US obligations under the international treaty governing trade in endangered species. Simple in conception, the US law was absolutist in valuing species protection above competing economic interests. Once a species was listed as endangered, no development could take place that would harm its "critical habitat"; nor could it be "taken" for any purpose, even if a taking was purely incidental to development. The US Supreme Court upheld the constitutionality of these draconian provisions in the celebrated case of *TVA* v. *Hill*, (1978) which stopped the construction of the Tellico dam in order to protect the snail darter, which had been declared an endangered species.

That an obscure and economically insignificant fish could block a multimillion dollar construction project carried enormous symbolic force, but the decision's pragmatic effects were slight. Congress soon legislated to allow completion of the dam and President Carter chose not to veto the decision. More generally, listing under the Act proved to be painfully slow and controversial, leaving environmentalists disappointed and angry. Opponents of the law argued, for their part, that less intrusive strategies than total bans on development could meet the Act's goals as effectively. Scientific opinion also shifted, suggesting that the Act's focus on single species was misguided and that attention should be directed instead toward more systemic goals such as ecosystem or biodiversity protection. Congress partly responded to these pressures in 1982. The Act was amended so that economic development resulting in a taking of endangered species could be permitted, provided that it was carried out under an approved "habitat conservation plan."

Unlike NEPA, which explicitly addressed environmental impacts, or the Endangered Species Act, which concerned non-human species, most US environmental laws enacted during the 1970s placed considerable emphasis on protecting human health. A notable example was the Clean Air Act of 1970, which directed the newly formed Environmental Protection Agency (EPA) to set primary national ambient air quality standards at levels sufficient to protect human health, allowing ample margins of safety (Melnick 1983). Laws governing pesticides, drinking water, industrial chemicals, and toxic or hazardous wastes also placed a high priority on the prevention of adverse health effects. A politically vulnerable EPA found that it could more easily win support by regulating on the basis of public health concerns than relatively diffuse and ill-defined concerns about the environment. The risk of cancer, in particular, captured both the public's and the agency's attention. Throughout the 1980s, the detection and prevention of cancer risks from environmental causes formed the centerpiece of EPA's regulatory efforts.

An important, if unintended, consequence of these policies was to reorient the bulk of federally sponsored scientific research towards health issues in the early decades of environmental management. US agencies committed far greater resources to testing chemicals for cancer, reproductive damage, and other health risks than did the governments of comparably industrialized countries. Private industry followed suit, in part to meet the risk assessment obligations created by law and regulation. This imbalance only began to be righted when global environmental issues rose to prominence on national and international policy agendas, while at the same time EPA's critics began questioning whether the risks associated with industrial chemicals justified the resources spent to study and regulate them (Breyer 1993).

Risk assessment and management

No single concept has been so central to the development of modern environmental law as *risk*. The term's widespread use, especially in US environmental law, signaled the legislature's commitment to preventive, not reactive, policy-making. Risk is commonly defined as the probability of a harm times the magnitude of its consequences. From the standpoint of social welfare, a low-probability, high-consequence risk may merit regulation just as urgently as one of higher probability but lower consequence. The term was borrowed into environmental legislation from the financial sector, where it refers to the quantifiable probability of an adverse outcome. In this context, risk is an actuarial construct. That is, risk measures have traditionally been based on statistical analyses of regularly occurring events whose frequency has been recorded over long periods of time. Because these numbers are reasonably reliable, one can estimate many risks with a fair degree of accuracy. Consequently, one can (indeed, in technologically advanced societies, one often *must*) insure oneself against risks for which actuarial data are available, such as fires, floods, earthquakes, catastrophic illnesses, or automobile accidents.

Transposed to the environmental domain, risk became an altogether more elusive concept. Sometimes the term referred to the probability of historically unprecedented events, such as meltdown in a nuclear power plant, the transfer of genetic material from an artificially modified to a wild species, or the effects of carbon dioxide and other greenhouse gases building up in the earth's atmosphere. In other cases, risk was the possibility of harm from human, animal, plant, or ecosystem exposure to toxic and hazardous substances at levels far below what could be directly observed and measured. In the case of environmental chemicals, risk could arise from long-term exposure, gradual accumulation in tissues or the food chain, or the synergistic effects of multiple exposures. For none of these cases was it possible to gather statistical data permitting a reliable estimate of the probability of harm. Environmental risks had to be assessed instead on the basis of projections from incomplete data or by means of models that simulated, however imperfectly, the detrimental impacts of human activity.

Since certainty was out of the question, regulators implementing risk-based laws perennially faced the problem of deciding when the evidence of harm was firm enough to justify regulation. Early in the environmental era, US industry representatives sought to establish a relatively high standard, arguing that regulation ought not to occur unless science provided conclusive or near-conclusive proof of harm. As with other important issues in American environmental law, the question of the appropriate standard of proof eventually came before the courts. In *Ethyl Corporation v. EPA* (1976), the Court of Appeals for the District of Columbia Circuit influentially concluded that an overly stringent level of proof would undercut the legislature's precautionary intent. Something substantially less than scientific certainty, the court ruled, could still serve as the basis for regulation, and decisions about the adequacy of evidence should be left to the discretion of administrative agencies.

Administrative discretion, however, had to be exercised within legally recognizable bounds. Otherwise, regulatory decisions were in danger of being overruled as "arbitrary and capricious" under US administrative law. To constrain their discretion, EPA and other US agencies chose to promulgate formal risk assessment guidelines applicable to a range of health and environmental risks. These provisions stipulated in painstaking detail how evidence from varying sources would be evaluated and compared, how uncertainties would be expressed, how risk estimates would be quantified, and what levels of risk would be sufficient to trigger regulatory action. In effect, the guidelines helped to establish default positions that would support regulation unless industry provided sufficient evidence to override the defaults.

As thresholds for action, the default principles were inevitably value-laden. EPA famously decided, for instance, that data from animal tests would be sufficient to justify regulation even if evidence from human populations was negative or inconclusive. Other choices that expressed a strongly precautionary attitude included decisions to act upon data from high-dose animal tests, in spite of evidence that effects occurring at these levels might not be repeated at lower doses, and to use linear models for extrapolating from high to low doses, although this method arguably overstated the risk. Not surprisingly, many of EPA's major legal battles through the 1980s centered on whether its default positions were too conservative, leading to unrealistically inflated estimates of risk, and thus to overregulation. Under persistent attack for using "poor science," EPA shored up its credibility by creating a network of advisory bodies to review its most controversial policy proposals, including risk assessment guidelines (Jasanoff 1990).

Difficulties in implementing risk-based laws led to several notable reforms that essentially bypassed the need for risk assessment. In US federal law, for example, the hazardous air pollutants provision of the Clean Air Act originally required EPA first to list and then to regulate such emissions on the basis of risks to public health. EPA's risk assessment methods, however, aroused so much controversy that the agency for all practical purposes failed to implement this provision for more than a decade. Congress amended the law in 1990, providing EPA with a list of 189 hazardous air pollutants which had to be regulated by means of the "maximum available control technology." At the state level, impatience with the slow pace of federal regulation prompted a 1986 citizen referendum in California, Proposition 65, which required state agencies to list all known carcinogens and reproductive toxins. Listing triggered regulation without need for further risk assessment. Businesses were prohibited from discharging listed substances into the water and were required to warn the public of their possible exposure to these substances.

European environmental regulation initially avoided many of the legitimation problems encountered in the United States by evaluating risks case-by-case. The task of assessment generally fell to multipartite expert committees, which served as forums for negotiating political as well as scientific differences among interested parties. Reliance on such expert bodies, coupled with the case-by-case approach, led to important differences between American and European environmental regulation. No European government promulgated risk assessment guidelines comparable in detail or explicitness to EPA's guidelines for health risk assessment. None singled out cancer as a health endpoint of especially acute concern. European regulators also relied far less than their US counterparts on quantitative estimates of risks to health or the environment. In their qualitative judgments about risks to public health, European agencies and their advisers gave greater weight to human epidemiological evidence than to animal studies. Expert committees, moreover, operated for the most part consensually and confidentially, so that the basis for their decisions was never exposed to public review. Consequently, public scientific controversies were extremely rare, and – until the British "mad cow" crisis and other environmental scares of the 1990s – European environmental agencies experienced little of the distrust and criticism that had long since become endemic in US policy-making.

The precautionary principle

Despite its technical difficulties and the value judgments it inevitably entails, the concept of risk seems to render environmental problems more tractable precisely because it is measurable. Risk retains the appearance of a phenomenon that can be quantified and hence managed. It is also appealingly comparable. Risks can be offset against benefits, and environmental laws often prescribe that policy-makers should regulate economic activity only when its benefits are outweighed by the risks it poses to health or the environment. Importantly as well, risks can be compared with one another, so that policy-makers can be instructed to focus on large risks over small ones and to ignore risks that are too small to matter.

Critics of risk-based policy have suggested that the managerial language of risk implicitly conceptualizes most human–environment interactions as harmless, or even positively beneficial. Risk is thought to be the exception, not the rule, in human engagements with nature. As such, it encourages rational solutions rather than radical questions about underlying philosophies of development, consumption, or resource use. By contrast, some legal systems have favored the concept of the *precautionary principle* as a basis for environmental action because it shows greater awareness of human ignorance and uncertainty. Historically, this term is a translation of the German *Vorsorgeprinzip*, one of five fundamental principles recognized in German law as the basis for environmental policy. Now quite generally accepted in European policy, the principle states in brief that policy-makers have a duty to avoid damage to the environment. As with risk, the principle emphasizes prevention rather than cure, but precaution, as used in a wide variety of European policy statements, seems to urge something more than mere prevention. It demands heightened caution in the face of uncertainty, to the point of inaction if the consequences of action are too unpredictable. Unlike risk, which invites and lends itself to calculation, precaution implies a greater need for qualitative judgment and, where necessary, restraint.

Precaution, to be sure, is never an absolute mandate. Just as risks are balanced against benefits, so the precautionary principle can be offset in practice by other moderating principles, such as the requirement that actions be proportional to the anticipated harm. Nonetheless, the very indeterminacy of the idea of precaution has kept it from being translated into formal assessment methodologies, such as quantitative risk assessment or risk-benefit analysis. Put differently, the concept of precaution has worked particularly well in cultural settings such as those in Europe that do not insist on mathematical proof of the rationality of policy decisions. The preference for relatively informal and judgmental techniques of decision-making is linked in this way to a more pervasive sense of uncertainty and contingency in environmental policy-making.

Responsibility and burden of proof

While the goals of environmental law have been contested and reformulated over the years, there has been general agreement that the burdens of environmental protection should be carried primarily by known polluters or by those proposing to alter the state of the environment in a potentially detrimental manner. In the United States, laws governing pesticides and toxic chemicals shifted to manufacturers and producers the burden of proving that their activities would not damage the environment. Secondarily, these laws also committed manufacturers to testing their products extensively before introducing them into the market. The so-called Superfund law, enacted in 1980 in response to public concern about abandoned hazardous waste disposal sites, required industry to pay for cleaning up these sites at costs that many later criticized as exorbitant (Landy et al. 1990). European and international bodies meanwhile recognized the "polluter pays principle" as one of the basic principles of environmental law. This provided the grounding for legal measures aimed at pre-market testing, monitoring, and clean-up.

There were, however, important exceptions to the decision to shift the economic and scientific costs of environmental protection to the private sector. In the case of most existing enterprises (US Superfund sites were a notable exception), or products already on the market, governments usually retained the burden of proving the existence of unreasonable risks to health or the environment. The difficulty of meeting this burden meant that many environmentally harmful activities were either allowed to persist or, especially in the United States, regulated only when EPA was successfully sued by an environmental organization. Litigation became the prod to action on a host of issues, including the regulation of organochlorine pesticides, asbestos, and toxic air and water pollutants. European legal frameworks, which likewise failed to shift the burden of proof for most existing products and facilities, provided fewer opportunities for public interest litigation against government agencies. Environmental groups in Europe adopted political strategies for attaining their objectives, ranging from the formation of Green parties in several countries to direct action, such as boycotts and demonstrations, against private companies.

Questions regarding the state's burden of proof arose in somewhat different form in conflicts between environmentally and economically beneficial uses of land in the United States. Land-use laws protecting wetlands and other environmentally sensitive areas initially allowed federal, state, and local governments considerable freedom to control development in the public interest. Beginning in the 1980s, however, a resurgent property rights movement challenged these measures on the ground that they constituted an unlawful taking of property without just compensation. In the 1994 case of *Dolan* v. *City of Tigard*, the Supreme Court awarded property owners a partial victory. Henceforth, the Court declared, governmental bodies placing environmentally motivated restrictions on development would have to show that the value to the public bore a "rough proportionality" to the costs imposed on developers. Although the Court stated that there would be no need for rigorous mathematical demonstrations, the decision clearly increased the government's burden of proof in takings cases.

Environmental standards

The functional heart of environmental law in most countries has been to establish and enforce standards that provide desired levels of protection against pollution, resource depletion, and other harms to nature. A key assumption underlying environmental standard-setting in the early years was that it would be relatively unproblematic to determine the right level of protection – in other words, that there would be little, if any, disagreement about "how safe was safe enough." A second assumption was that standards would be relatively uniform across legal jurisdictions. Standards, so conceived, were averaging instruments. They demanded a stated level of performance from all regulated industries and products, without regard to the locations, circumstances, or characteristics of individual members. Finally, it was assumed that environmental standards could effectively be implemented through a "command and control" approach that placed on government agencies the primary responsibility for monitoring behavior and enforcing compliance. Three decades of experience have cast doubt on each of these initial assumptions, thereby weakening the role of standards in environmental management.

Standard-setting, to begin with, has proved to be a profoundly value-laden process calling for both expert and normative judgments. Beginning with risk assessment, each step of standard-setting entails value choices. These include, significantly, how to value the economic benefits of industrial activity, whether to weigh risks against benefits, and how risk-averse to be in setting standards. Although legislation can offer guidance on these points, for example by stipulating whether or not economic benefits should be considered in standard-setting, many specific details must necessarily be resolved through administrative action. In the relatively open and transparent US regulatory system, standard-setting emerged early on as a major locus of controversy. In spite of EPA's increased reliance on scientific advice, and sometimes also on prior negotiation, economically significant environmental standards were hardly ever adopted without litigation.

A threshold question of great importance in establishing standards is who should be protected: everyone, from the most to the least vulnerable; the "average" person;

the sick or sickness-prone; children; the elderly; the economically disadvantaged; those already subject to above normal risks; the politically powerful? Occasionally, this choice is made by legislation. Thus, the US Clean Air Act Amendments of 1990 specified that standards for hazardous air pollutants should aim to protect the "maximally exposed individual" (MEI). Critics of the Act noted that such a policy would not automatically advance public health, since the maximally exposed individual was not necessarily the one most at risk. Highly directive though it was, this provision did not eliminate the need for administrative discretion. EPA was still required to define the MEI and to set standards at levels that would adequately protect this hypothetical, most exposed individual.

In the absence of explicit legal stipulations, political pressure sometimes forced the government to pay greater attention to the needs of one or another vulnerable population. In the mid-1980s, for instance, a controversy over the plant growth regulator Alar prompted EPA to reconsider its risk assessment policies for pesticides so as to make special provision for cancer risks to children (Wargo 1996). In a potentially more far-reaching development, economically disadvantaged minorities in the United States began arguing that government policies had failed to protect them against development patterns that disproportionately concentrated toxic and hazardous facilities in poor communities. Their demand for ENVIRONMENTAL JUSTICE bore fruit following the 1992 election, when President Clinton issued an executive order directing federal agencies to consider the impacts of their actions on environmental equity.

In countries other than the United States, public controversies over who should be protected and at what levels have been rarer, corresponding to the less open and transparent character of environmental standard-setting. Few other regulatory systems have gone so far toward making explicit the basis for administrative decisions. In particular, expert bodies in most countries meet in private sessions to recommend standards that governments should adopt. There is ordinarily no record of their internal deliberations or of ways in which they raised and resolved particular normative questions. Value judgments undoubtedly are made in these closed and consensual processes, but they remain hidden from public scrutiny and possibly unacknowledged by the experts themselves. The efficacy of such processes in bringing normative issues to the fore depends on the skills and commitments of individual expert advisers.

Standards can offer more or less discretion to regulated parties. Design standards that specify equipment or processes for meeting particular environmental requirements provide clear benefits to the regulator. They are relatively easy to monitor and enforce on an industry-wide basis. Performance standards, by contrast, are often preferred by regulated parties because they establish only the goals of environmental policy and not the means of achieving them. The "bubble policy" adopted by EPA in the 1980s represented an important concession to industrial demands for greater flexibility in meeting air pollution standards. Under this policy, EPA sets emission standards for complex industrial facilities as if they are encased in a virtual bubble. A company may then distribute its total emission reductions among individual stacks inside the bubble, consistent with its overall economic and technological capabilities.

Another development in environmental standard-setting that offers more maneuvering room to industry is the turn from pollution control toward the approaches collectively known as "pollution prevention." The definitions and objectives of this policy vary across countries. In some cases, pollution prevention efforts have centered mainly on reducing releases of toxic chemicals, whereas in others the objective has been to minimize waste in all its forms. The 1990 US Pollution Prevention Act, for example, added new reporting requirements for treatment, recycling, and energy recovery to the data on environmental releases already demanded of the chemical industry. In numerous European countries, waste minimization has received higher priority than chemical releases per se. Regardless of their precise scope, all pollution prevention programs build on the insight that it is generally more costly to install end-of-pipe controls on undesirable emissions than to design cleaner technologies that do not need subsequent retrofitting.

The relative uniformity of environmental standards, whether geared toward control or prevention, varies from one legal jurisdiction to another. Under US law, it is generally accepted that federal regulations provide a floor for environmental protection which states or regions may freely exceed if they deem it necessary. Severely polluted regions, such as the southern California air basin that includes the city of Los Angeles, have used this power to craft stricter control regimes than are mandated by federal law. On the other hand, regions that not only meet but exceed federally required minimum standards may not, pursuant to the Clean Air Act, permit significant deterioration of their air quality. In Europe, the growing integration of environmental policy has tended to force greater uniformity in standard-setting, although the principle of "subsidiarity" leaves considerable discretion to national regulatory bodies. Elsewhere in the world, constitutional or legal provisions may limit the role of national authorities with respect to particular environmental media or amenities; in India, for instance, air quality but not water quality is protected by national standards. Finally, in all nations of the world, regional differences in regulatory capacity introduce variations in actual compliance with environmental standards.

Market approaches

Dissatisfaction with command-and-control regulation grew through the first two decades of the modern environmental era (Melnick 1983; Landy et al. 1990; Breyer 1993). Economists complained that this approach led to significant inefficiencies and overregulation because centralized government agencies were more responsive to administrative and political pressures than to economics. Environmentalists, too, were disenchanted, although their criticism focused primarily on the "implementation gap" resulting from the government's inability to monitor and enforce its own regulations. By the 1990s, there was a new openness to the idea of market-based solutions to regulatory problems. Even committed environmentalists acknowledged that the private sector should begin to play a more proactive role in policy design and implementation instead of serving as passive or obstructionist targets of regulation.

Market-based approaches in the United States developed fastest and furthest under the federal clean air program. Soon after the passage of the Clean Air Act, EPA realized that special policies would be needed in so-called non-attainment regions that were unable to meet the national ambient air quality standards in timely fashion. Without special provisions, no new development could have occurred in non-attainment regions, since new facilities would have added to the already unlawful levels of pollution. The device used to mitigate this problem was the use of "offsets." New plants could offset their added emissions against reductions achieved through collateral means, such as buying and closing down inefficient plants producing higher levels of pollution.

The 1990 amendments to the Clean Air Act extended the use of market-based approaches to control acid rain caused by sulfur dioxide releases from power plants. EPA was authorized to issue allowances to plants covered by the acid rain program; each allowance was worth one ton of sulfur dioxide released from the smokestack, and bonus allowances could be given for measures such as using clean coal or renewable energy. To obtain reductions in sulfur dioxide pollution, the total amount of allowances was set below the current level of emissions. Plants thereafter could release only as much sulfur dioxide as permitted by their allowances. If a plant wished to release more, then it had to get more allowances; these could be bought from another plant that had reduced its sulfur dioxide emissions below its allowed number and therefore had extra allowances to sell or trade. These transactions did not have to be conducted directly between power plants wishing to engage in emissions trading. In effect, the law established a nationwide emissions market, in which allowances could be bought and sold by middlemen as in any other commodities market.

While economists and industries applauded the move toward market-based approaches, not all were equally sanguine that this was a desirable direction for environmental policy (Sagoff 1988). Some argued that the very act of placing a value on emissions, such as tons of sulfur dioxide, helped to legitimate pollution. Others were concerned that markets operating on the basis of imperfect information would fail to price emissions accurately. Moreover, as emissions markets become global in response to problems such as climate change, some worried that markets would operate in coercive ways to the advantage of economically powerful industries in the North and the detriment of their weaker counterparts in the South (see ECONOMICS).

Citizen participation and standing to sue

Perhaps more than any other legal development in the late twentieth century, environmental legislation has helped to draw ordinary citizens into the day-to-day administration of government. Citizen involvement in environmental policy takes many different forms and enjoys different degrees of legal sanction across countries, but certain broad principles have gained in force with the passage of time. These include the propositions that citizens have a right to know of environmental threats to their health and safety, that they should have access to the basis for the government's environmental policies, and that they should be able to participate meaningfully in the decision-making process. Less commonly, citizens have also been granted the right to take agencies and polluters to court for failing to meet environmental obligations.

Right-to-know provisions were enacted in many countries following the 1984 gas disaster at a Union Carbide pesticide factory in Bhopal, India, which killed on the order of 3,000 people and injured or disabled many thousands more. In the United States, chemical plants were required under a 1986 law to provide state and local governments with information about the locations and quantities of chemicals that they were storing on site. They were also required to produce a "toxics release inventory" (TRI) reporting to EPA the amounts of some 600 toxic substances that they were emitting into the environment. The information so provided proved a boon to environmentally concerned citizens and organizations nationwide. TRI data were routinely used by environmental groups to create chemical hazard profiles for communities throughout the United States. European laws also changed in response to Bhopal, but disclosure requirements in Europe more often subscribed to a "need to know" than a "right to know" philosophy: that is, companies and governments were required to disclose to citizens only the information that they needed in order to protect themselves in emergencies.

The transparency of environmental decision-making became a significant political issue over the years in both developing and industrialized countries. On the whole, the United States led the way in providing citizens full access not only to the information relied on by government regulators but also to the reasoning underlying their regulatory proposals. Citizen participation in US environmental policy occurs most commonly through the administrative rule-making process. Environmental laws generally require implementing agencies to maintain detailed records, publish proposed rules, solicit public comment (often through formal hearings), respond to those comments, and explain the basis for their final actions. Agencies, moreover, are subject to judicial review for procedural errors in their decision-making, as well as for substantive deficiencies that arguably render their policies "arbitrary and capricious."

Together, these provisions offer interested and affected parties virtually a license to litigate environmental decisions of any consequence, including, of course, decisions not to act. Lawsuits by citizens proved to be an essential component of US environmental management in the early decades. NEPA, in particular, might have remained little more than a paper aspiration in the absence of such litigation. A receptive judiciary construed the legal doctrine of "standing" liberally, so as to allow suits by citizens with recreational, esthetic, or other indirect and non-economic interests in projects requiring an EIS. Property ownership in affected areas was not a precondition for the award of standing. In this way, the law came as close as it formally could to realizing some environmentalists' dream that natural objects, such as rivers, trees, or parklands, would receive legal representation (Stone 1974).

Other major US environmental laws included explicit citizen suit provisions which permitted ordinary citizens to take polluters to court if government agencies were unable or unwilling to do so. Supplemented eventually by information from the TRI database, these provisions offered communities a powerful weapon against industries polluting their local environments. Energetic use of citizen suits led to the imposition of heavy fines and other sanctions on many facilities throughout the nation. Industry, however, complained about the irresponsible use of lawsuits to penalize what seemed from the corporate standpoint to be trivial or purely technical violations of environmental regulations. Judicial sympathy toward citizen suits waned during the 1990s. A series of federal court decisions, spearheaded by the Supreme Court, limited citizen suits during the 1990s in a silent retreat from the earlier era of judicial activism.

Participation in other western countries arguably took a wider variety of forms than in the United States, although there were fewer opportunities for litigation, and access to information in the regulatory process was more limited. In some European countries, most notably Germany, and in the European Union (EU), the electoral success of Green parties permitted environmentalists to participate directly in the legislative process, with results that were more durable in some respects than the victories won through lawsuits in the United States. In addition, a number of smaller European nations made use of public referenda on highly consequential environmental policies, such as whether or not to permit nuclear power or genetic engineering. Land-use decisions, including the siting of hazardous facilities, were often accompanied by public inquiries which resembled in formality the hearings held during US rule-making proceedings. In some cases, citizen juries were employed to pass on the desirability of particular environmental policies. Environmental interests were also increasingly represented in expert committees involved in risk assessment and standard-setting.

More generally, by the end of the 1990s, the need for greater transparency and public participation was commonly recognized in international environmental law and policy. The EU in 1990 adopted a directive, binding on all member states, assuring freedom of access to information about the environment. Principle 10 of the 1992 Rio Declaration on Environment and Development formally recognized the importance of involving concerned citizens in environmental decision-making. Building on this principle, the environmental policy committee of the Economic Commission for Europe drafted a Convention on Access to Information, Public Participation in Decision Making and Access to Justice in Environmental Matters.

International environmental law

The rapid internationalization of environmental law during the 1990s overtook in some respects the evolution of domestic law and policy to meet national and local challenges over the preceding two decades. The transnational nature of many environmental problems was officially recognized at the 1972 Stockholm Conference on the Human Environment. International agreements proliferated on a growing array of transboundary issues, such as acid rain, the transport of hazardous wastes, trade in endangered species, protection of regional seas, Antarctic development, and exploitation of deep seabed resources. The 1992 United Nations (UN) Conference on Environment and Development held in Rio de Janeiro both accelerated the pace of internationalization and reoriented policy-making toward the concept of SUSTAINABILITY. The term "sustainable development" is normally defined as "development which meets present needs without reducing the ability of future generations to meet their needs" (WCED 1987). A more dynamic and forward-looking concept than "pollution control," sustainability provides a basis for continually re-evaluating human–environment interactions with the goal of preventing irreversible harm or catastrophic changes in environmental quality.

Whereas older transboundary problems, such as acid rain, were adequately addressed by national governments fulfilling treaty obligations within their own borders, the newer class of global environmental issues presented deeper challenges to state sovereignty (Haas et al. 1994). Problems such as ozone depletion, acid rain, deforestation, and loss of BIODIVERSITY arose from a multitude of widely dispersed and decentralized activities; yet, collectively, they posed threats to the health and well-being of the earth's entire human population. It was apparent by the century's end that managing problems of this scope would alter environmental law-making and implementation in unprecedented ways, going beyond the relatively limited intrusions on sovereignty made by prior environmental accords (Weiss and Jacobson 1998; Benedick 1998).

Legal regimes for coping with global environmental problems differ from earlier systems of environmental regulation in several salient respects, all of which undercut the autonomy of nation-states. Participation in treaty-making is not limited to national governments but includes international organizations, as well as non-governmental organizations; the UN Environment Program, for instance, brokered the conventions on ozone, CLIMATE change, and BIODIVERSITY, among others. Important risk assessment tasks are carried out by international expert bodies, such as the Intergovernmental Panel on Climate Change, over which national governments have only limited control. Legal obligations reach beyond compliance with environmental standards to include numerous subsidiary issues, such as technology transfer and intellectual property rights; international controls affect and seek to globalize domestic resources, often without any apparent quid pro quo. And implementation calls for novel forms of cross-national and cross-sectoral collaboration, especially if market-based approaches are applied internationally. At the same time, the rewards of managing long-range and complex global problems are neither readily visible nor reliably measurable. The disparity between immediate, tangible costs and distant, hypothesized benefits has been a thorny problem even in domestic policy debates; together with the erosion of sovereignty, the incommensurable cost-benefit balance may raise even higher barriers to the development and implementation of international environmental law.

The future of environmental law

Whatever short-term disputes and dislocations it may entail, environmental law has established itself as an essential resource in humankind's struggle to achieve sustainable ways of living on the earth. Like any other system of laws, environmental legislation importantly articulates and enforces norms that society holds in high value, but this is not its exclusive function. Many of the political forces to which environmental legislation has given support – including movements toward greater access, participation, justice, and global cooperation – are forces that twentieth-century societies came to see as indispensable for their sustainability. The process of making and implementing environmental laws, moreover, brought the culture of increased citizen participation into convergence with deeper scientific and ethical reflection on the relations between human beings and other aspects of nature. It is by providing a framework within which the scientific, ethical, and political dimensions of human experience can be simultaneously and continuously deliberated that environmental law offers the greatest promise for humanity.

References

Andrews, Richard N. L. (1999) *Managing the Environment, Managing Ourselves: A History of American Environmental Policy* (New Haven: Yale University Press). [A sweeping survey of 400 years of environmental policy in America.]

Benedick, Richard E. (1998) *Ozone Diplomacy: New Directions in Safeguarding the Planet*, 2nd edn (Cambridge, MA: Harvard University Press). [An account of the negotiations leading to the Montreal Protocol on ozone depletion by the chief US negotiator, providing an insider's look at international treaty-making, highlighting the complexities of forging an international consensus even when the environmental issue is relatively well understood.]

Breyer, Stephen (1993) *Breaking the Vicious Circle: Toward Effective Risk Regulation* (Cambridge, MA: Harvard University Press). [A critique of EPA's use of risk analysis for regulatory purposes, arguing that the agency has been driven by tunnel vision and irrational public fears rather than by rational expert judgments.]

Haas, Peter M., Keohane, Robert O., and Levy, Marc A., eds. (1994) *Institutions for the Earth: Sources of Effective International Environmental Protection* (Cambridge, MA: MIT Press). [A series of case studies documenting the role and rising significance of international institutions in managing the environment, as well as an analysis of the factors that make these institutions more or less effective.]

Jasanoff, Sheila (1990) *The Fifth Branch: Science Advisers as Policymakers* (Cambridge, MA: Harvard University Press). [A study of expert committees advising the US government on environmental and health regulation, arguing that such bodies play a valuable role not merely by providing neutral expert advice but even more by validating the exercise of judgment in mixed domains of science and values.]

Landy, Marc K., Roberts, Marc J., and Thomas, Stephen R. (1990) *The Environmental Protection Agency: Asking the Wrong Questions* (Oxford: Oxford University Press). [A detailed investigation of several major regulatory programs at EPA arguing that the agency systematically mistook its priorities in trying to improve US environmental quality over nearly two decades.]

Melnick, R. Shep (1983) *Regulation and the Courts: The Case of the Clean Air Act* (Washington, DC: Brookings Institution). [A political scientist's account of judicial involvement in the first decade of implementing the US Clean Air Act, arguing that the courts misunderstood the nature of scientific uncertainty and therefore pushed EPA toward adopting unnecessarily stringent standards.]

Paehlke, Robert C. (1989) *Environmentalism and the Future of Progressive Politics* (New Haven: Yale University Press). [A strong argument that environmentalism represents the most promising avenue for progressive politics in our era.]

Sagoff, Mark (1988) *The Economy of the Earth* (Cambridge: Cambridge University Press). [An influential book on environmental ethics criticizing attempts to reduce environmental values to economic ones.]

Stone, Christopher D. (1974) *Should Trees have Standing?* (Los Altos: William Kaufmann). [A classic of the early years of American environmentalism reflecting an idealistic faith in the power of law to bring about fundamental changes in human relations with nature.]

Vig, Norman J. and Kraft, Michael E., eds. (2000) *Environmental Policy: New Directions for the Twenty-First Century*, 4th edn (Washington, DC: CQ Press). [An accessible, interdisciplinary review of American environmental policy-making, assessing the roles of major policy-making bodies and the emergence of new, private actors, such as industry and non-governmental organizations.]

Wargo, John (1996) *Our Children's Toxic Legacy* (New Haven: Yale University Press). [A critical review of a quarter-century of pesticide regulation in the United States, suggesting that law, science, and public policy have not succeeded in adequately controlling the health and environmental risks posed by pesticides.]

Weiss, Edith Brown and Jacobson, Harold K., eds. (1998) *Engaging Countries: Strengthening Compliance with International Accords* (Cambridge, MA: MIT Press). [A comparative study of compliance with five environmental treaties in ten countries showing huge disparities in the international community's ability and willingness to follow through on such obligations.]

WCED (World Commission on Environment and Development) (1987) *Our Common Future* (Oxford: Oxford University Press). [The report that helped to lay the groundwork for the 1992 Earth Summit in Rio de Janeiro and shifted the discourse of environmentalism from pollution and conservation to human development by introducing the concept of "sustainable development."]

PART IV

PROBLEMS IN ENVIRONMENTAL PHILOSOPHY

24

Wilderness

MARK WOODS

Introduction: The Badlands and wilderness philosophy

At the end of the Cretaceous period (approximately 70 million years ago), what is now western North Dakota in the United States was covered by an inland sea. Over time this area was dramatically altered by the draining of this sea; the uplifting of the mid-North American continent; sedimentation and erosion from rivers in nearby mountain ranges; volcanic activity; altered climate patterns; glaciation; and the colonization, migration, immigration, and extinction of a wide variety of species. Today this area contains geological and ecological formations found nowhere else in North Dakota: buttes, mesas, canyons, bentonite clay slopes, scoria deposits, naturally burning coal veins, petrified forests, perennial prairie grasslands, ponderosa pine forests, and riparian communities. Elk, bison, pronghorn antelope, bighorn sheep, ferrets, and prairie dogs that are now locally extinct over much or all of North Dakota can be found in this area. Called *"Mako Shika"* ("land bad") by the Lakota Indians who inhabited this area until the end of the nineteenth century and *"les mauvaises terres à traverser"* ("the bad lands to cross") by eighteenth-century French fur trappers, the "Badlands" have long been recognized as a unique area. The Theodore Roosevelt National Park now protects some of the remnants of the Badlands from developments such as mining and cattle grazing. In order to preserve some of the land within the park in a "wilderness condition," in 1978 the United States Congress designated a wilderness area in each of the two separate units of the park. In accordance with American environmental laws, these two wilderness areas were to be preserved forever in an untrammeled, pristine state of nature, uninhabited by people.

Several years prior to the designation of these two wilderness areas, about half a million acres of the Little Missouri National Grasslands that surround the two units of the national park remained roadless and suitable for wilderness designation. By the end of the twentieth century the blazing of roads, the drilling of numerous oil and gas wells, and extensive cattle grazing within these areas had reduced the roadless acreage to less than one-third of its original size, and further developments threaten to eliminate virtually all of the rest. A coalition of environmental groups champion the preservation of all the remaining roadless lands in the North Dakota Badlands and recommend the designation of eleven new wilderness areas. They face an uphill battle against mining companies, cattle ranchers, and others who wish to continue to develop and inhabit the Badlands. Should these eleven new wilderness areas be designated? Why or why not?

I raise these questions concerning the North Dakota Badlands because this is a paradigm case of wilderness protection in North America and in many other areas. Environmentalists who wish to protect some of the last remaining wild and natural areas in North Dakota are pitted against oil companies, ranchers, and others who wish to develop and use some of the last remaining unexploited natural resources in the state. The case of the Badlands also can be read as a textbook example of a central problem within environmental philosophy, as wilderness supposedly represents the quintessential non-human, natural world that, many argue, is deserving of our protection. Choices that are made about wilderness protection in the Badlands embody answers to further questions about wilderness in general: How should wilderness be protected? Why is it worth protecting? In what does its value consist? What precisely is wilderness?

According to the so-called "received wilderness idea" (Callicott, in Callicott and Nelson 1998), standard answers can be given to these questions. I begin by discussing this received idea and the role it has played in some of the early work in environmental ethics. More recently, philosophers and others have begun to question wilderness and the values associated with it, and a number of critical arguments have been made against the concept of wilderness and the philosophy of wilderness preservation (see many of the essays in Callicott and Nelson 1998). I outline five of these arguments and attempt to sketch some responses that wilderness advocates might make to them. I conclude by outlining some future directions for wilderness philosophy.

Before I begin, an important caveat is in order: much of my focus is directed toward American wilderness. Although the American model of wilderness preservation has been exported to areas beyond the United States, much of the current understanding of wilderness – the received wilderness idea – has been informed by and made in explicit reference to American wilderness. Accordingly, American wilderness is the central target of many of the anti-wilderness arguments I outline below.

The received wilderness idea

What is wilderness? One of the most cited and criticized answers to this question is the following:

> A wilderness, in contrast with those areas where man and his works dominate the landscape, is hereby recognized as an area where the earth and its community of life are untrammeled by man, where man himself is a visitor who does not remain. An area of wilderness is further defined to mean in this chapter an area of undeveloped Federal land retaining its primeval character and influence, without permanent improvements or human habitation, which is protected and managed so as to preserve its natural conditions and which (1) generally appears to have been affected primarily by the forces of nature, with the imprint of man's work substantially unnoticeable; (2) has outstanding opportunities for solitude or a primitive and unconfined type of recreation; (3) has at least five thousand acres of land or is of sufficient size as to make practicable its preservation and use in an unimpaired condition; and (4) may also contain ecological, geological, or other features of scientific, scenic, or historical value. (Wilderness Act of 1964, §1131(c))

This definition is largely directed towards qualifying wilderness for legal and practical management purposes, but the first sentence importantly defines an *ideal* of wilderness in terms of a natural area that is untrammeled and not permanently occupied by people. Although this definition is from American public land law, many argue that it enshrines a "received wilderness idea" that is historically shaped from western notions of wilderness and, in turn, shapes much of the accepted notion of what wilderness is today (Callicott, in Callicott and Nelson 1998).

Max Oelschlaeger (1991, p. 28) argues that the rudimentary idea of wilderness, as we have come to understand it today, emerged during the agricultural transition to the Neolithic age (approximately 10,000–8,000 BCE) when people began to make a distinction between the "domestic" and the "wild," as applied to lands, animals, and plants. Prior to this, Oelschlaeger claims, Paleolithic humans had no antagonistic idea of wilderness because they were too much a part of nature to conceive of nature as wilderness apart from themselves. Much later, biblical and European attitudes toward the idea of nature as pristine wilderness ranged from worship to hatred. In his classic *Wilderness and the American Mind*, Roderick Nash (1982) claims that wilderness in early Judeo-Christian thought was understood as a place of evil to be feared and conquered. The contemporary term "wilderness" can be traced back to the Old English term "wildeornes," meaning uncultivated or wild land inhabited by wild animals and uninhabited by people. Nash (ibid, pp. 8–43) claims that it was this meaning of wilderness that was in play when the first Europeans arrived in the new world of America and found themselves in a "condition of wilderness," empty of civilization and populated only by wild beasts and "savage men" (Native American Indians). The rest of Nash's story is well known. Hostility toward this wild land, manifest destiny, and drive for economic gain led to the conquest of wilderness and its transformation into pastoral and urban civilization until, by the late nineteenth and early twentieth century, so little wilderness remained that Americans began to romanticize it and see it as something good that should be preserved (ibid, pp. 44–83, 96–121, 200–37). Today, rather than putting up fences to cultivate wilderness and bring it under human control, Americans fence off their remaining wilderness areas to prevent themselves from harming it.

The ideal of wilderness as untrammeled, uninhabited land that should be preserved is now embodied in more than 600 federal, legally designated wilderness areas in the United States that comprise 4.5 percent of the land mass of the 50 American states. The American model of wilderness preservation has been exported to Canada, Australia, New Zealand, South Africa, and Zimbabwe (Hendee et al. 1990, pp. 45–90). The World Wilderness Congress exists as an international organization devoted to wilderness preservation all over the planet, and a wide variety of legal and political means are used to designate various land classification schemes for wilderness-type areas (some suggest thinking of biosphere reserves as international wilderness areas (ibid, pp. 54–5)).

These wilderness preservation efforts accord well with some of the early work done in environmental ethics in the 1970s and 1980s. Environmental ethicists rearticulated calls for wilderness preservation that were made by early wilderness champions such as Henry David Thoreau, John Muir, Theodore Roosevelt, Robert Marshall, Aldo Leopold, Sigurd Olson, and David Brower, who appealed to the primal, aesthetic, spiritual, recreational, symbolic, and scientific values wilderness held for people (see NINETEENTH- AND TWENTIETH-CENTURY PHILOSOPHY, THE LAND ETHIC). Traditional ethical theories were reinterpreted as ascribing instrumental values to wilderness, and various arguments were advanced to justify wilderness preservation (Nelson, in Callicott and Nelson 1998; Sessions 1992). Wilderness also figured prominently in non-anthropocentric environmental ethics. Paul Taylor's (1986) biocentric theory of environmental ethics was directed toward wild animals and plants that existed as natural species-populations independent of human control or intrusion. Holmes Rolston's (1988) ecocentric theory of environmental ethics found its fullest expression in wilderness ecosystems that existed largely apart from human culture. Robert Elliot's defense of the value-adding property of naturalness (originally published in 1982; see Elliot 1997) relied upon the significance of wilderness's causal continuity with its non-human past (see NORMATIVE ETHICS).

Let us return to the North Dakota Badlands and the questions about wilderness I raised above as a way of summarizing the received idea of wilderness. First, why should wilderness be protected? When we look at the two already existing and the eleven proposed wilderness areas in the Badlands, we can articulate a number of different reasons that might answer this question. Many visitors are struck by the area's beauty; some claim to have had intense spiritual experiences or to have found God there; hikers, horseback riders, backpackers, hunters, and canoeists find opportunities for a "primitive and unconfined type of recreation"; and many North Dakotans feel a sense of pride knowing that some of the state's most rugged lands still exist in a pristine condition. Protecting wilderness in the Badlands protects native animals and plants that have disappeared elsewhere in the state, and unique biotic communities and ecosystems found nowhere else in the state exist in a wilderness condition. Second, in what does the value of wilderness consist? Those who take an objectivist approach (see META-ETHICS) might claim that it can be found in the flora and fauna of the Badlands or in the region's biotic and ecological assemblages, while those who take a subjectivist approach might claim that it is associated with the unique wilderness experiences one can have there. Third, how should wilderness be protected? In the case of the Badlands, wilderness proponents argue that all the remaining de facto wilderness areas (existing wilderness areas that do not yet have formal legal status as protected areas) should be given federal protection as legally designated wilderness areas where human impacts, motorized travel, and permanent human habitation is banned. Finally, what is wilderness? In the Badlands, wilderness may be defined as untrammeled, uninhabited, pristine areas that have been affected primarily by natural, non-human forces.

This happy picture of untrammeled wilderness in the Badlands is in trouble. While legislators argue about the need for more wilderness, the amount of de facto wilderness that exists in the Badlands continues to shrink due to human impacts. The two existing wilderness areas may be too small to support viable populations of some of their resident species, and both are impacted by anthropogenic impacts ranging from oil wells on their borders to the specter of global CLIMATE change. Further, the received idea of wilderness that gives meaning to wilderness preservation in the Badlands also is in trouble. Five main anti-wilderness arguments may be identified.

The ecological argument

I shall call the first argument the "ecological argument against wilderness preservation." When we preserve wilderness somewhere such as in the Badlands, what precisely is it that we preserve? Although one of the central reasons that seems to justify wilderness preservation is the creation and preservation of opportunities for distinctive wilderness experiences for people, it seems difficult to claim that wilderness preservation is aimed primarily at preserving these experiences. Rather, what is it in wilderness that is preserved across time that in turn provides opportunities for the wilderness experiences of people? Individual organisms – this blacktail prairie dog, that golden eagle, this wild lily – come and go through migration and death. Species and populations of organisms change through evolution, extinction, and oscillations of their numbers. What about biotic communities and ecosystems that exist across time? Many have thought that wilderness preservation should be directed at preserving these kinds of holistic ecological assemblages and, more properly, at a general "balance of nature" as it exists in wilderness. However, three of the fundamental organizing models of modern ecological science that express this idea of balance – the organismic model, the community model, and the ecosystem model – are now in disrepute (Worster 1994). Ecologists tell us that nature exists in perpetual flux, where disturbances and stochastic changes are the norm and where any kind of stability or simple balance of nature is the exception (Botkin 1990). What then can be preserved in wilderness such as in the Badlands? What is the fixed referent for preservation? "Preservation" suggests that we protect something from disturbance and maintain it in a continuous state. Since this now seems contrary to what wilderness is, J. Baird Callicott (in Callicott and Nelson 1998) argues that wilderness preservation is paradoxical because it works against wilderness itself in order to keep it the same (see THE LAND ETHIC).

How might a wilderness advocate respond to the ecological argument? We should note that the argument relies upon the new science of disturbance ECOLOGY. Disturbance ecology is best characterized as a shift in attention away from stable equilibrium and simple balance in nature and toward disturbances and changes. Disturbances – thought to be the exception in nature – are now thought to be the norm. This does not mean, however, that "anything goes" in nature. Ecologists still tell us that organisms, species, and populations have functional, evolutionary, and historical limits that may be largely non-anthropogenic in origin (Pickett et al. 1992). Anthropogenic disturbances may or may not resemble non-anthropogenic disturbances. Insofar as anthropogenic disturbances do not, they can be deemed harmful to wilderness, and the protection of wilderness areas as natural areas meaningfully might include protection against unnatural disturbances and unnatural disturbance rates. Further, and perhaps equally problematic to the argument, many people acknowledge that past wilderness preservation efforts largely have been motivated and steered by value considerations independent of knowledge from ecological science (Callicott, in Callicott and Nelson 1998). The fact that most American wilderness areas have political boundaries that bear little correspondence to ecological boundaries bears witness to this. The new science of disturbance ecology is no obstacle to ecology playing a greater role in future wilderness protection efforts.

The conceptual argument

Protecting non-anthropogenic disturbances such as lightning-caused fires, natural colonization of new prairie dog towns, and flooding along the Little Missouri River in the Badlands presumes that we can make a meaningful distinction between what is anthropogenic and what is not. When we protect the top of the Big Plateau from anthropogenic impacts, we are protecting part of the Petrified Forest Wilderness Area as a place that fundamentally exists *apart* from people. If a tract of wilderness is developed or impacted by people, it may appear that we can no longer call it wilderness, as it now becomes a part of some human culture. Thus, in order to define wilderness as untrammeled, pristine nature, we must first presuppose that a firm boundary between it and us exists. What I shall call the "conceptual argument against the concept of wilderness" denies this. Because we as humans evolved from ancestors common to other species, Callicott (in Callicott and Nelson 1998) claims that wilderness perpetuates a pre-Darwinian myth that we exist apart from nature, and the concept of wilderness is grounded in a metaphysically untenable dualism between culture and nature. William Cronon (in Callicott and Nelson 1998) also is skeptical of the culture / nature distinction, and he claims that the concept of wilderness embodies a dualistic vision in which people are situated outside of nature. This vision is supposedly problematic, but the reasons why it is problematic are less than clear. Cronon vacillates between two different assertions. First, because the concept of wilderness (like any other concept) is socially or culturally constructed, it is problematic to say that it can refer to something – de facto wilderness – that exists beyond human culture. Second, because we exclude our human presence from the place of de facto wilderness, we cannot have a meaningful relationship with nature, and we deny our own naturalness. Both of these assertions seem to suggest that the concept of wilderness is flawed because it is defined as a place apart from us. The first (social constructivist) assertion leads to the conclusion that wilderness cannot be meaningfully defined apart from us, while the second (naturalistic) assertion leads to the conclusion that wilderness should not be meaningfully defined apart from us.

How might a wilderness advocate respond to the conceptual argument? Consider first Callicott's claim about the pre-Darwinian myth of wilderness. *Homo sapiens* may come from the same evolutionary lineage as other species, and from this evolutionary fact we might want to conclude that a sharp metaphysical distinction between the rest of nature and ourselves cannot be maintained. But rejecting a metaphysical distinction between wilderness and culture may not render a conceptual distinction completely meaningless. Just as there are some significant differences between coyotes and cottonwood trees below the Achenbach Hills in the Badlands, there also may be some significant differences between a lone backpacker and everything else below these hills. But what precisely are these differences, and why are they significant? Oelschlaeger (1991, p. 8) argues that we can only begin to understand ourselves in a positive sense as cultured, civilized beings by recognizing what we are not in a negative sense – wilderness. Kate Soper (1995, pp. 38–9) argues similarly that much of human discourse presupposes a distinction between ourselves and non-human nature as a precondition for the meaningful articulation of such discourse. Imagine, for example, the discourse of environmental philosophy (and many of the essays in this book) without some meaningful, distinct categories of "non-human nature" and "human culture." Like all other terms, "non-human nature" and "wilderness" have a cultural origin. But does this force us to conclude that they denote only cultural artifacts? Consider a bare bentonite clay slope I once traversed near Ekblom Spring in the Badlands. The creation of this slope – as far as anyone can tell – had nothing to do with people and human culture. Contrary to those who pose the conceptual argument, a wilderness advocate denies that the mere act of conceptualizing this slope as a (wilderness) slope turns it into a cultural artifact.

The no-wilderness argument

This bentonite clay slope may have been traversed by several hundred other hikers and backpackers since the creation of the Petrified Forest Wilderness Area in 1978. Prior to this, however, it may have been traversed by Paleo-Indians for thousands of years and, more recently, by Mandan, Crow, Cheyenne, Arikara, Gros Ventre, Assiniboin, Hidatsa, and Lakota Indians (as well as French fur trappers, British and Spanish explorers, European-American pioneers, the United States Army, and cattle ranchers, among others). If we define wilderness as untrammeled, unimpacted, uninhabited non-human nature (à la Wilderness Act of 1964 and the received view of wilderness), this slope may not count as such. In fact, as we step back and examine not just the Badlands but the entire North American continent, we are hard-pressed to find the condition of wilderness that Nash (1982) describes. As William Denevan (in Callicott and Nelson 1998) tells us, people have existed in North America for at least the past ten millennia. The original inhabitants lived and traveled virtually everywhere, built numerous structures, and actively managed many landscapes through such means as agriculture, hunting, and fires. Three to four million people inhabited what is now the United States and Canada in 1492. However, up to 90 percent of these people died, largely as a result of European-transported diseases, and by 1750 much of North America (excluding Mexico) beyond the eastern seaboard was devoid of people. Wilderness preservation efforts seem doomed because they ignore the historical fact that what we today preserve as wilderness has been impacted by people in the past. There is no such thing as de facto wilderness in North America, and all of our current wilderness areas as untrammeled wilderness are fake. I shall call this the "no-wilderness argument." It relies upon empirical evidence that people have impacted most of North America, and the argument can be made for virtually anywhere on the planet where we think that wilderness exists (perhaps barring Antarctica, which has remained unimpacted and uninhabited until only recently).

How might a wilderness advocate respond to the no-wilderness argument? Consider first the claim that all of North America was impacted by people prior to 1492. It's not clear that empirical evidence exists to support a claim of this magnitude. There certainly are many instances of Native American Indians modifying the landscapes of North America in the past, but how much impact did fewer than 4 million people have on a continent that currently supports more than 300 million Americans and Canadians? Native American Indians lacked much of the technology that exists today that can be employed on large scales to change entire landscapes. Although I lack the space here to discuss what we might call "traditional Native American Indian land conservation practices and environmental ethics," there is a growing body of evidence about pre-European contact peoples and their many and varied forms of land conservation. Just as the claim that all Native American Indians have been good land stewards is too broad, so the claim that Native American Indians highly impacted most or all of the North American continent and destroyed whatever wilderness condition it might have had also seems too broad. Second, and perhaps more telling against the no-wilderness argument, the empirical evidence about wilderness impacts is itself open to interpretation. If we define wilderness as "untrammeled nature," what counts as a trammeling? Does the mere fact that someone walked across Bullion Butte in the Badlands 300 years ago mean that Bullion Butte is forever trammeled? If we answer "yes" to this question, we are subscribing to what we might call a "purity" definition of wilderness: wilderness must be forever pure of human impacts to count as wilderness. It's not clear, however, that a purity definition of wilderness is viable, because it might rest upon an equivocation between a "trammeling" and an "impact." To trammel something means to hinder it or to impede its free movement, as when we trammel an animal by confining it and breaking its spirit to roam. To trammel wilderness suggests redirecting and destroying natural processes and eradicating natural, wild nature to suit our preferences and interests or, in short, to control nature. In contrast, to impact nature suggests altering it in ways that may not destroy it or diminish its independence from us, as when someone simply walks across Bullion Butte. In light of this distinction, it's not clear that past impacts in what we now call wilderness count as telling trammelings against it. Consider also a third point. Can a condition of wilderness re-emerge from past trammelings? The answer is "no" if we follow a purity definition of wilderness. If, as I am suggesting, the purity definition of wilderness is problematic, then it seems possible for a wilderness condition to re-emerge over time, in spite of past trammelings. I have argued elsewhere that this forward-looking nature of wilderness protection is at least part of the intent behind federal wilderness preservation efforts in the United States (Woods, in Callicott and Nelson 1998).

The moral argument

Cronon (in Callicott and Nelson 1998) argues that the creation of the National Wilderness Preservation System in the United States was accomplished at the expense of the aboriginal, native inhabitants of North America. Beginning in the sixteenth century and continuing to this day, Native American Indians have been killed and removed from landscapes for a variety of reasons, one of which was to create empty landscapes that were "suitable" for wilderness designation. Because the killing and removal of Native American Indians was and is morally wrong, the concept of wilderness that necessitated such killing and removal to create wilderness areas also seems to be morally wrong. I shall call this the "moral argument against wilderness preservation."

How might a wilderness advocate respond to the moral argument? With few exceptions, the intent behind the killing and removal of Native American Indians was not to make way for wilderness areas. Rather, in almost all instances they were killed or removed to make way for railroads, mines, livestock grazing, homesteads, farms, timber operations, water developments, cities, and the like. The real culprit here seems to be development, industrialization, cultivation, and manifest destiny, not wilderness. Lakota Indians were removed from western North Dakota and the Badlands in the late nineteenth century not to make way for 13 wilderness areas but as a result of land-use patterns; social, political, and economic structures; and genocide. But while the moral argument as applied to most cases of wilderness preservation seems questionable, there are cases where it may be applicable. In 1957 the United States National Park Service stopped all Papago Indian farming at the oasis of A'al Waipia in what is now Organ Pipe National Monument in southern Arizona and later in 1962 destroyed all non-historic Papago structures to make way for the Organ Pipe Wilderness Area (Nabhan 1987, pp. 89–93). Beyond North America, Ramachandra Guha (in Callicott and Nelson 1998) cites a similar case in India, where people were removed and forbidden to utilize certain areas so as to create a network of wilderness-type parks – Project Tiger – to make way for tiger reserves. Cases such as these force wilderness advocates to acknowledge that wilderness preservation in practice can be morally problematic by pitting people against wilderness. Perhaps what is needed is a case-by-case approach for any given or proposed wilderness area to determine whether the moral argument is applicable or not.

The values argument

Our reasons for preserving wilderness, however, might be tainted with questionable values. Callicott and Guha (both in Callicott and Nelson 1998) each have criticized the concept of wilderness as being ethnocentric, claiming that it is a peculiarly western idea that has ignored the presence of aboriginal peoples. Cronon (in ibid) claims that early wilderness advocates typically were in privileged positions of economic, social, and political power (that is, many were middle- or upper-class white men); to the extent that we value wilderness today for the same reasons they did – for its aesthetic, religious/spiritual, recreational, and symbolic values, our valuing of wilderness is "tainted" with values of problematic origin. Some feminists argue (Plumwood, in ibid) that the concept of wilderness is flawed because it is built around eurocentric, androcentric, and anthropocentric values. Carl Talbot (in ibid) argues that wilderness and its preservation are flawed because they are grounded in a problematic logic of capitalism and capitalism's questionable values. Collectively I shall call such critiques the "values argument against wilderness preservation": wilderness preservation is problematic because historically it has been informed and justified with questionable values, and the preservation of wilderness today carries these same values. We often hear this argument when opponents argue against wilderness preservation on the ground that wilderness benefits only a small constituency – namely urban backpackers – that can actually "use" any given wilderness area. Oil industry workers in western North Dakota have made this very argument against the creation of the 11 proposed wilderness areas in the Badlands which, supposedly, will benefit only "yuppie" backpackers from Fargo and other more populated towns in the eastern part of the state.

If wilderness preservation is justified primarily by reference to what wilderness "users" do in wilderness, the values argument seems to be well supported. But wilderness protection can also be justified by reference to something distinctive about wilderness itself that helps give rise and expression to wilderness experiences and the values used to articulate them. Such a non-anthropocentric justification might serve as a counter to different critiques made against wilderness under the rubric of the values argument. And while the values argument importantly directs wilderness advocates to examine the values they hold about wilderness and its protection, critiques of wilderness that rely upon questioning historically traditional wilderness values at the expense of ignoring new values that wilderness might embody or represent risk committing a genetic fallacy with respect to values.

But what about the ethnocentric values associated with wilderness and its pre-servation? Certainly some of what has been written about wilderness is ethnocentric. Nash's *Wilderness and the American Mind* (1982) is a case in point, as Native American Indians are conspicuously absent from much of his account. Because non-European native inhabitants of North America are not seen by Nash as "civilized men," he effectively defines them away and subsumes them under the "wilderness condition" of pre-European North America.

What do non-westerners have to say about wilderness? While there are no blanket claims for what all Native American Indians say about wilderness, some tribes have designated wilderness areas within their own Indian Reservations, modeled mostly after the National Wilderness Preservation System in the United States. This desig-nated wilderness includes the Mission Mountain Tribal Wilderness in western Mon-tana, where the Salish and Kootenai have decreed that all people – including Salish and Kootenai people – within this wilderness are "visitors who do not remain." There is much more that needs to be heard from various Native American Indians about their many different world-views and attitudes toward wilderness, as well as much more from various aboriginal peoples all over the world (see INDIGENOUS PERSPECTIVES).

One could, perhaps, argue that Native American Indian tribes such as the Salish and Kootenai are themselves guilty of perpetuating the ethnocentricity of the wild-erness idea and should abandon their practice of wilderness preservation precisely because it is ethnocentric. It's not clear, however, that we should cease practicing something merely because it's ethnocentric. Western philosophy is ethnocentric, but a simplistic directive that we should stop practicing it just because of its ethnocen-tricity doesn't seem to follow. Problematic values such as ethnocentricity need not lead to the conclusion that wilderness preservation must be abandoned, but the values argument should direct wilderness advocates to begin to rethink the justifica-tion of wilderness preservation by appealing to less problematic values.

Concluding remarks

Even if the concept of wilderness and the practice of wilderness preservation can survive the ecological, conceptual, no-wilderness, moral and values arguments, other challenges still exist. I conclude by mentioning several important directions for future discussions about wilderness.

First, I want to suggest that two neglected values, naturalness and wildness, may lie at the heart of the case for wilderness preservation. Both of these values long have been associated with wilderness, but relatively little work has been done to explore what these values are, how they are related to wilderness, and how they might help ground a wilderness ethic. I argue elsewhere (Woods forthcoming) that what is natural has a non-cultural origin and causal continuity with other non-cultural origins (following Elliot 1997), and what is wild exists as an expression of more-than-human autonomy beyond anthropogenic controls; both naturalness and wildness can be articulated as value-adding properties. Both of these properties, when found together in wilderness, might help give meaning to what wilderness is and why it has value. Given the obvious etymological association between wilderness and wildness and the common articulation of wilderness as a natural area, this approach appears to be very promising.

Second, there is much I haven't addressed here about the "how" of wilderness protection. Nelson (1996) argues that current wilderness preservation efforts are doomed because the amount of de facto wilderness continues to shrink. In response, Reed Noss and Dave Foreman (both in Callicott and Nelson 1998) each argue that wilderness protection efforts should be proactive and aimed not merely at protecting existing wilderness but also at helping restore a wilderness condition to many landscapes.

Third, questions about how wilderness ought to be protected lead us straight back to questions about why wilderness ought to be protected. Some, such as Callicott (in Callicott and Nelson 1998), argue that wilderness protection should be aimed at the protection of native BIODIVERSITY and that wilderness areas should be reconceived in terms of biodiversity reserves. As more philosophical work is done in the area of biodiversity, wilderness advocates would do well to discuss the relationship between biodiversity and wilderness.

Fourth, I have raised some of the problems of the relationship between wilderness and people. On a planet with six billion people, a rapidly growing POPULATION, and more resource use and resulting pollution than ever, there are numerous questions that will have to be addressed about wilderness in the twenty-first century and beyond. I cannot pretend to know what all of the questions are, but here are some that seem important: Should permanent human inhabitation of wilderness continue to be banned? When a culture or group has been oppressed and/or marginalized in the past, how should the value of their cultural survival be balanced with wilderness protection? Will our social, political, and economic problems overwhelm our concern for wilderness? How should we think of wilderness in light of global CLIMATE change?

Given persistent human impacts all over the planet, any wilderness that survives into the third millennium – however we define, value, or protect it – will survive precisely because we have chosen to allow it to survive. Places such as the Badlands of western North Dakota will directly reflect this choice.

References

Botkin, D. B. (1990) *Discordant Harmonies: A New Ecology for the Twenty-first Century* (Oxford: Oxford University Press). [While the ecologist Botkin remains sympathetic to wilderness protection, albeit with heavy-handed management, his critique of the ecological balance of nature has been used for the ecological argument against wilderness preservation.]

Callicott, J. B., and Nelson, M. P., eds. (1998) *The Great New Wilderness Debate* (Athens: University of Georgia Press). [This anthology is arguably the best single book on wilderness philosophy.]

Elliot, R. (1997) *Faking Nature: The Ethics of Environmental Restoration* (London: Routledge). [In this summary of some of his earlier work, Elliot discusses intrinsic value, ecological restoration, and the value of naturalness.]

Hendee, J. C., Stankey, G. H., and Lucas, R. C. (1990) *Wilderness Management*, 2nd edn (Golden: Fulcrum Publishing). [This "Bible" of wilderness management is an important primer for understanding the federal management of American wilderness areas.]

Nabhan, G. P. (1987) *The Desert Smells Like Rain: A Naturalist in Papago Indian Country* (San Francisco: North Point Press). [Nabhan's ethnographical account of some of his experiences with Papago Indians is a good example of some of the recent monographs written about Native American Indians and their varied relationships to nature.]

Nash, R. (1982) *Wilderness and the American Mind*, 3rd edn (New Haven: Yale University Press). [Although problematically ethnocentric, Nash's history of American wilderness is considered by many to be the definitive history of wilderness in the United States.]

Nelson, M. P. (1996) "Rethinking wilderness: the need for a new idea of wilderness," *Philosophy in the Contemporary World* 3, pp. 6–9. [In this mostly critical discussion of wilderness, Nelson succinctly raises five anti-wilderness arguments.]

Oelschlaeger, M. (1991) *The Idea of Wilderness: From Prehistory to the Age of Ecology* (New Haven: Yale University Press). [In one of the few books about wilderness written by an environmental philosopher, Oelschlaeger discusses some of the history of the idea of wilderness from the Paleolithic age to contemporary wilderness philosophy and develops a postmodern account of wilderness.]

Pickett, S. T. A., Parker, V. T., and Fiedler, P. L. (1992) "The new paradigm in ecology: implications for conservation above the species level," in *Conservation Biology: The Theory and Practice of Nature Conservation, Preservation, and Management*, ed. P. L. Fiedler and S. K. Jain (New York: Chapman and Hall). [Pickett, Parker, and Fiedler succinctly discuss the new science of disturbance ecology and offer a rejoinder to the ecological argument against wilderness preservation.]

Rolston III, H. (1988) *Environmental Ethics: Duties to and Values in the Natural World* (Philadelphia: Temple University Press). [One of Rolston's most extensive discussions of values in nature.]

Sessions, G. (1992) "Ecocentrism, wilderness, and global ecosystem protection," in *The Wilderness Condition: Essays on Environment and Civilization*, ed. M. Oelschlaeger (San Francisco: Sierra Club Books). [Sessions catalogues a number of wilderness preservation arguments, discusses zoning the planet for wilderness preservation, and presents a deep ecology position on wilderness.]

Soper, K. (1995) *What is Nature? Culture, Politics, and the Non-Human* (Oxford: Blackwell). [Soper discusses some of the contested politics of nature and argues for a position that is situated between realist and social constructivist views of nature.]

Taylor, P. W. (1986) *Respect for Nature: A Theory of Environmental Ethics* (Princeton: Princeton University Press). [A theory of environmental ethics grounded in respecting the inherent worth of wild animals and plants conceived of as teleological centers of life with goods of their own.]

Woods, M. (forthcoming) *Rethinking Wilderness* (Broadview Press). [Woods articulates responses to the ecological, conceptual, no-wilderness, moral and other anti-wilderness arguments; discusses legal and scientific paradoxes of wilderness preservation; and argues for conceiving of wilderness in terms of the value-adding properties of naturalness, wildness, and freedom.]

Worster, D. (1994) *Nature's Economy: A History of Ecological Ideas*, 2nd edn (Cambridge: Cambridge University Press). [The definitive social history of ecology, tracing ecology from its conceptual origins in the eighteenth century to contemporary developments.]

25

Population

CLARK WOLF

How many people are there?

While people have been concerned about human population growth for thousands of years, the existence of what we would now consider large human populations is a relatively recent phenomenon: the human population of the earth did not reach the first billion until the early nineteenth century – long after the publication of Thomas Malthus's famous *Essay on the Principles of Population* in 1798. Population did not reach two billion until the early twentieth century (between 1925 and 1935). The third, fourth, and fifth billions arrived around 1960, 1975, and 1990 respectively, the sixth arriving with the new millennium.

Most estimates put the current (turn of the century) human population of the earth quite near 6 billion. The present rate of population growth, however, is between 1.6 and 1.7 percent per year. If that rate of growth were to remain stable, we would expect an additional billion people in about ten years, and would expect the current population to double in size in less than fifty years. However, while most demographers expect population size to continue to grow well into the twenty-first century, many also predict that the *rate* of growth will decline during the next twenty years, and that world population may even stabilize at some time during the mid-twenty-first century. There is little agreement, however, about what mechanism is likely to cause the rate of growth to diminish, or about the population levels that may be achieved before we reach stability or decline in total population size. Some argue that human population is likely to keep growing until environmental destruction and consequent resource scarcity causes widespread famine, bringing the death rate high enough to compensate for the birth rate. Others more hopefully propose that fertility rates may fall as economic and human development give people (and especially women) more control over their reproductive lives.

Is the increase in human population a problem, and if so, what kind of problem is it? Concerns about population growth usually identify the problem in one of two ways: first, human population growth may imply proliferation of destitution and misery for present and future generations of human beings. Some theorists have argued that population increase will go hand in hand with increasing poverty, since there will be less of everything to go around. But those who find this view untenable may still have a (second) good reason to be concerned, since the growing human population may unsustainably exploit resources and destroy the earth's great ecosystems. There is a third important reason why population growth and high human fertility should be regarded as a serious problem: the high fertility rates that lead to rapid population growth impose inordinate personal costs and an unacceptably high risk of death on women in their reproductive years.

Important elements of the current population debate were first articulated in an exchange between the Marquis de Condorcet and Thomas Malthus at the end of the eighteenth century. I begin by exploring the main themes in this exchange, tracing the influence of this classical debate in contemporary theories of population, and examining the role these theories play in development economics, including consideration of the policy implications of contemporary theories. Next I discuss paradoxes that arise when we try to use common normative criteria to evaluate potential changes in population. Finally, I consider the significance of population growth for environmental philosophy and policy.

Classic discussions of population: Condorcet and Malthus

In 1793, Antoine-Nicolas, Marquis de Condorcet argued that the advancement of science and knowledge will lead to the continued improvement of human institutions, and that the human condition will approach perfection as our knowledge increases. Even the length of human life, claimed Condorcet, may be expected to approach infinity as knowledge of medical science becomes more perfect. Since increasing population size poses a potential threat to improvement, he considered the likelihood that the number of people in the world might eventually exceed the means of subsistence, and that this might lead either to "a continual diminution of happiness and population," or alternately to "an oscillation between good and bad" which would be "a perennial source of more or less periodic disaster." This problem, argued Condorcet, will be solved once

> the absurd prejudices of superstition will have ceased to corrupt and degrade the moral code by its harsh doctrines instead of purifying and elevating it. We can assume that by then men will know that if they have a duty towards those who are not yet born, it is not to give them existence but to give them happiness; their aim should be to promote the general welfare of the human race or of the society in which they live or of the family to which they belong, rather than foolishly to encumber the earth with useless and wretched beings. (Condorcet 1955 [1793], p. 189)

It is usually assumed (for example by Malthus) that by "the absurd prejudices of superstition," Condorcet meant to refer to puritanical attitudes toward the use of birth control. It is clear enough that this was at least part of his intent. But in the context of the *Sketch*, it is plausible to read him as meaning more than this: Condorcet believed that the progressive improvement of knowledge and human institutions, including especially the recognition of fully equal rights for women, would lead people to have greater control over their lives generally. Voluntary fertility reduction would, he believed, be a natural consequence of these improvements. It is because of this broader project that Condorcet is usually associated with the view that fertility reduction will naturally follow from human development and improvement in the conditions of life.

It was largely in response to Condorcet's *Sketch* that Thomas Malthus wrote the first edition of his *Essay on the Principles of Population* (1798). In this work (usually called the *First Essay*) Malthus argues that human population will increase geometrically until checked by some countervailing force, while the "means for subsistence" can be expected to increase only arithmetically. Because of this, the size of the human population will grow until it eventually reaches a plateau when the earth's capacity to meet needs has been stretched to its extreme limit. At this point, it will stabilize as starvation causes the death rate to rise to the level of the fertility rate. If the means of subsistence increase (due, perhaps, to colonization of new territories or increase in productive efficiency) population will again rise to a new famine equilibrium. Malthus recognized two categories of check on population growth: "positive checks" are causes of increased mortality, while "preventive checks" are the causes of decreased fertility. Elsewhere in the *First Essay*, he argues that these checks, both positive and preventive, "may be fairly resolved into misery and vice." When starvation, disease, or war increase the death rate, population is checked by misery. Of the other category, he remarks that "Promiscuous intercourse, unnatural passions, violations of the marriage bed, and improper arts to conceal the consequences of irregular connections are preventive checks that clearly come under the head of vice" (Malthus, 1989 [1803], p. 18).

Puritanical Malthus was shocked by Condorcet's suggestion that birth control would allow people to gain more rational control over their reproductive lives. But in later editions of the *Essay* he added "moral restraint" as a third category of preventive check, if people can acquire the moral fortitude to abstain from marriage and from "irregular gratifications." Still, Malthus seems to have regarded this last check as much too weak to counteract the forces leading to rapid population growth. So population should be expected to rise to the level permitted by the availability of "means of subsistence," at which point "misery and vice" will bring this growth to a stop. Even then, "misery" will be the most prevalent check on population growth, since "vice" is not very effective as a means of fertility reduction while starvation and deprivation can be cruelly efficient causes of increased mortality.

While this analysis was already quite bleak enough, it was his prescriptions for policy that brought Malthus undeserved notoriety as a gloomy misanthrope. He saw efforts to ameliorate poverty as doomed to ultimate failure since they must ultimately cause an increase in population and a consequent increase in misery and suffering. Improving the conditions of life for the poor, he argued in the *First Essay*, simply facilitates faster rates of reproduction, leading to a new and more populous famine equilibrium at a later date. Malthus's views have often been dismissed as "cruel," but his express aim was to describe policies that would minimize human misery. It can hardly be acceptable simply to argue that such a view is cruel: it must be shown that there are alternative policies that are likely to do better. While contemporary theorists have improved upon Malthus's analysis, key elements of his theory have yet to be disconfirmed.

The contemporary debate: population, development, and the environment

The Malthusian view of the population problem is still prevalent in popular discussions of population, and many still see the Condorcet–Malthus exchange as having set out the essential elements of the current debate. Two fundamental features of Malthus's analysis are carried on in contemporary discussion: the Malthusian view that resource availability sets limits to growth is carried on in the contemporary notion of a "carrying capacity" for the earth. And Malthus's insight that fertility should be analyzed in terms of the factors that influence individual decision-making is carried on in economic models of fertility. While Condorcet's enlightenment optimism has few contemporary adherents, an important insight of his analysis has been resurrected in recent work on population and development: as Condorcet implies, the best way to reduce fertility may well be to improve the circumstances of life for the poor and to work to guarantee equal opportunities for women. Environmental philosophers should pay particular attention to this insight, since it implies that human development must be a centerpiece of any effective plan for global environmental protection.

Carrying capacity

The concept of "carrying capacity" was developed by ecologists, who have used it to refer to the Malthusian notion of an upper limit on population size set by the availability of resources. One way to estimate the carrying capacity of an environment is as follows: first estimate the quantity of renewable resource necessary to support an individual organism (whether human or non-human). Then estimate the total quantity of renewable resources available. The carrying capacity of this environment is determined by dividing the total quantity of renewable resources by the quantity needed to support an individual organism.

So understood, the carrying capacity of an environment represents the maximum population level that can possibly be held stable over time. However, this possibility is only theoretical, not practical: once carrying capacity is reached, it can be held stable only if each organism consumes just barely enough to stay alive. Since such perfectly egalitarian distribution is as unlikely in non-human populations as it is in human populations, it is not practically possible to hold the carrying capacity maximum as a stable equilibrium. It would be far better for each organism if population could stabilize far below the carrying capacity limit. However, on this conception, environmental carrying capacity can even be *exceeded* for limited periods of time, while non-renewable resources are used up, or when renewable resources are consumed faster than they can be renewed. Such over-exploitation is bound to be followed by a "crash," during which resource scarcity and consequent increased mortality (Malthus's "misery") will reduce population to a level that can be supported. The dynamics of population growth and decline can be represented by a "flow chart" such as that given in Figure 25.1. Some, like the biologist Garrett Hardin (1993), continue to make the case for the Malthusian view by applying the notion of a carrying capacity to the human population of the earth.

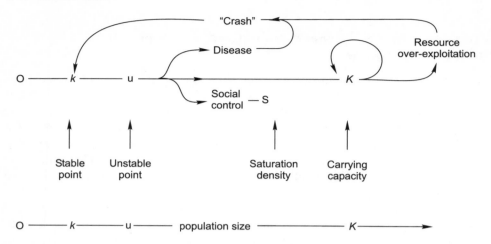

Figure 25.1 Carrying capacity understood in the context of population dynamics: "As population size increases from left to right, the population may reach one of two equilibria; k is the population size set by predation, while K is set by resources. Social control might cause a stable population to be maintained below K. Resource over-exploitation or disease might cause a population crash."

Source: Ron Pulliam and Nick Haddad, 1994, "Human Population Growth and the Carrying Capacity Concept." *Bulletin of the Ecological Society of America* 75 (1994)

But this conception of environmental carrying capacity was originally developed for demographic analysis of *animal* populations, and may not be easily applied to human populations. One reason for this is the ambiguity of the term "resource." Resources are not homogeneous, as the account above suggests, and in important respects resource availability is a function of technology. In particular, resource availability can vary when new technologies increase or decrease productive efficiency. Fertilizers can increase crop yields, shifts to reliance on new sources of energy may change energy needs, and improved communications systems may reduce travel needs. With technological change, we may be able to find substitutes for resources on which we now rely. For these reasons, the "human carrying capacity of the earth" is not a fixed quantity as the model above implies: carrying capacity varies with technology and with changes in productive efficiency (see ECONOMICS, CONSUMPTION).

Contemporary technological optimists rival Condorcet in their confidence that reason and human creativity will enable us to increase the carrying capacity of the earth so that shortages will not be a significant problem for the much larger human populations to come. Such considerations have led some to reject the notion of a "carrying capacity" altogether, since people themselves may be considered a resource for others. On this view, resources necessarily increase as populations grow, and the notion that resource scarcity could result from population growth becomes unthinkable. A moderate version of this view is reflected in ex-US President George Bush's observation that "Population growth itself is a neutral phenomenon... every human being represents hands to work, and not just another mouth to feed" (quoted in Cohen 1995, p. 38). A more extreme version is found in the work of the economist Julian Simon, who, like Condorcet before him, follows this technological optimism to its logical extreme: since human creativity is an "infinite" capacity, the set of resources available to human beings must itself be infinite. Applied to an infinite resource base, the account of "carrying capacity" given above implies that population may also grow infinitely. Population growth, urges Simon (1996), should not be inhibited. It should be encouraged.

While this optimistic view is often dismissed out of hand by economists and environmentalists, it is not all wrong, and it continues to have great influence in discussions of population. Simon is right to point out that the term "resource" is ambiguous, and that the earth's "carrying capacity" may increase (or decrease) with technological change. The ecological conception of carrying capacity, so useful in its application to animal species, may not neatly describe the demographic behavior of our own species. But neither creativity nor resources are "infinite" in the sense implied by Simon, and it would be premature to conclude that the carrying capacity concept is irrelevant for the analysis of human populations. For example, there is evidence that when fertility is higher, fewer resources are spent on education and nutrition for each child (Nancy Birdsall, in Lindahl-Kiessling and Landberg 1994, p. 178). If creative innovation requires education and resources, then there is reason to believe that per capita productivity may decrease as fertility and population size increase, as J. S. Mill (1806–73) predicted long ago: "It is vain to say that all mouths which the increase of mankind brings into existence bring with them hands. The new mouths require as much food as the old ones, and the hands do not produce as much" (J. S. Mill, *Principles of Political Economy*, Book 1, ch. XIII).

Beyond these internal problems with the optimistic view, there are external problems as well. Some "resources" are indispensable, and it is unlikely that technology will provide adequate substitutes (breathable air, for example). Others are valued in themselves, independently of their contribution to human well-being (ecosystems and wildlands). Their loss could not be compensated by replacement technologies, and we may have good reason to preserve and protect them independently of their contribution to human well-being. Even if the needs of an enormous human population could somehow be met without the earth's great natural systems, we would still have good reason to prevent environmental destruction (see NORMATIVE ETHICS).

The concept of carrying capacity will require revisions before it can be neatly applied to human populations. Still, those who are unconvinced by Condorcet's case for the infinite prospects for human reason and the perfectibility of the human condition will recognize that human and environmental limitations do ultimately impose upper limits on human population size, as Malthus recognized. For these reasons, it is quite clear that the concept of carrying capacity has continued relevance to issues concerning human population growth, and that it will be valuable to develop a conception of "carrying capacity" that is more readily applicable to human populations (Cohen 1995).

Focus on individual fertility decisions

A second Malthusian insight that retains considerable influence in contemporary discussions of population is that demographic change should be studied with an eye to the determinants of individual fertility decisions. While Malthus himself spent large portions of his later work investigating the factors that influence people's individual reproductive choices, Gary Becker and H. G. Lewis (1976) may be credited as the first to develop this Malthusian insight into a full theory by representing reproductive choice using the tools of microeconomic analysis. Becker and Lewis represent children as "consumer goods," and hypothesize that parents will "consume children" at efficient rates (that is, they will have an "efficient" number of them) balancing "quantity," the number of children they will have, against "quality," reflected in the resources they will be able to provide for their children. They assume that children who are provided with more resources will be "better children," and more satisfying to their parents. On these assumptions, it is possible to show that rational parents will make "optimal" choices, likely to benefit children and parents alike.

In spite of its virtues, the Becker–Lewis model does not provide any analysis of the criteria parents use in evaluating the "quality" of their children. They assume that the benefits children provide for their parents are primarily the "psychic benefits" of seeing their children prosper. This may reflect fertility choices in developed countries like the United States, but it leaves out a crucial fertility motive operant in developing countries, where children provide the primary means for old-age security. The difference matters a great deal, for if parents' concerns are primarily self-regarding (desire to have children who can and will support parents in old age), they will make quite different decisions from what they would if their concerns were altruistic (desire to see children prosper). The extent to which parents' rational decisions will reflect the interests of their children may thus be contingent on childhood mortality rates, on the likelihood that children will support their elderly parents, and on the existence of alternate means of economic security for the elderly. In less developed countries, where childhood mortality is high, where cultural norms assign children weighty obligations to care for their parents, and where there are no effective institutions providing support for older people, it may be rational for parents to have as many children as possible in order to maximize the likelihood that they will have children to care for them in old age. On the other hand, in developed countries where childhood mortality is low, where children do not generally bear financial responsibility for their parent's well-being, and where many people prepare financially for their retirement, parental choices may reflect the interests of children as suggested by Becker and Lewis.

The most helpful insight to come from this model of reproductive choice is that parents' reproductive decisions may be influenced by increasing the opportunity cost of fertility. The opportunity costs of a choice are measured by the value of the options one sets aside in making it. So the opportunity costs of fertility are measured by the value of the opportunities parents will be unable to use if they have additional children. The income that might have been gained if parents were wage-earners rather than child-caretakers is only one kind of opportunity cost of fertility. While programs such as China's one-child policy raise the direct costs of fertility by punishing parents and children alike, alternatives that provide parents with employment and social security improve their welfare, thus increasing the opportunity cost of fertility. When these opportunity costs are high, it is far more likely that parents will make reproductive choices with the welfare of their prospective children in mind. In such circumstances, it is far more likely that parents will choose to have fewer children and to provide each with a better start in life.

Among the most effective means for increasing the opportunity cost of fertility are the improvement of educational and employment opportunities for women, promotion of women's autonomy, and elimination of sexist barriers to equal opportunity. These means are desirable for their own sakes as well as for their implications for population. High fertility rates impose excessive burdens on women, including high mortality rates due to the stresses of pregnancy and childbirth as well as the labor involved in childcare. In most developing countries, maternal mortality is the largest single cause of death for women in their reproductive years: the maternal mortality rate in some areas in sub-Saharan Africa is as high as one in fifty. Since women in these areas typically have seven or more children during their reproductive years, the chance for each woman that she will not survive those years is about one in six. Partha Dasgupta grimly remarks that the reproductive cycle in this woman's life involves her "playing Russian roulette" (Partha Dasgupta, in Graham-Smith 1994, p. 157). This tragic state of affairs has hopeful implications for fertility policy, since fertility rates tend to fall toward stable levels when women have better opportunities for education and employment, access to effective birth control, and more autonomous control over their reproductive lives.

Here, Condorcet's hopeful analysis seems to have been correct: as he suggested, the best way to implement policies for fertility reduction may be to improve the conditions of life for the worst off members of society, and to work toward social and economic equality for women. Malthus was wrong to think that fertility will always increase when people are better off. Development theorists have taken Condorcet's hypothesis seriously, and have confirmed the causal connections among the problems of social inequality, poverty, women's rights, fertility, and environmental degradation. High fertility rates typically exacerbate poverty and social inequalities since fertility is strongly linked to affluence and class differences. In some developing countries, the fertility rate of the poor is twice that of the wealthy. Combined with data showing that fewer resources are used to provide for children in large families, this statistic reflects exacerbation of both poverty and social inequality, which in turn contribute to increased rates of environmental destruction. The popular slogan "Development is the best contraceptive" expresses Condorcet's optimism that this cycle may be broken by policies that improve the conditions of life for women and for the poor. Since we have good independent reasons for pursuing development efforts of this kind, this is a hopeful conclusion.

Fertility and development

The success or failure of this conclusion depends, however, on the nature of the development process. Economist Simon Kuznets famously hypothesized that initial income inequalities resulting from early stages of economic development should gradually level out as the benefits of economic prosperity are more broadly distributed. Frank Notestein proposed a corresponding hypothesis that fertility rates in developing countries will initially spike upwards, but that they too should level off or even decline as the changes due to economic development lead couples to choose smaller families. This second hypothesis (the "Notestein Demographic Transition Hypothesis") is based on the assumption that effective economic development will raise the opportunity costs of having children, since children will be selected among a broader range of desirable alternatives. Economic development is also supposed to diminish the motive to have children as protection for old-age security, as social institutions provide alternate means for protection of well-being in old age.

But like many efforts in "ideal theory," these optimistic economic hypotheses seem to apply poorly to the real world. As Lester Brown notes, many developing countries seem trapped in the second stage where fertility spikes upward, but are "unable to achieve the economic and social gains that are counted upon to reduce births" (Brown et al. 1987, p. 20). Perhaps it is the failure of Kuznets's hypothesis that explains the failure of Notestein's Demographic Transition Hypothesis: fertility rates do not fall in the poor sectors of the population, because the purported benefits of economic development are often not distributed widely within the population, and because economic development often increases social inequalities instead of alleviating them, when a powerful minority manages to reap the economic benefits.

What explains the frequent failure of Kuznets's hypothesis? No single explanation may apply in all cases where development has failed to improve the welfare of the poor. But there may be institutional barriers that were not adequately taken into account by optimistic development theorists: it is often in the interest of those who become wealthy in the early stages of the development process to do what they can to prevent the benefits of economic prosperity from being more widely distributed. In many cases, high profit margins and low production costs depend on the existence of a large and impoverished labor force. Furthermore, those who have an economic interest in perpetuating social and economic inequalities are often the same people who have power over social institutions, and can effectively put in place barriers that retard or prevent a broader distribution of development benefits. Thus we might expect to see the prosperous and the powerful working to thwart efforts to improve general welfare, and resisting efforts to more widely distribute democratic control of political institutions. When economic development does not bring the expected benefits for an impoverished majority, fertility and maternal mortality rates should not be expected to fall. Increasingly large and densely packed human populations in turn lead to increasing rates of environmental exploitation and destruction. This may explain much of what we see when we look at the developing world.

Unless development improves the lives of the poor, it is unlikely to have desirable effects on human fertility or population growth, nor is it likely to decrease the rate of environmental destruction. These considerations suggest an alternative model for development, quite different from the "top-down," large-scale industrial strategy that has traditionally been favored by organizations like the World Bank and the International Monetary Fund. Development projects that import large industries into developing regions rarely reduce social inequality, since the benefits may not "trickle down" to those who need them most. Such "development" sometimes makes the poor even worse off, since it can be highly destructive to traditional small-scale economies and ways of life. An alternative "bottom-up" approach would focus on improving the opportunities of the poor instead of focusing on industrial growth or increasing GNP.

If human development is sacrificed to economic development, fertility levels are unlikely to decrease.

Policies aimed specifically at population control have often been repressive, and have had high social costs. Amartya Sen (1994) distinguishes between "Collaboration" and "Override" as alternative strategies for addressing the population problem: the former changes fertility incentives by increasing opportunities, while the latter operates by limiting people's ability to make their own choices or by punishing those who have more children than policies permit. China's aggressive efforts to control population by imposing punitive sanctions on couples who exceed their quota of children is a prime example of a coercive strategy. Not only do such strategies penalize parents and their children, they are also likely to be less effective in the long run: when population policies are repressive, it is in each person's interest to attempt to skirt them and to avoid their effects and costs. In societies marked by traditional sexism, the costs of coercive policies are likely to fall most heavily on women. In China, this is reflected in the marked rise in female mortality rates following the imposition of family quotas. But when population policies endeavor to provide people with incentives and opportunities, to raise the opportunity cost of fertility, then lower fertility becomes individually rational. Three kinds of collaborative measure for fertility reduction are most clearly implied by this strategy of increasing the opportunity costs of fertility:

1. Efforts to expand women's educational opportunities are likely to have the effect of lowering fertility. Such access will not only improve women's employment prospects, but will also result in later marriage and reproduction so that each is likely to have fewer children overall.
2. Efforts to provide women with employment opportunities can have a similar effect: when women are prohibited from work, as they have traditionally been in much of the world, the opportunity costs of fertility are extremely low. Generally increased economic opportunity for both women and men will increase the opportunity cost of children, but since women have suffered radically diminished opportunities in every culture and every country in the world, and since women are still the primary caretakers for children worldwide, it is especially important to expand opportunities for women (see ECOFEMINISM).
3. Since the need for old-age security is a prime incentive to have children in most developing countries, institutions that increase the economic security of the elderly remove an important destructive incentive to have children. The motive to have children to provide for one's old age is destructive in the sense that it passes costs on to the succeeding generation, whose interests are not adequately represented in the decisions of their parents. There is empirical evidence that old-age pension and effective social security systems do indeed reduce fertility.

The account of the population problem given here has not emphasized the distribution of contraceptives as a means for population control, but of course the availability of contraceptives can be crucial for people's autonomous control over their reproductive lives. Where policies aimed at human development are accompanied by increased access to contraceptives, they will be more effective. But when efforts to control population growth focus on the distribution of contraceptives at the expense of attention to human development, they are unlikely to be effective, and are likely to be viewed with skepticism by those they are intended to help.

Population and moral theory

While population is a pressing practical problem, the articulation of sensible aims for population policy also raises serious theoretical difficulties: all contemporary moral theories and economic theories of social choice have paradoxical implications when they are used to evaluate population change or to compare prospective future populations. While these are problems for all moral theories, they can be most clearly presented as difficulties for utilitarianism.

In the context of population theory, it becomes necessary to distinguish between total and average versions of the utilitarian doctrine: according to total utilitarianism, the total surplus of happiness over misery should be as high as possible. To find this total, we simply add the utility levels of everyone together in one aggregate value. According to average utilitarianism, the average surplus of happiness over misery should be as high as possible. To find the average utility level, the total level is simply divided by the number of persons. Both versions of utilitarianism face daunting problems: total utilitarianism would force us to accept the "Repugnant Conclusion" that for any finite population of people who are all very well off, there is some much larger population of people all of whom have lives that are scarcely worth living, such that the latter is better than the former because the sum total of utility is greater (Parfit 1984, ch. 17). The average view implies that it would be wrong to have a child whose welfare level would be below the average level, no matter how high the average welfare level happens to be. On this view, the better off others are, the less likely it will be that having a child would be morally permissible. While many find these implications implausible, there is little agreement on how moral theories and economic theories of social choice should compare different prospective populations.

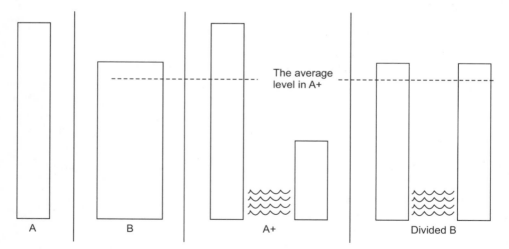

Figure 25.2 Parfit's "Mere-addition paradox."
Source: Derek Parfit, *Reasons and Persons* (Oxford: Oxford University Press, 1984.

The mere-addition paradox

One of the most perplexing of Parfit's paradoxes is the "mere-addition" paradox. (Parfit, 1984, ch. 19) The paradox arises in the comparison of the alternative populations represented in Figure 25.2. The width of the rectangles represents the number of people who exist, while height represents their level of well-being. Parfit stipulates that in A+ and Divided B an uncrossable sea separates two groups, whose numbers and levels of well-being are represented separately. One way to generate the paradox is to compare these alternatives to one another as follows:

1) *B is worse than A.*

Argument: All members of B are worse off than any member of A. Any principle that rejects this claim will imply the repugnant conclusion that for any finite population of very well-off people, there is some larger population of people each of whom has a life barely worth living, such that this larger population is better than the former (Parfit 1984, p. 388). Since we have good reason to reject this repugnant conclusion, we have good reason to accept that B is worse than A.

2) *A+ is not worse than A.*

Argument: The only difference between A and A + is that in A+ there exist more people, all of whom have lives worth living. It is implausible to suppose that the *"mere addition"* of their relatively happy lives constitutes a net loss, or that they make the overall situation worse or less choiceworthy. While there is inequality in A+ that is not in A, this inequality does not reflect injustice, for the two societies in A+ are separate and both redistribution and exploitation are impossible. So the existence of this inequality does not make A + worse than A. But this implies that overall A + is not worse than A.

3) *Divided B is just as good as B.*

Argument: The only difference between Divided B and B is that in Divided B there are two separate communities. Everyone is equally well off, and the number of people is the same. This division is not morally relevant, so Divided B is as good as B.

4) *Divided B is better than A +.*

Argument: In Divided B, the average level of well being is greater than in A+. If we imagine a gradual transition from A+ to Divided B, we see that the gainers have gained more than the losers have lost, while everyone is still adequately provided for. Those who accept a Rawlsian difference principle may note that such a principle would also favor Divided B over A+, since the worst off persons in B are better off than the worst off in A+. Finally, if equality has value, or inequality disvalue, Divided B has more equality, and less inequality than A +.

As long as the "better than" relation follows standard rules of ordering, we should be able to make some inferences from these four propositions. For example:

5) *B is better than A +* (from propositions 3 and 4).

6) *B is not worse than A* (from propositions 5 and 2).

But proposition 6 contradicts proposition 1. Which of the moves above should be rejected? There is no broad agreement about how this question should be answered. Some conclude from this paradox that the "betterness" relation must be intransitive (Temkin 1987). Some urge that we should accept total utilitarianism, or a variant of the total view, and that we should swallow the Repugnant Conclusion (Ng 1989; Broome 1992). Some argue for a negative utilitarian view that focuses on minimization of misery rather than the maximization of well-being (Wolf 1997). None of these solutions is without problems of its own, and none has more than a minority of adherents. The debate on these problems will undoubtably continue among theorists for quite a long time.

Fortunately, these theoretical paradoxes do not pose difficulties for the practical problem of population as a question of social and environmental policy. We are not faced with a choice between a small future population of very well-off persons (like A) and a much larger alternative population of less well-off people (like B). The population effects of policies are only predictable in vague terms, but in the real world we can confidently predict that increasing rates of population growth and fertility will lead to increased poverty, environmental destruction, and human misery. We do not need to solve the paradoxes of population theory before taking what steps we can to avert these consequences. Nor do we need to solve these paradoxes before we can support collaborative policies designed to reduce fertility by improving educational and employment opportunities for women, and by working toward the alleviation of current poverty and social insecurity.

Population ethics and environmental philosophy

Environmental philosophers have not generally devoted great attention to the growth of human population, but it is clear that population growth is one of the most important environmental problems of our time. Unless human population growth can be slowed and stabilized, it is unlikely that efforts to reduce the rate of environmental destruction can be successful. Many environmentalists naively accept the Malthusian argument that human development will simply provide grist for human population explosions in poor, environmentally stressed parts of the world. Some feed the misanthropic image of environmentalists by proposing that we should control the population problem by letting people starve. But if the best way to reduce fertility is to encourage human development in poor countries, then this Malthusian strategy is unlikely to achieve the desired aims. This is an important and hopeful implication for several reasons: first, it implies that the best way to address the population problem is to pursue social goals such as human development and women's equality. These are goals that we already have sufficient independent reason to support. Second, it implies that environmentalists must also be concerned with issues of social justice and human development. If it is true that the growth of human population is among the greatest of all threats to the world's ecosystems, and that this problem can most effectively be addressed by policies that work toward human development and social justice, then environmentalists must focus on social justice if we hope to preserve the fragile natural systems of the earth (see ENVIRONMENTAL JUSTICE).

References

Becker, Gary and Lewis, H. G. (1976) "Interaction between the quantity and quality of children," in *The Economic Approach to Human Behavior*, Gary Becker (Chicago: University of Chicago Press). [This groundbreaking paper argues that fertility control will arise naturally as parents make rational trade-offs between the number of children they will have, and the benefits they will be able to provide for each child.]

Broome, John (1992) *Counting the Cost of Global Warming* (Cambridge: White Horse Press). [This book presents a clear account of the economic problems of population choice.]

Brown, Lester R., Chandler, William, Flavin, Christopher, Postel, Sandra, Starke, Linda, and Wolf, Edward (1984) *State of the World: 1984* (New York: Norton). [Part of the 1984 edition of this annual report focuses on population growth and economic development.]

Cohen, Joel (1995) *How Many People Can the Earth Support?* (New York: W. W. Norton Company). [This is currently the most accessible and clear account of the "carrying capacity" concept applied to the earth's human population.]

Condorcet, Antoine-Nicolas (1955 [1793]) *Sketch for a Historical Picture of The Progress of the Human Mind*, trans. June Barraclough (Westport Ct: Hyperion Press). [Condorcet's *Sketch* was the goad that prompted Malthus to write his *Essay on the Principles of Population*, and is one of the classic sources on population theory.]

Graham-Smith, Sir Francis, ed. (1994) *Population: The Complex Reality* (London: The Royal Society). [This excellent collection contains a wide variety of papers on the causes and implications of human population growth.]

Hardin, Garret (1993) *Living Within Limits* (New York: Oxford). [One of the clearest contemporary "Malthusian" accounts of human population growth.]

Lindahl-Kiessling, Kerstin and Landberg, Hans, eds. (1994) *Population, Economic Development, and the Environment* (Oxford: Oxford University Press). [This collection contains many seminal papers on population growth and economic development.]

Malthus, Thomas (1989 [1803]) *An Essay on the Principle of Population*, ed. Patricia James (Cambridge: Cambridge University Press). [Malthus's work is the most famous source on population theory.]

Ng, Yew-Kwang (1989) "What should we do about future generations? The impossibility of Parfit's theory X," *Economics and Philosophy* 5, pp. 235–53. [Ng defends a total utilitarian theory of population.]

Parfit, Derek (1984) *Reasons and Persons* (Oxford: Oxford University Press). [Parfit's book brilliantly articulates the paradoxes of population theory, and is the source of most of the philosophical discussions of population.]

Sen, Amartya (1994) "Population: delusion and reality," *New York Review of Books* 41, no. 15 (September 22), pp. 62–71. [In this paper Sen explains the relationship between population growth and human development.]

Simon, Julian L. (1996) *The Ultimate Resource II* (Princeton: Princeton University Press). [Simon argues that population is not a problem, and that free markets will adequately meet human needs no matter how large the human population of the earth grows.]

Temkin, Larry S. (1987) "Intransitivity and the mere addition paradox," *Philosophy and Public Affairs*, 16, pp. 138–87. [This paper offers a tentative solution to one of the paradoxes of population theory identified by Parfit 1984.]

Wolf, Clark (1997) "Person-Affecting Utilitarianism and Population," in *Contingent Future Persons*, ed. Jan Heller and Nicholas Fotion (Dordrecht, Holland: Kluwer). [In response to Parfit's population paradoxes, this paper defends a complex negative utilitarian account of population and social choice.]

26

Future generations

ERNEST PARTRIDGE

We cannot escape history. We...will be remembered in spite of ourselves. No personal significance or insignificance can spare one or another of us. The fiery trial through which we pass will light us down in honor or dishonor to the latest generations....We...hold the power and bear the responsibility.

Abraham Lincoln

"Future generations" and "posterity" are terms that are frequently encountered in popular journalism, in political rhetoric, not to mention significant historical documents and literary works. For example, the Preamble to the US Constitution cites as one of its purposes, to "secure the Blessings of Liberty to ourselves and our Posterity." Scarcely a week goes by that one does not hear of "future generations" or "posterity" in the popular media.

And yet, serious philosophical attention to the issue of moral responsibility to future generations is quite recent. Of the approximately one million doctoral dissertations presently listed in Dissertation Abstracts, the first to contain either the term "future generations" or "posterity" in its title was completed in 1976: "Rawls and the duty to posterity" (by this writer). Since then, 19 dissertations have been completed which fit that description. The Philosophers' Index lists 134 items under "future generations" and "posterity." Of these, all but three have been published since the first Earth Day, April 22, 1970.

Why this apparent neglect, until very recently, by moral philosophers of an issue of such manifest interest to the general public?

The answer might be found in an analysis of the concept of moral responsibility. To say that a moral agent or a corporate body is morally responsible for his or her actions would seem to entail at the very least that the agent: (a) has, or is capable of having, knowledge of the consequences of those actions; (b) has the capacity to bring about these consequences; (c) has the choice to do otherwise; and (d) that these consequences have value significance. The second and third conditions reiterate the common meta-ethical insight that the realm of morality is found between the extremes of the impossible and the inevitable – or, to quote and then extend the maxim of the eighteenth-century philosopher, Immanuel Kant: "*ought* implies *can*," – and yet might not.

If this analysis of the concept of responsibility is accurate, then the reason for the emergence of the posterity problem becomes clear: the issue has arisen with the extraordinary advances in science (knowledge) and TECHNOLOGY (capacity). Before the mid-twentieth century, the very idea that human activities might seriously and permanently affect the global atmosphere and oceans, or the gene pool or our species and others, seemed preposterous. We were just too puny, we believed, and the planet too vast for such consequences. Now the sciences have disabused us of such assurances, as technology has produced chemicals and radioactive substances unknown to nature, and as evidence proliferates of permanent anthropogenic effects upon the seas, atmosphere, and the global ecosystem. Furthermore, such consequences of industrial civilization as ozone depletion, global warming, the contamination of aquifers, and the deposition of radwaste, while the by-products of benefits to the present generation, exact postponed costs to remote generations.

Not coincidentally, the posterity question arose alongside the emergence of the environmental movement. While not all posterity issues are necessarily environmental in nature (the preservation of landmark buildings and works of art come to mind as exceptions), the preservation of the natural environment is clearly the public and moral issue with the longest time entailments. And so, when in 1962 Rachel Carson's *Silent Spring* alerted the public to the moral implications of bioscientific knowledge and agro-industrial technology, and when, during the same decade, the Sierra Club and other organizations decried the loss of WILDERNESS, the consequences of these crises to future generations could not be ignored. Accordingly, the emergence of the posterity issue during "the environmental decade" of the 1970s was virtually assured.

In short, the accelerating advances of science and technology have made it compellingly clear that future generations are vulnerable to our acts and policies. Furthermore, through science we have come to understand the long-term consequences of these policies, and, through technology, we have acquired the capacity to affect these consequences, if only through forbearance. In our hands lies the fate, for better or worse, of future persons whose lives we will never share. This is a burden of responsibility that we cannot escape, so long as we willingly accept the enlightenment of science and the capacities of our technology. "To do nothing, is to do something"; namely, to assent to existing trends and entailments.

The moral status of future persons

At first glance, the posterity issue may appear to involve nothing more than a simple extension of our "moral community" to include, in addition to family, compatriots, distant contemporary victims of misfortune, and even ANIMALS and ecosystems, yet another category: persons who will be born after we have departed. By this superficial account, our responsibilities to future persons would not be significantly different in kind from our responsibilities to these contemporary "others." Put simply, it would seem that given our knowledge and capacities, future persons have the right to our responsible care and forbearance in their behalf.

A closer look reveals that the ontological and epistemological status of future persons raises numerous unique and extraordinary moral and meta-ethical problems. Among them:

- Most fundamentally, future persons, qua future, do not exist now, when the alleged burdens of responsibility fall upon the living. Thus the question arises:

can we have duties to non-existent beings? Still worse, what sense can be made of attributing rights to those who do not exist?

- Still more perplexing is the fact that by initiating a policy to improve the lives of future persons, we will be causing different individuals to be born in the future. But if so, then we can in no sense be said to be "improving the lives" of particular future persons, who, but for our provision (or neglect) would not exist (Parfit 1984).
- We cannot know future people as individuals. Instead, "posterity" is an abstract category containing unnumbered and undifferentiated members. And yet, much moral theory is based upon the principle of "respect for autonomous individuals."
- Our relationship with future persons is unidirectional and non-reciprocal. Future persons will be unable to reward or punish us, as the case may be, for our provision for their lives.
- How can we tell with any confidence just what might benefit future persons – i.e., what will or will not be "goods" to them?
- Who is entitled to act in behalf of future persons?

Clearly, by assigning moral significance to those not yet born, we are introducing problems that are unique to the history of moral philosophy.

What then, is the moral status of future persons? Just how much claim do they have upon us to make provision for them or, at the very least, to forbear from causing future harm? The responses of contemporary moral philosophers cover a broad scope of the moral spectrum. To some, the contingency and non-actuality of future persons virtually excludes them from moral consideration. If any attempt to improve the lot of future persons results in a population of different individuals, then, so the argument goes, no particular lives can be "improved" by present policies.

Other responses include:

Libertarianism Some libertarians insist that with the privatization of all resources, future generations will be well cared for – as a beneficent "by-product" of rational, self-serving behavior. Because, they argue, no rational property owner will deliberately degrade the value of his property, private individuals are, in effect, suitable surrogates of the interests of future generations. Accordingly, writes Martino,

> it is quite possible to take the needs of the future into account by permitting the establishment of markets in which assets with future values can be bought and sold ... [S]peculation in resources with an expected large future demand automatically results in conservation. Thus the interests of the people who will live in the future are actively protected. (1982, p. 33)

It follows that the libertarian society will leave "as much and as good" for successor generations, with little need for individuals, and much less for governments, to concern themselves about the fate of remote posterity. As for resources, optimistic economists such as Julian Simon argue that so long as human ingenuity is mixed with the profit motive, suitable resources for an abundant life will be found, developed, and utilized, as they are needed at the time.

Critics reply that this account disregards, first, the diminution of economic value through time (i.e., "the discount rate"), and second, that these optimistic forecasts favor abstract economic models over fundamental scientific facts and principles, most notably ecosystemic complexity and the laws of thermodynamics (see ECONOMICS).

Utilitarianism   Though future individuals are implicitly factored into Bentham's "hedonic calculus" (in particular, through the criterion of "social extent"), considerable difficulties in the utilitarian approach to the posterity issue have only recently entered into philosophical debate.

First, how far into the future does our provision for posterity extend? Do we "discount" the future, or are the interests and preferences of furthest generations to count equally to those of our own children and grandchildren? Both alternatives present difficulties. If all future generations count, then equal distributive shares with this indefinite but enormously large number leaves us with virtually nothing for ourselves. And yet as Derek Parfit (1984) and others have pointed out, there seems to be no moral justification for a "pure time preference" for nearer over further generations.

Second, how can we calculate the "utility" of our provision for future individuals whose tastes, preferences, and needs we do not and cannot know?

Third, among the decisions that we make regarding future persons is the very size of that future population. Do we harm "might-have-beens" by denying them existence by adopting stringent population control policies? And most profoundly, what do the utilitarians propose to maximize: the average utility of future persons or the total utility in a future population? This issue of average versus total utility, absent in utilitarian calculations regarding populations of fixed numbers (such as the present generation), arises with the question of population policy – i.e., how many future persons should we cause to exist? Full commitment to either average or total utility leads to counter-intuitive "repugnant conclusions." According to the average utility principle, Adam and Eve, before the fall, lived in a "better" world than a hypothetically later world of thousands or millions of individuals who, though quite happy on average, were slightly less so than the original couple. On the other hand, the total utility principle requires fertile couples to produce children whose lives will be on balance slightly happier than unhappy – an obligation which applies even in an overcrowded world. The average versus total utility dilemma leads to a question which lies at the very foundations of utilitarian philosophy: are we obliged to create people for happiness (total utility), or should we create happiness for people (average utility) (Warren, 1977; Sikora and Barry 1978; see also POPULATION)?

Communitarianism   Avner de-Shalit (1995) argues that we are morally bound to future generations through shared membership in a "community." This might appear to be an unpromising approach, for reasons now familiar to us: namely, that the present generation and its successors cannot interact – that their relationship is non-personal and non-reciprocal. Well aware of this difficulty, de-Shalit stipulates that just "one of three main conditions must be met in order for a group of people to count as a community: ... interaction between people in daily life, cultural interaction, and moral similarity" (ibid, p. 22). Clearly, the first condition is not applicable between non-concurrent lives. But, de-Shalit contends, in a figurative and restricted, yet significant, sense, the second condition, "cultural interaction," is applicable, as is the third condition, "moral similarity." These two conditions bind us with future generations into a "community."

De-Shalit explains that while we do not "converse" with non-concurrent generations, we do have "cultural interaction" with them. To understand this concept, consider the US Constitutional Convention in Philadelphia in 1787. As the Preamble states, the document was enacted "for ourselves and our posterity," and thus it is clear that the framers of that document understood that they were affecting the life conditions of future generations. Reciprocally, every case that is heard before the Supreme Court today is responsive to this document, which was framed by our predecessors. Similarly, as we make provision for the remote future, we fully expect that future generations will be mindful of and responsive to these (then past) provisions.

"Moral similarity," de-Shalit's third condition, does not mean full agreement among generations of all moral precepts; indeed, rational moral debate along with moral adaptation and evolution is essential to a vital transgenerational community. Consider once again the example of the US Constitution. That document was hotly debated and framed in the context of received moral and political presuppositions – a "frame of reference" or "form of life" (to use the twentieth-century philosopher Ludwig Wittgenstein's useful concept). It is within this context of agreement that moral debate takes place (or, to continue with our example, the Constitution is interpreted and occasionally amended). So long as this context of moral debate and interpretation remains essentially intact, de-Shalit argues, a "transgenerational community" can exist and continue. However, this concept carries with it the implication that this community across generations is time-contingent, and thus, as the moral "frame of reference" itself evolves, "the time will come when it becomes questionable whether [remotely] future generations will still speak of the same transgenerational community" (ibid, p. 47).

De-Shalit's book contains a sensitive and astute analysis of moral psychology – in particular an examination of the "time-binding" and "projective" aspect of human thought, action, and evaluation that is reminiscent of the twentieth-century philosopher, Martin Heidegger. Human life and experience, he argues, is incomprehensible without an awareness of the fact that we all, in an inescapable sense, live both in the present and the future, including a future that extends far beyond the span of our own lives (see NINETEENTH- AND TWENTIETH-CENTURY PHILOSOPHY).

Deontological views   These focus on the moral status of future persons and the moral categories that apply to them, in particular, the issue of the putative rights of and duties to the not-yet-actual. Can we, in fact, be said to "have duties toward" nonactual future persons? If so, do these duties correlate with the rights of these future persons? The answer to that question may bear upon the moral urgency of our responsibility toward the future. "Uncorrelated" duties (also called "imperfect duties") may have less priority than those duties which correlate with the rights of others. Richard deGeorge is among those who recognize "duties toward" future persons, but deny that these duties correlate with the rights, now, of future persons.

On the contrary, he insists, future generations "cannot now . . . be the present bearer or subject of anything, including rights . . . [They] should correctly be said to have a right only to what is available when they come into existence" (deGeorge 1979, pp. 95–6).

Partridge (1990) replies that this argument succeeds in denying only one category of rights to future persons: what Feinberg and others call "active rights" – i.e., rights "to do such and such." However, "passive rights" (e.g., the right not to be deprived of opportunities, or not to be harmed, etc.), are quite applicable to future persons before they become actual. This is so, since, unlike "active rights," the option to honor or to violate passive rights falls upon the correlative "duty bearer" – in this case, the present generation.

John Rawls and the "hypothetical contract"   One of the most influential and provocative treatments of the posterity issue appears in John Rawls's *A Theory of Justice* (1971), where Rawls proposes a "contractarian" approach to the question of what he calls "justice between generations." At first, a contractarian approach to the issue seems unpromising, for the very same reasons that it is troublesome for the communitarians: namely, that the "contractors," having non-concurrent lives, are incapable of bargaining and arriving at reciprocal agreements.

Fully aware of this difficulty, Rawls concedes at the outset that fundamental principles of justice cannot be arrived at through actual contract negotiations. Instead, the "contract" must be "hypothetical," and constructed through an elaborate thought-experiment which he calls "the original position." While we cannot describe here the details of Rawls's theory, suffice to say for our purposes that the "contractors," in drawing out the rules of "justice between generations," are denied knowledge of which generation in human history they belong to. Thus, the rules of intergenerational justice are devised in the original position to apply to all generations. Accordingly, the parties in the original position do not know whether, in the conditions of their actual lives, the rules of "just savings" will turn out to be a burden or a benefit. All they know is that, in either case, due to the conditions of "the original position," the rules will be "fair."

As a result of these deliberations in the original position (more traditionally, one might say, "from the moral point of view"), Rawls believes that the following rules of "just savings" would be adopted: "[1] preserve the gains of culture and civilization . . . , [2] maintain intact those just institutions that have been established . . . , [and 3], put aside in each period of time a suitable amount of real capital accumulation." He adds that "this saving may take various forms from net investment in machinery and other means of production to investment in learning and education" (1971, p. 285).

Conspicuously absent from this list is any direct reference to the conservation of natural resources or the preservation of the natural environment (though such considerations are not specifically excluded, and are arguably implicit in these principles). This omission is remedied by Edith Brown Weiss (1989), who stipulates as a fundamental "principle of intergenerational equity" that each generation leave to its successor a planet in at least as good a condition as that generation received it. Like Rawls, Weiss believes that principles of intergenerational justice should be drawn behind a "veil of ignorance" – without knowledge of which generation in the span of history is one's own. However, unlike Rawls, Weiss is attempting to derive principles that apply, not within a national entity, but to all nations – which is to say, will serve as a foundation of international law.

The motivation problem

Are human beings, either individually or communally, capable of making just provision for remotely future persons who they will never know and who cannot reciprocally reward or punish those of the present generation? While this question may seem to be more psychological and sociological than philosophical, it nonetheless is of profound concern to the moral philosopher.

Recall that one of the criteria of moral responsibility is capacity. While we earlier identified this as "technological capacity" to bring about or prevent foreseeable long-term consequences of our actions, "capacity" can also refer to psychological conditions. Rawls recognizes this issue as he asserts that moral principles, if they are to be valid, must be such that human beings are able to abide by them – they must, in Rawls's words, be capable of withstanding "the strains of commitment."

In an important paper, Norman Care presents doubts regarding "our ability to solve the motivation problem relative to what morality requires on behalf of future generations" (1982, p. 195). He argues that: (a) we can have no bonds of love or concern for indefinite future persons: "their interests cannot interest us"; (b) we have no "community bond" with future persons – no "sense of belonging to some joint enterprise"; and finally (c) we feel no "extended or unbounded shared-fate motivation," no "sense of common humanity" (ibid, pp. 207–9). Consequently, Care concludes:

> certain familiar sorts of motivation are not available to support policies demanding serious sacrifice for the sake of future generations, and we may well be discouraged by the further apparent fact that the cultivation of a form of motivation directly supportive of such policies might require something close to an overhaul of main elements in the makeup of our society which influence the moral psychology of citizens. (ibid, p. 213)

However, this conclusion does not completely close the door to a just provision for the remote future. Care does, after all, concede the possibility of a "moral overhaul" in society. Not only that, but the mere possibility of appropriate sacrifice for the sake of posterity is exemplified in the supererogatory acts of saints and heros.

Garrett Hardin, who largely shares Care's pessimism, nevertheless recounts two examples of extraordinary sacrifice in behalf of the future, both from the Soviet Union (1977, p. 78–9). In the first, during the 1921 famine, peasants in a starving village on the Volga refused to eat the seed grain stacked in an adjacent field. "We do not steal from the future," they said. In the second case, during the 900-day siege of Leningrad, while nearly a million residents starved, large stores of edible seeds in an agricultural research institute were untouched. Still, the essential question remains: notwithstanding known cases of extraordinary sacrifice in behalf of the remote future, can people in general and their established governments be persuaded to submit to "ordinary" constraints in order to make fair provision for posterity?

Rawls believes that to assure "just savings" for the future, the parties of his original position must understand themselves to be "heads of families," with parental ties and concerns for the immediately succeeding generation or two (1971, pp. 128–9). Provision for remote generations is thus accomplished through a "chain linking" of one generation to the next. This proposal immediately suggests two problems: first, it implies that childless individuals are incapable of caring for future generations, and thus are excused from making just provision. Second, Rawls's "heads of families" condition presents a "discounting" problem even more severe than that of the economists, for a parent's love and concern for a child is generally greater than for a grandchild, and so on, diminishing to insignificance within a very few generations.

A more positive account of the motivation question has been offered by Partridge (1981). Not only is significant "self-transcendent" concern for the remote future possible, he argues, it is in fact healthy – the result of normal processes of maturation and socialization. A "self-transcending concern" for persons, communities, locations, causes, artifacts, institutions, ideals, etc., arises from (a) the social origins of the self concept, (b) from the "objectification of values" (i.e., the perception of values as being "in" the valued objects), and (c) the universal awareness of one's mortality. All this leads to an interest in believing that these entities will continue to flourish beyond the span of one's lifetime. As further evidence of the claim that "self-transcendent concern" is healthy, Partridge points out that a lack thereof, described by clinical psychologists as "alienation" and "narcissism," is an unenviable condition (1981, p. 204).

In this account of self-transcendent concern we find an echo of an ancient yet timely moral insight, known as "the moral paradox": namely, that it is in one's own best interest not to seek deliberately one's own best interest – that the most fulfilling life is realized in outwardly directed activity and concern. If this condition is true of human nature, and if a widespread realization of self-transcending concern is available through educational and institutional reform, then the means of accomplishing Norman Care's "moral overhaul" may be at hand. Such an accomplishment may be difficult and even highly improbable given contemporary social conditions. However, mere possibility may suffice to prompt moral concern and involvement. Recall that capacity is a condition of moral responsibility, and that the arena of moral activity is found between the extremes of impossibility and inevitability.

Policy implications

We have explored the meta-ethical issue of whether future generations can be said to have rights, and have reviewed a variety of normative approaches to the posterity issue. Now we turn to the practical question of just what we might do to best fulfill our responsibilities to the remote future.

To begin, we should turn an acute critical eye toward the "business as usual" of public policy-making: "cost-benefit analysis" – an approach promoted by economists, widely endorsed by legislatures and administrators, and enshrined in the methodology of environmental impact analysis (see ECONOMICS). There are many criticisms of cost-benefit analysis. The most prominent among them are the following:

- By commensurating all values into cash (a non-moral value), morality is "factored out" of policy considerations.
- Cost-benefit analysis measures aggregated consumer preferences to the exclusion of community/citizen values.
- Economic analysis is descriptive – indicating what a consumer-public in fact values (economically), rather than prescribing what they should value (norma-tively). To put the matter bluntly, the economist asks: "What is the value? Tell me what are you willing to pay." The moral philosopher replies: "What am I willing to pay? First I must determine, independently, what is its value." This is a response that the economist cannot touch within the bounds of his discipline.
- Finally, and most significantly for the posterity issue, by measuring value in terms of cash, the future is discounted. Thus the costs and benefits to persons just a few generations into the future count for virtually nothing in economically based policy analyses.

The ignorance excuse   Before we proceed with policy recommendations, one more objection to provision for the remote future must be addressed. It is based upon the "knowledge criterion" of responsibility, and claims that we do not and in principle cannot, know what future generations will need or value, and thus can make no provision for them. How, for example, could previous generations have known of our need for rare semi-conducting elements such as germanium? And conversely, what if they had needlessly sacrificed by storing up vast quantities of whale oil, with no anticipation of the coming ages of petroleum and electricity? When we examine the predictions of 50 and 100 years ago, regarding life at the close of the twentieth century, how can we with any confidence forecast conditions of life in the remote future?

Granting all this, there are, nonetheless, some fundamental facts that we can know about future generations:

1. First, they will be humans, with well-known biotic requirements necessary to sustain their health.
2. Second, future persons for whom we are responsible will be moral agents, which means that they will be sentient and self-conscious, having a sense of themselves and other persons as continuing beings with the capacity to choose among alternative futures, and with the capacity to reason abstractly and thus to act on principle. All this entails that these future persons will be bound by familiar moral categories of rights, responsibilities, and the demands of justice.
3. Third, if these future persons are to live and flourish, they must be sustained by a functioning ecosystem.
4. And finally, they will require stable social institutions and a body of knowledge and skills that will allow them to meet and overcome cultural and natural crises that may occur during their lifetimes. (Partridge 1994)

Assuming then that we know enough about the welfare of future persons to act responsibly in their behalf, what guidelines might direct our policies toward future generations? Prominent among those proposed by philosophers and others, are the following:

"First of all, do no harm"   Because "the ignorance excuse" is not without some merit, an insight from the utilitarians would be very helpful to the policy-makers: namely, we should favor policies that mitigate evil over policies that promote good. This precept is supported by common-sense considerations. First, avoidable or treatable pain demands the moral attention of everyone, while "the pursuit of happiness" is the appropriate concern of the individual. Furthermore, it is much easier to identify and address the causes of misery than it is to promote the well-springs of happiness. This is especially so with regard to the future. The pains and tribulations of future persons, like those of ourselves, can often be traced to disruptions in the fundamental biotic, ecosystemic, psychological, and institutional conditions listed above. Their pleasures and satisfactions will come from a future evolution of culture, taste and technology that we cannot even imagine.

The "critical Lockean proviso"   According to John Locke (1632–1704), it is morally permissible to "take from nature," mix one's labor with the taking, and claim the result as one's private property, so long as one leaves "as much and as good for others." While this may have been true in a world of frontiers and homesteads, it is no longer possible. Once a barrel of petroleum is extracted from the earth and consumed, there is no longer "as much and as good" remaining for our successors. But if we were to share equally our petroleum resources with all generations far into the future, we would be allocated a cupful each. So we must, instead, adopt a "critical Lockean proviso," whereby we leave for the future, not the very resource that we deplete, but the opportunity to obtain whatever it was for which the original resource was utilized. Thus while future generations may not need petroleum (just as we no longer need whale oil), they will need what petroleum provides, namely energy. Thus it is our responsibility to find a replacement. The proviso also entails that we utilize recycling technologies and "interest-bearing" (i.e., renewable) resources, such as sustained yield forestry and fisheries. And this in turn validates the need to preserve natural ecosystems.

Preserve the options   This rule is clearly entailed by the previous two. While we cannot predict the technological solutions to future resource scarcity, we owe future generations a full range of options and opportunities for research and development of these technologies. This in turn entails a continuing investment in scientific and technical education and research. Happily, such an investment benefits our own generation and that of our immediate successors, as it also benefits the remote future.

Anticipation and prevention is preferable to cure   We should therefore keep an informed eye on impending impacts upon the future. "Earlier" is easier and cheaper than "later." Accordingly, our responsibility to future generations must include technological and environmental impact studies which will foresee, and expand the capacity to foresee, developing crises and the consequences of our projects and policies far into the remote future. Obvious examples of this "duty of anticipation" include studies of stratospheric ozone depletion, global warming, chemical hormone disruption, and nuclear waste disposal.

Just forbearance   This dimension of the duty to posterity clearly follows from the previous: for once we have determined, through scientific research, how our actions might affect the remote future, we may face a clear duty to forgo advantages for the sake of future generations. To cite our examples once again, studies of atmospheric physics and chemistry may determine that we face a choice between having our grandchildren protected from ultraviolet radiation or having our generation enjoy the convenience of aerosol sprays and supersonic aircraft. Similarly, due to the so-called "greenhouse effect," our voracious appetite for fossil fuel energy may be inconsistent with a tolerable CLIMATE for our successors. Accordingly, a decision to favor future generations would, in these instances, require just forbearances on the part of those now living. A policy of "just forbearance" is a conservative approach to provision for the future, which is often favored by environmentalists. The ecosystem, they argue, is a network of complex and subtle interrelationships, the intricacies and ramifications of which we can never fully comprehend. Rather than carelessly toss aside components of this system (e.g., species and nutrients), we should approach the planetary life community with humility and care. If our information is incomplete, it is better to postpone, or even to abandon, projects that threaten the integrity of the system.

Doing well by doing good   We should favor policies that work to the advantage of both us and the future – and which, other factors being roughly equal, are least burdensome to the present generation. This rule is responsive to the constant political problem of convincing the public to accept sacrifices now to bring about benefits that they will never see. On reflection, it seems that a significant number of our "duties to the future" also benefit us and those we directly care about – our children and grandchildren. Among these benefits are the control of pollution, population, and global warming.

Educational implications   None of the above will be accomplished unless succeeding generations acquire the moral stamina to face up to and carry out their moral responsibilities. This can only be accomplished through a carefully devised and generously funded program of environmental and moral education. Such a program would include the teaching of critical thinking, history, ecological principles, and a respect for free institutions.

The moral education here proposed is one, not of content but of process – not of answers, but of the skills to find the answers for oneself. As such, this approach prizes above all else the dignity and autonomy of the individual – qualities assaulted and threatened by our mass culture. Be that as it may, let us acknowledge that the youth will be "morally educated" somehow, if only by default. That is to say, they will have some set of values, for better or worse. Better that we assume the task deliberately, and do a good job of it.

Guardian for future generations   Such an arrangement should be established by the international community – preferably under the sanction of international law, but, failing that, with the widespread support of non-governmental organizations (Stone 1996; Weiss 1989). Christopher Stone suggests that such a guardian

> might be authorized: (1) to appear before the legislatures and administrative agencies of states considering actions with pronounced, long-term implications; (2) to appear as a special intervener-counsel in a variety of bilateral and multi-lateral disputes, and, (3) perhaps most important, even to initiate legal and diplomatic action on the future's behalf in appropriate situations. (1989, pp. 71–2).

As we noted at the outset, the posterity issue is new to the literature and debates of moral philosophy. But now, having made its appearance, the question of our responsibility to future generations cannot be returned to obscurity. For if our analysis of "moral responsibility" (as knowledge, capacity, choice, and value significance) is correct, the only plausible escape from this responsibility would be a disavowal of the knowledge provided by our sciences, and an abandonment of the capacity and choice bestowed by our technology. Few seem willing to pay that price to avoid the moral burden of our duty to posterity. If, on the other hand, we continue to support the advancement of science and technology, and yet ignore the long-term consequences thereof, we will not avoid our moral responsibility – we will be in default thereof, and will be properly condemned by the generations that succeed us.

References

Care, N. (1982) "Future generations, public policy, and the motivation problem," *Environmental Ethics* (Fall). [Raises serious doubts as to the psychological capacity of the present generation to make morally adequate provision for the future.]

de George, R. (1979) "The environment, rights and future generations," in *Ethics and Problems of the 21st Century*, ed. K. Goodpaster and K. Sayre (Notre Dame: University of Notre Dame Press). [Argues that while the current generation has some general duties toward future generations, future persons, qua "future," have no rights at the present time.]

de-Shalit, A. (1995) *Why Posterity Matters* (London: Routledge). [Proposes that there is an "intergenerational contract" binding present and future generations.]

Hardin, G. (1977) *The Limits of Altruism* (Indiana: Indiana University Press). [Hardin argues that altruism is possible among moderately prosperous individuals in small groups but improbable in conditions of acute scarcity now threatening mankind due to the population and environmental crises. "Institutional design" is more likely to do the trick than "individual morality."]

Martino, J. P. (1982) "Inheriting the earth," *Reason* (November). [A libertarian approach to the issue, which contends that future generations will be best served through the protection of property rights and the promotion of free markets in the present.]

Parfit, D. (1984) *Reasons and Persons* (Oxford: Clarendon Press). [Important book in ethical theory and the problem of personal identity, with significant insights into the problem of future discounting and the moral status of future persons.]

Partridge, E. (1981) "Why care about the future?," in *Responsibilities to Future Generations*, ed. E. Partridge (Buffalo: Prometheus). [Affirms the potential capacity of present persons to be motivated to act morally toward future generations.]

——(1990) "On the rights of future generations," in *Upstream/Downstream: Issues in Environmental Ethics*, ed. Donald Scherer (Philadelphia: Temple University Press). [Defends "passive" rights-claims of future generations (e.g., not to be harmed) upon the present generation, while conceding that future persons do not now possess "active rights" (i.e., "to choose among options") in the present.]

——(1994) "Posterity and the 'strains of commitment,'" in *Creating a New History for Future Generations*, ed. T. Kim, and J. Dator (Kyoto: Institute for the Integrated Study of Future Generations). [Public policy proposals aimed toward a fulfillment of the responsibilities of the present generation to its successors.]

Rawls, J. (1971) *A Theory of Justice* (Cambridge: Harvard). [A landmark work in political and ethical theory, offering a "hypothetical-contractarian" alternative to utilitarianism.]

Sikora, R. and Barry, B. eds. (1978) *Obligations to Future Generations*, (Philadelphia: Temple University Press). [One of the first anthologies on the subject, it deals specifically with discounting and the moral status of future persons, with prominent attention given to the defenses and criticisms of the utilitarian approach to the future.]

Stone, C. (1996) "Should we establish a guardian for future generations?," in *Should Trees Have Standing? and Other Essays on Law, Morals and the Environment* (Dobbs Ferry, NY: Oceana). [Defends the concept of a "guardian of the future" from the perspective of legal practice and theory.]

Warren, M. (1977) "Do potential people have rights?" *Canadian Journal of Philosophy* (June). [Addresses the questions of the status of future persons and of average vs. total utility, as these issues imply competing policies toward population and savings, affirming duties toward persons who *will* exist, while denying a duty to *produce* "merely potential" persons.]

Weiss, E. (1989) *In Fairness to Future Generations: International Law, Common Patrimony, and Intergenerational Equity* (New York: Transnational Publication and the United Nations University). [Proposes a theory of intergenerational justice from the contractarian perspective of Rawls's *A Theory of Justice*].

Further Reading

Laslett, P. and Fishkin, J., eds. (1992) *Justice Between Age Groups and Generations* (New Haven: Yale University Press). [Prominent attention to application of contract theory and discounting to intergenerational justice.]

Passmore, J. (1976) *Man's Responsibility for Nature* (New York: Scribners'). [Comprehensive historical and philosophical examination of "ecological problems and western traditions" with chapters on "Conservation" and "Preservation" that deal explicitly with issues of the motivation to provide for the future and of appropriate public policies toward future generations.]

27

Sustainability

ALAN HOLLAND

Introduction: birth of the idea

The twentieth century saw unprecedented environmental change, much of it the cumulative and unintended result of human economic activity. In the judgment of many, this change – involving the exhaustion of natural resources and sinks, extensive pollution, and unprecedented impacts upon CLIMATE, life-forms, and life-sustaining systems – is undermining the conditions necessary for the economic activity to continue. In a word, present patterns of economic activity are judged to be "unsustainable."

An initial response was to suggest that human society would have to abandon the attempt to improve the human condition through economic growth, and settle instead for zero growth. The response was naturally unwelcome, both to political leaders anxious to assure voters of better times to come, and to businesses anxious to stay in business. Its logic, moreover, is open to question. For even if we accept that economic growth has been the chief cause of environmental degradation, it does not follow that abandoning growth is the remedy. If zero growth led to global war, for example, there would be environmental degradation, and zero growth to boot. And genetic technology holds out the hope, at least, that we might provide for human needs with decreasing impact on the natural environment, and even reverse some of the degradation that has already occurred.

This is the hope expressed by the idea of "sustainable development" – or "sustainability," for short. The origin of the idea is commonly dated to a report produced by the International Union for the Conservation of Nature in 1980. Over the ensuing years, and especially since the publication of the Brundtland Report (WCED 1987), it has come to dominate large areas of environmental discourse and policy-making. Replacing more confrontational discourse between advocates of economic development, and those increasingly concerned over its environmental consequences, Brundtland advanced the (conciliatory) proposition that the needs of the poor (among the declared aims of economic development) were best met by sustaining environmental capacity (among the declared aims of environmentalism). Development, it was suggested, could be pursued to the extent that it was compatible with sustaining environmental capacity. On the assumption that environmental capacity can be expressed in terms of the capacity to satisfy human needs, this was formulated as a principle of "sustainable development" – "development that meets the needs of the present without compromising the ability of future generations to meet their own needs" (WCED 1987, p. 8).

There are formal analogies between the principle of sustainability, so framed, and J. S. Mill's (1806–1873) principle of liberty, which licenses the pursuit of liberty insofar as this is compatible with a similar liberty for all. The principle of sustainability in effect licenses the pursuit of quality of life insofar as this is compatible with a similar quality of life for all (including future people). Such a principle appears to safeguard the future of the environment, too. But far from abandoning the aim of economic growth, Brundtland (WCED 1987, p. 1) foresees "a new era of economic growth" and believes such growth is "absolutely essential" for the relief of poverty. On the other hand it holds that growth is not sufficient to relieve poverty, and sees the need for what it calls a "new development path" (ibid, p. 4), one that sustains environmental capacity. Its approach is notably human-centered, and aside from one reference to a "moral reason" for conserving wild beings (ibid, p. 13), the DEEP ECOLOGY perspective is absent. The loss of coral reefs, for example, is lamented simply on the grounds that they "have generated an unusual variety of toxins valuable in modern medicine" (ibid, p. 151); and hope is expressed that "The Earth's endowment of species and natural ecosystems will soon be seen as assets to be conserved and managed for the benefit of all humanity" (ibid, p. 160). Sustainable development is understood as development that sustains human progress into the distant future. At the same time, the human-centered reasons that are given are often as much moral as prudential. Poverty is declared to be an "evil in itself" and a strong thread of the argument centers on a concern that current economic activity imposes costs on the future: "We borrow environmental capital from future generations" (ibid, p. 8). In this way Brundtland clearly links issues of intragenerational equity with those of intergenerational equity. The implications for environmental protection, however, are less clear. Environmentalists may welcome the recognition that it is not environmental protection that stands in the way of future development so much as the fallout from existing patterns of development. But the fundamental issue is whether the protection that the environment requires serves to determine the "new development path," or whether it is the new development path that dictates the nature of the environmental protection required. In the latter event, it makes a difference – or rather it makes all the difference – what conception of the human good is to govern the development path in question.

Reception of the idea

In the world of policy, the concept of sustainability has been assimilated with remarkable speed, determining much of the agenda of the United Nations conference on Environment and Development held in Rio de Janeiro in 1992. Agenda 21, a programme to which governments all over the world have committed themselves, represents the agenda for putting sustainability into practice. At the local level, too, many sensible schemes are being put into operation in the name of sustainability, often under the auspices of Agenda 21, and the term figures increasingly as an overriding objective of environmental organizations, whether inside or outside the remit of government.

However, the appearance of consensus even at the highest policy levels continues to be accompanied by a sustained chorus of skepticism and suspicion. Environmentalists are suspicious that what is billed as a constraint on business as usual will turn out to be a cover for business as usual. Vandana Shiva comments on the paradox that development and growth – creatures of the market economy – are being offered as a cure for the very ecological crisis that they have served to bring about (1992, p. 188). "Nature shrinks as capital grows," she writes: the market destroys both the economy of nature, and non-market "survival economies" (ibid, p. 189). Business interests, on the other hand, are suspicious that the constraint on business as usual might be a cover for no business at all. The sustainability agenda is also a fertile source of suspicion between North and South – the poorer countries suspecting that the constraint on development now judged to be necessary as a result of patterns of economic activity from which they received little or no benefit is being used to justify a constraint on *their* development (see ENVIRONMENTAL JUSTICE). This was already a key issue ahead of the first ever world conference on Environment and Development held in Stockholm in 1972 (Landsberg 1992, p. 2).

At the theoretical level, too, the principle of sustainability faces criticism. It is said to be muddled, and even self-contradictory, and some question its moral stance if it means that the claims of the environment might override the claims of poor and hungry people (Beckerman 1994). Others argue that it encapsulates the very same values and assumptions as those it purports to challenge (Redclift 1987). Many detect new managerial aspirations behind the sustainability agenda; others see merely the continuation of older aspirations – for control or domination of world resources. Last but not least, there is the – skeptical – view, advocated for example by Julian Simon (1998), that there never was an "environmental crisis" to begin with, and that a sustainability agenda is therefore otiose.

We shall first briefly consider two such skeptical challenges, before turning to consider (1) the objectives of the sustainability agenda, (2) the criteria for its achievement, and (3) issues of implementation.

Challenges

Although it tends to receive short shrift from environmentalists, there is more to Simon's case than meets the eye. He claims that almost every trend that affects human welfare, if we take a reasonably long-term view, "points in a positive direction" (1998, p. 237). While some of the evidence he cites appears to be chosen very selectively, and in fact to be extremely short-term, he is on stronger ground in challenging claims about the "exhaustion" of sinks and resources and "threats" to life-support systems. For nature does not present itself as either resource, sink, or life-support system. "Resource," and "sink," too, are relational terms; and precious little of nature presents itself conveniently for our use without an untold input of human effort and contrivance. The so-called environmental "services" or natural life-support systems are, of course, necessary, but they are in no way sufficient to support human life, unless humans also support themselves. For this reason, increasing encroachment on the natural world does not in itself mean the exhaustion of natural resources; indeed, the very availability of nature as a resource requires and presupposes much destruction of the natural world. It should be remarked, for example, that BIODIVERSITY can only be counted as a "resource" at all because of the technology made possible by its (partial) destruction, and that without the sustained efforts of the human race, major segments of the natural world would still threaten rather than support its continuance. Whilst Simon is rightly taken to task for seeming to suggest that resources are therefore "infinite" (i.e. not finite), he is right to infer that they can at least be said to be "indefinite" (i.e. as having no fixed point of termination). And since humans can only hope for an indefinite rather than an infinite future, it could be argued that this is enough. In response, and appealing to the second law of thermodynamics, ecological economists such as Herman Daly have argued that increasing entropy sets an inescapable limit to economic growth. However, this does not rule out indefinite growth, if the increase can be slowed down sufficiently; nor does it take into account the extent to which solar energy might be increasingly used to "subsidize" such growth. Some analysts argue that, thanks to technological advance, levels of welfare can be maintained or even increased on the basis of reduced resource consumption. Unfortunately, it does not follow that more resources will be left intact (because fewer are needed); on the contrary, fewer resources may be left intact, and for the very same reason – that fewer are needed.

Another challenge, raised by Wilfred Beckerman (1994), concerns the validity of pursuing a sustained path, as opposed to one that exhibits more variation. He rightly points out that in our individual lives we are perfectly ready to anticipate declining fortunes in our later years as more than compensated for by earlier flourishing. Now the argument is admittedly not straightforward, because in the intergenerational case those who experience the decline are different individuals from those who flourish, which raises issues of justice not raised by the intra-personal case. But the point remains that the objective of a level path appears to privilege egalitarian conceptions of justice over more flexible ones, such as the notion of the political philosopher, John Rawls, that a situation is not unjust if everyone in it is no worse off than anyone in an alternative situation. It is conceivable that an uneven development path could leave everyone better off.

Objectives

For those who accept the need for a new, sustainable, development path, two immediate questions must be faced: (1) What values are affirmed by sustainability? (2) Are they all consistent?

The values most evident among the arguments advanced for sustainability are justice, well-being, and the value of nature "in its own right". The point of most interest to environmentalists is how far the claims of nature are going to be served by policies designed to secure human well-being and justice. For it is no foregone conclusion that some preordained "harmony" must obtain between these objectives. But equally of interest is the relation between sustainability and the pursuit of justice, both intragenerational and intergenerational. Sustainable development is sometimes defined as non-declining consumption per capita. However, non-declining per capita consumption is compatible with enormous per capita inequalities. And while it is true that a commitment to intergenerational equity appears logically to imply a commitment to intragenerational equity, realization of these two aims might in practice conflict. The opportunity costs of measures to "save" the environment that benefit

FUTURE GENERATIONS might happen to fall upon today's poor; and this just makes the point that although the poor suffer most from environmental degradation, because they depend more heavily than the rich on natural, as opposed to human-made resources, it does not follow that they will benefit most from its restoration. But if environmental protection is not sufficient to ensure social justice, i.e. to help today's poor, is it not at least necessary? A skeptic might wonder whether environmental damage – e.g. damage that results from development – is not also at least as necessary a condition of social justice. The relation between environmental protection and the well-being of future humans is also not straightforward. Environmental protection does not guarantee the well-being of future humans, without many enabling factors being in place. Whether it is necessary depends on how environmental protection is understood. If it is explained as "maintaining the capacity of the environment to serve human interests," then indeed the connection is assured – by fiat. But if environmental protection is given a more radical slant – allowing nature to "go its own way", for example – then again, it might be environmental damage that is required to ensure the well-being of future humans.

Whether long-term human economic interests and the long-term integrity of the natural world really do coincide is one of the deep underlying problems of the sustainability debate. Of particular interest in this connection is the way that the sustainability debate itself has prompted searching critiques of the growth model, and questionings of the relation between growth and the human good. Increasingly, the distinction is drawn between economic growth, on the one hand, and development on the other, the latter denoting a richer register of human aspiration. Amartya Sen (1987), for example, has explained development as "a process of expanding the capabilities of people," a notion that is intended to include expanded autonomy and greater access to justice. There are in fact sound conceptual reasons for claiming that human well-being, if this is understood as implying a conscious state of sensitivity, cannot be intelligibly specified without reference to external circumstances, including states of the natural world. Peace of mind is simply not an option if a baby is crying, or people are starving. And there are conceptions of the human good that make a concern for nature for its own sake a contributing or even constitutive factor in human well-being. In this way human interest and ecological integrity do not just happen to coincide, but exhibit an interlocking conceptual relationship. This prompts a more hopeful line of thought – that human aspirations for a better quality of life might be met even though there is decreasing reliance upon economic growth as such, and therefore decreasing impact on non-human life-forms. At least on one scenario, then, the leading objectives of sustainability might after all be made consistent.

A further question is how sustainability compares with environmental objectives of longer standing that it has tended to supplant, such as (a) nature conservation, (b) land health, and (c) ecological integrity.

Nature conservation Writing in the 1991 annual report of the Council for the Protection of Rural England, its Chairman David Astor voiced the opinion that "The great pioneers of CPRE in the 1920s did not use the term sustainable development but that is exactly what they stood for." But one might well take issue with this claim. For among these traditional nature conservationists one finds a concern for natural features that are indigenous, rare, venerable, fragile and irreplaceable. It is not clear, however, that a single one of these categories would be guaranteed a place on a sustainability programme.

Land health   Aldo Leopold's notion of land health – "the capacity of the land for self-renewal" – on the other hand, comes much closer (see THE LAND ETHIC). It embraces cultivated as well as natural landscapes and, like sustainability, anticipates the idea of future capacity. But one difference is suggested by an analogy with the human body. We can function in pretty much the normal way (sustain our activities) with spectacles, dentures, and a walking-stick. But the conditions which these aids help us surmount are incapacities. The same goes for agricultural systems, which can continue to function provided humans continue to supply the necessary fertilizers, etc., but it does not exactly have the capacity for *self*-renewal (as specified in Leopold's definition of land health). It is not clear that sustainability requires land health as such.

Integrity   The contrast between the goal of sustainability and that of ecological integrity – understood as a condition of minimum human disturbance – appears at first sight more marked. But the prospects for compatibility depend on which of two questions are asked. The first question is: how much integrity do we need? There are those who believe that a tolerable human future actually requires the maintenance of substantial portions of the globe relatively free of human influence. But whether they are right depends upon the character of the human future being envisaged; and it is hard to avoid the suspicion that certain sustainable futures at any rate would feature a natural world containing only species that can abide, or avoid, the human footprint. The second question is: how much freedom from human disturbance do non-human species need? This way lies a brighter prospect for the compatibility of the sustainability and ecological agendas. But its realization depends on whether human society is prepared to ask the question, and act on the answer.

The criteria

The issue of what will count as achieving sustainability, and what criterion will be used to map the new development path, is absolutely crucial. It will in effect determine the sustainability agenda. By far the most developed suggestions for measuring progress towards sustainability have come from economists (see ECONOMICS), and in a number of countries many so-called "green accounting" schemes are in operation. At the heart of the economic approach to sustainability is the concept of capital. The modeling of nature on the analogy of financial "capital," capable of yielding "interest," arises readily from earlier notions of "sustainable yield," found in resource economics. Applied to nature generally, the proposed criterion states that if each generation bequeaths at least as much capital to the next generation as it receives, then this will constitute a sustained development path. (Economists appear not to be deterred from using the model despite there being no clear sense in which non-renewable resources can "yield" interest.)

The theory proceeds to mark a distinction between two kinds of capital – natural and human-made (Pearce et al. 1989, pp. 34–5). Human-made capital comprises all artifacts, as well as human and social capital – people, their skills, intelligence, virtues, and institutions. Natural capital comprises all naturally occurring organic and inorganic resources, including not just physical items but also genetic information, biodiversity, life-support systems, and sinks. This distinction in turn generates two versions of the criterion: so-called "weak sustainability," which stipulates an undiminished capital bequest irrespective of how it is composed; and so-called "strong sustainability," which stipulates an undiminished bequest of natural capital.

The distinguishing feature of weak sustainability is indifference between natural and human-made capital, provided only that human needs continue to be met. It is often alleged, but on no very good textual evidence, that advocates of weak sustainability are committed to unlimited substitutability between natural and human-made capital. What they are committed to, as economists, is that the value of all kinds of capital is comparable. But this is quite different from the claim that the valued *items* can be substituted: a visit to the cinema might cost as much as a good meal, but it doesn't follow that it can replace a good meal. Moreover, advocates of strong sustainability, if they are committed to the principles of neoclassical economics, must also hold that the value of human-made and natural capital is comparable in terms of economic value; for this is ultimately reducible to the preferences of rational economic agents, and therefore capable of being expressed in monetary terms. Indeed, it is just this feature of the account that makes it possible for the level of capital to be measured, and therefore possible for there to be a criterion of sustainability. The distinguishing feature of strong sustainability is that it is not indifferent between natural and human-made capital, but requires natural capital to be maintained. So it requires natural capital to be maintained not only where substitution by human-made capital is not possible (this much weak sustainability would agree with, since if natural capital cannot be substituted its loss would be a loss to total capital, which weak sustainability does not allow), but crucially, where it is possible.

The impact of weak sustainability is not insignificant. Although it allows environmental loss to be offset against other kinds of economic gain, it at least acknowledges that environmental loss harbors economic loss, and must therefore be taken into account rather than regarded as an "externality" – something which purely economic accounting can afford to ignore. From the environmentalist perspective, however, the most obvious defect of weak sustainability is that it appears to countenance severing the connection between sustainability and environmental protection. It permits the natural environment to be degraded provided that human well-being can still be secured. But it should be noted that if the claim made by some advocates of strong sustainability is correct, and the presence of substantial features of the natural world is indispensable for human well-being, then certainly it will justify the claim that the level of natural capital should be maintained. But, far from justifying strong sustainability as a distinct position from weak, it actually shows that it is redundant.

The advantages of the economic approach are several:

1. It highlights the fact that environmental conservation carries economic costs and burdens; also – and crucially – that economic benefits carry environmental costs.

2. It offers a way of measuring the benefits of environmental conservation against those gained from other forms of expenditure, e.g. military, health.
3. It makes the case for compensating forgone income – e.g. "debt-for-nature" swaps (though this runs up against the problem that compensating "poor" countries may mean "compensating" individually rich people).
4. It offers a way of measuring the effectiveness of any conservation policy or program, which, however unclear its methods or contested its results, is vital for any durable program of implementation.
5. The concept of "natural capital" in particular makes the point that we should not regard our use of environmental resources as if we were living off *income*.

But how plausible is it to construe nature as capital? The account of the economists faces moral, methodological, ecological, and conceptual difficulties.

The moral objection, first, is that the natural world is not simply a resource but, for example, contains sentient creatures who have claims to moral consideration (see SENTIENTISM). An alternative, or additional, point is that the natural world embodies values other than its value to humans, values that are inherent rather than instrumental (see NORMATIVE ETHICS). A third objection stems from resistance to the idea that all values are commensurable, and especially resistance to the idea that they can be assessed according to a common economic numeraire.

Among methodological objections is the problem of how markets distorted by sociopolitical power structures can adequately reflect resource scarcity; and more generally, how the value of items and processes that span centuries can be adequately assessed according to the parochial and quotidian values of the day. Besides being presumptuous, the difficulty is that the slightest difference in evaluative criteria here and now – say a 1 per cent difference in the "discount rate" – will have enormous and amplified effects hereafter (see ECONOMICS).

Among ecological objections is the difficulty of mapping ecological realities – involving processes that are episodic, non-linear, unstable, and unpredictable – with economic indicators and criteria. A further objection to the resource approach is that it suppresses recognition of the historical character of the biosphere. Even where there is recognition that the biosphere is the result of complex events spanning many centuries, this tends to be construed as merely a technical problem of restoration. Time and historical process is construed, in other words, as nothing more than a technical constraint on the preservation of natural capital – an approach which completely misses what is at stake in loss of BIODIVERSITY. Irreversibility, too, is seen as an annoying impediment to the maintenance of capital, instead of being seen for what it is – the very stuff of natural process.

There are also severe conceptual difficulties. First, the concepts "natural world" and "natural capital" have quite different connotations. Natural capital is the natural world construed as an "asset": it is the natural world just insofar as it represents its capacity to service human needs. Large portions of the natural world therefore do not count as natural capital – for example, events such as volcanic eruptions and hurricanes, and species such as mosquitoes and locusts. On the one hand, degradation seems to abound: stunted tree development associated with deteriorating soil quality; premature leaf drop associated with air pollution; fish and aquatic mammals disappearing from rivers; thousands of miles of coral reef bleached or dying in the wake of 1998's highest sea temperatures on record. But the situation from the point of view of natural capital is far from clear. Is this a description of a decline in natural capital? The capacity of the natural world to serve human well-being appears unabated – perhaps *because* we have, for example, more efficient ways of destroying locusts. Hence, the economic criterion appears unable to identify what has gone wrong. If this is true, it cannot possibly function as a guide to the path that will put it right.

A second point is that the extent of natural capital depends on the availability of human-made capital. For our vulnerable ancestors, much of the natural world needed to be – and was – destroyed. Much else needed to be transformed – by fire, cultivation, and domestication. The implication is that natural capital relies so extensively on human-made capital for its capacity to be realized that it is by and large meaningless to talk of natural capital in abstraction from the human-made capital that mediates its use. Reflections of this kind lead Dale Jamieson to remark that "it is quite difficult to distinguish natural from human produced capital" (1998, p. 185). If this is true, then it will also be "quite difficult" to specify the requirements for strong sustainability. The amount of natural capital available simply cannot be judged independently of reference to human-made capital.

A third problem concerns the notion of substitution; for, levels of capital are supposed to be judged depending upon whether substitutions can or cannot be made. But the question whether A can or cannot be substituted for B is not intelligible in isolation; it depends on context – the purpose for which the substitution is made, the degree of precision required, and so forth (Holland 1997). Nor is it clear, in any case, how far these are empirical as opposed to normative questions. However, the real problem is not the proposed substitution between natural and human-made capital; it is the proposed substitution of capital for nature. Natural capital is not the yield of nature; on the contrary, it tends to be yielded through the destruction of nature.

One, final, difficulty with the economic approach is how we are to know, at any particular point along the "new development path," what the overall trajectory of the path is likely to be, and what "next step" will contribute to it. The source of the difficulty is both causal and epistemological, because each possible next step will have different outcomes, and these will rapidly become impossible to predict. It is hard to see how a sustainable path could be identified in any other way than retrospectively. This suggests that the condition or state of sustainability cannot be understood in terms of purely economic criteria, i.e. as measurable by any kind of efficiency or optimizing outcomes. It appears rather as an inter-temporal and path-dependent process which can only be maintained by procedures and traditions that are self-critical, self-renewing, and sensitive to distributional and historical concerns.

Implementation

A "new ethic," and new technologies, might both be seen as possible ingredients of a "new development path," but they cannot be realized in a vacuum. They require the presence of certain sorts of social and political institution, and above all a citizenry that is attuned to the demands of the new development path. Unfortunately, certain characteristics of the present global economy, for example, the mobility of labor and capital, and the centralization of knowledge and power, make transitions to environmental sustainability and to redistributive social and economic policies hard to envisage. The interests of multinational corporations, even though they put on a green costume and may sincerely speak of feeding the hungry, are not best served by widening access to natural resources and helping the hungry to feed themselves. Developments in science and technology, e.g. nuclear and genetic research programs, point to a similar conclusion. They are becoming less, rather than more, socially accountable, as their research agendas fall increasingly into private hands. The future looks set to belong to powerful and well-financed minorities rather than being held in common – the "common future" to which Brundtland aspired. For these reasons, the notion of a "technical solution" had best not be too readily dismissed, since from one perspective it appears the most likely eventuality. From the spinning jenny to the information revolution, TECHNOLOGY has shown a remarkable ability to lead society by the nose. In accordance with such reflections, it is now being increasingly recognized that "social" or "cultural" sustainability is likely to be crucial to the achievement of any kind of sustainability at all. Among the key elements of cultural sustainability that will need to be in place are: (a) resilient political institutions; (b) effective regulation; (c) appropriate social skills and habits; (d) accountable science and technology; and (e) a climate of trust (see LAW).

There are signs that the sustainability agenda itself may be capable of provoking certain sorts of political institution and vision, just as much as it requires them for its implementation. The very idea of intergenerational justice, for example, at least complements and may well presuppose and inspire notions of cross-generational community that are by no means new, but have been somewhat muted in the face of prevailing utilitarian and individualistic ideologies. In modern times they reach back at least to the eighteenth-century Irish philosopher Edmund Burke's notion of a diachronic community, a "partnership . . . not only between those who are living, but between those who are living, those who are dead, and those who are to be born." Skeptics doubt whether such a community can enjoy reciprocal relations, or shared values. But such doubts appear misplaced. Later generations can reciprocate by honoring their predecessors or striving to fulfill their hopes. And the importance of shared values can be overrated: absence of dissent and lack of change over time are more symptomatic of a moribund than a healthy community (see FUTURE GENERATIONS).

Certain alternatives to the economic approach to sustainability gain relevance here, such as the idea of patrimonial management developed by several French researchers (Lescuyer 1998). Inspired by relations between people and environment in non-market economies, the approach builds on gift and counter-gift exchanges that arise naturally among those whose livelihoods are invested in nature, and for whom, therefore, the environment itself is a medium of transaction and interaction over time. From this perspective, monetary transaction, far from being the key and measure of all environmental transactions, is a poor measure of the value of environmental resources, especially in the context of developing economies, besides also failing to capture the significance of transtemporal relations in developed market economies.

Conclusion

Sustainable development may be summarily defined as development of a kind that does not prejudice future development. It is intended to function essentially as a criterion for what is to count as acceptable environmental modification. Although we may not be able to predict future human needs with any precision, we can be sure that any future human development will require resources, sinks, and life-sustaining systems. We may be reasonably sure therefore that measures taken to minimize human impact on resources and sinks, and to minimize changes to life-support functions, will be steps toward sustainability thus understood. We can also be sure that measures taken to secure these environmental targets require a supporting social fabric. At the same time, it must not be forgotten that what any generation bequeaths to its successors is a package, including not only "costs," but also "benefits," such as technological expertise and other forms of human and social "capital," without which natural resources, sinks, and services would not have the value to humans that they do. But perhaps most crucial of all, its actions also shape and determine the very conditions under which succeeding generations will live. Hence, the question of whether any society is on a sustainable trajectory is at best an extremely complex one, and may well be in principle impossible to compute. What then, should we make of the attempts, especially by economists, to provide just such computations? It is true that environmental degradation has economic costs, and that these costs are a telling symptom of our environmental predicament. But it does not follow that these are the only costs, or that economic values can successfully measure these costs – for a variety of reasons. These include doubts about the various methodologies deployed, and difficulties of principle – about how to cost moral concerns, or how to cost features of the social fabric, such as a Royal Commission on Environmental Pollution, or the environmental habits of Swedish citizens. Above all, if our assessment of economic value is determined by the very economic system whose credentials are in question, it is hard to see how the translation of that value system into the environmental sphere can yield a just estimate of environmental value, or enforce the re-evaluation of environmental goods, as it is supposed to do.

The real importance of sustainability may lie in providing a new conceptual context within which issues of growth and environment can be debated, and in provoking us to reassess our notions of quality of life and environment. It answers also to a need, visceral as well as pragmatic, to do something in the face of loss. But as a guiding principle, it must be judged ultimately unsatisfying. It seems too closely locked in to conceptions of the world – a storehouse that must be kept filled, a machine that must be maintained – that are themselves no longer sustainable. In the wake of Darwin, the world looks much more like an open-ended historical process ill-suited for filling or maintaining. Our more modest task is how not to blight the interlocking futures of the human and the natural community that we have the power profoundly to affect but lack the capacity and the wisdom to manage.

References

Beckerman, W. (1994) "Sustainable development: is it a useful concept?," *Environmental Values* 3, pp. 191–209. [A sharp critique of the sustainability agenda.]

Holland, A. (1997) "Substitutability: or, why strong sustainability is weak and absurdly strong sustainability is not absurd," in *Valuing Nature? Economics, Ethics and the Environment*, ed. J. Foster (London: Routledge), pp. 119–34. [Explores some conceptual difficulties with the notion of sustainability.]

Jamieson, D. (1998) "Sustainability and beyond," *Ecological Economics* 24, pp. 183–92. [A sober assessment of the limitations of the sustainability discourse.]

Landsberg, H. H. (1992) "Looking backward: Stockholm 1972," *Resources for the Future* 106, pp. 2–3. [A brief, but useful backward glance at the Stockholm conference.]

Lescuyer, G. (1998) "Globalization of environmental monetary valuation and sustainable development: an experience in the tropical forest of Cameroon," *International Journal of Sustainable Development* 1, no. 1, pp. 115–33. [A timely reminder of the importance of non-market economies.]

Pearce, D., Markandya, A., and Barbier, E. B. (1989) *Blueprint for a Green Economy* (London: Earthscan). [A classic of environmental economics.]

Redclift, M. (1987) *Sustainable Development: Exploring the Contradictions* (London: Methuen). [An early critique of Brundtland.]

Sen, A. K. (1987) *On Ethics and Economics* (Oxford: Blackwell). [A seminal work on quality-of-life issues.]

Shiva, V. (1992) "Recovering the real meaning of sustainability," in *The Environment in Question*, ed. D. Cooper and J. Palmer (London: Routledge), pp. 187–93. [A brief but probing essay on sustainability.]

Simon, J. L. (1998) "Scarcity or abundance?," *The Business of Consumption*, ed. L. Westra and P. H. Werhane (Lanham: Rowman and Littlefield), pp. 237–45. [An outspoken critique of the sustainability agenda.]

WCED (World Commission on Environment and Development) (1987) *Our Common Future* (Oxford: Oxford University Press). [Also called "The Brundtland Report," the classic text on sustainability.]

Further reading

Daly, H. E. and Cobb Jr., J. B. (1994) *For the Common Good* (Boston: Beacon Press). [Presents the standpoint of "strong" sustainability.]

Jacobs, M. (1991) *The Green Economy* (London: Pluto Press). [An excellent guide to the subject.]

McQuillan, A. G. and Preston, A. L., eds. (1998) *Globally and Locally: Seeking a Middle Path to Sustainable Development* (Lanham: University Press of America). [A distinctive attempt to bring both local and global issues within a single framework.]

Rees, W. E., and Wackernagel, M. (1994) "Ecological footprints and appropriated carrying capacity: measuring the natural capital requirements of the human economy," in *Investing in Natural Capital: The Ecological Economics of Sustainability*, ed. A. Jannson, M. Hammer, C. Folke, and R. Costanza (Washington DC: Island Press). [Develops the influential notion of an "ecological footprint."]

28

Biodiversity

HOLMES ROLSTON III

When animals, birds, and plants vanish from the landscape, this raises public concern. Initially, the focus was on endangered species, which are still central, but in recent years attention has widened to other levels of biodiversity, such as types of ecosystems at a regional level, or genetic diversity at the microbiological level. Species are a more evident, mid-range, natural kind, which can be located in breeding populations. The US Congress, deploring the lack of "adequate concern (for) and conservation (of)" species, passed the Endangered Species Act (US Congress 1973, Sec. 2(a)(1)). The United Nations has negotiated a Biodiversity Convention, signed by more than 100 nations.

Such concern is unfamiliar to traditional philosophical analysis. John Rawls, for example, advocating his most perceptive contemporary theory of justice, admits that in his theory "no account is given of right conduct in regard to animals and the rest of nature." Nevertheless, he claims, "Certainly . . . the destruction of a whole species can be a great evil" (Rawls 1971, p. 512). But one will search past philosophical literature in vain for much help giving reasons why. This chapter first asks how far classical humanistic ethics can be applied to conserve biodiversity and then turns to explore novel problems in emerging human responsibilities of caring for endangered species.

The legislation to protect endangered species has often been used to protect as well the ecosystems of which they are part (such as the old growth forests of the Pacific Northwest, containing the spotted owl). An ecosystems approach is increasingly regarded as more efficient than a single-species approach. DNA sequencing and new possibilities in genetic technology have intensified concern for saving genetic diversity. At the same time, saving every genetic variant is evidently impossible even if it were desirable. Some recent studies find more diversity among microbes than among all the higher forms of life. Evaluating this spectrum of diversity, from genes through species to ecosystems to the biosphere, is one of the challenges in environmental ethics.

The implications of the Endangered Species Act have been unfolding over the last quarter century. The Act was passed mostly with the charismatic megafauna in mind (grizzly bears and whooping cranes), though the Act has always permitted listing less glamorous species. On rare inland dunes in California, the Delhi Sands Flower-loving Fly (*Rhaphiomidas terminatus abdominalis*), a huge and unusual fly, on the US endangered species list, is said (in the rhetoric of debate at least) to stand in the way of industrial development that would create 20,000 jobs, although the fly only needs about 300 acres of habitat (Booth 1997).

In later amendments Congress has increasingly extended protection to plants. Court decisions have protected habitat as essential to the survival of species. When the Act is applied to private lands, this has raised the "takings" issue, with land-owners claiming that compensation is due, and environmentalists replying the rights to land do not include the right to extinguish species.

Ethics is a matter of duty, in classical categories, or of appropriate caring, as some now prefer to say. Whether humans have duties to endangered species is a significant theoretical and an urgent practical question. Why ought we to care? In the larger picture, the question of duties to ecosystems will arise. It would seem awkward to ask about duties to genes, although proper to ask why we should care about preserving genetic diversity. We will focus on the species question, as this opens up these philosophical issues.

Few persons doubt that humans have some obligations concerning endangered species, because persons are helped or hurt by the condition of their environment, which includes a wealth of wild species. Taking or jeopardizing listed endangered species is illegal and, many think, immoral. But these might be all obligations to persons who are benefited or harmed by species as resources. Is there a human duty directly to species? An answer is vital to the more comprehensive question of the conservation of biodiversity.

Saving species for people

A rationale for saving species that centers on their worth to humans is anthropo-centric, where species have instrumental values. A rationale that includes their intrinsic and ecosystemic values, in addition to or independently of persons, is naturalistic, sometimes said to be biocentric. "The preservation of species," by the usual humanistic utilitarian account, reported by Stuart Hampshire, is "to be aimed at and commended only in so far as human beings are, or will be emotionally and sentimentally interested" (Hampshire 1972, pp. 3–4; see also NORMATIVE ETHICS).

This includes duties to future humans. Joel Feinberg says, "We do have duties to protect threatened species, not duties to the species themselves as such, but rather duties to future human beings, duties derived from our housekeeping role as tempor-ary inhabitants of this planet" (Feinberg 1974, p. 56; see also FUTURE GENERATIONS). Persons have a strong duty not to harm others (a duty of non-maleficence) and a weaker, though important, duty to help others (a duty of beneficence).

Many endangered species – which ones we may not now know – are expected to have agricultural, industrial, and medical benefits. Loss of the wild stocks of the cultivars leaves humans genetically vulnerable, so it is prudent to save the native materials. In an interesting example, an obscure Yellowstone thermophilic microbe, *Thermophus aquaticus*, was discovered to supply a heat-stable enzyme, which can be used to drive the polymerase chain reaction (PCR), used in a revolutionary gene-copying technique. The rights to the process sold in 1991 for $300 million, and the process is now earning $100 million a year.

According to this reasoning, the protection of nature is ultimately for the purpose of its enlightened exploitation. Norman Myers urges "conserving our global stock" (Myers 1979). But critics reply that examples of high economic value obtained from rare species are anomalous and that, on statistical average, most endangered species have little probability of significant economic value. Debates have also followed about who owns wild species, if anyone, or who owns rights to them or to products derived from them. These issues are especially problematic in many relatively species-rich and technologically poor developing nations, when wealthier nations come prospecting, or when development is curtailed to save biodiversity.

Where not directly useful, wild species may be indirectly important for the roles they play in ecosystems. They are "rivets" in the airplane, the earthship in which we humans are flying (Ehrlich and Ehrlich 1981). The loss of a few species may have no evident results now, but the loss of many species imperils the resilience and stability of the ecosystems on which humans depend. The danger increases exponentially with subtractions from the ecosystem, a slippery slope into serious troubles. Even species that have no obvious or current direct value to humans are part of the biodiversity that keeps ecosystems healthy. One team of economists estimates the value of the world's ecosystem services, though largely off the market, to be in the range of $16–54 trillion per year, compared to the global gross national product total of $18 trillion per year (Costanza et al. 1997). Even those doubtful of the numbers concede that the aggregate benefits are huge (see ECONOMICS).

Some benefits are less tangible. Species that are too rare to play roles in ecosystems can have recreational and aesthetic value. Biodiversity enriches the landscapes on which humans reside; people enjoy variety in wildlife and wildflowers. Those who see bears or wolves in Yellowstone report that this is the highlight of their experience. The aesthetic experience of nature differs importantly from that of artworks; seeing whooping cranes in flight is unlike visiting an art museum. The wealth of species is aesthetic, an amenity value, as much as it is economic, a commodity value. At least in developed nations, where consumer goods are not in short supply but opportunities to experience nature are diminishing, it seems probable that, in the decades ahead, the quality of life will decline in proportion to the loss of biotic diversity (see AESTHETICS).

Species can be curiosities. The rare species fascinate enthusiastic naturalists and are often key scientific study species. They may serve as indicators of ecosystem health. They can be clues to understanding natural history. Destroying species is like tearing pages out of an unread book, written in a language humans hardly know how to read, about the place where we live. This is the Rosetta Stone argument (named after the obelisk found at Rosetta in Egypt in 1799, which enabled the deciphering of forgotten languages of the ancient past). Humans need insight into the full text of natural history. They need to understand the evolving world in which they are placed.

Following this logic, humans do not have duties to the book, the stone, or the species, but to themselves – duties both of prudence and education. Such anthropogenic reasons are pragmatic and impressive. They are also moral, since persons are benefited or harmed.

An ethics for species?

Can all duties concerning species be analyzed as duties to persons? Many endangered species have no resource value, nor are they particularly important for the other reasons given above. Beggar's ticks, with their stick-tight seeds, are a common nuisance weed through much of the United States. However, one species, the tidal shore beggar's tick (*Bidens bidentoides*), which differs little from the others in appearance, is increasingly endangered. It seems unlikely that it is either a rivet or a potential resource. Its extinction might be good riddance.

Are there completely worthless species? If so, is there any reason or duty to save them? A primary environmental ethics answer is that species are good in their own right, whether or not they are any good for humans. The duties-to-persons-only line of argument leaves deeper reasons untouched. Those calling for a more objective, or biocentric, environmental ethics argue that the deeper problem with the anthropocentric rationale is that its justifications are submoral and fundamentally exploitive and self-serving, even if subtly so. This is not true intraspecifically among humans, when out of a sense of duty an individual defers to the values of fellow humans. But it is true interspecifically, since, under this rationale, *Homo sapiens* treats all other species as rivets, resources, study materials, or entertainments.

Ethics has always been about partners with entwined destinies. But it has never been very convincing when pleaded as enlightened self-interest (I ought always to act in my best self-interest), including class self-interest (we ought always to act in our group self-interest). This is true even though ethics makes a place for self-interest (myself and my group being treated justly, fairly). Ethics brings benefits to those who are ethical; it conveys mutual advantage; it is good for people. But it also enlarges spheres of care and concern. To value all other species in our human group's self-interest is rather like a nation arguing all its foreign policy in terms of national self-interest. Neither seems fully moral.

Nevertheless, those who try to articulate a deeper environmental ethic often get lost in unfamiliar territory. Natural kinds, if that is what species are, are obscure objects of concern. Species, as such, cannot be directly helped or hurt, though individual tokens of the species type can be. Species, as such, don't care, though individual animals can care. Species require habitats, embedded in ecosystems that evolve and change. Of the species that have inhabited earth, 98 percent are extinct, replaced by other species. Nature doesn't care, so why should we?

All the familiar moral landmarks of classical ethics seem to be gone. One has moved beyond caring about humans, or culture, or moral agents, or individual animals that are close kin, or can suffer, or experience anything, or are sentient. Species are not valuers with preferences that can be satisfied or frustrated. It seems odd to say that species have rights. Tom Regan says, for example, "The rights view is a view about the moral rights of individuals, and the rights view does not recognize the moral rights of species to anything, including survival" (Regan 1983, p. 359).

It seems odd to say that species need our sympathy, or that we should consider their point of view. Nor is it clear that species have interests. Nicholas Rescher says:

> Moral obligation is thus always interest-oriented. But only individuals can be said to have interests; one only has moral obligations to particular individuals or particular groups thereof. Accordingly, the duty to save a species is not a matter of moral duty toward it, because moral duties are only oriented to individuals. A species as such is the wrong sort of target for a moral obligation. (Rescher 1980, p. 83)

So it is hard to figure concern for species within the coordinates of prevailing ethical systems.

In fact, ethics and biology have had uncertain relations. An often-heard argument forbids moving from what *is* the case (a species exists) to what *ought to be* (a species ought to exist); any who do so commit, it is alleged, the naturalistic fallacy. On the other hand, if species are of objective value, and if humans encounter and jeopardize such value, it would seem that humans ought not to destroy values in nature, not at least without overriding justification producing greater value. A species is of *value* – this may be the intermediate premise. We might make a humanistic mistake if we arrogantly take value to lie exclusively in the satisfaction of our human preferences. What is at jeopardy and what are our duties?

The threat of extinction

Although projections vary, reliable estimates are that about 20 percent of earth's species may be lost within a few decades, if present trends go unreversed. These losses will be about evenly distributed through major groups of plants and animals in both developed and developing nations, although the most intense concerns are in tropical forests (Wilson 1992; Ehrlich and Ehrlich 1981). At least 500 species, subspecies, and varieties of fauna have been lost in the United States since 1600. The natural rate would have been about ten. Islands have been a special concern. In Hawaii, of 68 species of birds unique to the islands, 41 are extinct or virtually so. Half the 2,200 native plants are endangered or threatened. Covering all states, a candidate list of US plants contains more than 2,000 taxa considered to be endangered, threatened, or of concern. A candidate list of animals contains about 1,800 entries. Humans approach, and, in places, have even exceeded the catastrophic rates of natural extinction spasms of the geological past.

Questions of fact: what are species?

There are problems at two levels: one is about facts (a scientific issue – about species), one is about values (an ethical issue – involving duties). There are several differing concepts of species within biology. By some accounts any species concept is arbitrary, conventional – a mapping device that is only theoretical. Darwin wrote, "I look at the term species, as one arbitrarily given for the sake of convenience to a set of individuals closely resembling each other" (Darwin 1968 [1872], p. 108). Is there enough factual reality in species to base duty there?

No one doubts that individual organisms exist, but are species discovered? Or made up? Indeed, do species exist at all? Systematists regularly revise species designations and routinely put after a species the name of the "author" who, they say, "erected" the taxon. If a species is only a category or class, boundary lines may be arbitrarily drawn, and the species is nothing more than an artifact of the classifier's thoughts and aims. Some natural properties are used – reproductive structures, bones, teeth, or perhaps ancestry, or genes, or ecological roles. But which properties are selected and where the lines are drawn are decisions that vary with systematists.

Botanists are divided whether *Iliamna remota*, the Kankakee mallow in Illinois, and *Iliamna corei* in Virginia, which are both rare, are distinct species. Perhaps all that exists objectively in the world are the individual mallow plants; whether there are two species or one is a fuss about which label to use. A species is some kind of fiction, like a center of gravity or a statistical average. Almost no one proposes duties to genera, families, orders, phyla; biologists concede that these do not exist in nature, even though we may think that two species in different orders represent more biodiversity, with more genetic distance between them, than two in the same genus. If this approach is pressed, species can become something like the lines of longitude and latitude, or like map contour lines, or time of day, or dates on a calendar. Sometimes endangered species designations have altered when systematists decided to lump or split previous groupings.

A debate has continued over whether the red wolf is a species or a long-established hybrid of the gray wolf and the coyote. The distinction affects the considerable efforts to save this wolf in the southeastern United States. The tuatara is a large, iguana-like reptile with a third eye in the center of its head, which survives on a few islands off the coast of New Zealand. Because systematists earlier recognized one species rather than the three now claimed, tuataras have received inadequate protection, and one of the three species is now extinct. Depending on the degree to which species are or are not artifacts of those doing the taxonomy, duties to save them can seem more convincing or unconvincing.

There are four main concepts of species: (1) morphological, asking whether organisms have the same anatomy and functions; (2) biological (so-called), asking whether organisms can interbreed; (3) evolutionary, asking whether organisms have the same lineage historically; and (4) genetic, asking whether they have a common genome. But these concepts are not mutually exclusive; organisms that have enough common ancestry will have a similar morphology and function; they will be able to interbreed, and they can do so because they have similar genomes.

All these concepts combine for a more realist account. A species is a living historical form (Latin: *species*), propagated in individual organisms, which flows dynamically over generations. Species are dynamic natural kinds, historically particular lineages. A species is a coherent, ongoing natural kind expressed in organisms that interbreed because that kind is encoded in gene flow, the genes determining the organism's morphology and functions, the kind shaped by its environment. In one sense, the genes are what is reproduced, if one chooses to focus on that level; but in another sense the natural kind (species) is what is reproduced. There is genome producing genome producing genome, with genetic variation. There is also tiger producing tiger producing tiger. The coding is at the genetic level; the coping is at the native range level of organisms with adapted fit in ecosystems. A gene is an information-bit about how the species makes its way through the world.

In this sense, species are objectively there as living processes in the evolutionary ecosystem – found, not made by taxonomists. Species are real historical entities, interbreeding populations. By contrast, families, orders, and genera are not levels where biological reproduction takes place. So far from being arbitrary, species are the real evolutionary units of biodiversity. This claim – that there are specific forms of life historically maintained in their environments over time – is not fictional, but, rather, seems as certain as anything else we believe about the empirical world, even though at times scientists revise the theories and taxa with which they map these forms.

Species are more like mountains and rivers, phenomena that are objectively there to be mapped. The edges of such natural kinds will sometimes be fuzzy, to some extent discretionary. We can expect that one species will modify into another over evolutionary time, often gradually, sometimes more quickly. But it does not follow from the fact that speciation is sometimes in progress that species are merely made up, instead of found as evolutionary lines articulated into diverse forms, each with its more or less distinct integrity, breeding population, gene pool, and role in its ecosystem. It is quite objective to claim that evolutionary lines are articulated into diverse kinds of life. What taxonomists do, or should do, is "carve nature at the joints" (Plato).

G. G. Simpson concludes, "An evolutionary species is a lineage (an ancestral-descendant sequence of populations) evolving separately from others and with its own unitary evolutionary role and tendencies" (1961, p. 153). Niles Eldredge and Joel Cracraft insist, with emphasis, that species are "*discrete entities in time as well as space*" (1980, p. 92). The various criteria for defining species (recent descent, reproductive isolation, morphology, distinct gene pool) come together at least in providing evidence that species are really there. What survives for a few months, years, or decades is the individual animal or plant, what survives for millennia is the kind as a lineage. Life is something passing through the individual as much as something it possesses on its own. Even a species defends itself; that is one way to interpret reproduction. The individual organism resists death; the species resists extinction through reproduction with variation. At both levels, biological identity is conserved over time.

Questions of duty: ought species be saved?

Why ought species to be protected? One reply is that nature is a kind of wonderland. Humans ought to preserve an environment adequate to match their capacity to wonder. But nature as a wonderland introduces the question whether preserving resources for wonder is not better seen as preserving a remarkable natural history that has objective worth. Valuing speciation directly, however, seems to attach value to the evolutionary process (the wonderland), not merely to subjective experiences that arise when humans reflect over it (the wonder).

One might say that humans of decent character will refrain from needless destruction of all kinds. Vandals destroying art objects do not so much hurt statues as do they cheapen their own character. By this account, the duty to save endangered species is really a matter of cultivating human excellences. It is philistine to destroy species carelessly. It is uncalled for. But such a prohibition seems to depend on some value in the species as such, for there need be no prohibition against destroying a valueless thing. Why are such insensitive actions "uncalled for" unless there is something in the species itself that "calls for" a more appropriate attitude? If the excellence of character really comes from appreciating something wonderful, then why not attach value to this other? It seems unexcellent – cheap and philistine – to say that excellence of human character is what we are after. One ought to want virtue in the human beholder that recognizes value in the endangered species. Excellence of human character does indeed result, but let the human virtue come tributary to value found in nature. An enriched humanity results, with values in the species and values in persons compounded – but only if the loci of value are not confounded (see NORMATIVE ETHICS).

A naturalistic account values species, speciation, and the cumulative biodiversity intrinsically. Humans ought to respect these dynamic life forms preserved in historical lines. It is not *form* (species) as mere morphology, but the *formative* (speciating) process that humans ought to preserve, although the process cannot be preserved without some of its products, and the products (species) are valuable as results of the creative process. An ethic about species sees that the species is a bigger event than the individual organism. Biological conservation goes on at this level too; and in a sense this level is more appropriate for moral concern, since the species with its populations is a comprehensive evolutionary unit.

A consideration of species is both revealing and challenging because it offers a biologically based counterexample to the focus on individuals – typically sentient animals and usually individual persons – that has been so characteristic in western ethics. As evolution takes place in ecosystems, it is not mere individuality that counts. The individual represents (re-presents) a species in each new generation. It is a token of a type, and the type is more important than the token. A biological identity – a kind of value – is here defended. The achievement resides in the dynamic form; the individual inherits this, exemplifies it, and passes it on. The evolutionary history that the particular individual has is something passing through it during its life, passed to it and passed on during reproduction, as much as something it intrinsically possesses. Having a biological identity reasserted genetically over time is as true of the species as of the individual. That identity includes its evolutionary achievements, the know-how to perpetuate that kind in the midst of its perpetual perishing, its location as an adapted fit in its ecosystem, filling its niche in the biotic community; respecting this identity generates duties to species.

When a rhododendron plant dies, another one replaces it. But when *Rhododendron chapmanii* – an endangered species in the US Southeast – goes extinct, the species terminates forever. Death of a token is radically different from death of a type; death of an individual different from death of an entire lineage. The deaths of individual rhododendrons in perennial turnover are even necessary if the species is to persist. Seeds are dispersed and replacement rhododendrons grow elsewhere in the pinewood forests, as landscapes change or succession shifts. Latercoming replacements, mutants as well as replacements, are selected for or against in a stable or changing environment. Individuals improve in fitness and the species adapts to an altering climate or competitive pressures. Tracking its environment over time, the species is conserved, modified, and continues on.

With extinction, this stops. Extinction shuts down the generative processes, a kind of superkilling. This kills forms (*species*) – not just individuals. This kills "essences" beyond "existences," collectively, not just distributively. To kill a particular plant is to stop a life of a few years, while other lives of such kind continue unabated, and the possibilities for the future are unaffected; to superkill a particular species is to shut down a story of many millennia, and leave no future possibilities.

A species lacks moral agency, reflective self-awareness, sentience, or organic individuality. Some are tempted to say that specific-level processes cannot count morally. But each ongoing species defends a form of life, and these forms are, on the whole, good kinds. Such speciation has achieved all the planetary richness of life. Virtually all ethicists say that in *Homo sapiens* one species has appeared that not only exists but ought to continue to exist. Everyone concerned for children, grandchildren, and FUTURE GENERATIONS believes that. A naturalistic ethic refuses to say this exclusively of a late-coming, highly developed form and asks whether this duty ought not to extend more broadly to the other species – though not with equal intensity over them all, in view of varied levels of development.

The wrong that humans are doing, or are allowing to happen through carelessness, is stopping the historical gene flow in which the vitality of life is laid, which, viewed at another level, is the same as the flow of natural kinds, which is the drama of biodiversity. A shutdown of the life stream is the most destructive event possible. The duty to species can be overridden, for example with pests or disease organisms. But a prima facie duty stands nevertheless.

The question is not: What is this rare plant or animal good for? But: What good is here? Not: Is this species good for my kind, *Homo sapiens*. But: Is *Rhododendron chapmanii* a good of its kind, a good kind? To care directly about a plant or animal species is to be quite non-anthropocentric and objective about botanical and zoological processes that take place independently of human preferences.

Never before has this level of question been faced, which is why philosophical ethicists have been stuttering about it. Previously, humans did not have much power to cause extinctions, or knowledge about what they were inadvertently doing. But today humans have more understanding than ever of the natural world they inhabit, of the speciating processes, more predictive power to foresee the intended and unintended results of their actions, and more power to reverse the undesirable consequences. The duties that such power and vision generate no longer attach simply to individuals or persons but are emerging duties to specific forms of life.

A consideration of species strains any ethic fixed on individual organisms, much less on sentience or persons. But the resulting ethic can be biologically sounder, though it revises what was formerly thought logically permissible or ethically binding. When ethics is informed by this kind of biology, it is appropriate to attach duty dynamically to the specific form of life. The species line is the more fundamental living system, the whole, of which individual organisms are the essential parts. The appropriate survival unit is the appropriate level of moral concern. Concern for biodiversity will always, by this account, be concern centrally for species. Saving endangered species can even, at times, take priority over the preferences of persons – or even the lives of persons, as with the shoot-to-kill policies for poachers of elephants and rhinoceros (Rolston 1996).

Species in ecosystems

A species is what it is inseparably from the environmental niche into which it fits. Habitats are essential to species, and an endangered species often means an endangered habitat. The species and the community are complementary goods in synthesis, parallel to, but a level above, the way the species and individual organisms have distinguishable but entwined goods. From this viewpoint, it is not preservation of *species* that we wish, but the preservation of *species in the system*. It is not merely *what* they are, but *where* they are that humans must value correctly. Appropriate concern for species is impossible without concern for the diverse ecosystems that they inhabit.

This limits the otherwise important role that zoos and botanical gardens can play in conservation. They can provide research, a refuge for species, breeding programs, aid in public education, and so forth; but they cannot simulate the ongoing dynamism of gene flow over time under the selection pressures in a wild biome. They only lock up a collection of individuals; they amputate the species from its habitat. The species can only be preserved *in situ*; the species ought to be preserved *in situ*. That does move from scientific facts to ethical duties, but what ought to be has to be based on what can be.

Neither individual nor species stands alone; both are embedded in an ecosystem. Every species came to be what it is where it is, shaped as an adaptive fit. (A problem with exotic species, introduced by humans, is often that they are not good fits in their alien ecosystems.) The product, a species, is the outcome of entwined genetic and ecological processes; the generative impulse springs from the gene pool, defended by information coded there. But the whole population or species survives when selection by natural forces tests the member individuals for their adapted fitness in the environmental niche the species occupies.

In an ethic of endangered species, one ought to admire the evolutionary or creative process as much as the product, since these two are interwined. A species is an ongoing historical event, not just a collection of individuals produced. This involves regular species turnover when a species becomes unfit in its habitat, goes extinct, or tracks a changing environment until transformed into something else. On evolutionary timescales, species too are ephemeral. But the speciating process is not. Persisting through vicissitudes for two and a half billion years, speciation is about as long-continuing as anything on earth can be.

Natural and human-caused extinctions

It might seem that for humans to terminate species now and again is quite natural. Species go extinct all the time in natural history. But there are important theoretical and practical differences between natural and anthropogenic (human-caused) extinctions. In natural extinction, a species dies out when it has become unfit in habitat, and other existing or novel species appear in its place. Such extinction is normal turnover in ongoing speciation. Though harmful to a species, extinction in nature seldom impoverishes the system. It is rather the key to tomorrow. The species is employed in, but abandoned to, the larger historical evolution of life.

By contrast, artificial extinction typically shuts down future evolution because it shuts down speciating processes dependent on those species. One opens doors, the other closes them. Humans generate and regenerate nothing; they only dead-end these lines. Relevant differences make the two as morally distinct as death by natural causes is from murder. Anthropogenic extinction differs from evolutionary extinction in that hundreds of thousands of species will perish because of culturally altered environments that are radically different from the spontaneous environments in which such species evolved and in which they sometimes go extinct. In natural extinction, nature takes away life when it has become unfit in a habitat, or when the habitat alters, and typically supplies other life in its place. Natural extinction occurs with transformation, either of the extinct line or related or competing lines. Artificial extinction is without issue.

From this perspective, humans have no duty to preserve species from natural extinctions, although they might have a duty to other humans to save such species as resources or museum pieces. Some have claimed that the Uncompahgre fritillary (*Boloria acrocnema*), known from two alpine mountain peaks in Colorado, is going extinct naturally, and that, therefore, no effort should be made to save it. (Others claim that livestock are a decisive factor.) No species has a "right to life" apart from the continued existence of the ecosystem with which it is able to cofit. But humans do have a duty to avoid artificial extinction.

Over evolutionary time, though extinguishing species, nature has provided new species at a higher rate than the extinction rate; hence the accumulated global biodiversity. There have been infrequent catastrophic extinction events, anomalies in the record, each succeeded by a recovery of previous diversity. Typically, however, the biological processes that characterize earth are prolific. Uninterrupted by accident, or even interrupted so, they have rather steadily increased the numbers of species.

An ethicist has to be circumspect. An argument might commit what logicians call the genetic fallacy to suppose that present value depended upon origins. Species judged today to have intrinsic value might have arisen anciently and anomalously from a valueless context, akin to the way in which life arose mysteriously from non-living materials. But in an ecosystem, what a thing is differentiates poorly from the generating and sustaining matrix. The individual and the species have what value they have to some extent inevitably in the context of the forces that beget them. There is something awesome about an earth that begins with zero and runs up toward five to ten million species in several billion years, setbacks notwithstanding. Were the moral species, *Homo sapiens*, to conserve all Earth's species merely as resources for human preference satisfaction, we would not yet know the truth about what we ought to do in biological conservation.

Respect for life: biodiversity and rarity

Duties to endangered species will be especially concerned with a respect for rare life. Such respect must ask about the role of rarity in generating respect. Rarity is not, as such, an intrinsically valuable property in fauna and flora, or in human experiences (even though people take an interest in things just because they are rare). Certain diseases are rare, and people are glad of it. Monsters and other sports of nature, such as albinos, are rare, and of no particular intrinsic value for their rarity, curiosities though they sometimes become. Indeed, if a species is naturally rare, that initially suggests its insignificance in an ecosystem. Rarity is no automatic cause for respect. Nevertheless, something about the rarity of endangered species heightens the element of respect, and accompanying duty.

Naturally rare species, as much as common or frequent species, signify exuberance in nature; they add to the biodiversity. A rare species may be barely hanging on, surviving by mere luck. But a rare species may be quite competent in its niche, not at all nearing extinction if left on its own; it is only facing extinction when made artificially more rare by human disruptions. The rare flower is a botanical achievement, a bit of brilliance, an ecological problem resolved, an evolutionary threshold crossed. The locally endemic species, perhaps one specialized for an unusual habitat, represents a rare discovery in nature, before it provides a rare human adventure in finding it.

Naturally rare species – if one insists on a restricted evolutionary theory – are random accidents (as in some sense also are the common ones), resulting from a cumulation of mutations. But this mutational fertility generates creativity, and, equally by the theory, surviving species must be more or less satisfactory fits in their environments. Sometimes they live on the cutting edge of exploratory probing; sometimes they are relics of the past. Either way they offer promise and memory of an inventive natural history. Life is a many-splendored thing; extinction of the rare dims this luster. From this arises the respect that generates a duty to save rare lives.

A six-year study sponsored by the National Science Foundation surveyed environmental attitudes in the general public. The survey tested support for the claim: "Our obligation to preserve nature isn't just a responsibility to other people but to the environment itself"; and, perhaps surprisingly, found agreeing not only 97 percent of Earth First! members but also 82 percent of sawmill workers from the Pacific Northwest. The public average was 87 percent. For the claim: "Justice is not just for human beings. We need to be as fair to plants and animals as we are towards people," the agreements are similar: 97 percent, 63 percent, and an average of 90 percent. The survey authors conclude: "An environmental view of the world is more universal than previous studies have suggested" (Kempton et al. 1995, pp. 113, ix).

The seriousness of respect for biodiversity is further illustrated when the idea approaches a "reverence" for life. Surveys also show that for many this is the most important value at stake, often taking a monotheistic form. Species are the creation itself, the "swarms of living creatures" (biodiversity) that "the earth brought forth" at the divine imperative; "God saw that it was good" and "blessed them" (Genesis 1). Noah's ark was the aboriginal endangered species project; God commanded, "Keep them alive with you" (Genesis 6). Any who decide to destroy species take, fearfully, the prerogative of God. When one is conserving life, ultimacy is always nearby. Extinction is forever; and, when danger is ultimate, absolutes become relevant. The motivation to save endangered species can and ought to be pragmatic, economic, political, and scientific; deeper down it is moral, philosophical, and religious. Species embody a fertility on earth that is sacred.

On the scale of evolutionary time, humans appear late and suddenly, a few hundred thousand years on a scale of billions of years, analogous to a few seconds in a twenty-four-hour day. Even more lately and suddenly they increase the extinction rate dramatically, as we have done in this one last century among several thousand years of recorded history. What is offensive in such conduct is not merely the loss of resources, but the maelstrom of killing and insensitivity to forms of life. What is required is not prudence but principled responsibility to the biospheric earth. Only the human species contains moral agents, but conscience ought not to be used to exempt every other form of life from consideration, with the resulting paradox that the sole moral species acts only in its collective self-interest toward all the rest.

Several billion years worth of creative toil, several million species of teeming life, have been handed over to the care of the latecoming species in which the mind has flowered and morals have emerged. On the naturalistic account, the host of species has a claim to care in its own right. There is something Newtonian, not yet Einsteinian, besides something morally naive, about living in a reference frame where one species takes itself as absolute and values everything else relative to its utility.

References

Booth, William (1997) "Developers wish huge fly would buzz off," *Washington Post*, April 4, p. A1. [Unusual endangered fly in California troubles developers.]

Costanza, Robert, et al. (1997) "The value of the world's ecosystem services and natural capital," *Nature* 387, pp. 253–9. [A provocative estimate; nobody knows the dollar value, in large part because it is so high.]

Darwin, Charles (1968 [1872]) *The Origin of Species* (Baltimore: Penguin Books). [An original survey of biodiversity and its origins.]

Ehrlich, Paul and Ehrlich, Anne (1981) *Extinction* (New York: Random House). [Still one of the best general studies of extinction.]

Eldredge, Niles and Cracraft, Joel (1980) *Phylogenetic Patterns and the Evolutionary Process* (New York: Columbia University Press). [An analysis of species and speciation in evolutionary history.]

Feinberg, Joel (1974) "The rights of animals and unborn generations," in *Philosophy and Environmental Crisis*, ed. W. T. Blackstone (Athens, GA: University of Georgia Press), pp. 43–68. [A well-known philosopher puzzled about environmental ethics, including endangered species.]

Hampshire, Stuart (1972) *Morality and Pessimism* (New York: Cambridge University Press). [Includes an account of the utilitarian view of species preservation.]

Kempton, Willett M., Boster, James S., and Hartley, Jennifer A. (1995) *Environmental Values in American Culture* (Cambridge, MA: MIT Press). [Revealing survey, finding that many, even most, Americans value species intrinsically as well as instrumentally.]

Myers, Norman (1979) "Conserving our global stock," *Environment* 21, no. 9 (November) pp. 25–33. [Species as resources for human use.]

Rawls, John (1971) *A Theory of Justice* (Cambridge, MA: Harvard University Press). [A justly celebrated theory of human justice, noting that duties to species require further development of ethics.]

Regan, Tom (1983) *The Case for Animal Rights* (Berkeley CA: University of California Press). [The best analysis of animal rights, but rights do not extend to species.]

Rescher, Nicholas (1980) "Why save endangered species?" in *Unpopular Essays on Technological Progress* (Pittsburgh, PA: University of Pittsburgh Press), pp. 79–92. [Another philosopher troubled about the justification for saving species, other than for human uses.]

Rolston III, Holmes (1996) "Feeding people versus saving nature," in *World Hunger and Morality*, 2nd edn, ed. William Aiken and Hugh LaFollette (Upper Saddle River, NJ: Prentice-Hall), pp. 248–67. [Saving nature often coincides with the long-range interests of the poor, but sometimes the duty to save nature, especially species, overrides the duty to assist the poor.]

Simpson, G. G. (1961) *Principles of Animal Taxonomy* (New York, Columbia University Press). [Argues for the reality of species, found in nature, not made up by systematists.]

US Congress (1973) *Endangered Species Act of 1973*. 87 Stat. 884. Public Law 93–205. [The most famous public law protecting species and one of the most remarkable acts of the US Congress.]

Wilson, Edward O. (1992) *The Diversity of Life* (Cambridge, MA: Harvard University Press). [Life on global scales and in all its evolutionary and ecological richness.]

Further reading

Rolston III, Holmes (1988) "Life in jeopardy: duties to endangered species," in *Environmental Ethics* (Philadelphia: Temple University Press). [Expands the argument of this chapter.]

29

Animals

PETER SINGER

Introduction: choosing among non-speciesist ethics

In the 1970s, two related but distinct movements challenged the dominant human attitude toward nature. The environmental movement insisted that it was wrong to think of the natural world as existing solely in order to provide us with fields to till, beautiful sunsets to contemplate, building materials for our houses, and an ocean into which we can dump our wastes. Instead, environmentalists wanted us to value nature independently of the benefits that humans may reap from it. A forest is worth more than the timber it can yield us, more than the pure water that soaks through its soils and into our reservoirs, more even than the peace and joy we experience in hiking through it. It exists and has value for its own sake – or so the advocates of a new "ecological ethic" claimed.

In the same period, the animal liberation movement reacted against the traditional attitude that human interests always take priority over those of non-human animals. Consistent with this attitude, the established anti-cruelty organizations opposed the infliction of suffering on animals only when it was gratuitous or wanton. This view, the animal liberation movement argued, is a form of "speciesism," that is, an indefensible bias or prejudice against members of other species. They argued that all sentient beings have interests, and we should give equal consideration to their interests, irrespective of whether they are members of our species or of another species (see SENTIENTISM).

The environmental and animal liberation movements have often worked together on issues of mutual concern. Indeed, they are not even as clearly distinct as this way of putting it implies. Many organizations combine both environmental and animal liberationist objectives. Those seeking to protect whales or great apes, for example, will typically be concerned about the preservation of the species as well as about the welfare of individual animals. The membership of environmental and animal liberation organizations is also likely to overlap considerably. Nevertheless, just as rebels can make a common cause against a dictatorial government and then fall out among themselves when the revolution triumphs, so in the struggle against human arrogance it is easier for the critics to agree on their opposition to the dominant view than on what they would put in its place. This chapter explores the fundamental divide within this broad rebel camp between those who would limit intrinsic value to sentient beings, and those who seek to extend it beyond sentient beings.

The traditional view

I shall begin by stating the traditional view. We all know the key text:

> And God said, Let us make man in our image, after our likeness: and let them have dominion over the fish of the sea, and over the fowl of the air, and over the earth, and over every creeping thing that creepeth upon the earth.
>
> So God created man in his own image, in the image of God created he him: male and female created he them.
>
> And God blessed them, and God said upon them, Be fruitful, and multiply, and replenish the earth, and subdue it: and have dominion over the fish of the sea and over the fowl of the air, and over every living thing that moveth upon the earth. (Genesis 1: 26–8)

According to the dominant Western tradition, the natural world exists for the benefit of human beings. God gave human beings dominion over the natural world, and God does not care how we treat it. Human beings are the only morally important members of this world. Nature itself is of no intrinsic value, and the destruction of plants and animals cannot be sinful, unless by this destruction we harm human beings. The traditional Judeo-Christian view of the world is based on a creation myth that was decisively refuted more than a century ago. At least since Darwin, we have known that the forests and animals were not placed on earth for us to use. They have evolved alongside us. The assumptions that derived from that myth, however, are still with us. If we jettison them, the consequences for our way of living will be as far-reaching as any changes in human history have ever been (see JUDAISM, CHRISTIAN-ITY).

Going beyond the species barrier

In any serious exploration of environmental values a central issue will be whether there is anything of intrinsic value beyond human beings. To consider this question we first need to understand the notion of "intrinsic value." Something is of intrinsic value if it is good or desirable in itself; the contrast is with "instrumental value," that is, value as a means to some other end or purpose. Our own happiness, for example, is of intrinsic value, at least to most of us, in that we desire it for its own sake. Money, on the other hand, is only of instrumental value to us. We want it because of the things we can buy with it, but if we were marooned on a desert island, we would not want it – whereas happiness would be just as important to us on a desert island as anywhere else (see NORMATIVE ETHICS).

Now consider any issue in which the interests of human beings clash with the interests of non-human animals. Since we are here concerned especially with environmental issues, let us take as an example Australia's kangaroo industry, which is based on killing free-living kangaroos in order to profit from the sale of their meat or skins. As a community, Australians must decide whether to allow this industry to exist. Should the decision be made on the basis of human interests alone? For simplicity, let us assume that none of the species of kangaroos shot is in danger of extinction. The issue therefore is one about whether, and to what extent, we consider the interests of individual non-human animals. So, immediately, we reach a fundamental moral disagreement: a disagreement about what kinds of being ought to be considered in our moral deliberations.

Many people think that once we reach a disagreement of this kind, argument must cease. I am more optimistic about the scope of rational argument in ethics. In ethics, even at a fundamental level, there are arguments that should convince any rational person. Let us take a parallel example. This is not the first time in human history that members of one group have placed themselves inside a circle of beings who are entitled to moral consideration, while excluding another group of beings, like themselves in important respects, from this hallowed circle of protection. In ancient Greece, those they called "barbarians" were thought of as "living instruments" – that is, human beings who were not of intrinsic value, but existed in order to serve some higher end. That end was the welfare of their Greek captors or owners. To overcome this view required a shift in our ethics that has important similarities with the shift that would take us from our present speciesist view of animals to a non-speciesist view. Just as in the debate over equal consideration for non-human animals, so too in the debate over equal consideration for non-Greeks, one can imagine people saying that such fundamental differences of ethical outlook were not open to rational argument. Yet now, with the benefit of hindsight, we can see that in the case of the institution of slavery in ancient Greece, that would not have been correct.

Notoriously, one of the greatest of ancient Greek philosophers justified the view that slaves are "living instruments" by arguing that barbarians were less rational than Greeks. In the hierarchy of nature, Aristotle said, the purpose of the less rational is to serve the more rational. Hence it follows that non-Greeks exist in order to serve Greeks.

No one now accepts Aristotle's defense of slavery. We reject it for a variety of reasons. We would reject his assumption that non-Greeks are less rational than Greeks, although given the cultural achievements of the different groups at the time, that was by no means an absurd assumption to make. But more importantly, from the moral point of view, we reject the idea that the less rational exist in order to serve the more rational. Instead we hold that all humans are equal. We regard racism, and slavery based on racism, as wrong because they fail to give equal consideration to the interests of all human beings. This would be true whatever the level of rationality or civilization of the slave, and therefore Aristotle's appeal to the higher rationality of the Greeks would not have justified the enslavement of non-Greeks, even if it had been true. Members of the "barbarian" tribes can feel pain, as Greeks can; they can be joyful or miserable, as Greeks can; they can suffer from separation from their families and friends, as Greeks can. To brush aside these needs so that Greeks could satisfy much more minor needs of their own was a great wrong and a blot on Greek civilization. This is something that we would expect all reasonable people to accept, as long as they can view the question from an impartial perspective, and are not improperly influenced by having a personal interest in the continued existence of slavery (see THE CLASSICAL GREEK TRADITION).

Now let us return to the question of the moral status of non-human animals. In keeping with the dominant western tradition, many people still hold that all the non-human natural world has value only or predominantly insofar as it benefits human beings. A powerful objection to the dominant western tradition turns against this tradition an extended version of the objection just made against Aristotle's justification of slavery. Non-human animals are also capable of feeling pain, as humans are; they can certainly be miserable, and perhaps in some cases their lives could also be described as joyful; and members of many mammalian species can suffer from separation from their family group. Is it not therefore a blot on human civilization that we brush aside these needs of non-human animals so as to satisfy minor needs of our own?

It might be said that the morally relevant differences between humans and other species are greater than the differences between different races of human beings. Here, by "morally relevant differences" people will have in mind such things as the ability to reason, to be self-aware, to act autonomously, to plan for the future, and so on. It is no doubt true that, on average, there is a marked difference between our species and other species in regard to these capacities. But this does not hold in all cases. Dogs, horses, pigs, and other mammals are better able to reason than newborn human infants, or humans with profound intellectual disabilities. Yet we bestow basic human rights on all human beings, and deny them to all non-human animals. In the case of human beings we can see that pain is pain, and the extent to which it is intrinsically bad depends on factors such as its duration and intensity, not on the intellectual abilities of the being who experiences it. We should be able to see that the same is true if the being suffering the pain is not of our species. There is no justifiable basis for drawing the boundary of intrinsic value around our own species. If we are prepared to defend practices based on disregarding the interests of members of other species because they are not members of our own group, how are we to object to those who wish to disregard the interests of members of other races because they are also not members of our own group? The argument just presented shows that while the dominant western tradition is wrong on the substantive issue of how we ought to regard non-human animals, this same tradition has within it the tools – in its recognition of the role of reason and argument – for constructing an extended ethics that reaches beyond the species boundary and addresses the human/animal relationship. There is no objection of principle to this extension. The principle that must apply, on this view, is that of equal consideration of interests. The remaining difficulties are about exactly how this principle is to be applied to beings with lives – both mental and physical – that are very different to our own.

Is there intrinsic value beyond sentience?

The position just outlined can be criticized from two sides: from those who seek to defend a speciesist ethic, and from those who think that extending ethics to all sentient beings does not go far enough. The latter criticism, in particular, is the focus of this chapter. While animal liberationists and deep ecologists agree that ethics must be extended beyond the human species, they differ in how far that extension can intelligibly go. If a tree is not sentient, then it makes no difference to the tree whether we chop it down or not. It may, of course, make a great difference to human beings, present or future, and to non-human animals who live in the tree, or in the forest of which it is a part. Animal liberationists would judge the wrongness of cutting down the tree in terms of the impact of the act on other sentient beings, whereas deep ecologists would see it as a wrong done to the tree, or perhaps to the forest or the larger ecosystem. The question is whether it is possible to ground an ethic on wrongs done to beings who are unable to experience in any way the wrong done to them, or any consequences of those wrongs.

From the perspective of deep ecologists, an ethic limited to sentient beings seems to stick too closely to traditional ethical viewpoints (see DEEP ECOLOGY). It is, for example, compatible with classical utilitarianism, which judges acts as right or wrong by asking whether they will lead to a greater surplus of pleasure over pain than any other act open to the agent. As the great classical utilitarian writers – Jeremy Bentham, John Stuart Mill and Henry Sidgwick – all made clear, the boundaries of "pleasure" and "pain" do not stop at the boundary of our species. The pleasures and pains of animals must be taken into the calculation. This is not to say that a non-speciesist ethic concerned about individual animals must be a utilitarian ethic. Many different ethics are compatible with this approach, including an ethic based on rights, as Tom Regan (1983) has ably argued. Similarly, a feminist ethic based on the idea of extending our sympathy to others can reach a similar conclusion (Kheel 1985).

In practice, a non-speciesist ethic is so revolutionary that the question of whether it goes far enough often does not arise. But in other contexts it can seem restrictive rather than revolutionary. Some see the roots of our ecological problem as lying in the nature of the western tradition. They argue that it is enlightenment humanism that is responsible for a civilization that has, for the first time in history, changed the climate of our planet, put a hole into the ozone layer, and made species extinct at an unprecedented rate. And they claim that an ethic based on the interests of sentient beings has no way of accounting for the wrong done when an ancient tree is felled, a species pushed into extinction, or the integrity of an ecosystem is violated.

Whatever the historical merits of that claim, it invites us to ask what other approaches to environmental ethics might be put in place of an ethic that is broadly within the western tradition. The nub of the problem is that we typically understand value in terms of interests, typically consisting of conscious states, including states we find pleasurable or displeasurable, and states directed toward some end, such as wants, desires, preferences, and the like. The simplest way of extending this ethic beyond sentient beings, therefore, is to argue that entities such as a tree, a species, or an ecosystem can also have interests. But it is not clear if this makes sense. When we say that it is in the interests of a tree to receive water and light, are we speaking literally or metaphorically? In what sense is it in the interests of a tree to receive water and light, and not equally in the interests of an icicle for the temperature to remain below freezing? But to claim that the icicle has an interest in continued cold weather seems dubious.

Moreover, even if we can be persuaded that trees, species, and ecosystems have interests, it will be necessary for advocates of an ecological ethic to show that they have morally significant interests. One way of establishing that an interest is morally significant is to ask what it is like for the entity affected to have that interest unsatisfied. Imaginatively, we can put ourselves in the place of that being, and ask: how would I like it if I were in that situation? This works for sentient beings, but it does not work for trees, species, or ecosystems. There is nothing that corresponds to what it is like to be an ecosystem flooded by a dam. In this respect trees, ecosystems, and species are – in the case of the latter two, considered as wholes rather than as the parts of which they are made up – more like rocks than they are like sentient beings; so the divide between sentient and non-sentient creatures is to that extent a firmer basis for a morally important boundary than the divide between living and non-living things or holistic entities.

The problem is that to suggest that there is value beyond sentient beings opens the door so wide that we don't know what to let in and what to reject, or even what we are looking for. Should an ethic that goes beyond sentient beings be limited to living things, to something like Albert Schweitzer's (1929) ethic of a "reverence for life"? Schweitzer himself never really stated what this ethic amounted to, but one inter-pretation of it would be a form of "biocentric egalitarianism," in which every living thing has equal value. Paul Taylor appears to adopt this in his book *Respect for Nature* (1986), arguing that once we understand that every living thing is pursuing its own good in its own unique way, we should be ready to place the same value on their existence as we do on our own. But the notion of "pursuing one's own good" is radically different when applied to a being that is sentient and when applied to one that is not. The former has a subjective awareness of whether it has achieved "its own good" (perhaps it feels satisfied instead of frustrated, warm instead of cold, replete instead of hungry) and the latter has nothing corresponding to this. Is this difference something that can properly be ignored?

Even an ethic that extends to all living things will still leave most of nature outside its scope. So should we also seek value in rocks and streams, in mountains and lakes? Remember, we are not talking here about the value of the living things that depend upon the rocks, streams, mountains, and lakes, let alone about the humans who may wish to hike to them and enjoy their beauty, but upon those inanimate things themselves. We have to imagine that the existence of the rocks and streams makes no difference to any living things, and never will. Are they then still of value? If so, why?

One way of answering this puzzling question is to locate value at a larger, more "holistic" level. Thus Aldo Leopold developed an ethic based on the land, writing that "A thing is right when it tends to preserve the integrity, stability and beauty of the biotic community. It is wrong when it tends otherwise" (1949, pp. 224–5; see also THE LAND ETHIC). Deep ecologists such as Arne Naess and George Sessions (1984, p. 67) have asserted that "richness and diversity of life forms" are values in themselves; and Sessions, this time with Bill Devall, has claimed that "all organisms and entities in the ecosphere, as parts of the interrelated whole, are equal in intrinsic worth" (1985). The reference to "organisms and entities" seems to imply an equality of intrinsic worth not only between, say, aardvarks and single-celled organisms, but also been zebras and mountain ranges, or between the ecosystem of the Amazon basin and Boris Yeltsin.

It is difficult to know what such an equation of intrinsic worth could possibly mean. As these examples show, once we go beyond the boundary of sentience, we meet with increasing difficulties in deciding what we value, and how we are to trade off conflicting values. This makes it much harder to solve potential conflicts between the different approaches.

Practical problems

Animal liberationists and environmentalists can make common cause on most of the major environmental issues that we face. The environmental crisis is so grave that for many of these issues, even a traditional ethic that took a sufficiently long-term view of the interests of human beings – and nothing but human beings – could serve as the basis for a radically different attitude to the environment. The preservation of old growth forests serves as an example of an issue on which all three of the kinds of argument we have considered in this essay converge. Against the short-term economic benefits of cutting the forests down, one could argue in terms of the importance of forests for the preservation of our CLIMATE and the quality of our water supply, and of the loss to all FUTURE GENERATIONS if they are unable to walk in an untouched forest. It is an argument that has been based entirely on the interests of members of our own species, and it can be strengthened by the recognition that forests are homes to millions of animals who will die from starvation and stress when the trees are felled. The suffering and death of these wild animals makes the clearing of the forests even worse than it would be if only human beings benefited from them. Those who attribute intrinsic value to trees, or to the forest itself, or to the ecological system of which it is a part, would accept both the human-centered and the animal-centered arguments against cutting down the forests, and add their own arguments as well.

In the case of other environmental issues, the interests of individual sentient animals and the values that some environmentalists find in the preservation of ecosystems or species can come into conflict. One example of such a conflict occurs when an abundant population of grazing animals reaches a point at which it endangers rare plants in the area in which the animals live. Perhaps previously the plants and animals could both survive as part of the same ecosystem, because predators kept the population of grazing animals low. Or perhaps the range of the grazing animals has been restricted by land development and they can no longer circulate through their range slowly enough to allow the plants to recover. In these situations, should the animals be killed in order to protect the plants? Environmentalists are likely to support this action, while some who base their views on concern for the interests of sentient beings may oppose it. Conflict also often arises because of the introduction of feral animals into an ecosystem. The welfare of individual feral animals may be incompatible with the preservation of the environment in a state unaffected by modern civilization. The presence of the feral animals can also pose a threat to native animals. In California, for example, very large numbers of introduced fish have been poisoned in order to restore native fish to the streams that they used to inhabit. The Australian possum was introduced into New Zealand in order to establish an industry based on its fur. Instead, it adapted well to the forests of New Zealand, and is now regarded as a major threat to the native forests of that country. So possums, protected animals in Australia, are killed in large numbers in New Zealand. Ferrets, stoats, and rats have caused the extinction of some of New Zealand's unique ground-dwelling birds, and threatened others. Attempts have been made to rid off-shore islands of these feral predators, so that they can become refuges for endangered species. How many feral animals is it justified to kill in order to attempt to save a species?

Another example on an even larger scale is the problem of rabbits in Australia. Rabbits were introduced to Australia in the nineteenth century by Europeans who thought that they would be a useful food source. They reproduced so successfully that they became a major pest, eating grass that farmers wished to reserve for their more valuable sheep and cattle. The rabbits also change the nature of Australian native vegetation, cause soil erosion, compete all too successfully with some native animals, and prevent the regrowth of native plants in areas that have been cleared. Australian farmers and environmentalists are therefore united in attempting to reduce the number of rabbits in Australia. From the point of view of an ethic of concern for all sentient beings, however, rabbits are beings with interests of their own, capable of feeling pain and of suffering.

At present, attempts are made to control rabbit numbers by trapping, shooting, poisoning, the ripping up of warrens with tractors, the deliberate release of the myxomatosis virus, and, most recently, the spreading of rabbit calicivirus. The degree of pain and suffering inflicted on rabbits by these methods varies, but in every case there appears to be significant suffering. By all accounts, myxomatosis would rank as the worst of these methods, from the perspective of the suffering inflicted on the rabbit. Shooting by a professional shooter is probably the most humane way of killing rabbits in the wild, although even a professional cannot be accurate 100 percent of the time. Calicivirus is said to cause a quiet death, but there are conflicting reports on this, and it may be that the nature of the disease changes as rabbits develop some degree of resistance to it.

Farmers concerned for their livelihood are more likely to focus on the cost of methods of eradicating rabbits, rather than on the amount of suffering such methods cause to the rabbits. From this perspective, shooting is not likely to make much impact on the rabbit population. Myxomatosis was therefore hailed as the savior of Australian farmers, until rabbits developed resistance to it. Poisoning with 1080 has been widely used, and considerable hope has been placed in the recently released rabbit calicivirus disease, although it seems likely that it, like myxomatosis, will prove to be at best a temporary solution.

From the perspective of preservation of the Australian environment, any method is acceptable if it does not cause further environmental problems. Poisoning is problematic, because there is always a risk of poisoned bait being taken by native animals. Environmentalists have been concerned about the premature escape of calicivirus in Australia, before approval for its release had been given by the government bodies responsible. It is significant that some methods that inflict extremely distressing deaths on rabbits may in other respects be highly desirable, from an environmental point of view. Myxomatosis is specific to rabbits, and after many years' use in Australia it does not appear to have any adverse environmental consequences. The use of phosphorus gas in burrows also appears to kill nothing but rabbits, and to do no further environmental harm, but its mode of action – known from the trenches of World War I, where it was used in gas warfare – is extremely painful.

We therefore have a conflict between values that appear to be incommensurable: on the one hand, the preservation of endangered species and of those ecosystems that remain relatively unaffected by the impact of modern civilization; and on the other, the suffering and death that will be inflicted on sentient creatures in order to eliminate the effect they are having on the environment. Whether animals are native or feral, of course, does not affect their ability to suffer when they are poisoned, trapped, or infected with diseases.

One approach to such conflicts is to find a solution that protects the environment while minimizing harm to individual animals. If the area containing rare plants is small, perhaps the animals can be fenced out of it; if the number of grazing animals threatening the plants is small, it may be possible to relocate them. Sometimes fertility control can be used to control the numbers of animals in a specific area. Fertility control seems easier to reconcile with an ethic of concern for all sentient beings than lethal methods of reducing population. One question that could be raised, from this perspective, is whether the animals suffer in virtue of becoming infertile – that is, do they experience any unsatisfied need, or other adverse effects from not having off-spring? We would need to study each species carefully in order to answer this question; but even if the answer is affirmative, it may still be the case that fertility control is, if not acceptable from an animal-regarding standpoint, the least bad option.

If no compromise solution of that kind is available, what ought we to do? Here we have a clash of values of very different kinds. Those who maintain that all value must be related to the interests of sentient beings will claim that the value of preserving an endangered species of plant must be related to the present or possible future interests of sentient beings in the survival of that plant. Humans, for instance, may want to see it growing in the wild, or may simply want it to survive. Perhaps one day it will play an important role in the stability of an ecosystem on which both humans and non-human animals depend. Unless we preserve it, we will never know. These are important interests, and in some cases they could even outweigh the interests of a limited number of animals in continuing to live their lives undisturbed. But in other cases they will not.

Advocates of broader ethics will in any case think that such considerations are wrong-headed, because they fail to see the value in preserving the plant for its own sake. But if they consider it justified to inflict significant suffering on other sentient beings – something against which clear ethical arguments can be given – then they owe us an equally clear account of what it is that makes a plant or other (living or non-living) natural entity worth preserving. A simple egalitarianism between all living things is not enough to give us grounds for preserving organisms belonging to rare or endangered species in preference to those that belong to more common ones. Taking a holistic approach will help only if the survival of some larger whole is at stake. Arguably, this is the case when the integrity of an ecosystem is threatened by feral animals or plants. But ecosystems are constantly changing in more or less subtle ways to adapt to different forces that have an impact on them, so even here it is not always easy to say what will count as a threat to the integrity of an ecosystem, and what will count as an adaptation of it. Short of a total collapse of an ecosystem in which all or most living organisms die, how are we to decide that an alteration to an ecosystem makes it "worse" rather than just "different"? At what point does it lose its "integrity"? Should Australians just accept that rabbits are part of their country's ecosystems? Should New Zealanders be reconciled to the fact that their forests are now home to a tree-dwelling marsupial, and will adapt to it? And how much animal suffering can be justified by the preservation of an endangered species, or of the continued existence of an ecosystem in one form rather than another? Until those who find value beyond sentient beings can give us plausible answers to these questions, we have not yet reached the point at which we can hope to make any progress on ethical issues arising from conflicts between their position and a position based on equal consideration of the interests of all sentient beings.

References

Aristotle (1916) *Politics* (London: J. M. Dent and Sons). [Probably the most influential philosopher of the western tradition, and a supporter of a hierarchical view of nature.]

Bentham, Jeremy (1948) *Introduction to the Principles of Morals and Legislation* (New York: Hafner). [The founding work of English utilitarianism.]

Devall, Bill and Sessions, George (1985) *Deep Ecology: Living as if Nature Mattered* (Salt Lake City, Utah: Gibbs M. Smith). [A more extended presentation of the deep ecology view.]

Kheel, Marti (1985) "The liberation of nature: a circular affair," *Environmental Ethics* 7, no. 2, pp. 135–49. [A feminist view of animal liberation and ecological ethics.]

Leopold, Aldo (1949) *A Sand County Almanac* (New York: Oxford University Press). [An oft-quoted statement of "the land ethic."]

Mill, John Stuart (1976) "Whewell on moral philosophy," reprinted in Regan T. and P. Singer, eds, *Animal Rights and Human Obligations* (Englewood Cliffs, NJ: Prentice-Hall) pp. 131–2. [Here, the most widely read of the classic utilitarians makes his views on animals plain.]

Naess, Arne and Sessions, George (1984) "Basic principles of deep ecology," *Ecophilosophy* 6. [A summary statement by two leading proponents of "deep ecology."]

Regan, Tom (1983) *The Case for Animal Rights* (Berkeley: University of California Press). [The leading statement of the claim that animals have rights.]

Schweitzer, Albert (1929) *Civilization and Ethics*, 2nd edn, trans. C. T. Campion (London: A & C Black Ltd). [Here, Schweitzer states his ethic of "reverence for life."]

Sidgwick, Henry (1907) *The Methods of Ethics*, 7th edn (London: Macmillan). [Sidgwick's comprehensive work of moral philosophy, which includes a reference to the position of animals in the utilitarian view.]

Taylor, Paul (1986) *Respect for Nature* (Princeton). [An argument for a radical egalitarianism in our attitude to nature.]

Further reading

Singer, Peter (1990) Animal Liberation, *New York Review of Books*, New York, 2nd edn. [Sometimes referred to as "the Bible of the animal rights movement," this book argues for equal consideration of the interests of all sentient beings, and shows how our attitudes and practices towards animals fall short of this standard.]

30

Environmental justice

ROBERT FIGUEROA AND CLAUDIA MILLS

Introduction

The most industrialized nations of the world have produced enough CFCs to generate dangerous holes in the ozone layer of the atmosphere, with deleterious effects on the health of the entire world's plant, animal, and human population. One-fifth of the world's population consumes four-fifths of the world's resources, leaving four-fifths of the world's population with only one-fifth of the available resources. Indigenous groups such as the Waipai in Brazil defend the right to their traditional lands and practices against the invasion of multinational mining operations. The poor and developing nations around the world (primarily in the global South) attempt to satisfy their rights to development as the rich, industrialized nations (primarily in the global North) call for environmental protection against the same development practices that they themselves invented and used for decades and which introduced much of the environmental degradation we see around the world today.

In the United States, Native Americans suffer the negative health and environmental impacts of uranium mining that feeds the nuclear arsenal and sustains the nuclear power plants of a nation which has displaced their people; meanwhile, several economically desperate Native American tribes consider the economic benefits of hosting the nation's nuclear waste facilities. Places like Love Canal, New York, and Times Beach, Missouri, struggle to receive just compensation from toxic wastes. Downstream states along the Mississippi River are over-burdened with industrial wastes from upstream states: the lower Mississippi, occupied primarily by African-American residents, is renowned as "Cancer Alley," indicating the toxic impact on the health of residents. During the 1980s, several studies disclosed the greater likelihood of poor and minority communities suffering toxic landfill and facilities sitings compared to their white counterparts.

The response to inequities in the distribution of environmental burdens in nearly every nation around the world, and the failure of mainstream environmental groups and agencies to address the issues of inequitable distribution and representation, has culminated in the latest social movement addressing environmental issues – the environmental justice movement.

Environmental ethics focuses on the relationship between humans and nature; environmental *justice* emerged as a concern for both activists and academics when it was realized that this relationship is not constant across all humanity. Environmental practices and policies affect different groups of people differently, and environmental benefits and burdens are often distributed in ways that seem unjust.

Environmental justice refers to the conceptual connections and causal relationships between environmental issues and social justice.

A rough distinction can be drawn between domestic and global forms of environmental justice. Environmental policies, laws, and practices, along with political relations between different societal groups, may be specific to a particular nation-state or region. But many environmental impacts transcend national boundaries, such as air pollution, acid rain, toxic waste export, transnational corporation activities, and global warming. These impacts widen environmental justice to a global scope.

This overview of environmental justice provides a description of the vocabulary and history of environmental justice in terms of two dimensions of social justice – distributive justice and participatory justice – applied to both domestic and global environmental justice. Our discussion of domestic environmental justice will concentrate on the history and development of the United States environmental justice movement.

Two dimensions of environmental justice

Generally speaking, there are two different dimensions to environmental justice. The first is distributive justice: how are environmental benefits and burdens distributed? The second is participatory justice: how are these distributive decisions made? Who participates in their making?

Concerns for the distributive dimension of environmental justice begin with the observation that people of color, the poor, and under-represented groups such as indigenous tribes and nations are faced with a disproportionate amount of environmental burdens. The issue here is one of environmental equity. Examples of environmental burdens include exposure to hazardous materials and toxic wastes, pollution, health hazards, and workplace hazards, as well as the exploitation and loss of traditional environmental practices and depletion of local natural resources. Environmental benefits include a safe workplace, clean water and air, easy access to natural surroundings or parks, fair compensation for environmental burdens, and the preservation of traditional environmental practices connected to local natural resources. Not all inequities are unjust, but where inequitable distribution occurs according to some morally arbitrary characteristic or principle, we have an instance of environmental discrimination. Inequities based on racial characteristics are certainly morally suspect, as are most forms of socio-economic inequities in the distribution of environmental burdens. In the United States and many parts of the world, the most discussed and debated form of environmental discrimination is environmental racism, a concept that we will discuss in more depth below. However, environmental discrimination often concerns socio-economic discrimination. An individual or group consistently receiving significant environmental burdens, while others benefit as a result of circumventing these burdens, is being subjected to a social injustice or inequity; an individual or group targeted in virtue of moral arbitrary characteristics is experiencing discrimination.

The participatory dimension of environmental justice turns attention to the fact that people of color and the poor (domestically) and nations and people of the unindustrialized South (globally) have little representation in the environmental movement and in other arenas that bear on how environmental benefits and burdens are assigned. Lack of opportunity for democratic participation in the environmental movement can be referred to as "discriminatory environmentalism." In discriminatory environmentalism, representation and participation in mainstream environmental groups, participation in environmental policy-making, representation in local, national, and international environmental agencies, and decision-making power over the location of environmental burdens and benefits are either intentionally or unintentionally exclusionary.

Although discussions of both dimensions of environmental justice appear together in the literature, there has been a tendency to favor the distributive dimension of environmental justice. Peter S. Wenz, for example, defines "environmental justice" exclusively in distributive terms:

> chief topics related to environmental justice concern...the distribution of benefits and burdens among all those affected by environmentally related decisions and actions [including] the division of the burdens of environmental protection between poor and affluent people in our society, as well as the division of natural resources between rich and poor nations. (1988, p. 4)

However, other analyses of environmental justice focus on participatory inequities. Iris M. Young (1983) explicitly argues that what is called for by a community sited for a toxic waste facility is not distributive but participatory justice. She claims that any purely distributive theory fails to address the nature of the risks and harms associated with this type of environmental burden, which is why the decision-making process is often biased, top-down, and neglectful of democratic rights. Crucial here is a principle of self-determination which grounds the right of those most immediately affected to decide if such burdens and remedies are acceptable to them.

Indeed, the *Principles of Environmental Justice*, adopted by the First National People of Color Environmental Leadership Summit in 1991, include only 2 references to distributive justice in the 17 principles. The remaining principles emphasize participatory justice concerns of rights against discrimination, individual and group self-determination, and respect for diverse cultural perspectives (Hofrichter, 1993).

Both dimensions of environmental justice are clearly important and will shape the discussion of domestic and global environmental justice that follows.

Domestic environmental justice in the United States

In the United States the civil rights movement and the environmental movement experienced separate agendas, until the relationship between social justice and environmental reforms became the focus of political controversy and citizen protest, and the environmental justice movement was born.

There were many precursors to the movement, however. During the 1960s Martin Luther King, Jr., and other civil rights leaders observed that people of color suffer higher pollution and denigrated environments (Bullard 1993). The 1960s and 1970s also saw the struggle of Cesar Chavez and the United Farm Workers to protect

Chicano migrant farmworkers; studies of rural Appalachian living conditions revealing the connection between poverty and environmental burdens; the 1978 brochure
Our Common Concern, released by the federal government, indicating the disproportionate impact of pollution on people of color; and the 1979 City Care Conference in
Detroit, jointly sponsored by the National Urban League and the Sierra Club. However, it is widely agreed that the movement took root at Warren County, North
Carolina, in the community of Afton.

The Afton community had an 84 percent African-American population; Warren
County had the highest percentage African-American population in North Carolina.
At the time, Warren County suffered the second highest poverty level of North
Carolina counties, with 13.3 percent unemployment. In 1982, Dr. Charles E. Cobb,
a director of the United Church of Christ's Commission for Racial Justice (UCC-CRJ),
spoke out against the Warren County PCB landfill for making African-Americans and
the poor bear heavier environmental burdens than those borne by other communities. This inspired a campaign of non-violent civil disobedience culminating in a
protest blocking the trucks hauling PCB-laced soil, which led to more than 500
arrests and drew national media attention.

The Warren County protest represents the first public mobilization for environmental justice against environmental racism. Although it was unsuccessful at halting
the dumping of the PCB-contaminated soil, it incited the 1983 United States General
Accounting Office (US-GAO) study of hazardous waste landfill siting, which found a
strong correlation between sitings of hazardous waste landfills and race and socio-
economic status (US-GAO 1993). This study spawned later comprehensive studies,
including the UCC-CRJ's frequently cited *Toxic Wastes and Race in the United States*, a
national study which not only confirmed the disparate environmental burdens suffered by minorities and lower socio-economic groups nationwide, but centrally
located race in the disparity: "Race proved to be the most significant among variables
tested in association with the location of commercial hazardous waste facilities"
(UCC-CRJ 1987, p. xiii). Together with the Warren County protest, these studies
inspired conferences and meetings explicitly devoted to the relationship between
environmental values and the social justice concerns of the poor and people of
color. Often highlighted is the First National People of Color Environmental
Leadership Summit at Washington, DC, in 1991, which produced the document
Principles of Environmental Justice, outlining the agenda of the environmental justice
movement.

There is wide agreement that the term "environmental racism" was originally
coined by the Reverend Dr. Benjamin F. Chavis, Jr., in 1987, when the UCC-CRJ
presented its findings at the National Press Club in Washington, DC. Chavis offers a
definition of racism that includes the "intentional or unintentional use of power to
isolate, separate and exploit others" (UCC-CRJ 1987, p. x). He described environmental racism as:

> racial discrimination in environmental policy making, and the unequal enforcement
> of environmental laws and regulations . . . the deliberate targeting of people of color
> communities for toxic waste facilities . . . the official sanctioning of the life-threaten-
> ing presence of poisons and pollutants in people-of-color communities for toxic waste

facilities...the history of excluding people of color from the leadership of the environmental movement. (US House of Representatives, 1993, p. 4)

Robert Bullard, the leading author on environmental racism, provides a definition of environmental racism that agrees with that of Chavis: "any policy, practice, or directive that differentially affects or disadvantages, whether intended or unintended, groups or communities based on race" (ibid, p. 47).

Bullard and Chavis define environmental racism as involving both intentional and unintentional social injustices, comprising both the intent and effects of an act. This has sparked a major debate and a surge of scholarship on environmental racism. Defining environmental racism to include both intentional and unintentional racism may appear problematic at first because "racism" is a term of moral condemnation, and we generally do not criticize or condemn unintentional actions. But the 1960s civil rights movement in the United States raised consciousness about institutional as well as individual forms of racism that may be observable only through their effects. Intentional racism is more likely to be found in individual rather than institutional forms of racism, except where laws and policies explicitly discriminate on the basis of race (such as the Jim Crow laws that once mandated racial segregation of public facilities in the American South). These laws and policies have been officially repudiated, but unintentional institutional racism remains in the distribution of environmental burdens, as well as the exclusion of people of color from full participation in the institutions that are most responsible for this distribution.

US courts have shown themselves willing to address unintentional as well as intentional racism. In 1971, the US Supreme Court set a precedent in *Griggs* v. *Duke Power Company* for evaluating racism on the basis of disparate effects, as opposed to clear intent. The US Civil Rights Act of 1964 contains Title VI, which stipulates that racially disparate effects violate national laws against racism. However, several landmark civil cases charging environmental racism, such as *Village of Arlington Heights* v. *Metropolitan Housing Development Corporation*, *East Bibb Twiggs* v. *Macon-Bibb County Planning & Zoning Commission*, and *R.I.S.E.* v. *Kay*, have been judged according to the Fourteenth Amendment of the US Constitution, which requires racist intent for identifying racist acts. Despite precedents for applying the effect-standard to judge racism using Title VI, the courts in these cases declined the importance of disparate impact by showing preference for the intent-standard of the Fourteenth Amendment's Equal Protection Clause (Godsil 1991). Perceiving the intent-standard to be nearly impossible to prove in present-day civil courts and the blatant resistance to utilize the more appropriate effects-standard, proponents of environmental justice have worked vigorously to increase the awareness and use of Title VI in the civil courts. For example, the United States Environmental Protection Agency (US-EPA) has recently established policy using Title VI for interim guidance in assessing the distributive impacts of emissions-producing facilities sited for minority communities.

A further dimension of the controversy over environmental racism comes in the objection that environmental benefits and burdens are distributed primarily according to socio-economic considerations rather than on the basis of racial characteristics. Critics claim either that environmental burdens are not in fact assigned disproportionately according to race, or that, even if they do correlate with race, market forces best explain their assignment.

A University of Massachusetts study by Doug Anderton et al., sponsored by Chem Waste Management in 1994, claims that the UCC-CRJ's 1987 report fails to provide definitive evidence for the conclusions linking race to environmental burdens (Anderton et al. 1995). According to the Anderton study, Hispanic-Americans are the ethnic group most consistently located by hazardous waste facilities, not African-Americans, and the population most impacted are industrial workers, regardless of race or ethnicity. Anderton argues that in areas with higher populations of minorities, we should not be surprised to see more minorities living near hazardous waste facilities.

The Anderton study differs in crucial respects from the UCC-CRJ study. The latter observed both commercially controlled facilities and uncontrolled facilities, while the former observed only commercially controlled facilities. Moreover, Anderton's study does not measure communities with populations of fewer than 50,000 residents. Many communities making charges of environmental racism have populations of well below 50,000. Interestingly, by failing to include populations under 50,000, Anderton omits two of Chem Waste's largest hazardous waste facilities, in Kettleman City, California, a Latino community, and in Emelle, Alabama, a predominantly African-American community. Finally, the question remains why minorities are more often located by hazardous waste sites in areas of both high and low minority populations. Robert Bullard (1994) has written in rebuttal. He essentially argues that Anderton's study reveals only that different measuring tools reveal different results.

Other critics acknowledge that minorities are disproportionately assigned environmental burdens, but contend that the distribution of environmental burdens and benefits is nonetheless best explained by market forces, rather than by any kind of racism. Corporations determining where to place a hazardous facility may cite evidence that they based their decisions only on socio-economic factors, which form a legitimate basis for decision. An example of this is a 1984 report, *Political Difficulties Facing Waste-to-Energy Conversion Plant Siting*, written by Cerrell Associates, a private consulting firm for government planners in California. According to this report, opposition to hazardous waste facilities is most likely to come from liberal, college-educated, young residents, within high income brackets, living in urban areas. Non-opposition would likely be characteristic of lower socio-economic communities with high unemployment and lower levels of education (Bullard 1993; Russell 1989). For this reason, "communities that conform to some kind of economic need criteria should be given high priority" (Russell 1989, p. 26) and "middle and higher socio-economic strata neighborhoods should not fall within the one-mile and five-mile radius of the proposed site" (Bullard 1993, p. 18). Because the Cerrell Associates report provides evidence of discriminatory targeting of the *poor*, the corporation may claim that race was irrelevant.

Moreover, corporations focusing on socio-economic factors may claim that on balance they benefit the communities targeted for environmental burdens by providing adequate compensation, including community improvement plans and employment opportunities for local residents. According to law professor Vicki Been (Been 1995), there is a crucial difference between siting decisions that bring the nuisance of hazardous waste facilities to the communities and siting decisions in which the community chooses to come to the nuisance. Where communities come to the nuisance, Been argues that economic decisions made by minority populations in a competitive market better explain the results than racist practices.

We contend, however, that these lines of defense against environmental racism charges are often inadequate. First, even if it is true that corporations base their siting decisions explicitly on socio-economic rather than racial factors (and there is certainly ample opportunity for disingenuousness here, not to mention outright deception), we may nonetheless be deeply troubled about the disparate effects of the use of such factors on communities of color. The premise that minority communities are often economically disadvantaged and unable to offer organized resistance to the imposition of environmental burdens does not entail the conclusion that minority communities should suffer the disproportionate siting of hazardous waste facilities.

Second, the compensation argument faces the problem that economically desperate communities may be under considerable pressure to accept the package offered, however ultimately disadvantageous. This charge is one of environmental blackmail. The compensation argument can escape this charge only if those involved are aware of the nature of the risks and benefits to be traded off and participate in a genuine process of negotiation. But this seldom occurs. For instance, in compensation for the siting of the "Cadillac of toxic waste dumps" in Emelle, Alabama, Chemical Waste Management promised to provide more than 400 jobs and to pour millions of dollars into the community through paychecks and community support. However, the community was not involved in any of the negotiations leading to this compensation package. In fact, members of the community had no idea the dump existed, and rumors suggested it was a brick factory.

Finally, market forces can hardly be understood apart from the underlying racism of most contemporary societies. Been herself recognizes that race and socio-economic issues are interrelated. She points out that racist practices in loan agencies, housing, education, employment, and health care generate the socio-economic conditions that bring poor minorities to industrial centers where unemployment is greater and property values are less. Been accepts that racism exists, but secondarily to market forces: "as long as the market discriminates on the basis of race, it would be remarkable if LULUs (locally unwanted land uses) did not eventually impose a disproportionate burden on people of color" (Been 1995, p. 41). Part of the confusion here is where Been separates market forces from racism. Her argument can succeed only if we accept racism in nearly all institutions that are relevant to people's migration toward and away from environmental hazards. In effect, a socio-economic defense against the environmental racism charge only accentuates the complex relationship between race and class in the United States and other contemporary societies.

Beyond this particular environmental racism debate, which is most prominent in the literature, the US environmental justice movement addresses a myriad of controversies overlapping distributive and participatory dimensions of justice, such as women's leadership roles in the grassroots organizations, the plight of Native Americans in attempting to preserve environmental values in the face of economic challenges, the impact of lead poisoning on children of color, and the working conditions of many immigrants and poor people.

Concerns for environmental justice generally and environmental racism in particular have culminated in numerous conferences, academic publications, protests, and
grassroots mobilizations. Federal responses have also indicated the centrality of
environmental justice to environmental concerns: the US-EPA now maintains an
Environmental Justice Commission. These efforts at addressing environmental justice
culminated with President Clinton's Executive Order 12898: *Federal Actions to Address
Environmental Justice in Minority Populations and Low-Income Populations*, signed February 11, 1994. This Executive Order calls for federal commissions, interagency
cooperation, policy overhaul, research development, enforcement of right-to-know
laws, and judicial review. While its impact is yet to be assessed, it does represent a
clear legitimation of the charges from the environmental justice movement in the
United States.

Global environmental justice

Global environmental justice refers to the examination of distributive and participatory inequities among nations, in addition to emphasizing a variety of global political
issues which grow out of environmental concerns that transcend national boundaries
and defy the control of individual nation-states. There will, of course, be crossover
between domestic environmental justice and global environmental justice, as in the
case of environmental justice issues between the US and Native-American nations.

During the 1980s, environmental concerns began to appear as primary concerns
on the global political agenda. By the 1990s, "the global environment had emerged
as the third major issue area in world politics, along with international security and
global economics" (Porter and Brown 1996, p. 1). The concept of the global "commons," those parts of the earth's environment that all humans share and in principle
cannot be owned (e.g., the ozone layer, oceans, and climatic systems), emerged
during the 1980s. The first global summit on the environment in 1992, the United
Nations Conference on Environment and Development (UNCED or "Earth Summit"),
is a testimony to this level of interest in the global environment. Many commend this
shift in perception to a view of the earth as a system of environmental interactions
belonging to and affecting all the earth's creatures. However, defenders of global
environmental justice have grown increasingly suspicious of the social and political
implications of this global ecological outlook.

A first criticism is that global environmental problems are increasingly managed by
the few political powers that have what Vandana Shiva (1993) has called the "*global
reach*." Global players include national entities, multinational entities such as UN
agencies, transnational corporations, major non-governmental organizations, and
global institutions such as the World Bank. In addition, research in global ecology
is conducted by a group of relatively few scientists who assist global political entities
in making policy decisions. Thus, the politics of global ecology become another
instance of the very few ruling and making decisions for the very many.

Shiva argues that the "global" in "global environmentalism" does not refer only to
concern for the health of the entire planet, but instead to "the political space in which
a particular dominant local seeks global control and frees itself of local, national, and
international restraints" (Shiva 1993, pp. 149–50). She argues that a focus on global

ecological issues such as desertification, CLIMATE change, acid rain, and ozone depletion ends up turning over the world's environmental management strategies, trade control, and political power to elite institutions and political entities which determine the fate of the rest of the world. Unless participatory justice becomes a primary concern, the shift to global ecology may lead only to further de-democratizing of global politics.

Following World War II, the leading nations of the world initiated a policy of "development" that shaped the political purposes and identities of nations around the world. The first step was to label nations as "developed" versus "underdeveloped," labels which later grew into the divisions of "first world," "second world," and "third world" nations. Today, "underdeveloped nations" are standardly referred to as "developing nations" to suggest that all nations are moving and should move toward the same goal of first-world-style "development."

Wolfgang Sachs points out that the implied meaning behind such labeling is that "development" becomes identified with "civilization," and "society" becomes synonymous with "economy" (Sachs 1993). Thus, the maturity level of a society's civilization is measured according to its stage of industrial development and the strength of its political economy.

Once the development paradigm became widely accepted throughout the world, developing nations shifted their domestic political emphasis to try to achieve the benefits that wealthy industrial nations seemed to enjoy, such as rich economies, advanced technologies, high levels of consumption, and greater international political and military power. But in this paradigm shift, long-standing cultural traditions of indigenous groups, localized trade and agriculture, and many environmental values are sacrificed. Moreover, it is exceedingly unlikely that developing nations will ever achieve the lifestyle of the wealthy industrial nations. The South entered the development race when the North had already secured dominance in the global political economy. The figures illustrating the futility of the South's attempt to achieve equality with the North are devastating: "during the 1980s, the contribution of developing countries (where two-thirds of humanity live) to the world's GNP shrank to 15%, while the share of the industrial countries, with 20% of the world population, rose to 80%" (Sachs 1993, p. 5). As a result, the South is in real danger of being left behind in the global political economy and continuing to suffer the consequent vulnerability to exploitation.

The development paradigm has several critical implications for global environmental justice. First, it helps to explain the creation and maintenance of power differences between the global North and South. The South must struggle with the terms set by the North and must speak the vocabulary of economic and industrial "progress" rather than of other cultural and environmental values. Second, as economic and industrial development became central to nations, other interests such as indigenous environmental values and traditional resource management suffer. This has diminished the rights of indigenous peoples around the world and encouraged the exploitation of many resources they rely upon. Third, in order to keep up with the global political economy, the South has adopted many harmful environmental practices, such as reliance on mono-agriculture and excessive resource extraction. And as export markets wane, like cotton during the 1970s, developing nations attempt to recover by increasing export production at lower rates of return. Fourth, the South has become increasingly suspicious of the North, as shown by its insistence on its right to development and its resistance to environmental protection enforced by the North. Documents such as the "Declaration of Principles," adopted at the United Nations Conference on the Environment at Stockholm in 1972, *Our Common Future*, the report of the Brundtland World Commission on Environment and Development published in 1987, and the "Rio Declaration on Environment and Development" of 1992 express the sovereign right of nations to manage development practices, a right which developing nations charge has been curtailed, although the same right has been exercised for decades by the North. Clearly, these implications indicate that the development paradigm works against environmental preservation and management.

The main tension between the North and South arises from their different perspectives on how best to address pressing global environmental concerns. The North expects the South to recognize the global environmental issues that threaten the world's population such as ozone depletion, climate change, acid rain, and species depletion. It looks with alarm at the environmental implications of the South's growing industrialization, for example, the massive destruction of the tropical rain forests. The South, while recognizing these issues as a global responsibility, believes the North should respond by reducing its excessive level of CONSUMPTION (which ranges from 28 times more in cars, 13 times more in paper, and 45 times more in oil) and providing the South with compensation in the form of economic support and environmental technologies for its destruction of the global commons (Porter and Brown 1996). Moreover, the South has been reluctant to join in global environmental agreements to reduce the use of CFCs and carbon emissions, because it tends to perceive them as another way for the North to secure power over the world's natural resources, the majority of which lie in the South, and thus to retain northern hegemony.

Thus the dilemma of development. If the desire for development is a primary cause of both massive environmental degradation and massive inequities between North and South, it seems self-defeating of both North and South to look to standard forms of development to remedy the problem of global environmental degradation. Attempts to solve the dilemma usually come in the name of "sustainable development"; however, not only is this term unclear and vague, but the strategies to achieve sustainable development are not always successful (see SUSTAINABILITY). In order to achieve global environmental justice, an alternative to the development paradigm must be sought. Identifying and implementing such an alternative is an overarching goal of global environmental justice.

As with domestic environmental justice, one way of dealing with an inequitable distribution of environmental burdens is through compensation, in the form of needed economic and technological resources, provided by first world to third world nations. But such compensatory strategies face problems of their own, as when wealthy nations impose conditions on the transfer of resources to poor nations (Jamieson 1994). For instance, the South already suffers excessive economic debt to nations of the North and global lending institutions. Lenders often put environmental conditions on loans in order to persuade the recipient to adopt more environmentally safe technologies, practices, and policies. The recipient's interests, however, may not match those of the lender. Recipients may wish to exercise rights to choose development strategies that overcome poverty, while lenders prefer loans to be spent on other environmental advances. Jamieson argues, however, that unconditional transfers may be both dangerous to the environment and ineffective in helping those who need the economic resources the most. This practice pits distributive justice against participatory justice, as the transfer of monies for loans or compensation constrains the power of self-determination.

Domestic and global environmental justice come together in the environmental justice struggles of indigenous peoples. For centuries, indigenous groups which have maintained traditional, non-industrialized, self-subsisting, environmentally friendly, and spiritual lifestyles in their natural environments have experienced waves of colonial and industrial conquest, carried out for the explicit purpose of wresting away control over their natural resources.

In 1975, 100 percent of uranium mining in the United States was carried out on indigenous land. Winona LaDuke reports that worldwide, "Over one hundred million indigenous people will be relocated to allow for the development of hydroelectric dam projects in the next decade; and over fifty million indigenous people inhabit the world's resources" (1993, p. 99). Oil and mining companies are constantly discovering deposits on indigenous lands, and pharmaceutical corporations expand upon the environmental conquest of indigenous peoples through the usurpation of traditional environmental knowledge and other indigenous resources. Many global trade agreements provide patent protection for corporations which succeed in acquiring traditional environmental knowledge. Patenting imposes restrictions on indigenous groups that discovered the patented knowledge in the first place. Vandana Shiva (1997) refers to this as "biopiracy."

Since indigenous peoples are nations within nations, although they are often referred to as sovereign, they are actually only quasi-sovereign or domestic dependents. The sovereignty of indigenous peoples is recognized when treaties are made, since in principle treaties can be made only between two self-determining, sovereign powers. However, the quasi-sovereign status of indigenous peoples emerges when such treaties presume that indigenous nations have transferable title to their resources. Thus, in a patronizing double-speak on sovereignty, indigenous peoples frequently end up transferring their resources by treaties assuming equal sovereignty or their resources are taken away by allegedly legitimate governmental statutes which fail to recognize their sovereignty (Goldtooth 1995; see INDIGENOUS PERSPECTIVES).

Conclusions

The inequities in the distribution of environmental burdens, both domestically and globally, are often the result of a failure to respect participatory justice. Policies for global environmental justice are lagging behind domestic efforts in the United States, largely because the non-governmental organizations defending the natural environment and environmental rights lack the power of national governments and transnational corporations. However, there is increasing effort to create and implement global policies that address the overlapping problems of development, indigenous rights, human rights, environmental practices, transboundary environmental burdens, and the transportation of toxic hazards. But significant progress is unlikely to be achieved without explicit recognition of the importance of both domestic and global distributive and participatory justice.

References

Anderton, D. L., et al. (1995) "Studies used to prove charges of environmental racism are flawed," in *At Issue: Environmental Justice*, ed. J. S. Petrikin (San Diego: Greenhaven Press, Inc.), pp. 24–37. [This study represents a sociological challenge to key studies and assumptions that set the environmental racism charge into motion.]

Been, V. (1995) "Market forces, not racist practices, may affect the siting of locally undesirable land uses," in *At Issue: Environmental Justice*, ed. J. S. Petrikin (San Diego: Greenhaven Press, Inc.), pp. 38–59. [Been provides a fundamental challenge to the environmental racism charge by contending that people of color are drawn to the nuisance of environmental burdens according to market motivations.]

Bullard, R. D., ed. (1993) *Confronting Environmental Racism: Voices from the Grassroots* (Boston: South End Press). [A central collection on environmental racism from the leading author on the topic.]

——(1994) "A new 'chicken-or-egg' debate: Which came first – the neighborhood, or the toxic dump?," *The Workbook* 19, pp. 60–2. [A response to major critics of environmental racism.]

Godsil, R. D. (1991) "Remedying environmental racism," *Michigan Law Review* 90, pp. 394–427. [One of the earliest accounts of the Title VI debate for judging civil cases of environmental racism.]

Goldtooth, T. B. K. (1995) "Indigenous nations: Summary of sovereignty implications for environmental protection," in *Environmental Justice: Issues, Policies, and Solutions*, ed. B. Bryant (Washington, DC: Island Press), pp. 138–50. [This discussion gives a useful account of the ways in which sovereignty in environmental struggles is problematized for indigenous peoples.]

Hofrichter, R., ed. (1993) *Toxic Struggles: The Theory and Practice of Environmental Justice* (Philadelphia: New Society Publishers), pp. 237–9. [A collection which includes the first documented manifesto for environmental justice.]

Jamieson, D. (1994) "Global environmental justice," in *Philosophy and the Natural Environment*, ed. R. Attfield and H. Belsey (Cambridge: Cambridge University Press), pp. 199–210. [A detailed analysis of problems in the transfer of funds between nations struggling over environmental debts.]

LaDuke, W. (1993) "A society based on conquest cannot be sustained: Native peoples and the environmental crisis," in *Toxic Struggles: The Theory and Practice of Environmental Justice*, ed. R. Hofrichter (Philadelphia: New Society Publishers), pp. 98–106. [A compelling account of the environmental justice struggles of Native Americans and indigenous peoples worldwide.]

Porter, G., and Brown, J. W. (1996) *Global Environmental Politics* (Boulder: Westview Press). [A thorough and clear introduction to major global environmental issues.]

Russell, D. (1989) "Environmental racism: Minority communities and their battle against toxics," *Amicus Journal* 1, pp. 22–32. [A relatively early discussion of environmental racism presenting details of critical cases for understanding discriminatory siting procedures.]

Sachs, W., ed. (1993) *Global Ecology: A New Arena of Political Conflict* (Atlantic Highlands: Zed Books), pp. 3–20. [Sachs's collection is an excellent source of articles from international authors addressing global development philosophies, indigenous environmental struggles, and the politics of UNCED.]

Shiva, V. (1993) "The greening of the global reach," in *Global Ecology: A New Arena of Political Conflict*, ed. W. Sachs (Atlantic Highlands: Zed Books), pp. 149–56. [A poignant description of the power dynamics driving global environmental politics by one of the most important author/activists for global environmental justice.]

——(1997) *Biopiracy: The Plunder of Nature and Knowledge* (Boston: South End Press). [One of the few texts entirely devoted to exploring the cultural injustices brought on by the linkages between the motivation for genetic engineering, the global power associated with the pharmaceutical industry, and the politics of international trade and patent agreements.]

UCC-CRJ (United Church of Christ Commission for Racial Justice) (1987) *Toxic Wastes and Race in the United States: A National Report on the Racial and Socio-Economic Characteristics of Communities with Hazardous Waste Sites* (New York: Public Data Access, Inc.). [The seminal study of environmental racism in the USA.]

US-GAO (United States General Accounting Office) (1983) *Siting of Hazardous Waste Landfills and Their Correlation with Racial and Economic Status Surrounding Communities*, GAO/RCED-83-168. [One of the first studies conducted by the US government on the relationship between race, poverty, and hazardous waste sitings.]

US House of Representatives (1993) *Environmental Justice: Hearings Before the Subcommittee on Civil and Constitutional Rights, Committee on Judiciary*, 103rd Congress, 1st Session (Washington, DC: US Government Printing Office, March 3–4). [These pivotal hearings include definitions of environmental racism and testimonies of leading proponents and skeptics.]

Wenz, P. S. (1988) *Environmental Justice* (Buffalo: SUNY Press). [An introduction to liberal distributive approaches to environmental justice.]

Young, I. M. (1983) "Justice and hazardous waste," *The Applied Turn in Contemporary Philosophy: Bowling Green Studies in Applied Philosophy* 5, pp. 171–83. [One of the first philosophical arguments discussing hazardous wastes and environmental justice. A useful argument for participatory justice.]

31

Technology

LORI GRUEN

Environmentalists tend to view technology with suspicion. In the wake of the Exxon Valdez oil spill in 1989 and the catastrophes at Bhopal (1984) and Chernobyl (1986), such suspicion appears warranted. And opponents of technology are not only concerned about such massive environmental disasters, even though this is often the time that environmentalist criticisms of technology reach the general public. Critics of technology see such disasters as an inevitable result of measuring progress in terms of our ability to manipulate the environment through technology. And thus, while critical of the environmental damage caused by the use of various technologies, critics have also raised concerns about the social and political consequences of technological use and development. In the first part of this chapter, I will discuss these criticisms. Even when the consequences of technology are not particularly problematic, some critics nonetheless believe that technology is bad. In the second part of this chapter, I will assess the normative arguments mounted by critics against technology, and explore the value assumptions upon which the criticisms of technology depend.

The consequences of technology

Many of the objectionable environmental consequences of technology are obvious. In addition to the disasters just mentioned, one need only pick up a daily newspaper to see that human reliance on technology is a large contributing factor in the deterioration of the environment. To take a recent example, consider global warming, which is a predicted outcome of increased emissions of greenhouse gases that trap heat in the atmosphere. Emissions of one of the main greenhouse gases, carbon dioxide, has increased exponentially since the beginning of the Industrial Revolution. Ever-increasing human reliance on technologies that require fossil fuels is directly connected to the impending threat of global warming. And if some of the gloomier scientific predictions are right, such technologies will be implicated in significant damage to human and non-human health and life as well as the destruction of entire ecosystems (see CLIMATE).

Less obvious, but equally environmentally damaging, is the production of so-called "clean technologies" – computers and other high-tech equipment. The manufacturing process for microchips involves the use of many highly toxic chemicals, such as arsine, acetone, ethylene glycol, and xylene. These and other chemicals used by the high-tech industry have caused massive ground water contamination in the last thirty years. When a spill or leak of toxic chemicals occurs at the site of a high-tech company the pollution often spreads many miles from its origin and can affect vital sources of drinking water and precious wetlands. In Silicon Valley, the center of high-tech production, there are now more polluted sites prioritized for clean-up by the federal government than in any other county in the United States. So while the use of computers and other high-tech electronic equipment may not have particularly damaging environmental consequences, their production has proved destructive to humans, non-humans, and their environments.

It might be suggested that while the production and use of some technology is certainly responsible for a great deal of environmental damage, there are technologies that are not environmentally harmful. It might be argued that not all technology leads to bad consequences. With the development of environmentally friendly tech-nologies we may be able to maintain current levels of human productivity and the high quality of life that technologies allow in those nations that can afford them. So, the environmentalist criticisms might only apply to environmentally destructive technologies.

While many environmentalists believe that technology can be used in environment-ally sensitive and responsible ways, and may even be central in efforts to protect the natural world, others point out that there are additional negative consequences of its development and use that are often overlooked. These critics point to the economic and political organization of technology and the social consequences of technological "regimes." Neo-Luddites, ranging from journalist and author Kirkpatrick Sale (1995) and former advertising executive Jerry Mander (1991), to the "unabomber" Theodore Kaczinsky (widely available on the web), have highlighted the dangerous, undemo-cratic organization of virtually all technological advancements. They urge that the power relations that are implicit in technological development and use be examined. Critics point to the fact that technological development requires both highly organ-ized, hierarchical decision structures and the concentration of capital in the hands of a few. Nuclear power is a commonly cited example that illustrates this point. The development of nuclear power required massive capital, centralized control, and the establishment of governmental bureaucracies to monitor safety, distribution, and waste disposal. Communities that live in the areas that were to become sites for nuclear power facilities had little, if any, input into the decision process and the workers employed by the nuclear power industry often were not informed about the risks of their work.

The development of technology, the neo-Luddites also point out, plays a central role in the global economy with its fiercely competitive market expansion strategies. Not only does this contribute to environmental degradation, but it also leads to the destruction of small, localized, and environmentally sound ways of living. Vandana Shiva, Director of the Research Foundation for Science, Technology, and Natural Resource Policy in India, provides an interesting example of how first world techno-logy exports have contributed to social and political turmoil in Punjab. During the 1960s, technologically enhanced agricultural strategies were being touted as the way for struggling, famine-afflicted areas to attain abundance and peace. The "green revolution," as the new strategy was called, involved a shift from locally controlled peasant farming to a reliance on imported and expensive agrochemical and miracle seeds. As Shiva writes:

The Green Revolution technology requires heavy investments in fertilizers, pesticides, seed, water, and energy. Intensive agriculture generated severe ecological destruction, and created new kinds of scarcity and vulnerability, and new levels of inefficiency in resource use...the Green Revolution created major changes in natural ecosystems and agrarian structures. New relationships between science and agriculture defined new links between the state and cultivators, between international interests and local communities. (1991, p. 46–7)

According to Shiva, the green revolution created monocrops, new pests, new diseases, water shortages, economic debt, and dependence, and increased rather than decreased social instability. While the agricultural policies and political dynamics in Punjab, and throughout the third world, are complex, this example illustrates the way that even technologies that are meant to enhance well-being can permanently alter and damage traditional, sustainable ways of life.

The life-altering effects of technology extend beyond the agricultural practices and political life of various communities. Biotechnology also has the potential to physically change human and non-human beings. In the late 1980s, scientists began a multibillion-dollar, long-term project which attempts to identify and map all of the human genes. The ostensible purpose of the human genome project is to gain greater insight into human diseases. The basic goal is to identify genetic links to disease so that, eventually, individuals can be genetically tested for diseases and undergo treatment to prevent the diseases from manifesting. Two types of treatment, or therapy, are commonly discussed: somatic cell therapy and germ line therapy. Somatic cell therapy modifies or augments our non-reproductive cells; gene line therapy modifies or augments our reproductive cells. The former alters a particular individual and the therapy only affects that individual; the latter alters the genetic make-up of future generations. Critics of technology suggest that just as in the case of the green revolution, where the manipulation of seeds led to immediate, short-term gains in crop yield and productivity at the cost of far-reaching, and in some cases unanticipated, ecological and social consequences, so too biotechnological manipulation of human cells can have frightening consequences.

Critics of biotechnology do not have to rely on distopian fantasies about the imagined consequences of genetic manipulation for their concerns to be understood, however, as the actual results of genetic engineering are already being felt ecologically and socially. Genetically engineered organisms are being created in laboratories and released into the environment, creating a whole new category of pollution – "biological pollution." Unlike chemical pollution, which in many cases can be contained and cleaned up, biological pollution does not eventually dissipate, but rather reproduces and can overrun indigenous plant and animal life. In the social realm, human growth hormone, which was originally engineered from human pituitary hormones in order to help those suffering from dwarfism, has been marketed as a way to enhance the height of short children. Thousands of parents with the consent of their physicians are injecting human growth hormone into their children, usually the boys. Given that height enhancing technology is now available, parents who care about the social acceptance and success of their children (and who can afford it) now have a new option available to help their children get a good start in life. But what is the social cost? Parents who choose not to inject their children with growth hormones, either out of fear of unforeseen side-effects or because they do not want to condone what they perceive as groundless stereotypes, may be thought to be bad parents. Those who can afford the treatment, but forego it, may be thought to be selfish. If being a tall young man contributes to success in the world, those who can afford to provide their sons with the treatment put their children in a better social and economic position. What of the parents who cannot afford the treatment to help their shorter sons? The economic disadvantage their youngster faces will be multiplied by his height disadvantage.

The existence of human growth hormone raises interesting issues about the effects technology can have on what is considered normal. Though the consumption of technology appears to be optional, often the use of technology becomes very close to a social requirement. In most of the United States, for example, it is next to impossible to make a living without a car for transportation. In our high-tech society, individuals who do not have answering machines, faxes, pagers, or computers are excluded from certain forms of social and professional activities. And even if the individual without such devices is not excluded from these activities, she is often viewed as outside of the norm. The social pressure of failing to use certain technologies, even if not materially damaging, can nonetheless be intense (as anyone who doesn't have an answering machine or use email can testify). And once an individual is on the technological path, it is very difficult to step off. Many of us who use computers can hardly imagine what it would be like to go back to pen and paper. This technological mindset, as critics call it, is just one more damaging consequence of technology. Individuals in technological societies become dependent on technology and their ability to think and act outside of technology becomes limited.

All of the examples mentioned here raise complex questions which go beyond the scope of this brief discussion. The point these examples are meant to illustrate is that technology, even when it does not directly, immediately, or obviously affect the natural world, is nonetheless implicated in problematic social, political, psychological, and ecological consequences. But granting that the negative consequences outlined here exist, does that mean that all technology should be condemned? Or is technology that is organized in ways that avoid the undemocratic, capital intensive, socially, psychologically, and ecologically damaging consequences acceptable? In order to answer these questions, the value assumptions on both sides of the argument about technology must be explored.

Some of those who have analyzed technology, including those environmentalists who advocate "appropriate" technologies, have suggested that technology, in itself, is neutral, and they restrict their assessment of technology to the consequences that it brings about. They argue that recent technological advances, such as video cameras and the internet, can provide us with information about and glimpses of nature that will motivate people to work to protect non-humans and the environment. Their view is that when technology can aid in protecting the natural world and can be developed and implemented in a non-coercive and participatory way, then it is morally acceptable. When, however, technology is damaging to the environment or is undemocratically developed and forced on people it is open to criticism on moral grounds. The reasons for the moral condemnation are external to the technology itself. Other critics, however, have argued that technological neutrality is a myth and that there is something intrinsic to technology that makes it morally problematic. I will now look at two types of argument that might support such a view.

Nature versus culture

Technology is ubiquitous in human culture. It is so pervasive that technologies, those tools and devices used to shape and change the environment, have become the mark of culture. It is often thought that a culture can be defined and assessed by how successful that culture is at controlling nature through technology. Culture is thus opposed to nature, and technology is the means by which this opposition is maintained. When culture is understood in opposition to nature, technology itself can be viewed as unnatural. For many environmentalists, no matter how well intentioned human cultural activities and technological innovations may be, no matter what the consequences of such activities and innovations, they are always artificial, and thus have a value that is fundamentally different from that of natural processes. The cultural is understood as a disruption of the natural and thus antithetical to it.

According to this perspective, artificial things, artifacts of human invention, are less valuable than natural things. Many environmentalists believe that nature has value because it is natural, that is, because it is not the product of human construction or creation. Such products have value insofar as they are useful to humans; they serve human ends. Automobiles, nuclear power facilities, biotechnologically engineered seeds, and computers are all created to serve human needs. Nature, on the other hand, exists for itself and thus is an altogether different kind of thing. Ecological and evolutionary processes occur quite independently of human activities. Nature existed long before humans did, and will continue long after humans are gone (assuming some human-generated technological disaster does not destroy everything). Some argue that this independent genesis and existence is what gives nature its value, and while nature can be and often is taken over by human cultural activity to serve human needs, its value goes beyond its use-value to humans (see NORMATIVE ETHICS, BIODIVERSITY, WILDERNESS).

Technology, on this view, is the mechanism by which nature is disrupted and destroyed. It is not simply an artifact of human creation, and thus less valuable than the natural world, but it is also that which diminishes natural value. Technology is the means by which valuable nature is transformed into products for human use and consumption. Even when technology is used for protecting and preserving nature, such as when various technologies are employed to identify and protect endangered species, it is still thought to be problematic by some environmentalists. At best, technology is a device humans can use to attempt to repair what their use of other technologies has destroyed. But technology cannot restore the natural value of the environment, nor can humans improve it. Once that value is interfered with by humans, it is gone forever.

There are a number of problems with this criticism of technology that is based on a dichotomy between nature and culture. First, viewing nature as a category that is distinct and independent from culture fails to take into account the various ways in which we interpret "nature" rather than merely report on it. How we understand natural processes, species, and the differences between ecosystems and their states of "health," for example, all require interpretation by cultural beings. The very division between culture and nature, one could say, is a cultural artifact. And technology often helps us to gain information to better interpret the natural world and thus can aid us in acquiring knowledge about what is valuable in nature.

A second problem with this view is that it presupposes that things can be neatly divided into either the cultural or the natural and this doesn't seem to be the case. At the extremes, the division may be clear – a plastic necklace is clearly cultural and artificial, a thunderstorm is clearly natural. But what about second-growth forests that have existed for over one hundred years or non-indigenous plants that have lived in and adapted to their non-native environments over several centuries? What about El Niño storms? While the forest, the plants, and the climate have in some ways been interfered with by the use of technologies, they have since flourished, evolved, and reacted independently of humans. Do they belong in the realm of the cultural or the natural or both?

A third problem with the conceptual framework that divides culture from nature is that it poses a dilemma for environmentalists. Either they must believe that humans are part of nature and thus what they do is natural, or that humans are separate from nature and thus human activity is unnatural. If they believe the former, then they must view the destruction of nature through the use of various technologies as natural, just as predation is natural. But then it would be difficult to say why the destruction of nature is morally objectionable if what is natural is thought to be good. If they believe that humans are unnatural, then they would be committed to accepting a radical discontinuity between humans and other naturally evolved things (a view that has been convincingly challenged at least since the nineteenth-century British biologist Charles Darwin). This contradicts the notion that many environmentalists want to promote, namely that humans are a part of nature and that in order to solve our environmental problems we must recognize our connection to rather than separation from the natural world. This dilemma could be overcome by rejecting the normative implications of the culture/nature divide, that is, by denying the simple theory of value which maintains that what is natural is good and what is cultural is bad, and drawing on a more refined theory about what is valuable. Let me turn now to one such theory.

Technology versus authenticity

While many people view technology as a means to free us from the drudgery and tedium of thankless tasks, others argue that technology removes us from the work-ings of the natural world and in so doing mediates our experiences of it. What is wrong with technology, then, is not that it is a product of culture, but that it creates experiences that are unnatural or inauthentic. A thought experiment will help bring out the insight of this type of criticism of technology.

Imagine learning that your favorite place in nature is not what it seemed. The designated wilderness area you've been visiting every summer for the last ten years is not wilderness at all. The trees and mountains are synthetic, the lake is man-made, the "indigenous" wildlife has been farm-raised and then imported, and the fern, moss, and other plant life were manufactured in a factory outside of Gary, Indiana. The environmental engineers who created this place did a fine job. Their employers removed the natural resources in the area in order to make a profit, thereby destroying the original environment, and have replaced what was natural with a very good fake. For a decade you have enjoyed your time in what you thought was a pristine natural area. Only now you have learned that the wilderness was a technologically created copy.

What is wrong with this scenario? It might be argued that you will no longer enjoy your so-called wilderness experience, and since pleasure is what is ultimately valued, what is wrong here is that pleasure will no longer be generated from this experience. Assuming that no sentient beings suffered during the process of creating this place (an improbable assumption in a number of ways, but for the sake of argument let's assume that the native wildlife species of the area were removed and have now been released) and that human experiences of this area were not unpleasant, it looks like the only thing wrong with this scenario is that you and others experience disappointment upon learning that this natural area was not what it seemed. But is this really all that is wrong with faked nature?

Critics of technology can draw on the view that there is more wrong with this artificial environment than the mere disappointment you and others may experience. The value of the fake, they might suggest, is less than the value of real nature. This is, for example, how many environmentalists have responded to ecological restoration projects (see Elliot 1997). Environmental theorists have argued that when we destroy a natural area and then recreate or restore it through acts of technological wizardry, something of value is permanently lost. Some environmental theorists maintain that the value accompanying authentic wilderness cannot be restored, even when the area still provides positive "wilderness" experiences, because its value is not reducible to the experiences of valuers. The origin of a natural area contributes to its value and thus, because the faked wilderness area has a different origin, it does not have the same value as authentic or genuine nature. What is wrong with the above scenario, critics argue, is not that the subjective quality of our wilderness experience may have changed, but that the value of the actual objects of such experiences is diminished.

But is this view right? Consider the above scenario modified. Imagine that you never learned that the wilderness area you have so much enjoyed over the years is in fact fake. You continue to visit the area and experience much pleasure. Not only do you continue to maintain the false belief that you are experiencing authentic wilderness, but other visitors share this belief. Imagine further that rather than being employed by a for-profit company, the environmental engineers were employed by an environmental organization that believed that it was important for as many people as possible to experience what they thought was nature. They believed, quite plausibly, that if everyone did experience real nature they would undoubtedly destroy it, so the environmental engineers were hired to create an excellent and durable substitute.

According to those who hold that what is ultimately valuable is pleasurable experiences, it looks as though the modified scenario is not only acceptable, but may even be morally required (assuming that a world in which many people had pleasurable experiences of what they think is real nature is a better world). But, critics might argue, it is not any pleasant experience that is valuable, but the quality of the experience. An experience that is based on a false belief, while pleasurable and thus of some value, is not as valuable as an experience that is based on a genuine, unmediated encounter with the world. Another way of putting it is that what is valuable is not just the belief that we have satisfied our desires, but their actual satisfaction. A person who desires to make the world more just, for example, by engaging in activities to resist racial or gender discrimination, would presumably not be satisfied if they were to learn that though they thought they were succeeding in changing discriminatory institutions, their success was illusory. Similarly, if one desired to experience authentic nature, and then learned that what they thought was authentic was artificial, their desire would not actually be satisfied.

Part of what contributes to a meaningful life, and thus a pleasurable one, is making plans and setting goals that one hopes will be accomplished. Part of what is pleasurable is the making of such plans, and seeing a plan through to fruition generates tremendous satisfaction. If people knew that there was a possibility that they could be deceived into thinking that they had actually succeeded in achieving a goal, when in fact they were just strapped to electrodes in a tank or were being lied to by everyone they knew, there is a good chance that they might not set out to make a plan or try to accomplish a goal. Given that the making of plans and the setting of goals is part of what contributes to overall pleasure, deception will negatively affect that pleasure. If one were asked whether their lives on the whole would be better if they were deceived, but nonetheless happy, I suspect many would answer negatively. In the modified case of faked nature, it can be argued that the very possibility of there being faked nature will undermine individuals' enjoyment of the real thing. The satisfaction that individuals would have experiencing nature could be compromised if they believed that what they thought they were experiencing might be fake. Further, the possibility that the deception might exist may cause individuals to not plan to visit natural areas and thus lose out on what could be valuable experiences. Most of us value authentic experiences and would be disturbed to learn that we have been deceived.

Drawing on the insights of this thought experiment, critics of technology might suggest that our experiences of the natural world, because they are mediated by technology are inauthentic, that our understanding of ourselves and the natural world are based on deception. Even though the natural world has not been recreated by environmental engineers (and the possibility of creating a realistic ecosystem is very remote indeed given that scientists working on artificial life have yet to create a realistic model of moths or cockroaches), our modern lives are so saturated with technology that our day-to-day experiences are not unlike those we would have in a faked environment. This is one of the reasons why people seek out natural areas, to escape to a more genuine reality. What is wrong with technology, critics might suggest, is that it creates a false, unnatural world.

While this criticism of technology is in many ways quite compelling in that it allows us to understand why technologically mediated experiences are of questionable value, it nonetheless presupposes an absolute rejection of technology that is difficult to defend. Perhaps this can best be seen by considering the extreme, but not unrealistic, situation in which an individual has no chance at all of experiencing genuine nature.

Perhaps she is poor and lives in an overpopulated urban center. Most of her time is spent trying to survive and keep her children alive. On rare occasions, she and others like her are invited to view a nature video or experience nature in a "virtual" way. This experience provides her with genuine pleasure, even though she knows her experience is mediated through technology and, we can assume further, such an experience allows her to recognize the value of nature. One of her hopes is that her children, or their children, might be able to experience genuine nature someday. While she has little time and no resources to devote to protecting the natural world, she nonetheless is glad that others can, so that her children may experience it. Critics of technology, though rightly critical of the conditions that lead to this woman's impoverished situation, would have to tell a richer story about what is morally wrong with this mediated experience of nature, in order for their sweeping moral condemnation of technology to hold.

Conclusion

Technology is surely implicated in much environmental damage, as well as the destruction of politically and psychologically sustainable ways of life. In the fast-paced world of video games, cell phones, laser-guided missiles, and the like, it is indeed tempting to think that technology, in itself, is objectionable. Such an argument, however, is hard to sustain. If nature is valuable, as many have argued, then technology can be used to inform, educate, and assist in promoting its value. Critics have done a tremendous service in helping us to think more critically about the use and development of various technologies. They are right to have us examine most of our current technological trends. But ultimately, the strongest arguments for or against technology will be based on the consequences of its use for people, for animals, and for the natural world.

References

Elliot, R. (1997) *Faking Nature* (London: Routledge). [An important book that discusses both the meta-ethical and normative issues of natural value as well as carefully exploring problems with technological intervention in the natural world.]

Mander, J. (1991) *In the Absence of the Sacred* (San Francisco: Sierra Club Books). [The former advertising executive and author of *Four Arguments for the Elimination of Television* explores the dangerous consequences of technology on native cultures and society in general.]

Sale, K. (1995) *Rebels Against the Future: The Luddites and Their War on the Industrial Revolution* (Reading, MA: Addison-Wesley). [A history of the nineteenth-century opposition to technology and the lessons we can learn from it.]

Shiva, V. (1991) *The Violence of the Green Revolution* (London: Zed Books Ltd). [A carefully documented examination of the dangers of technological intervention in India.]

Further reading

Ellul, J. (1964) *The Technological Society* (New York: Vintage Books). [An early and thorough critique of technology.]

Ferré, F., ed. (1992) *Research in Philosophy and Technology: Technology and the Environment* (Greenwich, CN: JAI Press). [A wide-ranging book of essays that addresses both the theoretical and practical issues that technology raises.]

Mills, S., ed. (1997) *Turning Away from Technology* (San Francisco: Sierra Club Books). [Based on transcripts from the 1993 and 1994 international conferences on megatechnology, this volume contains insights from some of the leading critics of technology today.]

Sclove, R. (1995) *Democracy and Technology* (New York: Guilford Press). [Argues for the need for participatory technologies.]

Zerzan, J. and Carnes, A., eds (1988) *Questioning Technology* (London: Freedom Press). [A collection of sometimes fictional, always disturbing, reflections on technology.]

32

Climate

HENRY SHUE

Environmental challenges do not wear philosophical name-tags, and the judgment about what kinds of question they raise is more fateful, because more difficult to shake loose from, than any particular answers offered to the questions once assumed. Much philosophical writing about climate change so far has assumed that the fundamental issues are distributive: issues of justice between rich and poor and between present and future. Issues of distributive justice, trans-spatial and trans-temporal, are certainly important, but other kinds of question arise as well.

Inflicting harm

A change in the climate is a profound change, a modification in some of the interacting forces that, in combination with its distance from the sun, give this planet its distinctive environment. What may be harmed by human choices to bring about avoidable changes in the climate depends upon what is morally considerable, the range of things whose interests deserve to be taken into account (see SENTIENTISM, META-ETHICS). However, since the climate is a planetary-level phenomenon, virtually anything that is indeed morally considerable may well be affected by the extent or speed of climate change. For example, the species that flourish on earth now are species that found a hospitable spot in the climate we have now. Species adapt – some migrate – and speciations are constantly occurring, but natural adaptation and natural evolution occur on a timescale far slower than the timescale that appears likely if increases in the atmospheric concentration of anthropogenic greenhouse gases (GHGs) continue. Few species can adapt nearly as rapidly as the climate may change. The primary cause of species extinction is loss of habitat; rapid climate change could be the ultimate destroyer of habitats. Insofar as existing species, or the ecosystems in which they live, or the natural processes through which they would otherwise change, have some value and are worthy of protection from avoidable human destruction or distortion – insofar as anthropogenic extinction is an ethical issue – anthropogenic rapid climate change is morally suspect for the harm it will inflict beyond the human species (see BIODIVERSITY).

Here the focus will be on harm to humans, which comes in at least two kinds, the second somewhat less evident than the first. First is straightforward, if indirectly caused, physical harm of many kinds. Climate change will centrally involve relatively simple changes in weather, some of which will be dangerous. Consider water and then insects. Some locations that now have abundant rainfall will have inadequate rainfall; drinking water may become inadequate. Other locations that now suffer drought may receive heavy rains, producing flooding and causing people to drown. Changes such as deficits and surpluses in rainfall and drinking water are uncomplicated and utterly ordinary, but people – and crops and livestock, and thus indirectly more people – perish from droughts and floods. And wars, in which of course more people (and crops and livestock) die, are fought over access to water for drinking, irrigation, and manufacture.

Some insects, like certain mosquitos, cannot range farther than a certain distance from the equator because the winters are too cold or long for them. Those of us who live in the cooler temperate zones rather complacently think of the infections carried by these species as "tropical" diseases and invest far less in their prevention and cure than in diseases that now threaten us, in spite of the fact that some "tropical" diseases – like malaria – are among humanity's greatest scourges. One of the most likely components of climate change will be a lessening of the severity of the winters in some temperate areas, with the incursion of unfamiliar "tropical" diseases by way of an extension of the range of their vectors. Human illness and death is very likely to result. Changes in rainfall patterns and disease patterns resulting from weather changes which in turn result from changes in atmospheric concentrations of GHGs raise just as many – but no more – issues about causation, and about the relation between causal responsibility and moral responsibility, as more familiar cases such as second-hand cigarette smoke and cancer. If the smoker can be morally responsible for the cancer of his non-smoking children who inhale the smoke, it is not apparent why the sources of the avoidable GHGs cannot at least sometimes be responsible for the inundations or infections to which the increased atmospheric concentrations contribute. This appears to be the very long-distance but fully real infliction of physical harm on innocent strangers.

The second kind of harm is not so straightforward, but is, if anything, more serious: it is the harm of preventing people from obtaining the necessary minimum of a resource vital for their survival. Before explaining how in this instance some people make it impossible for others to secure a minimum needed, we should notice the nature of the resource in question here, which may initially seem odd. Every human being needs, in order to survive, some minimum quantity of certain obvious resources such as drinkable water and breathable air. The quantity of each resource needed obviously varies from individual to individual depending upon features of each individual, such as age and level of activity, and features of the individual's situation, including climate. Yet any given individual at any given place and time needs some minimum amount of essential resources such as safe water and safe air. Less obviously, most people now also need what amounts to a minimum amount of the planet's capacity to deal safely with GHG emissions. The vast majority of people alive today must, in order to survive, engage in economic activities that generate GHG emissions: they, for example, raise livestock or rice, both of which create methane, or they consume fossil fuel, which releases CO_2. It may seem slightly odd to treat absorptive capacity as a vital resource, but absorptive capacity for GHG emissions is not only a necessity but an increasingly scarce one, as the research on climate change has demonstrated.

The shortage of this absorptive capacity is of course not an unchangeable feature of the universe; on the contrary, it is an artifact produced by the energy regime on which we have based our economic system. At one technological extreme, denizens of a pre-industrial, tropical society might survive simply by gathering uncultivated fruits and vegetables, without heating or cooling their habitations and without transportation. They might produce no GHG emissions of any consequence, making their minimum need for GHG absorptive capacity effectively zero. At the other technological extreme, we might construct an advanced industrial (or post-industrial) economy powered by solar, wind, and/or geothermal energy that also produced no GHG emissions because, although it consumed large quantities of energy, none of the energy was carbon-based. There, too, GHG absorptive capacity would not be needed by everyone engaged in economic activity. Our current need for GHG absorptive capacity is, therefore, an avoidable necessity: it is perfectly possible for matters to become otherwise than they in fact are. It is avoidable, however, only on the social level, not the individual level. If, for example, one needs surgery, the surgeon will probably drive to the hospital in a vehicle powered by a combustion engine and the operating theater will be lighted by electricity more than likely generated by burning fossil fuel. An individual could forgo the surgery in order not to be responsible for the GHG emissions involved, but that would, given the kind of economy we have, constitute an insanely large sacrifice for a relatively small saving in emissions. Yet the society as a whole, with as advanced a medical technology as one likes, could be operated on non-carbon-based energy. The reasonable avoidability is only at the social level, and not a matter for individual martyrdom.

Consequently, whether an individual needs to generate GHG emissions in order to live – and thereby needs some minimum absorptive capacity for those emissions – is a function of the time and place, and specifically the energy regime, into which she is born. For practically everyone at present, and for the immediate future, survival requires the use of GHG emissions absorptive capacity. No reasonable, immediate alternative exists. Strange as it may initially sound, emission absorptive capacity is as vital as food and water and, virtually everywhere, shelter and clothing. The central finding of research about climate change, however, is that there is a global maximum on safe GHG emissions because there is a physical limit on the quantity of GHGs that can be absorbed without changes that affect surface climate. Emissions in excess of this safe maximum produce climate change; and, of course, current total emissions are already far in excess of the safe global maximum and rapidly growing every year (worse, at an accelerating rate of increase). The underlying logic of the situation is, then, abundantly clear: (a) the global total of emissions must (if we are to avoid climate change – in fact, increasingly rapid climate change) be reduced, while (b) every human being depends for survival on the production (direct or indirect) of a minimum amount of GHG emissions. So the global minimum total is the product of the per capita minimum (given the existing energy regime) times the existing population, while the global maximum total is the amount the planet can recycle safely, i.e. recycle without climate change.

Actually, three global emissions totals are in play: (1) the socially determined minimum total (for survival of current population with current energy regime); (2) the naturally determined maximum total (for a sustainable economy that does not produce climate change); and (3) the actual total (current emissions). The relations among the three totals are matters of fact. The research of the Intergovernmental

Panel on Climate Change (IPCC) has found that (3), the current total, is far in excess of (2), the sustainable total that would avoid climate change. The size of (1) depends critically on the energy sources on which the world economy relies. In a world economy driven by solar, wind, and geothermal (or nuclear) energy, (1) could be extremely low; agriculture, as we know it, will still produce methane, but the methane would not be a problem without CO_2 produced by electricity-generation and transportation. In a world economy like ours, driven by fossil fuels, (1) may be larger than (2).

Indeed, (1) may even be larger than (3); this depends on the ratio between the amount of energy now frivolously consumed, or carelessly wasted, by the affluent and the additional amount now needed by the desperately poor for decent lives. It is logically possible that sheer redistribution of current energy use could provide for everyone's basic needs, while keeping the existing fossil fuel regime, i.e. that (1) is no larger than (3), while (3) is now simply too unequally distributed. The obvious difficulties with taking consolation in the possibility that (1) is no larger than (3), provided that the distribution of energy consumption were sufficiently less unequal internationally than the current wildly unequal distribution, include: (a) the affluent and powerful would have to be willing to accept a redistribution of energy consumption that would severely reduce their current standard of living (given the existing carbon-based regime) – a willingness rarely in sight, whatever its ethical merits; (b) the redistribution would have to be feasible without throwing the world economy into a tailspin that made matters even worse for the worst-off (by, for example, large net elimination of jobs); and (c) none of this matters here in any case because (3) is much larger than (2) – redistributing emissions that are already in excess of what the planet can handle without changes in the climate would not prevent climate change (nor, over the long-run, help the poorest, who will be least able to afford to adapt to climate change).

Where is there any infliction of harm? The billion or so poorest human beings on the planet need sound and sustainable economic development. They need to engage in economic activity that will, given that the current world economy runs on fossil fuel, add GHG emissions to the earth's atmosphere by consuming fossil fuel. They need "space" for their increased emissions, and this space needs to be within a global total less than (2), the maximum sustainable total compatible with the avoidance of climate change. They need to use emission absorptive capacity, but no absorptive capacity is left because those of us in the affluent economies have taken it all (and much more). We are parked in their spaces, and no empty spaces exist. Our unnecessary emissions are blocking their vital ones, except at the price of speeded-up climate change, which will be most unmanageable for them. We are depriving them of a necessity for their survival, given the fossil fuel regime, which the poor, unlike the affluent, cannot change. The economic/energy system in which we thrive and indulge in excess prevents their enjoying a decent life. The energy regime that makes life opulent for Belgians and Saudis makes it impossible for Rwandans and Haitians, who are helpless victims of a complex global social institution in which they have absolutely no voice.

Suppose a picnic table is set with enough food for two dozen people, but only one dozen come. Any food not eaten will spoil. I "pig out," eating enough for two or three people. I have demonstrated that I am a glutton, lacking in self-discipline and perhaps civility. But I have harmed no one – no one else is worse off as a result of my excess (although I myself may be).

Now suppose that a picnic table is set with enough food for one dozen people, and one dozen eventually come. I arrive early and, being a glutton, eat enough for two or three people, as usual. The last one or two people to come have nothing to eat because I have eaten their share. I have harmed them because I have deprived them of what they were entitled to, unless we make some heroically implausible assumption such as that they have no right to be there or that I am so special that I have a right to double the share of ordinary folks. If we add the assumption that this meal was part of the minimum those deprived needed for their survival, which would make the picnic more analogous to GHG emissions, then I have injured them severely – arguably, I have killed them. I have certainly done them harm.

Increasing injustice

Physical necessity requires, if humanity is to break free from the spiral into rapid climate change predictable with business-as-usual, that practically every state in the world cooperate – most vitally, the states with the highest emissions (the USA has by far the highest) and the states with the largest populations (China's emission total, although not its per capita rate, will soon surpass that of the USA). Fairness requires that each state do its fair share. What are the criteria of a fair share in this case? This turns out to be a philosophically challenging question. For a start, fairness and unfairness arise at three theoretically separable but practically intertwined points: procedures, emissions, and costs. Further, costs will be incurred for different, though deeply interrelated, purposes.

Fair procedures   What, if anything, will be done to ward off rapid climate change is in fact now being decided under the *Framework Convention on Climate Change (FCCC)* (opened for signature at the Earth Summit, the United Nations Conference on Environment and Development, held in Rio de Janeiro on June 4, 1992; entered into force, March 21, 1994; and potentially modified by *Kyoto Protocol*, approved by the Conference of the Parties, December 11, 1997, and awaiting a sufficient number of national approvals, with the US Executive declining to submit it for US Senate ratification). The *FCCC* itself requires no action. The ratification process for the *Kyoto Protocol*, which would for the first time require some action by affluent states (results to be averaged across 2008–12, with "demonstrable progress" by 2005 required – Article 3), is heavily weighted, in a manner roughly similar to the weighted voting within the World Bank and the International Monetary Fund, in favor of the states with the highest current emissions of GHGs (entrance into force depends upon approval by states responsible for 55 percent of the CO_2 emissions in 1990 – Article 24). Any argument for the fairness of this ratification process seems to depend upon some claim that those who pay the piper should call the tune. While this practice is customary in international affairs, it tacitly assumes the absence of any prior grounds for responsibility for bearing costs. In other words, it prejudges the substantive questions discussed below.

The fundamental features of the *FCCC* procedures are that they are (a) negotiations among (b) radically unequal parties, namely national states, precisely the kind of procedure most likely to produce outcomes that merely reflect the enormous power differentials among the bargainers. The parties range from a nuclear superpower and the European Union with vast wealth and power, at one extreme, to the states most immediately vulnerable to the most indisputable results of climate change such as sea-level rise (e.g. Bangladesh and the small island states), which have no leverage, at the other extreme. Insofar as the leaders of the rich and powerful states construe their own "national interest" within a horizon that is narrow, the poor in the weak states are largely at their mercy; insofar as they construe "national interest" within a horizon that is short term, the poor (at least) of future generations are completely at their mercy. The actual procedure will permit as unfairly skewed an outcome as the USA, EU, and other most powerful players choose to give it; only stands on principle on behalf of the weak – current and future – taken by the bargainers with the leverage could enable this biased process to produce substantively fair outcomes.

The substantive principles need to cover both fair sharing of emissions and fair sharing of costs. One crucial complication is whether the allocation of emissions of GHGs and the allocation of costs of dealing with climate change ought to be settled separately, each on its own merits. The specific alternative to independent settlement of the two issues worth considering is allocating the costs of dealing with climate change precisely in order to bring about the allocation of emissions that is fair. This would mean treating the allocation of costs as an economic incentive structure designed to generate the allocation of emissions sought – using the allocation of costs as the means to the goal of attaining the fair allocation of emissions. First, note quickly why the allocation of emissions is an issue of fairness at all rather than a matter to be left entirely to markets.

Fair distribution of emissions   Morally permissible emissions of GHGs are extremely limited because of the harms being caused by emissions in excess of the quantity that can be recycled without climate change. Legally permissible emissions would also be extremely limited if negotiations under the *FCCC* ever led to serious attempts to achieve the original purpose of the treaty: gaining control over anthropogenic changes in the atmospheric concentrations. So, at least morally, and potentially legally, if we are to avoid the harms sketched above, total global emissions of GHGs are scarce. Given that they are also valuable, as long as economic welfare is kept dependent upon fossil fuel, their distribution poses a classic question of justice: what ought to be the distribution of a resource (absorptive capacity for GHGs, in this case) that is both scarce and vital for life?

As long as those in control choose not to leave behind the fossil fuel energy regime that makes GHG emissions essential to a decent life, powerful considerations support the following principle: the only morally permissible allocations of emissions are allocations that guarantee the availability of the minimum necessary emissions to every person, which entails reserving adequate unused absorptive capacity for those emissions. As already noted, the global total constituted by the minimum essential for each person might in itself equal or exceed the global total compatible with the avoidance of rapid climate change. This is a matter for scientific determination. It seems entirely possible that once every person was guaranteed minimum emissions from burning carbon-based fuels, the maximum safe global total of CO_2 would have been reached, so that no emissions beyond the minimum could be allowed to anyone. Presumably such an outcome would be completely unacceptable to the now wealthy and powerful, but then no one has a God-given guarantee that they can (1) burn fossil-fuel, (2) live the kind of lives they most enjoy, and (3) avoid climate change. It may turn out that burning fossil fuels was a primitive solution, feasible for only a brief, technologically unsophisticated period of human history on this planet, and ought now to be left behind as quickly as entrenched energy interests will permit.

The most obvious reason why every person born into a fossil fuel-based world economy would be entitled to a guaranteed minimum of the emissions essential to life is quite simply that to make the political choice to impose a ceiling on total emissions, while not guaranteeing a minimum to each person, would condemn to death the poorest people on the planet. To make the social choice to continue to rely on burning fossil fuel, while capping the total emissions of the GHGs that result, would be to impose upon the world a package of international institutions – an energy regime combined with a climate-change regime – that made it impossible for considerable numbers of the poorest people on the planet to survive, when there are alternative packages of institutions that would allow them to survive, and perhaps even flourish – human society need not choose to continue burning oil until the last barrel is gone. Setting up institutions, knowing in advance that they unnecessarily condemn large numbers of people to die, is as obviously morally wrong as human conduct can be. One would like to think that this option is as politically infeasible as it is morally outrageous and is accordingly not worthy of much discussion.

Inalienable minimum emission rights are perfectly compatible with the kinds of scheme for trading in emission rights that are currently popular among intellectuals who study environmental policy. Economic considerations support leaving as much of the distribution of emission permits to the market as is compatible with fundamental moral requirements. The minimum guarantee simply requires that, however many permits for emissions beyond the minimum necessary for a decent life could safely be made available for trading (which is of course a scientific/political question), no tradeable permits should be issued for vital emissions. Minimum vital emissions could be viewed as an inalienable private property right, or simply a human subsistence right. The vital minimum ought not to be marketable.

Food is vital for life and scarce, but – someone may say – we market all the food. Why not market all the emission permits as well? For a start, strong arguments are also available for a right to food – a right to the minimum sustenance essential to normal vitality. Decent societies do not in fact market all their food but, instead, reserve significant amounts of it to be distributed by way of food stamps, or their functional equivalent, which are not themselves supposed to be marketed but distributed according to need, and reserve other significant amounts of food for relief to victims of famines, refugees from war, and other desperately helpless victims. A society in which food is available only for payment is a brutal and uncivilized place. What is suggested here is merely the equivalent of food stamps on the global level for vital emissions.

Further, even if one thought, on the contrary, that food stamps and famine relief were somehow misguided and that people without money for food (including children presumably) ought for some reason simply to be left to starve, the case of CO_2 emissions in a carbon-based energy regime with a global ceiling on the emissions is a still more compelling case even than food. The imposition of the ceiling on emissions would create an extraordinary – to my knowledge, utterly unique – case. There is no global ceiling on the quantity of food that may be produced. Consequently, when confronted by a healthy adult with neither food nor money, one might persuade oneself that if only he rose earlier, worked harder, or both, he would be able to catch, find, or grow some food or earn some money with which to buy food. This is naive in all kinds of ways (not least, that desperately hungry people are not usually very healthy), but it is at least a conceptually coherent fantasy. The food supply legally can be, and physically can be, enlarged indefinitely; indeed, the global total is increasing constantly. It is possible to obtain more for oneself without taking it away from someone else. If there were a global ceiling on CO_2 emissions, by contrast, the supply of permissible CO_2 emissions would be strictly zero-sum: more for anyone would mean less for someone else, because the supply would be fixed. (If the worst fears of the scientists studying climate change are confirmed, the total sum would, even worse, need to be progressively diminishing over the years.) Prohibited emissions by those below their minimum would have to come either at the expense of someone else or at the expense of the climate – by exceeding the safe total. It would be as if the only way for the hungry to obtain more food were to steal it. No person in her right mind would cooperate with a set of institutions that imposed a ceiling on the total by refusing to grant her a minimum she needed and could obtain in no other non-harmful way, while others were allowed to exceed the minimum. Such institutions treat her with contempt. If she has any self-respect, she will evade or resist them. It is evident that the distribution of emissions must guarantee a minimum to every person unless the climate-change regime is simply to be forced upon the poor.

Fair distribution of costs: abatement   In the short term it will be expensive to take the measures necessary to reduce total global GHG emissions to a rate that does not constantly expand their atmospheric concentrations. Large quantities of emissions now result from sheer waste, so significant reductions can initially be made at a profit. The reductions in emissions possible from reductions in waste of energy are, however, not sufficient to bring the current rate down to a sustainable rate, even on optimistic scientific assumptions, so after the initial savings from reducing energy waste there will be significant costs for abatement of climate change through, for example, improved technology.

In addition to abatement costs, two other sets of costs will result from attempts either to avoid damage from components of climate change (for example, sea-walls to try to hold back rising sea levels) or to deal with damage (for example, build new inland cities to replace flooded or eroded coastal cities not saved by sea-walls). These two kinds of cost from attempting to deal with climate change that in fact occurs, as distinguished from the abatement costs of attempting to mitigate the climate change itself, are usually called adaptation costs. As mentioned earlier, adaptation costs and abatement costs must be considered both separately and in relation to each other.

First, however, is the other question already raised about the relation between the allocation of emissions and the allocation of – specifically – abatement costs.

If the abatement costs – the costs of measures taken to prevent or reduce climate change itself, rather than its economic and social effects – are to be structured in order to create incentives designed to bring about a fair distribution of emissions, then the greatest abatement costs will have to be borne by the states whose current emissions most exceed their fair share of emissions. The absolute quantity of a fair share depends in part, of course, on the research to determine the sustainable annual global total of emissions – one cannot calculate the absolute size of a share of a total without actually knowing the total. Nevertheless, if one accepts both (1) the finding of the research so far that whatever precisely is the sustainable rate of emissions, it is far lower than the current rate and (2) the suggestion above that every human is entitled to at least a minimum share of the total emissions, it is perfectly clear from the vast current inequalities in per capita rates of emissions that (3) in order for those below the economic minimum to reach it, those above it must reduce their emissions. Other things being equal, it would appear equitable that those with the highest per capita rates of emissions should make the largest reductions in emissions.

Whoever ought to make the largest reductions in GHG emissions – assume these are the people with the highest per capita rates – ought to bear the largest shares of the abatement costs, if the allocation of the abatement costs is to be used to create incentives that will motivate movement in the direction of a fair distribution of emissions. At least two questions immediately arise about this allocation of abatement costs: would it in turn be fair and is such a scheme likely to work, if it is fair to attempt it?

Allocating the heaviest financial burdens for abatement to those whose own emissions ought to be reduced the most would be unfair to them only if there are other grounds for the distribution of abatement costs that would yield a different distribution less burdensome to them. The most familiar alternative grounds are (1) the backward-looking considerations of (a) contribution to the problem – causal responsibility for climate change – and (b) benefit from the processes that have caused climate change, and (2) the forward-looking consideration of ability to pay. In theory it would be perfectly possible for these various grounds – contribution, benefit, and ability – each to point toward a different distribution of responsibility for contributing to the mitigation of the problem. Climate change, fortunately, is a case in which ethical reality is much less messy than ethical theory.

Consider contribution. The threat of climate change has been produced predominantly by the Industrial Revolution, fed first by coal and then by oil as well, and the consumerist societies which trade and use its products. Naturally, there are variations that matter, such as Japan's industrial production being less energy-intensive than the USA's and the USA's being less in turn than the ageing Stalinist installations in Eastern Europe. The chief contributors are the wealthy industrialized states, roughly the members of the Organization for Economic Cooperation and Development (OECD). Consider benefit. The primary beneficiaries of industrialization have been the states that have industrialized. A small exception exists to the extent that genuine benefits of industrial society have trickled down to non-industrialized states, but the lion's share of the benefits has gone to those which industrialized in pursuit of them: the OECD. Consider ability. The states that are the wealthiest and best able to pay for abatement measures mostly became so through the process of industrialization that created the excess concentrations of GHGs: the OECD. Contribution, resultant benefit, and consequent ability are largely coextensive in the states they select in this instance. The one exception worth noting consists of the major oil producers, which have become wealthy from selling oil mostly without industrializing; by not having industrialized, they have not contributed directly to the excess emissions they have fueled, but they have benefited greatly and are well able to contribute.

And the states that have contributed and benefited most from the last century and a half of massive CO_2 emissions, and are as a result most able to bear the costs of the abatement of the threat to the climate for which they are most responsible, are also in fact the states with the largest per capita emissions. No industrial state has yet managed to leave behind the fossil fuel-based economy that made it rich, so those which emitted the most in the past are for the most part those which are emitting the most now. As noted above, the oil producers have not in the past, and are not now, directly contributing high emissions. And insofar as the relatively less industrialized states, which of course include the two most populous, industrialize by adopting the fossil fuel-based technologies of the OECD, they can soon become the worst emitters ever. It is evident that while these poorer states must improve the quality of life of their people, they must not gain their wealth in the same way that the now-wealthy gained theirs. Yet only the now-wealthy can afford to create and spread the alternative energy technology needed by everyone.

Further reading

Banuri, T., Göran Mäler, K., et al. (1996) "Equity and social considerations," *Climate Change 1995: Economic and Social Dimensions of Climate Change*, Contribution of Working Group III to the Second Assessment Report of the Intergovernmental Panel on Climate Change, ed. James P. Bruce, Hoesung Lee, and Erik F. Haites (New York: Cambridge University Press), pp. 79–124. [Ethical issues as understood within UN process.]

Bolin, Bert (1998) "The Kyoto negotiations on climate change: a science perspective," *Science* 279 (whole no. 5349), pp. 330–1. [Inadequacy of Kyoto Protocol briefly explained by original head of IPCC.]

Broome, John (1992) *Counting the Cost of Global Warming* (Cambridge: White Horse Press). [Analysis of inter-temporal distribution construed as issue of discounting.]

Coward, Harold, and Hurka, Thomas, eds. (1993) *Ethics and Climate Change: The Greenhouse Effect* (Waterloo, Ont.: Wilfrid Laurier University Press). [Pioneering philosophical discussions.]

Grubb, Michael (1995) "Seeking fair weather: ethics and the international debate on climate change," *International Affairs* 71, no. 3, pp. 463–96. [The best single article integrating ethics, economics, and politics.]

Hayes, Peter, and Smith, Kirk, eds. (1993) *The Global Greenhouse Regime: Who Pays?* (London: Earthscan). [A book-length integrated interdisciplinary analysis.]

Houghton, J. T., Meira Filho, L. G., et al. (1996) *Climate Change 1995: The Science of Climate Change*, Contribution of Working Group I to the Second Assessment Report of the Intergovernmental Panel on Climate Change (New York: Cambridge University Press, 1996). [The most authoritative account of scientific findings.]

Kaiser, Jocelyn, and Schmidt, Karen (1998) "Coming to grips with the world's greenhouse gases," *Science* 281, (whole no. 5376), pp. 504–7. [Current situation.]

Kempton, Willett, Boster, James S. and Hartley, Jennifer A. (1995) *Environmental Values in American Culture* (Cambridge, Mass.: MIT Press). [Attitudes of citizens of most powerful state.]

Kyoto Protocol to U.N. Framework Convention on Climate Change (1998) (10 December 1997), 37 ILM, pp. 22–43. [The most recently proposed international treaty.]

McKibben, Bill (1989) *The End of Nature* (New York: Anchor Books), pp. 3–91. [An eloquent lament for the destruction of the autonomy from humans of climate.]

Paterson, Matthew (1996) "International justice and global warming," in *The Ethical Dimensions of Global Change*, ed. Barry Holden (London: Macmillan), pp. 181–201. [A survey of philosophical positions.]

Pogge, Thomas W. (1998) "A global resources dividend," *Ethics of Consumption: The Good Life, Justice, and Global Stewardship*, ed. David A. Crocker and Toby Linden (Lanham, Md.: Rowman and Littlefield), pp. 501–36. [A concrete constructive suggestion about how to lessen injustice.]

Reus-Smit, Christian (1996) "The normative structure of international society," in *Earthly Goods: Environmental Change and Social Justice*, ed. Fen Osler Hampson and Judith Reppy (Ithaca, NY: Cornell University Press), pp. 96–121. [International politics in brief.]

Schelling, Thomas C. (1997) "The cost of global warming," *Foreign Affairs* 76, no. 6 (November/December), pp. 8–14. [International economics in brief.]

Shue, Henry (1995) "Avoidable necessity: global warming, international fairness, and alternative energy," in *Theory and Practice, NOMOS XXXVII*, ed. Ian Shapiro and Judith Wagner DeCew (New York: New York University Press), pp. 239–64. [One in a series of complementary articles, all cited there.]

33

Land and water

PAUL B. THOMPSON

When ecologists and geographers discuss human impact on land and water, they begin with agriculture. The Food and Agriculture Organization of the United Nations (FAO) reports that 5,872,738 hectares of the world's 13,048,300 hectares (or slightly more than one third) of land is used for agriculture. According to FAO, another third is in forests and woodlands. The remaining 4,002,828 hectares comprise deserts, tundra, and swamps not habitable by human beings; wetlands and savanna set aside for recreation and wildlife preservation; lands used for mining and manufacturing; and urban areas. In the United States, agricultural uses account for nearly half of the total landmass. In the United Kingdom the figure is 40 percent, though that estimate does not include meadows used for grazing. Excepting multiple-use forests, American urban and recreational lands, plus uninhabited deserts, swamps, and high mountain ranges account for a mere 20 percent of the total.

Lester Brown, founder of the Worldwatch Institute and coiner of the phrase "sustainable development," believes that food production is the key to sustainable land use. Agriculture also uses the largest share of fresh water. Not surprisingly, a large percentage of the world's crops and pasturelands are located in areas of reliable rainfall. Rainfed farms and ranches get first crack at this water, taking their share before rainwater enters ground or surface systems. Brown writes, "There is a tendency in public discourse to talk about the water problem and the food problem as though they are independent. But with some 70 percent of all the water that is pumped from underground used for irrigation...the water problem and the food problem are in large measure the same" (1997, p. 31).

Any discussion of the environmental ethics for land and water is, thus, first and foremost a question of an adequate ethic for agricultural production. What environmental parameters should be considered in farming and ranching? Should food production operate within a framework of totally renewable resources, or should some consumption of non-renewable energy, soil, and water resources be regarded as an acceptable trade-off for the production of food for hungry mouths? What does it mean for farmers to be good stewards of nature, and how do economic or policy incentives affect their stewardship? Only when these questions have been answered does it become meaningful for those who are *not* directly involved in farming or ranching (98 percent of the population in the USA) to ask how their consumption choices can be made on a more ethical basis.

Threatened agro-ecosystems

Agriculture creates a human-dominated ecosystem. In many regions and for many centuries, agro-ecosystems have functioned well: soil fertility and water availability have been maintained, sustaining a diverse mix of flora and fauna (including humans). Worldwide growth of human population has placed the food-producing capacity of agro-ecosystems under pressure. Lands that should not be cultivated have come under the plow. As production systems have been intensified, habitat for wild species has been eliminated and the basic soil and water resources have been stressed. Yet population growth does not fully explain the current stress on agro-ecosystems. Waggoner (1994) believes that the land currently in production using current production technology could feed a population of 10 billion, double that of year 2000 estimates.

Many factors contribute to the current stress on land and water resources. Increases in wealth are often accompanied by dietary shifts toward greater consumption of grain-fed meat and poultry. Chickens, pigs, and cows eat between two and four grams of vegetable protein to produce a gram of edible animal protein, so the shift in diets stresses global food production capacity. Waggoner's projection of sufficiency is based on the assumption that grains currently used for animal feeds will be redirected to human use, but he also believes that new production will increase yields, creating an extra margin of available food. Commodity yields measured on a per acre basis have grown between 100 and 500 percent since World War II. Some continuation of that growth in yields is presumed in every projection of future food needs.

Although modern farming methods have increased the overall productivity of agriculture, they have tended to have a detrimental effect on soil fertility and water quality. Some effects are direct. Heavy farm equipment compacts soil, and even heavier equipment is needed to break it up. Soil texture is damaged and nutrients are lost. The powdery dirt left behind is more susceptible to erosion by wind and water. Chemical fertilizers (designed to combat declining soil fertility) and pesticides have polluted ground and surface water. Irrigation water has been pumped out of aquifers far faster than rain and run-off recharge these underground lakes. Manure from intensive "factory farms" has become an odor nuisance and a source of groundwater pollution. Though agricultural researchers were slow to respond to these threats, most agricultural technology now under development makes some attempt to mitigate or avoid unwanted environmental consequences.

Fortunately, not all yield-enhancing technologies are inimical to soil and water conservation. Improved seeds, multi-cropping techniques and well-designed fertilizers or chemicals can be made compatible with the basic principles of agro-ecology. However, indirect effects make higher-yielding, ecologically sound production systems difficult to manage. One problem is simply the shift in farmer incentives that seems to be a permanent feature of industrialized agriculture. Farmers have always faced short-run imperatives that are inconsistent with their long-term self-interest in preserving soil and water resources. The subsistence farmer must produce enough food each season to last the winter. Survival comes before soil loss. Now farmers introduce machinery, chemicals, and seeds into their production system with borrowed capital. They must earn enough to repay their loans or face the loss of their farms. Industrialized farmers do not fear starvation, but, ironically, the use of borrowed capital creates a short-run imperative that is just as powerful in diverting farmers from their long-term best interest.

Environmentally sensitive use of modern technologies is complex even on debt-free farms. Farmers can level slopes with terraces, reducing water use and erosion at the same time. But terraced fields may not be suitable for the most modern equipment. The farmer who diligently maintains terraces may find that neighbors with larger tractors or mechanical harvesters (machinery that cannot operate on terraces) have lower production costs. And modern farmers find that only those with the lowest production costs are able to survive. Some strategies for making agriculture more sustainable are mutually inconsistent. One can also reduce soil erosion by using a no or low till system. In these systems plant roots are left to hold soil after crops are harvested. The land is seldom (if ever) plowed and left in the exposed state where wind and rainfall can do their worst damage. However, no and low till systems rely on chemical herbicides to ensure that crops can compete with weeds for sunshine, water, and soil nutrients. The farmer must balance erosion against pollution of groundwater when choosing between these systems.

The optimization approach

How, then, are farmers to arrive at environmentally sensitive production practices? Some agricultural economists and producer organizations have promulgated the view that this is not an ethical problem at all. They have portrayed farm decision-making as a classical economic problem of optimization. Farmers manage inputs such as land, labor, water, and capital to produce outputs such as food commodities and environmental pollution. Costs occur on both sides of the production equation: purchased inputs and harmful outputs. Benefits are largely associated with the saleable commodities produced. A good farmer is one who minimizes costs and maximizes benefits.

The optimization approach presumes that the benefits of less expensive food compensate for the cost of pollution. If the value of these benefits is sufficiently large, pollution or soil loss should simply be accepted as the price one must pay for feeding hungry mouths. In the amoral view of this optimization procedure, one assumes that market forces will assign relative exchange values to costs and benefits. If soil loss or water pollution is profitable for the farmer, the cost is acceptable. The farmer need not trouble with moral deliberation, since the profitability of the production practice proves that society has judged the ready availability of food to be more valuable than long-term soil fertility or water quality. There is often an ethical philosophy at work in this view, since markets are presumed to aggregate and average out the moral preferences of all individuals who buy and sell. Tweeten (1987), for one, has pointed out that cheap food is especially important to the poor. Market forces that tolerate soil loss and water pollution reflect society's collective judgment that the immediate needs of the poor outweigh environmental imperatives (see ECONOMICS).

This use of market logic involves many assumptions that are controversial. It neglects the fact that markets probably fail to value pollution costs adequately, not to mention the fact that FUTURE GENERATIONS (who are most affected by soil loss and water pollution) are unable to express their preferences in present-day market trans-actions. Critique of economic optimization has been a frequent theme in environ-mental ethics, and it has been decried by critics of intensive agriculture as well (see Berry 1977; Jackson 1996). Yet mainstream environmental ethics has had little to say about agricultural use of land and water, and some main patterns of thought within environmental philosophy have tended to reinforce the view that agriculture should be understood as a complex optimization problem with no ethical dimensions of its own.

Agricultural environmental ethics: a neglected topic

Agriculture is critical to environmental quality and sustainability, yet it has been an infrequent topic in environmental ethics during the last 25 years. This is in part because threats to sustainable agriculture seldom make newspaper headlines. Yet agriculture is a frequent topic in other areas of environmental studies, including HISTORY and geography. Environmental philosophers have overlooked agriculture in part because they have assumed that land and water use simply represented special cases to which the broader theory could be applied. But the early history of the movement to establish national parks and to preserve wildlife framed much of the thinking in environmental ethics, and the framing assumptions of that debate have not been conducive to serious ethical analysis of agriculture.

The debate between John Muir (1838–1914) and Gifford Pinchot (1865–1946) over the future of American forest set the stage for an environmental ethics that has largely ignored the most extensive uses that humans make of land and water. Disciples of Muir believe in the preservation of woodlands and other wild areas. They argue for the intrinsic value of ecosystems, and have proposed non-anthropo-centric philosophies to account for the interests and integrity of natural areas (see NORMATIVE ETHICS). They decry those who would decide nature's fate by calculating the economic value of wild species or habitat, and they support political initiatives to remove natural areas from the threat of development by timber and mining compan-ies, or by public water projects. Disciples of Pinchot argue for conservation and wise use of nature, and see no problem in describing forests and protected areas as resources that must be set aside for future or alternative use. They think of environ-mental ethics in terms of duties to FUTURE GENERATIONS of human beings. As Pinchot and Muir were frequent political allies, anthropocentric conservationists may support many of the same political goals as their non-anthropocentric preservationist oppon-ents, but they see nothing intrinsically wrong with weighing nature's loss against humanity's gain.

Muir and Pinchot represent perspectives that also arose in debates over the future of African wildlife and European woodlands. The debate is crucial to that third of the world's landmass that is now forested. It also bears on the threats that urban encroachment, energy consumption, and thermal pollution pose to the large land areas in which human use still has only marginal and indirect effects on wildlife and ecosystem processes. Yet, by organizing philosophical debate around this dichotomy, environmental ethicists have fallen prey to two related dogmas which, if unques-tioned, limit our ability to ask the right philosophical questions about land and water.

The first is the dogma of pristine nature, that substantial land area exists where humans have had no significant effect on landscape or ecosystem processes. The second is the dogma of environmental impact, that the ethical issues for land and water use are best framed in terms of human impact on nature and natural processes.

The dogma of pristine nature

Michael Pollan (1991) recounts the story of Cathedral Pines, a natural preserve much loved by his fellow New Englanders. It seems that one year the pines fell prey to a particularly violent storm, and the once venerated park became an eyesore of rotting stumps and dense undergrowth. What to do? One contingent of townsfolk argues that fire and storm are natural events, and that the unsightly state of Cathedral Pines is entirely consistent with the preservationist goals that guided its establishment. Hence, do nothing; the pines will come back (eventually) on their own. Others stress the contribution of the Pines to local history and culture, note that the area will not return to its former state for 100 years, and urge a management scheme of reseeding and brush control.

Is Cathedral Pines another episode in the contest between non-anthropocentric preservationists and conventional conservationists? The story continues. Cathedral Pines, it turns out, was second growth forest. It replaced hardwoods that had been cleared by European settlers in bygone days. The Pines would have never established themselves without drastic human intervention. Even the hardwoods that had gone before had been managed by Native Americans. The pristine nature prized by every-one, it seems, was nowhere to be found.

Clearly, many preservationists have assumed that what they were preserving was nature untouched and unsullied by human management. This assumption was implicit in much of Muir's writing. Building on this approach, some have argued that agriculture is the natural enemy of environment. They believe that land areas shifted from forest to pasture or cropland are not merely changed; they are irrevoc-ably destroyed. If this is so, then the overriding imperative for land use ought to be one of making the most intensive use possible of those areas brought under human domination, so that more of wild nature can be preserved.

Yet, excepting the most extreme climates, pristine or wild nature (understood as a place where human projects play little or no role in the distribution of nature's resources among the various flora and fauna) is a myth. William Cronon (1984) has documented the environmental history of human impact on American environ-ments prior to European invasion, exposing the belief in pristine nature as a tool in European rationalization of conquest. If the New World was "empty," what fault could be found in its subjection by conquistadors and colonists? Perhaps Native Americans were savages whose very wildness rendered them incapable of thoughtful ecosystem management, and who deserve to be "preserved" along with the wild nature of which they were a part? The offensiveness of this speculation constitutes a *reductio ad absurdum* for the moral implications of belief in pristine nature (see WILDERNESS).

On a different view, even forests, like farmers' fields, should be understood as human-dominated ecosystems. It is obvious that intensive logging has brought many of the world's forests under human domination. What we may overlook is the role of forest gardens and slash-and-burn agriculture in the maintenance of global forests. In fact, many global forests are best understood in terms of agro-ecology, not pristine nature. In traditional systems, small patches of forests are cleared. Gardening and crop production take place until soil fertility declines, but Noble and Dirzo write: "These practices have occurred in many tropical forests for millennia without obvious signs of degradation" (1997, p. 523). Clearly, as human population grows and forest resources decline, traditional systems give way to practices that are far from benign. The problem, however, is less one of protecting forests from agricultural encroachment than of preventing the intensification that preserving pristine nature seems to support.

The dogma of environmental impact

The dogma of pristine nature calls to mind a beautiful and well-functioning ecosystem. This system is then sullied by human impact. Much of environmental policy in the United States has been guided by the preparation of environmental impact statements (EISs), and similar studies are used in most industrialized democracies. In these policy instruments, analysts use biology and economics to predict the consequences of a construction project, a management scheme, or a public policy. Consistent with themes from ethical theory, undertaking the activity in question is understood as a choice that humans, as autonomous agents, are free to accept or reject. The activity under review is implicitly understood as the proximate cause of these consequences. The economic and political acceptability of the activity is thought to turn on the acceptability of these consequences. We are expected to make a choice based on the projected impact of our actions.

Many credit Rachel Carson (1907–64) with sparking the modern environmental movement by calling the public's attention to the environmental impact of widespread (and often indiscriminate) use of pesticides. Her activism precipitated laws and regulations to protect the environment around the world. Her book *Silent Spring* is important for environmental ethics because it established the model for arguments intended to influence human action on environmental grounds. The best empirical science is used to establish the consequences of a human action (such as pesticide use) or to predict the likely or potential consequences of a planned activity (such as genetically engineered crops). The results of scientific studies are reported in professional journals and technical reports such as the EIS. These results are summarized in popular form by authors who, like Rachel Carson, hope to mobilize public outrage. The pesticide story has been pursued for three decades. Books such as Colburn, Myers and Dumanoski's *Our Stolen Future* (1996) follow Carson's lead in tracking the impact of pesticide use. Books such as Doyle's *Altered Harvest* (1985), or Rissler and Mellon's *The Ecological Risks of Engineered Crops* (1996) have applied Carson's model to genetic engineering.

Like *Silent Spring*, all these books describe actual and possible consequences accruing from human action. While they describe these consequences in a manner that is designed to provoke outrage and reform, they shrink from explicit statements about *why* the predicted consequences are morally unacceptable. In doing so, they allow readers to supply their own moral premises. The predicted consequences might be wrong for anthropocentric *or* ecocentric reasons. They might represent a poor trade-off of benefit and risk, *or* they might violate rights or other non-negotiable constraints on human practice. For the most part, environmental philosophers have been willing to accept this implicit division of labor, confining their deliberations to the debate over why impacts are significant, and whether economic pricing of outcomes is an adequate basis for decision-making. They leave the description and prediction of environmental impacts to scientists and science writers.

Pristine nature and environmental impact: implications for land use

The Carson model construes environmental ethics as an ethic of environmental impact. It has been the basis for a powerful analysis of many land and water issues during the last three decades. However, the prediction and ethical evaluation of environmental impact has been so successful for framing environmental issues that it has become dogma, an unexamined and uncritical doctrine or set of assumptions. This has led to an implicit consequentialism in environmental ethics. In its most blatant form, environmental consequentialism leads to philosophical and economic debates on valuation, such as the one conducted by Muir and Pinchot. What are the relative values of environmental impacts? How should they be compared to one another? And how should they be aggregated? These questions are summed in the process of choosing to accept or reject a planned activity. This debate echoes utilitarian philosophy, and many environmental philosophers have proposed theories of animal or ecosystem rights, or of nature's interests in hopes of putting some distance between environmental ethics and utilitarian thinking (see ANIMALS). The dogma of environmental impact usually overcomes these efforts, however, and the alternative fall prey to a "consequentialism of rights," meaning that the rights or constraint violation itself comes to be seen as a consequence of the planned activity. The dogma of environmental impact has also encouraged us to think of human action in terms of autonomous choice. This way of thinking can help us bring criteria of responsible action to bear on activities that might otherwise be undertaken with little reflective thought. However, it can also reinforce the belief in a radical separation between human consciousness and the natural environment (see NORMATIVE ETHICS).

When combined with an uncritical belief in the moral priority of pristine nature, the dogma of environmental impact leads to a disastrous ethic for agriculture. Agriculture by its very nature involves impact on nature. Whether ethical imperatives for land use are expressed in consequentialist (optimizing trade-offs) or non-consequentialist (respecting pristine nature) terms, the less agriculture the better. However, if agriculture is to be minimized on a per acre basis, it must be practiced as intensively as possible on those acres given over to it. This reasoning supports high-tech industrialized agriculture against organic or low-input alternatives. It reaches its logical conclusion in an agriculture that consists of slime pits where genetically engineered micro-organisms efficiently transform sunshine and nutrients into biomass, which is piped into factories and processed by more genetical engineering into edible substances that resemble conventional foods. Agro-ecosystems would be given over entirely to an industrial model, and could be managed to minimize pollution while maximizing the amount of land area spared from agricultural use. Yet such a scenario would so thoroughly transform the biological conditions of human existence as to complete the spiritual and psychological isolation of human consciousness, a prospect radically inconsistent with the main themes of environmental ethics (Busch et al. 1992).

The agrarian alternative

Critical consideration of agriculture demands a search for alternative philosophical models. Though abandoned by professional philosophers since J. S. Mill (1806–73), traditional agrarian philosophy may provide intellectual resources. Agrarian moral philosophy is aimed not at the justification of autonomous choice but at the incentive structure that frames human aspirations and cultural identity. So-called environmental impacts are often better conceptualized not as consequences or endpoints for human action, but as components in dynamic feedback systems that regulate both ecosystem process and human interest. Here it is useful to recall the difference between the moral theories of Immanuel Kant (1724–1804) and Mill, which place the individual decision-maker at the center, and classical Greek ethics, where the social environment in which human projects and interests are formed receives more stress (see NINETEENTH- AND TWENTIETH-CENTURY PHILOSOPHY and THE CLASSICAL GREEK TRADITION).

Victor Davis Hanson (1995) believes that the classical Greek philosophers such as Socrates, Plato, and Aristotle must be read in light of an agrarian moral tradition that characterized Greece in general and Athens in particular. The Greek view of society incorporates both nature and culture into an environment that aids or inhibits right action. There is no good person without a good environment. Agrarian thought places individuals within concentric webs: family, community, and nature. These webs form a hierarchy in which individuals experience the consequences of their practice through feedback that signals the overall health and integrity of their homes, their cities, and their environment. In a healthy moral environment, tensions between family loyalty, citizenship, and stewardship prevent the excessive or overriding pursuit of any one virtue to the exclusion of others. A balance of virtue and vice signals right action. Decline occurs when otherwise virtuous conduct tends toward excess.

In Hanson's view, the political events that spawned the golden age of Athenian philosophy were precipitated by changes in marine technology. Athens had enjoyed a dramatic economic and military expansion owing to its sea power, but these changes also created new economic interests in the polis. Unlike the old interests that had been rooted in ownership of land, these new interests argued for incessant expansion of the Athenian sphere of influence through trade and military conquest. In response, Athenian philosophers attempted to articulate moral philosophies that would express why moral and civic character needed to remain tied to Athens as a specific place; why, in other words, moral character needed to remain tied to the cultivation of land.

The notion that morality could be rooted in the work experience of farmers also occupied an important place in the thought of Thomas Jefferson (1743–1826) and

Ralph Waldo Emerson (1803–82). Jefferson's *Notes on the State of Virginia* describes how farmers make good citizens because ownership of land (as opposed to capital) prevents them from promoting irresponsible policies, then leaving for greener pastures when things go sour. In essays such as "Nature," and "Farming," Emerson writes that farmers are blessed because their work is naturally attuned to the soul's authentic capacity for creativity and expression. "Cities make men talkative and entertaining," writes Emerson, "but they make them artificial" (1904 [1870] p. 154). Each member of the farm family occupies a social role that makes the interdependence of self, family, and public interest transparent. Agrarian philosophy stresses the particular rather than the universal, as the individual is linked to the moral community by an extensive network of ties to specific others, family members, neighbors, and store owners in the nearby town. These relations depend on the specific people with whom one has commerce, and equally on the placement of social roles around the immovable geographic place of the farm, the land itself.

Traditional agrarian philosophy expresses specifically environmental claims by holding that farmers must be stewards of nature, must husband the plants, animals, and soil under their care, and that the virtuous will be rewarded with bounteous crops and litters. Berry (1977) describes how the ethic of the yeoman farmer requires sharing and camaraderie, but also presupposes a status of personal dignity and self-reliance. An agrarian would not diagnose contemporary problems in terms of environmental impact, but rather in terms of decay accruing from gradual but accelerating lack of balance. As agriculture intensifies under the pressure of industrialization, norms of sharing and generosity begin to erode. As described above, industrial technologies rearrange and complicate the incentives that align stewardship with self-reliance. Farmers respond less to the signals of nature than to the signals of commodity and credit markets.

Agrarian philosophy and environmental quality

In short, we see the traditional ethic that underlies rural communities being transformed from one in which equals seek to realize communitarian virtues within natural constraints by bringing forth the material requirements of life through self-reliant industry, to one in which property owners manage credit, labor, and technology to secure the cash income needed to survive in a monetized economy. In the latter view, environment enters the picture when regulations to limit the impact of farming introduce legal and economic constraints on the decision-making process. It is therefore possible to understand recent environmental deterioration associated with food and fiber production as a symptom of the moral decay that accompanies the disappearance of agrarian society. This diagnosis shares many social, political, and even spiritual goals with an environmental ethic construed in terms of preserving pristine nature from environmental impact, but its philosophical language of value and normativity is deeply at odds with that of recent western thought in environmental ethics.

The agrarian tradition represents a way of framing ethical issues for land use that places human transformation of nature within the material and conceptual framework of an agro-ecosystem. Stewardship is conceived less as a duty to God than as a virtue reinforced by the feedback mechanisms of nature itself (though our forebears probably saw little reason to separate the two). The agrarian conceptualization of humanity's place in nature develops its moral language in terms of virtues that are to be realized by humans, but it is not anthropocentric in the sense of according no value to nature, nor does it impute a right of human mastery or domination over nature. The idea that one might succeed at farming by subduing nature is a recent conceit. The agrarian world-view is thus at odds not only with environmental philosophy that frames issues in terms of a philosophical debate between anthropocentric and ecocentric philosophies, but with the line of thought that traces its origins to Lynn White's (1967) analysis of Christianity's meaning for environmental philosophy (see CHRISTIANITY).

Agrarianism represents an untapped source of ideas for an environmental ethics. However, there is no prospect of returning to the agrarian world-view as an ethic for land and water. For one thing, it presumed that many if not most people would be small-holding producers, a prospect that is now impractical. For another, it presumed a community organized entirely around the material production of food, an equally implausible suggestion for the twenty-first century. What is more, the very idea of a "return" to agrarian morality is deceiving, for much of the world's land has been farmed as large, landed estates and plantations for several centuries. And while the agrarian emphasis on stewardship may have been a serviceable ethic for land use, its emphasis on place, prosperity, and loyalty to one's fellow citizens fed xenophobic and insular attitudes toward other peoples. Agrarian moral arguments have been handmaidens to racism and fascism in their application.

From agrarianism to sustainable land and water use

As the twenty-first century begins, agricultural scientists, policy-makers, and farmers themselves are displaying a keen interest in environmental ethics. Many of these individuals gravitate naturally toward traditional agrarian views, views that stress the stewardship and the farmer's interest in maintaining soil fertility and water quality. At the same time, these practitioners are keenly aware that science-based prediction of environmental consequences from production technologies must be incorporated into future thinking. There is thus an active search for philosophical strategies that will synthesize the agrarian orientation of the past with the lessons of environmental impact studies. At present, only a handful of professionally trained philosophers have contributed to the debate over the future of agriculture. Crafting a new production ethic for agriculture is a task for the future of environmental ethics.

The debate over a new production ethic for land and water use is being framed in terms of sustainable agriculture and sustainable development. Two conceptions of SUSTAINABILITY are emerging. One conception is based on enlightened optimization. A production practice is deemed sustainable if the resources needed to carry it out are foreseeably available. In this resource sufficiency approach, soil and water are become scarcer. Land and water uses are made more sustainable when use of scarce resources becomes more efficient, or when adequate substitutes are found. But other resources used in agriculture are becoming scarce, too. Modern farming utilizes fossil fuels to power machinery and as the basis for many chemicals and fertilizers. Sustainability becomes a complex problem in optimizing trade-offs.

The alternative view stresses the functional integrity of agro-ecosystems. Here the ecosystem is seen as regenerating itself in a cyclic fashion. The emphasis is on mechanisms that reproduce key elements of the ecosystem for each cycle. In some production systems, for example, crop stubble and animal waste return nutrients to soil in a process that regenerates fertility. When fields are cleared or when animals are fed with grain hauled in railroad cars from distant places, this nutrient cycle is broken. In the functional integrity view, a system of farming is sustainable when key regenerative mechanisms are relatively stable. It becomes less sustainable when these mechanisms become brittle and vulnerable.

The functional integrity approach draws on classical ecology, but it is linked to agrarian philosophy because we are considering human-dominated ecosystems. As such, it becomes important to ask, "How will key human practices be regenerated or reproduced, year in and year out?" The optimization approach relies entirely on market mechanisms, but agrarians see custom, culture, and community embedded in a landscape where seasonal change and human practice are in constant dialog. Advocates of functional integrity protest against the wholesale disruption of agrarian systems in developing countries that are still regulating human practice in a sustainable manner. Industrialized countries face a more difficult path to functional integrity, but re-establishing solidarity between food consumers and producers may be one way to make land use more sustainable. Experiments in community-supported agriculture, for example, bind urban dwelling consumers in a trust with farmers who promise to utilize ecologically sensitive production methods. Farmers are assured of a market, and may concentrate on making their farms into environmentally healthy places, rather than achieving the lowest production cost.

Wes Jackson (1996) provides a vision of functional integrity that is deeply agrarian. His work uses careful environmental accounting and ecological models to predict environmental consequences, but he also advocates a change of mentality that departs from the optimization/environmental impact view of resource sufficiency. Instead, Jackson argues that human communities must concentrate on "becoming native" to the places they inhabit, on being attentive to landscape, and organizing life's rituals in a manner that will make consumers and producers alike more aware of ecosystem health. The cultural and personal identity of the native is attuned to environmentally sound practice. It does not require a series of discrete choices, each of which must be calculated to assess environmental impact. Though Jackson is a staunch advocate of leaving some land aside so that we may learn from nature, becoming native requires one to see the landscape as home. His philosophy thus rejects the dogmas of pristine nature and environmental impact, as it draws upon an ethic of community, identity, and solidarity to ground norms for the use of land and water.

References

Berry, W. (1977) *The Unsettling of America* (San Francisco: Sierra Club Books). [This early work by Berry, who is the current generation's leading voice on the moral and cultural significance of agriculture, provides the most systematic exposition of his view.]

Brown, L. (1997) *The Agricultural Link: How Environmental Deterioration Could Disrupt Economic Progress*. Worldwatch Paper 136, (Washington, DC: Worldwatch Institute. [This is one of many papers that Brown has published over the last three decades that are critical of industrial agriculture.]

Busch, L., Lacy, W., Burkhardt, R. J., and Lacy, L. (1992) *Plants, Power and Profits: Social, Economic and Ethical Consequences of the New Biotechnologies* (Oxford: Basil Blackwell). [This book blends the sociology of science with an "ethic of responsibility" in producing one of the first philosophically grounded critiques of agricultural biotechnology.]

Colburn, T., Myers, J. P., and Dumanoski, D. (1996) *Our Stolen Future: Are We Threatening Our Fertility, Intelligence and Survival? – A Scientific Detective Story* (New York: Dutton). [Like Rachel Carson's *Silent Spring*, this controversial book mixes science with an implicit utilitarian argument against pesticides.]

Cronon, W. (1984) *Changes on the Land: Indians, Colonists and the Ecology of New England* (New York: Farrar, Straus, and Giroux). [Cronon "debunks" the idea of pristine wilderness, arguing that Native Americans undertook transformations of the land as extensive as (though not equivalent to) those of European settlers.]

Doyle, J. (1985) *Altered Harvest: Agriculture, Genetics and the Fate of the World's Food Supply* (New York: Penguin Books). [An ecologically informed and clearly written overview of the ecological risks associated with plant breeding and biotechnology.]

Emerson, R. W. (1904 [1870]) *Society and Solitude* (Boston: Houghton Mifflin). [Ralph Waldo Emerson was the leading exponent of transcendentalism, a nineteenth-century philosophy that sought to reconcile spirituality and naturalistic metaphysics. With Henry David Thoreau, he developed moral, metaphysical, and aesthetic doctrines that are properly classified as "environmental philosophy."]

Hanson, V. D. (1995) *The Other Greeks: The Family Farm and the Agrarian Roots of Western Civilization* (New York: The Free Press). [This book by a classics professor and California raisin farmer is arguably the best contemporary exposition and defense of agrarian philosophy available.]

Jackson, W. (1996) *Becoming Native to This Place* (San Francisco: Counterpoint). [This book by an eccentric plant geneticist with the soul of a poet promotes the idea that traditional rural places (farms and small towns) deserve the same consideration that environmentalists have wished to extend to wilderness.

Noble, I. R. and Dirzo, R. (1997) "Forests as human-dominated ecosystems," *Science* 277, pp. 522–5. [This article provides a concise ecological account of what it means to be a "human-dominated ecosystem."]

Pollan, M. (1991) *Second Nature: A Gardener's Education* (New York: Dell Publishing). [This book by a gardening columnist, who has also written essays criticizing genetically engineered crops, poses a central dilemma in environmental ethics in a succinct and readily accessible way.]

Rissler, J. and Mellon, M. (1996) *The Ecological Risks of Engineered Crops* (Cambridge, MA: MIT Press). [As of 1999 this book by two Union of Concerned Scientists staff members is still the most complete and balanced overview of known risks from genetic engineering of crops.]

Tweeten, L. (1987) "Food for people and profit," in *Is There a Moral Obligation to Save the Family Farm?*, ed. G. Comstock (Ames, IA: Iowa State University Press), pp. 256–63. [A classically utilitarian argument for industrial agriculture.]

Waggoner, P. E. (1994) *How Much Land Can 10 Billion People Spare for Nature?*, CAST Task Force Report 121 (Ames IA: Council for Agricultural Science and Technology, February). [This is a key source for anyone who wants to understand the dynamics between world food needs and agricultural production.]

White, Jr., Lynn (1967) "The historical roots of our ecological crisis," *Science* 155, no. 3767 (10 March), pp. 1203–7. [An influential early article arguing that science and technology are the source of environmental problems, and that they have their source in the dominant traditions within Christianity.]

Further reading

Blatz, C., ed. (1990) *Ethics and Agriculture: An Anthology in Current World Context* (Moscow ID: University of Idaho Press). [This book collects essays that represent various perspectives on agricultural ethics.]

Thompson, P. B. (1995) *The Spirit of the Soil: Agriculture and Environmental Ethics* (London: Routledge). [This book provides a more in-depth analysis and discussion of some of the themes explored in this chapter.]

34

Consumption

MARK SAGOFF

Captain Planet, a television cartoon popular with children, airs on weekend mornings, while parents sleep. Children of various nationalities team up with the eponymous superhero to fight those who would wantonly exploit the earth. Each episode ends with the slogan: "Remember: the power is *yours!*"

Commercials aired on the program demonstrate that children possess the power to goad their parents into buying Combat Trolls, Barbie Dolls, Fruit Loops, Nintendo, and trips to Wild World. The Captain leaves vague the connection between environmental protection and Toys "ℛ" Us. The message, though, is clear: children, as they grow up, will indeed have to adjust their activities as consumers to the concerns of the global environment. The accompanying advertising, which advocates greater and greater consumption as the path to happiness, seems incongruous in this context.

Two concepts of consumption

The *Adventures of Captain Planet* connects two logically distinct concepts of consumption. First, consumption refers to getting and spending – that is, buying, using, and eventually discarding goods of the kind that are advertised on television. In this sense, America has become a consumer society; material possessions loom larger and larger in our lives. Second, consumption refers to the depletion of the earth's resources and the exhaustion of its capacity to safely absorb emissions and effluents. In this sense, consumption has to do with the flow of materials and energy from the earth through the economy and back to the earth and atmosphere as waste.

Many commentators believe that consumption in the first sense, i.e., the acquisition and use of material things, leads inevitably to consumption in the second sense, i.e., the depletion of the earth's limited resources. Indeed, nothing may seem more obvious than that the more consumer goods we buy, use, and discard, the more we overwhelm the capacity of the earth to provide materials and absorb wastes. If this is correct, we cannot sustain our standard of living, much less see the rest of the world rise to it, without running out of raw materials and destroying the ecological systems on which all life depends.

The connection between the two concepts of consumption, however, may appear more obvious than it actually is. Environmentalists such as Amory Lovins and William McDonough have suggested ways of designing consumer goods and services, such as housing and transportation, that will allow people to enjoy the same and even higher standards of living while treading more lightly on the earth. They argue that if the world adopts more sensible and efficient technologies, for example, by moving from fossil fuels to solar and other renewable forms of energy and by designing products to make them easier to recycle, it can greatly ameliorate the effects of affluence on the environment.

Even if higher levels of consumption worldwide are possible or sustainable, however, it does not follow that they are desirable. Many observers point out that as we work harder to earn the money to buy more things, we seem to enjoy our lives less. Juliet B. Schor, an economist at Harvard University, argues that "Americans are literally working themselves to death" (1991, p. 11). A fancy car, video equipment, or a complex computer program can exact a painful cost in the form of maintenance, upgrading, and repair. No one has written a better critique of the assault consumption makes on our lives than Thoreau (1817–62) provides in *Walden* (originally published in 1854). The cost of a thing, according to Thoreau, is not what the market will bear but what the individual must bear because of it: it is "the amount of what I will call life which is required to be exchanged for it, immediately or in the long run" (1965, p. 128). We are possessed by our possessions; they are often harder to get rid of than to get.

This chapter explores the relation between two concepts of consumption. The first concept refers to the acquisition, use, and disposal of the goods money can buy, such as those advertised by Captain Planet. The second refers to the movement of raw materials and energy from the earth through the economy back to the earth again as waste. It argues that advances in technology promise to make these conceptions of consumption compatible, for example, by allowing us to produce more of what people want to buy and use while using up less energy and material. Yet it also argues that after basic needs are met, consumption cannot justify itself, but must be justified in relation to some other good, such as human flourishing or happiness. To sustain high levels of consumption, moreover, we must transform the natural world to make it serve our purposes. We then sacrifice goods to be valued for their own sake for those we think will benefit us. This exchange may impoverish us – even as it makes us rich.

Historical background

It is hard to find anything in our cultural tradition that explains, much less justifies, the trend toward a commercial, materialistic, or mass-consumption society. Plato (428–347 BCE) taught that insofar as knowledge is the true food of the soul, humanity must try to limit or eliminate its other appetites. Any desire is unnecessary, Plato wrote, "from which a man could free himself from youth up, and whose presence in the soul does no good and in some cases, harm" (*Republic* 559a). For Aristotle (384–322 BCE), consumption was the reverse of noble; he did not regard it as a form of achievement. He taught the virtue of moderation: he thought that we should possess and consume only as much as necessary to get on with the worthwhile business of life, namely, political action.

Hardly any figure in our literary, cultural, or religious past defends a life dedicated to the acquisition and enjoyment of material things. The dominant American faith, CHRISTIANITY, is an other-worldly and ascetic religion. "Whosoever will come after me," Jesus said, "let him deny himself, and take up this cross, and follow me." The idea that "less is more" – whether as expressed by Plato, Aristotle, Jesus, or Thoreau – more accurately represents our philosophical and religious traditions.

One may suppose that our economic system, capitalism, is responsible for our increasing levels of consumption. The German sociologist, Max Weber (1864–1920), argued that capitalism at its inception offered a system of stewardship of natural resources as well as an ethic of social responsibility. Capitalism in the seventeenth century, Weber tells us, was not "unscrupulous in the pursuit of selfish interests by the making of money" (1958, p. 47). Weber argued, on the contrary, that capitalism rested on a Protestant calling to frugality and savings. This calling brings one dignity through productive work in the community here below. And one's success manifests one's prospect of salvation in the world to come.

As influential as Weber's theory has been, it remains a matter of debate how deeply early capitalism was infused with the ethics of Protestantism. There is little doubt, however, that from the seventeenth century onward, the dominant expressions of capitalism detached themselves from stewardship, hard work, and responsibility to the community, and became associated with the secondary effects Weber also described – extremes of wealth and poverty, an infatuation with making money, and conspicuous and often competitive consumption of material goods. This did not mean, however, that capitalism ceased to justify itself in religious terms. On the contrary, as social and economic elites in Europe and America lost interest in the world to come, they came to see in the Industrial Revolution the key to ending material scarcity and thus establishing a heaven on earth, primarily by applying reason to the management of social and natural resources. The continual conquest of nature would ensure limitless material progress; material plenty would then make it possible to set economic and social policy on rational principles, since scarcity would disappear as a cause of conflict.

Faith in material progress as the solution to social problems persisted up until the First World War. Moreover, as Christopher Lasch observes, this conception of progress brought with it not only rising expectations but also a limitless view of what people need:

> Instead of disparaging the tendency to want more than we need, liberals like Adam Smith argued that needs varied from one society to another, that civilized men and women needed more than savages to make them comfortable, and that a continual redefinition of their standards of comfort and convenience led to improvements in production and a general increase in wealth. There was no foreseeable end to the transformation of luxuries into necessities. The more comforts people enjoyed, the more they would expect. (1991, pp. 13–14)

Today, however, very few of us maintain the belief that the scientific principles of economics – Marxist or capitalist – may serve as directions to bring heaven to earth. The collapse of socialism in Eastern Europe, two world wars, persistent disparities in levels of income, and environmental destruction have turned all but the hardiest free-marketeers away from the Enlightenment faith in material progress, and a widespread pessimism about the prospects of humanity has taken hold of popular thought today.

Why do we consume so much?

The Enlightenment faith in technology and science was right about one thing: the immense gains in productivity associated with the Industrial Revolution. By the 1950s consumers were being taught to do their duty because consumption had to expand to keep pace with production even though it appeared to many to serve no other useful purpose.

Critics since Thoreau have pointed out time and again that people, after their basic needs are met, do not generally view themselves as happier after they have acquired some consumer good they coveted. As A. O. Hirschman points out, people "think they want one thing and then upon getting it, find out to their dismay that they don't want it nearly as much as they had thought . . . and something else, of which they were hardly aware, is what they really want" (1982, p. 21). A "dissatisfied consumer" rather than a satisfied one is exactly what industry needed to create, at least according to Charles Kettering, who introduced "planned obsolescence" at General Motors by creating a new model each year. He knew that industry, to sell its goods, required "the organized creation of dissatisfaction" (as quoted in Schor 1991, p. 120).

"Consumerism," Juliet Schor observes, "turned out to be full of pitfalls – a vicious pattern of wanting and spending which failed to deliver on its promises" (1991, p. 122). Schor and many other social critics reiterated Thoreau's conclusions: things *are* in the saddle and ride mankind; we *are* rich to the extent of the things we can do without. Empirical research bears out this common wisdom. Studies relating increased consumption to perceived happiness find that "rising prosperity in the USA since 1957 has been accompanied by a falling level of satisfaction. Studies of satisfaction and changing economic conditions have found overall no stable relationship at all" (Argyle 1987, p. 144). The competitive dilemmas involved with "keeping up with the Joneses," the vicious cycle of rising expectations, the dissipation of deeper values, and many other well-known defects of consumerism are obvious to nearly everyone – and have produced a rich commentary condemning our commercialism, materialism, and so on. If critics are correct – if consumption has no relation to contentment – why do levels of consumption seem inexorably to increase?

Miss Piggy, a muppet diva created by Jim Henson, believes the answer is obvious, summarizing it neatly in her credo, "More is More." Miss Piggy's assessment conforms with that of the economics profession generally, which holds that every consumer attempts to maximize utility and that a larger bundle of goods is always preferred to a smaller bundle. This is the so-called "nonsatiety requirement."

If want-satisfaction led to contentment, one might understand why a person would attempt to maximize it; however, according to the nonsatiety requirement, it does not. A person is more likely to achieve some sort of contentment or happiness, indeed, by overcoming or disciplining his or her desires than by satisfying them. In any case, hedonism cannot be the reason people find themselves on the treadmill of needing more money to purchase more things: The overworked American, "too tired for sex," is not having fun.

Anthropologists, sociologists, and cultural historians have offered a variety of insightful theories to explain the rise of mass-consumption. Commentators in the

Marxist tradition have argued that enormous gains in productivity required increases in consumption to keep up with them, or economies would cease to grow, and great social dislocation would result. Thus the production of consumption has always accompanied the consumption of production – to turn a phrase Galbraith (1984) has applied to our affluent society.

To create enough consumption to keep up with production, retailers linked traditional religious sentiments with consumer goods. Religious sensibilities when secularized, for example in the Romantic movement, easily became associated with fashions, novels, movies, cars, and other goods that promised people a kind of "salvation" – in other words, entry into the community of the elect. The cultural anthropologist Colin Campbell (1987) traces our patterns of increased consumption to the pouring out of religious feelings in the presence of certain secular symbols that stand in for religious icons. As a result, the way to "election" today is more likely to be found in the purchase of the right sneakers, stereo, or yacht than by the hard path of the Protestant ethic.

Consumption plainly has many explanations. To a large extent, we consume because others do; if they have telephones, so must we. Then answering machines. Then faxes. We must drive, have certain clothes, houses in particular locations, as well as familiarity with literature, music, films, magazines, and so on, to "fit in" with people we respect and whose respect we wish in return (Lichtenberg, 1998). There is the perennial problem of "keeping up with the Joneses," which is sometimes called the "Veblen Effect" and in other contexts the "Bandwagon Effect." We send out signals about ourselves, moreover, in the consumer choices we make. Robert Frank observes that many "of the most important decisions ever made about us depend on how strangers see our talents, abilities, and other characteristics. . . . The potential client who doesn't know better will assume that a lawyer with a battered car is not much sought after" (1985, pp. 148–9). Perhaps we are wrong to seek a single reason to explain why we seek to acquire so many material goods. It may be better to ask how much we really need to consume – how to justify consumption beyond basic needs – especially if consumption, after a point, is neither good for us nor good for the earth.

How much do we need to consume?

When Marx wrote in the *Critique of the Gotha Program*, "to each according to his needs," he quoted this phrase as an old saw going back to the Bible (Acts 4: 35). Marx recognized the paradox: since capital including technology causes production ever to increase, "needs" must also grow, to consume all that is produced. Imagine what would happen to the economy if consumers were all like Socrates, who, when looking at the mass of objects for sale, would say to himself, "How many things I have no need of!"

When Goneril confronts her father, King Lear, about his expenses, she asks him to reduce the number of his knights. How many did he need? Did he need even one? Lear's reply – "Oh, reason not the need" – helps us understand that needs are not "given" or "innate" – they cannot be numbered in terms of particular human functions. Rather, they are themselves constructed from social expectations and experiences, cultural aspirations, and human relationships. Galbraith argued that after basic needs are met, production "only fills a void that it itself has created" (1984, p. 127). Yet the most valuable and wonderful things – the music of Coltrane, the poetry of Yeats – create the need or desire that they satisfy. Almost all of us condemn not so much the *unnecessary* – whatever that may be – as the *wasteful*. And defining or characterizing wastefulness may be an essential task in determining what we most need to reform about the way goods are produced and consumed.

Economists often tell us that people become "better off" – their welfare improves – insofar as they have more of the things for which they are willing to pay. To see if this statement is true in any but a trivial tautological sense (i.e., because being "better off" is simply defined as having more of the things one wants to buy), we should need an independently defined concept of well-being or welfare. One promising proposal comes from Amartya Sen (1984) and Martha Nussbaum (1992), who have developed an account of "human flourishing" and the "capabilities" that are necessary to permit it. They recognize that under-consumption and some kinds of over-consumption might prevent human flourishing and reduce our capabilities. Having too little can obviously prevent flourishing; but wanting too much might alienate us from family, friends, and civil, political, and cultural life.

The capabilities approach promises a transcultural method for assessing levels of consumption, but much work needs to be done to flesh out the concept of "flourishing" and to investigate methodological challenges to the Sen–Nussbaum perspective. An emphasis on needs as opposed to manufactured or artificial desires has become an important strand in thinking about these matters; it is a way of fixing on certain essential, perhaps universal, minimum conditions that ought to be satisfied for all people. On the other hand, it is a mistake to think that needs are necessarily "given" or "innate." In part at least, they are themselves constructed from social expectations and experiences, cultural aspirations, and human relationships.

That needs are partly relative to community standards and expectations has been a commonplace among economists from Adam Smith to Amartya Sen. Smith wrote:

> By necessaries I understand not only the commodities which are indispensably necessary to support life, but what ever the custom of the country renders it indecent for creditable people, even the lowest order, to be without.... Custom ... has rendered leather shoes a necessary of life in England. The poorest credible person of either sex would be ashamed to appear in public without them. (1937 [1776], pp. 821–2)

We could put Smith's essential point in either of two ways. We might say that leather shoes became a necessity in Smith's England, although they had not been before. Or we might say that the satisfaction of a universal need – for self-respect, or for the avoidance of shame – required shoes in Smith's England where they had not been required before. Indoor plumbing provides another example of the way luxuries soon become decencies and then necessities. In 1900, only a quarter of American homes had running water and, of course, fewer had indoor toilets. By now, virtually all homes do. What was a luxury has become a necessity – and the same with cars, telephones, computers, and so on.

An escalation of perceived needs and, therefore, of the income necessary to satisfy those needs, may lie at the heart of the problem. Rising expectations encouraged by proliferating technologies have raised the ante – the minimum required for health care, education, transportation, housing, and so on, if one is to have even a moderately "decent" life. Thoreau's exhortation, "Simplify," is very good advice, but then Thoreau had no wife and no children. He had already simplified in that sense – but many of the rest of us cannot go it alone.

Consumption and the environment

Critics of consumption today rarely concern themselves with its moral or cultural effects. Rather, they call attention to its environmental effects, that is, its unsustainability in view of the earth's limited resources and capacity to process waste. In the 1970s, Paul Ehrlich and physicist John Holdren (1971) reduced the ecological critique of consumption to an equation which measures environmental impact (I) of a nation or society as the product of its population size (P) multiplied by per-capita consumption or affluence (A) and the technology (T) of production. These three factors, since they are all multipliers, are thought to compound the damage each causes to the natural environment. This equation has theoretical bite because it puts technological advance in the numerator and thus entails that the more technology progresses, the more it amplifies the environmental impact of affluence and population.

Critics of this position point out that a world of difference exists between clean and efficient technologies (such as compact fluorescent bulbs) and dirty and wasteful ones (such as incandescent bulbs). Mainstream economists contend that the environment does not impose physical limits to the growth of the global economy. Rather, societies can "grow" their economies indefinitely as long as they make intelligent policy and technological choices. From this perspective, the world's people can all have refrigerators, for example, provided that each unit uses a refrigerant that (unlike CFCs) poses no environmental hazard. Likewise, people can use automobiles, provided vehicles are powered by technology, such as fuel cells, that are more efficient and run on cleaner and renewable forms of energy. According to the World Bank, "The key to growing sustainably is not to produce less but to produce differently" (The World Bank 1992, p. 36).

Mainstream economists who agree with the World Bank position argue that richer is cleaner – affluence, rather than straining the ecosystem, allows society to invest in the technologies, such as waste-treatment plants, needed to protect the earth and the atmosphere. Affluent people have the time and resources to lobby for environmental protection; those in poorer countries are much less able to regulate industry or control pollution. Analyst Norman Myers observes that peasants who scratch a living from marginal lands "are often the principal cause of deforestation, desertification, and soil erosion" and the "mass extinction of species," but if impoverished peasants could afford kerosene, they would not denude forests for fuel. These people "can be helped primarily by being brought into the mainstream of sustainable development, with all the basic needs benefits that would supply" (1993, p. 306).

By placing affluence and technology in the numerator of the equation that measures harm to the environment, Ehrlich and Holdren (1971) make environmental models of the poor peasants who must burn rainforest for the sake of subsistence farming. The idea that high-tech farming, by vastly increasing yields, can spare land for nature seems to them a delusion.

Should we believe with Ehrlich and Holdren that affluence or consumption and technological advance inevitably hurt the natural environment? Our intuitions suggest this is true, since the more powerful technology becomes and the more goods and services it produces, the greater our ability to deplete the earth's resources and exhaust its capacity to absorb wastes. Yet we may acknowledge, too, that increasing affluence and advancing technology can also allow us to do more with less, to substitute plentiful for scarce resources, to recycle materials, and to control pollution. The way affluence and technology affect the environment, then, may not be a mathematical certainty but up to us, that is, the choices we make. If so, we should become concerned with society's "coping capacity" as much as with the earth's carrying capacity, since so much depends on our political and cultural will to move from inefficient and polluting technologies to technologies that are designed to protect the natural environment.

Are resources limited?

Technological pessimists like Ehrlich believe that natural resources exist in fixed amounts in the earth and therefore that consumption must deplete them. This intuitively compelling belief is found in the classical economists of the eighteenth and nineteenth centuries, including Petty, Cantillon, Quesnay, Smith, Malthus, Ricardo, and others, who insisted that the inelasticity of natural resources sets limits on economic growth. Adam Smith (1776) divided capital into two complementary kinds: fixed (which included land) and circulating (which included technology or machines). Ecological economists today present this view in more sophisticated and urgent terms, but it does not differ in its essentials from that of the older economists (see SUSTAINABILITY).

In 1890, Alfred Marshall summed up the view of the classical tradition by formulating a distinction between human-made capital and "natural agents . . . taken to include all free gifts of nature, such as mines, fisheries, etc." Land, in which Marshall included other natural resources, constitutes a "permanent and fixed stock while appliances made by man . . . are a flow capable of being increased or diminished." Marshall continued:

> Now, if the nation *as a whole* finds its stock of planing machines or ploughs inappropriately large or inappropriately small, it can redistribute its resources. It can obtain more of that in which it is deficient, while gradually lessening its stock of such things as are superabundant: *but it cannot do that in regard to land*: it can cultivate its land more intensively but it cannot get any more. (1920, ch. 4)

In the same vein, Herman Daly writes:

that material transformed and tools of transformation are complements, not substitutes. Do extra sawmills substitute for diminishing forests? Do more refineries substitute for depleted oil wells? Do larger nets substitute for declining fish populations? On the contrary, the productivity of sawmills, refineries, and fishing nets (manmade capital) will decline with the decline in forests, oil deposits, and fish. (1990, p. 3)

While Daly's argument is persuasive in relation to "hunting and gathering" operations, such as forestry and mining, it is less convincing when applied to other forms of production. Capture fisheries, to be sure, are in peril, but the supply of some of the most desirable species – salmon, for example – suffers from glut. Norway's immense salmon farming industry produced about 150,000 tons in 1989 and earned $1.35 billion. Similarly rising production in Scotland, Canada, Maine, and elsewhere has caused world prices to fall. Fishing fleets complement rather than substitute for wild fisheries. Both fleets and fisheries, however, may be replaced by industrial aquaculture – perhaps on the model of mass-production that works so well with hogs and chickens.

Whales and whaling vessels exemplify complementary forms of capital. The depletion of whale stocks during the nineteenth century confirms Herman Daly's insight that larger and more efficient fleets do not substitute for but at most complement the natural resource base. Those who believe that human capital can substitute for natural capital, however, have Thomas Edison (1847–1931) in mind, not Ahab. When Edison invented the electric bulb, he converted whales from resources to aesthetic marvels and cultural icons – which they remain to this day. Other resource substitutions tell the same story. The amount of paper we can produce is not limited by supplies of papyrus. Genetic engineers, by retooling the process of photosynthesis, are developing all-purpose poplar trees that process sunlight and nutrients so efficiently one can almost see them grow.

Mainstream economists today differ from their classical predecessors in that they offer three reasons to believe that resources do not represent a "fixed" stock but are better seen as variable artifacts of changing technology. First, with regard to subsoil resources, the world becomes ever more adept at discovering new reserves and exploiting old ones. Exploring for oil, for example, used to result in a lot of dry holes. Today, oil companies can use seismic waves to create precise computer images of the earth. Second, plentiful resources can be used in place of those that become scarce. Analysts speak of an Age of Substitutability and point, for example, to nanotubes, tiny cylinders of carbon whose molecular structure forms fibers a hundred times as strong as steel, at one-sixth the weight. As technologies that use more abundant resources substitute for those needing less abundant ones – for example, ceramics in place of tungsten, fiber optics in place of copper wire, aluminum cans in place of tin ones – the demand for and the price of the less abundant resources decline. Third, the more we learn about materials, the more efficiently we use them. The progress from candles to carbon-filament to tungsten incandescent lamps, for example, decreased the energy required for and the cost of a unit of household lighting by many times. Compact fluorescent lights are four times as efficient as today's incandescent bulbs and last ten to twenty times as long. Comparable energy savings are available across the board but especially in transportation. One can hardly pick up a magazine or newspaper without reading of new developments in science and technology that promise greater efficiency in the use of resources.

In spite of these arguments, the intuition that current levels of consumption are unsustainable – or physically impossible given the resource base – remains appealing. One reason for this may be the fear that societies will not adopt the technologies needed to make consumption compatible with environmental constraints. Another reason may be even more compelling. Even if clever technology can uncouple consumption from the depletion of resources, it cannot keep consumption from destroying the beauty and majesty of the natural world. Indeed, the less we have to fear from nature, the more quickly we may convert or transform it to an artifact. We will come increasingly to live in and depend upon not nature's own spontaneous course, but a world of our own making.

The difference between nature and the environment

The 1992 *World Development Report* poses this question: "Environmental damage – why does it matter?" Environmental damage matters, the *Report* concludes, because it involves "losses in health, productivity, and amenity" and therefore losses in human welfare. Environmental damage matters for economic reasons, that is, because it limits the amount of consumption the world could otherwise sustain. Thus any changes we make to nature – by converting pristine areas to highly developed ones – may not count as damage. Rather, by transforming nature for economic purposes, so the World Bank reasons, we may improve it by extending its capacity to bear the weight of a growing consumer economy.

Critics of economic growth, including ecological economists, appear to agree in defining environmental damage as any change in the environment that is bad for economic reasons. To damage the environment, for both sides of the debate, is to impair its ability to satisfy our wants. Mainstream economists, such as those at the World Bank, being technological optimists, believe that we do not damage the natural world when we transform it better to serve our purposes. Ecological economists, in contrast, believe the world has a fixed ecological order and a fixed supply of resources to which any human-caused change can be interpreted as damage. For them, nature as it comes is well organized to serve our purposes and so we should leave it alone.

The debate between mainstream and ecological economists ignores an important distinction which can be drawn between "nature" and the "environment." Nature comprises whatever humanity did not make, and something is "natural" to the extent that its qualities owe nothing to human beings. Yet the values nature inspires – religious, moral, and aesthetic – are all deeply human. These values impel us to appreciate and to protect nature for its intrinsic qualities and not for the ways it may benefit us. Our basic normative approach to nature, therefore, is not necessarily instrumental or even prudential. It is founded in religious experience, moral reflection, and aesthetic judgment (see AESTHETICS, NORMATIVE ETHICS, and PART I: CULTURAL TRADITIONS).

The environment, in contrast to nature, comprises just those aspects of nature that are useful and that we therefore value for welfare-related reasons. The environment is what nature becomes when we cease to believe in it as an object of cultural, religious, and aesthetic affection and regard it wholly as a prop for our well-being – as a collection of useful materials and as a sink for wastes.

If we value nature simply as a source of raw materials and as a sink for wastes, then we may welcome the technologies – including genetic engineering – that allow us to increase yields, extract minerals, etc. But to sustain consumption in this technological way, we may lose touch with and respect for the natural world. If the only reasons to care about nature, in other words, are economic and rooted in human well-being, then any change is beneficial that allows us to consume more over the long run. There would be no reason to protect or preserve nature except the fear that we will run out of resources or lose some service that ecological systems (rather than our own technology) may provide.

Many and perhaps most environmentalists, however, are not motivated solely by a concern with making consumption sustainable. They are also concerned with the authenticity – indeed the beauty and magnificence – of nature. They are moved by religious, ethical, cultural, and aesthetic considerations, and not simply by economic arguments. Indeed, in some contexts – the protection of biodiversity would be one – the aesthetic and religious arguments for environmental protection are so strong that economic concerns (the possibility of new medicines, for example) seem secondary and almost trumped-up in comparison. The fundamental reason to protect the diversity of nature is not necessarily to find economic uses for it. On the contrary, the reason to find economic uses for BIODIVERSITY may be to help protect it by offering an instrumental motive in addition to moral, religious, and aesthetic reasons to preserve threatened plants and animals.

This chapter has distinguished between two senses of the term "consumption." First, consumption refers to the economic activity of producing, acquiring, using, and discarding material things of the sort advertised on television. Second, consumption refers to the depletion of the earth's resources and exhaustion of its capacity to process wastes. The chapter has argued that at least in principle advances in technology can uncouple these two kinds of consumption. Improvements in design, in other words, may allow us to raise global living standards without overwhelming the carrying capacity of the earth.

To say that increasing consumption is feasible – to claim that it can be sustained in the context of the carrying capacity of the earth – is not to say that it is desirable. Indeed, a consumer culture, even if advances in technology might make it sustainable – cannot be justified in its own terms. To a large extent, what we consume – clothes, cars, even food – has a symbolic or expressive significance and so must be judged in aesthetic or cultural terms. Consumption cannot be considered an end in itself, but must serve a purpose, such as satisfying basic needs or embodying cultural aspirations and ideals.

Among those ideals, the appreciation of nature for its inherent qualities – rather than simply for the benefits it offers us – motivates many environmentalists. They may regard nature not simply as a system of resources or raw materials for our use or, at the other extreme, as a preserve apart from economic life, but as the habitat in which we and all other species live.

How to cultivate nature as habitat – rather than to exploit it as a resource – is the question before environmentalists today. To sustain our economy we must design and apply the kinds of technologies that make resources go farther, that substitute plentiful for scarce materials, and that recycle wastes. This is feasible. To sustain ourselves as a culture, however, we must also treat nature with respect – as having a good of its own not simply as serving our good. Our moral traditions make this possible, even essential. The power is ours, Captain Planet says (see ECONOMICS, TECHNOLOGY).

References

Argyle, Michael (1987) *The Psychology of Happiness* (New York: Methuen and Co.). [Presenting empirical evidence showing that perceived happiness does not vary with income once basic needs are met.]

Campbell, Colin (1987) *The Romantic Ethic and the Spirit of Modern Consumerism* (Oxford: Blackwell). [A brilliant historical and cultural analysis of the transference of religious sentiments, particularly feelings of ecstasy and election, from religious icons and symbols to those created largely by advertising to promote the consumption of material goods in the eighteenth and nineteenth centuries.]

Daly, Herman (1990) "Toward Some Operational Principles of Sustainable Development," *Ecological Economics* 2, pp. 1–6. [Argues that the global economy cannot grow indefinitely on a finite planet.]

Ehrlich, Paul R. and Holdren, John P. (1971) "Impact of population growth," *Science* 171, pp. 1212–17. [Introduces the "I = PAT" equation, which defines environmental impact as a function of population, affluence, and technology.]

Frank, Robert (1985) *Choosing the Right Pond: Human Behavior and the Quest for Status* (New York: Oxford University Press). [Argues that since happiness depends on relative status, people should have access to as many separate spheres as possible in which to compete, so that they can be content as big fish, albeit in small ponds.]

Galbraith, John Kenneth (1984) *The Affluent Society*, 4th edn (Boston: Houghton Mifflin). [Arguing that society does not become happier in any meaningful sense as it grows wealthier after basic needs are met because consumer wants are just as much products of industry as the goods intended to satisfy them.]

Hirschman, A. O. (1982) *Shifting Involvements: Private Interest and Public Action* (Princeton, NJ: Princeton University Press). [Hirschman persuasively describes a cycle in which people, growing weary and disillusioned with the search for private satisfaction, participate in public causes, then return to hoe their own gardens when those causes turn sour.]

Lasch, Christopher (1991) *The True and Only Heaven: Progress and its Critics* (New York: W. W. Norton). [A despairing, bleak, and well-argued analysis of the failure of the Enlightenment project to improve the human condition through scientific and economic progress.]

Lichtenberg, Judith (1998) "Consuming because others consume," in *The Ethics of Consumption*, ed. David Crocker and Toby Linden (Lanham, MD: Rowman and Littlefield), pp. 155–75. [An excellent discussion of consumption as a coordination problem.]

Marshall, Alfred (1920) *Principles of Economics*, 8th edn (London: Macmillan). [The standard statement of classical economics which includes land or natural resources along with capital as a basic and limiting element of production.]

Myers, Norman (1993) "The question of linkages in environment and development," *BioScience* 43, no. 5, pp. 302–10. [An analysis of the role of economic development in improving environmental conditions in impoverished countries.]

Nussbaum, Martha (1992) "Human functioning and social justice: In defense of Aristotelian essentialism," *Political Theory* 20, no. 2. [Defending a substantive and universal conception of the good based on human capacities and capabilities.]

Schor, Juliet B. (1991) *The Overworked American* (New York: Basic Books). [Arguing that Americans impoverish their lives spiritually and emotionally as they enrich them economically.]

Sen, Amartya (1984) *Resources, Values and Development* (Oxford: Blackwell; Cambridge, MA: Harvard University Press). [A collection of essays analyzing the goals of economic development in terms of human capacities and potential rather than in terms of the production of wealth.]

Thoreau, Henry David (1965) *Walden and Other Writings*, ed. Joseph Wood Krutch (New York: Bantam Books). [Understanding of oneself and of social and economic relationships achieved through a sympathetic sojourn in and study of nature.]

Weber, Max (1958) *The Protestant Ethic and the Spirit of Capitalism*, trans. Talcott Parsons (New York: Scribner's). [Arguing that the rise of capitalism depended on the social ethic of Protestantism, e.g., an ethic of frugality, saving, and productivity.]

The World Bank (1992) *World Development Report 1992: Development and the Environment* (Washington, DC: World Bank). [A lengthy rebuttal of the view that finite resources necessarily limit economic growth.]

Smith, Adam (1937 [1776]) *An Inquiry into the Nature and Causes of the Wealth of Nations*, ed. Edwin Cannan; intro. by Max Lerner (New York: The Modern Library). [Landmark eighteenth-century work articulating the case for capitalism.]

35

Colonization

KEEKOK LEE

Introduction

Humans have caused profound ecological changes. This chapter examines two different historical situations from which to evaluate some of them. The first, documented by literate observers, illustrates the deliberate process of producing neo-Europes in modern times. The second concerns the more controversial anthropogenic role in megafauna extinction in the late Pleistocene period involving preliterate people. This contribution also considers a possible and probable future scenario, the colonization of Mars. It teases out some philosophical problems which arise, in particular, on the one hand between the historical episodes of major colonization on earth and, on the other, the outcome of the contemplated terraforming of planets such as Mars.

Colonization and neo-Europes

Colonization (on earth) may be understood in terms of "the four horsemen of the environmental apocalyse" – overkill, habitat destruction and fragmentation, the introduction of exotic species such as cats and goats, and disease-bearing organisms carried in turn by them as well as by the human colonizers.

The creation of neo-Europes will be considered first, though it happened long after the Pleistocene episode. Methodologically, it does not present the same sort of problems as the latter, for which only fossil and archaeological evidence are available.

Neo-Europes (Crosby 1986) include North America, southern South America, Australia, and New Zealand and may be characterized as follows:

1. Like Western Europe, they are, by and large, temperate in climate.
2. The population today is predominantly European in descent – New Zealand has the highest proportion, nearly 90 percent. Europeans in each case have displaced the indigenes which now form minorities.
3. Europeans, who practiced mixed farming, generally cultivating wheat, and keeping mainly cattle and sheep, transplanted this tradition to the colonies.
4. However, their biota before European colonization were distinctly non-European in character in spite of their temperate climate.
5. But by the end of their transformation, their dominant biota and their landscapes have become distinctly European, satisfying European agricultural and other demands.

New Zealand: a neo-Europe

The brief account here of creating neo-Europes focuses only on New Zealand. About 180 or 200 million years ago, the modern continents began to form through the breaking up of Pangea, the supercontinent, bringing in its train the separate histories of natural evolution distinctive of each of them. But New Zealand itself broke off from Australia about 80 to 100 million years ago, which meant that its natural history evolved in isolation even from that of Australia.

The ecosystems in parts of New Zealand were not pristine when Europeans appeared, as the Polynesian colonizers (arriving about a thousand years ago) had already altered them to quite an extent. At the time of the Polynesian colonization, the country had no land mammals except two species of bat, but flightless birds. These occupied the niche which mammalian browsers could have occupied. There were 13 species of moas. The first Maoris killed the birds in excessive numbers for food, beginning in the northern parts of South Island and spreading southwards. The deposits of moa bones in South Island have been dated from 1100 to 1300 AD. Today the moa is extinct; some Europeans claimed to have seen the bird in the early 1800s, but these sightings have never been verified.

The moa apart, 20 other landbirds, 9 of which were also flightless, were also extinguished. Other species included the tuatara (the only living member of the Rhynchocephalia reptilian order), unique frogs, and flightless insects. Their disappearance was due in part to deforestation caused by the Polynesians and their hunting. But these colonizers also brought (unintentionally) with them their own rat – *rattus exulans* – which bred in great numbers and against which the native fauna had no or few defenses. Their dog, too, contributed to the destruction of the pristine ecosystems.

With the arrival of the first Maoris, New Zealand then had four mammals – its bat, the Maoris themselves, their domesticated dog which they brought with them mainly for food, and their rat, which turned out also to be a source of food. As for crops, they principally relied on kumara, a kind of Amerindian sweet potato which they had also brought. But as they came from a tropical to a temperate zone, their crops were not really suited for their new homeland.

The biota of New Zealand had been transformed by the first wave of colonizers, who used their stone ax and torch to clear vast areas of forests for their agriculture, and for timber to build their houses and boats. In North Island and the eastern side of South Island, forests had largely given way to scrub, fern, and grassland, although half of the total surface of the islands was still thickly forested at the time of the second colonization. But whether transformed or pristine, the ecology remained distinctly unEuropean to the eighteenth-century newcomers. Joseph Bank, the naturalist accompanying Captain Cook in 1769, could identify only 14 of the 400 or so plants he first encountered. This meant that 89 percent of New Zealand's flora then were unique to it, with ferns and their associates accounting for one-eighth.

But those forests were immensely tempting as magnificent timber to meet the European demand for masts and spars. As native trees were felled, new plants, weeds (here defined simply as opportunistic plants which capitalize on disturbed soil conditions) such as Canary grass and cow-itch brought by the Europeans spread with remarkable success; certain originally Amerindian crops, such as a variety of sweet potato which outproduced the Polynesian kumara, and the white potato flourished the whole length of New Zealand.

While the first Maoris merely hunted the seals primarily for food, the Europeans killed them off for their export trade in sealskins by the 1820s. By the late 1840s, inshore whaling (for whale oil), too, was destroyed by their unsustainable practice of harpooning first the calves and then killing the mothers. But on land, the transformation to become a neo-Europe consisted of introducing the usual Old World domesticated animals such as sheep, cattle, and pigs, and cultivars such as wheat. The native flora had to be replaced by imported ones before Old World farming could be established. The clover had a crucial role to play. The missionaries sowed the first seeds, but in spite of its exceptional flourishing, it did not seed itself as it did in the Old World; it had to be replanted annually. This was because New Zealand had no suitable insect pollinator amongst its native fauna. The honeybee was then introduced to solve the problem. The bees not only did this well, thereby rendering the country suitable for European livestock and their owners, but also produced abundant honey and wax. By 1861, Canterbury in the South Island had nearly 900,000 sheep, 33,500 cattle, and 6,000 horses, and Otago had 600,000 sheep, 34,500 cattle, and 4,800 horses. These great herds, in turn, provided ecological niches for Old World weeds such as cow grass, knotgrass, dock, sow thistle, quicksilver, etc. The clover, aided by the honeybees, grew everywhere. These exotica elbowed out the native grasses.

The pig went feral, overrunning the country. The Maoris regarded it favorably as a protein source. But they also lost an old supply; the Norwegian brown rat (landing around 1830) drove the Polynesian rat to the edge of extinction. Old World dogs and cats harassed and killed native birds. The native bluebottle fly was also driven into retreat by the initially inadvertent importation of the Old World housefly; but as the former took to laying eggs in the flesh of sheep, herdsmen took to carrying their own jars of the exotic fly into the bush to wage biological warfare against the indigenous species.

The Maoris themselves had to contend with Old World pathogens. Measles in 1854 killed 4,000 in the North Island. However, smallpox did not cause the havoc it did elsewhere because measures like quarantine and vaccination worked, fortunately, in this instance. By the 1850s they had succumbed heavily to scrofula and venereal disease. They also fell for the *pakeha*'s guns acquired for their intertribal warfare, killing many of themselves. But to pay for them, they had to work for the *pakeha*'s economy and its requirements.

One observes, then, that the Polynesian colonizers did engage in overkill, at least of the moas; the Europeans were similarly guilty as far as seals were concerned. But on land, systematically through habitat destruction and fragmentation, introduction of exotic biota (wild and domesticated), and the pathogens carried by themselves, the Europeans managed to transform the country into a very successful neo-Europe in terms of both its biotic and human populations.

The Clovis colonization

The Pleistocene epoch covers about 1.9 million to 10,000 years ago. Within it, major continental glaciations took place. But during the last 100,000 years, as the climate got warmer with the retreating ice, *Homo sapiens* emerged. Extinction of much megafauna occurred in the early Pleistocene in Africa, but by the late Pleistocene in Eurasia, North and South America as well.

Scientists, since the nineteenth century, have wondered what caused these extinctions. There were, and still are, mainly two rival explanations: the CLIMATE change and the overkill hypotheses. Recently, the main proponent of the latter is Paul Martin who defines "overkill" as follows:

> human destruction of native fauna either by gradual attrition over many thousands of years or suddenly in as little as a few hundred years or less. Sudden extinction following initial colonization of a land mass inhabited by animals especially vulnerable to the new human predator represents, in effect, a prehistoric faunal "blitzkrieg." (Martin and Klein 1984, p. 357)

On his view, *blitzkrieg* is a special case of overkill with four main characteristics: "1) rapid deployment of human populations into an area not previously inhabited by man, 2) man's possession of a big-game-hunting technology . . . 3) the virtual simultaneous and synchronous extinction of megafauna resulting from direct hunting by humans" (Marshall, in ibid, p. 799), and (4) where the individuals of the victim species were killed off at a rate which exceeded their maximum rate of reproduction or of growth. The term "megafauna" does not refer to a taxonomic group as such, but to large mammals, particularly, the genera of continental herbivores which became extinct during the late Pleistocene. Martin considers any animal which approximated or exceeded 44 kilograms in adult body weight to count as megafauna (ibid, p. 355).

The hypothesis has been challenged on several grounds: (a) that no particular explanation is called for, as species are mortal; the extinction of large numbers of genera may just be a coincidence, (b) it is irrelevant, as the normal non-anthropogenic changes in earth's climate alone are sufficient to account for the demise of those species which failed to adjust to the increase in temperature in the late Pleistocene, and (c) it lacks empirical evidence in key cases by way of fossil remains in which, in particular, human artifactual remains are implicated.

The overkill hypothesis, like its climate change rival, is intended as a global model. The controversy is technically complex. This chapter confines itself only to some overall comments about the dispute in the North American instance. Furthermore, it recognizes that while overkill as *blitzkrieg* is not appropriate elsewhere such as Australia where *sitzkrieg* may be more relevant, it may obtain in the case of North America (Diamond 1998).

The arguments, simplistically reconstructed, are as follows:

1. The timing of the arrival of the Clovis people and the extinction is more than a mere coincidence, as it is too exact.
2. The people needed food and the large mammals were tempting targets.

3. They had the weapons and the skills for big-game hunting.
4. Their prey were totally naive and unprepared in their evolutionary experience for such predators.
5. Archaeological sites have been found with the remains of the bones of mammoths, bison, and other large mammals mingled with human bones, the stone weapons of the Clovis culture, and charcoals from fires.
6. Collateral evidence shows that humans arriving upon ecosystems which had never confronted them before caused extinctions where there was no climate change. In the case of New Zealand, the Polynesian colonizers accomplished that. Other cases could also be cited, such as Madagascar, where the first human colonizers, the Malagache, arrived around 500 AD. No climate change occurred, yet megafauna extinction took place – six to a dozen elephant birds and the moas met their demise. As for the mammals, 17 genera of lemurs vanished. There is also archaeological evidence to implicate these people.
7. As the Rancholabrean extinction coincided with climate change, at best one could claim that the change was a necessary condition, but not both necessary and sufficient, for the megafauna demise. But in view of (2)–(6) above, there is a case for saying that anthropogenic activity alone was a necessary and sufficient condition in the Rancholabrean episode.

The controversy carries on apace; neither hypothesis as a research programme has run out of steam and not all the evidence is yet in. However, two notable biologists – Diamond (1998) and Wilson (1994) – have come down in favor of the overkill hypothesis, though the former refines it when applied especially to the more problematic case of Australia. Like them, this contributor, in assessing the overall evidence adduced so far, is inclined to favor it over its rival.

Philosophical significance of anthropogenic and non-anthropogenic extinctions

There are two kinds of extinction – non-anthropogenic and anthropogenic. Non-anthropogenic extinction had occurred on a massive scale in the geological past because of climate change, or following a meteorite striking earth; it also occurred (and still occurs) as just natural background extinction (calculated to be between one and ten species a year). But it is not really the concern of environmental philosophy; however, anthropogenic extinction is. To say so is to presuppose that anthropogenic environmental change, including species extinction, raises two related philosophical issues: (a) humans ought to be concerned with their impact upon the environment, and (b) the value individual organisms, species, and ecosystems may possess. These involve the basis of our moral responsibility to nature, the distinction between intrinsic and instrumental value, as well as the debate about anthropocentrism and instrumentalism on the one hand and non-anthropocentrism with its attendant rejection of instrumentalism as the basis of the human relationship to nature on the other (see NORMATIVE ETHICS and META-ETHICS).

The matter of moral responsibility to non-human others rests primarily on the admission that human consciousness is uniquely capable of grasping good and evil, and choosing to do good or evil. What is right or wrong is endlessly disputed, leading some to conclude that these notions reflect nothing more than subjective attitudes. Even so, it remains true that humankind, alone, is capable of such moral agonizing and debate. This is because human intelligence, in spite of similarities it shares with that of other species (especially fellow primates), is, nevertheless, distinctive in at least two ways. It is mediated by language and is capable of abstraction; it can foresee as well as take steps to ascertain and monitor the consequences of actions. These two aspects may be linked via the concept of the absent which human intelligence can entertain. By this is meant that we can imagine the situation to be other than what is confronting us at any one moment. We can work out solutions to hypothetical (which may or may not exist in the future) problems, where the context is merely abstract and theoretical in character. We first conceive of flying and then figure out eventually how to do so. Unlike birds, we are not beings evolved to fly; we fly by means of airplanes and spaceships. These artifacts embody in a material form our intelligence, which is at once capable of grasping the future, the abstract, the absent. A chimpanzee like Sultan may be capable of figuring out how to reach the food lying outside his cage after his accidental discovery of slotting two sticks together to make a longer one. However, Sultan's solution occurred to him only in the actual physical presence of the food and the poles. In their absence, he could not conceive of the problem as a purely hypothetical one for which there may be many conceivable hypothetical solutions.

This qualitative difference between human and non-human intelligence may be understood at the very least as a necessary condition for the human capability for morality. We can determine in advance of an act, to some extent, what consequences it might produce, whether it would harm the self only or others as well and in what way. We can imagine and hypothesize about possible futures which we could bring about. Options make choice intelligible. Choice to us humans is phenomenologically real even if some philosophers argue that it is an illusion.

Of course humans must cause environmental changes in order to live. Nevertheless, it remains meaningful for us to raise the question whether damaging or destroying individual organisms, their species, and their ecosystems could be said to promote good or bad, for us or for them, and in what sense of good or bad. However, this ability for moral inquiry and concern should not be mistaken for Cartesian arrogance. On the contrary, it can lead to the realization that humankind may have direct duties to non-human others which act as moral constraints upon its activities and their impact on the ecological homes and niches of non-human others.

Whether there are such moral constraints in the main turns upon the anthropocentric and non-anthropocentric axis regarded as crucial in environmental philosophy. Anthropocentrism, for the purpose of this chapter, is defined as follows:

1. The sole locus thesis – humans alone have intrinsic value (in virtue of their unique type of consciousness, their capability for language, and/or abstract reasoning).
2. The thesis of instrumentalism which is an entailment of (1), namely, that the biotic only has instrumental value for humankind, as it lacks the requisite characteristic(s) for ascribing intrinsic value to it.

3. Individual organisms, species, and ecosystems are of use to humans in several
    ways:
    (a) resource value (resource conservation) – the silo argument;
    (b) amenity value (resource preservation) – (i) a source of psychological, spirit-
         ual, or religious sustenance (the cathedral argument); (ii) providing recrea-
         tional opportunities (the gymnasium argument); (iii) a source of aesthetic
         pleasure (the art gallery argument);
    (c) biospheric value (resource preservation) – as provider of "public services
         and goods" by maintaining the great cycles such as the hydrological, and by
         acting as a sink to absorb the waste and pollution produced by human
         production and consumption, without which human life is not possible (the
         life-support system argument).

A quick gloss is called for. The operative word in (2) above is "only," as to admit
that humans do find certain non-human individual and species instrumentally valuable or need them for survival and flourishing is not equivalent to instrumentalism –
this admission is logically compatible with denying instrumentalism itself. It also
follows that (3) may be read in two ways, either as an entailment of (2) or independent of (2). In the context of anthropocentrism, (3) refers to the former, not the latter.

According to this philosophical perspective, the loss of species and well-established
ecosystems is worrying only because ultimately:

1. Human material well-being may be adversely affected.
2. Human physical well-being may be jeopardized as some of the biota lost might
    contain medicinally useful properties.
3. Human flourishing in terms other than physical and material may be under-
    mined.

This then calls for a philosophy of conservationism, for prudent and sustainable
policies in the harvesting, use, and management of biota not only to secure the all
round well-being of present but also of FUTURE GENERATIONS It also follows from such a
philosophy that (extant) biota are not necessarily to be saved as the species we know
them to be in the wild. Should technology provide the means, only their seeds, their
eggs, their sperms, their DNA need be saved and safely stored for future use and
exploitation; the species themselves and, indeed, not even the whole organisms need
be saved. Today biotechnology beckons down this road to cryotoria, which are much
more efficient than the old-fashioned seeds bank. Such engineering reductionism is
but the logical extension of the philosophy of conservationism when aided and
abetted by sophisticated science and its TECHNOLOGY. Neither do naturally evolved
species need be saved to discharge their life-support function. Research is being
conducted to engineer genetically a type of tree which is able to absorb more carbon
dioxide than extant tree species. From the standpoint of the philosophy of conservationism, there is nothing morally wrong with replacing the rainforests ultimately
with such biotic artifacts. After all, what really counts is the superiority of such
engineered plant life over naturally occurring ones in serving the end of biospheric
integrity for humankind.

Non-anthropocentrism may be presented as follows:

1. Rejection of the sole locus thesis – non-human organisms, species, and eco-systems are also loci of intrinsic value.
2. This rejection entails the rejection of instrumentalism.
3. But rejection of instrumentalism is compatible with maintaining the obvious, namely, that organisms, species, ecosystems, and landscapes have instrumental value of one kind or another for humans.
4. (1) and (2) entail constraints upon the use of the biota to advance human ends.
5. Non-anthropocentrism, therefore, embraces the philosophy of preservationism.

The extinction of non-human species is morally unacceptable precisely because it destroys beings which have come into existence and continue to exist independent of humans. In contrast, as we have seen, anthropocentrism at best recognizes limits to human exploitation of the biota on prudential grounds; at worst, given radical technological possibilities and innovations, no limits at all needs to be respected.

A gloss is necessary. The two opposing philosophies have been presented in stark contrast. But it has been said that no one (or no one who has been known to express a systematic view about the matter) falls either into one camp or the other. Three comments are called for. Methodologically, there is merit in such polar delineation, for it enables one to tease out systematically the theoretical and practical implications of these philosophies. Quite a few very influential writers have expressed views which approximate to these so-called "caricatures." Just to name two figures – Gifford Pinchot (1864–1914) on behalf of anthropocentrism and the philosophy of conservationism, John Muir (1838–1914) on behalf of non-anthropocentrism and the philosophy of preservationism (at least as defined above). Finally, public rhetoric today reinforces such delineation. On the whole, it is considered politically (in the largest sense) foolish for policy-makers and those who influence their thinking to argue in the public domain for the saving of (naturally evolved) species and ecosystems from extinction in pure preservationist terms, even though they themselves may privately have great sympathy with that philosophy. Even conservation biologists are on the whole cagey about this in public (Takacs, 1996). The justification for maintaining BIODIVERSITY is invariably conservationist, like the life-support argument. However, the latter invites a ready retort to it in conservationist coin – the cascading effect of biodiversity loss is feared and to be avoided, but this does not mean that a species rendered extinct here, and another species there, would undermine biospheric integrity. In other words, the argument cannot be used to save the snail-darter. It is not often easy to reconcile the two philosophies both on the theoretical and practical levels.

Terraformation: Mars

Except for Antarctica, humans have colonized earth's land surface either densely or patchily. (The deep ocean has so far resisted exploration either for science or development, but technology is now being developed for these purposes.) Space colonization next beckons. Mars is regarded as a possible first candidate amongst the planets of this solar system. But Mars does not look very tempting and is far from suitable as it stands.

Mars's surface area is about the same as earth's land masses. It is very cold with a surface temperature of $-53\,°C$ (compared to earth's $13\,°C$) which can go down to $-150\,°C$, and pressure at 0.0064 bar (as opposed to Earth's 60 bars). Carbon dioxide constitutes 95 percent of its atmosphere, nitrogen 2.7 percent, oxygen 0.13 percent; and there is no methane. (Earth's atmosphere consists of 0.03 percent carbon dioxide, 78 percent nitrogen, 21 percent oxygen and 1.7 ppm methane.) Its gravitational pull at the surface is about a third of that on earth. It has no surface water, although it did in the past and there may be frozen water underground. Its north pole is water ice with some carbon dioxide, while its south pole is frozen carbon dioxide. At the Martian surface is some ultraviolet radiation. The sun's heat stirs up great dust storms of up to 100 miles per hour. Unsurprisingly, it is lifeless, although claims, so far unsuccessful (based on a variety of evidence), have recently been made that Mars had, in the past, supported bacteria-like organisms; nevertheless, the hope remains that further exploration, made possible by technological advances, would bear out the hypothesis that Mars was once capable of sustaining life.

Given its totally inhospitable nature, it must be terraformed to render it fit for human colonization in any form. Terraformation is the process of consciously and deliberately transforming a planet which does not possess the conditions – chemical, physical, geological – necessary for life to become one which can support not only plant but also animal, including human, life. In other words, to create a biosphere where none exists, to turn Mars into an earth-like planet.

The first step is to raise the temperature to a level such that plants can thrive. This could take an estimated 100 or 100,000 years, depending on the method chosen. The shorter route proposes using a soletta, a very large mirror, to capture and concentrate the sunlight to melt the water and carbon dioxide as well as burning deep holes in the planet's crust to melt the permafrost. As both water and carbon dioxide produce the greenhouse effect, positive feedbacks would quicken the pace of warming up, eventually producing a thick enough atmosphere for the introduction of specially genetically engineered algae and bacteria. This would later be followed by genetically engineered plants which could survive and make use of the little oxygen in the atmosphere. As for the plant's requirement of nitrogen, this could be met by micro-organisms releasing it from the nitrites and nitrates already there. Genetically modified plants could also be established on the frozen polar surface, to make it darker, thereby absorbing rather than reflecting the sunlight. This would melt the ice, enabling lakes and oceans to be formed.

The next step of engineering a breathable atmosphere for humans is more difficult. The biological route through plants and their photosynthesis is a very long one, quite apart from the fear that it might not be powerful enough to prevent Mars from slipping back into being a frozen desert. The "hardware" route is much quicker – one proposal is to release the oxygen in the iron oxide deposits using atmospheric processors to do so.

From the perspective of environmental philosophy, whether terraformation will ever take place or when precisely it will happen is irrelevant, as such a project poses certain fundamental theoretical problems for the discipline itself, including the question of its scope. Up to now, theorists, with a few exceptions, have seen it as being earthbound. But should it? May be it should be astronomically bounded.

Abiotic nature: is it morally considerable?

The issues which have prompted the articulation of the study called environmental ethics/philosophy center around the polluting impact, up to now, of our predominantly ecologically insensitive processes of production and consumption, the destruction and fragmentation of habitat owing to pressure of human population, leading to the loss of biodiversity. Earth is unique, as far as one can ascertain, in possessing life in its numerous forms; so it is not surprising that environmental philosophers have been almost exclusively preoccupied with this salient fact in debating whether or not non-human life forms may be said to be valuable independently of the ends of humans instead of being merely instrumentally valuable to humans, a status assigned to them by the dominant anthropocentric paradigm. The abiotic is rarely examined in its own right. If the biotic – either as individual organisms, or as species – can be shown to be intrinsically valuable, then one can proceed straightforwardly to argue that the abiotic is simply instrumentally valuable to the biotic. In policy terms, to save the biotic involves saving the abiotic, as the latter is indispensable to the flourishing of the former. An alternative approach consists of arguing that ecosystems themselves are also intrinsically valuable. But either strategy avoids the more philosophically knotty issue of whether the abiotic, in the absence of its involvement with the biotic, could be said to be valuable apart from the instrumental value which it obviously has for humankind. However, terraformation challenges environmental philosophy to confront this issue, as Mars and other planets appear to have no life on them (see SENTIENTISM).

But if only life – human and/or non-human – is intrinsically valuable, and Mars has no life, then technology and resources permitting, there is nothing morally unacceptable to terraforming it. Furthermore, if life is intrinsically valuable, the possibility of more life being engendered by human manipulation, management, and control through terraformation would mean increasing more intrinsically valuable entities in the world. How could this beguiling line of argument be resisted? Can the intuition that such colonization is morally suspect be rationally backed?

Tackling the issue obliquely is initially called for, staying earthbound for the moment. Is it possible to develop a line of argument to defend earth's intrinsic value but without being obsessed with earth's unique characteristic, namely, that it possesses life?

An earthbound conception of intrinsic value consists first of all of denying the thesis of external teleology, namely, that non-human (biotic and abiotic) nature on earth came into existence or continues to exist simply to serve human ends, although this is not to deny that humans, as a matter of fact, find many non-human entities of use to them, just as some of these entities could, in turn, find humans very useful to themselves. It follows that there is a sense of intrinsic value which may be rendered by the term "independent value" which is shared by biotic and abiotic alike. Furthermore, humans as well as biotic nature strive to maintain their own respective functioning integrity (instantiating the thesis of immanent or intrinsic teleology) while finding one another of use in such pursuit, without it being true that either biotic nature exists solely for the sake of humans or humans solely for the sake of biotic nature. But the abiotic does not exhibit similar striving; nor would it be conceptually appropriate to say that it does. It follows then that there is a sense of intrinsic value which is shared by humans and biotic nature but which excludes abiotic nature – this sense may be represented by the expression "for itself". However, there is a more inclusive sense of that expression which applies to humans, biotic and abiotic nature alike and may be called "for$_a$ itself" which is simply entailed by the denial of the thesis of external teleology.

The next step consists of upholding what may be called the autonomy thesis. Earth did not come into existence, nor does it continue to exist because of humans. *Homo sapiens* appeared only about 100,000 years ago; earth itself is 4.5 billion years old, while life began about 3.6 billion years ago. The biosphere existed and functioned well before humankind evolved. It would continue to exist and function well should mankind become extinct in the future. But whatever existed and continues to exist independent of humans, and whatever exists "for$_a$ itself" constitute compelling reasons why humankind (which, with its peculiar type of self-consciousness and intelligence, may be said also to be uniquely intrinsically value "in itself") should recognize a duty not to destroy or undermine entities with such value.

The third step consists of affirming the asymmetry thesis. Causally speaking, without nature, humankind would perish; without humankind, nature would not perish but, conversely, would positively flourish. While we are totally dependent on nature, nature is not really dependent on us. This realization reinforces the argument from autonomy to establish the thesis that nature has a value which is independent of us.

In extrapolating from earth to Mars and other planets, the analogue of the denial of the external teleology thesis may be constructed by pointing out that Mars exists "for$_a$ itself," as it neither came into existence nor continues to exist for the sake of humans, although this is not to deny that Mars's existence is of use to humankind (in the sense of ensuring that the earth's orbit in the solar system remains stable).

An adaptation of the autonomy thesis consists of saying that Mars, the other planets, and the sun came into existence totally independent of humans, and continue to behave in the way they do, totally independent of human desires or designs. (It is true that human technology in the future threatens to alter their properties and/ or their behavior through terraformation, but that is a different matter which should be distinguished from the thesis of autonomy.)

Finally, the analogue of the asymmetry thesis shows that human flourishing depends on the earth's diurnal and annual rotations, its particular distance from the sun, and the mass and gravitational pull of the sun and the other planets. But the sun and all its planets do not depend on humankind in any way. Humans are causally and cosmologically insignificant and irrelevant.

There then appear to be sufficient reasons for holding that lifeless planets, too, have a value independent of us humans which we ought not to disregard. Terraformation is morally suspect precisely because such a process of humanization assumes that abiotic nature and its processes are only of instrumental value to humankind, and exist exclusively for the realization of our own projects.

Conclusion

Colonization on earth has invariably produced loss of BIODIVERSITY and led to the transformation of the biota of the regions into which the colonizers moved. The transformation, depending on the historical period in question, is either intentional or unintentional, or, more usually, a combination of both. It has also (in the absence of public health measures) reduced the indigenous people to minority status, not necessarily by outright slaughter but through the exotic pathogens the colonizers introduced. One may conclude that colonizers have often acted in a damaging way, whether consciously or unconsciously, both to the native peoples and the native biota (see INDIGENOUS PERSPECTIVES).

But colonization of other planets brings different problems, as these have neither people nor biota on them. Could it be morally wrong then to terraform them and make them fit for human and specially designed non-human life? The answer is "no" so long as one assumes that the abiotic cannot be said to be moral considerable.

References

Crosby, Alfred W. (1986) *Ecological Imperialism: The Biological Expansion of Europe, 900–1900* (Cambridge: Cambridge University Press). [On colonization, in particular the creation of neo-Europes.]

Diamond, Jared M. (1998) *Guns, Germs and Steel* (London: Vintage Books). [On domestication and the spread of cultures and civilizations.]

Martin, Paul S., and Klein, Richard G. eds. (1984) *Quatenary Extinctions: A Prehistoric Revolution* (Tucson: University of Arizona Press). [Standard text on late Pleistocene and recent extinctions of large mammals.]

Takacs, David (1996) *The Idea of Biodiversity: Philosophies of Paradise* (Baltimore and London). [On the recently emerging idea of biodiversity.]

Further reading

BBC (1993) *Mars Alive* (London: BBC Publications). [On terraforming Mars.]

Elton, Charles S. (1958) *The Ecology of Invasions by Animals and Plants* (London: Methuen). [On effects of colonization on native biota.]

Klein, Richard G. (1992) "The impact of early people on the environment: The case of large mammal extinctions," in J. E. Jacobsen and J. Firor, *Human Impact on the Environment* (Boulder, Colorado: Westview Press). [A recent update on the controversy about pre-historic extinctions.]

Lee, Keekok (1994) "Awe and humility: intrinsic value in nature, beyond an earthbound environmental ethics," *Philosophy and the Natural Environment*, ed. Robin Attfield and Andrew Belsey (Cambridge: Cambridge University Press), pp. 89–101. [On the moral considerability of abiotic nature.]

——(1999) *The Natural and the Artefactual: The Implications of Deep Science and Deep Technology for Environmental Philosophy* (Lanham: Lexington Books). [On ontological arguments for the moral considerability of nature.]

Wilson, Edward O. (1994) *Diversity of Life* (London: Penguin books). [A scientific account of biodiversity.]

36

Environmental disobedience

NED HETTINGER

Environmental theorists frequently paint a radical picture of the nature of environmental problems. The depletion of natural resources, global pollution, the destruction of ecosystems, and extirpation of species constitute, they say, an "environmental crisis." They believe that modern humans' relationship to the earth is unsustainable and that our environmental policies constitute a grave injustice to other humans and to non-humans as well.

What sort of practical response is warranted by this world-view? Henry David Thoreau (1817–62), a founder of the American conservation movement who spent time in prison for opposing governmental injustice, once wrote: "How can a man be satisfied to entertain an opinion merely, and enjoy *it*? ... Action from principle, the perception and the performance of right, changes things and relations; ... it divides the *individual*, separating the diabolical in him from the divine" (Thoreau 1991 [1849], p. 35). I suspect that many greens hold views about the severity of the environmental crisis and the nature of ecological injustice that justify (or require) forceful action. Given radical green rhetoric, one expects widespread boycotts, protests, and acts of civil disobedience. Such radical environmental activism has found expression around the globe, from protests against nuclear power plants in England to the blocking of logging roads by forest peoples of Southeast Asia. In some instances, less civil tactics are used. For example, the Sea Shepherd Conservation Society has rammed Japanese drift-net fishing boats and sunk Icelandic whaling vessels in an ongoing 20-year campaign to protect marine mammals and ocean ecosystems. Some admire these radical greens for acting on their convictions, while others accuse them of illegitimacy and even terrorism.

This chapter evaluates the moral legitimacy of illegal activities motivated by environmental concern. It explores why obedience to law is morally important, distinguishes between types of non-compliance with law, and examines justifications for such disobedience. It suggests that environmental activism beyond civil disobedience is very difficult to justify in a democratic society, but provides a rationale for such activism based on a critique of democracy as a humans-only institution.

The possibility and need for justification

Some might reject environmentally motivated disobedience of law out of hand because law-breaking is never morally permissible. This absolute legalism is counter-intuitive. On this view, the Penan of Malaysia ought to let their ancient forest homes be destroyed peacefully when local authorities grant logging rights to foreign timber companies for a percentage of the profits. Legal obligations (what the law demands) and moral obligations (what valid moral principles require) are conceptually distinct and it is not plausible that legal obligations invariably outweigh conflicting moral obligations. One might restrict absolute legalism to significantly just societies. On this view, the Penan may rightly resist the illegitimate laws of their corrupt local government, but Earth First! members in western democracies must obey the environmental laws they oppose.

Although the legitimacy of legislative institutions is an important factor in determining the moral force of resulting laws, even laws issuing from democratic political institutions need not invariably be obeyed. For example, it would seem to be acceptable to destroy another's property to prevent the spread of fire or to avert a chemical explosion at a factory near neighborhoods. It may also be morally permissible to disobey laws sanctioned by a democratic majority when they clearly violate minority rights. That a society is a substantially just democracy is no guarantee that all of its laws have sufficient moral legitimacy to outweigh countervailing moral concerns in all circumstances.

Not only should we reject the idea that democratically sanctioned law must always be obeyed, but we should also reject the opposing extreme that law qua law (including democratically sanctioned law) has no moral claim on us. In arguing for the independence of moral conscience from political obligation, Thoreau says: "It is not desirable to cultivate respect for law, so much as for the right. The only obligation which I have a right to assume, is to do at any time what I think is right" (1991 [1849], p. 29). Martin Luther King (1929–68), the great crusader for civil rights for African-Americans, appears to accept the more limited view that morally deficient laws (rather than all laws) lack moral weight. Responding to the charge of inconsistency in demanding that white segregationists obey laws requiring integration of schools, while encouraging Blacks to ignore remaining segregationist laws, he wrote, "There are two types of laws; there are *just* and there are *unjust* laws. I would agree with Saint Augustine that 'An unjust law is no law at all'" (1991 [1963], p. 73).

The suggestion is that bad laws (or all laws) lack moral weight entirely. But this makes the fact that an act breaks the law morally irrelevant. A more reasonable approach grants that laws (including bad laws) have moral weight, but makes the obligation to obey them "prima facie," i.e., overrideable by stronger moral considerations. On this view, sometimes a person can be morally required to obey morally deficient laws. Even when a person is morally justified in violating a law, some moral force must be overcome. One implication is that environmental disobedients cannot simply refer to the putative injustice or moral deficiencies of a particular law to justify their illegal behavior.

The ground for this prima facie obligation to obey the law in a substantially just society is a subject of long-standing and ongoing philosophical controversy. In Plato's *Crito*, Socrates (470–399 BCE) argues that just as we should be loyal and obedient to our parents because of all they have done for us, so too we owe a duty of loyalty and obedience to the state out of gratitude for its far greater provision of benefits. Typically, environmental activists have benefited from modern states and thus may have duties of loyalty and obedience to the rule of law that made this possible. Activists might, however, justifiably feel a greater sense of gratitude and loyalty to the earth, the wellspring of life.

Obedience to law is supported by a duty to promote just institutions, such as democratic majority rule and the resultant rule of law. Lawbreaking can damage democratic institutions by engendering disrespect for law and further lawbreaking. Unless they favor the overthrow of the democratic rule of law, environmental disobedients must be concerned with the effects of their actions on respect for and the rule of law.

The obligation to obey the law is also supported by a duty of fair play. The benefits of social living are made possible by a reciprocal sharing of the burdens of society, including obedience to law. The rule of law depends on citizens being willing to obey laws they do not like. In short, a functioning democracy requires reciprocal willingness to lose. If environmental activists expect timber companies to obey laws preventing stream-side cutting (for example), then it is prima facie unfair for activists to refuse to obey laws that they oppose.

Civil, militant, and revolutionary disobedience

The appeals to fair play and upholding just institutions support a prima facie moral duty to obey the outcomes of democratic procedures, and thus lawbreaking by environmentalists in reasonably just, democratic societies requires justification. One entrenched position in both the philosophical literature and popular mind is that "civil disobedience" can be justified relatively easily, whereas other forms of disobedience cannot. Whether environmental lawbreakers practice civil disobedience or some other form of non-compliance with law is important for morally assessing these activities.

In contrast to ordinary criminal lawbreaking that is motivated by self-interest, conscientious lawbreaking is motivated by a belief in the righteousness of some cause. Conscientious lawbreakers include the civil disobedient, the militant, and the revolutionary. The revolutionary finds the core principles of a political system corrupt and wants to supplant the entire system. In contrast, the civil disobedient remains faithful to the system as a whole, while objecting to particular laws and practices. Environmental activists aiming to replace global capitalist free trade between nation-states with self-sufficient bioregional communities are revolutionaries, while opponents of urban sprawl are not.

The civil disobedient is also not militant. Lawbreaking can attempt to improve democratic processes and outcomes or it can attempt to thwart them (Singer 1993, p. 303). The civil disobedient tries to educate and persuade the public that the cause is just and that laws must be changed, while the militant coerces them by bringing the desired goal into existence despite their opposition. Environmental activists who oppose logging an old growth forest might block the road into the forest to capture the imagination of the public, get the attention of authorities, and begin a dialog about the ecosystem's value. Contrast this educative and persuasive function of civil disobedience with militant action designed to compel the desired change. Environmental activists might hammer nails into trees or destroy logging equipment to make logging the forest unprofitable. Such activists impose their will on the public and its authorities.

As a way of testing and amending democratic procedure and outcomes by appealing to the public's sense of justice, civil disobedience remains faithful to the institution of democracy, even while violating particular laws. Practiced with care, civil disobedience can improve and strengthen democratic decision-making. John Rawls compares civil disobedience to "such things as free and regular elections and an independent judiciary" as a mechanism that helps to "maintain and strengthen just institutions" (1971, p. 383). In contrast, militant lawbreaking would seem to undermine, rather than promote, just democratic institutions. Because it bypasses even the attenuated democratic procedures used by civil disobedients, militant action has the substantial burden of justifying an outright rejection of the obligation to obey democratic decisions.

Disobedience may be civil or uncivil in manner. A lawbreaker who acts civilly acts submissively, courteously, and respectfully, rather than violently, rudely, or evasively. Activists who barge into a boardroom and dump trash on the table act uncivilly, while those who don a coat and tie and join the blockade act civilly. Many define "civil disobedience" to prohibit uncivil tactics. The civil disobedient, it is said, acts non-violently and accepts punishment. On this view, those who employ violence against persons or property, or evade arrest and punishment, are not engaged in "civil disobedience."

There are reasons for expecting civil disobedience to be practiced civilly. Because the civil disobedient is neither a revolutionary nor an ordinary criminal, one expects signs of fidelity to the system and a manifestation of sincerity and conscientiousness. Submitting to arrest and punishment is one way to manifest sincerity and an underlying respect for law, though it is not the only way. Additionally, civil disobedience as a mode of political speech aimed at educating and persuading the public is likely to fail when it involves rude, aggressive, or violent behavior. Such tactics tend to cloud the message and make it harder for the public to hear. Furthermore, the use of violence escalates tensions, invites violent retaliation by those against whom it is used, and often leads to repression by the government, rather than a thoughtful response to the ideas that underlie the protest.

Although there are good reasons for associating politeness, submissiveness, and non-violence with civil disobedience, to require that civil disobedience meet such constraints is a mistake. One could attempt to persuade the public and achieve a more genuine democratic decision by clandestine, evasive, and violent means. Sometimes such tactics are successful. For example, in 1984, the Animal Liberation Front broke into a head-injury lab at the University of Pennsylvania, and stole videotapes of struggling monkeys strapped to devices that inflicted head injuries (Singer 1993, p. 289–90; see ANIMALS). When the tapes were made public, widespread public revulsion and subsequent protests led to the closure of the lab. In certain cases, violence might be the best (or only) way to get people to listen. One defender of environmental sabotage argues that such acts can enhance democratic processes by insuring a serious public hearing for the views of those who have been effectively shut out of the debate: "Sometimes the use of violence serves to highlight an injustice in a way no other form of protest can match.... it is not until there is violent protest that any meaningful response to wrongs is likely to be made in many a society" (Young 1995, p. 206). Surreptitious lawbreaking and evading arrest may also be the only way to continue to present one's case to the public. Thus, although as a general rule the tactics of violence and evasion of arrest do not fit well with the conception of law-breaking to enhance democratic procedures and decisions, in some circumstances civil disobedients might resort to such uncivil tactics without inconsistency. Conversely, revolutionaries might employ civil and non-militant tactics of disobedience as a tool for their goals; Mohandas Gandhi's (1869–1948) use of non-violence as a means to undermine the British rule of India is an example.

Worries about violence and letting the individual decide

How are environmental activists to know if their cause justifies taking the law into their own hands, perhaps militantly and violently? The seriousness of this problem becomes evident when we reflect on the views of those with whom we disagree. Some people believe that abortion is such an enormous evil that breaking the law, even violently, to prevent it is justified. The Unabomber, a quasi-environmental anarchist, believed that the cause of dismantling the industrial-technological system justified sending letter bombs that killed individuals whose technical skills make the system possible (see TECHNOLOGY). Others apparently believed that their opposition to the US government justified blowing up buildings with children inside. These examples illustrate a substantial danger of allowing individuals to decide for themselves when and to what extent they may break the law.

John Rawls's defense of civil disobedience addresses this danger by not only eschewing violence, but also by limiting the type of justifications protestors can invoke. For Rawls, civil disobedients may not rely on their own narrow political allegiances, religious convictions, or private moralities, but must appeal instead to principles of justice that have widespread acceptance in society (1971, p. 365). Environmental activists thus could not use Rawls's justification for civil disobedience if they appealed to radical environmental world-views (such as deep ecology) that the public does not share. This leads one defender of radical environmental activism to dismiss Rawls's account of civil disobedience as irrelevant to non-anthropocentric environmental activists (List 1994). Peter Singer (1991 [1973]) has also criticized Rawls's limitation arguing that there is no reason why civil disobedients must rely on the existing sense of justice in the society and cannot also try to reform and improve that sense of justice. Allowing this broader appeal, however, sacrifices the public check on the protestors' reasoning that Rawls's constraint provides.

Unless we are willing to rule out in principle all instances of lawbreaking (or all lawbreaking of a particular type), I see no plausible alternative to allowing individuals to decide when a cause is sufficiently important to justify breaking the law and what means are permissible. People are ultimately responsible for what they do or fail to do, including complying with the law. This does not mean that we must accept any sincere act of a conscientious lawbreaker as morally permissible. The justifiability of breaches of law depends on substantive moral issues concerning the rectitude of cause, the appropriateness of the means used to pursue it, and whether the disobe-dient acts responsibly. It does not depend simply on whether there are ever justifiable

examples of lawbreaking of that type. For example, that civil disobedience is sometimes morally justifiable does not entail that every instance of it is. When Lester
Maddox (a famous segregationist) openly refused to obey laws requiring that he
permit African-Americans into his restaurant, his act of civil disobedience was not
justifiable. But this does not mean we should refuse to allow individuals to decide
when civil disobedience is morally appropriate. Similarly, leaving open the possibility
that militant action or violence in support of environmental goals may be permissible
does not require that we accept the Unabomber's use of violence.

Allowing violence as a tactic for social change is dangerous, and many would rule
it out entirely and in principle, especially in a democratic society. Such views too often
fail to distinguish between types of violence, equating all violent activity with terrorism, and condemning it all in absolute terms. Those who have written in defense of
the use of violence for environmental goals make a distinction between violence
aimed at persons and violence aimed at property and have (almost) universally
limited the "violence" they condone to property destruction or sabotage. Their stated
goal is to harm no living being (human or otherwise), but to destroy the machinery
that attacks the living earth. This distinction is important. In a democratic society,
violence aimed directly at persons is almost impossibly difficult to justify. Violence
against property does not confront nearly as high a hurdle. But we must not let this
distinction delude us into thinking that violence against property has no harmful
effects on people, as if only things are being hurt and not people (Morreall 1991
[1976], p. 133). Those who own property are going to be hurt by damage to it;
damaging property that no one cares about would be totally ineffective. Still, legal
activity and non-violent civil disobedience can inflict greater harm than do some acts
of property destruction. A massive road-blocking protest can inconvenience thousands and impose high costs on local governments who must arrest and prosecute
protestors. Businesses can be more threatened and injured by legal strikes and
boycotts than by small-scale sabotaging of equipment.

Those who believe that violent lawbreaking can sometimes be justified argue that
the absolute prohibitionists rely on an untenable act/omission distinction (Singer
1993, p. 307ff). They point to situations where only violent illegal activity can stop
others from committing much greater violence. The earlier mentioned case of the
Penan is an example. If people are responsible for acts of omission as well as for acts of
commission, then to refrain from violent activity in these situations might be wrong.
Arguing that one remains morally clean simply because one did not commit the
violent act oneself is implausible. Consider the case of the rancher who put up a 28-
mile-long fence that threatened the lives of 1,600 pronghorn antelope which were
blocked from their wintering grounds. Is it plausible to say that an activist who
refused to cut holes in the fence has clean hands because it was the rancher, and
not she, who killed the antelope?

Violent activity confronts a special and very high burden of justification, even when
it is employed as a tool of civil disobedience. Those considering violence have a solemn
responsibility to confirm their beliefs with morally sensitive and reasonable people
who are informed about the facts. They must seek out and seriously consider
the viewpoints and perspectives of their opponents. Mohandas Gandhi (1971
[1957]) argued that because our beliefs are subject to error, no one should be so

presumptuous as to inflict harm on others to further those beliefs. He also argued that violence degrades and brutalizes those who use it. Paul Watson of the Sea Shepards, who advocates the use of violent tactics (e.g., sinking whaling ships) for environmental goals, illustrates Gandhi's concerns:

> If you are a self-righteous tight-ass who gets morally indignant about correct tactics, you know, the "I agree with your motives, I just can't accept your methods" type – if you are one of THEM, then do yourself and us a favour and read *Time* or the *Greenpeace Examiner* instead. This article . . . advocate[s] the destruction of property because, and pardon me for my old-fashioned ways, I believe that respect for life takes precedence over respect for property which is used to take lives. . . . The killing of whales in 1986 is a crime. It is a violation of international law, but more importantly it is a crime against nature and a crime against future generations of humanity; Moreover, whaling is a nasty form of anti-social behavior and an atrocity which should be stamped out. So, I don't want any crappy letters about tradition, livelihood or Icelandic rights. (1993 [1986], p. 172)

Will those who believe they are justified in breaking the law violently invariably display such absolute assurance in their cause and firm conviction that their opponents are moral monsters? One need not disagree with Watson's cause to see the danger here of an arrogance that demonizes the opponents and fails to take seriously their perspective. Gandhi is right to focus our attention on human fallibility. Those who use violence must guard against the likelihood that they have an irresponsibly high level of confidence in the rectitude of their cause. We must require a more humble approach from those who pursue these most extreme of means.

Justifications for militant environmental activism

If we are unwilling to rule out in principle militant disobedience to democratically sanctioned law, then we must morally evaluate possible justifications for such activities. The most common justification offered is that the valuable consequences of these acts of militant disobedience are sufficiently good to outweigh their negative results (see NORMATIVE ETHICS). In his defense of the practice of sabotaging environmentally destructive projects, Robert Young suggests that "surely it is a mistake of major significance to value more highly a bulldozer or some marker pegs . . . than an intact ecosystem which provides support for a community of plants, insects and animals" (1995, p. 209). While such an evaluation is appealing, as Young points out there are other negative consequences of acts that destroy property, including loss of profits, potential loss of employment, and the possibility of contributing to the erosion of respect for the democratic rule of law. Another defender of militant disobedience, argues that "what they are fighting for is more important than respect for law. . . . respect for the law will be of little importance in a world with polluted air and water, devoid of natural wilderness, and depleted of most of its natural variety" (Martin 1990, p. 302).

Such consequentialist arguments are often buoyed by drastic assessments of the severity of the environmental crisis. If current environmental policies really are jeopardizing the life-support systems of the planet, as many environmental theorists claim, then the negative consequences of militant activism pale in comparison to the evils to be avoided. Of course, one must also argue that such tactics are effective in bringing about the desired results. Further, even if militant action is successful in stopping particular ecological insults, one must show that militant environmental disobedience does not turn the public against environmental causes, and thus damage the environmental movement as a whole. Michael Martin (1990) presents a thorough analysis of these consequentialist arguments for militant ecoactivism in the context of American environmentalism.

While this consequentialist approach to the justification of militant eco-activism raises important issues, it is of limited significance. By its very nature, it fails to consider non-consequentialist concerns, including the special burden of justification which acts of militant disobedience must bear. From a straight consequentialist perspective, that such acts are illegal and undemocratic is not itself directly relevant to the assessment of their legitimacy. Purely consequentialist justifications also fail to examine the relationship between environmental theory and the democratic basis of political obligation. But many green theorists argue that a commitment to participatory democratic procedures is part of the very substance of a deep environmental world-view. Those who practice militant, environmental disobedience which coerces the majority must respond to the charge that their practices are inconsistent with their own values.

An analysis of the relationship between democracy and environmental theory is thus crucial to the task of assessing militant environmental disobedience. If radical environmentalism were not committed to the democratic basis of political obligation, then militant tactics would not confront the significant burden of justification created by the democratic sanction of law. Is the deep bow ordinarily given to democratic procedures appropriate from a radical environmental perspective?

The critique of humans-only democracy

Non-anthropocentric environmentalists who accept the idea that humans are plain members and citizens of biotic communities – and not the one pre-eminent and privileged species – can mount a serious critique of modern democracies. Democracy is a humans-only political institution. It is a political procedure that arrogates all power, authority, and legitimacy to one out of millions of species. It is a system that legitimizes decision-making authority by reference to a set of abilities – namely, consent, voting, delegation – that non-humans are constitutionally unable to manifest. The vast majority of the interests, goods, and values that should count according to non-anthropocentric moral theory have no guaranteed standing in democratic procedure. Democracy does allow individual humans to set aside their own interests and cast their votes for non-human interests and value. But this merely highlights the injustice of a system that prohibits non-humans from counting politically in their own right (see POLITICS).

It might be objected that because non-humans are incapable of political participation, it is not democracy's fault that they are disenfranchised, for any way of structuring political participation would have this result. If the aim of political institutions is to find decision procedures that fairly adjudicate between all participants making *claims* on what should happen and to orchestrate decisions based on differing *views* about what should be done, then criticizing a political system for leaving out beings which make no claims and have no views is misguided. But if the aim of political institutions is to give fair, equal, and just consideration to all value, goods, and interests affected by a decision and to include in some fashion all beings which have a stake in the decision, then democracy can be criticized for not doing this adequately. A system that requires political participation as a prerequisite for inclusion in the determination of legitimate authority is not a just institution for those beings that cannot participate.

The suggestion that democracy is in principle unjust from a deep non-anthropocentric perspective can be evaluated by considering attempts to restructure democracy to include non-human nature (Mathews 1995). Robyn Eckersley proposes to "incorporate the interests of the non-human community into the ground rules of democracy" and "secure the protection, or . . . systematic consideration, of non-human interests that might be at odds with generalisable human interests" (1995, pp. 169, 179) Because non-humans cannot represent themselves, what is needed are institutional forms that create trusteeship roles by which humans carry out fiduciary responsibilities toward non-human beneficiaries. Such legal guardians might administer a trust fund, instigate legal action, and levy fines to prevent or make good injury suffered by non-humans. Eckersley suggests the establishment of an Environment Defender's Office, a well-funded independent agency that has legal authority to "scrutinise the implementation of environmental legislation and instigate actions against governments, corporations and individuals in cases where biodiversity interests are infringed" (ibid, p. 193).

An even more important strategy for including non-humans in political systems is to specify and legally enforce rights of non-human nature. Just as human rights limit what democratic majorities can do to other humans, non-human rights could be used to limit what democracies are allowed to do to non-humans. Eckersley puts the suggestion as follows:

> Certain fundamental rights of non-human species (such as the right to exist) should be incorporated and entrenched alongside fundamental human rights in a constitutional bill of rights to ensure that they are not "bargained away" by a simple majority . . . Any legislation, or any administrative or other decision, that authorised action that posed a threat to the survival of endangered species could be challenged as constitutionally invalid. (ibid, p. 181)

Assuming their scope was broad and their content was significant, rights of nature enshrined in the constitutions of modern democracies would be a serious step toward including non-humans in democracy.

Although rights for nature would prevent democratic abuse of basic goods and the value of non-human nature, such rights would fail to assure that political institutions consider non-humans in decisions that do not affect their constitutional rights. To rectify this deficiency, a truly non-anthropocentric democracy would set aside significant numbers of legislative seats to be held by human trustees of the interests, goods, and value of non-human nature. These nature guardians would vote on behalf of non-humans. To insure that these surrogates do not backslide and vote for human interests over non-human interests, their votes would have to be justified by reference to bona fide environmental values. While such a procedure would not insure unique solutions, it would rule out particularly self-serving votes. Christopher Stone (1974, p. 40), one of the first to propose legal rights for nature and who suggested giving additional representatives to regions that had more significant natural areas, found his own ideas so shocking that he said: "I am not saying anything as silly as that we ought to ... retreat from one man-one vote to a system of one man-or-tree one vote." But unless we advance beyond one human-one vote, claims that a democracy is not for humans only will be unpersuasive.

These structural changes in democratic decision-making include a non-anthropocentric perspective in the political arena and provide political standing for non-human nature. Such procedures should result in policies that respect the flourishing and self-unfolding of non-human forms of nature. Just as a human democracy manifests respect for human autonomy, so a more-than-human democracy would respect the self-determination of both non-humans and humans. Substantively, this respect would involve humans refraining from interfering with non-human lives and processes, except when required by fundamental human needs and values. Nature representatives would make non-interference their basic policy objective; they would lobby and vote to allow non-human nature to fulfill its own destiny, as far as possible independent of human manipulation and control. (Human involvement with nature that did not compromise nature's autonomy would be encouraged.) This conception of the fundamental value that humans ought to respect in nature addresses the concern that, in a more-than-human democracy, humans would have the epistemically preposterous task of determining what is good for or of value in non-human nature. It also addresses the worry that such a system would involve humans treating non-humans paternalistically, sometimes even deciding how to resolve conflicts between them. By insisting that respect for non-human nature requires letting nature unfold autonomously as much as is compatible with satisfying fundamental human needs and values, we avoid paternalist intervention and manifest the respect that we so value in our relation with other humans also in our relation with the non-human world.

Implications for militant disobedience

These suggestions for a more-than-human democracy show that non-anthropocentric environmentalists need not give up on democracy as an inherently unjust political system, and thus they need not strive to overturn democracy entirely. Nonetheless, modern democracies are far from embodying political structures compatible with non-anthropocentric environmentalism. Transcending humans-only democracy requires radical, some might say revolutionary, changes in current democratic structures.

Given this critique of modern democracies from a non-anthropocentric perspective, non-anthropocentric, environmental activists are not morally obligated to pursue only democratic means of change. Arguing that these radical environmentalists must limit themselves to lobbying and voting as their mechanisms for change, or claiming that civil disobedience is the outer limit of their permissible activism, ignores that, from their perspective, current democratic procedures are ecologically unjust. Why should they limit themselves to means sanctioned by a system they believe to be corrupt as currently constituted? If their use of civil disobedience to appeal to the sense of justice of the majority fails to move humans toward ecological justice and a more-than-human democracy, then militant tactics would seem to be a morally open option. The significant burden of justification against lawbreaking that democratic institutions create crumbles under this non-anthropocentric critique of democracy. The obligation to obey laws that protect the ongoing, drastically unjust, human treatment of nature is specious when such laws are sanctioned by a system that systematically excludes just consideration of the value, goods, and interests of non-human nature. In one way, radical environmentalists who engage in militant lawbreaking act undemocratically, though, as I have argued, with potential justification. In another way, however, they can be seen as acting under the guise and legitimacy of more-than-human democratic norms they believe ought to govern our society.

This does not mean that radical environmentalists may see all laws as lacking morally binding force. Rather, the illegitimacy is limited to those laws that importantly affect the human treatment of nature. Furthermore, that militant lawbreaking might be morally permissible does not mean that it should be undertaken. Practical questions must be addressed about whether such lawbreaking will successfully advance the cause of protecting nature and ultimately move human societies toward more environmentally just democratic systems. It is here that consequentialist and pragmatic reasoning become important.

Conclusion

I have argued that obedience to law is a serious prima facie obligation based on the duty to uphold and play fairly by democratic political institutions. Civil disobedience when practiced civilly is far less difficult to justify than are either militant action or uncivil disobedience. In particular, direct violence against persons faces an almost impossibly high justificatory burden. Letting individuals decide when to break the law, perhaps militantly, violently, or evasively, is a seriously troubling position, yet one that is preferable to ruling out these types of disobedience in principle. In the final analysis, whether an instance of lawbreaking is morally permissible depends on the substantive moral issues involved and on the responsibility and humility of those who so act. Justifications for eco-activism beyond civil disobedience must not only show that the consequences of such actions are good overall, but they must also address a substantial burden of justification placed on those who fail to comply with democratically sanctioned law. Until modern societies move toward more-than-human democracies, non-anthropocentric environmentalists can successfully respond to this burden by arguing that humans-only democracies are fundamentally unjust (see LAW).

References

Eckersley, R. (1995) "Liberal democracy and the rights of nature: The struggle for inclusion," *Environmental Politics* 4, pp. 169–98. [Thought-provoking suggestions for a non-anthropocentric democracy.]

Gandhi, M. K. (1971 [1957]) "Non-violence," in *Civil Disobedience and Violence*, ed. J. G. Murphy (Belmont, CA: Wadsworth Publishing Company), pp. 93–102 [Elegant and forceful defense of non-violence in an out-of-print but extremely useful volume.]

King, M. L. (1991[1963]) "Letter from Birmingham city jail," in *Civil Disobedience in Focus*, ed. H. A. Bedau (London: Routledge), pp. 68–84 [Most famous document of American civil rights movement and compelling defense of civil disobedience.]

List, P. C. (1994) "Some philosophical assessments of environmental disobedience," in *Philosophy and the Natural Environment*, ed. R. Attfield and A. Belsey (Cambridge, England: Cambridge University Press), pp. 183–98. [An assessment for eco-activism of Carl Cohen's and John Rawls's accounts of civil disobedience.]

Martin, M. (1990) "Ecotage and civil disobedience," *Environmental Ethics* 12, pp. 291–310. [A favorable utilitarian assessment of eco-sabotage.]

Mathews, F., ed. (1995) "Ecology and democracy," *Environmental Politics* (special issue). [Excellent volume on liberal democracy's ability to respond to the environmental challenge.]

Morreall, J. (1991 [1976]) "The justifiability of violent civil disobedience," in *Civil Disobedience in Focus*, ed. H. A. Bedau (London: Routledge), pp. 130–43. [Analysis of violence showing that if ordinary civil disobedience is acceptable, so is more violent disobedience.]

Plato (1991) "Crito," in *Civil Disobedience in Focus*, ed. H. A. Bedau (London: Routledge), pp. 13–27 [Classic defense of law abidingness.]

Rawls, J. (1971) *A Theory of Justice* (Cambridge, MA: Harvard University Press). [Most influential book on political philosophy in the second half of the twentieth century.]

Singer, P. (1991 [1973]) "Democracy as a plea for reconsideration," in *Civil Disobedience in Focus*, ed. H. A. Bedau (London: Routledge), pp. 122–9. [Critique of Rawls on civil disobedience.]

——(1993) *Practical Ethics*, 2nd edn (Cambridge, England: Cambridge University Press). [Chapter 11 is excellent on the ethics of lawbreaking.]

Stone, C. D. (1974) *Should Trees Have Standing? Toward Legal Rights for Natural Objects* (Los Altos, CA: William Kaufman, Inc.). [Sophisticated, environmentally motivated, legal philosophy.]

Thoreau, H. D. (1991 [1849]) "Civil disobedience," in *Civil Disobedience in Focus*, ed. H. A. Bedau (London: Routledge), pp. 28–48. [Skepticism about government and powerful plea for individual responsibility.]

Watson, P. (1993 [1986]) "Raid on Reykjavik," in *Radical Environmentalism: Philosophy and Tactics*, ed. P. C. List (Belmont, CA: Wadsworth, Inc.), pp. 172–6. [Reprinted from the *Earth First! Journal*.]

Young, R. (1995) "'Monkeywrenching' and the processes of democracy," *Environmental Politics* 4, pp. 199–214. [Best philosophical defense of eco-sabotage.]

Index

Abahu, Rabbi 85
Abbey, Edward 259, 260
Abe, Masao 61
abiotic factors 304, 495–6, 497
aboriginal peoples 5–7, 9, 12, 228–9; *see also* indigenous peoples; Maori culture; Native Americans
abortion 194
Acaraga Sutra 53
acid rain 344
activism: deep ecology 223–4, 230–1; ecofeminism 233; environmental 498, 499–500; militant 504–5; violence 502–4
Adam, Eden myth 115–16, 148
Adams, Carol J. 237
adaptation 309–10, 411
Aditi goddess 39
aesthetics 266–7, 272–3; biodiversity 404; community 253; conservation 264–6; deforestation 266; ecology 253–4; environmental literature 267–8; intentionality 268–9; intrinsic value 174, 265–6; intuition 271, 273; Kant 146, 268–9; nature 151, 264, 268–71, 274–5, 275; positive 271–3; psychological awareness 267, 270; wilderness 352
affiliations 4–6, 14
Afrocentricism, ecowomanist 245–6
Agenda 21, 391
Aggassiz, Jean Louis 150
Agni (light/fire) 40
agrarian philosophy 467–9
agricultural economists 462–3
agriculture 291; animal husbandry 87, 237; deep ecology 229; developing countries 238–9; environmental ethics 463–4; environmental impact 460; future generations 462–3; insecticide-resistant crops 333; irrigation 295; land usage 460; landscape changes 293–4; market forces 462–3, 468; morality 467–8; optimization approach 462–3, 470; production/consumption 461; rainfall 460; slash and burn 465; subsistence 293, 461–2, 480; sustainability 121, 469–70; technology 366, 440–1; treatment of workers 237
agro-ecosystems 461–2, 466–7, 470
ahimsa (non-violence) 43, 53
Aiken, William 210–11
Aitareya Upanishad 38
Ajahn Pongsak 57
Akash (space) 39
al-Marginani 124
Alar 339
alienation 81–3, 151, 384
Allen, E. L. 94
Ambrose, Saint 100, 101
American Buddhism 62–4
amr (universal principle) 118
anarchism: eco-anarchism 156, 323; ecofeminists 243; Godwin 152; Kropotkin 156, 159; Proudhon 151; and social ecology 227
Anaximander 68
Anaximenes 67–8
ancestors 9, 10, 16
ancestral lands 15–16
Andean peoples 14
Anderton, Doug 431
androcentrism 242, 244, 245
animal liberation 196–7, 416, 420

Animal Liberation Front   501
animal sacrifice   56, 114–15
animals   170, 179–80; agriculture   87,
   237; ecofeminism   236–7; God   97–8,
   99; Hinduism   45–6; incarnation   45;
   Islam   122–4; Jainism   46;
   Judaism   87, 88–9; moral standing   165,
   187, 242, 419; rationality   75–6, 78,
   100–1, 143; reincarnations   71;
   rights   197–8; suffering   106, 193, 420;
   treatment   123–4, 236–7, 298
anthropocentrism: Bacon   105;
   biodiversity   199; Buddhism   61;
   Calvin   104; Chinese philosophy   24, 31;
   Christianity   37, 417; deep ecology
   225–6; environmental ethics   158,
   177–9; extinction   308; instrumental
   value   166, 405, 491–2; intrinsic
   value   164, 166, 491–2; Judaism   82,
   93; nature   219, 222–3;
   oppression   244; Plato   70–1;
   sustainability   391; teleology   74
anthropogenic changes: climate   449–50;
   extinctions   411–12, 490–3;
   forests   464–5; landscapes   292;
   pollution   204–5; wilderness   273,
   355–6, 359
Antony of Padua, Saint   133
Antony the Great, Saint   104
Anuvrat Movement   54
Apah (water)   39
aparigraha (non-possession)   53
aquaculture   481
Aquinas, Saint Thomas   103, 111, 131,
   132, 142
Aridjis, Homero   251
Aristotle   75–6; Augustine on   102;
   consumption   474; De Anima   74–5;
   environmental issues   76–7; ethics   175;
   Meterorologica   76; nature   73–4; on
   Plato   69; reincarnation   74;
   slavery   418; virtue/vice   188
Ariyaratne, A. T.   58–9
Arrernte ownership   10
art   253, 297, 299
Ashoka, Emperor   46, 56
Asian Cultural Forum on Development   58
Assisi Declaration   42
asteya (not stealing)   53

Astor, David   394–5
astronomy   132
Athabascan Indians   12
Athanasius   101
Atharva Veda   39, 40–2
atomism   134, 135, 141–2, 327
Attica   73
Augustine, Saint: on Aristotle   102; God/
   nature   103, 131; Great Chain of
   Being   102; ordo amori   132; on
   Plato   102; rationality   98, 100–1;
   unjust laws   499
Australia: Canberra   12; green
   parties   318; introduced species   423;
   kangaroo industry   417–18; traditional
   owners   10; see also aboriginal peoples
authenticity   444–7, 483
authoritarianism   321–2
autonomy   187, 273, 359, 369, 496

Bacon, Francis   105, 111, 234
Bacon, Roger   133
Badlands   349–50, 352, 357–8
bal taschit (non-destruction)   90–3
Balguy, John   106
Bank, Joseph   487
Bartram, William   258
Basil the Great   100, 101
bass   310, 312
Bass, Rick   253, 260
Batchelor, Stephen   63
bats   313, 487
Bauckham, Richard   97, 98, 102
Baudelaire, Charles   151
Bayle, Pierre   143
Beardsley, Monroe   266–7
beauty   265, 266–7; see also aesthetics
Becker, Gary   368
Beckerman, Wilfred   393
Been, Vicki   431–2
bees   488
beggar's ticks   405
beholdenness   8–9, 13
Belkin, Samuel   85
belonging   7–8, 13
Benally, Alice   3, 4, 16
Benedictines   102, 103
beneficence   403

benefit-cost analysis 277, 280–2, 285–6, 384–5
Bentham, Jeremy 380, 420
Bentley, Philip J. 84, 85–6
Bergson, Henri 154
Berkeley, George 139–40
Berlin, Isaiah 301
Bernard of Clairvaux 102
Bernstein, Jeremy 82–3
Berry, Wendell 253, 260, 261, 468
Beston, Henry 260
Bhopal accident 342, 439
Biehl, Janet 241
biocentrism: egalitarian 220, 243, 245, 421, 424; intrinsic value 164, 166, 308; Protestantism 105; species preservation 403–4; Taylor 352; Theravada Buddhism 57
biodiversity 392–3, 404; aesthetics 404; anthropocentrism 199; colonization 497; conservationists 493; deep ecology 218–19; ethics 402; intrinsic value 421; mapping 397; Naess 421; rarity 412–14; respect 413; sentientism 199–200; species preservation 88, 402; valorized 410; wilderness 359
biological conservation 158, 409, 493
biophilia hypothesis 267–8
biopiracy 436
bioregionalism 151, 230, 301, 323
biospheric rights 186–7, 492
biotechnology 441, 492
biotic community: land ethic 209–10, 211, 213, 421; Native Americans 210; non-anthropocentrism 505–6; relationships 304
birds under threat 213–14, 313, 402, 407, 487
birth control 363–4, 371–2
birth rituals 6
Black, John 100
blood sports 106, 124
Bookchin, Murray 156, 227–8, 243
Boyle, Robert 134
Bradford, William 258
Bradstreet, Anne 258
brahmacarya (sexual restraint) 53
Brahman 38

Bright, April 10
Brower, David 351
Brown, Lester 370, 460
Brundtland Commission 289, 320, 390, 391, 399
Bruun, Ole 61
Budd, M. 269–70, 274–5
Buddha 52, 55, 56
Buddha-nature 34, 35
Buddhadasa Bhikkhu 57
Buddhism 58; anthropocentrism 61; Dharma 57; ecological issues 64; environmental philosophy 55–6, 58; forest hermitages 57; freedom from attachment 55; interpenetration 62; karma 56; self- purification 55; sexuality 58; vegetarianism 58
Buddhism, types: American 62–4; Chinese 34–5; Green 63–4; Hua Yen 61; Mahayana 52, 59–62; Theravada 52, 56–9; Tibetan 61–2; Vajrayana 52; Zen 60
Bullard, Robert 430, 431
Bundjalung beliefs 10
Burke, Edmund 399
burning of books, China 21
Burns, Robert, "To a Mouse" 148

Cabeza de Vaca 258
Callicott, J. Baird 196, 197–9, 200, 350, 351, 353, 354, 359
Calvin, Jean 104, 107
Cambodia 57
Campbell, Colin 477
capital: environmental 391; natural/ manufactured 289, 397, 398; Smith 480
capitalism 151, 289, 298, 475
Cappadocians 101
Captain Planet 473
carbon dioxide emissions 439, 492
Care, Norman 383, 384
care ethic 96, 108, 403
Carlson, A. 268, 270, 271
Carmell, Aryeh 87
Caro, Rabbi Yosef Hayyim 83
carrying capacity 311, 319, 365–7
Carson, Rachel, Silent Spring 378, 465
Cartesian philosophy 105, 135–8

Cathedral Pines 464
Catholicism 107, 133–4
Celsus 100
Cerrell Associates 431
CFCs 426
Chadwick, Owen 107
Charaka Samhita 46
Chavez, Cesar 428–9
Chavis, Benjamin F. Jr 429–30
chemical waste 342, 439–40
Chemical Waste Management 431, 432
Cheney, Jim 244
Cheng Hao 33–4
Cheng Yi 33–4
Chernobyl accident 439
Cherokee people 3
Chhandogya Upanishad 39
child-bearing 367–9; *see also* fertility
children 75–6, 368, 371, 473
China: Burning of Books 21; emperor's
  role 28; Mahayana Buddhism 59; one-
  child policy 368, 371; Three Gorges
  development 296
Chinese philosophy: anthropocentrism 24,
  31; Buddhism 34–5; cosmology 22–3;
  di (earth) 23–4; Han period 21, 22, 29,
  30; human–non-human world 22–3;
  Old/New Text Schools 29–30; *qi*
  (stuff) 33–4; *ren* (man) 23–4; *tian*
  (heaven) 23–7; *wuxing* (five
  elements) 27–8; *yin-yang* 28–9
Christianity 102–3, 106–7, 294;
  anthropocentrism 37, 417;
  care ethic 96; consumption
  474–5; environmental philosophy
  469; green 224; incarnation 82,
  132; nature 96–9, 100, 102; Old/
  New Testaments 96, 97–8;
  patristic writers 100; Reformation
  104–5; stewardship 96, 100, 103,
  105–6, 107; symbolism 256–7;
  theocentrism 98; vegetarianism 133;
  wilderness 98–9, 104, 106
Christianity, types: Catholicism 107,
  133–4; Green 224; Protestantism
  104–7; Puritanism 106
Chrysippus 78–9
Chrysostom, Saint John 101–2
Chunqiu Fanlu 25

Cisnero, Sandra 261
Cistercian orders 102
citizen participation 342–3
city 156–7, 298
civil disobedience 500–1, 503, 508
civil rights 428–9
Civil Rights Act 430
civil society: *see* society
civilization 298
class differences, pollution 219
Clean Air Act 333, 335
Clean Air Act Amendments 288, 339, 341
Clements, Frederic 309
climate changes: anthropogenic 215,
  449–50; disease 450; extinction
  489–90; global 215, 285, 328;
  insects 450; international debate 321,
  452; wilderness 352
clover 488
Clovis people 489–90
coal 292
Colburn, T. 465
Coleridge, Samuel Taylor, *The Rime of the
  Ancient Mariner* 148–9
Coles, Andrew 75–6
colonialism 155, 227
colonization: biodiversity 497; deep
  ocean 493; Mars 486; neo-
  Europes 486–8; New Zealand 487–8
commodity value 404
commons, tragedy of 280
communication, electronic 293, 294
communitarianism 380–1
community: aesthetics 253; future
  generations 380–1; individual
  208; local 322–3; moral 378;
  multiple membership 211–13;
  obligation 213; species 209–10,
  410–11
compassion 89, 106, 122; *see also*
  sympathy
compensation 281, 426, 431–2
computers, chemical waste 439–40
Condorcet, Marquis de 363–4, 367, 369
Confucianism 24–5, 27, 30–1
consciousness 137, 294
consequentialism 181–4, 188, 466–7,
  504–5, 508

conservationism 394–5, 492;
  aesthetics 264–6; biodiversity 493;
  biological 158, 409, 493;
  Buddhism 58; environmental 47–9,
  58, 189–90; plants 209, 405, 407, 409;
  pollution 204–5
consistency argument 169–70
consumerism 53–4, 299–300, 476, 477
consumption 474–5; agriculture 461;
  Aristotle 474; capabilities
  approach 478; capitalism 475;
  children 473; distribution 426;
  environment 479–80; future
  generations 394; industrialism 476;
  inequalities 320–1; mass 476–7;
  natural resources 473; nonsatiety
  requirement 476–7; North/South 435;
  overconsumption 91; per capita
  393–4; Plato 474; population 319;
  production 461, 477, 483; social
  expectations 477–8; Thoreau 474, 479
Cook, Francis 61
Copernicus 133, 234, 297
coral reefs 391, 398
Cosmas Indicopleustes 103
cosmic ecology 61, 68
cosmology: Chinese philosophy 22–3;
  correlative 29, 30; eco-cosmology
  227–8; Hinduism 42–3, 45; Plato
  72–3
cost-benefit analysis: see benefit-cost analysis
Council for the Protection of Rural
  England 394–5
Cracraft, Joel 408
Cree people 13–14
Cronon, William 354, 356, 357, 464
Crosby, A. W. 486
cruelty 174, 190
culture and nature 152–3, 154, 354,
  443–4
Cuomo, Chris J. 237, 238, 241, 242–3
Curtin, Dean 237
custodianship 10–12, 17, 229; indigenous
  peoples 10, 17; responsibility 10–12;
  see also guardianship; stewardship

Daishonen, Nichiren 61
Dalai Lama 61, 62
Daly, Herman 393, 480–1

dam building 3, 264, 296, 333, 436
Daniel, John 261
dao 30–2
Dao Sheng 35
Daoism 59; and Buddhism 34; dao
  30–2; holism 32; tian–di–ren 24, 26,
  27; zhiran 31–2
Darwin, Charles: and Aggassiz 150;
  ethics/society 206–7, 209–10;
  evolutionary theory 106–7, 152,
  205, 295; natural selection
  152–3; species 406; survival of the
  fittest 154–5
Dasgupta, Partha 369
de-Shalit, Avner 380
death rate 362, 368, 369, 371
debt-for-nature swaps 397
decentralization 321, 323
deep ecology 218–19, 220–4;
  activism 223–4, 230–1;
  agriculture 229; androcentrism 244,
  245; anthropocentrism 225–6;
  biodiversity 218–19; critiques 225–6;
  ecofeminism 224, 226, 243–4;
  gendered 229; human–non-human
  world 225–6; identification with
  224–5; Jainism 53; Naess 141, 186,
  218–19, 220–2, 243; non-sentient
  beings 420; normative ethics 163;
  rights of entitites 186; wilderness 228,
  229–30
deforestation: aesthetics 266; Attica 73;
  Ganges River 55; India 55, 56; New
  Zealand 487; Thailand 57
deGeorge, Richard 381–2
Delhi Sands Flower-loving Fly 402
Deming, Alison Hawthorne 261
democracy: ecology 317; Locke 138; non-
  human nature 506; participatory 317,
  321; rule of law 500
Denevan, William 355
deontological ethics 178, 184–8, 381–2
Derham, William 100
Derr, Thomas 37, 48
Descartes, René 105, 135–8
descendants 9–10; see also future
  generations
determinism 135, 141, 298
Deuteronomy 88, 90

Devall, Bill   222, 225, 239, 421
developing countries   238–9, 426, 434–5, 452–3
development: classified   434; economic   369–70, 371, 393, 482; patriarchy   239, 240; poverty   240, 370, 392; power relations   434–5; *see also* industrialism; sustainable development
Dharma   46, 57
di (earth)   23–4
Diamond, Eliezer   92–3
Diamond, Jared M.   490
Dillard, Annie   261
diminishing marginal utility   286
Diné people   6, 13, 17
Dirzo, R.   465
discount rate   380, 384, 397
disease   450, 488
distributive justice   319–20, 453–8
disturbance ecology   353–4
divinity   23–4, 44; *see also* God
Dobson, Andrew   325
Dodson, Mick   7
Dogen, Zen master   60
dogs   487
Dolan v. *City of Tigard*   338
domination   226, 227, 234; *see also* patriarchy
dominion   83–4, 103, 107, 148
Dong Zhongshu   29
Donne, John   297, 299, 302
Doyle, J.   465
drought   449
dualism   300; Descartes   137; domination   226, 227; materialism   67–8, 134–8; Plumwood   226, 227, 235; stewardship   108; theism   108; values   235–6; *yin-yang*   29
Dubos, René   103
Dumanoski, D.   465
Durham, Jimmie   15, 17
duty   211–13, 387, 404–6, 408–10; *see also* deontological ethics

Earth: Andean peoples   14; *di*   23–4; Hinduism   40–2; Poryphyry   79; as purification   120
Earth First!   225, 413, 499
Earth Summit   343, 391, 433, 453–4

East Bibb Twiggs v. *Macon-Bibb County Planning & Zoning Commission*   430
Eckersley, Robyn   506
eco-anarchism   156, 323
ecocentric ethics   308, 320, 325
ecocriticism   252, 258
eco-fascism   197, 211, 322
ecofeminism: activism   233; anarchism   243; animals   236–7; deep ecology   224, 226, 243–4; developing countries   238–9; ecowomanism   245–6; essentialism   239–40, 241; generalization   241, 242; vegetarianism   237; virtue ethics   189
eco-libertarianism   328
ecologism   325–6
ecology   214, 316; aesthetics   253–4; art   253; Buddhism   62–4; conservationists   209; cosmic   61, 68; Darwin   153; democracy   317; disturbance   353–4; diversity-stability   307; economy   277, 284, 288–9, 295, 403–4; environmental philosophy   304; hard/soft   304–5, 306, 310–11; integrity   306–7; knowledge   313; land ethic   214–16; practical   304, 312–14; reciprocity   11; reductionism   309; relationality   304–5, 317; second-order principles   212, 310; social   227–8, 243; value judgments   305–6
economics   277–81, 289; business cycles   296; discount rate   380, 384, 397; ecology   277, 284, 288–9, 295, 403–4; environmental   277, 340–1; integrity   394; preferences   277–8; species preservation   403; sustainability   286, 395–8, 400; values   282–4, 403–4
ecosocialism   224, 323
ecosophy   220–1, 225, 230–1
eco-spirituality   47–9
ecosystem   150, 254; change   307–9; local   323; as natural capital   289; species   410–11
ecowomanism, Afrocentric   245–6
Eden myth   115–16, 148
Edison, Thomas   481

egalitarianism: biocentric   220, 243, 245,
    421, 424; positive aesthetics   272–3;
    Rawls   393; relationality   222
Ehrenfeld, David   84, 85–6
Ehrlich, Paul   479, 480
Eiseley, Loren   259
Elder, John   252
Eldredge, Niles   408
Eleatics   68–9
Eleazar, Rabbi Simeon ben   98
elements: Chinese philosophy   27–8;
    Hinduism   38–40
Eliot, T. S.   299
Elliot, Robert   352
Elton, Charles   208
Emerson, Ralph Waldo   106, 468
emissions: absorptive capacity   450–2;
    carbon dioxide   439, 492; chief
    contributors/beneficiaries   457–8; costs of
    avoiding   456–8; distributive
    justice   453–8; sulfur dioxide   288, 341;
    trading in   341, 455; see also greenhouse
    gases
empiricism   138–40, 141
employment   237, 283, 432
Encompassing Nature: A Sourcebook   252
Endangered Species Act (USA)   200, 307,
    333, 402
energy sources   291–3; alternative
    technologies   458; business cycles   296;
    fossil fuels   292–3, 296, 387, 439;
    industrialism   292–3, 296;
    renewable   452, 479; restrictions
    450–1
Enlightenment   130, 142–3, 219, 319,
    475, 476
entropy   393
environment   279–80; consumption
    479–80; influences on   273–4, 283, 299;
    instrumental value   482–3; mixed
    274–5; nature   482
Environment Defender's Office   506
environmental activism: see activism
environmental degradation:
    agricultural   460; costs   283–4, 400;
    economic growth   482; ethics   177;
    Islam   116; natural   397–8; North-
    caused   435; poverty   394;
    technology   392–3, 439; violence   503–4

environmental ethics   187, 189; agrarian
    philosophy   468–9; agriculture   463–4;
    anthropocentrism   158, 177–9;
    attitudes   413; consequentialism
    181–4, 466–7; deontology   184–8; future
    generations   320, 463; human–non-
    human world   426–7; instrumental
    value   164; intrinsic value   164, 174,
    405, 416; meta-ethics   164;
    misanthropy   158; poetry   148–9;
    rights   185–6; sentientism   196–202,
    495–6; thin/thick concepts   173–5;
    virtue-based   140, 178, 188–90;
    wilderness   350–2
Environmental Ethics   194
environmental impact statement   332–4,
    465
environmental issues   291–5;
    Aristotle   76–7; global   344;
    Islam   112–13, 116, 121–2;
    Judaism   87
environmental justice   413; distribution of
    burdens   436–7, 449; distributive/
    participatory   427–8; global   433–6;
    inequalities   392, 426–7, 453–8; Native
    Americans   432; participatory   434;
    pesticides   339; and sustainability   320,
    323–4, 392
environmental law: see laws
environmental literature   251–4, 465–6;
    aesthetics   267–8; exploration   261–2;
    human–non-human world   258–9;
    impact   259–60; liberal arts   257–8;
    poetry   148–9; social critique   261
environmental philosophy:
    agrarianism   468–9; Buddhism   55–6,
    58; Christianity   469; ecology   304;
    instrumental value   242; intrinsic
    value   171; Jainism   52–4;
    population   365, 374–5;
    utilitarianism   466–7
environmental protection   506–7;
    developing countries   426, 434–5;
    Hinduism   42; Judaism   86–8;
    regulations   336
Environmental Protection Agency: bubble
    policy   339; Clean Air Act   333;
    emissions   430; Environmental Justice
    Commission   433; law suits   335, 337;

scientific advice   335, 338; striped-
    bass   310
environmental racism   429–31, 432
environmental studies   251
environmentalists: benefit-cost
    analysis   285–6; forest protection
    264–5; instrinsic value   416;
    instrumental value   242;
    misanthropy   374–5; Muir   106;
    neighborhood   260–2;
    sentientism   200–1; sustainability   392;
    wilderness   350–2
Epicureans   100, 297
Epicurus   77–8
equal opportunities   371
essentialism   239–40, 241
ethics: Aquinas   142; Aristotelian   175;
    biodiversity   402; consequentialist/
    deontological   188; ecocentric   308,
    320, 325; evolutionary theory   205–6;
    hierarchy   180, 212–13; human
    rights   207–8; Islam   122; and meta-
    ethics   163–4, 167–8; non- speciesist
    416, 420; normative   119–24, 163–4,
    173–5, 204; philosophers   204;
    Qur'án   116–17; realism   171–2;
    second-order principles   212, 310; self-
    interest   405; society   206–7, 209–10,
    286; species   409; virtues/
    rationality   140; see also environmental
    ethics
ethnocentrism   358
Ethyl Corporation v. EPA   335
Europe   336, 337–8, 340, 343
evil   131, 132, 143
evolutionary theory   106–7, 152, 205–6,
    295
Exclusive Economic Zones   300
existentialism   212–13
expansionism   142–3
exploitation: economic   280; nature   40,
    105, 321, 403–4; over-exploitation   365;
    race   237; women   321
expressivism   163–4, 166
extensionism   180–1, 190, 242
externalities   280, 396
extinction: anthropocentrism   308; climate
    change   489–90; mass   214–15;
    natural/anthropogenic   214–15, 254,

405, 411–12, 490–3; overkill   489–90;
    rates   406; species   307–8, 409, 449–
    50,
    490–3
Exxon Valdez oil spill   259–60, 283–4, 439

fair play   500
Family of Earth and Sky: Indigenous Tales of
    Nature from Around the World   251–2
famine   362
Feinberg, Joel   192, 193–4, 403
feminism   243, 357, 420; see also
    ecofeminism
fengshui (geomancy)   61
Ferré, Frederick   211
fertility rates   362, 367–70, 371
fertilizers, chemical   461
Fichte, Johann   150
fiqh (Islamic law)   120, 123, 125–6
fire use   292
First National People of Color summit   428,
    429
fish, threatened   310, 312, 333
fish farming   481
flooding   450
flourishing   168–70, 180, 186, 478
Food and Agriculture Organization   460
Foreman, Dave   359
forest hermitages   57
forests: anthropogenic   464–5;
    environmental protection   264–5; future
    generations   422; old growth   402, 422;
    second growth   464
fossil fuels   292–3, 296, 387, 439
Fox, Matthew   102, 108
Fox, Warwick   226–7, 243–4
Framework Convention on Climate
    Change   453–4
Francis of Assisi, Saint   103–4, 133
Frank, Robert   477
freedom   327, 328–9
Freudenstein, Eric G.   90
Fromm, Harold   262
Fuller, Buckminster   304
Fung, Y. L.   34
future generations   286, 377–8, 385–8;
    agriculture   462–3; community   380–1;
    consumption   394; contractarian
    approach   382; deontological

future generations (*cont*)
  ethics   381–2; environmental
  ethics   320, 463; Feinberg   403;
  forests   422; green politics   317;
  libertarianism   379–80; moral
  standing   378–83; population   380;
  speciation   410; sustainability   399;
  utilitarianism   380

Gaard, Greta   233, 237
Gablik, Suzi   253
Galbraith, John Kenneth   478
Galileo Galilei   133–4, 297
Gandhi, Mohandas   53, 221, 502, 503–4,
  504
Ganges River   47, 55
garden city movement   156, 157
Gare, Arran   298, 299
gas, natural   292
Gaudi, Antoni   151, 152
Geddes, Patrick   156–7, 159
Geist   150–1
gender factors   226, 229, 239–41
genealogies   4–6, 7, 8–9, 10
generalization   241, 242, 311, 313
generational changes: *see* future generations
Genesis   100
genetic technology   293, 402, 407, 441–2,
  481, 483, 494–5
geocentrism   234
geology   153–4
geomancy   61
geometry   133–4, 135–6
gift exchanges   399–400
Gilson, Etienne   131
Giorgione   297
Gita   42
Glacken, Clarence J.   100, 102
global warming   215, 439
globalization   294, 300–1, 473
Glotfelty, Cheryl   252, 262
Gnosticism   100
God   82, 104, 138–9; Augustine,
  Saint   103, 131; creator   96–9, 100,
  114–15, 117; Descartes   136; evil
  132; Islam   114; Judaism
  81–2; Merciful   118; *see also*
  theism
Godwin, William   152

good   173, 265, 282; *see also* virtue
Goodpaster, Kenneth   196
goods   168, 169, 170, 171
Gordis, Robert   81, 84, 89, 91, 92, 93
Gordon, Pauline   10
government intervention   280–1
Gray, Asa   107
Great Chain of Being   98, 102, 132
Great Lakes Water Quality Agreement   306
Greek philosophy: Aristotle   69, 73–7, 102,
  175, 188–90, 418; instrumental/intrinsic
  values   418; nature   68, 72–3, 78;
  Plato   69–73; post-Aristotelian   77–9;
  Presocratics   67–9; reincarnation   70–1;
  society   467; soil erosion   297;
  vegetarianism   71–2
Green, T. H.   327
green accounting   395
green conditionality   435–6
green parties   318, 337, 343
green politics   316–17, 320;
  ecologism   325–6; freedom   328–9;
  hybrids   324; liberal democracy   322;
  liberalism   327–9; practice/theory   326;
  society   325–6; sustainability   317,
  318–19, 320
green revolution, India   440–1
greenfly example   168, 170
greenhouse gases   293, 387, 439, 449–51;
  see also emissions
Gregory of Nazianzus   101
Gregory of Nyssa   101
Griffin, Susan   233
Griggs v. *Duke Power Company*   430
Grotius, Hugo   142–3
Gruen, Lori   237
guardianship   9, 17, 388; *see also*
  custodianship; stewardship
Guha, Ramachandra   357
gurrutu (beholdenness)   8

Habermas, Jürgen   300
habitats   410, 483–4
Hadith, Islam   112, 113, 119–24
Haeckel, Ernst   150–1, 155
Hakamaya, Noriaki   61
Hale, Sir Matthew   105–6, 107
Hampshire, Stuart   403
Han period   21, 22, 29, 30, 34

Hanina, Rabbi 91
Hans, James S. 252
Hanson, Victor Davis 467
Hardin, Garrett 280, 365, 383–4
Hargrove, E. C. 265
harm, inflicting 449–53
harm prevention 331–2, 386, 450–1; see also ahimsa; non-destruction
Hassidic traditions 82
Haudenosaunee chiefs 9
Hawaii, extinction rates 406
hazardous wastes 427, 431–2, 439–40
health 131, 237, 251, 332–4
Hebrews, Book of 99
hedonism 77–8
Hegel, Georg W. F. 150–1
Heidegger, Martin 154, 159, 381
Helfand, Jonathan 85, 87
heliocentrism 130, 133–4, 234
Heraclitus 68, 73
herbicides 462
hierarchy: anthropocentrism 225–6; Daoism on 32–3; Darwin 107; ethics 180, 212–13; Great Chain of Being 98, 102, 132; moral 220, 235–6; nature 321; society 207, 430–2
Hildegard of Bingen 102
Hill, T. Jr 189–90
hima/haram (sanctuary) 112–13, 120–1, 125–6
Hinduism: ahimsa (non-violence) 43; animal life 45–6; cosmology 42–3, 45; Dharma 46; divinity 44; Earth 40–2; elements 38–40; environmental conservation 47–9; environmental protection 42; Karma doctrine 43; nature 37–8, 42–3; non-alienation 221; pollution prevention 46–7; rebirth 43; sanctity-of-life principle 44–6; stewardship 49; transmigration of souls 43; tree worship 43; Vedic period 38–42; vegetarianism 43; water 46–7
Hirschman, A. O. 476
history 291, 294, 295
Hobbes, Thomas 134–5, 138, 147
Hogan, Linda 4, 8
Holdren, John 479, 480

holism: Daoist 26, 32; ecology 308–10; environmental ethics 196; land ethic 208–9; sentientism 202, 421; Smuts 155
honeybee 488
Hourani, George 119
housefly 488
housing, environment 283
Howard, Ebenezer 156, 157
Hua Yen Buddhism 61
Huainanzi 29, 33
Huang-Lao School 22
Hudson River, striped-bass 310, 312
Hughes, George 104–5
Hui Yuan 35
human–non-human world: affiliations 14; animal liberation 416; Chinese philosophy 22–3; Confucianism 25; deep ecology 225–6; democracy 506; Descartes 137–8; environmental ethic 426–7; environmental literature 258–9; epistemology 254–5; Fox 226–7; genealogies 7; goods 170, 171; Greek philosophy 68; indigenous people 4–7; intelligence 491; interests 179, 420; intrinsic value 222–3; Islam 111–12, 115–16; Judaism 81, 83–6, 88–9; kinship 258–9; moral standing 165, 187, 242, 419; morality 187, 221, 491; reciprocity 10; respect 259–60; rights 193–4; Rousseau 147; Zen Buddhism 60
human-centred: see anthropocentrism
human genome project 441
human growth hormone 441–2
human rights 207–8, 211, 419
human waste 86–7
humanitarianism 106
humanity 139, 298–9; asymmetry thesis 496; creation of 115–16, 118–19; dominion over earth 83–4, 103, 107, 148; in God's image 96–7, 100; moral responsibility 108, 414; moralilty 153, 491; population density 210–11, 292, 299–300, 319; rationality 75–6, 78, 100–1, 243; see also human–non-human world
Humboldt, Alexander von 295

Hume, David: empiricism 140;
  ethics 206, 207; qualities 172;
  race 143; self-interest 208–9; and
  Smith 140, 206
hunter-gatherers 291, 292, 293, 298, 481
hunting 197, 198, 237
Husserl, Edmund 154
Hutcheson, Francis 106, 267
Huxley, T. H. 157
hybridization 87–8
hylozoism 68
hypothetical contract, Rawls 382

Illich, Ivan 156
immanentism 82, 104
imperialism 142–3
incarnation 45, 82, 132
Index of Biological Integrity 306–7
India: agricultural technology 440–1;
  development 238–9; Ganges 47, 55;
  green revolution 440–1; Narmada
  dam 296; reforestation 54;
  wilderness 357
indicator species 306
indigenous peoples: belonging 7–8; as
  custodians 10, 17; human–non-human
  world 4–7; knowledge/land 3–4; land
  use 470; multinational mining 426;
  non-interference 228–9; ownership 7,
  10; relocated 3, 17, 436; respect
  13–15; responsibility 10–12;
  sovereignty 436; Tasmania 13;
  water 470; see also aboriginal peoples
indiscernibility of identicals 136–7
individual/community 208, 310, 322–3,
  327, 367–9
industrial zoning 87
industrialism: consumption 476;
  energy 292–3, 296; green
  critique 319; migratoriness 261;
  Morris 151–2; nature 291, 295, 298;
  species protection 402
inequalities: consumption 320–1;
  social 207, 370, 430–2
insects threatened 168, 170, 402, 450,
  488
Institute for Social Ecology 243
instrumental value: anthropocentrism 166,
  405, 491–2; environment 482–3;

environmental ethics 164;
  environmental philosophy 242; Greek
  philosophy 418; Muir 242;
  nature 265, 443–4
integrity: agro-ecosystems 470;
  ecological 306–7; economic
  interests 394; respect for 317–18, 326,
  495–6; species preservation 425;
  sustainability 317–18, 395
intelligence 491
interdependence 219, 323–4
Interdisciplinary Studies in Literature and
  Environment 252
interests 179, 193–4, 212, 213, 420–1
Intergovernmental Panel on Climate
  Change 452
International Monetary Fund 370
intrinsic value 164–5; aesthetics 174,
  265–6; anthropocentrism 164, 166,
  491–2; biocentrism 164, 166, 308;
  biodiversity 421; consequentialism
  181; environmental ethics 164, 174,
  405, 416; environmental
  philosophy 171; expressivism 166;
  Greek philosophy 418; human–non-
  human world 222–3; Moore 167;
  moral standing 201–2; nature 265,
  318, 443–4; non-sentience 419–22
intuition 239–40, 271, 273
Irenaeus 100
Iriquois people 13
Isavasya Upanishad 44
Ishimure, Michiko 251
Islam: amr 118; animals 122–4;
  compassion 122; environmental
  issues 112–13, 116, 121–2;
  ethics 122; fiqh 120, 123, 125–6;
  God 114; Hadith 112, 113, 119–24;
  hima/haram 112–13, 120–1, 125–6;
  human–non-human world 111–12,
  115–16; nature 111–12, 113–19;
  ownership of natural resources 121–2;
  self-injury 116; wasteland 113, 126
island biogeography 306
Italy, Cinque Terre 274
Izzi Deen, M. Y. 117, 126

Jackson, Moana 11
Jackson, Wes 470

Jainism: animal life 46; Anuvrat
    Movement 54; deep ecology 53;
    environmental philosophy 52–4;
    karma 53; *mahavrata* (great vows) 53;
    non-violence 53, 64; Tirthankaras 52;
    vegetarianism 53
Jamieson, D. 436
Janah, Rabbi Jonah ibn 86
Japan 59, 60, 61
Jeffers, Robinson 259
Jefferson, Thomas 258, 467–8
Jesus 96–9
Job, Book of 92, 94
John, Saint 99
Johnson, Edward 197–8, 202
Johnson, Liz 15
joy 230–1
Joyce, James 299
Judaism: alienation 81–3; animals 87,
    88–9; anthropocentrism 82, 93; *bal
    taschit* 90–3; compassion 89;
    diaspora 83; environmental issues 87;
    environmental regulations 86–8; food
    blessings 85; God/nature 81–2;
    Hassidic traditions 82; human–non-
    human world 81, 83–6, 88–9;
    hybridization 87–8; Kabbalistic
    tradition 93; love 93; nature 81–2,
    84, 93; over-consumption 91;
    plants 89; sabbath 85–6; species
    preservation 88; stewardship 84–5, 86,
    93–4; theocentrism 85–6, 92–3;
    vegetarianism 84; wilderness 94
justice: distributive 319–20, 453–8;
    intergenerational 382–3;
    principles 502; Rawls 402;
    social 427; *see also* environmental justice

Kabbalistic tradition 93
Kabilsingh, Chatsumarn 58
Kaczinsky, Theodore (Unabomber) 440,
    502, 503
kaitiaki (guardianship) 9, 15
Kakadu National Park 9
Kalpa Sutra 52
kangaroo industry 417–18
Kant, Immanuel: aesthetics 146, 268–9;
    idealism 150; knowledge theory 150;
    moral distinction 221, 467;

nature 146; rational autonomy 187;
    responsibility 377
Kantians 169–70, 187
karma: Buddhism 56; Hinduism 43;
    Jainism 53
Kautilya's Arthasastra 46
Kautsky, Karl 295–6
Kellert, S. 267
Kepler, Johann 133
Kettering, Charles 476
King, Martin Luther Jr 428
King, Ynestra 243
King Lear 477
Kingsley, Charles 107
Kirkwood, Carmen 9
Kitaro, Nishida 61
Kittredge, William 252–3
knowledge 385–6; ecology 313;
    embedded 16–17; gendered 239–40;
    genealogies 5; intuition 239–40, 271,
    273; Kant 150; land 3–4; natural
    history 313; philosophy 155, 298,
    300; respect 15
Krishna, Lord 42
Kropotkin, Peter 156, 159
Kuznets, Simon 369, 370
Kyoto Protocol 288, 453
Kyoto School 61

LaDuke, Winona 436
LaFleur, William 60
Laguno Pueblo stories 15–16
Lakota people 9
Lamm, Norman 84, 91
Lancaster, Lewis 55
land ethic: biotic community 209–10, 211,
    213, 421; Callicott 196–7; Diné 17;
    ecology 214–16; holism 208–9;
    Leopold 158–9, 196, 204–5, 207–8,
    209, 421; overpopulation 210–11;
    respect 209–10; sustainability 395;
    wilderness 353
land use 12–13, 15–16, 308, 460, 466–7,
    470
landscape changes 292, 293–4, 297, 299,
    355–6
Lane, E. W. 123
Laos 57
Laozi text 26, 30–1, 32

Lasch, Christopher   475
last man example, Routley   166, 200–1
law-breaking   498–9, 500, 502–3, 508
laws   499; environmental   331–4, 340–1,
    343–4; environmental standards
    338–40; just/unjust   499; Maori   11;
    risk assessment   331, 334–6;
    science   335, 338; *see also fiqh*; natural
    laws
Leibniz, Gottfried Wilhelm   141–2, 166–7
Leopold, Aldo: accretions   211;
    holism   194; land ethic   158–9, 196,
    204–5, 207–8, 209, 421; *Sand County
    Almanac*   204–5, 260;
    sustainability   395; wilderness   351
Leviticus   87–8, 100
Lewis, C. S.   132
Lewis, H. G.   368
liberal arts   251, 257–8
liberalism   327–9
libertarianism   379–80
liberty, Mill   391
Liezi text   32–3
life force   15
Liji text   24
'limits to growth' debate   318, 319
Lincoln, Abraham   377
literature: *see* environmental literature
*Literature of Nature: An International
    Sourcebook*   252
Little Missouri National Grasslands   349
living things: autonomy   187;
    flourishing   168–70, 180, 186; potential/
    actual   199; *see also* sentientism
local community   260–2, 322–3
Locke, John   106; compassion   106;
    empiricism   138–9; natural
    resources   386; property rights   138–9,
    327–8; slavery   143; wilderness   139
logging   213–14, 499, 500–1
Logos   68, 69, 78, 99
Lopez, Barry   253
Los Angeles Times   259–60
love, Judaism   93
Lovins, Amory   473–4
Luhmann, Niklas   300
Lunyu text   33
Lushi Chunqiu   27–8
Luther, Martin   104

Lyons, Oren   4, 9, 17
McDonough, William   473–4
McGee, W. J.   158
Machaca, Modesto   14
Machievelli, Niccolò   234
McIntosh, R. P.   311–12
Mackie, J.   172
Macrina   101
Maddox, Lester   503
Magee, Alan   253
Mahabharata   45, 47
Mahabhutas (elements)   38–40
Mahapragya, Acharya   54
Mahavira   52, 53
mahavrata (great vows)   53
Mahayana Buddhism   59–62
Maimonides   91
Major, J. S.   22, 29
maldevelopment   240
mallow species   407
Malthus, Thomas   152–3, 362, 363–4, 367
Mander, Jerry   440
Mannison   268, 269
Manusmriti   45, 47
Maori culture: ancestors' stories   16; as
    colonizers   487–8; human–non-human
    world   6, 7; *kaitiaka*   8, 15; law   11; life
    force   15; *whakapapa*   5; *whenua*   6
Maracle, Lee   9
marginalization   240, 321, 427
marine technology   467
Maritain, Jacques   107
Mark, Saint   99
market failures   279–80
market forces: agriculture   462–3, 468;
    compensation/waste   432;
    efficiency   278–9; pollution   278–9,
    280–1, 287–8
Mars   486, 493–5, 496
Marshall, Alfred   480
Marshall, Robert   351
Martin, Michael   505
Martin, Paul   489–90
Martino, J. P.   379
Marx, Karl   151, 295, 477
materialism   67–8, 134–8, 150–1, 155,
    301–2
matrimonial ethics   207
Matthew, Saint   100

Mayan customs 5, 6, 11
mechanism 134, 155; *see also* industrialism; technology
media 252
medical science 308
medicinal herbs 11, 16, 56
medieval era 102–3, 130–3, 297
Mehta, Raychandbhai 53
Mellon, M. 465
Menchu, Rigoberta 5
Mengzi 25, 30
Merchant, Carolyn 233–4, 298
Mere-Addition paradox 372–4
meta-ethics 163–4, 166, 167–8
metaphysics 159, 266–7
Metropolitan Edison v. *People Against Nuclear Energy* 332
Milesian philosophers 67–8
militant disobedience 500, 504–5, 507–8
Mill, John Stuart 327; agrarianism 467; animal pain 420; liberty 391; morality 155; population 367
misanthropy 158, 364, 374–5
moas 487
Mohawk people 11
Momaday, M. Scott 9
Monet, Claude 299
Montaigne, Michel de 143, 147
Montreal Protocol 435
Moore, G. E. 167, 265
moral community 378
moral education 387
moral psychology 381
moral responsibility: future generations 377–8; harm prevention 450–1; humanity 108, 414; motivation 383–4; species extinction 490–3
moral standing: abiotic factors 495–6, 497; future generations 378–83; hierarchy 220, 235–6; instrinsic value 201–2; interests 420–1; Kant 221, 467; natural entities 201–2; non-human animals 165, 187, 242, 419; Regan 194; species 410
morality 206, 209; agriculture 467–8; civil disobedience 503; human–non-human world 187, 221, 491; humanity 153, 491; judgment 173;

law-breaking 508; Mill 155; population 372–4; rights 194–5
Morris, William 151–2, 271
mortality: *see* death rate
Muddinan, John 96
Muhammad, Prophet 119, 120, 124
Muhsin Kahn, M. 121, 122
Muir, John: environmental philosophy 242; non-anthropocentrism 106, 463, 493; wilderness 106, 157–8, 351
Mulholland, William 264
multinational mining 426
Mumford, Lewis 156–7
Muriwhenua Land Report 8
Murphy, Patrick D. 252
mutual aid 151, 156
Myanmar 57
Myers, J. P. 465
Myers, Norman 403–4, 479

Nabhan, Gary Paul 260–1
Nachmanides 84, 88
Naess, Arne: biodiversity 421; deep ecology 141, 186, 218–19, 220–2, 243; ecosophy 220–1, 230–1; self-realization 244–5; and Sessions 222, 223
Nagatomi, Masatoshi 61
Nagila (common ancestry) 9
Narmada dam 296
Nash, Roderick 351, 355, 358
nation-states 142–3, 323
National Academy of Sciences 311, 312–13, 314
National Environmental Policy Act 332–3, 342
National Science Foundation 413
National Urban League 429
National Wilderness Preservation System 356
Native Americans: biotic community 210; conquistadors 142; environmental justice 432; uranium mining 426; wilderness 355–7, 358, 464
natural entities 180–1, 185–6, 194, 201–2
natural history 313
natural laws 142–3, 152–3
natural resources: consumption 473; correct use of 91–2; limitations 480–2;

natural resources: (cont)
  Locke 386; ownership 121–2;
  population growth 364, 365;
  sustainability 392; value 282–4, 492
natural selection 153, 309–10
naturalism 143, 152–4, 155, 406,
  410
nature 256; aesthetics 151, 264,
  268–71, 274–5; anthropocentrism 219,
  222–3; anthropogenic changes 214–16;
  Aristotle 73–4; art 297;
  authenticity 483; balance 307, 353;
  capitalism 151; Chinese
  philosophy 21–2; Christianity 96–9,
  100, 102; culture 152–3, 154, 354,
  443–4; domesticated 201;
  environment 482; Epicurus 78;
  experience of 270–1; exploitation 40,
  105, 321, 403–4; flux of 215–16, 353;
  geometry 133–4; Greek philosophy 68,
  72–3, 78; habitat 410, 483–4;
  Hinduism 37–8, 42–3; industrialism
  291, 295, 298; intrinsic/instrumental
  value 174, 222, 265, 318, 443–4, 482;
  Islam 111–12, 113–19; Judaism 81–2,
  84, 93; Kant 146; legal rights 507;
  paganism 100, 101; pristine 464–5;
  Romanticism 146–7; Rousseau, Jean-
  Jacques 146–7; scala naturae 78–9;
  value of 297–8, 359; women 233–4,
  239–40; Zen Buddhism 60; see also
  wilderness
naturism: see naturalism
Neidjie, Bill 7
neighborhood environmentalism 260–2
Nelson, M. P. 359
Nelson, Richard K. 259–60
neo-Confucianism 24–5, 33–4
neo-Daoism 34
neo-Darwinians 309
neo-Europes 486–8
neo-Luddites 440
Neoplatonists 79
New York utility companies 310
New Zealand 318, 422–3, 487–8
Newton, Sir Isaac 144
Ngarinman land 12
Nicholas, Darcy 8
Noble, I. R. 465

non-anthropocentrism 493, 505–6
non-destruction 90–3, 185, 386, 403,
  408–9; see also harm prevention
non-interference 223, 228–9, 507
non-sentient beings 379, 419–22
non-speciesist ethic 416, 420
non-violence 43, 53, 64
Norman, Waerete 6
normative ethics 119–24, 163–4, 173–5,
  204
North Dakota 349–50, 352
North/South divide 392, 434
Noss, Reed 359
Notestein, Frank 369–70
nuclear power 440
nuclear waste 426
Nussbaum, Martha 478

obligations: community membership 213;
  deontological ethics 187–8; legal 500;
  moral 405; non- destruction 185;
  ranked 212
ocean, colonization 493
Oelschlaeger, Max 295, 351, 354
oil 292, 357–8, 458, 481
oil spills 259–60, 283–4
Olson, Sigurd 351
omission, acts of 503
one-child policy, China 368, 371
Onondaga people 9
oppression 226, 244
Organ Pipe Wilderness Area 356–7
organicism 152, 154
Origen 100, 102
Orr, David W. 251, 257, 258, 260
Ostfeld, R. S. 215
otherness 258, 273
overkill 489–90
ownership 7, 10, 121–2; see also
  property
ozone layers 254, 426

paganism 100, 101
Palmer, Clare 100
panpsychism 142
pantheism 101, 148–9, 150
paper mills 287–8
paradigm shift 220
Pareto Optimality 278–9

Parfit, Derek   372–3, 380
Parmenides   68–9
Parsons, H. C.   295
Parsvanatha   52
Partridge, Ernest   382, 384
Pascal, Blaise   143
Passmore, John   97, 100, 103, 190
patriarchy: development   239, 240;
   ecofeminism   226, 227, 236; gender
   roles   240–1
patrimonial management   399–400
patristic writers   100
Paul, Saint   99
Pearce, D.   396
Penan people   498–9, 503
perception   139–40
perfectionist ethics   178
permaculture   230
pesticides   342, 461, 465
Peters, Robert Henry   305
Petrified Forest Wilderness Area   355
phenomenology   154
Philo of Alexandria   97
philosophy   155, 204, 298, 300; see also
   environmental philosophy
photosynthesis   284, 481
Phra Prajak   57
Pickettt, S. T. A.   215
Pinchot, Gifford   157, 158, 463, 493
plants: biotic community   199;
   conservation   209, 403, 405, 407, 409;
   extinction   406; Judaism   89;
   Montaigne   147; photosynthesis   284,
   481; sentientism   72
Plato: anthropocentrism   70–1; Augustine
   on   102; consumption   474;
   cosmology   72–3; Critias   73;
   Forms   70; and Heraclites   69–70;
   law   499; Laws   73; Phaedrus   70;
   Philebus   72–3; Republic   71;
   Statesman   71, 72; teleology   72–3;
   Timaeus   71, 72–3, 101
Plotinus   79
Plumwood, Val: dualism   226, 227, 235;
   rationality   243; self-realization   244–5;
   suffering   240; see also Routley, Val
Pollan, Michael   261, 464
polluter-pays principle   287–8, 337

pollution: anthropogenic   204–5;
   biological   441–2; class differences   219;
   compensation   281; conservation
   204–5; global   216; ground water
   439–40, 461; health   251, 332, 333–4;
   market forces   278–9, 280–1, 287–8; oil
   spills   259–60, 283–4; race   238, 426,
   427, 428–9, 431; toxics release
   inventory   342; trading   300, 341; see
   also emissions
pollution prevention   46–7, 287–8, 340
Pollution Prevention Act   340
population   362; Condorcet   363–4;
   environmental philosophy   365, 374–5;
   future generations   380; Malthus
   363–4, 367; Mere-Addition paradox
   372–4; Mill   367; moral theory   372–4;
   natural resources   364, 365;
   overpopulation   210–11; poverty
   362–3, 364; utilitarianism   372–3
population density   210–11, 292, 299–300,
   319
Porphyry   79
positive aesthetics   271–3
possum   422
postcolonialism   228–9, 238
posterity: see future generations
postmodernism   300
poverty   238–9; capitalism   475;
   development   240, 370, 392;
   environmental degradation   394; natural
   laws   152–3; population   362–3, 364;
   sustainable development   391, 452–3
Powell, Lake   264, 266
power relations   434–5
practical ecology   304, 312–14
Prakriti (nature)   42, 44
prana (breath)   39
Pravascitta Tatva   47
predators   215–16
preservationism   493; see also conservation;
   environmental protection
Presocratics   67–9
Prithvi (earth)   38, 39
Prithvi Sukta   40–2
production, consumption   461, 477, 483
properties: see qualities
property ownership: citizen
   participation   342; land   280;

property ownership (*cont*)
  liberalism   327–8; Locke   138–9,
  327–8; violence against   503, 504
Protestantism   104–7, 475
Proudhon, Pierre-Joseph   148, 151
psycho-history   293
Ptolemy   132
Puketapu-Hetet, Erenora   5, 14
Pulkara, Daly   12
Pure Land sect   35
Puritanism   106
Pyle, Robert Michael   253, 261
Pythagoreans   70

qi (stuff)   33–4
qualities   134, 138, 171–3
quality of life   319, 394
quantum mechanics   172
Qur'ān   111, 113–14, 116–17

rabbits   423
race: exploitation   237; imperialism   143;
  pollution   238, 426, 427, 428–9, 431;
  women   237
racism   229, 236, 238, 418, 430–1;
  environmental   429–31, 432
Rahman, F.   115–16
Rancholabrean extinction   490
rarity of species   412–14
rationality: animals/human   75–6, 78, 98,
  100–1, 243; Augustine   98, 100–1;
  autonomy   187; Descartes   105;
  economic   328; empiricism   141;
  Kant   187; Plumwood   243;
  Stoics   100
rats   487, 488
Rawls, John: civil disobedience   501, 502;
  egalitarianism   393; hypothetical
  contract   382; just savings   384; justice
  theory   402; technological capacity   383
Ray, John   100
realism   164–5, 174–5; environmental
  history   291–3; ethical   171–2;
  goods   168, 169; meta-ethics   166;
  metaphysical   266–7
rebirth   43
reciprocity   10, 11, 13–14
recycling   287–8, 322–3, 386
reductionism   309

Reed, Christopher   63–4
reflexivity   291, 298–9
reforestation   54, 57
Reformation   104–5
Regan, Tom: *The Case for Animal
  Rights*   194; eco- fascism   197, 211;
  rights   194–5, 405, 420;
  sentientism   192, 196
Regier, Henry   306
reincarnation   70–1, 74
reinhabitation   323
relationality   6, 220, 222, 304–5, 317, 318
religion   37, 298; *see also* Buddhism;
  Christianity; Hinduism; Islam; Jainism;
  Judaism
relocation   3, 17, 436
ren (man)   23–4
Renaissance   104, 297
reproduction, control over   362, 368,
  371–2
Rescher, Nicholas   405
respect   318, 421; biodiversity   413;
  human–non-human world   259–60;
  indigenous peoples   13–15;
  integrity   317–18, 326, 495–6;
  knowledge   15; land ethic   209–10
responsibility   414; art   253; future
  generations   286, 385–7; indigenous
  peoples   10–11; Kant   377; knowledge
  criterion   385–6; personal   322–3; risk
  assessment   337–8; social   320; *see also*
  moral responsibility
Revelation, Book of   99
revolutionary disobedience   500
rhododendron species   409
Rig Veda   39, 40, 44–5, 46–7
right-to-know legislation   342
rights: abortion   194; active/passive   382;
  animals   193–4; biospheric   186–7,
  492; deep ecology   186; environmental
  ethic   185–6; human–non-human
  world   193–4; moral   194–5;
  Regan   194–5, 405, 420; species   405–6
Riley, Shamara Shantu   245–6
Rio Declaration: *see* Earth Summit
R.I.S.E. v. *Kay*   430
risk assessment: costs   283; law   331,
  334–6; precautionary principle   336–7;
  responsibility   337–8

Rissler, J. 465
road-blocks 503
road building 332
rocky intertidal zone 307
Rodman, John 192, 196, 201
Rolston, H. III 271, 352
Romanticism 143, 146–8, 149
Roosevelt, Theodore 351
rootedness 261
Rousseau, Jean-Jacques 143, 146–7
Routley, Richard 196; last man
   example 166, 200–1
Routley, Val 196, 200–1; see also
   Plumwood, Val
Ruskin, John 151, 152, 271
Russia, self-sacrifice 383–4

sabbath 85–6, 97
sabotage 501–2, 504–5
Sachs, Wolfgang 434
sacrificial animals 56, 114–15
Sagoff, M. 265, 312
Saigyo, Zen Buddhist monk 60
St John de Crevecoeur, Hector 258
Sale, Kirkpatrick 440
Salleh, Ariel Kay 239
salt marsh example 307
sanctity-of-life principle, Hinduism 44–6
sanctuary, Islam 120–1, 125–6
Sanders, Scott Russell 253, 261
sanitation 46, 86–7
Santmire, H. Paul 102
Sartre, Jean-Paul 212–13
Sarvodaya 58–9
satya (truthfulness) 53
scala naturae 78–9
Scheler, Max 154
Schelling, Friedrich 150
Schor, Juliet B. 474, 476
Schwartz, Eilon 90, 91
Schwarzschild, Steven 81–2
Schweitzer, Albert 421
science 133–4; Enlightenment 319;
   experience 271; future generations
   378; industrialism 294–5, 298;
   law 335, 338; theism 133; women's
   status 233–4; see also technology
Scott, Sir Walter 148
sea levels 398, 456

Sea Shepherd Conservation Society 498,
   504
seals 488
Sedley, David 74
Seed, John 244
self-determination 428
self-injury, Islam 116
self-interest 135, 208–9, 219, 267, 405
self-knowledge 69, 79
self-purification, Buddhism 55
self-realization 221–2, 243, 244–5
self-sacrifice 383–4
self-sufficiency 323–4
self-transcendence 384
Sen, Amartya 371, 394, 478
sensory experience 133–4
sentient beings 35, 59, 102, 209, 416
sentientism 192–5; anthropocentrism
   179–81; biodiversity 199–200;
   environmental ethics 196–202, 495–6;
   environmentalists 200–1; holism 202,
   421; moral standing 397–8, 495–6;
   plants 72; utilitarianism 192–3
Sequohay, Ammoneta 3, 4, 16
Sessions, George 222, 223, 225, 228, 421
sexuality, Buddhism 58
Sforno, Obadiah 84
Shang dynasty 23–4
Shapiro, David S. 93
Shay, Kee 13
Shepard, Paul 293, 294
Shi Huangdi 21
Shiva, Vandana 238–9, 240, 392, 433–4,
   436, 440–1
Shrader-Frechette, Kristin 211, 212
Shujing 28
Shvetashvatara Upanishad 38–9
Sibley, F. 269
Sidgwick, Henry 420
Sierra Club 378, 429
Silko, Leslie 11–12, 13, 15–16
Simon, Julian 366–7, 379, 392
Simpson, G. G. 408
Singer, Peter: Animal Liberation 192–3,
   201, 242–3; Practical Ethics 193;
   Rawls 502; sentientism 192;
   utilitarianism 242
Singh, Karan 42, 47
Singhvi, L. M. 54

sinks 392, 492
Sivaraksa, Sulak 58
slavery 143, 158, 418
Slicer, Deborah 243–4
Smith, Adam: capital 480; and
    Hume 140; market forces 278; moral
    sentiments 206, 209; necessaries 475,
    478
Smuts, Jan 155, 156
snail darter 333
Snyder, Gary 253; 'Ripples on the
    surface' 255–6
Sober, E. 265–6
social Darwinism 155, 298
social ecologists 227–8, 243
social justice 427
social welfare 279, 281, 286
society 132; coping capacity 480;
    Enlightenment 219; ethics 206–7,
    209–10, 286; fair play 500; Greek
    philosophy 467; green politics 325–6;
    inequalities 207, 370, 430–2;
    responsibility 320; technology 399
sociobiology 159
sociology 152, 155
Socrates 69, 71, 477, 499
soil erosion 297, 397, 423, 462
Soka Gakkai movement 61
Soper, Kate 354–5
sovereignty, indigenous peoples 436
speciation 214–15, 409, 410, 449
species 406–8; change 353;
    community 209–10, 410–11; duty
    to 404–6, 408–10; ecosystem 410–11;
    endangered 402, 403; ethic 409;
    exotic 411, 487–8; extinction 307–8,
    409, 449–50, 490–3; indicators 306;
    individual 310; introduced 422–3;
    moral agency 410; rights 405–6;
    value 404, 405
species preservation: biocentrism 403–4;
    biodiversity 88, 402; conflict 422–4;
    economic benefits 403; industrial
    development 402; integrity 425;
    Judaism 88; rarity 412–14; Rosetta
    Stone argument 404
speciesism 193, 416
Spencer, Herbert 154–5
Spinoza, Baruch 82, 141, 230–1

spotted owl/logging example 213–14, 402
Sri Lanka 58–9
standing to sue 342–3
Stegner, Wallace 261
Stevenson, C. L. 166
stewardship: agrarian philosophy 469;
    Christianity 96, 100, 103, 105–6, 107;
    dualism 108; Hinduism 49;
    Judaism 84–5, 86, 93–4; Maori
    culture 8, 15; Romantics 148, 149; see
    also custodianship; guardianship
Stockholm Conference 343–4
Stoics 77, 78, 98, 100
Stone, Christopher D. 194, 201, 211, 388,
    507
storytellers 5, 16
striped-bass 312
Stubbes, Philip 106
Sturgeon, Noel 233
subsistence economies 238–9
subsistence ethos 229–30
subsistence farming 293, 461–2, 480
substitutability 278, 282–3, 398, 481–2
suffering 106, 193, 194–5, 198–9, 240,
    419
sulfur dioxide emission 288, 341
Superfund law 337
survival of the fittest 154–5
sustainability 393–5, 484;
    agriculture 121, 469–70;
    anthropocentrism 391; Brundtland
    Report 390; conservation 394–5;
    criteria 395–8; economic
    approach 286, 395–8, 400;
    environmental justice 320, 323–4, 392;
    environmentalists 392; future
    generations 399; green politics 317,
    318–19, 320; implementation 398–400;
    integrity 317–18, 395; land ethic 395;
    laws 343–4; Leopold 395; liberal
    arts 251; natural resources 392;
    poverty 391, 452–3; weak/strong 396
sustainable development 460; Brundtland
    Report 289, 390; developing
    countries 435–6, 452–3; eco-
    spirituality 47–8; environmental
    justice 435–6; poverty 391, 452–3
Suzuki, D. T. 60, 63
Swamp, Jake 11

Swimme, Brian 239–40
sympathy 140, 209, 420; *see also* compassion
systemists 406–7

Talbot, Carl 357
Tall Mountain, Mary 12
Talmud 90
Tasmanian indigenous people 13
Tattvarthasutra 53, 54
Taylor, Paul 187, 352, 421
technology: agriculture 366, 440–1; alternative 458; appropriate 442–3, 473; authenticity 444–7; carrying capacity 366; consequences 294, 295–6, 383, 439–43; conservationism 492; determinism 298; efficiency/waste 479; Enlightenment 319; environmental destruction 392–3, 439; natural value 443–4; society 399; *see also* industrialism
teleology 72–3, 74, 78
terraformation, Mars 486, 493–5, 496
Tetsuro, Watsuji 61
Thailand 57
Thales 67–8
Theater 253
theism 108, 131, 158; science 133; *see also* God
theocentrism 85–6, 92–3, 98
Theodore Roosevelt National Park 349
Theravada Buddhism 56–9
Thermophus aquaticus 403
Thich Nhat Hanh 61–2
Third World: *see* developing countries
Thomas, Keith 100, 106, 297–8
Thomists 107
Thompson, J. 265, 268–9, 272–3
Thoreau, Henry David 260, 498; consumption 474, 479; law/right 499; *Walden* 106, 254, 258–9, 474; wilderness 228, 351
Three Mile Island 332
tian–di–ren 24–5, 26, 27
tian (heaven) 23–7
Tibetan Buddhism 61–2
Tirthankaras, Jainism 52
Tobias, Michael 53
Tongass National Forest 264–5

Torah 82, 83
Torrance, Robert M. 252
toxics release inventory 342
tradable discharge permits 287–8
trade-offs 279–80, 283, 284
transcendence 34–5, 82
transmigration of souls 43
transnational corporations 300–1, 399, 426
transport 293
tree worship 43
Truganinny 13, 15
truth value 167
Tryon, Thomas 106
tuatara species 407, 487
Tulsi, Acharya 54
TVA v. *Hill* 333
Tweeten, L. 462–3
tyrants example 170

Umasvati, *Tatttvarthasutra* 53, 54
UN Biodiversity Convention 402
UN Conference on Environment and Development: *see* Earth Summit
UN Environment Program 344
UN Food and Agriculture Organization 460
UN Law of the Sea 300
Unabomber (Kaczinsky) 440, 502, 503
Union Carbide pesticides 342
United Church of Christ, Commission for Racial Justice 429–30, 431
United Farm Workers 428–9
Upanishads 38–9, 44
uranium mining 426, 436
US Constitutional Convention 381
utilitarianism: animal pain/pleasure 420; consequentialism 182; consistency argument 169–70; environmental philosophy 466–7; future generations 380; non-harming 386; population control 372–3; sentientism 192–3; Singer 242; social welfare 281

value: aesthetic 266–7, 272–3; amenity 404, 492; anthropocentrism 164, 166, 405, 491–2; biospheric 492; consequentialism 183; dualisms 235–6; economic 282–4, 403–4;

value (*cont*)
 extrinsic   165; media   252; natural
 resources   282–4, 492; nature   297–8,
 359; non-instrumental   164–5, 166;
 objective   165, 229, 352, 406, 408;
 realism   165; species   404, 405;
 transpersonal   300; truth   167; *see also*
 instrumental value; intrinsic value
value judgments   305–6
vampire-bats   313
vandalism   174
Varner, Gary   200, 208–9
Vayu (air)   39
Vedas   44
Vedic period, Hinduism   38–42
vegetarianism: animal liberation
 197; Buddhism   58; Christianity
 133; ecofeminism   237; Epicurus
 77–8; Greek philosophy   71–2;
 Hinduism   43; Jainism   53;
 Judaism   84; Plotinus   79;
 Rousseau   143
Village of Arlington Heights v. *Metropolitan
 Housing Development Corporation*   430
violence   502–4
virtual nature   447
virtue ethics   140, 178, 188–90
vitalism   154
Vitoria, Francisco de   142
von Wright, G. H.   168–9
Vyaddha Jataka   56

Waggoner, P. E.   461
Wainburranga, Paddy   5
Walker, Alice   236–7
Wallace, Alfred Russel   153–4
Wang Chong   29–30
Wardy, Robert   74
warfare   135, 142, 147
Warren, Karen J.   236, 240
Warren County protests   429–30
waste: chemical   439–40;
 compensation   431–2, 432;
 hazardous   427, 431–2; toxic   342
waste dumping   238, 427
waste-treatment plants   479
wasteland: Islam   113, 126; *see also*
 wilderness
Wat Plak Mai Lai monastery   57

water: climate changes   449–50;
 Hinduism   46–7; indigenous
 peoples   470; pollution   439–40, 461
water technology   296
Watson, Paul   503–4
Weber, Max   475
Webern, Anton von   299
Weiss, Edith Brown   382–3
Wenz, Peter S.   428
whakapapa (genealogy)   5
whaling   481, 498, 504
whenua (land/placenta)   6
White, Lynn Jr   37, 63, 83–4, 97, 103, 469
Whitehead, Alfred North   155–6
Wideman, John Edgar   261
Wihonhi, Dell   8
wilderness: aesthetics   352; anthropogenic
 factors   273, 355–6, 359;
 authenticity   444–5; autonomy   359;
 Badlands   349–50; biodiversity   359;
 Christianity   98–9, 104, 106; climate
 changes   352; deep ecology   228,
 229–30; environmental ethic   350–2;
 feminists   357; Judaism   94; land
 ethic   353; Leopold   351; Locke   139;
 loss of   264–5, 378; Muir   106, 157–8,
 351; Native Americans   355–7, 358,
 464; non-interference   223; objective/
 subjective values   229, 352;
 pristine   351, 352, 354, 356;
 Thoreau   228, 351
Wilderness Act   350
wilderness preservation   350, 352–8
wildlife management   209
Williams, Bernard   273
Williams, Duncan   59
Williams, Terry Tempest   253;
 "Redemption"   256–7
Willson, E.   267
Wilson, Edward O.   490
witch hunts   234
Wittgenstein, Ludwig   381
wolf species   407
Wollaston, William   106
women: equal opportunities   371;
 exploitation   321; intuition   239–40;
 and nature   233–4, 239–40; race   237;
 see also ecofeminism; feminism; gender
Wong, Hertha D.   252

woodpeckers, red-cockaded   313
working conditions   237, 432
World Bank   370, 479
World Development Report   482
World Parliament of Religions   63
World Wilderness Congress   351
Worldwatch Institute   460
Wright, Frank Lloyd   156
wuxing (five elements), Chinese
   philosophy   27–8

Xenophanes   70
xenophobia   469
Xunzi text   24–5

Ya'akov, Rabbi   82
Yajnavalkya Smriti   45–6

yin-yang   28–9, 157
Yin-Yang School   28, 30
Yolngu people   8
Yosemite National Park   264
Young, Iris M.   428
Young, Robert   504
Yunupingu, Galarrwuy   7

Zen Buddhism   60, 63
Zhang Zai   33–4
zhiran (natural)   31–2
Zhuangzi text   26, 30, 32
Zimmerman, Michael E.   243, 244
Zionism   82
zoos   274–5, 411
Zou Yan   28, 29
Zuozhuan   27, 33